OXFORD MONOGRAPHS ON
LABOUR LAW

*General Editors*: Paul Davies,
Keith Ewing, Mark Freedland

WOMEN AND THE LAW

*Oxford Monographs on Labour Law*

*General Editors*: Paul Davies, Fellow of Balliol College, and Professor of Law at Oxford University; Keith Ewing, Professor of Public Law at King's College, London; and Mark Freedland, Fellow of St John's College, and Professor of Law at Oxford University.

This series is the first new development in the literature dealing with labour law for many years. The series recognizes the arrival not only of a renewed interest in labour law generally, but also the need for a fresh approach to the study of labour law following a decade of momentous change in the UK and Europe. The series is concerned with all aspects of labour law, including traditional subjects of study such as industrial relations law and individual employment law, but it will also include books which examine the law and economics of the labour market and the impact of social security law upon patterns of employment and the employment contract.

**Titles already published in this series**

*The Right to Strike*
K. D. EWING

*Legislating for Conflict*
SIMON AUERBACH

*Justice in Dismissal*
HUGH COLLINS

*Juster Pensions, Employment, and the Law*
RICHARD NOBLES

# Women and the Law

SANDRA FREDMAN

CLARENDON PRESS · OXFORD
1997

*Oxford University Press, Great Clarendon Street, Oxford* OX2 6DP
*Oxford New York*
*Athens Auckland Bangkok Bogota Bombay*
*Buenos Aires Calcutta Cape Town Dar es Salaam*
*Delhi Florence Hong Kong Istanbul Karachi*
*Kuala Lumpur Madras Madrid Melbourne*
*Mexico City Nairobi Paris Singapore*
*Taipei Tokyo Toronto Warsaw*
*and associated companies in*
*Berlin Ibadan*

*Oxford is a trade mark of Oxford University Press*

*Published in the United States by*
*Oxford University Press Inc., New York*

*British Library Cataloguing in Publication Data*
*Data available*

*Library of Congress Cataloging in Publication Data*

*ISBN 0-19-876322 0*
*ISBN 0-19-876323-9 (pbk)*

*Typeset by Best-set Typesetter Ltd., Hong Kong*
*Printed in Great Britain by*
*Bookcraft Ltd., Midsomer Norton Somerset*

# Women and the Law

SANDRA FREDMAN

CLARENDON PRESS · OXFORD
1997

Oxford University Press, Great Clarendon Street, Oxford OX2 6DP

Oxford New York

Athens Auckland Bangkok Bogota Bombay
Buenos Aires Calcutta Cape Town Dar es Salaam
Delhi Florence Hong Kong Istanbul Karachi
Kuala Lumpur Madras Madrid Melbourne
Mexico City Nairobi Paris Singapore
Taipei Tokyo Toronto Warsaw

and associated companies in
Berlin Ibadan

Oxford is a trade mark of Oxford University Press

Published in the United States by
Oxford University Press Inc., New York

British Library Cataloguing in Publication Data
Data available

Library of Congress Cataloging in Publication Data

ISBN 0-19-876322 0
ISBN 0-19-876323-9 (pbk)

Typeset by Best-set Typesetter Ltd., Hong Kong
Printed in Great Britain by
Bookcraft Ltd., Midsomer Norton Somerset

*This book is dedicated to my children*

*Jem, Kim and Dan*
*and to my husband, Alan.*

*You have been the source of all my inspiration.*

# Editors' Preface

This is sixth title in the series of Oxford Monographs on Labour Law, established to promote the publication of books which will make a distinctive contribution to the study of labour law. The contemporary publication of the fifth and sixth titles will, we hope, represent a recognition and affirmation of the central importance of discussion of the treatment of women to the study of labour law at the present day.

Having always maintained an open-ended and multi-disciplinary approach to this series, we are particularly pleased to be able to publish in the series a text which both in title and in substance extends widely beyond the traditional confines of labour law.

For the real point which is made by this text, and by its inclusion in our series, is that we can fully and adequately understand the treatment of women in employment law only from the perspective of an analysis of the situation of women in the legal system at large.

It is that analysis which Sandra Fredman carries out very powerfully in this text, not least because she establishes an effective theoretical basis for it in her first, foundational, chapter. It quickly becomes apparent how helpful that exercise is towards the general task of identifying the modern theoretical basis for labour law as a whole, this being the very enterprise to which our series seeks to contribute.

PLD KDE MRF
10 July 1997

# Preface

I come to the topic of Women and the Law without attempting to conceal my passionate concern for the subject. In the spirit of modern feminism, I draw explicitly on the personal as well as the academic. Delving into women's recent history, I am touched profoundly by the knowledge that even partial freedom has come so recently. Delving into the philosophical and political underpinnings of the law, I am astounded by the tenacity of oppression against women. There has certainly been significant change: a woman at the end of the nineteenth century would have been astonished at the freedom experienced by her counterparts at the end of the twentieth. Yet a closer look reveals the stubborn persistence of women's disadvantage. Women predominate among the lowest earners of society, and amongst the poorest sections of the population. There remains a yawning gap between men and women's pay. While many of the old obstacles have been surmounted, new and equally challenging barriers have arisen. This book attempts to understand why the advent of juridical equality has had so little impact on these tenacious manifestations of disadvantage. I argue that this is no coincidence: instead, it is closely related to the inherent limitations of the conceptual structure underpinning the legal system. The lofty ideals of equality, rationality and autonomy in fact obscure the concerns of women and hinder real progress. Moreover, they co-exist with stereotyped assumptions about women which continue to limit the reach of the law, particularly in the welfare system. It is only by refashioning the legal tools available and by moving beyond legal strategies that further progress can be achieved. I argue that the concerns of women need to be brought centre stage, while at the same time being profoundly aware that there is no 'essential' woman, and that the needs and demands of different groups of women may well differ or even conflict. By a synthesis of philosophical analysis, sociological insights and detailed legal examination, I hope to contribute something to women's ongoing struggle.

There are a great many people who have helped in the formulation of the ideas in this book. My thanks are especially due to Paul Davies, Mark Freedland and Keith Ewing, as editors and colleagues, whose contributions have been invaluable. I have also gained enormously from many years of discussions with Bob Hepple and Chris McCrudden. Many others have assisted too, including Marilyn Butler, Nicola Lacey, Jane Hanna, Paul Slack and the students in successive BCL seminars on comparative human rights and international employment law. I owe an especial debt to Sandra Cooper, without whom this work would never have been completed, and to the British Academy, for their assistance in funding my research. Outside of the academic environment have been the numerous women whose life experiences have contributed to my perception of the issues here. I owe especial thanks to Shirley Litt. This book comes too with love and gratitude to my parents, Naomi and Mike Fredman. Finally, and most importantly, I dedicate this work to my children, Jem, Kim and Dan Fredman Stein and to my husband, Alan Stein.

# Contents

# Abbreviations

| | |
|---|---|
| ACAS | Arbitration, Conciliation and Advisory Service |
| APP | Approved Personal Pension |
| CA | Court of Appeal |
| CAC | Central Arbitration Committee |
| CCT | Compulsory Competitive Tendering |
| CRE | Commission for Racial Equality |
| DSO | Direct Services Organisation |
| EAT | Employment Appeal Tribunal |
| EC | European Community |
| EEOC | Equal Employment Opportunities Commission |
| ECJ | European Court of Justice |
| EOC | Equal Opportunities Commission |
| EOR | Equal Opportunities Review |
| EqPA | Equal Pay Act |
| EPCA | Employment Protection (Consolidation) Act |
| ERA | Employment Rights Act |
| EU | European Union |
| GLC | Greater London Council |
| HL | House of Lords |
| ILJ | Industrial Law Journal |
| ILO | International Labour Organisation |
| IRS | Industrial Relations Service |
| IRLR | Industrial Relations Law Review |
| JES | Job Evaluation Study |
| LIFO | Last in first out |
| MOD | Ministry of Defence |
| NAACP | National Association for the Advancement of Coloured People |
| NES | New Earnings Survey |
| NHS | National Health Service |
| QB | Queen's Bench |

| | |
|---|---|
| RRA | Race Relations Act |
| SDA | Sex Discrimination Act |
| SERPS | State Earnings Related Pension |
| SMP | Statutory Maternity Pay |
| TEC | Training Enterprise Council |
| TfW | Training for Work |
| TUC | Trades Union Congress |
| TUPE | Transfer of Undertakings and Protection of Employees Regulations |
| TURER | Trade Union Reform and Employment Rights Act 1993 |
| UK | United Kingdom |
| US | United States |

# Table of Cases

# Table of Statutes

**Statutory Instruments**

# Table of Material

# [1]
# Myths and Messages: Theoretical Perspectives

## INTRODUCTION

Legal systems throughout the centuries have treated women as subordinate to men. It is only in recent times that women have been granted equal rights with men; explicit anti-discrimination statutes are yet more recent. Yet even now, women remain substantially disadvantaged, in the work-place, in political life, and in the home. This chapter explores the perplexing persistence of disadvantage, by unravelling some of the myths and assumptions about women which permeate the legal framework. The critical analysis which emerges will be used as a basis for assessing the substantive law in later chapters.

Before we embark on the substance of the chapter, it is useful to clarify the way in which the topic will be approached. Most importantly, it is necessary to examine the notion of law itself. Law has the aura of truth and justice about it; making us believe that truth and justice are objective realities incorporated into law. The power of law, and the deference accorded it, are centrally related to its ability to appear to be neutral and superior to individuals and society.[1] In fact, however, law is not a disembodied force. It is made by people in power, traditionally monarchs, now politicians, bureaucrats and judges, and is therefore strongly influenced by prevailing economic and political conditions and ideologies. Moreover, new laws are superimposed on old, resulting in a complex amalgam of differing elements. The recognition that law is a product of social forces enables us to pierce the veil of objectivity and neutrality, and assess the extent to which law represents and reinforces the interests of particular groups in society. These interests have always been predominantly male; not only because the vast majority of law-makers have been male, but also because men have dominated over women. One of our chief tasks, therefore, is to unmask the male perspective in law, enabling us to give due weight to that of women.

However, in the excitement of revealing the male perspective in law, it is easy to fall into the trap of simply substituting a different perspective and asserting that this is now objective truth. White middle-class feminists of the 1960s and early 1970s enthusiastically set off down this road, claiming to speak in the 'voice of women'. However, the business of revealing perspectives has its own momentum. As Spelman argues: 'The focus on women "as women" has addressed only one group of women—namely, white middle-class women of Western industrialised countries.'[2] Thus it is important to use the feminist critique of objectivity as a way of recognising that all stances are based on a particular point of view; and to scrutinise critically our own. In this book, then, no claim is made for a unitary female perspective. The nature of subordination differs between women, depending on other factors such as race, class, sexual orientation, marital status, parenthood. Women can be subordinate to other women: women servants and slaves are the paradigm example. Nevertheless, it is argued here that gender is an important and at times determinative feature in patterns of domination, and needs to be studied, not to the exclusion of other features of domination, but in conjunction with them.

As a final preliminary point, it is important to stress that domination usually results from social structures and institutions, rather than individual activities by individual men. Many men find themselves in positions of power or privilege in respect to women, rather than choosing to be there. This is not to say that such men do not benefit from their position, and in some cases take advantage of it. In that sense, they bear responsibility for

---

[1]  See, e.g., C. Smart, *Feminism and the Power of Law* (Routledge, 1989), ch. 1.
[2]  E. V. Spelman, *Inessential Woman* (Women's Press, 1990), p. 3.

women's disadvantage. But this book does not aim to attribute individual moral blame for entrenched social structures of domination.

A useful way of examining the continuing disadvantage of women is to identify the assumptions and stereotypes which have been central to the perpetuation and legitimation of women's legal and social subordination. Such assumptions have roots which stretch deep into the history of ideas, yet continue to influence the legal and social structure of modern society. Indeed, the continuity is startling, given the extent and fundamental nature of change in the political and economic context. Six schools of thought will be examined below:

(a)  patriarchy in the pre-capitalist period;
(b)  social contract and early liberal theories;
(c)  liberal feminism;
(d)  critiques of liberalism;
(e)  modified liberalism and the Welfare State; and
(f)  neo-liberalism.

The influence of each of these schools of thought is still noticeable in the modern legal framework.

a) Patriarchy in the Pre-capitalist Period

It is with Aristotle that we begin, since his depiction of women has been a central influence on later thinkers, and his arguments resonate throughout the ages. Like many later thinkers, Aristotle based much of his argument on biological differences between men and women, translating empirical observations of difference into normative arguments for inferiority. Central to his position was his thesis that females were merely defective or mutilated males.[3] His purported empiricism, however, concealed his normative assumptions, namely, that man was the paradigm and the yard-stick against which all others are measured.[4] From this premise, it appeared logical to argue that difference was deviation and deviation inferiority.

Also highly influential were his arguments about rationality. The human being, in Aristotle's schema, only attained its purpose by exercising reason to make moral choices. Women, however, were depicted as less than rational: the female's faculty of deliberation was 'inconclusive'[5] and lacking authority, suitable only for those who are ruled, rather than those who rule. Hence, he maintained, 'the male is naturally fitter to command than the

---

[3]  Aristotle, *The Generation of Animals*, 737a 28, 775a 15, in J. Barnes (ed.), *The Complete Works of Aristotle* (Oxford University Press, 1982).

[4]  See e.g. *History of Animals* 608 a22, where he argues that the nature of free man is the most rounded off and complete.

[5]  *The Politics of Aristotle* translated by E. Barker (Clarendon Press, 1946), 1260 a7; on the meaning of 'inconclusive' or *akuron* see A. Saxonhouse, 'On Aristotle' in M. L. Shanley and C. Pateman (eds.), *Feminist Interpretations and Political Theory* (Polity Press, 1991), p. 38.

female'.[6] Aristotle used these arguments to develop a set of dualisms: the male is active, the female passive;[7] the male contributes the soul, the female the body;[8] the male is strong, the female weak.[9] The highly effective technique of depicting the world in terms of dichotomies is again one that is constant currency among later thinkers. Its particular power lies in its polarisation of alternatives: the dichotomy obscures the possibility of elements of both poles in the same individual. In reality, of course, soul and body, activity and passivity, and strength and weakness are not mutually exclusive, but often happily co-existing elements of the same individual.

From these assumptions, Aristotle was able to justify the subordination of women both in the family and the State. He depicted the family as the site of at least three sets of power relations: that of master and slave, that of husband and wife, and that of parents and children.[10] In all these relationships, the free male householder was dominant.[11] Equally important was women's exclusion from political life, despite its key importance to Aristotle's view of human perfection. Although 'the *polis* completes and fulfils the nature of man',[12] women's reproductive functions were used as a pretext to deny them political participation. Nor was Aristotle arguing in abstract: his philosophical assertions endorsed the legal status quo in ancient Athens, where women of all classes were treated as mere chattels.[13]

Plato forms an interesting contrast with the thinkers of his time. His insistence that the biological differences between men and women did not preclude equality of intellectual and moral faculties set him apart from almost all contemporary and subsequent philosophers.[14] Most importantly, he argued that women could be Guardians or Philosopher Queens, the elite rulers of the State. It is significant too that for him such egalitarianism could only occur in conjunction with the abolition of the family as we know it, to be replaced by communal wives and children.[15] Indeed, as Okin argues, Plato's argument demonstrates the importance of the family in women's subordination: Plato can only envisage equality in that part of the State in which private property and the family have been abolished.[16] Moreover his egalitarianism was limited to the ruling class. In the rest of his ideal society,

[6] Aristotle, *Politics*, above n. 5, 1259 b1.

[7] Aristotle, *The Generation of Animals*, above n. 3, 729 a29.

[8] *ibid.*, 738 b25.

[9] Aristotle, *Economics* 1343 b6 in J. Barnes (ed.), *The Complete Works of Aristotle* (Oxford University Press, 1982).

[10] Aristotle, *Politics*, above n. 5, 1253 b1.

[11] *ibid.*, 1259 a37, 1259 b10.

[12] Aristotle, *Politics*, above n. 5, 1252 a15.

[13] Saxonhouse 'On Aristotle' in Shanley and Pateman, above n. 5, p. 35; S. M. Okin 'On Plato' in Shanley and Pateman, above n. 5; Spelman, *Inessential Woman*, above n. 2, pp. 14–17.

[14] Plato *The Republic*, translated by R. Waterfield (Oxford University Press, 1993) Book V, pp. 454, 456.

[15] *ibid.*, p. 457.    [16] Okin in Shanley and Pateman, above n.13.

he continued to equate women with property and relegate them to subordinate status.[17]

Equally important and possibly more influential with ordinary people were biblical rationalisations of women's inferiority, particularly the story of the creation of Adam and Eve. The Genesis story of the creation of Eve out of the rib of Adam to be his companion has been used to justify the subordination of women in religious as well as political contexts. Possibly the best-known rendering is that of the seventeenth century patriarchalist, Sir Robert Filmer. 'We know,' he wrote 'that God at the creation gave the sovereignty to the man over the woman, as being the nobler and principal agent in generation.'[18] Similarly, Sir Thomas Aquinas argued for the 'natural inequality and subordination of women to men, who are by nature more reasonable and discerning', a difference clearly 'intended by God, the author of nature as a whole'.[19]

It is interesting to contrast the Adam and Eve story, with the alternative, egalitarian, myth of creation, the story of Lillith. According to the story, it was Lillith not Eve who was the very first woman, and she was created equal to Adam. 'They quarrelled immediately. She said: "I will not lie below you." He said "I will not lie below you, but above you. For you are fit to be below me and I above you." '[20] The fact that Eve rather than Lillith became the accepted first woman shows the extent to which biblical stories reflect and reinforce social domination. This view is fortified by the fact that mythology soon turned Lillith into an evil, vengeful witch.

It is important to note that for the thinkers we have discussed, the portrayal of women as inferior to men was consistent with their general philosophy. Equality was not the primary value; to the contrary, order and hierarchy were the ideal. Thus, argued Aristotle, 'there is a principle of rule and subordination in nature at large'.[21] For Aristotle, then, only a small group of people were in a position to achieve the highest good: the male ruling class. A host of other groups was denied participation in the *polis* and, in varying degrees, denied rationality.[22] For example, Aristotle saw slavery as a beneficial and just system, provided the slave was naturally best fitted to be ruled by his or her master.[23] The non-existence of equality as a value also explains Plato's apparent 'feminism' in opening the doors of the elite class to women. As Spelman argues, 'the equality of some women to some men was inextricably intertwined with an argument for the superiority of

---

[17] *ibid*; Spelman, *Inessential Woman*, above n.2, ch.1.

[18] Sir Robert Filmer, *Patriarcha and Other Writings*, J. P. Sommerville (ed.), (Cambridge University Press, 1991), p. 192; see also p. 225.

[19] Thomas Aquinas, *Summa Theologiae*, T. McDermott (ed.) (Eyre & Spottiswoode, 1989), 1, q.92, art. 1.

[20] Alphabet of Ben Sira 23A-B, cited in Aviva Cantor 'The Lilith question' in S. Heschel (ed.) *On being a Jewish Feminist* (Schokcen Books, 1983), p. 40.

[21] Aristotle, *Politics*, above n. 5, p. 11.

[22] *ibid.*, 1253 b32, 1274 b32 (slaves); 1277 b24 (artisans and labourers).

[23] Aristotle, *Politics*, above n. 5, 1255 a25.

that group of men and women to all other people.'[24] Similarly, Filmer and other patriarchal writers of the early seventeenth century expressly repudiated suggestions of the natural equality of all individuals.[25]

## b) SOCIAL CONTRACT AND LIBERAL THEORISTS

It was the intense political and economic upheaval accompanying the loosening bonds of feudalism that brought notions of equality to the fore. Under feudalism, each person's destiny was dictated by his or her position in the pre-ordained hierarchy. By the seventeenth century feudal hierarchies had largely dissolved, and been replaced by mercantile capitalism, which required individual mobility in pursuit of trade. It was in this context that notions of individual autonomy and equality became dominant. As the liberal thinker John Stuart Mill argued, 'human beings are no longer born to their place in life and chained down by an inexorable bond to the place they are born to, but are free to employ their faculties, and such favourable chances as offer, to achieve the lot which may appear to them most desirable.'[26] Together with economic change, came political transformation. Most importantly, the new notions of individual freedom challenged the absolute authority of the monarch, to be replaced by greater powers for Parliament. In the new social order, 'contract and individual choice supplanted birth and divine designation as crucial factors in social and political analysis.'[27]

Liberalism was the ideology which justified and extolled the emerging capitalist order. Central to this ideology were notions of individualism, autonomy and equality before the law. In the memorable words of Locke: 'Men [are] by Nature all free, equal and independent.'[28] Underlying these notions was the pivotal concept of rationality. The intrinsic value of the individual was predicated on the assumption that all individuals have an equal potentiality for reason.[29]

Politically, this meant that as much as possible should be left to the individual's own choice.[30] This in turn entailed a particular model of the State and legal regulation. Political authority, comprising as it did an important abdication of autonomy, was only legitimate if based on individual consent.[31] Once established, moreover, the State should intrude as little as possible on individual choices, its main function being to act as a neutral umpire between conflicting interests. This notion of the State is at

[24] Spelman, *Inessential Woman*, above n. 2, p. 35.
[25] M. Butler 'On Locke' in Shanley and Pateman, above n. 5, p. 74.
[26] J. S. Mill, *The Subjection of Women* (2nd edn., Longman, 1869), pp. 29–30.
[27] Butler 'On Locke' in Shanley and Pateman, above n. 5, p. 75.
[28] John Locke, *Two Treatises of Government* P. Laslett (ed.), (Cambridge University Press, 1988) 'The Second Treatise', para. 95.
[29] A. M. Jaggar, *Feminist Politics and Human Nature* (Harvester 1983), p. 33.
[30] Mill, above n. 26, p. 31.
[31] Locke, above n. 28, 'Second Treatise', para. 95.

the basis of a dualism central to liberal thought, known as the 'public–private' divide. The 'public' State should intrude as little as possible on the sphere of individual autonomy, or the 'private' sphere. In capitalist terms, the State should not attempt to regulate the 'free' market.

Thus five central characteristics of early liberalism can be discerned, characteristics which have had an important influence on the law. They are

(i)   rationality;
(ii)  autonomy;
(iii) individualism;
(iv)  equality before the law; and
(v)   an abstentionist, neutral State, respecting a divide between public and private and based on consent.[32]

The reflections in the legal structure are striking. For example, rationality is an important attribute of legal subjects; children and the insane are not full legal subjects because of their purported lack of rationality. This was frequently the reason given for denying rights to women. Rights are attached to individuals rather than groups, and individuals are said to be equal before the law. Finally, the law claims neutrality. Like the State, which, after all, produces law, law is seen as an objective umpire between conflicting interests.

On the face of it, then, the new ideology held great promise of liberation for women. Yet both the legal position and the philosophical rationalisation of women's subordination continued in the patriarchal vein. This is epitomised by the law of marriage. Under the common law of coverture, marriage signified the obliteration of a woman's legal personality, giving the husband near-absolute control of both her property and her person. Far from subsiding, coverture grew and strengthened (see further Chapter 2). The recharacterisation of marriage as contractual did nothing to displace the reality of that subordination. Politically, despite the increased participation of ordinary citizens in political life, women's exclusion remained complete. Indeed, women's life chances were as fully determined by their status as those of women in feudal times. And in political theory, the depiction of women bore closer resemblance to Aristotle's ideas than to liberal assumptions. Locke, like Aristotle, set out to consider a 'Master of a Family with all these subordinate Relations of Wife, Children, Servants and Slaves'.[33] As between husband and wife, he argued, it 'being necessary that . . . the Rule, should be placed somewhere, it naturally falls to the man's share, as the abler and the stronger'.[34] His appeal to nature was all the more striking in light of his repeated assertions that all men are naturally free and equal.

---

[32] See the helpful summary in Jaggar, above n. 29, pp. 28–35.
[33] Locke, above n. 28, 'Second Treatise' 86.
[34] *ibid.* 82; and see 'First Treatise' 47, 48.

There was some small advance over the earlier theorists, in that Locke placed express limits on the husband's power.[35] However, the structure of domination remained intact.

Locke's views on women are surprising not only because they contradict his proclamations of freedom and equality for all. They also seem to contradict his apparent rejection of patriarchy. Indeed, the first of his two Treatises is devoted to refuting Filmer's patriarchal arguments. However, on closer examination, it becomes clear that the debate over patriarchy was not about the power of men over women, but about justifications for absolute monarchy. Indeed, it was only because Filmer chose to justify monarchical power by extrapolating from paternal power, that patriarchy became a focus for debate. Locke, for his part, opposed patriarchal arguments in the political sphere. But he avoided the logical consequences of this opposition by deftly separating the family from political life. This meant that, whereas political power required justification, power within the family did not.[36] In addition, he gave 'conjugal society' a measure of legitimacy on his own terms by stating that it was made by a voluntary compact between husband and wife.[37]

Rousseau was more explicit than Locke in his depiction of the subordination of women, and the parallels with Aristotle are even closer. Like Aristotle, Rousseau purported to argue empirically from the respective roles of each of the sexes in copulation. 'One ought to be active and strong, the other passive and weak. One must necessarily will and be able; it suffices that the other put up little resistance. Once this principle is established, it follows that woman is made specially to please man.'[38] How then, did he reconcile his views on women with his lofty proclamations of freedom and equality? The answer was simple: he asserted that women did not have the intrinsic rationality necessary to count as individuals.[39] Whereas men were endowed with reason, women had only modesty.[40] The subordination of women within the family was justified by two further assertions. First, women were credited with a rampant sexuality, which was not sufficiently controlled by their modesty.[41] Civil order therefore depended on the right of the husband over the wife[42] and the confinement of women in a separate sphere.[43] Secondly, Rousseau was deeply concerned with overcoming the

---

[35] Locke, above n. 28, 'Second Treatise' ch. VII 78. At first sight, Locke appears to be moving towards equality, for he argues in relation to parental rights that the mother has equal power over the children as does the father. However, it soon becomes clear that this is intended to refute Filmer's attempt to justify absolute monarchy on the basis of paternal power, rather than to challenge the power structure within the family.

[36] C. Pateman, *The Sexual Contract* (Polity Press, 1988), p. 21.

[37] Locke, above n. 28, 'Second Treatise' 78.

[38] J.-J. Rousseau, *Emile* translated by A. Bloom (Penguin, 1991), p. 358. On Rousseau, see generally L. Lange 'On Rousseau' in Shanley and Pateman, above n. 5, ch. 5.

[39] Pateman, *The Sexual Contract*, above n. 36, pp. 52, 90.

[40] Rousseau, *Emile*, above n. 38, p. 359.

[41] Pateman, *The Sexual Contract*, above n. 36, p. 97.     [42] *ibid.*, pp. 53–4.

[43] Lange in Shanley and Pateman, above n. 38, p. 102–3.

uncertainty of paternity. This entailed strict subordination of women to their husbands, the exclusion of women from political life and the requirement that they live a domestic and retired life.[44]

It should be noted that women were not the only group excluded by liberals from full political participation. Locke argued that those who did not own property had no opportunity to develop their powers of reason;[45] this justified restricting full civil rights to property owners. Nor did he argue for a comprehensive notion of equality.[46] His equality of 'every Man . . . to his natural Freedom, without being subjected to the Will or Authority of any other Man' permitted other kinds of inequalities, including those of birth and merit.[47] Moreover, his theory of equality did not entail democracy; implicit consent to government was assumed unless an individual emigrated or rebelled. Rousseau's commitment to democracy was more thorough-going than that of Locke,[48] and his notion of equality more far-reaching.[49] Nevertheless, like Locke, his equality was not 'that the degrees of power and riches are to be absolutely identical for everybody; but that, power shall never be exercised by virtue of rank and law, and that . . . no citizen should ever be wealthy enough to buy another, and none poor enough to be forced to sell himself.'[50]

## c) First Wave or Liberal Feminism

Despite these limitations, the rhetoric of liberalism signalled a radical philosophy, with the potential to embrace the highest ideals of humanity. It was this which turned liberalism into a crucial trigger for change. Once notions of freedom and equality of all individuals became legitimate currency, feminists gained the necessary vocabulary to argue for women's emancipation. 'As the new bourgeois man held up the torch against absolutist tyranny and argued for freedom and equality, the new bourgeois woman wondered why she was being left out.'[51] In particular, the inconsistencies in the liberal position could be exposed.[52] Thus Mary Astell, as early as 1700, could ask: 'If all men are born free, why are women born slaves? If absolute sovereignty be not necessary in a state, how comes it to be so in a family?'[53] Nearly a century later, Mary Wollstonecraft took on the liberal

---

[44] *ibid.*, p. 106.

[45] Locke, *An Essay Concerning Human Understanding*, B IV, ch. XX, section 2 (Clarendon Press, 1975).

[46] Locke, above n. 28, 'Second Treatise' 54.     [47] *ibid.*

[48] G. D. H. Cole 'Introduction' to Jean-Jacques Rousseau, *The Social Contract and Discourses* translated by G. D. H. Cole (Dent, 1986) p. xxi.

[49] Rousseau, 'A Discourse on the Origin of Inequality' in *The Social Contract and Discourses* p. 117; Rousseau, 'The Social Contract' in *The Social Contract and Discourses* p. 199 and see introduction to the above, p. xxi.

[50] Rousseau 'The Social Contract', above n. 49, p. 225.

[51] J. Mitchell 'Women and Equality' in Mitchell and Oakley, *The Rights and Wrongs of Women* (Penguin, 1976), p. 387.

[52] C. Smart, *Feminism and the Power of Law*, above n. 1, p. 140.

[53] M. Astell, 'Reflections upon Marriage', in Astell, M. and Hill, B. *The First English Feminist* (Gower, 1986).

theorists, particularly Rousseau, on their own ground. Wollstonecraft accepted the basic liberal tenet that human beings' pre-eminence consisted in reason.[54] But she refused to accept the liberal assertion that women lacked rationality, arguing instead for internal consistency within liberalism. 'The nature of reason must be the same in all,' she maintained.[55] Women appeared irrational only because they were socialised into such behaviour. Indeed, one of Wollstonecraft's major contributions was her recognition that the portrayal of women as 'naturally' passive, weak or frivolous was no more than an ideological construct, which not only justified female subordination but maintained and reinforced it.

The need for internal consistency within liberalism finally reached the heartland of liberal thinking with the eloquent advocacy of liberal feminist views by John Stuart Mill. Mill recognised that women's subjection had outlasted other forms of unjust domination[56] and that, apart from royalty, only women were still ordained a status by law at birth. He made at least three fundamental contributions to the debate. First, he recognised the contradiction between proclamations of equality on the one hand and the reality of women's subjection on the other. 'The disabilities . . . to which women are subject from the mere fact of their birth, are the solitary examples of the kind in modern legislation.'[57] His second major contribution was his perception of the central importance of marriage in perpetuating women's subordination. Most importantly, he depicted marriage as 'the only legal bondage known to our law'.[58] A married woman 'vows a lifelong obedience to [her husband] at the altar and is held to it all through her life by the law . . . She can acquire no property but for him; the instant it becomes hers, even if by inheritance, it becomes *ipso facto* his. In this respect, the common law of England is worse than that of slaves in the laws of many countries.'[59] Indeed he argued, in some respects, a wife was in a worse position than a female slave; since even a slave can refuse to have intercourse with her master, a right denied to a wife.[60] Moreover, only the husband had any legal rights over their children. This was particularly problematic, since the family was the primary source of education in moral values. 'The family is a school of despotism . . . the family, properly constituted, would be the real school of the virtues of freedom.'[61] Thirdly, Mill was able to make concrete proposals aimed at the achievement of equality for women. At the centre of his reform programme was the call for equality of married persons before the law. From this, other central rights would follow, including property ownership, equal suffrage, and open competition for occupations. In these respects, Mill was far ahead of his contemporaries.

---

[54] M. Wollstonecraft, *Vindication of the Rights of Women* (Penguin Classics, 1983), p. 91.
[55] *ibid.*, p. 142.     [56] Mill, above n. 26, p. 20.
[57] Mill, above n. 26, p. 35.     [58] *ibid.*, p. 157.
[59] *ibid.*, p. 55.     [60] *ibid.*, p. 58.     [61] *ibid.*, p. 81.

However, Mill's vision remained in some important respects circumscribed by the inherent limitations of the school of liberalism to which he belonged. Most importantly, his concept of equality was restricted to formal legal equality, with no real recognition of the realities of social power. Thus, he argued, even under conditions of legal equality, 'the common arrangement, by which the man earns the income and the wife superintends the domestic expenditure, seems to me in general the most suitable division of labour.'[62] In this respect, Mill seriously underestimated the importance of access to independent income in the maintenance of true equality for women, both in the family and in society. For him, the power of earning was sufficient; as long as this possibility remained open to a wife, it was not necessary that she made use of it. Resorting to the old liberal notion of choice, he argued that 'when a woman marries, it may in general be understood that she makes choice of the management of the household and the bringing up of a family as the first call upon her exertions . . . and that she renounces, not all other objects and occupations, but all which are not consistent with the requirements of this.'[63] Moreover, he assumed that only wives could properly do the work involved in caring for children and keeping house. Because the possibility of men sharing in domestic work simply did not occur to him, he maintained that a woman who worked outside the home would merely incur a double burden of work, with the result that children and the household would not be properly cared for.

d)  THE LIMITS OF LIBERALISM

The extent of the contribution of liberal feminists to the emancipation of women should not be under-estimated. The slow but consistent movement towards removal of formal legal impediments against women was achieved partly because of the effective harnessing of liberal concepts to the cause of women's emancipation. This approach reached its apotheosis with the extension in 1928 of equal suffrage to women, signifying the admission of women into full civic citizenship. This was potentially an achievement of momentous importance, opening up to women the possibility of political participation and power. However, the fact that this potential has scarcely been realised prompts further and deeper questions. Under such scrutiny, it can be seen that the central concepts of liberalism are inherently limited and incapable of pushing the boundaries of emancipation any further. The critique which follows focuses on the five main characteristics of liberalism set out above:[64]

(i)  rationality, particularly rationality as the pursuit of one's own self-interest;

---

[62] *ibid.*, pp. 87–8.      [63] *ibid.*, p. 89.
[64] For a very valuable discussion, see Jaggar, above n. 29, pp. 39–48.

(ii)   autonomy, or the right to pursue one's own good, free from interference;

(iii)  individualism, in that individuals are prior to society;

(iv)   formal equality before the law, based on the presumption of equal rationality of all individuals;

(v)    the State as a neutral umpire, with State interference on individual autonomy requiring special justification.

Two further issues require scrutiny: first, the liberal feminist reliance on law as an instrument of change; and secondly, the age-old technique of reducing debates to discussion of dichotomies. At least three main dualisms have continually dogged the debate: mind–body; equality–difference; and public–private.

## i) **Rationality**

As we saw above, liberal thinkers saw the potentiality for rationality as the essential attribute setting human beings apart from animals. There are two points of criticism of liberal rationality: first, the notion of rationality as egoism; and secondly, the mind–body dualism.

(1) *Rationality as Egoism*   In tune with the emerging capitalist free market economy, the liberal notion of rationality was closely associated with the pursuit of one's own self-interest or conception of the good.[65] However, the conception of rationality as egoism ignores a central reality of human existence, namely the dependence of young children on their parents,[66] and the dependence of the aged, sick and disabled on others. As Pateman argues, the logical conclusion of pure pursuit of self-interest, as seen for example in Hobbes' work, is that no-one would care for children.[67] It is not an accident that the altruism ignored by this conception of rationality has historically been primarily the function of women. More worrying even has been the equation of caring functions with emotionality and therefore irrationality, thus depriving women of the key characteristic necessary for full humanity.

(2) *The Mind–Body Dualism*   The notion that the body is separable from and inferior to the mind is not solely a liberal conception; we have seen its operation as far back as Aristotle. It was, however, reiterated and strengthened by liberal reliance on the Cartesian assumption that the mind is separable from the body.[68] Its problems are epitomised by Descartes' well-known aphorism: 'I think, therefore I am.' The idea that human existence is founded entirely on rational capacities ignores the crucial role of repro-

---

[65] Jaggar, above n. 29, p. 33.      [66] *ibid.*, p. 45.
[67] Pateman, *The Sexual Contract*, above n. 36, p. 49.
[68] Jaggar, above n. 29, p. 40; Smart, above n. 1, pp. 90–1.

duction and bodily needs. Again, it is no accident that these are primarily the function of women. The aphorism is also essentially class-based: had the working classes not laboured to produce his food and clothing, there is little doubt that Descartes' existence would have been in jeopardy.

The problems of the mind–body dualism are deepened by the consistent equation of women with body and men with mind. Clearly the major difference between men and women is biological, namely their reproductive capacities. By associating women with the body and portraying body as inferior to mind, reproduction is devalued or ignored, and women by definition are considered irrational. A further twist is seen in the reflection of this dualism in law. As we have seen, earlier denials of rights to women were in part predicated on the assumption of incapacity and irrationality. However, even with the removal of such assumptions, the denigration of the body and the assumed irrationality of women continue to influence law. This is particularly true in the context of a rape trial, as Smart so tellingly demonstrates.[69] Women are portrayed as inescapably irrational: 'no' may well be a woman's way of saying 'yes'. As recently as 1990, a judge, in his summing up to a jury in a rape trial, was reported as saying 'When a woman says no, and the gentlemen of the jury will understand this, she doesn't always mean it.'[70] Since absence of consent is the key to the definition of rape, such formulations are crucial in rape trials. Moreover, women's bodies, being irrational, are considered as potentially unruly and in need of legal regulation. We have already seen that Rousseau depicted women in terms of a rampant sexuality which required strict regulation. Similar assumptions appear repeatedly in legal regulation. For example, the Contagious Diseases Acts of 1864 and 1866 addressed the problem of the spread of venereal disease by intrusive and punitive measures against women, leaving men untouched.[71] Similarly, concern with reproductive hazards has resulted in laws excluding women from the work-place rather than regulating the source of the hazard. Finally, new technology enabling surrogate motherhood has also brought allegations that the biological mother must be unstable and irrational to have entered into a surrogacy agreement, whereas the biological father's actions remain above comment.[72]

## ii) **Autonomy and Choice**

The notion of autonomy is closely related to the liberal concept of rationality. Since each individual is best placed to make her or his own choices of life-style, there should be as little as possible intrusion on the freedom to do so. Yet this conception over-estimates the range of choices genuinely open

[69] Smart, above n. 1, pp. 34–49.
[70] The *Daily Express*, 12 April 1990; for further similar examples, see Smart, above n. 1, p. 35.
[71] M. L. Shanley, *Feminism, Marriage and the Law in Victorian England, 1850–1895* (Tauris, 1989), pp. 82–6; Smart, above n. 1, p. 94.   [72] *ibid.*, p. 103.

to individuals. As was mentioned above, Mill argued that even in conditions of legal equality, married women would still make the 'choice' to give
whole-hearted priority to child-care and domestic work. Marxists have
pointed out that such freedom takes no account of the constraints on
people dictated by the economic circumstances. As Mitchell has argued, for
the ordinary worker, the 'freedom to work is little more than the freedom
not to go hungry'.[73] From the feminist perspective, these constraints relate
particularly to women's role in child-care and domestic work. As will be
seen forcefully in Chapter 3, women's ability to compete in the labour
market has been severely restricted by these factors; indeed, this has been
a major reason for their continued disadvantage.

Legally, the concepts of autonomy and choice, as well as their limitations,
are epitomised in the idea of contract. As we saw above, contract became
a pervasive legal instrument with the rise of mercantile capitalism and the
emerging 'free market' economy. It was also a central symbol in political
theory: the subjection of individual autonomy to the State could only be
justified by conjuring up the idea of a 'social contract' whereby individuals
agreed to limit their freedom. In theory, at least, contract stands for freedom and choice: a party to a contract is only bound by its terms if the
contract was freely entered into. However, as with the general concept of
autonomy, contract law rarely takes into account social and economic
pressures, assuming instead that the fact of entry into a contract is sufficient
evidence of free choice. This has frequently been demonstrated in relation
to the contract of employment;[74] the economic inequality of bargaining
power as between worker and employer makes a mockery of the purported
equality of contract. The gulf between the legal characterisation and the
social reality is even greater in respect of the marriage contract.[75] It is
striking that liberal thinkers such as Locke could assert the contractual
nature of marriage while at the same time reiterating the dominion of
husband over wife. As Pateman points out, there are two central contradictions to the notion of marriage as a contract. First, the terms are not open
to negotiation but are dictated by the State.[76] Secondly, and even more
surprisingly, one of the parties to the marriage contract, the woman, was
presumed to lack the capacity to contract in all other contexts.[77]

### iii) **Individualism**

For liberals, the individual is the central and primary unit and society is no
more than a conglomerate of individuals. There are several levels of criticism of this conception. First, as Jaggar argues, such a view ignores the way

---

[73] J. Mitchell 'Women and Equality' in Mitchell and Oakley (eds.), *The Rights and Wrongs
of Women* (Penguin, 1976), p. 384.

[74] See for example Engels 'The Origin of the Family and Private Property' in Marx and
Engels *Selected Works* (Lawrence and Wishart, 1968), p. 500.

[75] Engels, above n. 74, pp. 500–1, p. 507.

[76] Pateman, *The Sexual Contract*, above n. 36, p. 166.      [77] *ibid.*, pp. 167–8.

in which individual desires and interests are shaped by the society in which they live.[78] We have seen the importance of such a recognition in the work of Wollstonecraft and Mill, who perceived that much of women's supposed irrationality was due to socialisation. Secondly, it ignores the mutuality of individual needs, and their reliance on community for survival and psychological and social growth. Most importantly, individualism conceals the central role of the family, and thus obscures men's domination of women within the family.[79] Indeed, the family becomes an individual by equation with the 'head of household'.[80] Usefully for capitalism, women can 'disappear' into the family when their work is not needed in the workforce. Individualism is particularly important in legal terms, since it is to the individual that legal rights generally attach. This makes it difficult for the law to conceptualise and address group wrongs. As will be seen in later chapters, even rights not to be discriminated against and rights to equal pay attach to the individual, despite the fact that discrimination is due to the individual's *status* as a woman, or her group membership.

## iv) **Equality**

The critique of the concept of equality will be developed and expanded throughout this book. Two major points should be made at this point. First, the concept of formal equality utilised by liberalism is limited to the removal of formal legal impediments against women. While this is clearly a necessary condition for change, it is far from sufficient, since it ignores the reality of social power structures. Indeed, by pretending that structures of domination do not exist, formal equality both perpetuates and legitimates them. Secondly, as MacKinnon has forcefully argued, the use of a notion of equality as a mechanism for change immediately raises the question 'Equal to what?' and the answer, inevitably, is 'equal to a man'.[81] The Aristotelean formula, that likes should be treated alike, begs the central question—when are two people sufficiently similar to qualify for equal treatment? The problem with relying in this way on a male norm is that the existing values in a male-dominated world are accepted without challenge, and women are required to compete on their terms. For example, women with child-care obligations are simply unable to conform to working patterns which assume that the family obligations of the worker are dealt with outside of the market.[82] The most graphic example is drawn from pregnancy: early caselaw in both the UK and US refused to hold that detrimental treatment on grounds of pregnancy was unlawful sex discrimination because there were no pregnant male comparators. (See further Chapter 5.)

---

[78] Jaggar, above n. 29, p. 42.
[79] Engels, above n. 74, p. 501.
[80] J. Rawls, *A Theory of Justice* (Oxford University Press, 1972).
[81] C. MacKinnon, *Feminism Unmodified* (Harvard University Press, 1987), p. 33.
[82] S. Fredman 'European Equality Law: a Critique' [1992] ILJ 119.

It is here that the difference–equality dualism, like a two-headed monster, raises its ugly heads. If the notion of equality is rejected because of its presumption of a male norm of comparison, perhaps one should argue that women should be treated differently from men? The ramifications of this dualism are explored in detail later. At this stage, two main points should be made. First, differential treatment of women has its own dangers, most importantly, in perpetuating stereotypical assumptions about women and therefore entrenching subordination. For example, in a well-known American case, women were prevented from working as prison guards in a high risk prison because it was assumed that they were vulnerable to rape.[83] Secondly, and centrally, the assumption that equality and difference are the only two alternatives is misleading and counter-productive. Many feminist thinkers have found themselves hopelessly trapped in its dilemmas. The dualism needs to be abandoned, and instead the underlying power structures need to be challenged and reformed.[84]

## v) **The State**

The notion of the State as a non-interventionist neutral umpire is the final central characteristic of the liberal paradigm. It is closely related to the legal paradigm, which portrays the law as neutral and objective, and finds its most graphic illustration in the well-worn arguments about a public–private divide. There are two major points of criticism. First, the characterisation of the State as non-interventionist and neutral is difficult to square with reality even in the nineteenth century: witness intrusive legislation such as the Contagious Person's Acts and the common law of coverture in marriage. Secondly, the legal claims to neutrality and objectivity disguise the latent perspectives and biases within law. Law is not a disembodied, impersonal force. It is made by legislators and judges and therefore reflects the current balance of power within society.

Possibly the most controversial spin-off of the notion of State neutrality has been the depiction of society in terms of a division between the public and the private. A chief source of difficulty lies in the ambiguity of the terms themselves. In liberal and free market discourse, the public–private divide signifies the autonomy of individuals and the market from State regulation. Thus the public is the State, while the private is civil society or the marketplace. At the same time, the public–private divide has been used to signify the difference between the family (the private sphere) and social relations outside of the family (the public sphere) which includes both political life and the market or workplace. On this second rendering, women are held to belong only in the private sphere, having no part in political or economic life. Thus what functions as the private for men is characterised as the

---

[83] *Dothard* v. *Rawlinson* 433 US 321 (1977).
[84] MacKinnon, *Feminism Unmodified*, above n. 81, pp. 32–45; D. Rhode, *Justice and Gender* (Harvard University Press, 1989).

public for women.[85] This conceptual ambiguity has led to dangerous con-
fusion, particularly in legal debates. For example, it has been argued that
because the family is private (the second meaning), it is outside the realm
of legal regulation by the State (the first meaning). This rendering (which
also confuses the normative and the descriptive) has been selectively used
to justify refusal to 'interfere' in family relations. For example, it was argued
until quite recently that because the law has no place in family relationships,
it should not intervene to prevent domestic violence against wives. Yet by
refusing to intervene, the law actually reinforces and legitimates the power
of husbands over wives. Such a rendering also conceals the very real and
extensive nature of regulation of the family, in areas such as the old
common law of coverture.[86]

Apart from the ambiguity of its terms, the notion of a divide between the
public and the private in the second sense has had serious substantive
implications in the debate about the role of women at law and in society,
which will be raised again and again in later chapters. Three major pointers
to the later discussion may be set out here. First, and most importantly, the
implicit assumption is that the private sphere is inferior to the public
sphere. This renders invisible the value and significance of reproductive
labour and ignores the role of the family as one of the chief means of
educating and socialising future citizens.[87] Secondly, it is based on the false
premise that the public is fully insulated from the private. The idea that the
family (the private sphere) is separate from work merely hides the family
from the market. This means that working patterns in the market make no
concessions to family needs, the assumption being that child-care, domestic
work and care of the elderly are taken care of in the private sphere. Yet
participation in work outside of the home has come to be essential both for
social status and power, and for economic reasons. The relegation of family
responsibilities to a private sphere makes it particularly difficult for women
to participate in this way. Finally, it is only from a middle-class perspective
that the divide appears in any sense historically accurate. Working-class
women have always participated in the paid labour force. The public–
private divide was, in their case, used in order to put moral pressure on
them, and to blame them for neglect of their children.[88] By contrast, for
middle-class women, until well into the 1960s, confinement to the private
sphere was a reality, leading to isolation, ill-health, passivity, frustration and
lack of education.[89]

[85] M. O'Brien, *The Politics of Reproduction* (Routledge, 1981), pp. 163, 178; Pateman, above
n. 36, p. 11.

[86] Okin, *Justice, Gender and the Family*, (Basic Books, 1989), pp. 128–30.

[87] *ibid.*, ch. 2.

[88] J. Lewis, *Women in England 1870–1950: Sexual Divisions and Social Change* (Wheatsheaf,
1984) chs. 2 and 4.

[89] M. Wollstonecraft, *Vindication of the Rights of Women* (1792) p. 143, and see generally B.
Friedan, *The Feminine Mystique* (Penguin, 1963).

e) THE WELFARE STATE AND MODIFIED LIBERALISM

The key tenet of the Welfare State is the recognition of the role of the State in mitigating the inequalities which would otherwise arise from the operation of the free market and representative democracy. 'It does this by regulating private institutions, by the direct provision of benefits and services, and by limited economic and social planning.'[90] Whereas formal equality before the law corresponds roughly to early liberal and social contract theories, the Welfare State generated two further, and different, kinds of law, namely (a) social welfare law; and (b) anti-discrimination law. Laws of this sort took shape in the late nineteenth and early twentieth centuries; and the Welfare State became the dominant mode after the Second World War. There is a diversity of theories underpinning the Welfare State, but for our purposes, it is worth concentrating on two types of theory. I shall call the first 'modified liberalism' and concentrate on three theorists, Dworkin, Rawls and Raz, who have had a crucial impact on both law and jurisprudence. The second group of principles has its roots in democratic socialism. While distancing themselves from Marxism, theorists from this tradition consciously refute the basic tenets of liberalism. I shall concentrate here on the sociologist T.H. Marshall, and Sir William Beveridge, who was one of the chief architects of the modern Welfare State.

i) **Modified Liberalism**

Modern liberals, while retaining the core concepts of early liberalism, have moved a long way towards accommodating the critiques identified above. Most importantly, they no longer argue for an abstentionist State, but regard the State as having a legitimate role in intervening in society to redistribute resources, opportunities and power to those who are disadvantaged. Correspondingly, significant progress has been made in the legal structures relating to women, most notably through anti-discrimination statutes. However, as will be argued below, the theories remain flawed in some key areas. Since similar flaws appear in the legal framework, we are able to begin to formulate an explanation for the persistence of gender disadvantage.

(1) *Dworkin*   One of the foremost proponents of modified liberalism is Ronald Dworkin. Dworkin's first major premise (and he argues that this is a substantive, not a neutral, moral position) is that the State should treat all individuals as entitled to equal concern and respect. Secondly, he asserts, individuals differ in their conception of the good life. The combination of these two principles yields a distinctively liberal position: the State must not prefer one conception to any other, for if it did, it would not be treating

---

[90] R. Cranston, *Legal Foundations of the Welfare State* (Weidenfeld, 1985), p. 2.

citizens as equals. Like the early liberals, Dworkin sees the market as a useful means of ensuring that those with expensive preferences are not able to use up more than their fair share of resources. At the same time, however, he recognises that wide disparities due to unequal talent, inheritance, education, and similar factors are unjust. 'It is obviously obnoxious to the liberal conception . . . that someone should have more of what the community as a whole has to distribute because he or his father (sic) had superior skill or luck.'[91] Thus it is legitimate for the State to intervene, both to redistribute directly, and to prevent discriminatory acts by private individuals against each other.

It can be seen from this very brief description that Dworkin's theory retains some central characteristics of early liberalism, albeit in modified form. The liberal conception of *rationality* is reflected in his belief that a person's own conception of the good is of fundamental value. *Autonomy* is endorsed by the principle of respect by the State for each such conception. *Equality* reappears, although in the far more sophisticated version of equal treatment.[92] Dworkin's theory is *individualistic* to the extent that it is each *individual's* conception of the good that matters; and his State is *neutral* in that it must not prefer any one conception to any other.

At the same time, Dworkin has carefully modified his theory to take account of many of the criticisms identified above. First, he disputes the idea that his version of rationality is necessarily self-interested; it is perfectly possible for an individual's conception of the good to involve work for the community.[93] Secondly, his emphasis on personal autonomy takes into account material constraints on the exercise of choice; hence the role of the State in facilitating choice. Thirdly, he accepts that people's opinions about their lives are not self-generated but are influenced by their social and economic context. He nevertheless defends liberalism by arguing that the content of preferences is irrelevant to fairness in distribution, so that eccentric and non-conformist preferences are entitled to equal respect.[94] So far as his individualism is concerned, he dismisses as nonsense the idea that liberals posit a world of autonomous individuals, arguing that most liberals accept that people are normally interested in each others' fates and certainly are able to share values sufficiently to sustain social institutions.[95] Again, his sophisticated conception of equality goes beyond formal equality in recognising that treatment as equals does not imply that each individual is treated equally in all contexts. Finally, of course, his State is permitted limited intervention.

Modified in this way, Dworkin's theory is attractive in some respects. Most importantly, his principle of respect by the State for each individual's

---

[91] R. Dworkin 'Liberalism' in *A Matter of Principle* (Clarendon Press, 1985), p. 195.
[92] This concept is dealt with more comprehensively in chapters 5 to 9.
[93] Dworkin 'Liberalism', above n. 91, p. 203.    [94] *ibid.*, p. 204.
[95] R. Dworkin, *Law's Empire* (Fontana Press, 1986), p. 440 n. 19.

version of the good life yields a valuable principle of tolerance, protecting against discrimination and persecution against people because, for example, of their sexual orientation or religion. Possibly his most important contribution in the context of women is his use of the principle of personal autonomy to support freedom of choice in abortion. Dworkin argues persuasively that women have a right to procreative autonomy, a right which derives from the fundamental belief in individual human dignity. 'People have the moral right—and the moral responsibility—to confront the most fundamental questions about the meaning and value of their own lives for themselves, answering to their own consciences and convictions.'[96] Central to this argument is his rejection of the view that the foetus is a constitutional person with rights of its own, an argument which almost inevitably leads to anti-abortion laws. Instead, he locates the abortion debate in the universal belief in the sanctity of human life. As such, the degree of respect due to a growing foetus is a question of personal moral (and even religious) choice by the pregnant woman, a choice which States have no legitimate right to proscribe. His version of personal autonomy in this context is a strong one, proscribing not just laws against abortion but also restrictions which in practice make it impossible for a woman to have an abortion or which deter women who would otherwise have made the moral choice in favour of abortion.[97] Indeed, he usefully suggests that a failure to finance abortion in a context of State provision for medical care during pregnancy might well contravene the right to procreative autonomy.[98]

However, outside of the abortion issue, Dworkin's theory remains fundamentally problematic. This is because his notions of rationality, autonomy and individualism fail to recognise, and therefore to value, relations of dependence and care, the paradigm example being that of mother and child. Despite the modifications referred to above, Dworkin still takes the individual and his or her conception of the good life as his central value, attracting protection from the State. This simply fails to capture a relationship whereby one person's activities are dictated by another's needs for care, particularly if the dependant could not otherwise survive. None of Dworkin's responses to criticism meet this point: for example, a mother whose activities are responses to a baby's needs is not choosing a version of the good life which includes caring for babies, since her response is dictated by those needs. Nor is this a constraint on choice; choice simply does not feature. It is indicative of his lack of appreciation of this issue that Dworkin remarks (in a footnote) that parents can choose whether to have children.[99] In an ideal world of perfect contraception, education and rationality, this might possibly be true, but any woman who has anxiously awaited her next period knows the fallacy of this point.

---

[96] R. Dworkin, *Life's Dominion* (Harpes Collins, 1993), p. 166.

[97] Dworkin, *Life's Dominion*, above n. 96, p. 173.   [98] *ibid.*, p. 176.

[99] Dworkin, *Law's Empire*, above n. 95, p. 437, n. 20.

The above analysis may appear abstract or extreme. However, it is fully borne out by Dworkin's description of the family. Dworkin uses the family as one of the models of association from which he develops his theory of legitimacy of political obligation. Obligations arise in such associations, he argues, because of a sense of reciprocity. In other words, each member has obligations to the group even if he or she did not choose to belong, but loses those obligations if others in the group do not extend to that member the benefits of belonging.[100] This is a strange sort of family indeed. In reality, mothers do not care for their children because they expect reciprocity; they do it because the child is dependent on them.[101] Dworkin's denial of the very existence of parent–child relationships is epitomised by the fact that he refers to familial obligations as fraternal,[102] and sums up the essence of such obligation as follows: 'I have special responsibilities to my brother by virtue of our brotherhood, but these are sensitive to the degree to which he accepts such responsibilities toward me.'[103] It is true that at another point in the text, in the context of political fraternity, he makes a gesture of apology for the fact that the word 'fraternity' is 'etymologically masculine' and offers to include sorority.[104] Nevertheless, his concept of a family fails entirely to include relations of dependence, and therefore wholly negates what is often a core role of mothers.

Thus Dworkin's schema renders invisible the role of primary carer for a child, a role which has always been and continues to be performed predominantly by mothers. It will be argued throughout this book that the undervaluing or ignoring of child-care is a key to women's continuing disadvantage. Caring responses to dependence should be considered as primary values in themselves, rather than squeezed into a paradigm of self-interest.

(2) *Rawls*   Possibly the most influential of modern liberal works is John Rawls' *Theory of Justice*. Rawls' central project is to define principles of social justice. He does this by positing his well-known 'original position'. In this position, free and rational persons concerned to further their own interests are placed behind an imaginary 'veil of ignorance' which hides their future position in society. This means that they are ignorant of their class position, social status and their natural assets and abilities, such as strength and intelligence. 'Since all are similarly situated and no one is able to design principles to favour his particular condition, the principles of justice are the result of a fair agreement or bargain.'[105] The original position

---

[100] *ibid.*, p. 196.

[101] Similarly, Dworkin argues that, while family relationships can be hierarchical, no-one's life may be more important that any one else's: *Law's Empire*, above n. 95, p. 200. Yet a parent might well choose to sacrifice his or her own life for that of a child.

[102] Dworkin, *Law's Empire*, above n. 95, p. 198, p. 437 n. 20.

[103] *ibid.*, p. 198.      [104] *ibid.*, p. 437 n. 13.

[105] Rawls, *A Theory of Justice*, above n. 80, p. 12.

is therefore set up so that, although each individual is motivated by self-interest, he or she lacks the necessary information to choose principles of justice which will advance his or her own interests at the expense of another. After all, thinks the rational person behind the veil of ignorance, it could be me who is disadvantaged. The result is that rational persons behind the veil of ignorance will judge economic and social inequalities in terms of the expectations of the least advantaged social group.[106]

In the original position, thus constructed, rational individuals would choose two central principles. First, each person has an equal right to the most extensive total system of equal basic liberties compatible with a system of liberty for all. Secondly, social and economic inequalities are to be arranged so that they are to the greatest benefit of the least advantaged and attached to offices and positions open to all under conditions of fair equality of opportunity.[107] The second principle, therefore, permits some inequalities; but excludes the utilitarian possibility that some should have less in order that others prosper.[108]

This brief description gives only the bare bones of a sophisticated and attractive theory. As with Dworkin, the key elements of liberalism can be discerned in a carefully developed form. Liberal *rationality* is central to the structuring of the original position. Rawls' original individuals are rational in that they will make choices of principles necessary to further their own interests.[109] However, the implications of their egoism are fundamentally altered by their ignorance as to class and natural abilities. Although the original individuals are mutually disinterested in that they do not take an interest in one another's interests,[110] they are forced by the risk of landing up in the most disadvantaged positions to imagine everyone's interests and to cater for them. Rawls' original position caters too for *autonomy*, in that the veil of ignorance permits individuals to make decisions *autonomously*, following the Kantian definition of autonomy as meaning that 'a person's principles of action are chosen as the most adequate possible expression of his nature as a free and equal rational being'.[111] Like his liberal predecessors he stresses the importance of choice by using contract terminology: the principles of justice are binding because they are principles which would be freely chosen by autonomous agents in the original position. At the same time, he considers contract as a symbol of reconciliation of conflicts of interest and social co-operation.[112] Rawls' starting point is clearly *individualistic*, partly because of his concern that each individual should be respected and his opposition to utilitarian claims that some individuals could be sacrificed to the greater good. But the importance of community is clearly central to his work; indeed, the whole project in the *Theory of Justice* is to work out just principles of community life. Finally, his notion of *equality* is complex. He acknowledges that institutions of

---

[106] Rawls, *A Theory of Justice*, above n. 80, p. 44.
[107] Rawls, above n. 80, p. 302.   [108] *ibid.*, pp. 15, 28.   [109] *ibid.*, pp. 11, 13.
[110] *ibid.*, p. 13.   [111] *ibid.*, p. 252.   [112] *ibid.*, p. 16.

society favour certain starting places over others, arguing that such inequalities cannot possibly be justified by an appeal to notions of merit
or desert. It is to these inequalities that principles of justice must be
applied.[113] Yet he condones inequality provided it is to the benefit of the
least well off. Thus his theories are fully compatible with an advanced
welfare state and a legal system which includes welfare and anti-
discrimination legislation.

What then is the implication of his theory for women? It is striking that
nowhere in the *Theory of Justice* is this question expressly addressed.[114]
Indeed, as Okin trenchantly argues,[115] Rawls' theory omits to address the
fact that 'modern liberal society to which the principles of justice are to be
applied is deeply and pervasively gender structured'.[116] This is seen in two
central parts of his theory. The first relates to his depiction of the family.
Like Dworkin and unlike Mill, Rawls wholly disregards the possible role of
the family in reflecting and perpetuating systems of gender disadvantage. In
most contexts, he equates the individual with a head of family.[117] This is
primarily because of his desire to ensure that future generations will be
considered in the course of choosing principles of justice. Similarly, in his
discussion of market systems as the basis for distribution of resources, he
refers interchangeably to the individual and the household.[118] This assumes
that the interests of all members of the family necessarily coincide, thus
ignoring the important effects of imbalance of powers between men and
women in the family. Like Locke, therefore, he is 'trapped into the traditional mode of thinking that life within the family and relations between the
sexes are not properly to be regarded as part of the subject matter of a
theory of social justice.'[119] This is even more disturbing in that he regards
the family as the earliest school of moral development.

The second point of criticism of Rawls' theory goes to the heart of the
conceptual plausibility of the original position itself. This is his assumption
that the fact of being stripped of knowledge of one's own class, intelligence,
wealth and (as an afterthought)[120] gender is sufficient to imbue one with a
real understanding of 'what it must feel like' to be a member of a group
disadvantaged in one or more of these respects. Okin has argued that far
from being an abstraction from all contingencies of human life, the original
position is in fact much closer to an appreciation of human differences.[121]
However, this ignores the fact that each person's perspectives on life are
so profoundly influenced by her or his class, race or gender, that it is

---

[113] *ibid.*, pp. 7, 15.

[114] His fleeting references on pp. 99 and 149 are not further developed.

[115] Okin, *Justice, Gender and the Family*, above n. 86, ch. 5.       [116] *ibid.*, p. 89.

[117] e.g. Rawls, above n. 80, pp. 128, 292.       [118] e.g., *ibid.*, pp. 270–4.

[119] Okin, *Justice, Gender and the Family*, above n. 86, p. 184.

[120] Gender, not included in the *Theory of Justice* in the list of unknown factors, was
mentioned in a later publication: John Rawls 'Fairness to Goodness' (1975) *Philosophical
Review* 84, p. 537.

[121] Okin 'Reason and Feeling' in C. Sunstein (ed.), *Feminism and Political Theory* (University of Chicago Press, 1982), p. 32.

impossible to reach a full understanding of the concerns of those in positions of disadvantage simply by positing a position of ignorance. This can only genuinely be achieved by incorporating members of such groups into the decision-making process.[122]

(2) *Raz*   The version of modified liberalism most sympathetic to the aims of this book is that of Joseph Raz as set out in his book *The Morality of Freedom*.[123] While ultimately reaffirming the liberal emphasis on the core value of personal autonomy, Raz departs radically from the traditional rendering of this conception. Most importantly, he severs the deep-rooted links between personal autonomy and moral individualism. The notion that each individual should be free to pursue her own self-interest as determined solely by herself is roundly rejected. Instead Raz recognises that personal well-being is based as much on collective public values as individual values. Such collective goods are valuable in themselves; they are not simply instrumental in enhancing individual self-interest.[124] Personal autonomy and well-being can only be enhanced within a social context, one which not only provides a range of acceptable options, but also includes the institutions and network of human relationships which are essential to human existence. In his view, it is crucial for the development of normal personal relationships that an individual understands his or her own tastes and goals in ways which relate to others, and which incorporate the mosaic of values inherent in social life.[125] Raz's acknowledgement of the crucial role of personal interaction and collective values enables him to avoid the artificiality of Dworkin's attempt to incorporate altruism into his schema. Indeed, it exposes the falsity of the dualism between egoism and altruism which plagues traditional liberals. The significance of this for our purposes is to facilitate the recognition of the fundamental and intrinsic value of childcare, a value which need not be related to a notion of the pursuit of narrow self-interest, but which instead is shown to be part of the achievement of human well-being.

Raz also departs from traditional liberals in his rejection of the notion that a neutral State is essential for the protection of individual autonomy. The traditional view posits a neutral State as an essential protection against the coercive imposition by the State of a particular set of values on individual citizens. This is based on the assumption that there is no universal or objective 'good' and therefore that individuals should be free to choose any set of values for themselves. Raz, however, is unashamedly 'perfectionist', arguing that the good can be distinguished from the bad, and that the State

---

[122] Lacey 'Theories of Justice and the Welfare State' *Social and Legal Studies* vol. 1 (1992) 323 at p. 338.

[123] J. Raz, *The Morality of Freedom* (Clarendon Press, 1986). The following analysis concentrates exclusively on Raz's theory as represented in this book.

[124] See Raz, above n. 123, pp. 18, 193–206.     [125] *ibid.*, p. 215.

has a positive role in promoting the good. The traditional liberal fear that such a substantive view of morality will inevitably lead to authoritarian imposition by the State of a particular value system is counteracted by his argument that the good is not unitary, but consists in a plurality of sets of values, which may indeed be incompatible or in conflict with each other. This pluralism does not, however, mean that all sets of values are acceptable. Instead, the State is justified in preventing the pursuance of morally bad goals. This preparedness to endorse a substantive view of the good is a useful general basis for the view advanced in this book of the core importance of substantive distributive fairness, rather than formal legal justice.

Equally important is Raz's recognition of the inherent constraints on choice. Personal autonomy, in his view requires the existence of a range of acceptable and realistic options, options which can in fact be pursued by the individual. This in turn necessitates a positive State, whose duties go far beyond refraining from coercion, to ensuring the availability of an adequate range of options.[126] In other words, the rejection of value neutrality is accompanied by a strong vision of the positive role of the State, entailing a rejection of the liberal view that the State is necessarily coercive and unjustifiably restrictive. Instead, freedom for him is robustly positive, rather than negative.

While Raz introduces principles which are valuable in the analysis of women's position, he does not actively use these principles for a feminist purpose. This is left to more explicitly feminist theorists. So far as the legal framework is concerned, modified liberalism is to some extent reflected in the movement away from an abstract endorsement of formal equality before the law and towards a more positive legal duty to treat men and women equally. This receives legal expression in the various anti-discrimination statutes, which require men and women to receive equal pay for equal work and which prohibit direct or indirect discrimination against women. However, as the detailed discussion in later chapters reveals, the limitations of liberalism in almost all its forms are inherent too in anti-discrimination legislation. Most problematic are its strong endorsement of individualism, equality, and neutrality and an overriding deference to market forces.

## ii) Democratic Socialism and the Welfare State

The political development of a Welfare State is not the product of any one unitary political theory, but rather a series of pragmatic responses to modern social problems and based on strands from differing political theories, including liberalism, social democracy and socialism. Although its roots were in the alleviation of the worst excesses of poverty and exploitation

---

[126] *ibid.*, p. 408.

thrown up by the industrial revolution, the idea of the Welfare State soon developed into a much broader concept, based on the essential interaction between individual and community, generating mutual obligations of care and support and a wide sharing of available social goods. These perspectives made it inevitable that the foundation stones of traditional liberalism should be overturned or reshaped. Thus individuals are not depicted as characterised only by their rationality. Although rational choice remains crucial to a full personality, independent value is attributed to other aspects, including physical, psychological and emotional needs and incorporating in an organic fashion both social and individual needs.[127] Nor are individuals depicted as abstract moral agents. Instead individuals are organically bound together in a community, which has a profound influence on their needs, aspirations and opportunities. Also crucial to the development of the ideology of the Welfare State is the recognition that the operation of the capitalist market can undermine civic or juridical citizenship by making it impossible for many citizens, particularly those who find themselves in poverty, to exercise their civic rights to the full or indeed to any extent.[128] This makes a mockery of the liberal ideals of freedom of the individual or equality before the law.

These key insights are most eloquently expressed by T. H. Marshall. Writing in the immediate post-war period, Marshall asserted confidently that 'our modern system is frankly a socialist system' operating within a limited market context.[129] Marshall's pivotal concept was that of citizenship. In contrast with liberal individualism, he believed that citizenship entailed a direct sense of community membership and carried with it both rights against the State and responsibilities to fellow members of the community. Nor was he bound to a formal vision of equality. From 'an appreciation that the formal recognition of an equal capacity for rights was not enough' there developed 'a conception of equality which overstepped these natural limits, the conception of equal social worth, not merely of equal natural rights.'[130] It was this recognition that led to a conception of rights which extended beyond liberal and political rights, to the granting of social rights. Social rights necessarily enlisted the positive contribution of the State, to ensure that citizens enjoyed 'the whole range from a modicum of economic welfare and security to the right to share to the full the social heritage and to live the life of a civilised being according to the prevailing standards'.[131] Education and social services epitomised these rights. Crucially, however, Marshall did not advocate quantitative or economic equal-

---

[127] M. Freeden 'Rights, Needs and Community' in A. Ware and R. Goodin (eds.), *Needs and Welfare* (Sage, 1990), p. 55.

[128] C. Pateman 'The Patriarchal Welfare State' in *The Disorder of Women* (Polity Press, 1989), p. 182.

[129] T. H. Marshall 'Citizenship and Social Class' in T. H. Marshall and T. Bottomore, *Citizenship and Social Class* (Pluto, 1992), p. 7.

[130] *ibid.*, p. 24.    [131] *ibid.*, p. 8.

ity. His crusade was directed only against those inequalities which restrict full civic participation. Once this qualitative inequality had been eliminated, quantitative inequality would lose its sting; even more optimistically, it could be said that what used to be qualitative political differences have become mere quantitative economic ones.[132]

Marshall's approach is, on one level, full of promise for women. The recognition that civil and political rights are illusory without social rights is particularly appropriate for women. Moreover, it inevitably legitimates a positive interventionist State, which is permitted to treat its citizens differently according to their different needs. As embodied in the Welfare State, these principles have clearly been of immense value to women, both as recipients of benefits and services, and as workers within the Welfare State apparatus. The threats to the concepts of social citizenship in the 1980s and 1990s make it important to value these achievements. At the same time, substantive intervention by the State has, in practice, proved highly ambiguous for women. As Lewis points out, 'In practice the basis for claiming [social] rights and the nature of entitlements [are] not universal, but rather differ profoundly for men and for women.'[133] In Marshall's writings, women are conspicuous by their absence. Not only does he date the attainment of civil rights to the eighteenth century and political rights to the nineteenth century, with only a cursory reference to the fact that neither were available to women until much later. In addition, his conception of social rights, while claiming to be universal, is profoundly male. Thus, he argues, 'What matters is that there is a general enrichment of the concrete substance of civilised life, a general reduction of risk and insecurity, an equalisation . . . between the healthy and the sick, the employed and the unemployed, the old and the active, the *bachelor and the father of a large family*.'[134] (my italics) This legitimated the development of a Welfare State which was based on explicitly patriarchal presumptions about the family and women's role in it.

This central ambiguity is exemplified in the Beveridge Report of 1942,[135] which established some of the central principles of welfare law. Beveridge's proposals enshrined the paradigm of a family in which the wife was primarily occupied in child-care and domestic work, and the husband was the main breadwinner. His vision of women's role had a positive and a negative face. On the positive side, he insisted that women's unpaid work in the home should be valued and rewarded: 'the great majority of married women must be regarded as occupied on work which is vital though unpaid, without which their husbands could not do their paid work and

---

[132] See R. Dahrendorf 'Citizenship and Social Class' in M. Bulmer and A. Rees (eds.), *Citizenship Today* (1996), pp. 36–7.

[133] J. Lewis, *Women in Britain since 1945* (Basil Blackwell, 1992), p. 114.

[134] Marshall, above n. 129, in Marshall and Bottomore, p. 33.

[135] *Social Insurance and Allied Services* Report by Sir William Beveridge (Cmd. 6404) 1942.

without which the nation could not continue.'[136] In addition, he not only believed that child-bearing and -rearing were essential to the future of the nation, but that women should be particularly valued for that role, arguing that it was imperative to give first place in social expenditure to care of childhood and the safeguarding of maternity.[137] Thus he recommended that all married women be entitled to a maternity grant, and that women who did undertake gainful employment be entitled to a maternity allowance (for thirteen weeks) intended 'to make it easy and attractive for women to give up gainful occupation at the time of maternity'.[138] On the negative side, however, although he argued that married women should be considered as equal partners in a 'man and wife team', and not as dependants, his scheme made it inevitable that they would be unequal and dependent. This is because, like Mill, he failed to acknowledge that power relations within the family were strongly related to women's access to a means of income independent of their husbands. Nor did he see the implications for women of the fact that social citizenship in the modern State had become closely correlated with status in the work-place.

Thus, he proposed, a woman on marriage should acquire a new economic and social status. Her first line of defence was her legal right to maintenance by her husband; in return, she undertook to provide 'vital unpaid service', subject to the risk of widowhood or separation. Even if a married woman undertook paid employment, her earnings were not considered a means of subsistence.[139] For national insurance purposes the husband's contributions were to be treated as made on behalf of himself and his wife. A married woman who did undertake paid employment could opt to pay no contributions, but even if she chose to contribute, she would only receive benefits at a reduced rate.[140] He justified his proposals to pay lower benefits to 'housewives who are also gainfully employed' by arguing that their needs were less than single women, their houses being provided by their husbands' earnings or benefit.[141]

The evolution of the Welfare State since Beveridge has sharpened the ambiguity inherent in the Beveridge Report. In some respects women have made significant gains. Women have constituted the majority of recipients of many welfare benefits, largely because of the fact that women are more likely than men to be poor.[142] All women, regardless of class or wealth have benefited specifically from the more general availability of health care, particularly in relation to gynaecology and obstetrics. In addition, entitlements to income from the State have constituted a small but crucial step for women away from total financial dependence on men. To this extent, gender relations in society have been modified. However, in other impor-

---

[136] *ibid.*, para. 107.   [137] *ibid.*, para. 15.
[138] *ibid.*, para. 341.   [139] *ibid.*, para. 108.
[140] *ibid.*, para. 111.   [141] *ibid.*, para. 112.
[142] Pateman, *The Disorder of Women*, above n. 128, p. 180.

tant respects, women's secondary status has been perpetuated. There are two dimensions to the Welfare State which have this result: the focus on the family as the basic unit of support and maintenance, and the stress on paid work as the key to full social citizenship. Post-war welfare provision has largely followed Beveridge in constructing a family form which assumes that married women would take responsibility for unpaid domestic work, and that any paid work undertaken would be secondary to that of their husbands or other male members of the family.[143] For example, a woman's entitlement to claim benefits in her own right is almost always subordinate to the expectation that she should first rely on men. This is true even outside of marriage. According to the cohabitation rule, which operates in many Welfare States, a woman who is believed to be cohabiting with a man is disqualified from certain important benefits either directly or indirectly, by requiring that her resources be aggregated with his.[144] The second dimension, the stress on paid work, is reflected in the insurance principle, according to which the most valuable benefits depend on a record of contributions made as a result of paid work.

The combination of the assumption of the family as the basic unit, and the stress on paid work as a key to citizenship, has two main implications for women. First, the assumption of the family as the basic unit of society presumes that any measure to improve male welfare is shared by women and children.[145] Research, however, shows that the balance of power within the family makes this far from inevitable.[146] Secondly, the stress on paid work disadvantages women, whose continuing responsibility for child-care and domestic work means that they are unable to participate in paid labour on the same terms as men. This is reinforced by the structure of benefits. For example, pension benefits are based on lifetime earnings, which are necessarily reduced by periods out of the labour market for the purposes of child-care[147] (see Chapter 8). The result is a significant narrowing of the concept of social citizenship. As Pateman argues, men, as participants in the market are considered to have made a contribution which entitle them to the benefits of the Welfare State. Paradoxically, women's direct contri-bution of welfare in the form of domestic and caring work in the home, is not treated as sufficient to attract the rights of social citizenship.[148] The Welfare State has failed to reflect Beveridge's positive side, namely, his attempt to ensure that women's unpaid work was properly valued. Benefits which are not related to paid work, such as child benefit and maternity grant, have been kept at very low levels.

The final impact of the Welfare State has been on the public–private divide. As has been noted above, this notion has two separate meanings,

---

[143] Lewis, above n. 133, p. 92.

[144] Cranston, *Legal Foundations of the Welfare State* above n. 90, p. 194.

[145] Lewis, above n. 133, p. 94.     [146] *ibid.*, pp. 100–2.     [147] See ch. 8.

[148] Pateman, *The Disorder of Women*, above n. 128, p. 192.

distinguishing first between the State and civil society, and secondly between the world outside the family, and the family. In both dimensions, the Welfare State has redrawn the boundaries between the public and the private. The legitimacy of State intervention in the market is a central tenet of the ideology of the Welfare State, although the importance of a residual 'private' sphere relatively free from State regulation has never been undermined. In addition, the Welfare State has changed the contours of the family–market divide, but, as in the other characteristics of the Welfare State, in a complex and ambiguous way. In some important respects, the family has 'gone public',[149] with the transfer of traditionally domestic tasks to the public sphere. Thus education and aspects of caring for the ill and elderly have been accepted as social responsibilities. However, this has not changed women's responsibilities as much as might be expected, for three main reasons. First, the socialisation of family work has been far from complete; indeed, the Welfare State has presupposed that certain aspects of welfare, such as care of very young children, should continue to be provided in the home.[150] Secondly, even where the State provides services or benefits, women perform important mediating roles between the family and welfare provision. Links with schools, well baby clinics, health visitors and social workers are normally provided by mothers rather than fathers.[151] Thirdly, much of the work previously performed by women unpaid in the home continues to be considered as 'women's work'. Although it now attracts pay in the public sector, such work is generally at the bottom of the reward hierarchy, demonstrating the continuing undervaluation of 'women's work'. It should also not be forgotten that the redrawing of the public–private divide also worked in the opposite direction, permitting greater intrusiveness on people's personal lives. For example, the cohabitation rules have brought with them a significant element of social control by the State, most importantly, by surveillance and other extensive intrusions on privacy.[152]

### f) Neo-Liberalism and the New Right

The last two decades of the twentieth century have witnessed a marked change in government policy. Spearheaded by Margaret Thatcher and reinforced by successive Conservative governments, new policies have focused on the systematic dismantling of the Welfare State and the dismembering of the public sector. In order to legitimise its political agenda, the New Right has drawn heavily on the ideological power of classical liberal principles. However, the use of liberal vocabulary in the context of a greatly changed social order has obscured its originally lofty ideals and highlighted instead its harsh discordance with reality. As we have seen, the most

---

[149] H. Hernes 'Women and the Welfare State' in A. Sassoon (ed.), *Women and the State* (Routledge, 1987), p. 73.

[150] Pateman, *The Disorder of Women*, above n. 128, p. 192.    [151] *ibid.*, p. 181.

[152] Cranston, *Legal Foundation of the Welfare State* above n. 90, p. 198.

important contribution of classical liberalism was in creating the philosophical underpinning for individual liberation from hierarchical social
bonds and authoritarian power structures. By contrast, in the modern
context, the vocabulary of liberalism is used primarily to justify the withdrawal of the State from its social responsibilities to its citizens. On an
ideological level, this has proved a remarkably successful strategy. Indeed,
the hijacking of liberal terminology by the New Right has frequently left
opponents of its policies without the vocabulary to defend their cause.[153]

Possibly the most articulate and well-known proponent of neo-liberal
ideology is Hayek. Central to Hayek's political philosophy is his concern
with liberty, which he defines as the 'state in which a man is not subject to
coercion by the arbitrary will of another or others'.[154] As Hayek acknowledges himself, this definition is derived from the original context which gave
liberty its significance: the distinction between slaves and free people. True
to this context, he limits his definition solely to the question of coercion by
one person of others. This immediately renders his definition one which is
formal and abstract; the extent to which a person can exercise real choice
among a range of acceptable options is irrelevant. 'Liberty describes the
absence of particular obstacles—coercion by other men . . . It does not
assure us of any particular opportunities, but leaves it to us to decide what
use we shall make of the circumstances in which we find ourselves.'[155] The
correlative of this narrow conception of liberty is a definition of coercion
which is confined to the imposition by one agent of its will upon another.
Institutional forces, including collective and class pressures, are thus excluded entirely from consideration as significant elements limiting individual liberty. The narrowness of this conception of coercion is particularly
evident in his discussion of trade unions.[156] Hayek floridly depicts trade
unions as the wielders of an inordinate power of coercion, without once
mentioning the institutional factors making it inevitable that workers will be
subject to the coercive power of employers, a power which can only be
counterbalanced by collective organisation.

Hayek moves quickly from this conception of liberty to an equally narrow
definition of the role of the State. The only way to prevent coercion by some
individuals over others, he argues, is to confer a monopoly of coercion on
the State, a power which is itself limited in its use to the prevention of
coercion by private individuals against others. Most important among the
means to limit the power of the State are that it should only be permitted
to act according to known general rules, which do not differentiate between
individual citizens. This version of the neutral State is complemented by
the re-emphasis of the public–private divide and the abstract notion of
formal equality before the law: 'What distinguishes a free from an unfree

[153] See S. Fredman 'The New Rights. Labour Law and Ideology in the Thatcher Years'
[1992] *Oxford Journal of Legal Studies* 24.
[154] F. A. Hayek, *The Constitution of Liberty* (Routledge & Kegan Paul, 1960), p. 11.
[155] *ibid.*, p. 19.      [156] *ibid.*, c. 18.

society is that in the former each individual has a recognized private sphere clearly distinct from the public sphere, and the private individual cannot be ordered about but is expected to obey only the rules which are equally applicable to all.'[157]

Central too to his notion of freedom of the individual is his emphasis on the spontaneity of the market order. Only within a situation in which each individual can make his or her own choices without direction from the State, is he or she really free, and only the market order fulfils this requirement. The essential spontaneity of the market order is underpinned by an intensely individualist conception of justice. Hayek argues that only human conduct can be just or unjust, with the result that justice is essentially about rules of procedure and cannot refer to the outcome, individual or collective.[158] From these premises, he is able to conclude that the concept of social justice is meaningless, and its use a potential threat to individual liberty. 'The demand for "social justice" is addressed not to the individual but to society—yet society . . . is incapable of acting for a specific purpose.'[159] The demand for 'social justice' therefore becomes a demand that the members of society submit to the power of co-ordination or direction necessary to distribute shares in the product of society to different individuals. This is an illegitimate coercive power. Hayek admits that the manner of distribution of the market could well be regarded as unjust if it were the result of deliberate action by particular people. However, because justice only refers to individual actions, it is 'clearly absurd' to demand justice from the market process.[160] Similarly, he concedes that in the existing market order not only the results but also the initial chances of different individuals are often very different, affected by circumstances beyond the individual's control. But he maintains that any attempt to achieve real equality of opportunity would require that the government control the whole physical and human environment of all persons, a process which would clearly infringe individual liberty.[161]

It is not surprising, given the restrictions on legitimate State power, and the avowed meaninglessness of social justice, that Hayek should declare it illegitimate for any government to act in pursuit of distributive or social justice.[162] He does not deny an essential service role to the State, in areas which do not involve coercion; and he concedes that the community has a duty to make provision for those 'threatened by the extremes of indigence or starvation due to circumstances beyond their control'.[163] Both are justified in terms of individual pursuit of self-interest, the former being necessary for the smooth running of the market and the latter on the desire of

---

[157] Hayek, *Constitution*, above n. 154, pp. 207–8.
[158] F. A. Hayek, *Law, Legislation and Liberty* vol. 2 (Routledge and Kegan Paul, 1976), pp. 31–3.
[159] *ibid.*, p. 64.     [160] *ibid.*, p. 65.
[161] *ibid.*, pp. 84–5.     [162] Hayek, *Constitution*, above n. 154, p. 231.
[163] *ibid.*, p. 285.

individuals 'to protect themselves against the consequences of the extreme misery of their fellows'.[164] However, he argues, the chief aim of the social security system quickly extended beyond these aims, to include a redistribution of incomes. This, in Hayek's view, constitutes a critical threat to freedom: 'while in a free society it is possible to provide a minimum level of welfare for all, such a society is not compatible with sharing out income according to some preconceived notion of justice.'[165]

The links between Hayek's theories and the political agenda of Thatcherism are clear.[166] Under the banner of individual freedom from State coercion, and the reassertion of the private sphere of individual agency, the government has purported to 'roll back the boundaries of the State' by cutting public spending and radically reshaping the public sector. The primacy of the individual is constantly proclaimed; indeed Thatcher is quoted as asserting that 'there is no such thing as society'.[167] The savage reductions in universal welfare services, such as health care and education, and the marked shift towards means-tested rather than contribution-based welfare reflect Hayek's views of the illegitimacy of State responsibility for any more than provision for the destitute. In the name of the primacy of the market order, and the centrality of individual freedom, government has removed minimum wage controls, and radically undermined trade union powers. The obsession with the market has indeed been so strong as to lead to its imposition in a wide variety of formerly public arenas. Local authorities are now required to subject all their services to market testing, leading to contracting out to the private sector. Similarly, an expensive and cumbersome 'internal market' has been introduced within the health service and education systems. This again has generally been justified in terms of individual freedom of choice. 'The main objective of [Thatcherism] was to shift power from producers to consumers and extend as much choice as possible.'[168]

However, the impact of these policies on society has accentuated the deeply flawed nature of the neo-liberal principles at their core. By deliberately refusing to consider the injustice of market outcomes, and by negating the significance of social bonds, the government has rapidly increased imbalances of power in society. Yet the cloak of liberal terminology enables it to escape moral blame. For example, the removal of minimum wage controls and the reduction in trade union power have simply left unchallenged the power of employers over their workers. The stress on individual freedom of contract only reinforces such imbalances. Similarly, the notion

---

[164] *ibid.*, p. 286.

[165] *ibid.*, p. 303.

[166] Lord Wedderburn 'Freedom of Association and Philosophies of Labour Law' [1989] ILJ 1.

[167] D. Willetts 'The Family' in D. Kavanagh and A. Seldon (eds.), *The Thatcher Effect* (Clarendon Press, 1989), p. 268.

[168] *ibid.*, p. 265.

of choice is reduced to empty rhetoric by the definition of choice as freedom from coercion from other individuals without insisting on the availability of a range of desirable choices, as any parent wishing to exercise her choice in favour of high quality State education for her children, or rail commuter wishing to choose a high standard of railway services, or ill person wishing to choose speedy and effective health care, soon discovers. Perhaps most disturbing is the fact that the fundamental rationale, that of protecting individuals from State intrusion on their freedom of action or thought, has not been achieved. Instead, the power of central government has been vastly increased: the internal affairs of free trade unions are now subject to detailed and authoritarian controls; schools are required to follow rigid normative educational rules; and local authorities, which even Hayek considered to be preferable as sources of regulation to central government, have been stripped of much of their autonomy, even at the cost of an inability to respond to local electoral demands.

For women, the rhetoric and reality of Thatcherism and its successors has been particularly problematic. Deregulation of the labour market has led to a dramatic deterioration in terms and conditions of work. The large numbers of redundancies in industries characterised by high union density, reasonable levels of pay and some measure of job security have been complemented by the growth of marginal, flexible employment with low pay, little job security and few fringe benefits. The gendered nature of these trends is striking: traditionally male jobs have been savaged while women have been propelled into low paying, low status work. While there are clearly positive aspects to the exponential increase in the number of married women in the paid work-force, it is not clear that this carries with it a corresponding increase in the much-vaunted personal freedom of choice of the New Right. Instead, the focus on the individual as no more than an economic agent within the market has obscured the real constraints on choice caused by women's continuing family responsibilities. The value of parenting, not as a dimension of self-interest but as an intrinsic social value, is inevitably ignored by a set of values so explicitly based on the centrality of the pursuit of self-interest. This is not to say that the family has received no attention by New Right theorists or policy-makers. To the contrary, New Right governments in both the UK and the US have proclaimed themselves to be the parties of the family. This is because the family, in its neo-liberal construction, fits neatly into the framework which prohibits the State from pursuing distributive justice. The family has two main values in neo-liberal terms. The first is its perceived independence from the State. Indeed, it is viewed as 'the most powerful social institution outside the political sphere'.[169] The second is its utility as a repository for the functions devolved from the State. One of the most important policy mechanisms for implementing this stress on the value of the family has been 'to identify

---

[169] Willetts, in Kavanagh and Seldon (eds.), above n. 167, p. 265.

ways in which greater power and responsibility can be passed to the family away from the State'.[170] A central example concerns policies in relation to health care. Policy-makers have stressed that 'publicly provided services constitute only a small part of the total care provided to people in need. Families, friends, neighbours and other local people provide the majority of care in response to needs which they are uniquely well placed to identify and respond to.'[171] In other words, it is argued, the welfare function is returned to its rightful place: the tender loving care of the family. Hence the thrust of community care policies has been to reduce the role of State institutions in favour of care by the family or equivalent. Despite some gestures in policy documents to the need to support carers,[172] it is unsurprising that this has been left out of account.

The implications of these policies for women are clear. The family itself is individualised: instead of a group of separate individuals, it becomes a single undifferentiated person with unitary interests. Principles of freedom, choice and rationality are therefore not applied to relationships within the family; indeed, it appears unnecessary to examine the question of justice within the family. In practice, of course, Thatcherite policies have significantly increased the burden on women, who already bore a disproportionate responsibility for caring for children, the ill, and the elderly. At the same time, the ostensible withdrawal of the State from distributive justice has meant not only that the socialisation of some key family functions has been reversed, but also that little or no State assistance is available to help women discharge these responsibilities. Again, far from increasing women's autonomy, such policies have significantly constrained the range of real choices available. Nor has the New Right been true to its promise of preventing State incursion on the private sphere reserved for the individual. Because the reality of a pluralist, organically inter-related society has resisted the imposition of a unitary individualist ideology, the government has been required to assert its values in authoritarian forms. Paradoxically, therefore, the New Right espouses conservative and authoritarian moral values. In the US, a major symbol of this view has been in the form of an attack on women's reproductive freedom, particularly, their rights to abortion. In the UK, it has manifested itself in the crusade against single mothers, the rejection of gay rights, the coercive powers of the Child Support Agency, the toughening of divorce laws, the dictatorial attitudes towards education, and many others.

g)  BEYOND LIBERALISM

This chapter has demonstrated that, despite radical changes in political philosophy and practice, there are striking continuities in the ways in which

---

[170] *ibid.*, p. 266.
[171] Sir Roy Griffiths *Community Care: Agenda for Action* (HMSO, 1988), p. 5.
[172] *Caring for People* Cm 849 (HMSO, 1989), para 1.11.

women are characterised. The ascriptions which were explicit in pre-liberal philosophies were obscured but not obliterated by the promises of liberalism and democratic socialism. These themes have profoundly influenced the shape of the laws which govern women's lives.

The insights drawn from this chapter form the basis of the critical structure which informs the remainder of the book. It will be evident that while the removal of explicit inequalities between men and women has signified a measure of progress, women remain disproportionately disadvantaged in society. I shall argue that this is no coincidence. Instead, the law has been intrinsically limited in its ability to achieve true progress. This is in large part due to the tension between the tenacious status ascriptions to which the law continues to subscribe and the liberal tenets which underpin much of the legal framework. Liberalism is a complex ideology to challenge, because it speaks in the language of equality and individual freedom, ideals to which we all aspire. Thus in order to understand the impact of liberalism on the laws governing women, it is essential to unpack the specific meanings of its basic tenets. Six such tenets exert a particularly powerful influence on the law: rationality; autonomy; individualism; equality; a neutral State and legal system; and a free market. Even in the modified form espoused by Dworkin and Rawls, these concepts have frequently sidestepped or even undermined the concerns of women. Nor have women fared better under democratic socialism. It is true that democratic socialists have shared the feminist recognition that individual autonomy and equality are rendered meaningless by insufficient access to power or wealth. Nevertheless, the Welfare State and its theorists have left in place the very patriarchal status ascriptions which liberal promises claimed to dislodge.

It is only by remoulding the basic assumptions of both liberalism and democratic socialism that progress can be made. The aim is not simply to slot more women into the existing structures. This would merely reinforce the notion that success is comprehensively determined by the individualistic pursuit of self-interest in the paid market, to the obliteration of personal and family concerns. Nor is it sufficient to prop up the market by a welfare system which ameliorates women's dependence only by reinforcing it. Instead, I will argue, the principles of individualism, rationality, autonomy and neutrality need to be replaced by a recognition of the individual as part of a community of inter-relationships, which constrains as well as facilitates his or her choices and opportunities. In place of the paradigm of a 'rational individual' who should be left free to pursue his or her pursuits without constraints by the State, it is critical to acknowledge the key role, both positive and negative, of emotionality, care and responsibility for others. Crucially, account needs to be taken of the family, not as a quasi-individual, but as a dynamic set of interactions, a power structure and a source of both energy and restraint. Such an approach exposes too the shallowness of the liberal concept of equality. Liberal equality offers women some of the entitlements available to men; but only on condition that women refashion themselves in the image of men. Instead, I argue, it is the underlying structures which must be refashioned so that the world of paid work accommodates and values parenting functions.

To go beyond liberalism requires a sensitivity to the real distributions of power in society as well as the close interaction between power on the one hand, and gender, race and wealth on the other. It replaces the ethic of self-interest with one of responsibility, both by people for each other, and by the State for its citizens. Most urgently, the responsibility and care for children need to be both valued and accommodated within the public as much as the private sphere. The result would be a relaxation of the rigid boundary between unpaid and paid work, between the family and the market place, with the duty on formal structures to accommodate responsibilities towards children and others. In this way both men and women, and the broader community, are made to take responsibility and share the cost of ensuring the continuity of the human species.

# [2]
# Past and Present: Legal Developments

## INTRODUCTION

The discussion in chapter 1 illustrated the striking contradictions in eighteenth and nineteenth century political theory. Deep-seated assumptions of the natural subordination of women remained impervious to ringing proclamations of freedom and equality for all individuals. Equally striking is the extent to which these contradictions were mirrored in legal developments since the late eighteenth century. This is exemplified by the work of Dicey, the leading nineteenth century constitutional lawyer. Dicey is probably best known for his formulation of the central principles of the British Constitution, foremost of which were his assertion of the primacy of the rule of law and equality. Yet Dicey was also implacably opposed to the extension of the suffrage to women.[1]

[1] A. V. Dicey, *Letters to a Friend on Votes for Women* (John Murray, 1909), p. 75.

Throughout the nineteenth and twentieth centuries, legislative reforms gradually incorporated political ideals of equality and autonomy into the legal framework. These were certainly developments of great importance. However, an assessment of the impact of such legal changes reveals the limitations of the principle of formal equality. Most importantly, formal equality frequently ignored material inequalities, and thus had the effect of reinforcing rather than replacing existing power structures. Similarly, the emphasis on individualism and autonomy, exemplified in contract and property law, failed to account for inequalities in bargaining power, and thus merely cemented those inequalities. This chapter uses the conceptual framework developed in chapter 1 to analyse critically the developments in the law in the following areas: (I) Marriage and Property Law; (II) Suffrage; (III) Employment; and (IV) Welfare Legislation.

## I.   MARRIAGE AND PROPERTY LAW

### a)   COVERTURE: WOMEN'S LEGAL BONDAGE[2]

It was in respect of marriage that the contradictions of the post-feudal legal system were at their most strident. Liberal principles of individual freedom from feudal status ascriptions were not extended to married women until deep into the twentieth century. Instead, the Diceyan ideal of formal equality of all individuals before the law unabashedly excluded married women from the category 'individuals'. This truth is epitomised by the common law of coverture which entailed that 'the very being or legal existence of the wife is suspended during the marriage or at least incorporated and consolidated into that of the husband under whose wing, protection and cover she performs everything.'[3] Coverture gave the husband near-absolute control over the wife's property as well as her person. Married women were perpetual legal minors, divested of the possibility of economic independence. Any property which a married woman had owned as a single woman became her husband's property on marriage: personal property vesting absolutely, real property during the lifetime of the husband. Similarly, he had absolute rights to all property which came into her hands during her marriage, including all her earned income. Moreover, money given to her by him as housekeeping money remained his property at all times. 'For if the wife out of her good housewifery do save any thing out of it; . . . he shall reap the benefit of his wife's frugality . . . because when the husband agrees to allow his wife a certain

---

[2]   This account draws heavily on W. Blackstone, *Commentaries on the Law of England* (1809), pp. 441–5; O. Kahn-Freund in W. Friedmann (ed.), *Matrimonial Property Law* (Stevens & Son Ltd, 1955); J. H. Baker, *An Introduction to English Legal History* (Butterworths, 1979), pp. 395–400, W. H. Cornish and G. de N. Clarke, *Law and Society in England* (Sweet & Maxewll, 1989), ch. 5.

[3]   Blackstone, above n. 2, Book I Ch. XV p. 430.

sum yearly, the end of this agreement is, that she may be provided with clothes and other necessaries, and whatsoever is saved out of this redounds to the husband.'[4]

Control over her person reached into every aspect of legal dealings. A married woman could not sue or be sued unless her husband were a party to the suit; in tort, for example, she retained her liability but her husband had to be joined as a defendant. An important implication was that she could not sue him in tort. She could not make a valid will unless her husband consented to its provisions, and he could withdraw his consent at any time until probate.[5] He decided where the family would live and had ultimate authority over where and how the children were raised. He could 'correct' her physically;[6] but he was so much her sovereign that if she killed him she committed treason, not simple murder.[7] Contractual capacity was similarly denied her: a married woman could not enter into a contract except as agent for her husband, and then only with his express authority. This was especially harsh if a wife was evicted or neglected by her husband. Courts in the seventeenth century were prepared to imply authority for a wife to pledge her husband's credit for necessaries for her own support;[8] but this was of limited assistance, since the husband could displace implied authority by expressly warning traders not to contract with the wife.

The persistence of married women's legal disabilities was at the heart of their general inferiority. For example, it was frequently argued that it was impossible to grant married women equal voting rights if they remained legal minors. Their inability to own their own property or even retain their own income made it impossible for them to achieve economic independence. At the same time, the economic pressures on single women to marry were intense:[9] marriage was not an institution which could be avoided by most women.

It is true that, in a gesture to liberal individualism, marriage was now characterised as a contract,[10] thus formally incorporating the ideology of freedom and autonomy. Yet this did no more than highlight the inherent contradictions of women's legal position. As Pateman argues, women were presumed to have the capacity to enter into the marriage contract itself but as soon as they were married they were denied the capacity to enter into any other contract.[11] Moreover, 'unlike all other contracts, there was no way of

[4] *Lady Tyrrell's Case* (1675), Freeman's Reports 1660–1706, p. 304.
[5] She had limited power to dispose of her property in any case; freehold land reverted on her death to her kin.
[6] This power was doubtful by Blackstone's time.
[7] Blackstone, above n. 2, editor's note 23, p. 455; Baker, above n. 2, p. 395.
[8] Blackstone, above n. 2, p. 442; Baker, above n. 2, p. 399.
[9] M. L. Shanley, *Feminism, Marriage and the Law in Victorian England 1850–1895* (Tauris, 1989), p. 9.
[10] 'Our law considers marriage in no other light than as a civil contract.' Blackstone, above n. 2, p. 433.
[11] C. Pateman, *The Sexual Contract* (Polity Press, 1988), pp. 6, 156.

escaping from [the contract of matrimony] if it proved unsatisfactory.'[12] Similarly, the notion of consent was emptied of meaning by the extensive use of implied consent. Women were held to have impliedly consented not only to their own legal obliteration on marriage, but also to every act of sexual intercourse demanded by their husbands. Indeed, until as recently as 1991, a husband who forced his wife to have intercourse against her will could not be found guilty of rape except in limited circumstances.[13] Married women's legal subordination was also frequently justified by means of the familiar technique of asserting that the family was outside the political arena and therefore authority need not be legitimated by consent.[14] Blackstone went further and confidently asserted that these restrictions actually benefited women. 'Even the disabilities which the wife lies under, are for the most part intended for her protection and benefit. So great a favourite is the female sex of the laws of England!'[15]

Why then was marriage the focus of women's legal subordination? A central factor was the difference in women and men's reproductive capacities. Since it is the woman who becomes pregnant and bears the child, only her parenthood can ever be absolutely certain. No man can be biologically secure that he has fathered a particular child: paternal security can only be achieved socially.[16] This appropriation of paternity has traditionally required elaborate legal mechanisms,[17] designed to ensure the husband's absolute rights to the wife's sexual fidelity and the children of the marriage. Most explicit was the double standard of adultery, whereby the wife's adultery, but not the husband's, was treated as so serious an infringement of acceptable social standards as to warrant harsh penalties.[18] As Lord Chancellor Cranworth explained to the House of Lords, 'No-one would venture to suggest that a husband could possibly [condone an act of adultery by the wife], and for this, among other reasons . . . that the adultery of the wife might be the means of palming spurious offspring upon the husband, while the adultery of the husband could have no such effect with regard to the wife.'[19] The law of divorce was specifically structured to reinforce the husband's rights to certainty of paternity. Before 1857, a marriage could only be ended by ecclesiastical annulment or Private Act of Parliament.[20] The latter was a clear example of the 'double standard' of

[12] Baker, above n. 2, p. 401. The possibility of divorce by consent was extinguished by medieval canonists, who regarded marriage as indissoluble.
[13] R v. R [1991] 4 All ER 481; see further below.    [14] Shanley, above n. 9, p. 11.
[15] Blackstone, above n. 2, p. 455 contrast editor's note 23, p. 455.
[16] M. O'Brien, *The Politics of Reproduction* (Routledge and Kegan Paul, 1981), p. 53.
[17] Pateman, above n. 11, p. 35.
[18] U. Vogel 'Whose property' in C. Smart (ed.), *Regulating Womanhood* (Routledge, 1992), pp. 147–8.
[19] Quoted in M. Finer and O. R. McGregor 'The History of the Obligation to Maintain' Appendix 5, *Report of the (Finer) Committee on One-Parent Families* (Cmnd. 5629-1) (1974), para. 18. This was possibly more true of the middle than the aristocratic classes: para. 59.
[20] The ecclesiastical courts would also give an early equivalent of judicial separation: a divorce *a mensa et thoro* on the grounds of cruelty, adultery or unnatural sexual indulgence, was available to either spouse.

adultery. Adultery was the sole ground for a private divorce act, but whereas a wife's adultery was sufficient to earn her husband a divorce, she could not succeed on the grounds of his adultery unless it was 'aggravated' by bigamy, incest or unnatural vice. 'Short of this she suffered "no very material injury" and she ought not to resent her husband's unfaithfulness.'[21] Thus while only four women succeeded in securing a divorce in the period up to 1857, a total of 318 men did so in the same period.[22] Parliamentary divorce operated unevenly, not only between husbands and wives, but also between classes, being available only to the powerful sectors of society. In other parts of society, as O'Donovan shows, divorce was often a private matter arranged by the couple themselves.[23] When it was manifested in public, it was as much a sanction against adultery as an explicit expression of men's control over women. This is most clearly seen in the practice of wife selling,[24] whereby a husband, regarding his wife as 'his goods and chattels, . . . puts a halter around her neck and thereby leads her to the next market place, and there puts her up to auction as though she was a brood-mare or a milch-cow.'[25]

Protection of the father's legal rights to parenthood were further bolstered by draconian custody laws favouring the father in almost all circumstances. Until the limited reforms of 1839, a married woman had no rights of custody whatsoever over her children.[26] 'The basic premise of both law and equity in custody disputes over legitimate children was one of strict patriarchy—"the sacred right of the father over his own children".'[27] As Blackstone put it: 'A mother as such is entitled to no power, but only to reverence and respect.'[28] The courts would order a mother to surrender a child to the father even if the child was still being breast-fed. Thus in a nineteenth century case, the court upheld the father's rights to custody over the child even though he had forcibly snatched the baby from its mother's breast and taken it away almost naked in an open carriage in bad weather.[29] The court did not even hold that this fell within the exception for cases where a child required judicial protection: Lord Ellenborough CJ could see no reason to believe that the child had been 'injured for want of nurture or in any other respect'.[30] Nor would the courts consider that the father had given up his rights to children just because he was living in adultery.[31] Even after his death, the father's rights remained intact. He had absolute right to name a testamentary guardian to take care of his children after his death, and if he chose to name someone other than the mother, she had no rights whatever over her children.

---

[21] Cornish and Clarke, above n. 2, p. 379.
[22] Finer and McGregor, above n. 19, paras. 13–18.
[23] K. O'Donovan, *Sexual Divisions in Law* (Weidenfeld, 1985), p. 51.
[24] For details see Cornish and Clarke, above n. 2, pp. 380–1.
[25] Anon., *The Laws Respecting Women* (1777), cited in O'Donovan, above n. 23, p. 51.
[26] Shanley, above n. 9, p. 25.   [27] Cornish and Clarke, above n. 2, p. 370.
[28] Blackstone, above n. 2, p. 453.   [29] *R* v. *De Manneville* [1804] 5 East 221.
[30] *ibid.*, p. 223.   [31] *R* v. *Greenhill* (1836) 4 A. & E. 624.

The quest for certainty of paternity was particularly fervent in periods in which property passed by inheritance. However, this cannot fully explain the legal subordination of married women. Even when forms of wealth shifted to moveable capital and market accumulation, the potential for instituting freer forms of marriage was slow to be realised. As important as certainty of paternity was the validation of men's proprietary demands on women's sexuality and person,[32] clearly reflected in the marked reluctance of the law to restrain violence by husbands against wives.

When considering the position of married women, it is crucial to note that the experiences of women were far from uniform across classes. Indeed, in many respects, the law had very different implications for women from the upper and middle classes from its implications for their working-class counterparts. For example, restrictions on property ownership affected women from the propertied classes but barely touched working-class women. By contrast, the inability to retain her own earnings was a crucial disability for a working-class married woman. Similarly, the expense and complexity of divorce laws made divorce a possibility for wealthy women, but wholly out of reach of women without the necessary resources. It is therefore clear, as argued in chapter 1, that to regard women as a unified group with identical interests is to ignore the importance of other types of domination.

## b) Reform of Coverture

In this section, four central arenas are examined: (a) property, tort and contract; (b) custody; (c) divorce; and (d) rights of control over the wife's person, including marital rape and other sorts of violence.

### i) **Property, Tort and Contract**

Legal disabilities of married women continued well into the twentieth century, and progress towards reform was slow and painstaking. Not all change was directly aimed at women's emancipation, but instead aimed to protect men from the power of husbands over their wives' property. Thus wealthy fathers found ways of protecting their property against their daughters' husbands. Merchants demanded ways of preventing husbands from avoiding their wives' debts. The possibility of women owning separate property could cushion husbands against insolvency. In respect of the working classes, the retention by working women of their own income was proposed as a way of decreasing the burden on public assistance.[33] At the same time, nineteenth century feminists challenged the internal inconsistencies of liberal theory, demanding equal autonomy for women. The focus of their campaigns was legal change; for them formal legal equality appeared as both a necessary and sufficient condition for women's emancipa-

---

[32] Vogel, above n. 18, p. 163.     [33] Shanley, above n. 9, pp. 15–16.

tion. Their achievements were certainly important; but their neglect of material inequalities, of the sex-based division of labour in the home, and of the role of industrial capitalism in general meant that progress was no more than partial.[34]

The earliest reforms reflected the conflict between claims to property by the wife's father's family and those of her husband, rather than a principled desire for equality. As Kahn-Freund put it: 'Equity did . . . not [act] in the name of the principle of equality of the sexes . . . The purpose of equity was to keep the family (kinship) property intact and to preserve it from being sacrificed to the husband's speculative undertakings or extravagant habits or fancies.'[35] As early as the sixteenth century, equitable rules had been formulated to assist a wealthy father to protect his property against his son-in-law by ensuring that his daughter's property descended to her children, or, in the absence of children, reverted to her father's family. This could be done by settling property on trust for the wife's 'sole and separate use'. However, this did not have the effect of giving the wife full control over her own property, as can be seen by the rapid development of rules limiting her interest during the husband's life to the income on the capital.[36] Such restraint clauses were partially intended to prevent a husband from undermining the protection provided in the trust by forcing his wife to dispose of her equitable estate to him. But because the first priority was to protect descendants' interests, the restraint clause also prevented her from exercising any rights to deal with her property. In addition, she was subject to the supervision of trustees, who would have had her family's interests directly in mind.[37] In the event, such settlements became commonplace among the wealthy: indeed, few men of property would allow their daughters to marry without one.[38] But since settlements were too expensive to benefit any but the wealthy propertied classes, they exacerbated the division between wealthy wives, for whom some modicum of independence was available in law, and working-class wives who were entirely legally subjugated to their husbands.[39] Equity did not find it necessary to assist working-class women, whose earnings were deemed by the common law to be the automatic property of their husbands: it was left, belatedly, to legislation to achieve this effect.

Legislative reform was slow and halting and when it came was not motivated by a principled commitment to equality. Instead, the main thrust of the Married Women's Property Act of 1870 was to reduce the ostensible burden on the Poor Law by protecting the earnings of working-class wives from their allegedly wasteful husbands.[40] As a result, change was modest: as

[34] *ibid.*, pp. 10–14.    [35] Kahn-Freund, above n. 2, p. 274.
[36] Baker, above n. 2, p. 397; Cornish and Clarke, above n. 2, pp. 368–9.
[37] *ibid.*, p. 369.    [38] Shanley, above n. 9, p. 70.
[39] A. V. Dicey, *Law and Opinion in England* (MacMillan, 1914), p. 383.
[40] Baker, above n. 2, p. 397.

Dicey put it, the Act did no more than extend some of the rules of equity, framed for the daughters of the rich, to the daughters of the poor.[41] Married women did not gain full property rights. Instead, the Act merely treated a married woman's earned income as separate property for her own use only.[42] Also included as part of her separate property were personal property inherited on an intestacy, legacies not exceeding £200, income from real property coming to her on an intestacy, and, if she requested, certain investments.[43] All other property still passed to her husband on marriage unless the traditional equitable settlement was used. Such limited gains were achieved at a cost. Consistent with the primary aim of relieving the burden on the Poor Law, the Act placed wives under the same Poor Law obligations to maintain their husbands and children as their husbands owed to them.[44] In addition, a husband was no longer liable for his wife's prenuptial debts.[45] Because only her separate property was available to meet these debts, anxious traders lobbied for an amendment leaving the husband liable for pre-nuptial debts to the extent that he received her property.[46]

Campaigners were forced to wait another twelve years for substantial change, this time in the form of the Married Women's Property Act 1882. This Act, unlike its predecessor, made genuine strides towards formal equality for married women. The Act still did not explicitly treat a married woman as if she were single; instead, her enhanced property rights continued to take the legal form of a statutory settlement of property for her separate use.[47] Nevertheless, 'separate' property now included all real and personal property, and she now had complete power to 'acquire, hold and dispose by will or otherwise' of that property.[48] In addition, she was given the power to enter into contracts in respect of her separate property and was capable of suing and being sued in contract without joining her husband.[49]

The Act was the first great leap towards formal equality in property rights as between husband and wife. However, it did not sweep away the whole edifice of coverture. Significant elements of the legal incorporation of the wife into the person of the husband retained a tenacious grip on the common law,[50] and the limitations imposed by the artificial concept of a separate trust continued to obstruct progress. A clear example of the tenacity of the assumptions behind coverture concerns the extent of the wife's liability in tort. After some ambiguity in the caselaw, the House of Lords in 1925 reasserted that the doctrine of the unity of husband and wife remained alive unless specifically excluded.[51] As Lord Sumner put it:

---

[41] Dicey, above n. 39, p. 395.       [42] Married Women's Property Act 1870, s. 1.
[43] *ibid.*, ss. 2–5.       [44] Married Persons Property Act 1870, ss. 13, 14.
[45] Married Women's Property Act 1870, s. 12.
[46] Married Women's Property (1870) Amendment Act 1874.
[47] Shanley, above n. 9, pp. 125–7.
[48] Married Women's Property Act 1882, s. 1.       [49] *ibid.*, s. 2.
[50] Kahn-Freund, above n. 2, p. 280.       [51] *Edwards* v. *Porter* [1925] AC 1 (HL).

To assume that [the 1882] Act was intended to revolutionise the law of Baron and Feme and to dissolve their legal unity so completely that in litigation at any rate they twain should no longer be one flesh is to beg the questions . . . The Act carefully avoids saying that . . . a husband is not liable for his wife's post-nuptial torts, and, . . . it seems to me to preserve his liability for her torts committed during marriage for the benefit of those who would otherwise have no remedy if she has no sufficient separate estate.[52]

Nor did a wife gain the right to sue her husband in tort for wrongs done to her; and the equitable power to impose restraints on the wife's ability to use her separate property was not outlawed.

It took decades for the gaps in the 1882 Act to be filled. The most important reform was contained in the Law Reform (Married Women and Tortfeasors) Act 1935, whose main purpose was to free the law from the shackles of equity[53] by finally dropping the device of a statutory trust for the wife's separate property. Only then did the law genuinely afford a married woman the same property rights as a man or a single woman.[54] In addition, she was given capacity to sue or be sued in all respects as if she were a single woman; thus ending the husband's liability for her torts whether prior to or during the marriage.[55] Even then, however, formal equality was incomplete. For example, the rule that one spouse could not sue the other in tort remained intact until 1962.[56] New equitable restraints on a married woman's powers of alienation were forbidden in the 1935 Act[57] but existing restraints were not abolished until 1949.[58] Indeed, it was only in 1982 that Lord Denning could confidently assert: 'Nowadays, both in law and in fact, husband and wife are two persons, not one . . . The severance in all respects is so complete that I would say that the doctrine of unity and its ramifications should be discarded altogether, except in so far as it is retained by judicial decision or by Act of Parliament.'[59]

One of the most important features of this period was that formal equality and individualism were considered inseparable. Thus in filling the gaps in formal equality left by the 1882 Act, later legislation simultaneously entrenched the doctrine that each spouse should own his or her separate property. This is epitomised by the 1935 Act, which gave a married woman full ownership rights over all property which she owned at the time of the marriage or which was acquired by her or devolved upon her during the marriage.[60] In this respect, the law reflected the values attached to individual autonomy and equality before the law so passionately advocated by

---

[52] *ibid.*, *per* Lord Sumner at p. 46.    [53] Kahn-Freund, above n. 2, p. 287.
[54] Law Reform (Married Women and Tortfeasors) Act 1935, s. 1(a).
[55] *ibid.*, ss. 1, 3.
[56] Law Reform (Husband and Wife) Act 1962.
[57] Law Reform (Married Women and Tortfeasors) Act 1935.
[58] Married Women (Restraint upon Anticipation) Act 1949, s. 1(1).
[59] *Midland Bank Trust Co* v. *Green (No 3)* [1982] Ch. 529, at pp. 538–9.
[60] Law Reform (Married Women and Tortfeasors) Act 1935, s. 2(1).

Mill and other liberal feminists (see Chapter 1). However, the principle of separation of property clearly demonstrates the limits of formal equality and liberal individualism. Most importantly, material inequalities within a marriage have in many ways been reinforced. This is because the social division of labour within the family usually makes it far more difficult for the wife to accumulate her own separate property than the husband. The principle of separation of property assumes that each partner functions as a separate individual; whereas in reality the family operates as a community based on a division of labour. In practice, in most families, most or all of the work done by the wife is unpaid and therefore she does not directly accumulate her own resources. At the same time, it is only because of her unpaid work that her husband can paricipate fully in the paid labour force. The individualistic doctrine, however, has no means of recognising the value of unpaid work in the home. As a result, as the Law Commission put it in 1971,

Equality of power, which separation of property achieves, does not of itself lead to equal opportunity to exercise that power; it ignores the fact that a married woman, especially if she has young children, does not in practice have the same opportunity as her husband or an unmarried woman to acquire property; it takes no account of the fact that marriage is a form of partnership to which both spouses contribute, each in a different way, and the contribution of each is equally important to the family welfare and to society.[61]

This may be true even if the wife is able to undertake paid employment: in many cases she will be forced into low paid, part-time work; and frequently will use her income on consumables, such as food and clothing, or childcare, and therefore be unable to accumulate significant separate property.

The absence of legal recognition of the value of a woman's unpaid work in the home is further endorsed by the common law's retention of the principle that money received by the wife from the husband for housekeeping was deemed to be his money alone, and any savings belonged to him. Indeed, as recently as 1949, the Court of Appeal held that the wife had no right to a share in profits earned on savings from housekeeping money, even though the profits were a result of a joint investment.[62] Only in 1964 was this amended, by legislation which provided that such savings should be treated as belonging to the husband and wife in equal shares in the absence of any agreement between them to the contrary.[63]

As Kahn-Freund has argued, the achievement of full equality between spouses is not inevitably linked to a doctrine of separation of property. It was only because of the 'connection at common law between inequality of status and the combination of both spouses' property in the hands of the

---

[61] Law Commission, *Family Property Law*, Working Paper No. 42 (1971) London, para. 0.12.

[62] *Hoddinot* v. *Hoddinot* [1949] 2 KB 406.

[63] Married Women's Property Act 1964, s. 1; for criticisms of this Act, see J. Dewar, *Law and the Family* (Butterworths, 1989), p. 119.

husband [that] the idea of separation of property became . . . interwoven with that of equality, with which it has very little to do.'[64] Yet the alternative doctrine of community of property, whereby property acquired by each spouse is to a greater or lesser degree regarded as the property of the partnership, has never taken root.[65]

## ii) **Custody**

Advocates for reform of the father's absolute rights to custody were faced with dilemmas which differed in some respects from those occurring in respect of property rights. It was tempting for feminists to rely on arguments based on the unique role of mothers in respect of their children in order to tip the balance at least marginally in their favour, rather than to base their case on strict spousal equality. This was a manifestation of the perennial debate as to whether women should campaign for equality, or assert special rights on the grounds of their difference from men.[66] This controversy tended to merge too with arguments about the extent to which the child's welfare should be considered, an argument which gained ground as the sources of wealth shifted away from inheritance, and psychological theories became more influential.

Whichever argument prevailed, progress towards even minimal rights for the mother was painstakingly slow. The Custody of Infants Act of 1839 gave a mother the right to petition courts of Chancery for custody of children under seven, and for access to children over seven. It took more than three decades for this to be broadened to allow mothers to petition for custody of children under sixteen.[67] In any case, both Acts were only available to women who were rich enough to afford proceedings in the Chancery Division, and were not guilty of adultery.[68] Moreover, patriarchal assumptions about the father's absolute rights over his children remained so strong in the minds of the judges that the impact of the 1873 Act was largely undermined. In *In re Besant*,[69] for example, the Court of Appeal held that a refusal by the mother to bring up the child in the religion of the father was a good reason for removing the child from her custody. A further small step was taken in 1886, when mothers were first given the power to appoint guardians after the death of both parents, or to appoint a guardian to act jointly with the father after her death.[70] Similarly, the court was given the power to make custody and access orders 'having regard to the wishes as well of the mother as of the father'.[71] Cautious recognition was also given to the welfare of the child. But the link between rights of custody and matrimonial offences meant that spousal equality remained elusive so long as the grounds for divorce were unequal (i.e. adultery for women but 'aggravated'

---

[64] Kahn-Freund, in W. Friedmann (ed.), *Matrimonial Property Law*, above n. 2, p. 278.
[65] For detailed discussion, see B. Hoggett and D. Pearl, *The Family, Law and Society* (Butterworths, 1983).
[66] Shanley, above n. 9, pp. 145–6.   [67] Custody of Infants Act 1873, s. 1.
[68] Shanley, above n. 9, p. 137.   [69] [1879] 11 Ch. 508.
[70] Guardianship of Infants Act 1886, s. 3.   [71] *ibid.*, s. 5.

adultery for men). According to the 1886 Act, the court retained a discretion to refuse custody to the parent whose misconduct grounded the divorce; and this meant that that parent had no rights over the child even after the death of the custodial parent.[72] This approach was reinforced in divorce proceedings: although the 1857 Divorce Act gave the court broad discretionary powers to make such provision as it deemed just,[73] in practice, the courts would refuse to order custody in favour of a 'guilty wife'.[74]

The twentieth century was well under way before a legislative commitment to parental equality was manifested. The preamble to the Guardianship of Infants Act 1925 refers explicitly to the 'expedience' of applying the principle of equality in law between the sexes to guardianship issues. It thus provides that in cases involving the custody or upbringing of a child, the claims of the father should not be considered superior to those of the mother, nor should those of the mother be considered superior to the father. Indeed, the welfare of the infant should be 'the first and paramount consideration'.[75] Even then, 'to abandon any presumption in favour of the father was to ask the courts to show a Solomonic wisdom.'[76]

This commitment to equality between the spouses has remained central to the legislative structure during the course of the century. However, paradoxically, the judicial and social values which have infused the concept of the welfare of the child have turned the abstract commitment to equality into a strong presumption in favour of the mother.[77] In particular, post-war psychological theories emphasising the central importance of the mother–child bond[78] have proved highly influential, resulting in a shift in the caselaw away from strict equality and towards a preference in favour of awarding custody of the children to the mother. Necessarily, too, the courts have ceased to regard the mother's adultery as a bar to an award of custody in her favour.[79] In effect, then, the 'equality' approach has given way to a 'difference' approach based on the assumption of a mother's special role in relation to children. Recent decisions appear not to be based so much on a preference for the mother, as on a judicial policy not to remove children from the parent who has custody at the time of decision. However, because the vast majority of children remain with their mothers on separation, and because mothers appear to be more tenacious than husbands in attempting to obtain custody, the effect is little different.[80] While this certainly signifies progress when compared to earlier policies, it has been an ambiguous

---

[72] Guardianship of Infants Act 1886, s. 7.
[73] Divorce and Matrimonial Causes Act 1857, s. 35.     [74] See below.
[75] Guardianship of Minors Act 1925, s. 1; now the Guardianship Act 1973.
[76] Cornish and Clarke, *Law and Society in England*, above n. 2, p. 404.
[77] Hoggett and Pearl, above n. 65, p. 354.
[78] See for example, J. Bowlby, *Child Care and the Growth of Love* (2nd edn.) (Penguin, 1965), pp. 13–15.
[79] See, e.g., *Re K (Minors)* [1979] 1 All ER 647 (CA).
[80] J. M. Eekelaar and E. Clive with K. Clarke and S. Raikes, *Custody after Divorce* (Oxford University Press, 1977), paras. 3.6; 13.7.

victory for women. In practical terms, this assumption, together with the exponential rise in the divorce rate, has led to a large class of single mothers with primary responsibility for child-care.

### iii) **Divorce**

Judges were first given the power to adjudicate divorce in 1857. However, the new provisions were clearly aimed at continued protection of husbands' rights to assure their own paternity, rather than at spousal equality. Thus the Matrimonial Causes Act 1857 gave statutory authority to the 'double standard of adultery': 'simple' adultery would be a matrimonial offence if committed by the wife; but not if committed by the husband. Instead, a wife petitioning for divorce would need to prove that the husband had committed 'aggravated' adultery, that is incestuous adultery, bigamy with adultery, adultery with desertion for two years, adultery with cruelty, or rape, sodomy or bestiality.[81] Moreover, the newly created Divorce Court simply reinforced current assumptions. Even though the Act gave the Court a wide discretion to make such provision as it deemed just, regardless of the guilt of the parties, 'guilty' wives were almost invariably refused custody and access. 'It will probably have a salutary effect on the interest of public morality, that it should be known that a woman, if found guilty of adultery, will forfeit as far as this court is concerned, all rights to the custody of or access to her children.'[82] This was the case even if the court acknowledged that the husband's conduct towards the wife had precipitated the adultery.[83] This attitude continued well into the twentieth century.[84]

The Act did attempt to redress some of the imbalance between rich and poor, by creating a new Divorce Court to deal with divorce petitions instead of the ecclesiastical courts or highly inaccessible Parliament. However, its success in this respect was limited. Because all petitioners had to travel to the court in London, and because costs remained high, such proceedings were still out of the reach of people of ordinary means. As a result, the number of decrees granted annually never exceeded 583.[85] In practice, a two-tier system became entrenched, with poorer petitioners forced to rely on the limited powers given to the magistrates' courts in 1878 to protect wives against severe marital violence; in such cases, the magistrates could order what was in effect a decree of judicial separation for wives, and, where appropriate, weekly maintenance and legal custody of children under ten in favour of the wife (see below).[86] The result, according to the Finer Report was that 'the concern for extending to a larger population the benefits which the 1857 reforms had afforded to the wealthy bore fruit in the

---

[81] Divorce and Matrimonial Causes Act 1857, s. 27.
[82] *Seddon* v. *Seddon and Doyle* (1862) 2 Sw. & Tr. 640 at 642.
[83] *ibid.*       [84] Cornish and Clarke, above n. 2, p. 390.
[85] Finer and McGregor, above n. 19, para. 34.
[86] Matrimonial Causes Act 1878, s. 4.

creation of a secondary system designed for what were considered to be the special and cruder requirements of the poor.'[87]

It was not until 1923 that formal equality between wife and husband finally achieved statutory recognition. According to the Matrimonial Causes Act of 1923, either party could petition for a divorce on the grounds of simple adultery.[88] However, the fact that this matrimonial offence remained the sole ground made it impossible to divorce for other reasons, particularly, cruelty and desertion. It was left to the Matrimonial Causes Act 1937 to broaden the grounds for divorce to include three years' desertion and cruelty. Nevertheless, divorce remained a costly affair for most women, given their very limited access to resources of their own; indeed, as the Finer Report shows, it was not until the legal aid scheme of 1949 that wives won practical equality of access to the court.[89] The idea of a matrimonial offence as the main ground for divorce was even more intractable, and more open grounds of divorce were not introduced until the Divorce Reform Act 1969.

## iv) **Control over Women's Bodies**

For many married women, one of the most problematic aspects of marriage was the day-to-day reality of their husbands' legal rights to control their bodies. This control was reinforced by a married woman's lack of rights in other spheres. In particular, her inability to own property, and the restraints on access to paid employment, made it financially impossible for her to escape from a cruel or abusive husband. Possibly the clearest illustration of the law's endorsement of male domination over women was the legal sanctioning of violence and rape against married women. As in other areas, prevailing political ideals of personal liberty and equality made little impact on the position of married women. Here the public–private divide was put to work, firmly insulating relationships within the family from the reach of political rights.

As we have seen, one of the many powers of seventeenth century husbands was the power to 'correct' their wives. Blackstone justified this by asserting that 'as [the husband] is to answer for [the wife's] misbehaviour, the law thought it reasonable to intrust him with this power of restraining her, by domestic chastisement, in the same moderation that a man is allowed to correct his apprentices or children.'[90] Although 'in the politer reign of Charles the second',[91] this power came to be doubted, the court would still permit a husband to restrain his wife in order to ensure that she continued to cohabit with him. 'For the happiness and the honour of *both* parties, [the law] places the wife under the guardianship of the husband, and entitles him, for the sake of both, to protect her from the danger of

---

[87]   Finer and McGregor, above n. 19, para. 36.
[88]   Matrimonial Causes Act 1923, s. 1.
[89]   Finer and McGregor, above n. 19, para. 43.
[90]   Blackstone, above n. 2, p. 444.       [91]   *ibid.*, p. 445.

unrestrained intercourse with the world, by enforcing cohabitation and a common residence.'[92] Blackstone himself saw little contradiction between this power and the rights of personal security and personal liberty which he classified as two of the three principal or primary rights of the people of England.[93] This myopia could be achieved by assigning the family to a 'private' sphere which should not be invaded by the State. The result was to endorse substantial levels of violence perpetrated against wives. When feminist leaders turned their attention to the issue in the mid-nineteenth century, their efforts revealed the extent and severity of wife battering. As Mill vividly declared in the House of Commons:

I would like to have a Return laid before this House of the number of women who are annually beaten to death, kicked to death or trampled to death by their male protectors; and in an opposite column the amount of the sentences passed in those cases in which the dastardly criminals did not get off altogether . . . we would then have an arithmetical estimate of the value set by a male legislature and male tribunals on the murder of a woman . . .'[94]

Cobbe estimated that some 1,500 cases for brutal assaults against women were brought annually during the 1870s; a figure which covered only gross physical injury or the use of a dangerous weapon,[95] and ignored common assaults and those which were never reported or never prosecuted.

In campaigning on behalf of battered wives, feminist leaders recognised that a key issue was the inability of working-class wives to leave their marriages.[96] Legal constraints aside, the lack of financial independence made it impossible for a woman, especially if she had children, to contemplate separation from her husband. Indeed, there is evidence to show that where women had some financial independence, they were much more likely to prosecute their husbands for ordinary common law assault. Clark has pointed out that many working-class women in the late eighteenth century in London still participated actively in the family economy, and it was they who were most likely to utilise what limited legal remedies were available to them.[97] However, these remedies were limited indeed; and even such women were substantially hampered by their inability to own even their own earnings. It was because of this that campaigners shifted the debate from punishment of the offender to the provision of relief for the victim.[98]

Limited legislative intervention was achieved in 1853, when magistrates were given the power to impose six-month sentences on those found guilty

---

[92] *R* v. *Cochrane* (1840) 8 Dowl. 630 at p. 636.
[93] Blackstone, above n. 2, vol. 1, p. 129.
[94] Hansard Parl Deb. vol. CLXXXVII (20 May 1867), col 826.
[95] Shanley, *Feminism, Marriage and the Law in Victorian England*, above n. 9, p. 162.
[96] *ibid.*, p. 160.
[97] A. Clark 'Humanity or Justice' in Smart (ed.), *Regulating Womanhood*, above n. 18, p. 193.
[98] Shanley, above n. 9, p. 167.

of aggravated assaults on women and children.[99] Such light sentences meant that it was still true to say 'how much safer it was to stab one's wife than to defraud one's master.'[100] Moreover, the movement for protection of battered wives found itself in an unholy alliance with class prejudice against working-class men. Wife abuse was portrayed as a problem only of the working classes; and working-class wife batterers were correspondingly portrayed as irresponsible drunk brutes, who did not deserve the right to privacy from the law.[101] This was then extrapolated to discredit working-class claims to equal suffrage.

The Matrimonial Causes Act 1878 added some protective powers to existing punitive provisions by providing that if a husband was summarily convicted of an aggravated assault upon his wife, the court or magistrate which heard the case could order a judicial separation, and, in its discretion could order custody of children under ten in favour of the wife. Equally important on a practical level was the power to order the husband to pay a weekly sum of maintenance.[102] However, the ambivalence of the law to-wards violence against wives was clearly evidenced in that a conviction of aggravated assault on the wife was not in itself sufficient; in addition, the court or magistrate had to be satisfied that her future safety was in peril. In practice, this extra discretion was used by magistrates to send wives back to their husbands despite a proved history of wife beating.[103] Moreover, the institutional condemnation of adultery by a woman remained strong enough to displace her rights to protection: the Act also prohibited custody or maintenance orders in favour of a wife who had committed adultery (unless it had been condoned) and any future adultery could result in the discharge of both orders.

Shanley shows that evidence of the effect of the 1878 Act on the extent of wife beating was ambiguous. What is clear, however, is that law as an instrument of social reform was far from the panacea which nineteenth century feminists saw it as. Because a battered wife was reliant on a court order,[104] which could only be issued by a male judge or magistrate, the law could be subverted by continuing adherence within the judiciary to as-sumptions about the acceptability of violence against women. Magistrates were clearly reluctant to grant separation orders, and sentences for assault remained light, particularly if the magistrate considered it to have been justified by a 'shrill and shrewish wife'.[105] Without a separation order, the wife was singularly unprotected. If she left her husband, she would be guilty

---

[99] Aggravated Assaults on Women and Children Act 1853.
[100] *Daily News*, 24 August 1846, quoted in Clark, above n. 97, p. 199.
[101] Clark, above n. 97, p. 201; see J. S. Mill, *The Subjection of Women* (2nd edn.) (1869); Shanley, above n. 9, p. 166.
[102] Matrimonial Causes Act 1978, s. 4.
[103] Shanley, above n. 9, p. 169.
[104] *ibid.*, p. 174.
[105] *ibid.*, p. 171.

of desertion, and, prior to 1884, could be forced to return to him under threat of a prison sentence (see below). In addition, she would forfeit custody of her children and have no means of support.

Some of these defects were remedied in subsequent statutes. Most importantly, an 1895 statute allowed a wife to leave her husband *before* applying to court for orders of separation and maintenance. Grounds for application included not only, as before, a conviction of aggravated assault, but also one of ordinary assault. Moreover, even in the absence of a conviction, she could show that she had left him because of his persistent cruelty to her or his wilful neglect to maintain her or her children.[106] Custody orders were extended to encompass children under sixteen. However, adultery by the wife remained an absolute bar to the granting of an order, mitigated only by the exception in cases where the husband's wilful neglect or misconduct led to the adultery.[107]

The problem of marital violence received little attention during most of the twentieth century;[108] and it was only relatively recently that protection for battered wives was enhanced. The main judicial weapon was to develop the injunctive remedy. This remedy has always been available to the High Court as an interim protective measure during divorce or separation proceedings. In 1976, the County Court was given wider powers to issue injunctions outside of divorce proceedings, including the power to order the respondent not to molest the complainant, to depart from the home (even if he owns it) and to remain outside of the area in which the home is situated.[109] A power of arrest may be attached to the order if the judge is satisfied that actual bodily harm has been caused to the applicant by the respondent and that this is likely to recur.[110]

It took even longer for the law to recognise the right of a married woman not to be raped by her husband. For two-and-a-half centuries, and with little dissent, the law consistently held that a husband could not be guilty of raping his wife. Nor were the contradictions between prevailing theories of individual freedom of contract and the realities of the wife's subordination permitted to undermine the principle. Rather, the contradiction was purportedly overcome by deeming that the wife, in marrying the husband, had consented to having intercourse with him at his whim. This consent, moreover, was of an unusual kind: it could not be withdrawn. Thus, as far back as 1736, Sir Matthew Hale declared: 'The husband cannot be guilty of rape committed by himself upon his lawful wife, for by their mutual matrimonial consent and contract the wife hath given herself up in this kind

---

[106] Summary Jurisdiction (Married Women) Act 1895, s. 4.

[107] *ibid.*, s. 6.

[108] J. Eekelaar, *Family Law and Social Policy* (2nd edn., Weidenfeld & Nicolson, 1984), p. 158.

[109] Domestic Violence and Proceedings Act 1976, s. 1.

[110] *ibid.*, s. 2. Similar, although somewhat more complex, powers were given to magistrates under the Domestic Proceedings and Magistrates' Courts Act 1978.

unto her husband which she cannot retract.'[111] Similarly, a later commentator stated: '. . . a husband cannot by law be guilty of ravishing his wife, on account of the matrimonial consent which she cannot retract.'[112] This principle was judicially endorsed in the late nineteenth century case of *R* v. *Clarence*,[113] where Stephen J firmly reiterated his belief that a husband could not be convicted of raping his wife.[114] Such endorsement, indeed, was not withdrawn until 1991. Even in the 1950s a judge could state that, although a husband was not entitled to use force or violence to achieve intercourse, he 'has a right to marital intercourse and the wife cannot refuse her consent'.[115] Judges in the mid-twentieth century did begin to formulate exceptions in extreme circumstances, holding, for example, that consent could be revoked by a judicial separation order;[116] or by a decree nisi;[117] but as recently as 1990, a court held that a wife could not be considered to have revoked consent simply because a family protection order preventing the husband from using or threatening violence against her was in force.[118]

Nor was legislative reform forthcoming. Here, the debate focused less on the issue of consent, and more on the alleged importance of privacy and the sanctity of marriage. This debate is well reflected in the report of the Criminal Law Revision Committee in 1980. The minority favoured retention of the marital rape immunity on the grounds that if a wife could invoke the law of rape in all circumstances of non-consensual intercourse, the consequences for the family, including both wife and children, would be grave. Calling in the police, it was argued, would end any remaining chance of marital conciliation and the police would have to make distasteful inquiries into the details of married life. Indeed, this argument went so far as to blame the wife: 'a marital breakdown caused by a wife who had sought the protection of the criminal law would be particularly painful.'[119] The majority, while proposing that rape should be a crime within marriage, nevertheless accepted some of the arguments based on the privacy and sanctity of the family. 'If wives were to be treated in relation to rape in the same way as other women, that might lead to prosecutions which some would think were not desirable in the interest of the family or the public.'[120] They thus proposed that the consent of the Director of Public Prosecutions be required for prosecutions of marital rape. Even this diluted recognition was not acceptable. The statutory definition of rape, which

---

[111] Sir Matthew Hale, *History of the Pleas of the Crown*, 1 Hale PC (1736) 629.

[112] East, *Treatise of the Pleas of the Crown* 1 East PC 446.

[113] [1889] 22 QB 23.        [114] At p. 46.

[115] *R* v. *Miller* [1954] 2 All ER 529 at 533–4.

[116] *R* v. *Clarke* [1949] 2 All ER 448.

[117] *R* v. *O'Brien* [1974] 3 All ER 663.

[118] *R* v. *Sharples* [1990] G.M.L.R. 198.

[119] Criminal Law Revision Committee, *Working Paper of Sexual Offences* (1980) London HMSO, para. 33.

[120] *ibid.*, para. 42.

defined rape as having 'unlawful' intercourse with a woman without her consent[121] was widely construed as meaning that only intercourse outside of marriage was covered, thus giving statutory endorsement to the marital rape exception.

It was left to the common law finally to recognise that the assumptions behind the marital rape exception could no longer be sustained. The immunity was rejected first in 1989 by the High Court of Justiciary in Scotland,[122] and eventually, in 1991 by the House of Lords.[123] Lord Keith, with whom all the judges agreed, rejected the argument that 'unlawful' in the statute meant extramarital only; and held that the common law should now recognise that the status of married women had changed out of all recognition since Hale set out his proposition. Most importantly, he declared, 'marriage is in modern times regarded as a partnership of equals, and no longer one in which the wife must be the subservient chattel of the husband.'[124]

The final area of control over women's bodies, an area which may not necessarily involve violence, has concerned the ancient right, derived from canon law, of either party to claim restoration of conjugal rights. The Divorce Act 1857 gave statutory force to this right providing too that refusal to obey an order to cohabit was contempt, enforceable by imprisonment. The duty to cohabit was never held to include the duty to have intercourse.[125] However, the fact that a husband who forced his wife to have sex could not be charged with rape under the criminal law meant that in effect intercourse could be compelled. 'The physiological differences between men and women often made it possible for a husband to force sexual relations on his wife while neither she nor the court could force them upon him: gender neutral language marked very real differences in power between men and women.'[126]

As was so often the case with law reform, it was the attempt by a woman to enforce the duty to cohabit against her husband[127] that prompted Parliament to remove the sanction of imprisonment and deem instead that noncompliance with a decree for the restitution of conjugal rights amounted to desertion without reasonable cause, entitling the court to proceed immediately to a decree of judicial separation.[128] However, it remained unclear whether the husband had the right to detain his wife against her will. In 1840, Coleridge J had stated that 'there can be no doubt of the general

---

[121] Sexual Offences (Amendment) Act 1976, s. 1(1).
[122] *S* v. *HM Advocate* [1989] SLT 469.
[123] *R* v. *R* [1991] 4 All ER 481.
[124] *R* v. *R* [1991] 4 All ER at p. 484.
[125] *Forster* v. *Forster* (1790), Haggard's Reports vol. 1 144 at p. 154.
[126] Shanley, *Feminism, Marriage and the Law in Victorian England*, above n. 9, p. 178.
[127] *Weldon* v. *Weldon* [1883] 9 P.D. 52.
[128] Matrimonial Causes Act 1884, s. 4. In other circumstances, judicial separation could only be ordered if a period of two years had elapsed.

dominion which the law of England attributes to the husband over the wife'.[129] He therefore held that it was lawful for a husband to confine his wife in his own home, provided he used no cruelty. By the end of the century, however, even the courts had come to see the injustice of such a principle. Lord Halsbury LC, faced in 1891 by a husband's claim that he had the right to imprison his wife, was sufficiently outraged to declare that 'such quaint and absurd dicta as are to be found in the books as to the right of a husband over his wife in respect of personal chastisement are not, I think, now capable of being cited as authorities in a court of justice in this or any civilized country.'[130] In the same case, Lord Esher MR referred to 'a series of propositions . . . which, if true, make an English wife the slave, the abject slave of her husband . . . I do not believe that this was ever the law.'[131] Thus the Court of Appeal agreed to issue a writ of habeas corpus in favour of the detained wife.[132] The decision was hailed as a great victory by feminists and criticised as a betrayal of the fundamentals of marriage. However as Shanley shows[133] the victory was more symbolic than real. The action for restitution of conjugal rights was not abolished until 1970; in the meantime, noncompliance by a wife constituted desertion, which, in a divorce action, would deprive her of any rights to maintenance and custody.

## II.  SUFFRAGE

The refusal to extend political rights to women was possibly the most strident assertion of the internal contradictions of formal liberal theory. Until well into the twentieth century, women, far from being included in the category of rational individuals worthy of political rights, continued to be barred from political participation. The well-worn justifications were rehearsed over and over again. Women belonged in the private sphere not the public; they were emotional and irrational, allied with the body and not the mind, and temperamentally unsuited to the rough and tumble of political life. It was frequently argued, too, that women did not really want the vote, and were content to be represented by fathers and husbands. Underlying this was the politically expedient numerical argument: the apparently unacceptable scenario of men being numerically inferior to women.[134] Asquith exemplified these arguments when he declared in 1892:

[Women's] natural sphere is not the turmoil and dust of politics, but the circle of social and domestic life . . . The inequalities which democracy requires that we should fight against and remove are the unearned privileges and the artificial

---

[129]  *In re Cochrane* (1840) 8 Dowling 630.
[130]  *R* v. *Jackson* [1891] 1 QB 671 at 679.
[131]  *ibid.*, at p. 682.
[132]  *ibid.*
[133]  Shanley, above n. 9, p. 184.
[134]  D. Morgan, *Suffragists and Liberals* (Basil Blackwell, 1975), p. 15.

distinctions which man has made, and which man can unmake. They are not those indelible difference of faculty and function by which Nature herself has given diversity and richness to human society.[135]

These attitudes were even more apparent among the judiciary than the legislature: as will be seen below, concessions wrested from Parliament were frequently undermined by the courts.

As in marriage laws, gender domination interacted in a complex and significant manner with class divisions. Arguments about the extension of the franchise to women were frequently divided on class lines, particularly during the nineteenth century, when the extent to which working-class men were to be allowed to vote was still a matter of political controversy. Thus feminist groups were often divided over whether to insist on the franchise for all adults, regardless of property, or to press only for formal equality with men, thus limiting the suffrage to propertied women. Similarly, representatives of single women were prepared to advocate the exclusion of married women from any proposed extension. These issues are examined in more detail below.

The struggle for women's suffrage must also be examined in the context of the historical development of democracy in general. As was noted in Chapter 1, the demise of feudalism and its replacement by liberal political economies was by no means inevitably accompanied by democracy. At the beginning of the nineteenth century, the franchise was largely limited to male property owners, and even within this group, the system was ramshackle and unfair. An elector who qualified in two or more ways could exercise his vote two or more times: Chamberlain, for example, had six votes in 1885.[136] In the 'rotten' boroughs, consisting of towns which had decayed away, the few remaining property owners could wield total power.[137] Constituencies varied widely in size, so that the value of each vote was by no means equivalent. At the same time, the unelected House of Lords was a central source of power; and the monarch retained an important role.

During the 1820s and 1830s, the need for reform became apparent. But, although equal political rights for women had been advocated as early as 1792 by Mary Wollstonecraft and others, this aspect of reform was not on the political agenda. A petition presented to Parliament during the debates on the 1832 Reform Act received no Parliamentary support: notably too, it sought the franchise only for unmarried, qualified women.[138] Even this was totally disregarded; to the contrary, the 1832 Representation of the People

---

[135] Hansard Parl Deb. 4th Series vol. III, 27 April 1892, c. 1513; see also Hansard Parl Deb. vol. CLXXXVIII (20 May 1867), col 832, 839.

[136] J. P. D. Dunbabin, 'Electoral Reforms and their Outcome in the United Kingdom 1865–1900' in T. R. Gourvish and A. O'Day, *Later Victorian Britain* (Macmillan, 1988), p. 94.

[137] Cornish and Clarke, *Law and Society in England*, above n. 2, p. 9.

[138] Morgan, above n. 134, p. 10.

Act, which extended the franchise to limited categories, referred specifically to male persons.[139]

It was not until the 1860s that campaigners for the female suffrage could be regarded as an organised movement, a movement which received an important fillip by the election to Parliament of John Stuart Mill in 1865. In the run-up to the Second Reform Act,[140] however, the suffrage campaign was fought largely on grounds of formal equality between single propertied women and men. Thus a petition presented to the House in 1866, containing the signatures of 1,499 women, demanded the enfranchisement of 'all householders, without distinction of sex, who possess such property or rental qualification as your Honourable House may determine'.[141] Married women were clearly excluded, since, as we have seen, they could not at that time own property in their own right. Similarly, Mill's submission during the debates in Parliament was firmly based on the admission of women on the same property conditions as men.[142] In the event, the 1867 Act represented a major extension of the male suffrage, symbolising the important recognition by the dominant classes of the need to incorporate the 'respectable working class' into political life: 'the skilled workers who by earnings and an eagerness for education had marked themselves out as an "aristocracy of labour" '.[143] The Act gave the vote to all male householders in the towns, and decreased the rating limit for occupiers in the counties to £12.[144] However, the idea that political maturity was signified by householdership did not reach into the deep-seated stereotypes about women. Still, the fact that Mill's amendment, seeking to remove the word 'man' from the bill, attracted 73 votes, as against 194, gave some encouragement to the embryonic suffrage movement.[145]

Nor did the suffragists' attempts to draw the courts onto their side of the battle meet with any success; indeed, subsequent history shows that such attempts were doomed to failure. In *Chorlton* v. *Ling*,[146] it was argued that women were incorporated into the 1867 Representation of the People Act by virtue of an earlier statute, known as Lord Brougham's Act, which provided that 'words importing the masculine gender shall be deemed and taken to include females, unless the contrary is expressly provided.'[147] However, in a stance that proved characteristic of the judiciary for the next sixty years, the court rejected the argument. Although women had clearly not been expressly excluded from the extension of the suffrage, Willes J

---

[139] See e.g. ss. 19, 20, 27.
[140] Representation of the People Act 1867.
[141] Cited in A. Rosen, *Rise Up Women* (Routledge, 1974), p. 6.
[142] Hansard Parl Deb. vol. CLXXXVII (20 May 1867), col 829.
[143] Cornish and Clarke, above n. 2, p. 16.
[144] Representation of the People Act 1867, ss. 3–6.
[145] Morgan, above n. 134, p. 12.
[146] (1868) 4 L.R.C.P. 374 at 386.
[147] Lord Brougham's Act (13 & 14 Vict. c. 21), s. 4.

refused to accept that they were impliedly included by virtue of Lord Brougham's Act. On his view, Lord Brougham's Act, in stating that women were included unless the contrary is 'expressly provided', obviously meant that women could also be excluded by 'what is necessarily or properly implied' by the statute. Here the exclusion of women was necessarily implied. Although it is arguable that this was a credible position in the light of the express opposition to the extension of the suffrage to women, it also demonstrates the absence of sympathy among the judiciary for women's enfranchisement.

At local level, somewhat more credence was given to women's claims, possibly because local issues such as the Poor Laws and education were seen to be within the female, caring sphere.[148] Women with the relevant qualifications had been eligible to vote for Poor Law Guardians since 1834.[149] They had been, somewhat paradoxically, denied the right to vote for local government in 1835.[150] However, in an important victory, women ratepayers were given the municipal franchise on the same terms as men in 1869,[151] reflecting grudging acceptance of the principle of 'no taxation without representation'. Once again, however, the judiciary were quick to grasp at semantic niceties to pare down women's rights. The 1869 statute clearly provided that 'words importing the masculine gender . . . shall be held to include females for all purposes connected with . . . the right to vote'.[152] Nevertheless, within three years of the passing of the 1869 Act, the Queen's Bench Division held that married women were excluded.[153] 'Marriage is at common law a total disqualification, and a married woman, therefore, could not vote, her existence for such a purpose being merged in that of her husband . . . [The 1869 Act] only removes the disqualification by reason of sex, and leaves untouched the disqualification by reason of status.'[154] Nor was this the last of judicial incursions. When a new structure of local government was established during the 1880s, women were included among those entitled to vote, using the usual provision that 'for all purposes connected . . . with the right to vote at municipal elections words . . . importing the masculine gender include women.'[155] This time, the judges turned from the right to vote to the right to be elected. On the face of it, the intention of Parliament seemed clear: the Act provided that those entitled to elect should also be entitled to be elected.[156] Nevertheless,

[148] P. Thane 'Late Victorian Women' in Gourvish and O' Day, above n. 136, p. 207.

[149] Poor Law Amendment Act 1834.

[150] Municipal Corporation Act 1835: in fact, this disentitled some women in the older boroughs who had technically had the vote before.

[151] Municipal Franchise Act 1869, ss. 1, 9.

[152] ibid., s. 9.

[153] R v. Harrald [1872] L R VII QB 361.

[154] ibid. per Mellor J at p. 363.

[155] Municipal Corporations Act 1882, s. 63, incorporated into Local Government Act 1888.

[156] Municipal Corporations Act 1882, s. 11.

the Court of Appeal held,[157] the right to be elected did not extend to women. This was because, in providing that the masculine gender referred also to women, the Act only referred to the right to vote, not the right to be elected. The common law rule that women could not hold public office could not be shifted. 'Unless a statute expressly gives power to women to exercise [public functions], it is to be taken that the true construction is that the powers given are confined to men and that Lord Brougham's Act does not apply.'[158] This was reiterated two years later. 'By the common law of England' stated Lord Esher MR, 'women are not in general deemed capable of exercising public functions' and only express words in a statute could change this.[159] Similarly, maintained Fry LJ: 'As the law stands, a woman is absolutely disqualified by nature from being elected to a county council and her election is a mere nullity.'[160] Nor could the Married Women's Property Act 1870, which gave married women limited property rights, be construed to extend women's political rights by a side-wind.

The judicial restrictions were not reversed by the legislature until the Local Government Act of 1894, which expressly provided that no-one should be disqualified by reason of her sex or marriage from being elected as a member of a parish or district council or as a Poor Law Guardian.[161] Women with the municipal franchise could also vote and stand for school boards;[162] and by 1900 there were 200 female members of school boards and 1,975 female Poor Law Guardians.[163] Progress was, however, uneven: the Education Act of 1902 which established a new system of education, paradoxically removed education from the hands of the School Board system, through which women had, for the past 32 years, been able to exercise an active influence.[164]

At national level, progress was far slower. Both the major parties of the late nineteenth century, the Liberals and Conservatives, were largely opposed to female suffrage. In particular, the continued opposition of Gladstone and Asquith made progress almost impossible.[165] When the householder vote was extended to include rural areas in 1884,[166] thus extending the franchise to two in three adult males, women remained in the wilderness. Indeed, the attempt to introduce suffrage for women as an amendment to the Representation of the People Bill of that year was defeated by 136 votes, including that of Gladstone.[167]

[157] *Beresford-Hope* v. *Lady Sandhurst* [1889] 23 QBD 79.
[158] *ibid.*, at p. 96 (*per* Lord Esher MR).
[159] *De Souza* v. *Cobden* [1891] 1 QB 687 (CA) at p. 691.    [160] *ibid.*, at p. 692.
[161] Local Government Act 1894, ss. 3(2), 20(2); 23(2); and see London County Council Election Qualification Act 1900.
[162] Elementary Education Act 1870, s. 29.
[163] Thane, above n. 148, p. 207.
[164] Morgan, above n. 134, p. 32.
[165] See generally Rosen, above n. 141, p. 11ff.
[166] Representation of the People Act 1884.
[167] Rosen, above n. 141, p. 10.

Rather greater encouragement was given by the Independent Labour Party, which allowed women to play a more central role in its affairs than other parties. Moreover, the trade union members whose donations kept the Labour Representation Committee alive included a substantial number of women.[168] However, the nascent Labour Party found itself caught in the basic dilemma of the suffragists: in taking a determined stand in favour of universal suffrage, it found itself opposing any proposal for female suffrage based on property or other qualifications. Indeed, it was argued that extending the franchise to women on the basis of the existing property qualifications would harm the working class, since a disproportionate number of those enfranchised would be women of property who were unlikely to support Labour candidates.[169] This was reflected in the Resolution carried at the 1905 Labour Party Conference, which stated:

That this Conference, believing that any women's enfranchisement bill which seeks merely to abolish sex disqualifications would increase the political power of the propertied classes by enfranchising upper and middle class women and leaving the great majority of working women still voteless, hereby expresses its conviction that Adult Suffrage—male and female—is the only Franchise Reform which merits any support from the Labour Members of Parliament.[170]

Faced with a large Liberal victory in 1906, after an election in which women's suffrage was not even remotely an issue,[171] an important part of the women's movement took the crucial decision that attempts to persuade male politicians to concede power were doomed to failure unless more shocking tactics could be utilised. Thus the Suffragette movement, led by Emmeline Pankhurst and her daughters, resorted to increasingly militant action, which steadily escalated in the pre-war period from passive resistance to campaigns of arson, window-breaking and stone-throwing. Hundreds of women were arrested, imprisoned and subjected to police abuse during the next eight years.[172] There is no doubt that the activities of the suffragettes made an immense impact on the political scene, and later developments could probably not have happened without them.[173] However, there was little direct effect, especially after Asquith, an implacable opponent of the suffrage for women, took office in 1907.

When war broke out in 1914, some of the momentum was lost. There were deep divisions within the women's movement over the legitimacy of

---

[168] Rosen, above n. 141, p. 26.

[169] *ibid.*, p. 54; Morgan, above n. 134, p. 30.

[170] Cited in Morgan, above n. 134, p. 34.

[171] *ibid.*, p. 40.

[172] For extended accounts of the suffragette movement, see M. Fawcett, *Women's Suffrage* (T. C. and E. C. Jack, 1912); E. Pankhurst, *My Own Story* (Routledge, 1914); C. Rover, *Women's Suffrage and Party Politics in Britain 1866–1914* (Routledge and Kegan Paul, 1967); Morgan, above n. 134; Rosen, above n. 141.

[173] Morgan, above n. 134, p. 149.

the war, with some leading figures passionately committed to pacifism, and others equally committed to supporting the war effort.[174] Pankhurst and her followers, for example, called off their militant campaign and took a remarkably patriotic stand.[175] At the same time, the economic and political expediencies of war did more for the cause of women's suffrage than all the previous decades of campaigning. Women were drafted into the economy in large numbers, defusing all remaining caricatures of female fragility, emotionality and necessary confinement to home life. The number of women employed rose from 3.23 million in 1914 to 4.18 million by January 1918, with women routinely doing such 'male' work as bank clerks, bus conductors, munitions work and ship-building (see Chapter 3).[176]

By 1917, even Asquith had to acknowledge that women's suffrage could no longer be consigned to the political backwater. However, even then, with the prospect of women returning to their traditional roles to make way for returning war veterans, the battle was far from won. An abiding fear among the male Parliamentarians was the possibility of an electorate in which women had numerical superiority. It soon became clear that women could not expect to be granted the franchise on equal terms with men, a higher age limit being the most likely extra restriction. Nor was reform of the franchise even on the political agenda until it became clear that huge numbers of men who were serving in the armed forces at home or abroad had been inadvertently disenfranchised by the residence requirements of the 1884 Act.[177] When legislation was introduced to address this issue,[178] it was politically impossible to exclude women. Thus when the Representation of the People Act 1918 received the Royal Assent, it included a section granting women the franchise. However, as predicted, the Act did not provide for equality between women and men, but imposed the additional requirement that women could not vote until they had attained the age of thirty.[179] Ironically, this excluded many of the women whose war effort was said to have 'earned' them the vote: the vast majority of munitions workers, for example, were under thirty. In the event, the age qualification ensured that women remained a minority: the first register of electors under the 1918 Act included 12,913,166 men and 8,479,156 women. Judicial back-sliding was to some extent prevented by another Act of the same year which stated expressly that women should not be disqualified by sex or marriage from being elected as a Member of the House of Commons, or of sitting or voting as such a member.[180] This became law just in time for the election of 1918: paradoxically, too, it contained no age restriction, so that women

[174] J. Alberti, *Beyond Suffrage* (Macmillan, 1989) pp. 38–9.
[175] Rosen, above n. 141, pp. 248–51.
[176] *ibid.*, pp. 255–6.
[177] *ibid.*, p. 257.
[178] Representation of the People Act 1918, s. 5.
[179] *ibid.*, s. 4.
[180] Parliament (Qualification of Women) Act 1918, s. 1.

under thirty could stand for Parliament without being qualified to vote in their own right.

Women's suffrage was, however, slow to produce women MPs. In the 1918 election, about eleven women stood as candidates. The only one who was elected was, ironically, a member of Sinn Fein which, because it did not recognise the Westminster Parliament, was fielding candidates with no intention of taking up their seats.[181] It was not until the next year that a woman did become an active MP: Lady Astor was elected in a by-election after her husband, who had previously held the seat, was elevated to the House of Lords.[182] In 1923, eight women were elected, but this dropped back to four in the election of 1924.[183] In the meantime, Parliament proved as frustrating an arena as ever. In 1919, the House of Lords refused to pass a Women's Emancipation Bill which proposed to equalise the suffrage and admit women peeresses to the House of Lords. Instead, the Sex Disqualification (Removal) Act 1919 was passed. This was far less sweeping than the original Bill, but did take some important steps towards formal equality by providing that a woman should not be disqualified by her sex or marriage from the exercise of any public function, including the holding of judicial office and the liability to serve on juries.[184] Even this, however, was easily undermined by tenacious opponents of equality for women. This was clearly evidenced in 1922, when Lady Rhondda, a hereditary peeress, claimed that the 1919 Act meant that she could no longer be disqualified by her sex from the exercise of the public function of membership of the House of Lords. However, the Committee of Privileges of the House of Lords decided by a majority of twenty-two to four that the Act did not entitle her to sit as a peer.[185] Semantic niceties were pushed to their extreme: it could not be denied that membership of the House of Lords was a public office, and therefore a woman could not be disqualified on grounds of her sex. But, argued Viscount Cave, women had never had the right to sit in the House; and therefore there was no 'disqualification' in the strict sense of the Act. 'The 1919 Act', he stated, 'while it removed all disqualifications, did not purport to confer any right.'[186] The Committee also resorted to the familiar artifice of 'Parliamentary intention' to reinforce the point. Since Parliament had not expressly given women the right, it must be assumed that the intention was not to confer such a right. It was not sufficient that the Act specifically used the words 'a person shall not be disqualified by sex or marriage from the exercise of any public function.'[187] According to the Lord Chancellor, Viscount Birkenhead: 'The Legislature . . . cannot be

---

[181] Alberti, above n. 174, p. 82.
[182] *ibid.*, p. 96.
[183] *ibid.*, pp. 144, 160.
[184] Sex Disqualification (Removal) Act 1919, s. 1.
[185] *Viscountess Rhondda's Claim* [1922] 22 AC 339.
[186] *ibid.* at p. 389; and see Lord Dundedin at p. 390.
[187] Sex Disqualification (Removal) Act 1919, s. 1.

taken to have . . . employed such loose and ambiguous words to carry out so momentous a revolution in the constitution of this House.'[188]

True equality was not fully conceded until 1928, when the voting age for women and men was equalised at twenty-one.[189] Although the Bill had a relatively easy passage through the House of Commons, with only ten dissenting votes, there remained vocal opponents. At this stage, explicit references to women's lack of suitability for the franchise were relatively scarce. However, the familiar assertion that women did not really want the vote was regularly repeated, and the fact that the Act would give women a numerical majority in the country was a source of great concern for some members of Parliament. For example, one MP declared 'It [the Bill] means that we shall have a majority of 2,200,000 women over men. But it means something more; it means that in a place like South Kensington, where there are two women to every man, that, if women require the vote because they have different political views from men, men have only half a vote. It means that the men there will be disenfranchised.'[190]

These views notwithstanding, the Act came into effect on 2 July 1928. It certainly marked the end of an epoch. But it was also only the beginning, for even formal equality was still far from realised. Women were still barred from the House of Lords and the diplomatic service; it was not until 1963 that formal equality in the Upper House was finally achieved.[191] Discrimination against women on the grounds of sex remained wholly lawful until 1975 (see Chapter 4). Political rights for women would begin to facilitate change, but it would take decades before the effects would fully be felt.

## III.   EMPLOYMENT

Thus far, we have dealt with the slow and painful process of rooting out legal provisions which explicitly disadvantage women. The Diceyan ideal of formal equality before the law is still not fully achieved, but great progress has been made. The labour market, however, poses different challenges for liberal theory. Formal equality before the law is wholly compatible with extreme inequalities in the labour market. Indeed, the gradual equalisation of women's property rights and political rights did little to change the extent of their disadvantage within the paid labour force. It is here that substantive notions of equality clash with some of the primary doctrines of liberalism, most importantly, those of individual autonomy, abstention of the State and a public–private divide. Only by active interference with freedom of contract can the State have any impact on substantive inequalities in the market place. The history of employment legislation demonstrates the

---

[188]  [1922] 22 AC at p. 375. See now Peerages Act 1963, s. 6.
[189]  Representation of the People (Equal Franchise) Act 1928.
[190]  Hansard Parl Deb. 5th Series vol. 215 (19 March 1928), col 1390.
[191]  Peerages Act 1963; Life Peerages Act 1958.

extreme reluctance of the liberal State to do so. What intervention there was was often piecemeal and half-hearted, and indeed, it was not until the 1970s that legislation requiring equal pay and opportunities was enacted. Employment legislation will be assessed by considering: (a) protective legislation; (b) wages legislation; and (c) anti-discrimination law. (Maternity rights will be considered in Chapter 5.)

### a) PROTECTIVE LEGISLATION

An examination of nineteenth century employment legislation reveals both the barren nature of the concept of autonomy epitomised by freedom of contract, and the crudity of strict notions of equality. Freedom of contract, the symbol of free market capitalism, makes no allowances for inequality of bargaining power. As Ramm argues, the 'history of the realisation of liberalism . . . belongs to the darkest pages of human history.'[192] The relentless exploitation of workers, be they men, women or children, began to be recognised in the nineteenth century as a fundamental challenge to liberalism. There were two possible responses. The first was to demand State intervention in the market, anathema to adherents of a public–private divide. The experience of feudalism, it was argued, demonstrated that State interference would necessarily stultify the newly-found individual freedom. The second response was collective organisation in trade unions and pressure groups, anathema to the individualists, who saw collectivities as oppressive of individuals and interfering with the smooth running of the market. The harshness of capitalist exploitation of workers nevertheless precipitated both these responses, albeit in a highly diluted form.

Most importantly, for our purposes, the two strategies, State intervention and collective organisation, generally yielded different results for men and for women. Collective organisation was the preferred option for men, since the relatively late enfranchisement of working-class men led to an entrenched scepticism about the possibilities of Parliamentary support. Thus the pressure for shorter working hours and better working conditions for adult men came primarily from collective bargaining, especially after the easing of criminal restrictions on trade union activities in 1824.[193] However, Parliamentary support was more easily forthcoming in the case of women and children and collective action more difficult. The result was that statutory protections such as maximum working hours and safety regulations generally applied to women and children only. This differential treatment led into a further and central controversy. Was protective legislation a manifestation of further discrimination against women, or was it a sensible strategy in the face of numbing oppression of women workers in mines

---

[192]  T. Ramm, '*Laissez-faire* and state protection of workers' in B. Hepple (ed.), *The Making of Labour Law in Europe* (Mansell, 1986), p. 75.

[193]  Combination Laws Repeal Act 1824; and see Combination Act 1825; and later Trade Union Act 1871, ss. 2 and 3; Conspiracy and Protection of Property Act 1875, ss. 3 and 7.

and industry? Liberal feminists tended to prefer the first view, insisting that there should be no derogation from the principle of equality with men in all respects. Many working-class women by contrast favoured protection,[194] on the grounds that it went some way towards alleviating the harshness and danger of their working lives. Formal equality for them meant equal misery for all members of the working classes; instead their aim was to achieve better conditions for women in the belief that better conditions for working-class men would follow. It will be argued here that this controversy demonstrates again the hollowness of an unqualified application of formal equality; and the risks of a crude dichotomy of equality as good and difference as bad. Protective legislation requires a more complex critical approach, which asks whether the differential treatment in fact increases or decreases the disadvantage suffered by women in the specific context. Nor does this mean that equality has no role: a richer concept of equality could argue that protection for women should be extended to men, rather than that all be stripped away in blind adherence to the myth of freedom of choice.

Nineteenth century protective legislation thus needs to be understood both in relation to the relentless burgeoning of industrial capitalism and to the disenfranchisement of the working classes. Manufacturing and mining in the eighteenth and nineteenth centuries depended on a large supply of low paid and essentially expendable workers, with the pursuit of profit unchecked by the huge cost to the health, education, and quality of life of the workers. Children were employed from under five years old, either at home with their parents or in factories, workshops, and mines. They worked six days a week, often from five or six in the morning until ten at night, with infrequent meal breaks and no opportunities to attend school.[195] These conditions were endemic in the whole system: for men, women, and children alike, hours were excessively long, leisure time almost non-existent, and pay low. In addition, the work itself was extremely hazardous. Unfenced machinery was the frequent cause of serious accidents and deaths; and constant exposure to dust, lead, and other harmful substances caused long-term and chronic disabilities. The absence of the working-class franchise meant that opportunities for Parliamentary pressure were limited. The alternative, voluntary pressure through trade unions, was often effective, but organisation was patchy, particularly for women, who tended to work in occupations which were difficult to organise.

Campaigners during the first few decades of the nineteenth century were primarily concerned with achieving legislative protection for children, and it was not until 1833 that demands for its extension to women were first heard. By then, the contours of the debate were well established, but its

---

[194] J. Lewis, *Women in England 1870–1950* (Wheatsheaf, 1984), p. 188.
[195] Much of this account is drawn from B. L. Hutchins and A. Harrison, *A History of Factory Legislation* (P. S. King & Son Ltd, 1911), e.g. pp. 7ff.

implications for women were extremely complex. In fact, among the opponents of protection, liberal feminists found themselves in an uneasy alliance with strident advocates of laissez faire capitalism. On the other hand, supporters of statutory protection were clearly ambiguous as to whether their chief motivation was to improve the condition of women in the work-force, or to exclude them from the paid labour market altogether. More complex still was the fact that many active women trade unionists were in favour of limiting women's participation in the work-force in order to relieve their arduous double burden of work in the home and work in the factory. These various arguments need to be considered more carefully.

Most unambiguous was the approach of the free marketeers. These opponents of legislative intervention drew on a strong combination of the doctrines of individualism, autonomy and State neutrality, in support of the contention that the State should not interfere with individual freedom of contract in the market. As one Member of Parliament put it, the interference with the labour of adult men would constitute an 'interference with the only property they had to dispose of—namely, their labour'.[196] This was an effective and useful position for factory and mine owners, since individual freedom in effect meant freedom only for themselves, as the most powerful bargainers, to set the price and conditions of labour. In addition, it was a highly influential argument in a Parliament consisting largely of members of their own class. A very different set of arguments was used by liberal feminist opponents of protective legislation for women. This group, which included John Stuart Mill and Henry Fawcett, viewed protective legislation as merely reinforcing women's inequality in society. They too drew on central liberal concepts, although with a different dimension. Thus, the argument went, protective legislation interfered with women's autonomy, particularly their right to choose whether or not to undertake paid work, and what kind of work to do. Moreover, there should be no deviation from the principle of equality with men. On a more pragmatic level, they believed that protective legislation excluded women from essential means of livelihood.[197] This argument was shared by active members of the women's movement, both within trade unions and in the middle classes.[198]

The motivations of proponents of legislation were far more complex. Apart from humanitarians and enlightened capitalists such as Robert Owen, the major source of pressure for protective legislation came from working-class men, who, from 1831 organised themselves into vocal 'Short-time Committees'. It was clear that one of their primary aims was the achievement of a statutory ten-hour working day for all workers. However, they soon recognised that the strength of the laissez-faire argument

---

[196] Cited in Hutchins and Harrison, above n. 195, p. 89.     [197] ibid., pp. 185–6.
[198] A. John (ed.), Unequal Opportunities. Women's Employment in England 1800–1918 (Blackwell, 1986), pp. 16, 214.

was such that universal limitations on working hours were unattainable. It was for this reason that they concentrated initially on limiting the hours of children. There was also a pragmatic side: since the machinery required the work of the children, it was believed that shorter hours for children would force employers to shorten the hours of everyone.[199] They met with some success: in 1833, a forty-eight-hour working week was introduced for children.[200] However, it soon became clear that there was little prospect of an extension to adults. As a result, the campaigners decided to fight the battle 'behind women's petticoats',[201] again with the partial aim of achieving better conditions for all. At the same time, the motivations of the Short-time Committees were not wholly benevolent. It is clear that the influx of cheap female labour into the market (partly as a result of the restrictions on child labour) was a source of concern to male workers, who believed that women were a threat to their jobs and levels of pay. Thus a deputation to Parliament in 1841 explicitly requested the 'gradual withdrawal of all females from the factories' on the grounds that 'home, its cares and its employment is women's true sphere'.[202] As well as arguing for shorter hours, they proposed limits on the proportions of women relative to men and the prohibition of the employment of married women in factories during the life-time of their husbands. Later in the century, in 1877, a leading trade unionist insisted that the job of unionists 'as men and husbands [was to] use their utmost efforts to bring about a condition of things, where their wives should be in their proper sphere at home, instead of being dragged into competition for livelihood against the great and strong men of the world.'[203] This approach was not, however, universal. In industries where a 'family wage' was not paid, it is very likely that male workers recognised the essential contribution to the family economy of working women. In such cases, competition from women could be avoided, not by excluding them, but by reinforcing well established patterns of job segregation[204] (see Chapter 3).

Within Parliament, yet another set of reasons led to the support of protective legislation for women. Apart from the Tory landed gentry who wished to undermine the new class of industrialists,[205] there was a strong group of supporters whose primary concerns were moral and eugenic. Faced with descriptions of women dragging heavy chains on their necks or wielding sledge-hammers, the response was one of moral outrage at the indecency of women performing hard manual work in public,[206] rather than

---

[199] Hutchins and Harrison, above n. 195, pp. 51–2.      [200] Factory Act 1833.
[201] Hutchins and Harrison, above n. 195, p. 65.
[202] Quoted in *ibid.*, p. 65.
[203] Cited in Lewis (1984), above n. 194, p. 174.
[204] *ibid.*, p. 176.
[205] Ramm, above n. 192, p. 83.
[206] See e.g. S. Webb and B. Webb, *Industrial Democracy* (Longmans, 1897) vol. ii, p. 497, n. 1.

sympathy for the arduousness and degradation of their work. Equally explicit was a eugenic concern at the quality of the children such women could bear or rear. Any regard for their plight as workers would have logically entailed the extension of protection to all adult workers. Nor was any attention paid to occupational welfare in areas such as domestic service, when conditions did not relate directly to issues of female morality or motherhood.[207]

However, cynicism about the motivation of those who campaigned for protective legislation should not be allowed to obscure the very real misery of women in the mines and factories. In 1842, the highly influential First Report of the Children's Employment Commission depicted the horrendous conditions of women working underground in mines, where from an early age they were set to work dragging trucks of coal to which they were harnessed by a chain and girdle in conditions of inhuman heat and dirt.[208] They often worked in water underground, and their working day was twelve to fourteen hours long.[209] There is no doubt that many working-class women and trade unionists supported protective legislation, and believed that they should be extended to all workers. Thus in 1875, there were over 95,000 signatories of a petition in favour of the Factories Acts Amendment Bill of that year, and only 10,693 against.[210] Similarly, several important women's organisations, such as the Women's Trade Union Association, the Women's Industrial Council, and later the Women's Labour League supported effective protective legislation, provided it did not put women at an unfair disadvantage, and campaigned actively for its improvement.[211]

In the event, the balance of power was strongly in favour of employers; and each piece of protective legislation was the result of dispute and compromise. The result was that its coverage was patchy and the enforcement machinery was weak, often leading to the worst of all worlds. For example, when legislation was finally introduced in 1819, it merely prohibited the employment of children under nine and introduced a twelve-hour day for children between nine and twelve years old.[212] Even then, the Act was restricted to cotton-mills, and enforcement was left in the hands of Justices of the Peace, who were frequently employers themselves. Protection for children was strengthened in minor ways, culminating in the 1833 Act, which introduced the forty-eight-hour week for children in the textile industry, and, possibly more importantly, established the first independent factories inspectorate to enforce the Act. Nevertheless, as Ramm points out, 'it is likely that technological changes in manufacturing methods

---

[207] Lewis (1984), above n. 194, p. 188.
[208] Hutchins and Harrison, above n. 195, pp. 81–2.
[209] Ramm, above n. 192, p. 82.
[210] John (ed.), above n. 198, p. 17.
[211] E. Mappen 'Strategists for Change' in John (ed.), above n. 198, pp. 242–3.
[212] Factory Act 1819.

played a far greater role in the decline of children's labour than the legisla-tion.'[213] Extension to women came later. In 1842, the Mines Act was passed, prohibiting the work underground of women and children; but here too, supervision was almost non-existent and the Act was largely ineffective. Soon afterwards, in what was considered a major victory for the Short-time Committees, the Factory Act of 1844 covered women as well as children and young people. It is notable that the agreement of the industrialists to the 1844 Act was only achieved because the recession had led to short-time working in any case in many of the mills.

The Act of 1844 could be seen as the first major attempt to exclude women from paid work. However, an examination of the Act reveals quite a different dimension: that is, the clear and urgent need for protection of this sort for all workers. What is striking, therefore, is not so much the inclusion of women, as the exclusion of men. For example, the Act prohib-ited the practice of cleaning machinery while in motion, but only in respect of children, young persons and women. It restricted hours of work for these groups to twelve hours a day; required that no protected person be allowed to remain in the work-room during meal-times, thus prohibiting the prac-tice of keeping workers back to clean machinery at these times, and re-quired the fencing of machinery which children or young people would be likely to pass during the working day. The refusal to extend the legislation to adult men was justified by reference to individual freedom of choice.[214]

The rest of the century is characterised by slow and fragmented exten-sions of the Factories Acts. Provisions setting upper limits on working hours were complex and easily evaded. Working hours, which were limited to twelve hours a day in 1844, were decreased to ten in 1847,[215] coinciding with the reduction in hours forced on employers in any case by the reces-sion.[216] Even so, extensive evasions were widespread.[217] Nor was there significant improvement on this score for the rest of the century: in 1901 the working day in textile factories was still ten hours, with the maximum working week marginally reduced to fifty-five and a half hours from the earlier fifty-eight. In non-textile factories, the daily maximum was higher, at ten-and-a-half hours; with a maximum weekly sixty hours. Attempts to extend protection beyond textiles met with only limited success, and small workplaces, homeworkers and family workers were protected only sporadi-cally. For example, women working at home in non-mechanical work in which only members of the family were employed were not subject to limitations on their hours of work at all.[218] The stated reason for this was that it is 'desirable to interfere as little as possible with the habits and

---

[213] Ramm, above n. 192, p. 79.
[214] Hutchins and Harrison, above n. 195, pp. 88–9.
[215] Ten Hours Act (10 & 11 Vict, c. 29).
[216] Hutchins and Harrison, above n. 195, p. 97.
[217] *ibid.*, p. 112.
[218] Factory and Workshop Act 1878, s. 16.

arrangements of families'.[219] Yet some of the worst abuses of sweated labour took place in these workshops. Finally, enforcement measures of all the statutes were weak. The introduction of the inspectorate to replace magistrates was certainly a major advance, and the reports and investigations of a committed inspectorate were highly influential in the drafting of subsequent legislation. But the overall impression is one of wide-spread evasion.

What, then, can we conclude about the respective arguments for and against protective legislation? Certainly, the weak and fragmented nature of the legislation itself indicates that its effects, whether positive or negative, were limited. However, the impact is necessarily complex. Ironically, the restriction on the employment of children led to an immense increase in the number of women working in the factories, largely because they were cheaper to employ than men. It was this that led to fears by male trade unionists that women's labour was displacing that of men. However, it is not clear that women ever were a genuine threat to men's jobs. As a start, during the course of the century, trade unions representing male manual workers secured limitations on hours of work in key areas of employment through collective bargaining without the aid of legislation. Thus the argument from equality could be turned on its head, and it could be maintained, as Kahn-Freund has, that protective legislation merely extended to unorganised workers the gains made by their counterparts with more industrial muscle.[220] In industries where in practice men and women were subject to the same limitations on their hours, the effect of the legislation could not be detrimental to women. In addition, the deeply entrenched nature of job segregation, usually meant that women were doing jobs which men would refuse to do on any conditions. This was clearly revealed by a report in 1903–4 by the Women's Industrial Council which showed that men and women did not compete for the same jobs and that the legal limit on women's hours did not lead to a reluctance by employers to employ them.[221] Nor is it clear that protective legislation had the effect overall of decreasing women's participation in the workforce. Data collected by the Inspectors of Factories show that, after the introduction of restrictions on women's labour, the percentage of women and girls above thirteen working in the textile industries grew, while that of adult males decreased.[222]

Apart from the empirical evidence, the liberal feminists' arguments in favour of freedom of choice and strict equality must be critically examined. It is clear that many of these arguments were coloured by middle-class concerns. Middle-class women were justifiably angry about the numerous

---

[219] Hutchins and Harrison, above n. 195, p. 180.
[220] O. Kahn-Freund 'Labour law' in M. Ginsberg (ed.), *Law and Opinion in England in the 20th Century* (Stevens, 1959), pp. 221–2.
[221] Mappen, above n. 211, in John (ed.), pp. 243–4.
[222] Hutchins and Harrison, above n. 195, p. 110.

obstacles in the way of their right to work in a wide variety of professions and occupations. However, for working-class women, paid work per se was not necessarily a liberation. As Hutchins and Harrison argue, it is a 'blank and unfruitful individualism'[223] which places unquestioning value on the 'right to work' fourteen hours a day doing laundering or tailoring in dreadful conditions.[224] It is also a single dimensional view of equality, which prefers lowering women's standards to that of men in the name of equality, and does not consider the importance of raising men's conditions to those of women. In practice, the right to work lay on the employers' side: it was a right to work women as long as suited the employers. In the regulated industries, by contrast, women were able to spend their extra energy in organising and educating themselves. In fact, therefore, regulation by the State facilitated self-protection and real choice on behalf of the women; whereas lack of regulation in the name of formal freedom of choice simply weakened and degraded women workers. The laundry industry, which was almost exclusively a women's industry, is a good example. The proponents of 'women's rights' strongly opposed the inclusion of laundries in the net of protective legislation, with the result that the 1895 Act permitted women to work fourteen hours a day. It is difficult to see such abstentionism as enhancing freedom of choice.

b) PAY

As will be seen in more detail in Chapter 3, low pay was one of the most consistent characteristics of women's paid work throughout the nineteenth and most of the twentieth century. This was both absolute and relative: absolute in that many women earned below the subsistence rate, even when it was defined in women's terms; and relative to men. Thus where men and women did the same work, the women's 'rate for the job' was almost invariably lower than that of the men. In addition, in many industries, women were deliberately segregated into different, and lower paying, types of work from their male counterparts. There were several contributing factors which will be explored in more detail in the next chapter. Briefly, women were often considered to be naturally less productive than men or inferior as workers;[225] or their needs were thought to be lower, requiring a lower wage to support their quality of life. Also an issue was the male workers' claim to a 'family wage', which necessarily entailed that women were only working for 'pin money'. The facts that many men had no dependants, and many women were breadwinners, were never sufficient to dislodge this claim. In addition, women tended to have less industrial muscle: they were frequently excluded from unions, or worked in scattered occupations, such as the sweated trades, which were difficult to organise.

---

[223] Hutchins and Harrison, above n. 195, p. 198.
[224] *ibid.*, p. 184.
[225] See e.g. Webb and Webb, *Industrial Democracy*, above n. 206, vol. II p. 507.

Where they were organised, as in the textile industry, their wages were significantly better. Job segregation also played a significant role: indeed, the Webbs advocated deliberate segregation so that women could continue to demand a share of the market by offering their labour at lower pay without undermining the pay of men. Many of these characteristics are epitomised in respect of home-workers. A House of Commons Select Committee on Home Work in 1909 reported that 'the earnings of a large number of people—mainly women who work in their own homes—are so small as alone to be insufficient to sustain life in the most meagre manner, even when they toil hard for extremely long hours.'[226] One of the chief causes noted by the committee was the lack of organisation of the workers, especially when these were women, which the majority were.

State intervention to correct pay levels was, however, anathema to the political and economic culture of laissez faire capitalism. The repeal in 1813 of the relevant provisions of the Statute of Artificers 1563 ended wage-fixing by organs of the State and heralded the pre-eminence of the contract of employment. This in turn symbolised a 'free', mobile labour market, where the price of labour was determined by market forces rather than the dictate of the State. At most, the State would intervene through the Poor Laws or social security to prevent total destitution of those out of work. However, as will be seen, policy-makers were always concerned to ensure wage-setting in the market was unaffected by welfare benefits, by setting such benefits lower than earnings.

Against this background, the struggle for a statutory minimum wage or equal pay legislation seemed unlikely to succeed. Certainly, in the last two decades of the nineteenth century, there was still a strong belief that the only effect of regulation of the poorest paid workers would be inflation and unemployment[227] and Hutchins and Harrison, writing in 1902, declared emphatically that 'opinion is not yet converted to the legal regulation of wages, nor likely to be for a considerable time yet.'[228] However, in the first decade of the century, the misery of workers within the sweated trades suddenly caught the political eye. One reason was humanitarian: a large exhibition on sweating in London in 1906 did a great deal to bring into the public domain the extent of exploitation of workers, and a concerted campaign, led by the National Anti-Sweating Campaign followed. However, other arguments were probably more influential. As was the case with protective legislation, proponents of regulation were concerned both with morality and eugenics. The link between low wages and prostitution was stressed, as was the effect of impoverishment on infant health and welfare.[229] Probably the most effective were the economic arguments. The

---

[226] Report of the Select Committee on Homework 246 of 1908, p. vi.
[227] Hutchins and Harrison, above n. 195, p. 214.
[228] *ibid.*, p. 216.
[229] Lewis (1984), above n. 194, pp. 200–1.

Select Committee which reported in 1908 stressed that 'low-priced labour is a great obstacle to improvement. It discourages invention and removes or prevents the growth of a great stimulus to progress and efficiency.'[230] Thus the Committee concluded that wages regulation was as desirable and legitimate as minimum standards of sanitation, cleanliness and hours of work. This stand attracted support across party lines, and the first Trade Boards Act, which established wage-setting machinery in a select number of trades, passed both houses with little opposition in 1909.

The Act was an important symbolic victory. Kahn-Freund states that it was 'considered as a revolutionary step, an interference by the legislature with the sacred law of demand and supply.'[231] This was true in that the State would now intervene to set minimum wages, with penal sanctions for failure to comply. At the same time, however, the Act was deliberately formulated to minimise the extent of State intervention. This is most clearly seen in the two central characteristics of the scheme. The first was its selectivity: it applied only if the rate of wages in a particular trade was considered to be 'exceptionally low' relative to other wages.[232] The Act itself specified only four trades, box-making, lace mending and finishing, chain-making and the making of ready-made clothing,[233] in all of which pay and working conditions were abysmal. The Act made provision to extend the scheme further,[234] by means of a complex procedure. The second crucial characteristic was the nature of the wage-setting machinery. Wages were not set by central government but by Trade Boards established for particular categories of workers. Boards were structured to mimic to a degree formal collective bargaining structures: they consisted of representatives of employers, representatives of trade unions, and independent members.[235] It is notable that women were explicitly eligible as members,[236] despite the fact that this predated both enfranchisement and the Sex Disqualification (Removal) Act 1919. In addition, where workers covered by a board were predominantly women, one of the independent members had to be a woman.[237]

The impact of the Act is difficult to measure precisely. Early effects were encouraging. The first Trade Board to set a minimum wage, in chain-making, where women received as little as 5s. for a hard week's work, promulgated in an increase of over 100 per cent[238] and the other three Trades Boards made equivalent improvements. In addition, the Trade

---

[230] Select Committee on Home Work 1908, p. xiv.

[231] P. Davies and M. R. Freedland (eds.), *Kahn-Freund's Labour and the Law* (2nd edn., Stevens, 1983), p. 47.

[232] Trade Boards Act 1909, s. 1(2).

[233] *ibid.*, Schedule.

[234] *ibid.*, s. 1(2)–(6).

[235] *ibid.*, s. 11.

[236] *ibid.*, s. 11(2).

[237] *ibid.*, s. 13(2).

[238] Hutchins and Harrison, above n. 195, p. 268.

Boards appear initially to have stimulated significant increases in the level of organisation among the women in the relevant trades, a phenomenon which was repeated when the statutory minimum wage was extended in 1913 to a further six trades.[239] However, there were also problems. The women who sat on the Trade Boards were often middle-class trade unionists with no direct experience of work in the trades they represented.[240] More problematically, Trade Boards never broke free from the assumption that low wages were an integral characteristic of women's work. Despite the dramatic increases ordered by the Boards, women's pay in protected trades remained low compared to men working in the trade. Indeed, the Trade Boards simply perpetuated the existing ratio whereby women's average wages in the trade were about half the male average.[241]

In 1918, the aims of minimum wage legislation were changed somewhat, to include the active promotion of collective bargaining. Thus to establish a Trade Board, the Minister had to be satisfied not only that wage rates were low, but also that there was no adequate voluntary machinery for the effective regulation of wages.[242] In the hope that Trade Boards would themselves germinate into collective bargaining structures, the Minister was given express power to abolish the relevant Board once voluntary machinery was in place. By this time, there was general acceptance of the idea of such minimum wage regulation, and Trade Boards mushroomed: by 1921, there were forty-two, covering about three million workers, mainly in the manufacturing industry.[243] However, their impact was ambiguous. Minimum wages remained low; and for women workers in particular, the minimum tended to be the actual wage paid, rather than a safety net. The structure of the Trade Boards system was such that the wages set tended merely to reflect the existing market, and therefore there was little impact on differentials. Nor did they, after the first surge, encourage collective bargaining.[244] Most problematically, they institutionalised inequality by explicitly setting lower rates for women than for men.[245] In addition, the fact that Trade Boards were established to deal only with specific industries meant that existing patterns of job segregation were untouched. As will be clear from later chapters, one of the most important contributory factors to women's disadvantage is the fact that they are assigned different jobs from men. Trade Boards could do no more than reflect this.

Despite its weaknesses, the minimum wage-setting machinery played a useful role in underpinning women's pay in the worst areas of exploitation.

---

[239] S. Webb and B. Webb, *The History of Trade Unionism* (2nd edn., Longmans, 1920), pp. 494–5; see also p. 475.
[240] D. Thom 'The Bundle of Sticks' in John (ed.), above n. 198, pp. 274–5.
[241] Thom, above n. 240, p. 275.
[242] Trade Boards Act, 1918, s. 1(2).
[243] Department of Employment Consultative Paper, *Wages Councils* 1985.
[244] Report of the Donovan Commission, Cmnd. 3623, para. 234.
[245] J. Morris 'The Characteristics of Sweating' in John (ed.), above n. 198, p. 119.

It also symbolised a recognition that the State could legitimately intervene to correct pay abuses. Far less was achieved in the struggle for equal pay between women and men, an ideal which remained elusive until 1970. The contradictions within liberal theory are strikingly apparent in the debate about equal pay. The free market and freedom of contract did not produce fairness or equality of treatment; to the contrary the market continued to generate differential wage rates. In allowing the ideals of freedom and State abstentionism to eclipse the value of equality, policy-makers were in fact reinforcing yet again the age-old status ascriptions of women as inferior, ill-suited for the 'public' world of the market, and 'naturally' reproductive rather than productive beings. This is demonstrated by the extent of adherence on all sides of the political spectrum to the notion of a 'woman's rate for the job'. Even the Webbs were convinced that women constituted a distinct class of workers, necessitating differentiation of task, effort and subsistence.[246] Within the trade union movement, the equal pay debate revealed most of all the extent to which male trade unionists were concerned to protect their own position. The TUC perceived that a demand for equal pay would be a crucial line of defence against the possibility of employers using women at lower rates of pay and therefore undermining wages in general. This led to the passing of a resolution in favour of equal pay for women in 1888. However, this went hand in hand with a policy of excluding women wherever possible from male preserves; or, where this proved impossible, insisting on a strict segregation of work which ensured that women did not effectively compete with men.[247] In addition, equal pay was considered to be incompatible with male demands for a 'family wage'. Feminist campaigners too took different stances. Many trade union women were concerned that, although equal pay was desirable in principle, its harmful effects on women's employment would outweigh its benefits.[248] Others believed that unemployment was a reasonable price to pay for equality, the underlying assumption being that women's exclusion from the work-place was not undesirable in itself. Both these stances reflected the pervasiveness of the assumption that women workers were less efficient than men. As one active feminist put it: 'I am persuaded that if, when you pay men and women alike, women are driven out, it will be because the work is really better done by men, and in that case it is for the advantage of . . . the whole community that the men should do it.'[249] However, there were vocal proponents of equality for its own sake, the foremost among them being the National Union of Women Teachers.[250] The idea of a family allowance paid by the State from taxation, for example, was

---

[246] Webb and Webb, *Industrial Democracy*, above n. 206, vol. II, p. 505.
[247] *ibid.*, pp. 495–9.
[248] Lewis (1984), above n. 194, p. 202.
[249] Cited in Alberti, above n. 174, p. 150.
[250] *ibid.*, p. 151.

actively promoted in order to counter male demands for a family wage (see below).

Equal pay suddenly became a real possibility during the First World War. Male workers drafted into the army insisted that, if women were to be allowed to do their jobs while the men were away, they had to be employed on equal pay. Otherwise, they feared, cheap female labour would permanently undermine wage rates. Government conceded to this demand; and women's pay during the war was higher than it had ever been. However, the fact that the vast majority of women were pushed back out of the workforce after the war ended meant that equal pay could be ignored again.[251] Female civil servants and teachers for example remained on explicitly lower pay scales than men working on the identical job and the possibility of equal pay legislation remained a mirage, despite positive resolutions by the House of Commons in 1920 and 1921.

The Second World War heralded a renewed campaign for equal pay as a matter of social justice; and equal pay for women teachers very nearly received statutory endorsement when it was passed as part of the Education Bill 1944 by one vote. However, Churchill successfully obstructed this, and promised to set up a Royal Commission instead. Certainly, male trade unionists seemed to have resolved their ambiguity. With family allowances and full employment, it was felt that equal pay could be instituted without threatening male workers. However, they remained suspicious of any State intervention into wage setting, which was now firmly in the province of voluntary collective bargaining. Still, legislative intervention remained elusive: the Labour government refused to institute legislation after the war because of the cost. Indeed, it was not until 1970 that the right to equal pay for equal work reached the statute book.

Legislative inaction was reinforced by the judiciary. Indeed, the judges went further. Whereas the legislature refused to intervene to correct unequal pay, the judges went so far as to strike down employers' voluntary institution of equal pay, in the public sector at least. In the seminal case of *Roberts* v. *Hopwood*,[252] the House of Lords was asked to consider the case of the Poplar Borough Council, which had decided to pay all its lowest grade of workers, both male and female, the same minimum subsistence pay. 'The vanity of appearing as model employers of labour, . . . [and] ardent feminists'[253] was not something the House of Lords would tolerate. The Council's statutory power to pay 'such wages as [it] may think fit' had to be exercised reasonably; and, according to the court, equal pay was clearly not within the bounds of reason. The council had exceeded the bounds of its legitimate power by allowing itself, in the words of Lord Atkinson, 'to be guided . . . by some eccentric principles of socialistic philanthropy, or by a

---

[251] Lewis (1984), above n. 194, p. 204.
[252] [1925] AC 578.
[253] *Per* Lord Atkinson at p. 591.

feminist ambition to secure the equality of the sexes in the matter of wages in the world of labour.'[254]

## c) Anti-discrimination Law

The labour market throughout the nineteenth and twentieth centuries was characterised by an all-pervasive segregation of women and men workers. This manifested itself in a wide variety of ways. In the hosiery industry, for example, men were generally employed on mechanised processes in centralised workshops, while women did hand-work at home.[255] In clerical work, the boundary between men and women was 'constant and absolute. . . . Women worked with women, under women and in women's jobs, processes or parts of processes.'[256] In the sweated trades, such as tailoring, a constant splitting up of the production process consistently reinforced a sexual division of labour.[257] Such segregation was not simply caused by employers, but also actively promoted by male workers. The Webbs had no doubt about 'the intensity of the resentment and abhorrence with which the average working man regards the idea of women entering his trade'.[258] Trade unions frequently reacted with uncompromising policies of exclusion of women; but when they realised that this would not succeed in keeping women out of their trade, they accepted strict segregation on the basis of different job classifications for men's and women's work respectively.[259] Whatever form job segregation took, it was invariably accompanied by lower pay and an undervaluation of women's work.[260]

Among the middle classes, discrimination manifested itself most often as a total exclusion of women, particularly married women, from certain occupations. These included top posts in the civil service, and, prior to 1870, medicine. When there were no formal bars, women were frequently denied access because of their lack of adequate education or training. Such exclusion was bolstered by the ideology of motherhood which became dominant during the twentieth century. Between the wars this ideology operated actively in the form of marriage bars, or the automatic termination of women's employment on marriage.

As in the case of pay, the notion of State intervention to correct sex discrimination in the market remained anathema for most of the twentieth century. There was only one major gesture in favour of equality, namely, the Sex Disqualification (Removal) Act of 1919, a compromise measure

---

[254] [1925] AC at p. 504.
[255] N. Osterud 'Gender Divisions in the Leicester Hosiery Industry' in John (ed.), above n. 198, p. 50.
[256] M. Zimmek 'Clerical Work for Women' in John (ed.), above n. 198, p. 159.
[257] Morris, above n. 245, in John (ed.), p. 111.
[258] Webb and Webb, *Industrial Democracy*, above n. 206, vol. II, p. 496.
[259] *ibid.*, p. 501.
[260] Lewis (1984), above n. 194, pp. 171ff.

after the failure of the wide ranging Women's Emancipation Bill in 1919. The Act made it unlawful to disqualify anyone on the grounds of sex or marriage from the exercise of a public function, the holding of a civil or judicial office, the entry into a civil profession or vocation, and jury service.[261] Women could now, in theory, become Justices of the Peace; they could be appointed to public bodies from which they had previously been excluded, and they were given the right of access to male-dominated professions. In particular, section 2 permitted a woman to be admitted as a solicitor when the university at which she had studied had refused to grant degrees to women. This reversed *Bebb* v. *Law Society*,[262] in which the Court of Appeal had held that women were disqualified at common law from becoming solicitors. However, the Act was severely limited by the wide exception allowing women to be excluded by regulation from any branch of or posts within the civil service or foreign service and permitting restrictions to be placed on the mode of admission of women into the civil service.[263] This permitted the entrenchment of the marriage bar. Treasury regulations of 1921 required women to resign from the civil service on marriage.[264] Similar caution characterised the Act as a whole. For example, while universities were permitted to make provision for the admission of women, even if their statutes or charters decreed the opposite,[265] they were not required to do so. In any event, as Creighton comments, the Act was a dead letter.[266] A central reason was the absence of explicit enforcement methods. Although the courts could have used their equitable powers of injunction and declaration to fill the gap, they were reluctant to do so.[267] As a result, very little use was made of the Act.

Indeed, the courts played a highly limiting role in interpreting the Act as a whole. In a series of cases in the 1920s, teachers attempted to rely on the Act to overturn the rigid marriage bar which had been instituted by various local education authorities. The pretext given by the authorities was the high unemployment among teachers, and the 'periodic temporary absences of married teachers', which, they argued, was 'most inconvenient'.[268] This policy was found to be quite reasonable by the courts, in striking contrast with the judicial decree in *Roberts* that equal pay for women was unreasonable and *ultra vires*. 'It would in my view be pressing public policy to intolerable lengths to hold that it was outraged by this Authority expressing a preference for unmarried women over married women as teachers, in view

---

[261] Sex Disqualification (Removal) Act 1919, s. 1.
[262] [1914] 1 Ch. 286.
[263] s. 1(a).
[264] S. Fredman and G. Morris, *The State as Employer* (Mansell, 1989), p. 307.
[265] Sex Disqualification (Removal) Act 1919, s. 3.
[266] W. B. Creighton 'Whatever happened to the Sex (Disqualification) Removal Act 1919?' [1975] ILJ 155.
[267] Creighton, above n. 266, pp. 164–5.
[268] *Price* v. *Rhondda UDC* [1923] 1 Ch. 372 at 379.

of the fact that the services of the latter are frequently . . . liable to be interrupted by absences extending over several months.'[269] Nor did the 1919 Act apply. According to Eve J, the fact that the Act prevented disqualification on grounds of sex or marriage did not prohibit public employers from specifying a particular sex or marital status for a job! This precedent was followed by the Court of Appeal. In *Short* v. *Poole*,[270] the education authority argued that a marriage bar was reasonable because the duty of the married woman was primarily to look after her domestic concerns, making it impossible to do so and act as an effective teacher at the same time.[271] The court upheld this line of reasoning as reasonable and wholly within the bounds of the council's authority. Again, the contrast with *Roberts* is striking, particularly since in both cases the local authority was acting under the same statutory power, namely to employ teachers under such conditions as it thought fit.[272]

It was not until 1975 that more effective anti-discrimination legislation was enacted (see Chapters 4 and 7). In the interim, some small changes could be detected in judicial attitudes. For example, the marriage bar was challenged again in 1957 by a health services worker who had been dismissed as part of a policy by the Northern Ireland General Health Services Board of requiring female employees in her grade to resign on marriage. Here the House of Lords was prepared to construe her terms of service strictly: her contract of employment stated that she could only be dismissed for misconduct or incompetence, and neither of these was made out. Thus the court declared her dismissal invalid.[273] A similar softening of judicial attitude can be detected in *Nagle* v. *Fielden*,[274] in which a woman race-horse trainer challenged the policy of the Jockey Club to exclude women by refusing them licences to train horses.[275] Although the Court of Appeal decided no more than that she had an arguable case, the judges' approach demonstrated a welcome advance on the earlier cases. It was held in particular that where a body had a monopoly power over entry into a profession or vocation, such a body was under a public law duty to act reasonably and without caprice. Lord Denning was prepared to hazard his opinion that exclusion of women from horse training was indeed arbitrary and capricious. However, he was not wholly free from the shackles of stereotyping: he was still of the view that women could be excluded from occupations which were 'unsuitable' for women, such as that of a jockey or a speedway rider.[276]

---

[269]   *Per* Eve J [1923] 2 Ch. at 391.
[270]   [1926] Ch. 26.
[271]   *ibid.*, p. 84.
[272]   See also *Fennell* v. *East Ham Corporation* [1926] Ch. 641.
[273]   *McClelland* v. *Northern Ireland General Health Services Board* [1957] 1 WLR 594.
[274]   [1966] 2 QB 633.
[275]   CLJ 165.
[276]   [1966] 1 All ER at 695.

## IV.   WELFARE LEGISLATION

As was seen in Chapter 1, themes of individualism, equality, and autonomy have played a complex role in the history of welfare legislation. Welfare laws are based on principles of distributive justice which recognise the limits of formal equality and individualism. However, the concern with redistribution has not extended into gender relations. Indeed, far from correcting gender inequalities, the history of welfare legislation is dominated by the promotion and reinforcement of gender divisions in society. From the earliest days of the Poor Law through to the advanced twentieth century, women have been excluded from the class of autonomous individuals who are treated as contributing to society through their paid work, and who thereby reap the benefits of social citizenship. Instead, women are treated as dependent on men, and their entitlements to welfare benefits are similarly derivative. Crucially, dependence is not simply a description. It has also frequently been a prescription, the forces of welfare and employment law pushing women inexorably into the mould of appendages to their husbands.

These patterns are clearly evident throughout the nineteenth and most of the twentieth centuries. As the Webbs repeatedly show, the major policy documents and legislation of nineteenth century Poor Laws consistently omit to refer to women as a class. The central category of the 'able-bodied' implicitly refers to men alone; and 'nowhere do they mention, in recommendation or by way of illustration, . . . the independent woman worker.'[277] Instead, 'the wife is treated exactly as is the child',[278] expected to share her husband's entitlements and restrictions. Beveridge, in his seminal work on unemployment in 1909, was more explicit: society's 'ideal unit is the household of man, wife and children maintained by the earnings of the first alone.'[279] The result is a series of legislative provisions, requiring lower contributions from women and giving them lower benefits than men.[280] The progression from description to prescription is then inevitable. Beveridge considered that the option of women undertaking paid work merely operated to the detriment of men. For example, he noted that casual employment and underemployment among men frequently forced their wives into low paid sweated work. But this, he argued, worsened the position of the family: husbands were less mobile and could not seek work far away from their wives' occupations, and women drove wages down because, 'unskilled and unable', they competed in low-grade professions.[281]

---

[277] S. Webb and B. Webb, *English Poor Law Policy* (Longmans, 1910), p. 3; and see p. 6.
[278] *ibid.*, p. 6; and see pp. 15, 36, 100.
[279] W. H. Beveridge, *Unemployment* (1909; Longman's, 1931), p. 1.
[280] See e.g., National Insurance Act 1911.
[281] Beveridge, above n. 279, p. 109.

As a result, welfare policies for men and women have been framed to work in opposite directions: men are expected to work for a livelihood, and welfare legislation should never act as a disincentive to work. On the other hand, welfare policies have often been explicitly formulated to discourage women from engaging in paid work. Those women who do take up paid employment find that their benefits are lower than those of men. This is particularly true of unemployment benefit. Indeed, the very definition of 'unemployment' changes radically when applied to women: since they are not 'naturally' employed in the paid labour market, they are not considered to be unemployed if out of paid work, even if they want such employment. Their entitlement to unemployment benefit is correspondingly undermined. In an early version of the familiar modern invective against 'welfare scroungers', Beveridge complained bitterly about the phenomenon of 'the woman who having worked till marriage, ceases after marriage to be regularly attached to industry or dependent on her earnings, but not unnaturally tries to get all that she can out of the unemployment fund, by registering as unemployed.'[282] In twentieth century welfare legislation, the paradigm of the dependent wife and breadwinner husband is particularly disturbing. One of its primary manifestations is in the fact that until very recently the wife was largely 'dependent' on her husband's contributions and her husband's entitlements. This suspension of the married woman's social security personality has disturbing resonances of coverture, which, it was so confidently hoped, had largely disappeared by the middle of the twentieth century.

It is important at this point to draw out the complexities of the issues in this context. Treating women as dependants appears to exacerbate their second-class status. Yet formal equality between men and women in welfare provision might have the same effect: by ignoring the reality of women's dependence, it may well perpetuate it. Indeed, in the discussion on matrimonial property, I argued above that the principle of separation of property between spouses reflects an adherence to individualism and formal equality which reinforces inequalities of power because it ignores the interdependence of spouses. The recognition of women's dependence could, on this line of argument, be seen as a virtue of welfare law. Indeed, Kahn-Freund argued that social security laws are 'more realistic than property law because they address the needs of the family rather than the individual'.[283]

Yet in practice the abandonment of notions of equality between spouses has had a detrimental effect on women. Why is this? It will be argued here that the problem lies in the dichotomy between equality and difference

---

[282] Beveridge, above n. 279, p. 294.
[283] Kahn Freund, in W. Friedmann (ed.), *Matrimonial Property Law*, above n. 2.

itself. To take the view that, *a priori*, women are necessarily dependent on men, is as inaccurate and damaging as the opposite view. The result of either preconception is necessarily prescriptive rather than descriptive: instead of responding to the diversity of social reality, it imposes a preconceived picture onto that reality. When embodied in legislation, it in fact changes social realities to correspond to its norms. This can be illustrated clearly in respect of welfare legislation. Welfare legislation only rarely recognises women's unpaid labour by allowing them to accrue independent entitlements to maintenance by virtue of that labour. Instead, it generally uses the recognition of women's unpaid labour to reinforce dependency, by channelling any entitlements through their husbands. This in turn depends on a simplistic view of the family as a single unit, personified in the form of the male breadwinner. However, research has shown that men do not necessarily share family resources equally. Even more significantly, welfare legislation has generally evinced a bias against women attaining their own independence by undertaking paid labour, as reflected in differential benefits and eligibility qualifications. This discussion shows that the defects of welfare legislation cannot simply be corrected by substituting formal equality for difference: this would then, like matrimonial property laws, simply ignore dependency where it exists. The solution is to avoid dichotomising and prescribing, but instead to respond to the reality of power relations. The history of welfare legislation clearly illustrates this argument.

I turn now to a brief analysis of the Poor Laws, followed by a consideration of two branches of modern welfare legislation, namely, welfare targeted at unemployment and sickness. Old age and maternity are considered in later chapters. The chapter ends with a brief note about tax.

## a) Poor Laws

The role of the State in providing maintenance for the destitute and ill dates back to the Poor Laws of 1597 and 1601, which placed the responsibility for financing and administering relief on the shoulders of local parishes. Such intervention was precipitated by both the increased risks to health and welfare caused by industrial capitalism, and the inability of the traditional sources of welfare, the church, the family, and charities, to absorb these costs.[284] From its earliest days, the Poor Law involved a combination of control and maintenance, as evinced in the requirements that vagrants be disciplined and the able-bodied set to work. By the nineteenth century, when the ramshackle policies of Elizabethan times were reconstructed, the element of control became paramount under the influence of the strident laissez faire individualism of the time. The underlying principle of the

---

[284] See generally B. Hepple 'Welfare Legislation and Wage-Labour' in B. Hepple (ed.), above n. 192, p. 114ff; Cornish and Clarke, *Law and Society in England*, above n. 2, pp. 412ff.

Report of the Royal Commission in 1834, and the consequent Act of 1834 was the unshakeable conviction that unemployment and poverty were a result of individual idleness which invited stern deterrent and punitive action. Thus a destitute able-bodied person could only obtain relief if he or she agreed to enter the workhouse, a deliberately dismal, highly restrictive institution, and be put to work.[285] The intention of the framers of the 'New Poor Law' was that the ill, aged and mentally defective be treated differently; but, in practice, all classes of paupers were treated in the same parsimonious manner.

As noted above, references to women in Poor Law policy documents are conspicuous by their absence, reflecting the prevailing legal doctrine that women were merely appendages of their husbands. In practice, however, women could not be ignored in this way. Apart from the many unmarried women struggling to eke an existence out of a restrictive labour market (see Chapter 3), there were a large number of women whose husbands were killed or permanently disabled during the course of increasingly hazardous capitalist work. As the Webbs point out: 'With regard to the really baffling problems presented by the widow, the deserted wife, the wife of the absentee soldier or sailor . . . the [1834] Report is silent.'[286] Absence of central guidance meant that, at least during the mid-century years, policies regarding women differed widely. In some parishes, the local authorities retained the discretion to give relief to independent women without insisting they enter the work-house (out-door relief). In others, all out-door relief was prohibited, and able-bodied women, like their male counterparts, were forced into the workhouse as a condition for obtaining relief.[287] With time, however, this last policy proved so difficult to enforce that wide exceptions developed, so that in effect out-door relief was regularly granted to deserted wives, widows and wives whose husbands were, for various reasons, out of contact.[288] Married women, however, were treated as mere appendages of their husbands. Interestingly, although outside the workhouse the woman's treatment depended entirely on her status with regard to a man, once she entered the workhouse, this became irrelevant. Instead, she was classified according to such criteria as whether she had children under seven, whether she was aged, and whether she was of 'good character'.[289]

This varied treatment of women changed after 1871, with the general tightening up of the punitive element of Poor Law policy. The gradual relaxation of the compulsory nature of entry into the workhouse was reversed, and a strict policy against out-door relief was instituted. It is notable that it was as part of the restrictive approach of the inspectorate

---

[285] See generally Webb and Webb, above n. 277.
[286] ibid., p. 6.
[287] ibid., p. 31; for specific exceptions, see pp. 36–7.
[288] ibid., pp. 40–2.
[289] ibid., p. 43.

between 1871 and 1907 that a policy with regard to women as women was first established, with the Central Authority strongly discouraging outdoor relief to any able-bodied woman, whether she be a widow, the wife of an able-bodied man or a single woman without children.[290] The result was to halve the number of able-bodied women granted out-door relief. It is highly significant that this policy coincided with the Married Women's Property Act 1870, which, it will be recalled, was passed largely with the aim of protecting working-class women's earnings against allegedly wasteful husbands and thereby reducing the drain on the public purse (see above). At the same time, married women were given equal Poor Law obligations to maintain their husbands as their husbands had previously held.[291] This strongly suggests that the belated recognition by the Central Authority of the existence of able-bodied women was primarily motivated by a desire to decrease costs and set working-class women to work for wages wherever possible. The flawed assumption that employment or unemployment was an individual choice unaffected by general economic conditions continued to hold sway; implying that even if women had young children, they would find paid employment under threat of the workhouse.

b) Welfare Legislation

The turn of the century signalled a softening of the stridency of the doctrine which viewed individuals as responsible for their own poverty. Instead, unemployment came to be seen as a social and economic problem, warranting not punitive but supportive responses from the State. Thus the Royal Commission appointed in 1905 to examine the Poor Laws stated emphatically that it was no longer possible for the State to 'adopt the simple principle of the Act of 1834, that, in order to drive men (sic) into independent labour, we need only apply a test that shall be sufficiently deterrent . . . Not only is there cyclical dislocation . . . but going on all the time . . . there is this normal underemployment of casual and seasonal workers.'[292] In addition, a clear distinction had come to be drawn between the involuntary able-bodied unemployed, and the sick, aged and disabled. The result was that the individualism of the nineteenth century was complemented by a new and explicit acknowledgement by the State of its responsibility to provide for those in need.

The main twentieth century manifestation of individualism in welfare law has been the insurance principle.[293] At the heart of the insurance principle is the notion that the individual 'earns' his or her entitlements to welfare as a reward for individual efforts in the labour market, reflected in

---

[290] Webb and Webb, above n. 277, pp. 174–9.
[291] Married Persons Property Act 1870, ss. 13, 14.
[292] Majority Report (Cmd. 4499 of Session 1909), Part VI, p. 437.
[293] See B. Abel Smith 'Social Security' in Ginsberg (ed.), above n. 220, p. 354.

contributions towards national insurance. The alternative principle of State responsibility for the needy has taken the form of non-contributory means-tested benefits. In the case of married women, however, both principles were moulded to reflect and perpetuate their dependence on their husbands. The individualistic insurance principle has consistently worked to the detriment of women, particularly mothers and married women, who have been limited in their ability to contribute through their paid employment and have correspondingly been unable to 'earn' their entitlements. Nor did the State extend its support to women in need, expecting instead that they be supported by their husbands. Only if the husband was dead or incapacitated would a married woman gain independent entitlements to State welfare. Thus the paradox of individualism remains: the assertion of individual autonomy refers mainly to men and hides the insistence on female dependence. Similarly, the attainment of formal equality in the field of marital property and the suffrage did little to dislodge the tenacious assumption that women are the natural economic appendages of men. These points are well-illustrated by the development of welfare provision for unemployment and sickness.

(a) **Unemployment**

The most important initiative of the early twentieth century in respect of unemployment was the introduction of compulsory insurance. Voluntary insurance was already a familiar practice, administered by trade unions and friendly societies. The novelty of the new scheme was in its compulsory nature, and in the obligation on employer and the State to supplement the contributions of the worker.[294] Despite the fact that compulsory unemployment insurance was highly innovative for male workers, the various schemes introduced since 1911 have all been based on the clear assumption that women's role in the world of paid work should be secondary or non-existent. This has been manifested in provisions that have become familiar over the decades. First, women's contributions were generally lower than those of men, but so, correspondingly, were their benefits. Secondly, the requirement that a worker show that he or she was willing to take up suitable alternative employment has been used to squeeze women out of their entitlements, either by forcing them into specific occupations, such as domestic service, or by presuming that they do not genuinely want to desert their rightful place in the home for paid employment. Finally, the customary exclusion of domestic service from the insurance and benefit system meant that one of the few ready markets for female labour was entirely outside of the welfare system.

The earliest scheme for unemployment benefits, found in the National Insurance Act of 1911, was, because of its experimental nature, confined to

---

[294] See e.g., National Insurance Act 1911, s. 85(1).

specific trades, including building, construction of works (such as railways), shipbuilding, mechanical engineering, iron founding, and saw-milling.[295] Needless to say, workers in these trades were almost entirely male.[296] After the First World War, the principle of compulsory insurance was extended to all trades. However, the entry on a massive scale of women into the civilian work-force during the war, and the granting of the limited suffrage, were not sufficient to establish them as a permanent part of the paid work-force. To the contrary: women were expected to retreat to their homes to make space for returning soldiers in the work-force. This was reflected in the plethora of Acts which were enacted in the period of dislocation and high unemployment which followed the war. Thus the Unemployment Insurance Act of 1920 provided for lower rates of benefit for women than for men,[297] a pattern which was sustained through the Acts of 1921,[298] 1924,[299] 1927,[300] 1930,[301] and indeed, 1946.[302] Similarly, women paid lower contributions than men, and a correspondingly lower rate was set for contributions from the employer and the State.[303] Equally important in these early years was the requirement that the person be genuinely seeking work,[304] a qualification which was explicitly targeted at married women. Beveridge for example, was quite open about the fact that the 'genuinely seeking work' condition was used as a 'weapon of offensive defence . . . against claims by women who on marriage had practically retired from industry and were not wanted by employers, but tried . . . to get something for nothing out of the fund and add to the family income.'[305] A further serious restriction was the exclusion of domestic service.[306]

These statutory policies were reinforced by practice and opinion in the inter-war period. During the 1920s, feelings ran high against women munitions workers who were entitled to draw the dole but who, it was alleged, had no intention of carrying on working. One way of dealing with the perceived threat of abuse by married women was to propel them into domestic service, for which middle-class demand was high. During the 1920s and 1930s all women who applied for benefit under the Unemploy-

---

[295] National Insurance Act 1911, Sixth Schedule.
[296] Cornish and Clarke, above n. 2, p. 451, n. 43.
[297] Unemployment Insurance Act 1920, Second Schedule, para. 1.
[298] Unemployment Insurance Act 1921, s. 1.
[299] Unemployment Insurance (No. 2) Act, 1924, First Schedule Part II.
[300] Unemployment Insurance Act 1927, Third Schedule.
[301] Unemployment Insurance Act 1930, First Schedule.
[302] National Insurance Act 1946, Second Schedule.
[303] Unemployment Insurance Act 1920, Third Schedule; Unemployment Insurance Act 1921, First Schedule and s. 2(1); Unemployment Insurance Act 1922, First Schedule; Unemployment Insurance Act 1927, Second Schedule.
[304] Variously formulated: see, for example, 1920 Act, s. 7(1)(iii); 1921 Act, s. 3(3)(b); 1924 (No. 2) Act s. 3(1)(a).
[305] Beveridge p. 280 Unemployment Insurance see also p. 413.
[306] Act 1920 First Schedule Part II(b).

ment Insurance Acts could be required to train as a domestic servant.[307] Another was by way of the means-test, which aggregated the income of married women and their husbands.[308] The result was that between 1925 and 1928, two-and-a-half times as many women as men were disqualified for benefit.[309] Even these measures were not considered adequate to allay fears of married women 'scroungers'. The Royal Commission of 1930[310] insisted that married women were still receiving benefit although they had no intention of working after marriage. They therefore suggested that, as well as proving that they had not withdrawn from paid employment after marriage, women should have to show that they could reasonably expect to get insured employment in their district. This recommendation was accepted: regulations under the Anomalies Act of 1931 required a married woman to prove not just that she was actively seeking work but also that she had a reasonable expectation of finding work. This was a particularly difficult hurdle. Married women were often the first to be fired in times of economic downturn, and in the inter-war years, employers frequently refused to hire married women at all[311] (see Chapter 3). The result was that in the first quarter of 1931, 48 per cent of women's claims were disallowed as against 4 per cent of men's.[312]

A new dimension was introduced in 1921, with the institution of dependant allowances, or the right to an extra payment in respect of a dependant family. This provision too was based on the paradigm of the husband as breadwinner. Thus a man who qualified for unemployment benefit was entitled to the allowance in respect of his wife if she was not in regular wage-earning employment. By contrast, a qualified woman was only entitled to allowance in respect of a husband if he was 'prevented by physical or mental infirmity from supporting himself and [was] being maintained wholly or mainly by her.'[313] Interestingly, the allowance was available to both qualified men and women in respect of a resident 'female person for the purpose of having the care of his [or her] dependent children'.[314]

The advent of the Welfare State after the Second World War did nothing to change the presumption that married women's participation in the paid labour force should be secondary. As shown in Chapter 1, Beveridge, while recognising the importance of married women's unpaid labour, insisted

---

[307] J. Lewis 'Dealing with dependency' in J. Lewis (ed.), *Women's Welfare Women's Rights* (Croom Helm, 1983), p. 25.

[308] *ibid.*, p. 26.

[309] *ibid.*

[310] *First Report of the Royal Commission on Unemployment Insurance* Parliamentary Papers (1930–31) Cmd. 3872 XVII, 885, p. 43.

[311] Lewis, above n. 307, p. 27.

[312] *Final Report of the Royal Commission on Unemployment Insurance* Parliamentary Papers (1929–30) Cmd. 4185 XIII 393 p. 472.

[313] Unemployment Insurance Act 1922, ss. 1(1) and 16(1).

[314] Unemployed Workers' Dependants (Temporary Provision) Act 1921, s. 1; Unemployment Insurance Act 1922, s. 1(1); Unemployment Insurance (No. 2) Act 1924, s. 2.

that this should be their main function. Thus the dependant status of married women was strongly reinforced in the National Insurance Act 1946. As before, contribution rates for women were lower than those for men; and benefits for married women living with their husbands were substantially lower.[315] Similarly, dependant allowances were paid to a married man whose wife was not employed, or who was earning less than 20s a week; but a married woman was only entitled to the allowance if her husband was incapable of self-support.[316] The extent to which this view was entrenched is reflected in the fact that both these provisions were re-enacted in almost identical form in 1965.[317] As will be seen in Chapter 4, it was not until the late 1970s that these discriminatory provisions were removed. The Social Security Act 1975 finally equalised both contribution rates and benefits. The restriction of dependant allowances for women to cases where the husband was incapable of self-support remained un-changed until as recently as 1980 when equality was forced on an unwilling UK Government by EC law.

There were some important diversions from this pattern, however. One of the more positive reflections of Beveridge's view that women's unpaid work should be recognised was the introduction in 1945 of family allow-ances, that is, a special benefit for families with two or more children, now known as 'child benefit'. This was the culmination of a controversial campaign begun in 1917 by feminists who argued that mothers should be directly remunerated for mothering, in order to 'cut the Gordian knot of dependency'.[318] There were several different reasons why a family allow-ance was favoured by some early feminists. One was as a means of justifying equal pay for women and men doing the same work. If direct provision was made by the State to women for the benefit of their children, men could no longer justify higher pay on the grounds that they needed to support their families.[319] This argument never, however, had the desired effect, and was later overtaken by the view that women deserved State support for their activities as child-bearers and rearers without having to depend entirely on men. Other proponents were concerned with the health of children, either for their own sake or as eugenists.[320] Opponents of this view were found in both the feminist and non-feminist camps, the main argument being that such allowances would act as a disincentive on husbands to work and therefore to fulfil their obligation to maintain their wives. It was also feared that such demands would undermine men's claims to a family wage. In fact, when family allowances were finally instituted, the motivation was not so

---

[315] 1946 Act, Second Schedule.

[316] *ibid.*, s. 24.

[317] National Insurance Act 1965, s. 43 and schedules 1 and 3.

[318] Lewis, above n. 307, p. 32.

[319] Alberti, *Beyond Suffrage*, above n. 174, p. 77.

[320] H. Land 'The Introduction of Family Allowances' in C. Ungerson (ed.), *Women and Social Policy* (Macmillan, 1985), p. 11.

much the recognition of the importance of economic independence for women working in the home, but a desire to keep down male wage demands, and therefore to stem inflation.[321] It was also cast in eugenic terms. Beveridge, indeed, advocated family allowances as a means of raising the birth-rate and diminishing child poverty, rather than giving women any independence. Nevertheless, this was an extremely important benefit in that it was the only one to which married women had direct access in their own right. Indeed, the Act provided expressly that in the case of a husband and wife living together, the allowance belonged to the wife (although either party could claim it).[322] Moreover, entitlement was based on neither a contributions record nor a means test, with the result that most women could benefit. For women who in reality were primarily occupied with unpaid work in the home, this was an important recognition of the value of their work, as well as a crucial independent source of support, reducing reliance on husbands. Indeed, it could be 'the financial life-line in times of marital crisis and breakdown.'[323] At the same time, as Lewis points out, it did not challenge the view that married women's primary role was in the home.[324]

### (b) **Sickness**

The industrial revolution ushered in new hazards and new illnesses but very little new health care provision. The punitive character of the Poor Laws was not, despite the policy of 1834, reserved for able-bodied people: the ill and the aged were shepherded into workhouses and treated much the same as their able-bodied counterparts. This policy changed, as we have seen, by the end of the nineteenth century, resulting in the gradual transformation of workhouses for the ill into public hospitals. However, hospital provision of this sort catered for only a tiny proportion of medical needs.[325] Medical provision for the wage-earning population and middle classes was provided by clubs such as friendly societies and trade unions, funded by members' contributions, who contracted with a doctor. As Titmuss notes, this system was essentially a system for men in regular work, and generally excluded 'wives and other dependants, the old, the disabled and other "bad risks" '.[326] Partly as a result of complaints from doctors, the State for the first time took responsibility for some aspects of health care in 1911, with the passing of the National Insurance Act of that year. As with unemployment benefit, the scheme was based on the insurance principle, providing

---

[321] Lewis, above n. 194, p. 52.
[322] Family Allowances Act 1945, ss. 4(1) and (2); repeated in the Family Allowance Act 1965, ss. 4(1) and (2).
[323] Land, above n. 320, p. 31.
[324] Lewis, above n. 307, at p. 32.
[325] R. Titmuss 'Health' in Ginsberg (ed.), above n. 220, p. 306.
[326] *ibid.*, p. 307.

access to medical care and fixed weekly sickness benefit for employed people on the basis of their contributions record. This meant that a married woman who was not earning was generally not covered, either in her own right or through her husband. Wage-earning women could become insured in their own right, but, again as with unemployment benefit, their contributions were lower and so were their benefits.[327] The clear assumption was that an ill woman needed less to cover her needs than a man: men received 10s a week and women only 7s 6d. Single men with no dependants therefore were necessarily better off than women, whether they had dependants or not. Married women were considered to be a special class: if an insured woman married and gave up paid work, she was suspended from receipt of sickness benefits. If she later came back into paid employment, her pre-marital contributions were ignored, and she was treated as if she had never been an insured person.[328]

Even these statutory disadvantages did not prevent married women from being considered problematic. Within the insured classes, sickness rates among women were far higher than those among men. Thus by 1932, married women were overshooting their expected sickness rate by 140 per cent; and unmarried women by 25 per cent; whereas male sickness rate was lower than anticipated.[329] These figures merely confirmed the prejudices of policy-makers: it was suggested that women had a greater incentive to absent themselves from work, either to do their housework, or because their benefit was much closer to their average wages.[330] Such allegations missed the basic point, which was that married women genuinely suffered more illness than men, partly because of their triple role as paid workers, mothers and domestic workers, partly because of the generally low standards of obstetric and gynaecological health care, and partly because their working conditions were frequently dismal, particularly for those who worked in the sweated trades, domestic service and laundry work. Nevertheless, it was decided in 1932 that women constituted too great a risk to the scheme and married women's benefits were cut.[331]

A fundamental change occurred after the Second World War, when universal public health provision was introduced by the National Health Insurance Act 1946. Titmuss maintains that this 'gave to the middle-classes and to women and children what the working-man had received in 1911.'[332] However, it did more than that. Health care was no longer contributory; nor was it means-tested. Crucially, therefore, entitlements were equal, regardless of the individual's relationship with the paid labour force. It is

---

[327] National Insurance Act 1911, Second and Fourth Schedule.
[328] *ibid.*, s. 44. If she was a member of an 'approved society' she could elect to make voluntary contributions and receive reduced benefits, but not otherwise.
[329] Lewis, above n. 307, p. 28.
[330] *ibid.*
[331] *ibid.*, p. 29.
[332] Titmuss, above n. 325, p. 300.

notable that this equality of access revealed the far greater need, on average, of women. Women were found to make more use of the system, a reflection of the fact that they continued to experience higher levels of morbidity than men, particularly resulting from mental illness. The payment of financial benefits, in the form of sickness benefit, however, remained within the national insurance scheme, with all its concomitant inequalities.

### (c) Tax

The final aspect of the Welfare State which is worthy of consideration concerns tax laws. This has proved to be one of the most tenacious remnants of the doctrine of the wife's legal incorporation into the personality of her husband. Thus, for most of this century, income tax law has aggregated the resources of both spouses and treated them as those of the husband.[333] From 1918 a married man received an allowance higher than that given to a single person, 'in recognition of the special legal and moral obligations he has to support his wife.'[334] If the wife worked, the husband received an extra allowance, namely the wife's earned income allowance. Although a couple could jointly elect to have the wife's earned income taxed separately from that of the husband, this option was not available in respect of her investment income, which in all circumstances was treated as belonging to her husband for tax purposes. The husband was responsible for completing returns of both his and his wife's total income. Moreover, because the husband's allowance was greater than that of a working wife, and because other allowances, such as mortgage interest relief, were set against his income and not hers, his take-home pay was necessarily higher than hers even if they were earning the same.[335]

The legal incorporation of the wife into the husband's person for tax purposes was not reformed until 1990.[336] Under the new scheme, each spouse is now responsible for paying the tax on his or her own income. As a result, for the first time, the wife has her own personal allowance; any repayments of tax relating to her income are paid to her and, because she is responsible for her own tax return, she is able to keep her financial details private. However, the egalitarianism is not thoroughgoing. The married couple's allowance, available to married couples living together, is still payable to the husband in the first instance. Only so much of it which cannot be deducted from the husband's total income can then be deducted from the wife's.[337] Married persons are now also taxed independently on their capital gains.

[333] Income and Corporation Taxes Act 1970, ss. 37–42.
[334] Inland Revenue, *The Taxation of Husband and Wife* (Cmnd. 8093) (1980) HMSO para. 14.
[335] *ibid.*, paras. 20, 32.
[336] Finance Act 1988, ss. 32–35 and Sched. 3, which came into effect on 6 April 1990.
[337] Finance Act 1988, s. 33 substituting a new s. 257A into the Taxes Act 1988.

# CONCLUSION

A historical perspective on women and the law is crucial for a full under-standing of the current legal framework. This chapter reveals the painfully slow and conflictual process by which women were incorporated into liberal principles considered axiomatic in other contexts. Most salient has been the eventual victory in the struggle for juridical equality. The significance of this victory cannot be denied: a nineteenth century woman would view her counterpart in the late twentieth century as liberated indeed. Yet looking back, a woman approaching the twenty-first century might be astonished to discover how long it took for the liberal promise of formal equality to be fulfilled. Women were denied an equal right to vote until 1928; lower pay for the same work was sanctioned until 1975, as was explicit sex discrimi-nation; and the legal incorporation of married women into their husbands' personality for tax reasons remained intact until 1990. Nor has the victory of equality been total. Status ascriptions inherited from the pre-liberal period have been remarkably resilient, most obviously in welfare law. This is particularly paradoxical, given that welfare consciously sets out to redress some of the harsher results of liberalism.

The historical examination reveals too the limits of juridical equality, tied as it is to liberal notions of individualism, rationality, autonomy and a neutral State in a free market. Equality allied with individualism led to the principle of separate ownership of property by each spouse within the marriage. But the constraints on the wife's earning power, combined with her invisible support for her husband's income generation, have frequently perpetuated her financial inferiority. Equality allied with deference to the free market yielded equal pay legislation which skated over most of the real causative influences for women's low pay. An equal vote has not, six decades down the road, yielded equality in social power. In neither 'equal-ity' nor in 'difference' has the law been capable of going beyond the complex amalgam of liberalism and status ascription, to achieve a substan-tive recognition of the constraints on women's choices or the value of their unpaid caring work. To understand more fully the nature of these con-straints, and why they have proved impervious to legal intervention, it is necessary to examine women's social history. It is to this that I now turn.

# [3]
# Past and Present: Women's Work

I: THE NATURE OF WOMEN'S WORK
II: ORIGINS: LATE 18TH CENTURY TO WORLD WAR I
a) Women and the Family
b) Women in the Workforce
   i) Low Pay
   ii) Job Segregation
   iii) Trade Unions
   iv) Education
III: 1914–1945
a) The First World War and its aftermath
b) The Interwar Period
   i) Women in the family
   ii) Women and Paid Work
      (1) Low Pay
      (2) Job Segregation
      (3) Education and Training
IV: WORLD WAR II
V: POST-WAR PERIOD: 1945–1980
a) Women in the Family
b) Women and the State
c) Women in the Work-Force

A glance at the social and economic position of women at the end of the twentieth century reveals a striking persistence of disadvantage. Wide pay disparities persist and women remain segregated in low paying, low status jobs. It is true that a handful of women have progressed into positions of importance in politics or commerce. But the underlying structure has scarcely changed. Even more disturbing is the fragility of progress, as was starkly illustrated during the 1980s, when a woman Prime Minister designed and hammered into place a policy framework which significantly undermined what progress had been achieved for women. This illustrates starkly the limitations of legal equality. As was seen in the previous chapter, most legal impediments based on gender have now been removed. The stubborn persistence of disadvantage makes it crucial to look beyond the law to social relationships, and in particular, to women's position in relation to work and the family respectively.

Once again, a historical analysis is invaluable in tracing the sources of disadvantage. Such an examination reveals two themes which are disturbingly persistent. The first is that women remain primarily responsible for child-care and domestic work and the second is that such work is consistently undervalued or ignored, whether it is unpaid or paid. This is underpinned by the pervasive ideology seen in the previous chapters. Gestures towards formal equality, autonomy and neutrality in the law have co-existed with preconceptions of women as primarily reproductive, emotional rather than intellectual, and best fitted for the 'private' realm of the family rather than the public domain of the paid labour force. Such images reflect and perpetuate women's continued disadvantage both in the family and in the paid labour force. This chapter traces the patterns of social disadvantage from the industrial revolution to the present, focusing both on the family and the public sphere. But in order to appreciate fully the social history of women and work, it is necessary first to consider the nature of women's work.

## I.   THE NATURE OF WOMEN'S WORK

The key to a proper understanding of women's work is to consider paid and unpaid work simultaneously. Consideration of paid work alone obscures the extent to which women's opportunities have always been constrained by their unpaid responsibilities. Not only do women's continued responsibilities for unpaid work invariably restrict their ability to obtain well-paid work, but women frequently land up with the double burden of paid and unpaid work. This has had important effects on their ability to improve their position, through, for example, training or trade union organisation, as well as detrimentally affecting their emotional and physical health.

The interaction between paid and unpaid work was brought into focus by the Industrial Revolution, which largely stripped the family of its function as a unit of production.[1] Whereas previously, the family's joint industry had produced goods for the market, industrialisation split family work into different categories, only some of which were now regarded as productive and worthy of pay. Women remained primarily responsible for child-care and domestic work, which was generally unpaid and necessarily confined to the home. Although this did not prevent women from participating in paid labour (indeed, in working-class families women's paid labour was crucial to the survival of the family), it certainly meant that their participation was on unequal terms. For example, in a fascinating study of the Leicester hosiery industry in the nineteenth century, Osterud shows how women

---

[1] C. Delphy, *Close to Home* (edited and translated by D. Leonard) (Hutchinson, in association with the Explorations in Feminism Collective 1984), p. 67.

inevitably earned less than their husbands in framework knitting because their 'domestic responsibilities constantly interfered with their paid labour, limiting the hours they spent at the frame, the quantity of work they turned out, and the amount of money they earned.'[2] So long as workers were paid as families rather than as individuals, the gender division of labour remained a background factor. But once significant parts of the productive process moved out of the home and the amount each family member earned was individually computed, the difference between women's and men's work became clearly visible. 'The services that married women performed within the household were crucial to the family's well-being, but they carried no cash value. Male knitters recognised that such domestic responsibilities limited women's earnings, but that did not prevent them from regarding women's labour as less valuable than their own.'[3] This division remains central to women's continuing disadvantage to the present day.

Once unpaid work is included in the analysis, it becomes important to analyse the nature of such work. As Delphy has argued, housework is not by its nature value-less or unproductive. Aspects of housework, such as preparation of food, are frequently integral parts of work which are considered worthy of pay and therefore 'productive'. For example, the labour involved in preparing food in a restaurant is considered productive labour, as is that in cooking and canning foodstuffs for sale as commodities on the market. The notion that housework is not productive is, in fact, relatively modern. It was not until 1881 that the census excluded women's household chores from the category of productive work, and housewives were classified as 'unoccupied'.[4] It could be argued that housework differs because it produces goods or services which are intended for consumption by the household itself, rather than in the market.[5] But this is not in itself a reason for regarding it as intrinsically unproductive. The labour used in baking a loaf of bread should be regarded as productive labour whether it is baked for home consumption or for the market, since home consumption merely releases for a different use the money which would have been spent on buying the bread. Instead, Delphy argues:

The reason why housework is not considered to be productive . . . is because it is done, within the confines of the home, for free . . . And this is not because of the nature of the services which make it up, because one can find any and all of them on the market; nor is it because of the nature of the people who do it, because the same woman who cooks a chop unpaid in her home is paid when she does it in another household.

[2] N. Osterud, 'Gender Divisions in the Leicester Hosiery Industry' in A. V. John (ed.), *Unequal Opportunities. Women's Employment in England 1800–1918* (Blackwell, 1986), p. 55 and see pp. 55–7.
[3] *ibid.*, p. 56–7.
[4] J. Lewis, *Women in England 1870–1950: Sexual Divisions and Social Change* (Wheatsheaf, 1984), p. 146.
[5] Delphy, above n. 1, p. 84.

Instead, she maintains, the real reason stems from the nature of the contract which ties the wife to her husband.[6] Instead of attracting pay relative to the effort required, housework by a wife generally only attracts a right to maintenance from her husband,[7] thus entrenching dependency rather than self-sufficiency. Even more problematic is the fact that the classification of women's family work as unproductive severely depresses the value and status of that work even when performed in the market. It is therefore not surprising that laundry, catering, domestic service and child-care work have always been among the lowest paid occupations.

This discussion reveals too that, in the case of women, the general categories used to define employment are often inadequate.[8] Prostitution, for example, defies traditional categorisation. For women more generally, the boundaries between paid and unpaid work, between work in the home and work in the market and between light and heavy work are shifting and elusive. Particularly deceptive is the purported equation of paid work with work in the market, and conversely, of unpaid work with work at home. Paid work has frequently been performed at home: caring for other people's children, and taking in laundry work or lodgers are activities perennially undertaken by women as a means of earning money. In addition, manufacturing and service industries have always made use of homeworkers. In the nineteenth century, the use of the home as a workplace was particularly problematic, as the main room of the family house often doubled as a work-room and living room. An 1863 report on the hosiery industry, for example, noted that: 'Many of these rooms are squalid beyond what is usual in the country dwellings of the poor, and of necessity in [the same rooms] crowded as they are with frames, furniture and inmates, and noisy with the rattle of frames, meals such as can be had are cooked and eaten, infants nursed or put to sleep and other housework done.'[9] Similarly, in sweated trades such as dressmaking, work-rooms were often used as bedrooms at night, although ventilation was defective and the dust and shreds of fibre which filled the air caused serious lung irritation.[10] Conversely, unpaid work can just as easily be done out of the home as in it. Many women spend a great deal of time doing such work, whether it be caring for elderly relatives in their own homes, or organising play-groups and toddlers groups, servicing school parent–teacher associations, or straightforward charity work. Middle-class women of the nineteenth century were frequently engaged as unpaid social workers. Nor is there a clear dichotomy between 'reproductive' and productive work. In particular, the assumption that reproductive work is private and unpaid, while productive work takes place in the public sphere for pay is a distortion of the reality.

[6] Delphy, above n. 1, p. 88.    [7] *ibid.*, p. 70.
[8] John 'Introduction', above n. 2, p. 3.
[9] H. C. 1863, XVIII, White's Report, p. 264, cited in B. L. Hutchins and A. Harrison, *A History of Factory Legislation* (1911), pp. 157–8.    [10] *ibid.*, p. 163.

Child-care, for example, has always been work which can be paid or unpaid, and performed in the home or out of it.

The inappropriateness of rigid categorisation is thrown into relief by considering domestic work, which straddles several different categories. Domestic work is most often performed unpaid by women in their own homes. However, it has also been a major source of paid work for women, whether in the homes of others, or in homes of relatives. Even in the present century, cleaning remains a significant source of employment for women, usually in commercial rather than domestic premises.[11] The example of domestic work also reveals the erroneousness of characterising women's work as light work. Domestic work, whether paid or unpaid, is frequently arduous and dirty. Carrying coal or pitchers of water for domestic use must certainly be considered as heavy work. Although in modern times, domestic technology has made housework easier, it remains physically exacting, particularly when it includes the care of children, or disabled or elderly people.

The importance of unpaid work in women's lives also makes it inappropriate to apply straightforward economic models to women's activity in the labour force. Economic models assume that individuals make rational choices from sets of competing goals in an attempt to advance their own self-interest. As Maclean argues, a comprehensive analysis of women's search for income through employment requires us 'to add to the traditional economist's perspective something of the social scientist's approach, which sees the action of individuals in the context not just of money transactions but also of social relationships.'[12] When this perspective is taken into account, it becomes clear that women forego economic gain in order to meet their family responsibilities, and therefore do not necessarily maximise their earned income. Instead, 'they negotiate a series of conflicting demands caused by the complexity which the caring perspective adds to women's ways of allocating their time. These demands on them fluctuate over time, as the needs and capabilities of those in their caring network change.'[13]

In discussing the nature of women's work, it is important to emphasise again that it is a mistake to attempt to present a unitary view of women's experience of work. Feminist writing in recent decades has often assumed that paid work out of the home is the key to women's liberation. Yet this ignores the fact that women's experience of work has always been closely affected by their class, parental or marital status and race. For working-class women, black women, single mothers and many other women, paid work has frequently been an onerous necessity added to a considerable burden of domestic work. Nor, for the same reason, is the work itself liberating. Too often, women's domestic constraints, their limited

[11] For an account of nineteenth century domestic service, see Higgs 'Domestic Service and Household Production' in John (ed.), above n. 2, pp. 130–1.
[12] M. Maclean, *Surviving Divorce* (Macmillan, 1991), p. 34.    [13] *ibid.*

opportunities for training and the institutional discrimination within the market prevent them from obtaining work which is fulfilling or satisfying. For example, as will be seen below, the nature of the work available to working-class women in the nineteenth century was generally so difficult and unpleasant that it could not be regarded under any circumstances as liberating. Moreover, it will be recalled that married women could not retain their own earnings until 1870 (see Chapter 2), so that paid work did not even achieve financial independence for them.

It is necessary, however, to be extremely cautious before drawing conclusions from these negative aspects of paid work for women. Policy-makers through much of the period under consideration recognised women's double burden of work only by insisting that married women be 'freed' from paid work,[14] entirely ignoring the possibility of freeing them from their unpaid work. The result was to trap married women into financial dependence on their husbands. The alternatives, of spreading the burden of domestic work, and of changing the structure of the labour market to accommodate such work for all workers, have scarcely been contemplated.

At the same time, the potential liberating effects of paid work should not be forgotten. Middle-class women of the nineteenth and early twentieth century, and increasing numbers of women of all classes through the inter-war and post-war period, have been subject to a suffocating ideology of 'femininity', preventing them from engaging in fulfilling work outside of the home. In the earlier period, even domestic work in their own homes was considered demeaning for middle-class women. This, of course, ignores the contradictory nature of such a notion, which maintains middle-class 'femininity' only by harnessing the energies of working-class women into domestic service. For middle-class married women sentenced thus to a life of idleness, the strongest aspiration was to escape the narrow confines of the home into the liberation of useful work. As John puts it: 'The fervour with which so many middle-class women undertook philanthropic ventures speaks volumes about their constraints.'[15] In the later period, the ideology of femininity changed. Married women were expected to do all their own domestic and child-care work, but in the isolation of their own homes. The sense of negation and alienation this produced led to an important surge of feminist writing urging paid work as the chief liberating force in women's lives.[16] Single women, on the other hand, have come up against yet another face of 'femininity': they have usually had to undertake paid work to survive, but their opportunities have been limited to work which is 'suitable' or 'respectable' for women.

A final and highly significant point to emphasise is that relations of domination do not simply relate to the relationship between men and women. There are many more cross-currents of domination which should not be ignored. Thus women may dominate over other women, the para-

[14] John, above n. 8, p. 2.   [15] John, above n. 8, p. 3.
[16] See e.g. B. Friedan, *The Feminine Mystique* (Penguin, 1963).

digm being the relationship of mistress and servant. Similarly, the plight of disadvantaged men should not be ignored. Although such men have some control over their wives, they usually have very little control over their lives in general. For example, for most of the nineteenth century, working-class men struggled in miserable working conditions to eke out a survival income for themselves and their families. In the late twentieth century, there remains a significant group of disadvantaged men, thrown onto the margins of society due to high levels of unemployment or institutional racism or both. This has meant, as we have seen before, that allegiances of women are not necessarily first with other women: many working-class women in the nineteenth century would have seen their oppression first in terms of class and only second in terms of gender. Similarly in modern times, many black women would ally themselves with black men before white women. Conversely, there are striking examples of successful women, whose allegiances lie with successful men rather than with the disadvantaged, whatever gender they may be. Margaret Thatcher and the few female Cabinet members in the years of Conservative rule since 1979 exemplify this.

Having set out the main characteristics of women's work, I turn now to a more detailed analysis of the history of such work. Four main characteristics can be discerned. First, low pay for women has been a constant feature. Until 1975, this was partly due to differentiated pay scales, with women being paid less than men despite doing the same job. The Equal Pay Act 1970 has all but eradicated explicit differentials of this sort; but the persistence of women in the low paid category reveals that other factors are, and always have been, equally significant. The second characteristic is chronic job segregation, with women clustering in 'women's' jobs which are almost invariably low paid and low in status. Segregation has taken various forms: either an occupation has been predominantly male or female (vertical segregation) or women have congregated in the lowest grades of mixed jobs (horizontal segregation). The third characteristic is women's marginal role in trade unions. Although there are significant instances of militant women trade unionists, they have in general been less likely to be members of trade unions than men, either because of explicit exclusionary policies by male unionists, or because the nature of 'women's work' has militated against trade union organisation. Where women have been unionised, they have rarely had sufficient influence in the union for it to prioritise their requirements. Finally, women's education and training opportunities have tended to reinforce their position in the work-force.

In the remainder of this chapter, the relationships of women to the family and paid work will be discussed in more detail in the periods (i) up to the First World War; (ii) 1914–1945; and (iii) the post-war period. In each of the three periods, women's role in the family will first be described, followed by an examination of their participation in the paid work-force, highlighting the recurrence of low pay, job segregation, low unionisation and differentiated education and training.

## II.  ORIGINS: LATE EIGHTEENTH CENTURY TO THE FIRST WORLD WAR

Women reaped few benefits from the fundamental social and economic transformations of the eighteenth and nineteenth centuries. Instead, the traditional status ascriptions of women were reformulated in new ways, entrenching women's disadvantage both within and outside of the family. With the gradual breakdown of the family as a unit of production, the gender demarcations within the family were transposed into the world of paid work. The effects were felt differently for different classes. Married middle-class women were gradually excluded from participation in paid labour, finding themselves ultimately trapped in the idealised world of the home and domesticity. Other women were pemitted a continued role in the paid labour force, but always on inferior terms, with lower pay, worse conditions and inferior job content. All women, regardless of class, remained primarily responsible for domestic work and child-care, either unpaid in their own homes or for low pay in other people's homes. Advancing technology was slow to reduce the burden of domestic work, which remained heavy and thankless. Advancing medical science was only beginning, towards the end of the period, to reduce the high risks of child-birth, both to the infant and the mother. In this section, I consider first women's role in the family, before describing in more detail the nature and extent of their participation in the paid labour force.

a)  WOMEN AND THE FAMILY

During this period, the experiences of women were strongly determined by marriage and child-birth. Marriage conferred both social status and a measure of economic security. Women who did not marry were considered a failure, facing a lonely and often marginal life in the home of a relative and eking out subsistence wages from a hostile labour market. Demographic factors meant that many did not marry: the imbalance in the sex ratio increased steadily from 1871 to 1911, a pattern which was inexplicably more marked among the middle classes. Nevertheless, the vast majority of women did marry. In the late nineteenth century, 88 per cent of women who reached their later forties were or had been married, and this figure remained above 80 per cent through to 1921.[17]

Marriage, however, was far from a panacea for women. As we have seen from the previous chapter, married women faced a host of legal disabilities, which were only gradually being removed in the late nineteenth century. They could not own their own property, retain their own earnings or refuse consent to intercourse. They had no rights to custody of their children and

---

[17] Lewis (1984), above n. 4, pp. 3–4. The following account is drawn from Lewis (1984), above n. 4; B. S. Anderson and J. P. Zinsser, *A History of Their Own* vol. II (Penguin, 1990); and the essays in John (ed.), above n. 2.

little protection against marital violence. Companionate marriage had not yet displaced marriage as an economic and practical necessity, so that within marriage, child-birth and domestic work were the most important determinants of their life experience.

However, the nature of this experience differed markedly as between classes. For middle-class women, the rising prosperity of the nineteenth century meant an increasing distance from the world of paid work. Women who would previously have been active in the family business, and who would even have taken over their husbands' professional or business role on the latter's death, were now increasingly expected to withdraw from the 'rough and tumble' of the market place. Instead, their role was to create a home, a serene refuge for their men-folk, adorned with the 'feminine' virtues of patience, love and care. Within the home, increasing prosperity also meant the possibility of shedding some of the hard physical labour of domestic work, by hiring other women as domestic servants. By hiring one domestic servant, a woman entered the lower middle-class; by hiring three, she was considered an unassailable member of the upper middle-class. The extra time thus gained was expected to be used in more attentive child-care and, increasingly, in accomplishments of little practical value such as fine sewing or playing cards. Nevertheless, the reality of middle-class women was far removed from the idealised visions of home and femininity current at the time. Their world was intensely parochial, and their energies continuously restricted, by everything from their education to their clothes. Fragile high-heeled shoes, tight corsets and wide skirts made even short excursions in the street close to impossible. Moreover, the liberation of the middle-class woman from hard physical labour was achieved only at the cost of the working-class woman, on whom the burden fell with ferocity. Domestic service increasingly became a predominantly female occupation, and also one of the chief sources of employment for single women. Work was exceedingly difficult, including hauling coal, fetching water and emptying slop buckets. Even more serious was the extent to which the patterns of domination were reproduced by women over women: middle-class women, having few opportunities for self-fulfilment and scarcely any social power, were nevertheless in a position to dominate over other women. This power was often used to its limits: hours of domestic servants were long and unremitting, accommodation mean and uncomfortable and job security non-existent: a minor illness could lead to immediate dismissal, and old age certainly signalled termination of employment without a pension.

Indeed, notions of femininity were never applied to working-class women. Working-class women were never expected, and indeed never able, to retire from the world of paid work. Yet, their domestic commitments were so extensive as to severely limit their opportunities in the paid labour force. Living conditions were poor: large families had to be cared for in tiny houses, without running water or proper sewerage facilities. The basics of survival were extremely labour-intensive: cooking and heating required wood to be gathered, coal to be hauled and fires lit; washing, both of persons and of laundry, required water to be fetched and heated, and basic clothing required sewing to be done in poor light at the end of difficult days. Laundry was an all-consuming exercise: only families with a man in regular employment could afford a copper to heat water over the fire. Soap was difficult to obtain and very expensive; shoes even more so: indeed, few working-class married women had footwear which could take them more than a few hundred yards from their homes. Moreover, many such women were seriously undernourished: the best food in the house was reserved for husbands and then for children, women were expected to get by with the remaining scraps. At the same time, such women were forced by economic necessity to find paid work. Often the only way to do so was by home-work such as renting out rooms to lodgers, taking in laundry or doing piece work at home for workshops or factories.

It was the experience of child-birth which was common to most women regardless of class. Fertility rates continued high until 1870, ensuring that a large number of women spent most of their adult life involved in pregnancy, child-birth and child-care. Child-birth was painful and dangerous. It was not until the closing decades of the nineteenth century that analgesia in child-birth was introduced, and only later were soluble sutures and surgery advanced enough to make Caesarian birth possible without the certain death of the mother. Midwifery became an increasingly male profession, but hospitals were so dirty and crowded as to be a significant source of infection. Indeed, births at home were marginally safer: the propensity of middle-class women to use hospitals meant that middle class maternal mortality rates were higher than those of the working classes until well into the nineteenth century.

It was in the latter years of the nineteenth century that marked changes in family size first became clear. The decline in fertility rates, which was to continue steadily until modern times, began about 1870, with the birth rate in England and Wales dropping from 35.2 per 1,000 in that year to 29.1 in 1899. Here too, women's experience differed according to their social class, with higher social classes experiencing a faster decline than other classes. Thus, the size of families headed by professionals and higher administrators fell by 33 per cent between 1850 and 1880; while those of skilled and semi-skilled workers fell by about 20 per cent, and those of unskilled workers by 15 per cent.[18]

Such gains were achieved as a result of a considerable struggle by women for control over their sexuality and reproductive capacity. During the nineteenth century, birth-control remained fraught with difficulty for women, particularly working-class women who had little privacy and an

---

[18] Thane in T.R. Gourvish and A. O'Day (eds.), *Later Victorian Britain* (1988), pp. 175–6.

almost total ignorance about the reproductive process.[19] Contraception was rudimentary, expensive and disliked by many men; indeed decreasing family size pre-dated widespread use of contraception, and therefore must have been largely achieved by abstinence or abortion.[20] The rhythm method was not available because of the lack of understanding of the precise timing of ovulation. Deliberate abstention was impossible without the co-operation of the husband; in practice, real limitation of family size only became possible once the husband himself began to fear the prospect of another child enough to exercise self-discipline. Where, as frequently happened, a husband did not co-operate, the only route open to a woman faced with an unwanted pregnancy was abortion. The extent to which women were prepared to face the high risks of abortion reflects their fierce determination to take control of their lives.[21] However achieved, the drop in family size led to a slow improvement in the lives of women, reflected in increased life expectancy, and a decrease in infant mortality.

b) WOMEN IN THE WORK-FORCE

Although it is commonly thought that one of the most important phenomena of recent decades has been the rise in women's participation rates in paid work, in fact, significant numbers of women have always participated in the paid work-force. This has certainly been true for single women: statistics for formal participation consistently reveal an important contingent of single women in the work-force. So far as married women are concerned, formal participation rates obscure the real extent of their paid work. Throughout the period, large numbers of married women sought some sort of paid work. This was often casual and unrecorded:[22] women would take in washing or lodgers or undertake child-minding or cleaning work for other families. Thus it is more useful to concentrate on the characteristics of women's paid work, focusing, as mentioned above, on low pay, job segregation, union organisation, and education and training.

i) **Low Pay**

Possibly the most striking feature of women's work before the First World War is the pervasiveness of the principle that women's work attracted only a women's rate. Even when men and women were engaged on identical work, the women were paid less than the men; and in absolute terms, women's rates were invariably low. Although there is evidence of women agricultural workers being paid half the male rate as early as the thirteenth century, differential rates for women were not marked until industrialisation, when individual rates replaced the 'family' wage paid to the head of

[19] See W. Seccombe, 'Starting to Stop' in *Past and Present* (1990) 126, 151.
[20] Anderson and Zinsser, above n. 17, p. 286.
[21] Seccombe, above n. 19, pp. 156, 161, 187.
[22] Lewis (1984), above n. 4, p. 55ff.

the household for the whole family's work.[23] By the nineteenth century, the principle of a women's rate was widespread, with women's average pay trailing well behind that of men in almost all occupations. Statistics gathered by the War Cabinet Committee on Women in Industry in 1919 are depressingly consistent: in 1833 women earned well under half of men's average pay in almost all industrial occupations, including cotton, paper, metal trades and engineering.[24] This remained true even if women were doing identical work with men. For example, Hunt's study of women in the London bookbinding trade revealed that although 'women bookbinders were female labour aristocrats in an "honourable trade" . . . at the turn of the century the sewers and folders earned 10/6d a week compared to the men who earned 17/– to 18/–.'[25] In the textile industry, women working side by side on similar work and machinery as their male colleagues were paid at rates which were up to 15 per cent less than those of the men.[26] This was no less true in the sweated trades, where men's wages were already dismally low. In the London ready-made tailoring trades, women's average pay was a mere 7/9d for an average of four days, compared to men's 24/1d.[27] Similarly, women shop assistants earned only 65 per cent as much as men in 1900, again despite being engaged on identical work, and often on longer hours.[28] Low pay was even more evident in all-women occupations, such as nursing and domestic service. It is ironic that prostitution remained one of the most lucrative of women's occupations in this era. A prostitute could earn in a day what other working-class women made in a week.[29] In fact, women's low pay was one of the main reasons why many women became prostitutes.[30]

Low levels of pay for women were justified in several ways. Possibly the most influential derived from the notion, already seen in so many contexts in this book, that a woman's 'natural' role was that of mother and housewife. This had various implications. The first was that a woman should be dependent on her husband for income.[31] Paid work by women was thus considered to be merely supplementary to that of their husbands, with the result that women's wages need not be regarded as anything more than 'pin money'. The pervasiveness of this principle is revealed by the fact that contemporary researchers set higher subsistence levels of pay for men than for women, based on the assumption that a woman's wage did no more than supplement her husband's income.[32] The converse of the notion of women as dependent on men is, however, that men should be paid enough

[23] *Report of the War Cabinet Committee on Women in Industry* (HMSO) Cmd.135, 1919, para. 37.

[24] *ibid.*, paras. 41–7.

[25] F. Hunt 'Opportunities Lost and Gained' in John (ed.), above n. 2, p. 74.

[26] J. Bornat 'Lost Leaders' in John (ed.), above n. 2, p. 210.

[27] J. Morris 'The Characteristics of Sweating' in John (ed.), above n. 2, p. 99.

[28] Lewis (1984), above n. 4, p. 166.      [29] Anderson and Zinsser, above n. 17, p. 263.

[30] *ibid.*, p. 264.      [31] See e.g. *Women in Industry*, above n. 23, para. 81.

[32] Morris, above n. 27, p. 96.

to support a family: hence the notion of the 'family wage'. This principle has been fundamental to the continuation of differential rates of pay for men and women, partly at least because it has created in male workers a vested interest in its retention. Any move away from the women's rate must logically entail abandonment of the family wage and therefore of a key to the maintenance of male wage levels. These interlocking reasons are summed up graphically by the Webbs: 'The facts that women have a lower standard of comfort than men, that they seldom have to support a family, and that they are often partially maintained from other sources all render them, as a class, the most dangerous enemies of the artisan's Standard of Life.'[33] It is interesting to note that even the concept of equality was used to justify the women's rate. Zimmeck shows how employers explained the practice of paying low wages to women by arguing that this was entirely in pursuit of an 'equal Standard of Comfort for people doing equal work. If you pay a single woman the same wage as you pay a family man, you are giving her a much higher standard of comfort than you are giving him.'[34] In reality, however, the twin notions of the family wage for men and pin money for women are no more than a justification for women's continuing subordination. As a start, despite giving the impression of a wage system which is based on the needs of the worker rather than her productivity, these notions are founded on stereotypes of the worker's family relationships which bear no relation to their real needs. Not only were men entitled to a family wage even if they had no dependants, but women breadwinners did not qualify for the higher rate of pay. Yet in reality, a significant number of women have always been breadwinners. For example, Morris notes that in 1891 in the clothing trades there were 82,000 heads of households, of whom as many as 30,000 were women.[35] This phenomenon was not confined to unmarried women: at times of unemployment of male workers, the woman of the house had no option but to go out to work. Nor was the family wage paid to men generally sufficient to support a family.[36] A final problematic feature of the notion of the family wage is its assumption that the male breadwinner would necessarily distribute his income fairly within the family. Yet it was relatively common for husbands to keep their wives' allowances low, or to retain some of their earnings for their own use.[37] The result was that women were poorly nourished and clothed.[38]

Another justification offered for women's low pay related to the alleged limitations of women as workers. Even Sidney Webb maintained that lower pay for women was justified by the 'fact' that their productive power was inferior to that of men.[39] The 1919 Report of the War Cabinet Committee

[33] S. and B. Webb, *Industrial Democracy* Vol. II (Longmans, 1897), p. 497.
[34] Cited by M. Zimmeck 'Clerical work for women' in John (ed.), above n. 2, p. 163.
[35] Morris, above n. 27, p. 100.
[36] For statistics, see Lewis (1984), above n. 4, p. 48.
[37] *ibid.*, p. 26.    [38] *ibid.*, p. 31.
[39] S. Webb 'the Alleged Differences in the Wages paid to men and women for similar Work' *Economic Journal* 1 (December, 1891), pp. 635–62.

concluded that because the idea that women are weaker than men has come down through the ages, it must have some origin in nature. However, the same committee did make the interesting observation that women are frequently required to expend time and strength on domestic tasks from which men are exempt and noted that girls are usually given smaller food allowances than men.[40] The relation of such social facts to ideas about women's 'nature' was not, of course, explored.

Because of assumptions about their reproductive role, women were also considered to be unstable as workers and lacking in ambition. The War Cabinet Committee maintained that this view was not simply based on prejudice: women's anticipation of marriage meant that both the women and their employers saw their participation in the work-force as no more than transient. Marriage, therefore, was a 'natural' disability.[41] Similarly, the Webbs declared that 'the well-brought up daughter of the artisan . . . owing to the fact that she so often is not wholly dependent on her wages, . . . is apt to accept any rate of pay rather than leave a comfortable and well-conducted factory, and employers often complain that no stimulus . . . will induce such women-workers to increase their effort beyond a somewhat low maximum.'[42] Again, this took no account of the fact that, through choice or demography, significant numbers of women would never marry, or would be sole breadwinners in their families.

More objective but equally linked to women's reproductive role are explanations which relate to the differences between the working lives of men and women respectively. In occupations where women tended to leave on marriage, or where a marriage bar operated, women workers were generally young. By contrast, men might stay in the occupation until retirement. In the textile industry for example, the majority of women workers at the end of the nineteenth century were under twenty-five. Although skills could be learned quickly, pay levels were often related to seniority.[43] In addition, aspects of the work reserved for men were specifically rewarded. For example, the heavy work of lifting beams in the textile industry was performed by men only, and, although it took no more than a few minutes, it was used to justify increments of 10 to 15 per cent.[44]

## ii) Job Segregation

One of the keys to the maintenance of low pay for women was the constant reinforcement of job segregation. In 1911, for example, men outnumbered women 10 to 1 in metal industries, 6 to 1 in paper and printing, and an astounding 37.5 to 1 in government establishments.[45] In domestic service

---

[40] *Women in Industry*, above n. 23, paras. 81 and 84.
[41] *Women in Industry*, above n. 23, para. 83.
[42] Webb and Webb, *Industrial Democracy*, above n. 33, p. 698 n. 7.
[43] Bornat, above n. 26, p. 211.   [44] *ibid.*, p. 210.
[45] *Women in Industry*, above n. 23, para. 14.

by contrast, over 80 per cent of employees were women. The few men who did work in domestic service tended to cluster in all-male work, usually outdoor labour.[46] Job segregation occurred in a variety of different ways. One common type resulted from the way in which job processes were split up, so that parts became 'women's' work and parts the sole preserve of men. There were numerous examples. Agricultural work was one: from about 1750 women became increasingly marginalised as a result of the replacement of the light sickle with the scythe in areas of grain production. Because of its weight, the scythe was seen as a tool suitable only for males. By the end of the nineteenth century, tasks had become 'so gender-specific that the small number of women workers tended to be in separate fields from the men engaged in their own special tasks of weeding, hoeing and stone picking'.[47] The hosiery industry in Leicester provides a similar example. In the early nineteenth century, when most production took place within the home, there was a relatively flexible division of labour between men and women. As production moved out of the home, around the middle of the century, a rigid division of labour developed, with men working at knitting in workshops and women seaming stockings by hand at home.[48] The women's work was invariably of lower status and pay. A similar pattern is seen in the sweated industries. Morris shows that the 'causes of low wages in the tailoring trade [in the late nineteenth century] lie with the sexual division of labour—the ability of employers to split up the work process into many different parts and to employ semi-skilled and unskilled female labour on these new processes at low and very low wages.'[49] This phenomenon was complicated by the diverse effects of mechanisation. Although mechanisation could either increase or decrease women's work opportunities, it was invariably accompanied by a lowering of standards of pay and conditions. For example, mechanisation in the clerical field increased women's job opportunities, but only because it had the effect of de-skilling the occupation and was accompanied by a decrease in pay and status. On the other hand, mechanisation in the hosiery industry, as we have seen, pulled part of the work out of the home, leaving the women at home with the least valued parts of the job.

A different type of segregation resulted from the exclusion of women altogether from certain spheres of work. Professional work was largely barred to women until well into the twentieth century. The medical register was not open to women until the 1870s and women were only permitted to be factory inspectors from 1894.[50] Even when women were formally allowed into various professions, de facto segregation persisted. There were only 212 female doctors in 1901,[51] and by 1911, women comprised only 6

---

[46] ibid., para. 26.      [47] John, above n. 8, p. 4.
[48] Osterud, above n. 2, p. 54.
[49] Morris, above n. 27, p. 119.
[50] Thane in Gourvish and O'Day, above n. 18, p. 192.      [51] ibid.

per cent of the professions,[52] most of whom would have been teachers. Exclusion was also a consequence of legal prohibitions. For example, as we have seen, women were prevented from working underground in mines in 1842. The result was the concentration of women in a small number of female-dominated occupations. This in turn depressed their wages even further: women crowding into a limited number of occupations created an oversupply which meant that they were forced to accept whatever wages were offered.[53]

Where women were permitted into male occupations, they were corralled into the low paying, low status jobs at the bottom of the hierarchy, a segregation which was actively maintained by employers. For example, although the statistics for commercial workers in 1911 show 25 per cent women, in reality these were almost all low paid shop assistants and clerks.[54] In the civil service, women were directly excluded from top posts,[55] and there were separate grades and entrance examinations for women and men. Segregation in clerical work received concrete expression in the insistence on entirely separate accommodation. 'In all but the smallest offices, women were kept strictly apart from men—on women's floors, in women's rooms or in women's sections complete with partitions to prevent even eye contact . . . In pursuit of a low profile for women, many employers did not permit women to leave the premises at lunchtime.'[56] In fact women in the Post Office only secured the right to fresh air at lunchtime in 1911 after a strenuous campaign.[57] Such segregation was reinforced by rigid hierarchical boundaries. There was no hope of promotion for women, whatever their length of service, and their work remained of the most routine kind. This was reinforced by well established marriage bars, which prevented women from accruing seniority unless they remained unmarried.

There are several important inter-related explanations for job segregation. Again, the most pervasive related to assumptions about women's natural role and capacities. The Webbs, for example, rejected any notion of equality between men and women as 'unfair and even cruel'. Instead, they argued, in manual work at least, 'women constitute a distinct class of workers, having different faculties, different needs, and different expectations from those of men. To keep both sexes in the same state of health and efficiency, implies often a differentiation of task, and always a differentiation of effort and subsistence.'[58] It was also considered important that women's work should prepare them for their future 'natural' role as housewives and mothers. A related contemporary explanation concerned male hostility. The Webbs describe 'the intensity of the resentment and abhor-

[52] Lewis, (1984), above n. 4, p. 194.    [53] *Women in Industry*, above n. 23, para. 86.
[54] *ibid.*, para. 27.    [55] Lewis, (1984), above n. 4, p. 195.
[56] Zimmeck, above n. 34, p. 160.    [57] *ibid.*, p. 160.
[58] Webbs, *Industrial Democracy*, above n. 33, p. 505.

rence with which the average working man regards the idea of women entering his trade.'[59] This was partly related to the issues of morality: 'The respectable artisan has an instinctive distaste for the promiscuous mixing of men and women in daily intercourse.'[60] Similarly, the segregation of women in as diverse occupations as clerical work and copper mining was justified by reference to the need to preserve moral standards.[61] Clerical work in particular was relatively 'respectable' and therefore a convenient source of employment for single middle-class women, who were regarded as 'surplus' and a significant source of embarrassment.[62] The Webbs, in an interesting aside, recognise the dangers of what would now be considered sexual harassment which necessarily result from women working in a position of subordination to that of men working with them. However, their solution was not to prevent the men from exploiting the women's weakness, but to exclude the women from the job in question.[63]

Job segregation and low pay were locked into a vicious cycle. From a trade union point of view, job segregation comprised a neat answer to the risk that women would undercut men's pay. Women could not underbid men if the competition for men's jobs was confined to men. 'So long as the competition of men is virtually confined to the men's jobs, and the competition of women to the women's jobs, the fact that the women sell their labour at a low price does not endanger the men's Standard Rate.'[64] There was clearly no recognition of the way in which job segregation and low pay were mutually reinforcing. If male trade unionists had demanded equal pay for women, there would have been no need to insist on women doing different work. I return to this point in the next section.

### iii) **Trade Unions**

The attitude of trade unions played a significant part in maintaining women's disadvantage in the labour market. Although there were some historical encounters between organised women workers and their employers, trade unions more often acted as obstacles to women's advancement than protectors of their interests. The initial response was to exclude women entirely from trade union membership. Eighteenth century trade clubs, such as hatters, basketmakers or compositors would have immediately gone on strike if an employer had attempted to employ women in their trades.[65] In the printing industry, this policy of rigid exclusion continued well into the nineteenth century. For example, in bookbinding, the women were consistently excluded from membership of the union, the London Society of Bookbinders, which had actively promoted the men's cause throughout

---

[59] *ibid.*        [60] *ibid.*, pp. 496–7.
[61] See e.g. G. Burke 'The Decline of the Independent Bal Maiden' in John (ed.), above n. 2, pp. 189–90.
[62] Zimmeck, above n. 34, p. 156.
[63] Webbs, *Industrial Democracy*, above n. 33, p. 497.
[64] *ibid.*, p. 506.        [65] *ibid.*, p. 498.

the first half of the nineteenth century.[66] It is ironic that pressure for change came from employers, determined to employ lower paid women workers, even if this meant setting up a separate, non-union establishment. In 1886, the union finally faced the challenge and recommended acceptance of women provided that they were paid at the same rates as men. Although the Webbs hailed this as an important development,[67] Hunt points out that the likelihood of women attaining equal rates with men was remote, and that the union made no attempt to organise the women in an attempt to ensure that equal rates were achieved.[68]

The alternative to explicit exclusion was to insist on rigid job demarcations, preventing women from actively competing with men. This meant, as the Webbs remarked, that 'nine-tenths of the Trade Unionists have never had occasion to exclude women from their organisations.'[69] For example, in the hosiery industry, by agreeing that women should only work small frames, the union and employers allowed the women to 'retain their privilege of working at a farthing per dozen less than the men'[70] while preventing them from undercutting the men's rate. On these terms, and following a wave of militancy in the late 1880s, trade unions began to open up membership to women.[71] In addition, women began to form their own unions, encouraged by the Women's Trade Union League, which had been formed in 1874 to encourage women to join and organise unions.

Despite these changes, women remained marginalised in unions, and indeed there was a shared assumption that women were a 'problem'.[72] Although no-one doubted women's willingness to join unions, they found it more difficult to sustain membership or to reach positions of leadership in the union. As Bornat shows, this was largely due to the continuing presumption that women's role in production was secondary to their 'natural' role in the home. 'Segregation and marginalization were sustained by social and ideological controls which were imposed by employers and leading trade unionists.'[73] In the textile union, for example, women comprised almost half the membership in the years up to 1914, and there were significant examples of women's militancy in defence of their interests. However, leadership was concentrated among the men. The importance of social pressures was emphasised by a leading woman unionist in 1900: 'The political world preaches to women submission, so long as it refuses them the Parliamentary franchise, and therefore ignores them as human beings.'[74] Even more important was the insistence that married women belonged at home, a principle which, as we have seen, was crucial to male

---

[66] Hunt, above n. 25, in John (ed.), p. 75.
[67] Webbs, *Industrial Democracy*, above n. 33, p. 500.
[68] Hunt, above n. 25, in John p. 81.
[69] Webbs, *Industrial Democracy*, above n. 33, p. 496.
[70] *ibid.*, p. 503.     [71] Bornat, above n. 26, in John (ed.), p. 207.
[72] *ibid.*, p. 207.     [73] *ibid.*, p. 208.
[74] Cited in Bornat, above n. 26, in John (ed.), p. 222.

demands for a family wage. This led to the contradictory stance of the TUC on the issue of equal pay. The perception that equal pay would prevent women from undermining wage rates led to the passing of a resolution in favour of equal pay for women in 1888. Yet equal pay was also considered to be incompatible with male demands for a 'family wage'. The policy of exclusion and segregation seemed to achieve both these aims at once.

## iv) Education

Education has always been a key factor in the socialisation of girls into the role considered appropriate for their future lives. Notions of 'femininity' in the nineteenth and early twentieth centuries led to marked differences in the treatment of girls and boys,[75] with the result that few women received an education which fitted them to compete equally with men in the labour market. It should be stressed too that 'femininity' was a deeply class-bound concept, leading to very different educational experiences for girls of different classes.

Prior to 1870, education was the preserve of upper-class or socially aspiring families. Children were usually taught at home in the early years; when they did go to school, between the ages of twelve and fifteen, the gender demarcations were rigid. Whereas boys were educated in large, professionally staffed schools, with curricula dominated by the classics, girls were sent to small, fashionable schools, whose aim was the inculcation of 'femininity'. This had a highly specific meaning, entailing 'a certain delicacy, a strength not competent to walk more than a mile, an appetite fastidious and easily satisfied joined with that timidity which commonly accompanies feebleness . . . all are held more ladylike.'[76] The prevalence of chronic invalidity in middle-class women of the nineteenth century is no surprise in the light of the fact that schools expected them to 'develop delicate complexions aided by starvation diets, to improve their posture with aids like straight laces, back boards, iron collars and wooden stocks, and to keep their feet firmly in position while repeating information learned by rote.'[77] As an astute observer noted as early as 1864: 'I cannot find that any part of the training given in ladies' schools educates them for a domestic life or prepares them for duties which are supposed to be especially womanly.'[78]

Working-class girls had a very different experience. It was not until 1870 that a statutory right to education was introduced, covering boys and girls alike. In these schools, 'femininity', far from being associated with physical weakness and delicate accomplishments, meant training girls for a future as

---

[75] See generally, P. Marks 'Femininity in the Classroom' in J. Mitchell and A. Oakley (eds.), *The Rights and Wrongs of Women* (Penguin, 1976).
[76] Cited in Marks, above n. 75, p. 182.
[77] *ibid.*, p. 182.
[78] *ibid.*, pp. 182–3.

domestic servants, and, on marriage, housewives who would create the kind of home which would discourage male drunkenness, poverty and wife-beating.[79]

The opening up of elementary education prompted a serious debate about the role of secondary education. Substantial changes began to be implemented in the latter part of the nineteenth century, with the establishment of girls' schools with curricula similar to those in equivalent boys' schools. Nevertheless, notions of natural differences between girls and boys dominated the choice of curriculum. Pseudo-scientific and medical theories prevailed: a 'boy's' education, it was said, would harm women's reproductive organs, produce amenorrhoea and make it impossible for women to breast-feed babies.[80] For example, the view that adolescent girls needed to conserve their energies for reproduction led to such practices as those of the Girls' Public Day Schools Trust, whose schools were only open in the mornings so that girls would not be subject to too much strain.[81] As the Principal of the first proprietary girls' school in England put it, the aim was to train girls 'so that they may best perform that subordinate part in the world to which, I believe, they have been called.'[82]

It was only gradually and with some reluctance that universities opened their doors to women. Colleges for women were opened at Cambridge in 1870, and Oxford in 1879; and London University (apart from the medical school) admitted women students to examinations in 1878. In Oxford, however, it was considered necessary to 'protect' girls from rigorous examination schedules: it was not until 1884 that women were permitted to take any university examinations, and proposals to allow women to take degrees were repeatedly rejected until 1909.[83] Yet even such gradual change stirred up intense controversy. Senior members of Oxford University continued to stress the 'more refined, delicate and domestic nature of women, and the dangers of an unrestricted course of reading and study to the future mothers and teachers of our race.' Dean Burgon declared in 1884 that the statute admitting women to examinations was 'a reversal of the law of Nature which is also the law of God concerning women . . . Inferior to us God made you and inferior to the end of time you will remain.'[84] Even modern historians refer to the early principals of women's colleges in Oxford as 'women of great, in some sense masculine, character, . . . ruling their charges in an autocratic but paternalistic way.'[85] Hostility to women medical students was particularly rampant. Despite the opening of the medical register to women, none of the major teaching hospitals would accept

[79] Marks, above n. 75, p. 190.
[80] *ibid.*, p. 189.
[81] Lewis (1984), above n. 4, p. 90.
[82] *ibid.*, p. 91.
[83] V. H. H. Green, *A History of Oxford University* (Batsford, 1974), pp. 185–9.
[84] Both cited in Green, above n. 83, p. 186.
[85] *ibid.*, p. 187.

women as residents, leaving their training to smaller hospitals which had predominantly female staff and specialised in obstetrics.[86] In an important breakthrough in 1874, the Royal Free Medical School was founded specifically to enable women to qualify as doctors, and for many years, it was the only medical school to admit women students. Women who attempted to apply to other medical schools found numerous obstacles placed in their paths. For example, in 1875, the University of Edinburgh won a law-suit which entitled it to refuse to award degrees to a group of seven women who had succeeded in completing their medical studies.[87]

The notion of women as primarily reproductive also meant that employers regarded it as unproductive to train them. Even when young women were formally offered apprenticeships, the training was in the hands of employers or senior workers whose overriding view was that women belonged at home. As a result, the training was so poor as to be a mere disguise for cheap labour.[88]

## III.   1914–1945

a) The First World War and its Aftermath

The First World War brought radical changes to the position of women. Mobilisation of most of the male work-force necessitated the drafting of women into the war-time economy: the number of working women leapt by 22.5 per cent between 1915 and 1918.[89] Stereotypes of women's natural role gave way to necessity, and women were accepted as workers in a wide range of occupations, including such traditional male spheres as armaments and ship-building. Conversely, traditional female spheres were depleted: the number of domestic servants plummeted by 400,000 during the war years, as women were pulled into the armaments industry.[90] This had repercussions in all spheres of women's lives. Child-care was now recognised as a social responsibility, and war-time creches mushroomed. Organised male workers responded to the fear of undercutting by insisting, not on exclusion, but on equal pay for women, thus preserving existing pay rates until their return from war.[91] There was even change on the education front: most of the large London teaching hospitals began to take women as students and residents in response to the shortage of doctors.[92]

However, these changes were only superficial, and were not to be sustained after the war. War-time employers, who relied so heavily on female

---

[86] Lewis, (1984), above n. 4, p. 195.
[87] Anderson and Zinsser, *A History of Their Own*, above n. 17, p. 189.
[88] *Women in Industry*, above n. 23, para. 84.
[89] *ibid.*, para. 92.
[90] *ibid.*, para. 107.
[91] *ibid.*, para. 120.
[92] Lewis (1984), above n. 4, p. 195.

labour, continued to consider them to be a merely transient replacement. The fact that production in the munitions industry improved enormously was attributed to new processes rather than to women's input; and women's work was still seen as less valuable than that of men.[93] The usual preconceptions about women's role proved remarkably resilient despite the reality. Thus employers gave no credence to the fact that women were moving into jobs for which they had no training, but instead complained of the extra cost of supervision and separate accommodation.[94] Nor was account taken of women's continued heavy domestic burdens. Employers criticised women for bad time-keeping, or expressed dismay at absenteeism necessitated by domestic tasks such as laundry.[95] Yet this left out of account the fact that the low wages paid to such women left them no way of paying for domestic help. Where wages were somewhat higher, as in cotton weaving, absenteeism and bad time-keeping were hardly a problem.[96] Employers also continued to assume that women would leave the labour force on marriage, with the result that it was not considered worth the cost of training. Again, the vicious circle thus created was ignored: women were penalised for lack of training; yet it was considered wasteful to train them. Finally, although women's pay did improve enormously, the differential narrowing from one-half to two-thirds of male pay,[97] there was widespread refusal to implement the principle of paying women the same as men would have been paid had they not been drafted into the army.[98]

After the war, the ideology of women's natural role in the home, never far below the surface even in war conditions, reasserted itself with a vengeance. Women were expected to leave the labour force to make way for returning veterans; indeed, the Treasury had agreed in 1915 that any substitution of women for men should last only for the currency of the war. In addition, the armaments industry, which had absorbed so many women during the war, was now being significantly scaled down.[99] The result was a rapid loss of jobs for women, mitigated only slightly by the brief boom in consumer goods industries where agreements with the unions had not been made, or where jobs were unattractive to men. By the spring of 1919, half-a-million women were unemployed.[100] Initially, women refused to return to traditional 'women's work' such as domestic service, laundry and dressmaking; but as the slump of the 1920s set in, economic necessity forced them back into such jobs. Indeed, women lost any claim to benefit if they refused a

[93] *Women in Industry*, above n. 23, para. 93.
[94] *ibid.*, para. 114.
[95] *ibid.*, paras. 96, 115.
[96] *ibid.*, paras. 96, 115.
[97] *ibid.*, para. 178.
[98] B. Webb Minority Report to *Women in Industry*, p. 256.
[99] *Women in Industry*, above n. 23, para. 191.
[100] M. Pugh, *Women and the Women's Movement in Britain 1914–1959* (Macmillan, 1992), p. 82.

post in domestic service. By 1921, domestic service was, once again, the largest occupation of women.[101]

This marginalisation of women from the paid work-force was defended strenuously on grounds of women's natural role in the home and ineptitude in the labour force. This can be seen clearly in the report of the 1919 Cabinet Committee on Women in Industry, which assumed that women were necessarily less productive workers than men. For example, it accepted without question that equal pay for women without regard to their output would render women unemployable and the net result would be their wholesale exclusion from the work-force. In this the committee received the full support of employers and unionists alike.[102] Popular polemic was more strident. Newspaper headlines in 1919 described as scandalous the retention of 'flappers' while ex-servicemen could not find jobs.[103] Although a substantial majority of the unemployed in 1919 were women, unemployment was characterised as a male problem; indeed, in 1919, the Ministry of Labour stopped reporting separately on women's employment.[104]

b) THE INTER-WAR PERIOD

### i) Women in the Family

The inter-war period saw some improvement in women's material conditions, but advances were patchy and did not necessarily affect all women. Marriage continued to be central to the experience of adult women. Although the imbalance between men and women was exacerbated by the huge male losses during the First World War, the rate of marriage among women was only slightly reduced during the 1920s and began to climb steeply in the 1930s.[105] Within marriage, however, conditions had changed to some extent. Most important was the enhanced possibility of control over child-birth. Average family size dropped from 3.4 in 1911 to 2 in 1941.[106] A central contributory factor was the increasing availability of contraceptive devices, such as the condom and the diaphragm. For example, Marie Stopes opened the first birth-control clinic in London in 1921, and found herself deluged by appeals for information.[107] A second clinic was opened in south London in the same year, and in 1925–26, several clinics were opened in towns outside London.[108]

Progress towards limitation of family size was, however, achieved in the

---

[101] *ibid.*, pp. 81–3.
[102] *Women in Industry*, above n. 23, para. 213.
[103] Cited in Pugh, above n. 100, p. 82.
[104] *ibid.*, p. 83.
[105] *ibid.*, p. 222.
[106] Lewis, (1984), above n. 4, p. 5.
[107] Anderson and Zinsser, above n. 17, p. 286.
[108] S. Rowbotham, *Hidden from History* (1973), p. 149.

face of strong contrary pressures. One manifestation was the 'under-population' scare. This was clearly underpinned by strongly racist and elitist tendencies. Some critics argued that middle classes would be swamped by the working classes, who continued to reproduce at a faster rate; and others declared that the separation of sex from procreation would lead to moral degradation and the spread of venereal diseases.[109] In 1935, the Chancellor of the Exchequer, Neville Chamberlain, appealed for more babies to bolster the imperial power of Britain.[110] Thus birth-control advocates were forced to argue that birth-control would not lead to very small families, but to better planned families and healthier mothers and children. Even Marie Stopes reflected this, by calling her society the Society for Constructive Birth Control and Racial Progress.[111] State support for contraception was therefore slow in coming: it was not until 1930 that the government agreed to allow local authorities to make contraceptive information available, and then only to women for whom pregnancy was deemed detrimental to health. By 1937, less than a quarter of maternal and child welfare centres had established birth-control clinics.[112] Abortion remained illegal;[113] indeed, there was little support for abortion law reform until the 1930s.

Pressures on women to sustain their reproductive role and increase family sizes were not accompanied by medical or financial support for women in pregnancy and childbirth. The benefits of developments in medicine were painfully slow to reach mothers: the maternal mortality rate, which stood at 4.8 maternal deaths for every 1,000 live births in 1870, had only dropped to 4.3 in 1935. The high risks to mothers were clearly related both to the rudimentary care offered them and to poor nutrition and housing conditions.[114] Governments were reluctant to introduce family allowances and home helps; indeed, they were quick to blame mothers themselves for high infant mortality rates, on the grounds that fewer women breastfed their babies.[115]

Possibly the most marked feature of this period was the development of a strong ideology of maternity and domesticity.[116] Bolstered by contemporary women's magazines, this ideology represented marriage as the 'best job of all'[117] and housework as a profession to be proud of. However, rosy portrayals of domestic bliss masked the continuing drudgery of housework. There were certainly improvements, both in the standards of housing and

---

[109] Rowbotham, above n. 108, p. 149; D. Rhode 'Reproductive Freedom' in P. Smith (ed.), *Feminist Jurisprudence* (Oxford University Press, 1993), p. 307.
[110] Cited in Pugh, above n. 100, p. 88.
[111] Lewis, (1984), above n. 4, p. 32.
[112] *ibid.*, p. 33.
[113] Offences against the Person Act 1861 ss. 58, 59.
[114] Rowbotham, above n. 108, p. 145.
[115] Pugh, above n. 100, p. 89.
[116] Lewis, (1984), above n. 4, p. 32.
[117] Pugh, above n. 100, p. 222.

the availability of domestic appliances. But these were not an unmitigated benefit to women. Indeed, housework became more time-consuming for middle-class women. The decline in popularity of domestic service meant that middle-class women would have to do the work themselves; and for families who could afford vacuum cleaners and washing machines, the appliances simply reduced the dependence on domestic servants without in any way diminishing the burden on the housewife.[118] At the same time, standards of housekeeping had risen. This was partly to do with greater knowledge of the importance of cleanliness; but was also fuelled by manu-facturers of household goods, who found in women a fertile market.[119] For working-class women, housework remained arduous, requiring the all-consuming activities of making fires, heating water, doing laundry, sweeping, cooking and cleaning.[120] Labour-saving appliances were simply too expensive; the sewing machine was the most common piece of machin-ery, and this involved much time-consuming activity. In addition, the recession of the 1920s forced many men out of work, and shortage of money placed severe strains on the women, who were generally responsible for budgeting.

Improvements in housing, although significant in this period, were slow to reach women in the lowest income groups. Running water remained a luxury in some areas: Lewis shows how, as late as 1925 in Lancaster, 475 houses shared a single tap. In Manchester in 1931, up to fifty people in a tenement building were still sharing one tap. Indoor lavatories remained unusual until well into the twentieth century; outdoor privies being crude and unsanitary. A bathroom was possibly the greatest aspiration of work-ing-class women after the First World War.[121] There were, of course, many working-class families who could afford to purchase one of the four million new houses which were built during the period, especially in the 1930s, and this represented significant progress for working-class women, as it did for their middle-class counterparts. But this development too was not un-equivocally beneficial. Many of the new homes were on estates outside the centre of town, and tended to weaken the traditional ties of community, increasing the isolation of women within their homes. Only two-thirds of the new houses were wired for electricity, and even then many still included a traditional kitchen range, so that the heavy work of solid fuel fires remained unmitigated. The notion of housework as a profession may have increased women's pride in their homes, but it also increased their work by raising the standards and expectation of themselves and their neighbours.

Child-care too remained an all-consuming activity, although there were important changes in its nature. With the end of child labour, children were

---

[118] *ibid.*, pp. 219–21.    [119] *ibid.*, pp. 218–22.
[120] See e.g. the accounts in E. Roberts, *A Woman's Place* (Basil Blackwell, 1984), pp. 125–8.
[121] Lewis, (1984), above n. 4, pp. 28–31.

at home and dependent for longer periods. Day care for pre-school children, which had mushroomed during the war, dropped drastically in the inter-war period, and did not re-emerge as a significant resource until the Second World War.[122]

ii) **Women and Paid Work**

In the inter-war period, the patterns of low pay, job segregation, lower trade union organisation and different education and training persisted, bolstered by continued adherence to assumptions about women as primarily reproductive, belonging in the home, and inferior workers in the productive sphere.

(1) *Low Pay*    After the First World War, pay differentials between men and women were institutionalised across the public and private sectors, often reinforced by collective agreements and Trade Boards. In the civil service, for example, the '20 per cent' rule prevailed, ensuring that the maximum rate on the women's scale was pegged at about 80 per cent of the maximum male scale.[123] This applied even when men and women were doing identical jobs, and had the effect that a woman promoted to a particular grade would still earn less than a man on a grade beneath her. This had spin-off effects throughout a woman's lifetime: pensions for example were partially determined by maximum pay in the final years of service, ensuring that women pensioners were less well-off than their male counterparts. Similarly, in the armed forces, the ratio of women's to men's pay was maintained at about 2 to 3, and in the police force, rates of pay for constable and sergeant were prescribed in statutory instruments with women earning only 88 per cent of the male rate.[124] The principle of a woman's rate extended throughout the public services. In teaching, a woman's rate of 80 per cent of the male rate was recommended from the inception in 1919 of the official pay setting machinery, the Burnham Committee, and enshrined in delegated legislation.[125] Although women medical and dental officers in the civil service received equal pay with men, there was an express policy of paying women nurses less than men on the same grade.[126] Nor was this confined to the public services: indeed, the differential was generally wider in the private sector. Thus in manual work in manufacturing, adult women's weekly earnings were a mere 47 per cent on average of those of men in 1938; and minimum weekly rates, even those set by Trade Boards, stood at one-half to two-thirds the male rate. Women shop assistants could expect to earn only 60 to 70 per cent of their male colleagues' earnings in the pre-war

[122] A. Clarke-Stewart, *Day Care* (Fontana, 1982), p. 42.
[123] Report of the Royal Commission on Equal Pay 1944–1946 (Cmd. 6937, October 1946), paras. 41–48.
[124] *Equal Pay*, above n. 123, paras. 62 and 67.
[125] *ibid.*, para. 90.
[126] *ibid.*, paras. 126 and 130.

period; and separate pay scales for clerical workers generally set the women's rate at about 65 per cent of those of men.[127]

Explanations of pay differentials in the 1940s scarcely differ from those intoned by employers, trade unions and government commissions in the earlier decades of the century. Employers continued to assert that women were less productive than men, and entailed greater overhead costs on supervision and accommodation.[128] The greater physical strength of men, and their allegedly greater adaptability and versatility were called in aid to support this contention. The facts that new technology had by the 1940s largely undermined the importance of physical strength, and that women's education and training were geared to routine rather than flexible working were wholly ignored. This was linked to the assertion that women saw their primary role as home-makers, and their work in the labour market as secondary. As evidence, women's higher absentee rate was often cited. As one employer representative told the 1946 Royal Commission on Equal Pay: 'Men generally regard their work in a more serious light and have a greater economic urge as traditional breadwinners to keep at work. Women will often stay at home for more trivial causes . . . and will arrive just a little later in the morning and leave a little earlier in the evening.'[129] Again, as their First World War predecessors had done, this body wholly ignored the extra fatigue caused to women by their double burden of domestic and paid work. Moreover, as the TUC pointed out, on the low pay earned by women, they had less to spend on food and were likely to be less well-nourished than their male counterparts. Finally, the fact that they spent relatively short periods in the paid labour force was relied upon as a justification for paying women less. Again, this ignored the fact that widespread marriage bars forced women out of the work-force on marriage.

When women were clearly equal or better than men at the job, other justifications were found. The man, it was asserted, was the 'natural' breadwinner, and therefore in greater need of better pay. Thus in nursing, despite the admitted excellence of women, higher pay for men was justified on the grounds that they were usually married with family responsibilities.[130] In teaching, the 1919 Burnham Committee simply stated that the scale of salaries which were adequate for women would not be adequate for men,[131] a principle which was maintained throughout the inter-war period. Also an important contributing factor to women's low pay was the fact that they tended to be, on average, younger than men. Thus whereas 45 per cent of women between fifteen and twenty-four were in the paid

[127] ibid., paras. 144, 239, 246.
[128] ibid., para. 346.
[129] ibid., para. 353.
[130] ibid., para. 130.
[131] ibid., para. 86.

labour force, this dropped off to 20 per cent in the thirty-five to sixty-four age group.[132]

(2) *Job Segregation*    Despite the shake-up of the First World War, patterns of segregation soon reappeared, with women concentrated in low paying, low status jobs. As with differential pay, this was institutionalised in the public service, with clearly demarcated 'women's' and 'men's' grades. This in turn contributed to low pay for women, since the women's grades were invariably lower than those of the men. In the non-industrial civil service, for example, clerical and typing jobs were exclusively female, accounting for 54 per cent of all women in the service. By contrast, women constituted a puny 1.5 per cent in the professional, scientific and technical grades, and a mere 4 per cent of the administrative grades. Policies of total exclusion continued to operate: women were not admitted into the foreign service until after the Second World War and even then were subject to a 10 per cent quota at the recruitment stage.[133] A similar picture emerges in the teaching profession. Although women formed the vast majority of the profession as a whole, they clustered in the lowest grades. The 1946 Royal Commission on Equal Pay noted the 'natural primacy of women in the education of the youngest pupils',[134] so that children under seven were invariably taught only by women, and women predominated in schools for seven to eleven-year-olds. In the better paid secondary school sector, the numbers of men tended to equal those of women, with men teaching in boys' schools and women in girls' schools. More revealing still are figures concerning head teachers. Even in elementary schools, men were dispro-portionately represented in the ranks of head-teachers: in 1938, men formed only 29 per cent of the total number of elementary school teachers, but as many as 43 per cent of heads. In secondary schools, where men slightly outnumbered women in the category of teachers as a whole, they constituted nearly double the number of head-teachers.[135] In nursing, women did hold most of the senior positions, but this, paradoxically, was used as a reason to pay men in more junior positions more than women on the same grade.[136] In all other professions, women continued to constitute a minuscule proportion: only 7,200 out of 44,359 doctors in 1944; a mere 549 out of 15,404 dentists in 1943, and an insignificant 150 out of about 3,500 barristers in 1939.[137]

In private industry, job demarcations were equally marked, with patterns scarcely altered in the entire inter-war period. Women predominated in 'women's' trades: forming 75 per cent of all workers in hosiery and laun-

[132] *Equal Pay*, above n. 123, para. 138.
[133] *ibid.*, paras. 30, 32 and n. p. 10.
[134] *ibid.*, para. 79.
[135] *ibid.*, paras. 79–81.
[136] *ibid.*, para. 130.
[137] *ibid.*, p. 43.

dries, and as much as 90 per cent in dress-making. Similar predominance was clear in food, catering, and distribution. In so-called heavy industries such as mining, metal manufacture and shipbuilding, women constituted a mere 0.1 million out of a total of 3.9 million. Not unexpectedly, the men's work tended to be in relatively higher paying industries, and the women's in lower.[138] Nor was job segregation a phenomenon unique to the manual trades. In non-manual work in private industry and commerce, a high degree of segregation was maintained. For example, fewer than 2.5 per cent of typists were men in the inter-war period, whereas only about 10 per cent of draughtsmen were women. Very few women reached the higher administrative grades.[139]

(3) *Education and Training*   As in the pre-war period, stereotypes about women's natural role and capacities were central to the education and training provided. The result was to turn stereotypical assumptions into self-fulfilling prophecies. For example, marriage bars and the assumption that women would leave the work-force on marriage led to employers refusing to train women in the same way as they did men, who, they assumed, were intending to embark on careers for life. The result was that relatively few women reached senior positions.[140] In schools, the assumptions about femininity had changed very little during the inter-war period, although the general availability and quality of education had improved substantially. A small but highly able elite was identified among girls, and given an academic education similar to boys, qualifying them for university education. However, the number of girls having such an opportunity remained far smaller than boys, and often the price of a good education was considered to be the forfeiture of opportunities for motherhood.[141]

In higher education, some of the gains made during the First World War were quickly lost again. Medical schools, which had briefly opened for women during the war, closed their doors again after 1918.[142] In other universities, pre-war advances were consolidated and some small advances made, but only in the teeth of much resistance. For example, in Oxford, the resolution to admit women to full membership of the university passed in 1909 was not implemented until 1920. Women were now permitted to matriculate and to take all degrees, although the degree of theology was barred to them until 1935. However, the Student's Union continued to express vociferous opposition, and, in November 1928 passed a resolution that women's colleges should be levelled to the ground. In 1926, senior members convinced the University's Hebdomadal Council to impose a

---

[138] *ibid.*, paras. 139 and 146.
[139] *ibid.*, paras. 240, 243.
[140] *ibid.*, paras. 243–4.
[141] Marks, 'Femininity in the Classroom' above n. 75, in Mitchell and Oakley (eds.), pp. 193–4.
[142] Lewis, *Women in England* (1984), above n. 4, p. 195.

limitation on the number of women to be admitted to the university, a quota which remained in force until 1956.[143]

## IV.  THE SECOND WORLD WAR[144]

As in the First World War, the Second World War proved a major catalyst for the entry of women into the work-force. This time, however, there was some reluctance on the part of women. During the first years of the war, there was a mere trickle of women into the workforce, prompting the introduction in 1941 of conscription for single women between twenty and thirty. This, together with financial hardship and some measure of patriotism, precipitated an influx of women, so that by 1943, 90 per cent of single women and 80 per cent of married women between eighteen and forty worked in industry or the armed forces. Government did not, however, make life easy for such women. Women in factories worked long hours, frequently on twelve-hour shifts, and under dangerous conditions. Yet compensation was less than that for men doing the same jobs. A law of 1939 provided that women who were injured in war-related accidents should receive compensation at rates which were 25 to 50 per cent below that of men; this was only changed in 1943 after a public outcry. Nor was equal pay guaranteed. Government resisted any large-scale equalisation; and although some employers gave the rate for the job, equal pay was often avoided on the pretext that women needed extra supervision or help from male colleagues. On the railways and in government training centres, an explicit policy of lower pay for women was maintained. Where equal pay was achieved, as at Rolls Royce in 1943, it was often only after a strike and with the support of male colleagues. Most disappointing was the campaign for equal pay among teachers: when a clause in the 1944 Education Bill guaranteeing equality in pay was passed by a majority of one in Parliament, Churchill called a no-confidence vote and so succeeded in reversing it. At the same time, women were given little help in the task of feeding and caring for their own families. Despite vigorous protests by working mothers, government nurseries were inadequate, catering for only about one-quarter of the children of working mothers and often providing shorter hours than the mother's working day. In addition, finding food for the family in conditions of scarcity and rationing was a time-consuming and frustrating enterprise, requiring long hours of queuing.

The impact of war work on the post-war period was mixed. Policy-makers, like their First World War counterparts, generally assumed that women's paid employment was only for the duration of the War. After the

---

[143] Green, *A History of Oxford University*, above n. 83, p. 189.
[144] This section draws on Pugh, above n. 100, ch. 9; J. Lewis, *Women in Britain since 1945* (Basil Blackwell, 1992), pp. 69–71, p. 79; Anderson and Zinsser, *A History of Their Own*, above n. 17, pp. 309–10.

War, however, there were strong pressures in conflicting directions. Women were urged to return home to rebuild the family, and war-time nurseries were gradually closed. The ideology of full-time motherhood and domesticity, which had never fully receded, was resuscitated with vigour. On the other hand, it was clear that the labour force without women fell substantially short of industry's needs, prompting the Ministry of Labour in 1947 to appeal to women to enter industry if they were in a position to do so. The result was that the exit of women from the labour force was nowhere near as complete after the Second World War as it had been after the First World War, and the pattern of increasing participation by married women was set in place. One of the most important results was that policy-makers became convinced that it was possible for women to combine a limited amount of paid work with marriage and motherhood. Part-time work was seen as an ideal solution, thus sowing the seeds of one of the most significant elements of women's position in the modern work-force.

## V.  THE POST-WAR PERIOD: 1945–1980

The post-war period is characterised by a paradoxical combination of change and stasis, progress and regression. Women achieved formal equality within marriage and greater reproductive freedom. Technology gradually eased the burden of housework, and participation in the paid work-force grew common-place. Universities began to open their doors to women, as did the professions and the trade unions. Yet social equality remained elusive. There was little change in the patterns of low pay and job segregation seen throughout this chapter. Women's participation in positions of power in the State barely increased. Most importantly, women's increased participation in the paid labour force did not have the effect of changing the division of labour in the home. Women's primary responsibility for child-care, domestic work and care of the elderly and ill continued unabated, as did the social and political undervaluation of this function.

The post-war period was also characterised by a change in the pattern of social distinctions between women. There was a greater convergence between the experiences of working-class and middle-class women, as middle-class women faced the domestic chores and the imperatives to undertake paid work that their working-class sisters had always known. However, two important new divisions appeared. One was based on ethnic background: women from different ethnic backgrounds faced differing obstacles to advancement. In particular, black women were frequently confronted with a noxious combination of racism and sexism. Secondly, a major gulf opened up between women with children and those without. Childless women were increasingly able to penetrate traditionally male occupations, while women with children remained in positions of disadvantage.

The remainder of this Chapter will briefly highlight the central themes of the post-war period by considering women's role in the family, in the State and in the paid work-force. A detailed analysis of the position of women in the present will follow in Chapter 4.

## a) WOMEN IN THE FAMILY

The paradoxical combination of change and continuity, progress and regression, can be illustrated by considering three central determinants of women's life experience in the family: marriage, maternity and housework. The first of these, marriage, has remained a central social institution through most of the modern period. Although the number of marriages per year fell by about one-fifth between 1971 and 1991, statistics from the mid 1980s show that 90 per cent of UK adults married at some time during their lives.[145] At the same time, the number of couples choosing to live together without marrying has increased. In 1989, nearly 1 in 10 couples were cohabiting instead of or as a prelude to marriage.[146] However, marriage as an institution has changed fundamentally. As was shown in Chapter 2, the legal disabilities attached to marriage have gradually been dismantled: indeed, spouses are now in a position of formal equality. Of central importance too has been the greatly increased freedom of access to divorce (see Chapter 2). The rate of divorce has risen steeply: by the end of the 1980s, 1 in 3 marriages in the UK were expected to end in divorce.[147] It is striking that almost 75 per cent of those seeking divorce are women.[148] Nor is marriage any longer in itself an obstacle to paid employment. The Education Act 1944 formally ended discrimination against married women teachers, and the Civil Service abandoned the marriage bar in 1946.[149] Consequently one of the most significant characteristics of the post-war period has been the large increase in the formal participation of married women in the work-force.

However, not all of these changes have signalled unmitigated advances for women. For example, equal rights to property ownership have not yielded equality in practice. Because women tend to earn less than men and to have less stable working lives, building societies regard them as a bad risk on grounds of their earning capacity and thus are frequently reluctant to grant women mortgages on their own.[150] Moreover, formal equality in marriage is undermined by the fact that in general, women have a lower earning capacity than men. Within an intact family unit, allocation of

---

[145] Maclean, *Surviving Divorce*, above n. 12, p. 13.

[146] R. Lister, *Women's economic dependency and social security* (EOC Research Discussion Series No. 2, 1992) p. 5.

[147] Maclean, *Surviving Divorce*, above n. 12, p. 12.

[148] *ibid.*, p. 12.

[149] A. Carter, *The Politics of Women's Rights* (Longman, 1988), p. 13.

[150] H. Austerberry and S. Watson 'Women and Housing Policy' in C. Ungerson (ed.), *Women and Social Policy* (Macmillan, 1985), p. 96; Carter, above n. 149, pp. 42–3.

income between the partners is an important determinant of power relationships within the family. For example, in two-earner families, the man's
income may be used for permanent ends, such as mortgage payments,
whereas the woman's may pay for transient requirements, including weekly
shopping or child-care bills.[151] Where there is only one income, or the
woman's income is far smaller than that of the man, he might make
the crucial decisions in the family. Indeed, recent research has shown that
'the orthodox model of households as egalitarian decision-making units,
within which resources are shared equally, applied to only a fifth (20 per
cent) of the households in our sample.'[152]

Neither is divorce an unqualified benefit for women: the freedom to exit
marriage has not been correlative with freedom of opportunity. Instead, as
Maclean puts it, 'the evidence describing the adverse economic circumstances of the mother-headed family after divorce is now overwhelming.'[153]
The loss of the male wage tends to precipitate the new mother-headed
family into poverty, an effect which has worsened in recent years. Thus
official statistics show that in 1979, 29 per cent of lone-parent families had
incomes (after housing costs) which were below 50 per cent of the average.
By 1987, this proportion had soared to 47 per cent.[154]

Equally paradoxical has been the development of the second major
determinant of women's experience, maternity. In what O'Brien has described as a 'fundamental historical change of the kind which Hegel called
a world historical event',[155] the advent of widely available contraception and
abortion has given women a large measure of control over their own
reproduction. The struggle for access to birth-control was long and hard.
Central government support had still not been achieved by the 1950s,
although the Family Planning Association had by then succeeded in setting
up 500 clinics in conjunction with local authorities. Local authorities had
since 1930 been able to provide advice on contraception but only on
narrow medical grounds; and it was not until 1967 that local authorities
were given the power to assist women with contraception on social as well
as medical grounds.[156] Even this did not yield the desired results: a year
later only one-quarter of local authorities were providing a full family
planning service.[157] Finally, in 1973 free contraceptive advice was made
available to all women and the next year saw the introduction of free
contraceptive supplies under the NHS. This was augmented in 1975 by the
provision of family planning services by General Practitioners. Similarly,

[151] Maclean, *Surviving Divorce*, above n. 12, p. 21.
[152] C. Vogler, *Labour Market Change and Patterns of Financial Allocation within Households*
(ESRC, 1989), p. 20.
[153] Maclean, *Surviving Divorce*, above n. 12, p. 16.
[154] Cited in Lister, above n. 146, p. 14.
[155] M. O'Brien, *The Politics of Reproduction* (Routledge, 1981), p. 21.
[156] National Health (Family Planning) Act 1967.
[157] Carter, above n. 149, p. 67.

abortion was legalised in the Abortion Act 1967. The Act was particularly important in that it authorised abortion on grounds of a woman's general physical or mental health, taking account of social circumstances, rather than narrowly defined medical grounds. This had an impact on thousands of women: in the decade of the 1970s, over 50,000 women received abortions on the NHS, and many more were given legal abortions in private hospitals and clinics.[158] In addition, women have finally benefited from improvements in medical care: maternal mortality rates dropped to 0.15 maternal deaths for every thousand live births in 1976.[159]

The effect of widely available birth-control on women's lives has been of fundamental importance. Apart from the short-lived post-war baby boom, the general trend in birth rates continued downward until the 1970s, with a gentle upward movement in the last two decades.[160] The impact on women's lives is dramatically illustrated by contrasting the experience of women at the turn of the century with their counterparts seventy years later. In 1900, the average European woman could expect to spend twenty-five out of a life expectancy of fifty years in raising children. By 1970, the average woman would be spending only eighteen years in child-rearing, and her life expectancy had risen to seventy-five years.[161] Since the mid-1970s, there has been the added tendency for women to leave a shorter period between births, thus compressing the child-bearing years. At the same time, the number of childless women is increasing.[162]

These crucial changes in women's life experience have, however, had surprisingly little impact on gender roles in society. The child-rearing function has remained strongly associated with women, while at the same time continuing to be seriously undervalued. In particular, ideological and political pressures have continued to corral women in the child-rearing role, while refusing adequately to reward them for it. The ideology of domesticity was particularly influential in the decade-and-a-half after the war. Governments, for demographic reasons, frequently tried to encourage women to increase the birth-rate, usually by incentives provided by the Welfare State: we have already noted that Beveridge viewed the introduction of family allowances as a means of encouraging the birth-rate. State policies such as these were augmented by psychological theories such as those of John Bowlby, which stressed the negative effects on children of separation from their mothers. Although Bowlby's observations were based on the extreme experiences of children separated from their parents during war-time evacuation, they were used in subsequent decades to dissuade mothers from going out to work while their children were young. It was

---

[158] Carter, above n. 149, p. 68.
[159] A. Oakley 'Wisewoman and Medicine Man' in Mitchell and Oakley (eds.), above n. 75, p. 39.
[160] Pugh, above n. 100, pp. 293–4.
[161] Anderson and Zinsser, *A History of Their Own*, above n. 17, p. 322.
[162] Lister, above n. 154, p. 2.

reflected too in popular culture: women's magazines with wide readerships strongly discouraged married women from going out to work. This was, in Betty Friedan's words, the 'feminine mystique' in action: domestic life was portrayed as the primary ideal of women.[163]

The third central aspect of women's experience is that of housework, and again, important changes in technology have had surprisingly little impact on gender roles. It took a decade-and-a-half for the wounds of war to fully heal, but from the 1960s, standards of living rose for all classes. Indoor toilets, running water and electricity slowly permeated through to most dwellings and domestic appliances, such as washing machines, refrigerators and ovens, became accessible to many families.[164] These advances certainly made domestic work easier. However, they did not necessarily reduce the extent of household work or the burden on women. There were at least three reasons for this. First, the virtual disappearance of the female domestic servant meant that the burden of housework fell entirely on the shoulders of individual women. This particularly affected middle-class women who found themselves working harder than their pre-war counterparts.[165] Secondly, all women faced rising expectations of standards of household management and child-rearing. Thirdly, domestic appliances and better housing all required sufficient family income; in fact, as Pugh notes, the key to the improved standard of living was the spread of the two-income family in the period of relatively high employment of the 1950s and 1960s.[166] Thus the imperative to undertake paid employment came from within the family itself.

It is also important to note that modern housing policy has not been unambiguously positive for women. Traditional public housing policy has been to stress the need for a house with a garden, and by 1980 over three-quarters of all British households lived in such houses. Although life in such houses is materially more comfortable, it has also led to isolation and depression for many middle-class women primarily engaged in child-care and home-work. Conversely, in densely populated urban areas, high rise blocks of flats became the preferred option during the 1950s and 1960s. For women in these flats, life is a constant struggle with inadequate play-space for their children, communal facilities which are frequently out of order or vandalised and crime-ridden surroundings.[167] The rapid decline in public housing standards in recent decades has its primary effect on women and children. Indeed, research has shown that living in poor and over-crowded housing conditions with small children is a major cause of depression in women.[168]

[163] Carter, above n. 149, p. 18.
[164] Anderson and Zinsser, *A History of Their Own*, above n. 17, p. 122.
[165] *ibid.*, p. 222.
[166] Pugh, *Women and the Women's Movement*, above n. 100, p. 290.
[167] Ungerson (ed.), above n. 150, p. 85.
[168] G. Brown and T. Harris, *The Social Origins of Depression* (Tavistock, 1970).

## b) WOMEN AND THE STATE

The growth of the Welfare State after 1945 has played a central role in improving women's experiences and opportunities. Comprehensive health care offered through the National Health Service has possibly been the most unmitigated advantage. In addition, the availability of welfare payments has given women an important measure of financial independence. Family allowances and later child benefit, being a fixed allowance payable directly to the mother, regardless of her own or her partner's work history, have been particularly significant in this regard. Welfare payments have also played a crucial role in making divorce a real option for women with young children and only a tenuous link with the paid labour force. During the 1980s, statistics showed that almost half of all lone parents in the UK relied on welfare payments as their main source of income.[169] Finally, the Welfare State has been an important source of employment for women.

These changes, however, have not been unambiguously positive for women. Independence from male partners has to some extent been bought at the price of dependence on the State. As Chapter 2 illustrated, State policies towards women have not necessarily been egalitarian. Indeed, successive governments have often used the welfare system to promote or entrench gender divisions in society. The Beveridge heritage ensured that, until the mid-1970s at least, the structure of welfare payments was designed to promote and perpetuate women's role as primarily mothers and housewives. Despite attempts to challenge this model, new benefits introduced in the mid-1970s continued to rely on it.[170] A watershed was reached in 1979, as a result of European Community legislation insisting on equal treatment in social security, leading to the removal of explicit discrimination in most areas of the UK social security system (see Chapter 4). Nevertheless, the structure of the modern social security system, like that of the paid labour force, continues to reflect a male norm.

State policy towards women's employment has also been ambivalent. In periods of short supply of labour, women have been encouraged to enter the labour market. But there has been little direct support for working mothers. War-time nurseries were quickly closed after hostilities had ended, and there has never again been a proper commitment to State-funded child-care. In the early 1980s, only 19 per cent of British children under five had places in day-care or nursery schools. In Denmark, by contrast, 70 per cent of children under five are provided for in this way. The importance for women is obvious. In Denmark, 80 per cent of mothers with small children were in the labour market in the 1980s. In the UK, the activity rate of mothers is clearly correlated with the number of children,

---

[169] Maclean, *Surviving Divorce*, above n. 12, p. 40.
[170] Lister, above n. 154, p. 26.

particularly those under five. Thus it has been calculated that each pre-school child lowers women's participation rate by 35 per cent.[171]

It is also important to note that at the level of policy-making, women's voices have been muffled. Women MPs have remained scarce throughout the post-war period. In the first seventy-three years after women were admitted to the House of Commons, there were only 164 women Members of Parliament. The 1997 election returned the largest number of women ever (120 Members of Parliament). The effect on the House remains to be seen. Senior positions have been even more elusive: from 1919 to 1992, only forty-five women held Government office, a mere ten at Cabinet level.[172] Only one woman judge sits in the Court of Appeal and none has reached the House of Lords. Disproportionately few women are in top business positions or hold leadership positions in trade unions. The right to sit as a life peer in the House of Lords was only introduced in 1958, and as a hereditary peer in 1963, but even then few women made the grade (see further Chapter 4).

c) WOMEN IN THE WORK-FORCE

The position of women in the paid work-force continued to be strongly determined by their role in the family throughout the post-war period. Although women's economic activity rates increased dramatically, the nature of their paid work and their patterns of working have been closely correlated with the extent to which they have caring responsibilities, either for young children or for elderly or ill relatives. The result, as Carter notes, has been mixed for women: 'their right to go out to work and the importance of their economic role has been strengthened, but the work the majority have to take up is unskilled and ill paid.'[173] This is borne out by the fact that, despite the fact that many more women have access to income from paid work, they remain significantly over-represented among the poorest groups in society.[174]

During the post-war period, women became a far more visible part of the paid work-force than in earlier periods. As has been seen above, women, both single and married, have always been active in the paid work-force, but the extent of their participation has not been fully recorded because much of it has been casual and part-time. In the decades after the war, however, women's formal participation increased markedly. After a static period between 1931 and 1954, where women formed about 29 per cent of the recorded labour force, this figure rose steadily thereafter, reaching 34.4 per

---

[171] Lewis (1992), above n. 144, p. 75.

[172] A. Adonis, *Parliament Today* (2nd edn., Manchester University Press, 1993), p. 55.

[173] Carter, above n. 149, p. 106.

[174] S. Webb 'Women and the UK Income Distribution' in R. Lindley (ed.), *Labour Market Structures and Prospects for Women* (Equal Opportunities Commission, 1994), p. 95.

cent in 1971 and 38.4 per cent in 1981.[175] This general figure conceals some important underlying trends. Most significant has been the increase in married women's participation. In 1951, a mere 26 per cent of married women under sixty were part of the paid labour force; in 1971 this figure had jumped to 49 per cent.[176] Equally important has been the growth in part-time work. For many women, particularly those with young children, part-time work came to represent the only possible avenue to paid working. Part-time working rose slowly during the 1960s, but by 1971 it was estimated that 1 in 3 women employees were part-time, nearly three million women.[177] As will be seen in Chapter 4, this figure has continued to rise steeply.

Increased participation in the workforce has not, however, ameliorated the problem of low pay: in fact, the pattern of low pay for women workers has faded little in the post-war period. The position actually worsened between 1950 and 1965, when women's pay as a proportion of men's actually dropped. In the mid 1960s, the average hourly earnings of full-time women workers stood at only 59 per cent of that of men, and this figure remained obstinately stable until the early 1970s.[178] A major cause of the differential was blatant discrimination: differential pay scales remained rampant. The government refused in 1947 to introduce equal pay for women in the public sector; indeed, a Treasury spokesman asserted that 'the principle of sex differentiation, whether right or wrong, is at present a matter of government policy'.[179] Only a sustained campaign led the Conservative Government to agree in 1955 to introduce equal pay in the civil service, and even then it was phased in over seven years.[180] In the private sector, differential pay scales frequently remained in place even longer.

It was not until the 1970s that the pay gap began to narrow, with women's average hourly earnings increasing from 61.8 per cent of that of men in 1970 to 74.2 per cent in 1977. A major reason for the improvement was the coming into force of the Equal Pay Act 1970 which required equal pay for men and women doing like work (see Chapter 6). The effect of the Act was augmented by trade union action in raising minimum wage rates of women to those for men, and by government income policies permitting flat rate increases rather than percentage increases in wage rates.[181] However, the effect was soon exhausted and the ratio fell back to 72.4 per cent in 1980.

Nor has increased participation diluted job segregation. At the turn of the

---

[175] Wilson in Lindley (ed.), above n. 174, p. 24.
[176] Lewis (1992), above n. 144, pp. 65–6.
[177] Carter, above n. 149, p. 28.
[178] Lewis (1992), above n. 144, p. 80.
[179] Cited in Lewis, *Women in England* (1984), above n. 4, p. 163.
[180] Carter, above n. 149, p. 16.
[181] J. Rubery and R. Tarling 'Women's Employment in Declining Britain' in J. Rubery (ed.), *Women and Recession* (Routledge, 1988), p. 120.

century, 88 per cent of women were in female-dominated occupations; the corresponding figure in 1951 was 86 per cent and 84 per cent in 1971.[182] Job segregation in the post-war period has been particularly marked among some groups. For example, research has shown that Asian and Afro-Caribbean women in Britain remain largely confined to the jobs available to them or their mothers on entry to Britain. Part-time women workers are similarly concentrated into low paid jobs.

Continued segregation has been largely a result of the convergence of women's needs to combine paid work and family, and economic factors. Women were initially drawn into the labour market by the severe labour shortages of the period 1946 to 1959. This increase was sustained because of the shift in the economy away from heavy industry towards service industries. Continued job segregation is unsurprising. As Lewis remarks: 'The changing occupational structure towards a rapidly expanding service sector, which has in turn been intimately related to the expansion of the welfare state, has made particular call on women's labour because of profoundly gendered ideas as to what kind of work is appropriate for women.'[183]

The increased participation of women in the paid work-force has high-lighted too the causal link between the quality of education and training on the one hand and the nature of job opportunities on the other. In the post-war period, significant strides were made towards formal equality at all levels of education and training, and women's participation rates increased substantially. However, gender differentiation in subjects studied remained marked, laying the foundations for the deeply segregated labour market ahead.

This pattern is clearly evident in the development of compulsory school-ing. The duty to provide education for all children up to at least fifteen was established in the Education Act 1944, thus ensuring equal access for girls and boys to schools. However, gender differentiation continued in subtler but equally pervasive forms. This was clearly signalled by the Norwood Report of 1943, which still portrayed girls' chief interest as marriage and motherhood, whereas boys were assumed to be primarily concerned with a job or career. Further divisions were created by the selective system, which distinguished between 'able' and 'less-able' pupils. As a start, girls were allocated fewer grammar school places than their performance merited. County councils, noting that girls did proportionately better than boys at 11 plus, gave boys 'handicap' grades to equalise the numbers of boys and girls getting into grammar schools.[184] Grammar schools did not formally differ-entiate between boys and girls, but the allocation of resources to secondary

---

[182] Lewis (1992), above n. 144, p. 81.

[183] *ibid.*, p. 68.

[184] Carter, above n. 149, p. 37. For the legal challenge to this, see *R* v. *Birmingham, ex p. EOC*, described in ch. 7.

schools favoured boys' schools, particularly in provision of science and technical subject facilities. There were also clearly discernible differences in the education of girls compared with boys. Girls were likely to leave school earlier, to choose arts rather than science subjects and to have lower career aspirations. For the 'less-able' children, sex-based stereotypes were more explicit. For example, the Crowther Report of 1959 noted that for 'less-able girls, . . . we think schools can and should make adjustments to the fact that marriage now looms larger and nearer in the pupils' eyes than ever before.'[185]

During the 1960s, the selective system was gradually replaced by non-selective comprehensive secondary schooling, the aim being to ameliorate the glaring class bias within the school structure. Removal of gender in-equalities was not, at that stage, on the agenda. The impact on girls was ambiguous. On the one hand, they benefited from the expansion of subject matter which came with comprehensive schools. However, this often meant that girls were offered typing, short-hand or domestic sciences, while boys were offered quite different subjects. It was clear even during the 1970s that substantial numbers of comprehensive schools were restricting some sub-jects to one sex only. In addition, the shift away from single sex to mixed schooling has clearly had some disadvantages for girls.

Similar patterns are evident in respect of tertiary education. There was little improvement in the numbers of women reaching university during the 1950s; indeed, medical schools operated a quota system of 80 per cent men to 20 per cent women at least until 1970.[186] However, the expansion of university provision in the mid-1960s opened up wider opportunities to women, and many of the women who graduated during this period were to become leading feminists in the 1970s. The numbers of women in univer-sities jumped from only 27.6 per cent of undergraduates in 1965–6 to 39 per cent in 1980–1 and to 44 per cent of university full-time undergradu-ates in 1987. Formal barriers to women's participation have been largely removed, and women are now qualifying in increasing numbers for previ-ously male-dominated professions such as law and accounting.[187] At the same time, however, there have been severe cuts in the number of teacher training colleges, traditionally the most important source of further educa-tion for women. As a result, the proportion of women acquiring advanced further education fell from 50 per cent of all students in 1970 to 43.6 per cent in 1980.

The trade union movement was surprisingly slow to reflect the increased participation of women in the paid work-force. In 1948, a mere 18 per cent of trade unionists were women; by 1961, this figure had crept up to only 20

---

[185] *Report of the Central Advisory Council for Education '15–18'* Ministry of Education, HMSO, 1959, para. 51.
[186] Carter, above n. 149, p. 33.
[187] Lewis (1992), above n. 144, p. 87; Clarke-Stewart, above n. 122, p. 9.

per cent.[188] Progress was faster during the 1960s, with the growth of white collar trade unionism. During this period, trade unions systematically recruited workers in occupations dominated by women, especially in the public sector. As a result, by 1970, about one-quarter of trade unionists were women.

It is clear from these figures that open hostility towards women by male trade unionists had receded during the post-war period. However, there remained three important obstacles to women's progress in trade unions. First, women tended to work in occupations which were difficult to unionise: scattered work-forces such as domestic and catering work, high turnover (often due to lack of opportunities for promotion), part-time working and lack of job security are all well-known factors militating against the spread of trade unionism. Secondly, women's domestic responsibilities made it difficult for them to participate actively in a union. This was reflected in the fact that even when women did constitute significant numbers of trade union members, they were seriously under-represented among trade union leaders. Thirdly, while open antagonism had certainly waned, unions were still dominated by male concerns, reflecting the marginalisation of women from the policy-making echelons of the union. For example, unions frequently demanded percentage increases rather than the flat-rate increases which would assist low paid women workers. In addition, the maintenance of differentials between workers was often a key union demand: yet this merely perpetuated the distinctions between women and men workers. Finally, it is often said that women tend to be less militant than men. However, there are sufficient examples of militancy among women to undermine this point.[189] Possibly the best-known is the three week strike by 300 women sewing machinists at Ford in 1968 (see Chapter 4).

## CONCLUSION

It has been argued in this chapter that it is not sufficient to analyse the legal forces affecting women's position in society. It is crucial also to expose the social currents and cross-currents with which the law must engage. The chapter has shown in detail the power and continuity of these forces both as they have accrued historically and in their on-going effect on women. It has been argued too that the key to a proper understanding of these social forces is the simultaneous examination of women's role in the family and in the public sphere, always taking note of their dynamic interaction. Indeed, the tension between the two spheres constitutes a central factor in the explanation for the constraints under which women find themselves.

In many respects, as this chapter reveals, there has been dramatic

[188] Carter, above n. 149, p. 46.
[189] See for examples, J. Beale, *Getting it together* (Pluto Press, 1982).

progress, both in the family and the market place. Within the family, women's lives have been transformed by the availability of contraception and abortion, the dramatic progress in domestic technology and the crucial steps forward in obstetric and gynaecological care. These gains have been underpinned to some extent by the State, most notably in the provision of universal and comprehensive health care, and the facilitation of the availability of contraception. Within the paid work-force, progress has manifested itself in the opening of many different opportunities for women, such as increased availability and diversity of education, the abolition of the marriage bar, and the removal of formal barriers in access to the professions. However, despite these gains women continue to suffer disadvantage. There remains a yawning gender pay gap, women continue to be segregated into low paid, low status jobs, and education and training are still highly gender specific.

The historical assessment in this chapter provides a valuable insight into why this is the case. In particular, the chapter reveals the tenacity of the forces constraining progress, whether as present effects of past discrimination, or as a result of unchanged structural influences, or indeed spawned by new social pressures overlaid upon older ones. This is particularly true of pre-liberal status ascriptions. Most influential has been the presumption that the woman is primarily reproductive, and therefore 'naturally' best equipped to perform unpaid labour within the family and remain financially dependent on her husband. This presumption continues to exercise a powerful influence on pay structures and paid work opportunities. For example, although the principle of a 'family wage' for men, but only 'pin money' for women has now been rejected, it has had lasting effects in the form of continuing undervaluation of 'women's work'. Similarly, the assumption that women are less productive than men continues to dictate policy choices. As will be seen in later chapters, modern neo-liberal economists argue that lower pay for women simply reflects their lower productivity, and therefore that legislation requiring equal pay for work of equal value or minimum wages would put both the woman and her prospective employer at a competitive disadvantage. This has had a significant limiting effect on equal pay and minimum wages legislation (see further Chapter 6).

It is at this point that the need for careful and subtle analysis arises. It is crucial to puncture the presumption that women are naturally best equipped to take prime responsibility for family work. However, the response should not be to ignore social realities as liberal individualism and formal equality have tended to do. While this is not their inevitable or natural role in life, it remains disturbingly true that women do, in fact, continue to bear the primary responsibility for children and family work. Their job opportunities and pay levels are accordingly constrained. Nor on the other hand should the law respond, as welfare law has done, by recognising dependent status only to reinforce and perpetuate it. Instead, the complex interaction of family and the paid workforce need to be appreciated by the development of sensitive legal mechanisms which facilitate the combination of paid and unpaid work for all citizens, male or female.

The historical examination has also been striking in its revelation of the differences between the experiences of different groups of women. Throughout the nineteenth century and well into the twentieth century, it has been necessary to analyse the position of working-class women quite separately from their middle- or upper-class counterparts. While class divisions are now less marked, new divisions have appeared, such as those between women of different ethnic groups, women with or without children, women who are or become single parents and those with continuing partnerships, and young or elderly women. Not only does this underscore the argument made in Chapter 1 against an assumption of an 'essential woman', it also means that legal tools which appear universal in their application might have very different effects in practice on different social groups.

# [4]
# Women Today

## INTRODUCTION

Having traced in detail the history of legal developments on the one hand, and of social forces on the other, it is necessary now to draw these together to present a full picture of women in the present and the visible future, both socially and legally. Social aspects are considered in the first part of the chapter. Following the pattern of previous chapters, I begin with the current position of women in the family and society in general, drawing in at this point the highly problematic interaction between race and sex. I turn then to assess the current position of women in the paid workforce, focusing on patterns of participation and the 'flexible' workforce; pay; job segregation; education and training; and trade unions. The legal framework is dealt with in the second part. It will be seen that legal concerns have moved beyond the removal of express legal impediments, to positive laws attempting to address the social forces described. The aim of this section is to give an overall view of current legal provisions in the employment and welfare fields, so that the reader embarks on subsequent detailed chapters with a general map in mind.

## I. WOMEN IN THE PRESENT

a) FAMILY

Women's social and economic position remains, as it always has been, heavily dependent on their role within the family. During the last thirty years, the rapid increase in divorce and remarriage has led to a transformation of family structure. Although 90 per cent of UK adults will marry at some time during their lives, and will have children by that marriage, the nuclear family of two parents living with their children is less common. Indeed the proportion of households containing a traditional family of a married or cohabiting couple with dependent children fell from 32 per cent in the early 1980s to 24 per cent in 1992 and 1993.[1] By contrast, the proportion of families in Great Britain with dependent children headed by a lone mother has soared from 7 per cent in 1971 to 20 per cent in 1993. It is estimated that by 2001, 29 per cent of all households will be headed by a woman, either as a lone parent, or as a solo woman. In addition, during the 1980s, there was a rapid increase in couples who live together without marrying, either as a prelude to marriage or as an alternative.[2] As Maclean comments: 'The individual no longer characteristically passes from childhood to single adulthood, to marriage to child-rearing, to seeing children leave the home, to some portion of working life without children followed by retirement. Instead, marriage is likely to be preceded by cohabitation and followed by separation, then cohabitation, remarriage, possibly stepparenting and possibly redivorce.'[3] So far as children are concerned, on average women are tending to delay child-bearing until their late 20s, and to have small families with shorter periods between births.[4] The result has been a compression in child-bearing years. The average number of dependent children in the family has stabilised at about 1.8,[5] with Pakistani and Bangladeshi households including a much higher proportion of children under sixteen than Indian, Afro-Caribbean and white households.

It is in the interaction between family and paid work that the key to the understanding of women's position in the modern period lies. On the one hand, economic pressures have created a centrifugal force, pushing women out into the paid labour force as an essential part of the family's income generation. On the other hand, there has been little or no diminution of their responsibility for unpaid family work. A recent survey of the distribu-

---

[1] General Household Survey 1993, para 2.4.1.
[2] R. Lister, *Women's Economic Dependency and Social Security* (EOC, 1992), p. 5. (*Women's Economic Dependency*).
[3] M. Maclean, *Surviving Divorce* (Macmillan, 1991), p. 15.
[4] Lister, above n. 2, p. 2.     [5] General Household Survey 1993, para 2.3.2.

tion of unpaid labour in the home in London suggested that women spend an average of forty-two hours a week on housework and child-care compared to eighteen hours for men. Asian women spend considerably more time on housework, with less input from men, than any other group of women.[6] This is not confined to women who do not engage in paid work. Time–budget studies of families in which both adults earn income outside the home show that women consistently do more housework and child-care than men, often as much as six times more.[7] The inequity in distribution of household work is compounded when care of the elderly and disabled people is taken into account.

Women have responded in different ways to these discordant forces. Some have re-entered the labour force as soon as possible after the birth of their children. Between 1980 and 1991, the economic activity rate of mothers whose youngest child was under five jumped from 27 per cent to 50 per cent, with 43 per cent actually working, either full-or part-time.[8] In the period 1991–93, as many as 63 per cent of married women with dependent children were working full-time or part-time. However, in many cases, the hours and nature of work have had to reflect the demands of the family. The percentage of mothers of dependent children working part-time is double that of mothers working full-time.[9] Others have responded by remaining out of the formal workforce. In fact, despite recent increases, the economic activity rate for women still lags well behind that of men: in the age bracket thirty to thirty-four, 95 per cent of men but only 69 per cent of women were economically active in the period 1991–93. It is striking too that over half[10] the women who were economically inactive in 1995 gave as the main reason the fact that they were looking after a home or family, as against only a handful of men.[11] This was particularly marked among Pakistani and Bangladeshi women, over three-quarters of whom are not in the labour market because they are looking after a home or family full-time.[12]

The crucial interaction of family structure and paid work is vividly illustrated by contrasting women with children with their childless counterparts. The labour force participation of women with children is still well below those without children (40 per cent compared to 78 per cent in 1991).[13] Once in the labour force, women without children are increasingly able to penetrate traditional male occupations, particularly management.

[6] Cited in Lister, above n. 2, p. 11.
[7] B. S. Anderson and J. P. Zinsser, *A History of Their Own* vol II (Penguin, 1990), p. 327.
[8] EOC *Some Facts about Women* (1994).
[9] General Household Survey (1993), tables 2.28 and 2.29.
[10] 2.5 million out of 4.8 million.
[11] 125,000 out of 2.7 million. Labour Market Trends, December 1995, Labour Force Survey Helpline, 3.
[12] D. Owen, *Ethnic Minority Women in the Labour market: analysis of the 1991 census* (Equal Opportunities Commission, 1994), pp. 51–3.
[13] P. Elias and T. Hogarth 'Families, Jobs and Unemployment' in R. Lindley (ed.), *Labour Market Structures and Prospects for Women* (Equal Opportunities Commission, 1994), p. 92.

The impact of changing family structure is particularly acute in the case of lone mothers. Lone mothers are far less likely to be working in the paid labour force than other mothers: in 1993, 40 per cent of lone[14] mothers were working compared to 63 per cent of other mothers. They also tend to be less qualified: 38 per cent of lone parents had no qualifications in 1993 compared with 25 per cent of other parents. Most seriously, lone mothers are particularly likely to be living in poverty: whereas only 5 per cent of married couples have an income less than £100 a week; a startling 60 per cent of single (i.e. never married) mothers fall into this category.[15] Without the buffer of a second income in the house, women's dual role as homeworker and breadwinner becomes increasingly difficult to sustain.

The burdens on women within the family have been compounded by the antagonism of the Conservative government towards the participation of the State in social life. As was seen in Chapter 1, Conservative claims to 'roll back the boundaries of the State' have been manifested in cuts in service provision and welfare payments. The demonisation of the State has been accompanied by a corresponding elevation of the family as the primary source of welfare. These policies have had a particularly severe effect on women. The heavy cuts in welfare provision have sharply curtailed their traditional employment opportunities in the State sector, while the same cuts have increased their burden in the home, particularly in respect of care of the elderly and the ill. As a result, work which many women had previously been paid to do as employees of the Welfare State, has now been forced upon other women in an unpaid capacity.

Nor has the rise in male unemployment combined with the increase in opportunities for flexible women workers (see below) had the effect of reversing gender roles within households, as might have been expected. Instead, almost the entire increase in female employment has occurred in households with working partners.[16] Paradoxically the 1990s have witnessed a simultaneous rise in both the proportion of the population in two-earner households (work-rich) and those with no-earners (work-poor). The explanation for this lies in the combined effects of women's poor employment opportunities and the benefit system. A family on benefit will only be better off if one or both partners can find jobs with reasonable pay and job security. Poorly paid and insecure part-time jobs will therefore lead to no net gains. By contrast, in a family which already has one earner, there is usually no loss of benefit if the other partner seeks work. All extra income is retained. Even poorly paid work can therefore function as a useful or essential addition.

---

[14] This includes single and once-married women.
[15] General Household Survey 1993.
[16] P. Gregg and J. Wadsworth 'Gender Households and Access to Employment' in J. Humphries and J. Rubery (eds.), *The Economics of Equal Opportunities* (EOC, 1995), p. 346.

b) Multiple Discrimination: Race and Sex

It has been seen above that general statistics mask specific differences between the lives and opportunities of women. In particular, women with children differ markedly from women without, while among those with children, women with partners need to be considered separately from women without. In this section, an even more fundamental and less contingent difference is considered: that of ethnic origin. Although women of different ethnic origin share many similar experiences of discrimination, the intersection of racism and sexism yields a combination which is more than merely cumulative. Indeed, it has been argued that the familiar tools used to analyse women's position simply reflect a white, middle-class or patriarchal norm and therefore are incapable of incisively analysing the position of women as a whole. As the American feminist writer Patricia Hill Collins argues, in order to depict the experience of black women accurately, it is essential to challenge the 'very constructs of work and family themselves'.[17] Any analysis of ethnicity must also take into account the multiple cross-currents of class, religion and national origin. Thus the experience of women of Afro-Caribbean origin differs from that of women of Pakistani or Bangladeshi origin; middle-class women from those of the working class; and Christian women from Muslim, Jewish or Hindu women.

Such complexity should not be used as a pretext for continuing the invisibility of many black and ethnic minority women. Racism, both historically and in the present, is pervasive. For women of Afro-Caribbean origin in particular, the heritage of slavery and colonial exploitation has been reinforced by recent experience as new immigrants, and later as first and second generation citizens. As Bryan et al tellingly narrate:

It was this climate of grinding poverty and unemployment, coupled with our stubborn and centuries old tradition of refusing to be crushed, which laid the basis for the emigration of thousands of West Indian women and men in the post-War years. Britain, having lost many of its industries, homes and workers during six years of war, needed a cheap and ready supply of labour. And we needed jobs . . . Little could we have known the realities which we would have to face, as we entered a society so steeped in its racist past.[18]

Racism is, moreover, self-perpetuating, as continuing racial discrimination against black men as well as women leads to impoverishment of the family and the community as a whole. The common experience of racism against both men and women, together with the cultural heritage of strong kinship and communal support systems requires a reshaping of the notion that the division of labour within the family is central to women's continuing disadvantage. As Patricia Hill Collins argues:

[17] P. Hill Collins, *Black Feminist Thought* (Routledge, 1991), p. 47.
[18] B. Bryan, S. Dadzie and S. Scafe, *The Heart of the Race* (Virago, 1986), pp. 15–16.

The family life of poor people challenges the assumptions about universal nuclear family forms because poor families do not exhibit the radical split equating private with home and public with work. In order to survive, the family network must share the costs of providing for children . . . African-American families exhibit these fluid public/private boundaries because racial oppression has impoverished disproportionate numbers of black families.[19]

Similarly, the value of paid work is not necessarily equated with the value of the individual who performs it. Because both black men and black women have had to accept whatever work comes their way in order to survive, it has been crucial to divest paid work of the status assumptions commonly attached to it. Such an argument has strong resonances for Afro-Caribbean families in the UK. Black women, like working-class women of all ethnicities, have always been expected to undertake paid work; the ideology of passive femininity of the 1950s and 1960s having been applied exclusively to white middle-class women. At the same time, the burden of domestic work and child-care has traditionally fallen exclusively on the women of the family, particularly in lone parent households. Although it is important to recognise that a significant number of black and ethnic minority women have escaped the strictures of poverty, the level of disadvantage in general is disturbingly high. In particular, in 1995, the ILO unemployment rate for ethnic minorities was as high as 17.1 per cent compared to 6.1 per cent, more than double those of whites.[20]

Not only does sexism operate within racism but racism can operate to explode any bonds of gender. Thus, the privileges of being white may well invest white women with the power to dominate black women. The result is that many women find that their allegiances with men of the same ethnic origin are greater than those with white women. The extent to which this is reflected in labour market statistics is, however, controversial. The Labour Force Survey of 1994 shows that full-time women from ethnic minorities[21] earn roughly the same as white women, with black women earning on average somewhat more per hour than white women,[22] and Pakistani/Bangladeshi women earning significantly less. Smaller scale studies, however, contest these findings. Studies focusing on specific geographical areas show wide disparities between ethnic minority women and their white counterparts. For example, a 1990 study in Leicester found that Asian women were at the very bottom of the earnings heap, earning an average of £113.00 per week compared to the £148.22 earned by white women. Significantly, Asian men, at £167.60, earned more than white women, and

---

[19]  Hill Collins, above n. 17, p. 47.

[20]  F. Sly 'Ethnic groups and the labour market' [1995] *Employment Gazette* 251; Labour Force Survey, Dec 95: 7.23.

[21]  Defined as Black (Black Caribbean, Black African, Black other), Indian, Pakistani/Bangladeshi; Other (Chinese, other non-mixed, other mixed, Black mixed).

[22]  [1991] *Employment Gazette*, pp. 258–9.

white men were far ahead, with £209.85 a week.[23] More generally, it is well known that ethnic minority women are over-represented in former wages councils sectors. Also of significance is the conspicuous wage gap between white men and men from ethnic minority groups, with the latter earning only 89 per cent on average as much as white men. One important result of this is that the pay gap between ethnic minority men and women is narrower than that between white men and women. Indeed, the greater the disadvantage based on race, the smaller is the gender gap. Thus whereas Bangladeshi and Pakistani women working full-time earned as much as 95 per cent of the hourly earnings of men in the same ethnic group, the earnings of both men and women in that group lagged significantly behind white workers.[24] In other words, for Bangladeshi/Pakistani workers, the detrimental effects of racial discrimination draw men and women together in disadvantage.

c) THE WORK-FORCE

i) **Patterns of Participation**

The last two decades of the twentieth century have witnessed a remarkable confluence of two trends. Economic restructuring has led to an intense demand for 'flexible' labour, a demand which has been matched by the exponential increase in the number of women seeking paid work which meshes with their family responsibilities. The result has been a steady increase in the level of women's participation in the paid work-force, even in the face of deep recession and high unemployment. Women are clearly no longer a reserve army of labour, but an established part of the work-force. Employers' reasons for favouring flexible working are not, however, a response to the need to accommodate family work in the paid labour market. Instead, flexible working is favoured by companies because it allows an immediate response to fluctuations in available work, thereby reducing total labour costs and related overhead or fixed costs. It is inevitable therefore that from the demand side, flexibility is associated with absence of job security, low pay and lack of non-wage fringe benefits. Thus, as Rubery and Tarling perceptively note, women's employment has expanded 'not because women are progressively overcoming their relative disadvantage in the labour market, but because of the continued existence of these disadvantages which causes them to be an attractive source of labour supply to employers for particular types of jobs.'[25] Moreover,

increasing employment for women in fact now involves the sharing out of work over a larger number of women . . . Instead of a progressive improvement in both

---

[23] B. Patel, 'Racial Discrimination and Equal Pay', unpublished paper for National Pay Equity Conference 1991.    [24] *Employment Gazette*, June 1995, p. 260.
[25] J. Rubery and R. Tarling 'Britain' in J. Rubery (ed.), *Women and Recession* (Routledge, 1988), p. 126.

employment opportunities and the terms and conditions of women's employment, we may now be experiencing a trend towards a more intensive form of labour exploitation for a substantial part of the female labour force.[26]

The trend towards greater flexibility in the workforce is a direct result of the transformation in the nature of the British economy in the post-war period. Most marked has been the decline in manufacturing: the UK's share of world manufacturing trade plummeted from 25 per cent in 1950 to 8 per cent in the 1980s.[27] Employment in manufacturing fell from 7.12 million in 1976 to 3.85 million in 1995;[28] thus undermining the hard-won gains of a traditionally highly unionised sector. The simultaneous expansion in service sector industries has meant that more than 75 per cent of total employment is now in the service sector.[29] These macro-economic trends were repeated at the level of the firm. As Coyle notes: 'Driven by economic recession, increased global competition and constraints on public expenditure . . . organisations have been "downsizing", "delayering" and "decentralising" and along the way have created the demand for a highly flexible workforce.'[30] The most common form of flexible working is part-time working. Since 1971, a net 2.6 million new part-time jobs have been created, and the proportion of jobs that are part-time jumped from 15 per cent in 1971 to 28 per cent in 1994.[31]

These changes are deeply gendered. While unemployment in general has climbed steeply, largely as a result of the Thatcher government's deflationary policies, the number of women in the work-force has progressively increased. Thus in 1981 women formed 38.4 per cent of total employment, a figure which grew to 42 per cent in 1993, and was projected to reach 43 per cent in the year 2000.[32] Black Caribbean women show the highest participation rates: with an economic activity rate of 61.2 per cent in 1995, compared with 53.4 per cent for white women and only 23.2 per cent of women of Bangladeshi or Pakistani origin.[33] Yet this increase has been largely attributable to an increase in part-time working. By 1995, over 5 million women were working part-time, and the modest increase in employment projected for the last decade of the century will primarily be in

[26] Rubery and Tarling, above n. 25, in Rubery (ed.), p. 122.

[27] See generally, P. Armstrong, A. Glyn and J. Harrison *Capitalism since 1945* (Blackwell, 1991); R. C. O. Matthews, C. H. Feinstein and J. C. Oddling Smee, *British Economic Growth 1856–1973* (Clarendon Press, 1982).

[28] This was part of a general increase in unemployment, which soared from a maximum of 1.5 million in the 1970s to a peak figure of 3.41 million (12.3 per cent of the working population) in 1986. Official figures put the number of those unemployed and claiming benefit in October 1995 at 2.256 million, but this figure probably underestimates the real number of unemployed by as much as 1.1 million.

[29] Labour Market Trends 1996, p. S10.

[30] A. Coyle, *Women and Organisational Change* (EOC, 1995), p. iii.

[31] [1994] *Employment Gazette* 473–84.

[32] R. A. Wilson, 'Sectoral and Occupational Change: Prospects for Women's Employment' in R. Lindley (ed.), above n. 13, p. 24.

[33] EOC, *Women and Men in Britain 1993* (1993), p. 1.

part-time jobs, of which women are likely to take the lion's share. By contrast, male full-time employment is likely to fall by 500,000 between 1991 and 2000.[34] The predominance of women in part-time work is striking: 44 per cent of women employees worked part-time in 1995 compared with only 7 per cent of men.[35] Notably, however, this trend may well benefit white women more than women from ethnic minorities. Only 20 per cent of Black Caribbean women worked part-time in 1991, compared to 40 per cent of white women.[36]

Homeworking provides a further example of the extent to which the confluence of supply and demand factors have depressed women's pay and conditions. Statistics are almost by definition difficult to collect, but it is clear that significant numbers of women throughout the post-war period have taken in homework. Traditional types of homeworking have persisted: the clothing industry employed 8,800 homeworkers in the mid-1980s. These have been augmented by newer processes such as electrical component assembly and packaging of goods. In addition, advances in technology have facilitated the movement of much clerical work away from the office into the home, including word-processing, addressing envelopes and proof-reading.[37] As in other areas, the pattern of homeworking is carved along deeply gendered lines. In 1995, about two-thirds of the total of 631,000 homeworkers were women. Moreover, the type of work done by home-workers depends largely on gender: whereas 81 per cent of male home-workers were managers, administrators, professionals or in associated professional and technical occupations, only 42 per cent of women homeworkers fell within this category. By contrast, while over one-quarter of women homeworkers were in clerical and secretarial occupations, there were too few men in these occupations to represent a useful statistic. The same is true for patterns of employment: almost two-thirds of women homeworkers work part-time, less than one-quarter of their male counter-parts do so.[38] These divisions reflect the fact that many women work at home to accommodate domestic responsibilities. Homeworking has also been an avenue to paid employment for immigrant women, for whom language difficulties and cultural constraints have made it difficult to un-dertake paid work out of the home. Thus women from Cypriot, Bangla-deshi, Pakistani, Indian and East African communities have been recruited in the heartland of sweated labour such as the East End of London.[39] Other important means of meshing home and paid work include shift-working, which is more common than part-time working among ethnic minority

---

[34] Wilson, above n. 32, in Lindley (ed.), p. 16.
[35] Labour Market Trends, January 1996, Labour Force Survey Helpline.
[36] EOC, *Women and Men in Britain*, above n. 33, p. 9.
[37] S. Pennington and B. Westover, *A Hidden Workforce: Homeworkers in England 1850–1985* (Macmillan, 1989), pp. 158–9 (*A Hidden Workforce*).
[38] Labour Market Trends, December 1995, Labour Force Survey Helpline.
[39] Pennington and Westover, above n. 37, p. 160.

women, and working in family businesses, which is common among Asian women.

The move towards a more flexible work-force has been facilitated by measures taken by the Conservative government since 1979 to promote a low-wage economy within a deregulated market. Changes in employment law have dramatically diminished the power of trade unions and removed the lower thresholds in pay provided by wages councils and Fair Wages Resolutions. Employment protection rights have been limited to those working full-time with two or more years continuous service. Part-timers have until very recently been disqualified unless they worked for the same employer for five or more years. Similarly, the government actively encouraged the trend towards individualised pay, manifested in a dramatic weakening of centralised systems of pay setting and the rise of pay supplements such as incentive bonuses and similar premia. This trend is a vivid illustration of the influence of neo-liberal policies identified in Chapter 1, with its emphasis on market-based notions of individualism, free choice and rationality. Yet because individual autonomy is stressed only in a formal sense, deliberately ignoring the constraints of powerlessness, the result has been to strengthen employer prerogatives in pay-setting. Research shows clearly that such prerogatives have been used in a deeply gendered sense.[40] Individualisation in pay setting has been complemented by the imposition of market ideologies in the public sector, a major source of employment for women. A crucial manifestation has been the requirement of compulsory competitive tendering, which has led to contracting out of many services traditionally performed by women. Because the major incentive for contracting out is in order to cut costs, it is not surprising to find that the chief target has been women's pay.

The national insurance system has also actively contributed to the low pay and status attached to part-time flexible work. It does so by creating an incentive to employers to keep pay low in order to remain below the threshold above which national insurance contributions become payable. Employers are encouraged to avoid both the liability to pay employers' national insurance contributions on behalf of their workers and the administrative costs of national insurance returns.[41] As a result, there has been a surge in the incidence of part-time working for less than sixteen hours a week: low hours contracts grew by as much as 66 per cent between 1979 and 1987, to reach 11 per cent of people in employment.[42] The impetus to employers to maintain very low pay is also triggered by the system of family benefits, which uses the benefit system to top up low pay. Indeed, the

---

[40] Industrial Relations Services, *Pay and Gender in Britain* Vol. 1 (1991), p. 78.

[41] S. Deakin and F. Wilkinson, *The Economics of Employment Rights* (Institute of Employment Rights, 1991), p. 19.

[42] Compare the 30 per cent increase in part-time working of thirty or fewer hours a week: Deakin and Wilkinson, above n. 41, p. 19.

government explicitly believes that the system of family credit (which gives benefits to low income families) will off-set any fall in wages due to the abolition of wages councils (see below).[43] As Deakin and Wilkinson argue, the social security system is being used as a direct subsidy to low paying employers.

It is clear from the above discussion that from employers' perspective, the reason for the intense demand for flexible workers is their cost saving potential. Why then have women predominated among those prepared to accept paid work on such terms? The key to this remains the interaction between paid work and unpaid family work. As we have seen, the greater participation in the paid work-force has not carried with it an associated decrease in women's responsibility for housework and child-care. Nor has the structure of paid work been altered to create a more 'family friendly' working environment. As Coyle demonstrates, in fact a key feature of the 1990s is the intensification of working time. Reduced staff levels combined with an ever-increasing volume of work has meant longer hours for both white collar and manual workers. 'Flexibility' exists to suit operational needs rather than those of women with children: thus part-time hours or shifts are often extremely inflexible for the women concerned. Moreover part-time working and job sharing are rarely a real option at more senior levels.[44]

The bias towards a 'male' pattern of work is manifested in a multiplicity of ways. Many benefits of employment, such as training, promotion, and bonuses are dependent on continuous full-time working. In other words, the paradigm worker is either single, or a married man with a wife who carries the prime responsibility for family work. This is clearly evidenced by considering the different patterns of lifetime earnings of men and women respectively. Thus, while the gender pay gap is relatively narrow during the teens and twenties, it widens rapidly in mid-life, with women in their late forties earning on average only 62 per cent of the gross hourly earnings of men in the same age group.[45] This divergence is clearly associated with differing responsibilities for children. Women's earnings decline steeply in their early thirties, the period of family formation, a decrease which co-incides with a sharp fall in levels of full-time employment. By contrast, men's employment remains fairly constant from their early twenties to their late forties, family formation notwithstanding.[46] Moreover, the effect of time out of the labour market is long-lasting. Women who have taken time out of the labour market in order to look after children find that their pay levels are likely to remain low: indeed, the greater the number of years of full-time domestic experience the greater the likelihood of low pay.[47] The result is to create a widening gulf between women with and without

[43] *ibid.*, p. 20.      [44] Coyle, above n. 30, p. vii.
[45] EOC, *The Life Cycle of Inequality* (1995), p. 37.      [46] *ibid.*, p. 33.
[47] S. Dex and A. McCulloch, *Flexible Employment in Britain* (EOC, 1995), p. 50.

children: 58–62 per cent of women with three or more children are low paid, compared with 39 per cent of women with no children.[48]

This is not to say that all women are in a position of disadvantage in the paid work-force: it is clear that a minority of women have now successfully moved into high positions in the social hierarchy (see below: job segregation). Yet the underlying structure is little changed. Indeed most of those who have succeeded in breaching the male–female divide, have done so either by remaining childless, or by employing other women to look after their children and their homes—and these women are invariably low paid and afforded low social status.

The disadvantaged position of women in the workforce is clear from their low pay, both relatively and absolutely, the extent of job segregation into low status jobs, the nature of education and training, and their role in trade unions. Each of these is considered in turn.

## ii) **Pay**

Given the nature of women's paid employment, it is perhaps not surprising that the pattern of low pay, so clearly evidenced throughout the century, should have remained depressingly consistent. By 1995, gross hourly earnings of full-time women had inched up to only 79.6 per cent of those of men, a mere 0.1 per cent better than the previous year. Even these figures are deceptively optimistic. While a few highly paid women have narrowed the gap, a disaggregation of the total indicates a stubborn resistance to change. Thus in 1995 female manual workers earned only 72.8 per cent of their male counterparts while female non-manual workers earned as little as 68.2 per cent of their male colleagues. Nor has there been significant progress since 1994: both manual and non-manual women saw the gender gap narrow by a mere 0.3 per cent. Even more telling is the weekly differential. In 1995, women manual workers' gross weekly pay stood at only 64.6 per cent of that of their male colleagues, while the corresponding figure for women non-manual workers was as little as 65 per cent. Again little progress can be detected: the overall weekly differential widened fractionally (from 72.2 per cent in 1994 to 72 per cent in 1995) thus reversing a gradual convergence over the previous ten years.

Of even greater concern is the fact that these figures refer only to employees working full-time on adult rates. When part-time working and young women are taken into account, the differential worsens appreciably. Indeed, Rubery and Tarling demonstrate that consideration of the whole earnings distribution of women reveals a significant deterioration in women's earnings. Most importantly, the switch to higher levels of part-time working has in fact substantially lowered average female earnings. This is not only true for weekly earnings, which reflect the shorter hours worked.

[48] L. Corti and S. Dex, 'Highly Qualified Women' [1995] *Employment Gazette* 115 at p. 121.

It is also true for hourly earnings. According to the 1994 New Earnings Survey, women part-time workers earned a mere 58.7 per cent of the gross hourly average earnings of male full-time workers in 1994.[49] Moreover, these figures are likely to overestimate part-time women workers' pay: the New Earnings Survey omits workers who earn below the tax threshold or work in small workplaces, thereby excluding about one-fifth of all part-timers.[50] Here too the gap has barely narrowed: in 1993, women part-timers earned 58.5 per cent of male full-timers.

Most disturbing is the extent of low pay in absolute rather than relative terms. Not only do women comprise the majority of those defined as low paid;[51] but the average pay of women in substantial areas of the economy falls below the poverty threshold. This is true of average hourly earnings of female full-timers in most manual and some non-manual occupations, and of average hourly earnings of female part-timers in almost all manual occupations.[52] Women bunch at the bottom of the earnings distribution: as many as 43.4 per cent of women in 1995 earned less than £220 per week, compared with 19.8 per cent of men. This figure jumps to 74.2 per cent if manual full-time women are considered separately, compared to 28.5 per cent of manual full-time men. Not surprisingly, part-time jobs are over-represented in the low paid category, with 61 to 71 per cent of part-time jobs classified as low paid compared with 34 to 35 per cent of full-time women's jobs.[53] The extent of low pay among women is particularly prob-lematic because of its long-term effects. Since pension entitlement is largely dependent on lifetime earnings, significant numbers of women are destined to spend their retirement years in poverty (see Chapter 8).

Why, then, has low pay persisted despite fundamental changes both legal and economic? Until 1975 some of the differential was clearly due to 'women's only' rates or separate pay structures for men and women doing equal work. The impact of the Equal Pay Act 1970 was therefore initially dramatic. Largely as a result of the virtual elimination of women-only rates from collective agreements and wage structures,[54] full-time women's hourly pay jumped from 64 per cent of that of men in 1971 to 74 per cent in 1977. But the effect of the Act was soon exhausted. For a full decade, the ratio remained largely static: indeed, in 1987, it had dipped to 73.4 per cent, inching up, as we have seen, to a mere 79.6 per cent in 1995. Even more disturbing is the fact that new legal provisions requiring equal pay for work of equal value (see below) have had no immediate impact on differentials.

[49] Dex and McCulloch, above n. 47, p. 59.
[50] EOR No. 61 May/June 1995, p. 24.
[51] EOC (1993), above n. 33, p. 21. This follows the Low Pay Unit definition of low pay as earnings which fall below two-thirds of the median weekly earning of adult male full-time employees.    [52] ibid., p. 21.
[53] Dex and McCulloch, above n. 47, p. 59.
[54] L. Dickens 'Anti-Discrimination Legislation' in W. McCarthy (ed.), Legal Intervention in Industrial Relations (Blackwell, 1992), p. 109.

As Dickens notes: 'organisations which undertook limited revision of their pay structures following the original equal pay legislation have not necessarily been moved to reconsider them following the Equal Value Regulations.'[55]

The fact that the elimination of separate and inferior pay structures has not closed the gap suggests that the causes are deeply embedded in the social structure. One key factor is the continuing and pervasive influence of status in pay determination. Contrary to the neo-liberal assertion that low pay reflects low productivity, research has shown clearly that the labour market status of those doing the work colours the value attached to that work. Craig *et al*, for example, found that in many industries, the sex of the workers was the main influence on payment structures and employment systems.[56] 'Jobs are regarded as unskilled because they are feminised and not feminised because they are unskilled.'[57] This is particularly marked in secondary sector firms which are economically weak. Such firms rely on employing workers with little status or bargaining strength, but whose efficiency is in fact greater than their wage levels.[58] Women who are restrained by their child-care responsibilities constitute an ideal source of labour for such firms, particularly those who have no option but to accept low paid jobs because of low household income and absence of appropriate training. Homeworkers are a good example of this phenomenon. Despite their utility to a firm in providing fluctuating labour to meet irregular demands and in avoiding the overhead costs of direct employment, their rates of pay tend to be extremely low.[59] Nor is the influence of status confined to the secondary sector. Firms in the primary sector also exploit women's low status in the labour market: cleaning and catering workers even in relatively high paying firms remain low paid and segregated because of the low status of women workers.[60] The downward pressure exercised by labour market status is particularly evident from a comparison between educational achievements and levels of pay. Thus 45.7 per cent of women with A-levels are low paid, compared with 19 per cent of men.[61]

Status or stereotypical assumptions are also manifested in the persistence of the principle that men should be paid a 'family wage' while women only need 'pin money' (see Chapter 3). Even where basic pay has been equalised, the notion that women have family structures to rely on for income continues to influence the availability of earnings protection for sickness or holidays.[62] Such traditional assumptions have survived the reality of women's central role in maintaining their families. As we have seen, substantial numbers of women are single, lone parents or primary

---

[55] Dickens, above n. 54, in McCarthy (ed.), p. 109–10.
[56] C. Craig, J. Rubery, R. Tarling, and F. Wilkinson, *Labour Market Structure, Industrial Organisation and Low Pay* (Cambridge University Press, 1982), p. 84.
[57] *ibid.*, p. 77.    [58] *ibid.*, p. 83.    [59] *ibid.*, p. 85.
[60] *ibid.*, p. 82.    [61] Dex and McCulloch, above n. 47, p. 48.
[62] Craig et al, above n. 56, pp. 91–2.

breadwinners. Moreover, even where women do have partners, this does not mean they have a source of support, particularly in the climate of galloping unemployment. Indeed, women who most need a 'family wage' because their partners are unemployed are likely to be among the lowest paid.[63] Other important contributing factors include job segregation; education and training; and the role of unions, all of which are considered below.

### iii) **Job Segregation**

The pattern of job segregation in the 1990s reveals an increasing polarisation of women in the paid workforce. While some women have clearly progressed up the job hierarchy, this is matched by the fact that women's share of traditionally feminine jobs continues to rise. Nor is the progress at the higher levels unambiguously positive; the entry of women into such jobs often occurs at a time when the pay and status of the occupation is being down-graded.

The persistence of highly gender-specific job distribution emerges clearly from the statistics. Secretarial work, for example, remains a wholly female enclave: in 1991, 96.6 per cent of all secretarial workers were women, a figure which has remained stable at least since 1971. By contrast women constituted barely 10 per cent of craft and related workers, and just over 20 per cent of plant and machine operatives. Figures for employment by industry show a similar pattern of unwavering segregation. Thus women are still seriously under-represented in the construction industry, forming just over 10 per cent of employees in construction and scarcely 20 per cent in the energy and water supply industry. By contrast almost 70 per cent of employees in public administration, education and health are women.[64] Indeed, there has been a decline in women's participation in manufacturing: whereas women formed nearly one-third of manufacturing employees in 1954, this figure dropped to 28.4 per cent in 1991.[65] Within the feminised sectors there is further segregation between women of different ethnic groups. In particular, black women tend to be concentrated in catering, cleaning and in the lowest grades of the health service, a pattern established in the 1950s when West Indian women were actively recruited into these jobs. For example, a study of a London hospital in 1987 found that 61 per cent of nursing auxiliaries were of Caribbean origin, compared with only 12 per cent of the better paid and higher status State Registered Nurses.[66] Similarly, a large proportion of ethnic minority women are employed in the clothing and footwear manufacturing sector. In the West Midlands in particular, a high proportion of workers are Asian women,

---

[63] Dex and McCulloch, above n. 47, p. 60.
[64] Labour Market Trends, January 1996, Labour Force Survey Helpline 5.
[65] Wilson, above n. 32, in Lindley (ed.), pp. 24–5.
[66] EOC *Equality Management: Women's Employment in the NHS* (1991), p. 37.

many of whom are new to the labour market and therefore open to exploitation.[67]

Women have been somewhat more successful in penetrating male strongholds in higher levels of employment, particularly managerial occupations and professionals. Although women are still seriously under-represented, their share has improved in the past twenty years. For example, women in 1993 comprised 13 per cent of section leaders compared to only 2 per cent in 1974. The proportion of women department heads has increased from just over 2 per cent to 9 per cent in the same period. Significantly, though, this pattern is not repeated at the top of the hierarchy: women formed a mere 3 per cent of chief executives, deputy chief executives and other directors in 1993, an increase of only 2 per cent in two decades.[68] Moreover, it is not clear that the upward trend is continuing. One recent survey found that in large organisations, the number of women managers and directors has in fact declined, from 10.2 per cent in 1993 to 9.5 per cent in 1994.[69]

Nor are the gains made in higher level jobs without caveats. Within managerial and professional occupations, a significant degree of segregation has reappeared. Thus women constitute the majority of managers in financial institutions, of office managers and of Civil Service executive officers, but a puny 6 per cent of production managers in manufacturing, construction and related industries. A similar pattern is evident in respect of professions. Not surprisingly, women are well represented in teaching and librarianship, forming 62 per cent of teaching professionals and 69 per cent of librarians in 1992. This figure, however, plummets to a mere 5 per cent of engineers and technicians and 25 per cent of business and financial professionals.[70] Moreover, even where women are well represented in a profession, they tend to cluster in the lower grades. This is particularly stark in the teaching profession. Women teachers continue to cluster in nursery and primary schools (see Chapter 3), while men predominate in the higher status secondary school sector. In 1990, women comprised 9 out of 10 primary and nursery school teachers, but less than one-half of all head-teachers. In secondary schools, 60 per cent of teachers on the main scale were women, but women formed only 20 per cent of head-teachers. Moreover, at secondary level, women tend to teach subjects in which the majority of pupils are females, and men tend to teach subjects in which the majority of pupils are male.[71] A similar pattern is evident in the legal profession. Women's representation in the legal profession has increased: in the 1980s, the female proportion of practising solicitors more than doubled, and in 1992 as many as 41 per cent of those called to the Bar in England and Wales were women. Nevertheless, women are still under-represented

[67] Patel, above n. 23.     [68] EOC (1993), above n. 33, p. 25.
[69] EOR No. 55 (1994) p. 4.     [70] EOC (1993), above n. 33, p. 25.
[71] *ibid.*, p. 29.

in both parts of the profession, comprising only 25 per cent of practising solicitors, and a mere 20 per cent of practising barristers in 1992. In addition, women remain concentrated in lower levels; in particular there are still only a handful of women judges. In 1993, only 5 of the 91 High Court judges were women, and there were only 28 women out of 496 circuit judges.[72]

Of even greater concern is the fact that the entry of women tends to coincide with a downgrading of the pay and status of an occupation. For example, in hotels and catering women now account for nearly 50 per cent of managers, a figure which is likely to continue to rise. However, the pay of female managers in hotels and catering is surprisingly low, frequently less than average female earnings.[73] This pattern is evident too in respect of managers and directors in the largest organisations in the UK. A survey conducted in 1994 showed that women managers were earning on average nearly £5,000 (22.5 per cent) less than their male colleagues, while at director level, the differential was a massive £19,000 (about 26 per cent). Women in managerial positions are also less likely to have perks such as company cars. Overall, in 1992, female managers and administrators employed full-time earned only two-thirds of the average weekly earnings of their male counterparts. This tendency was confirmed in a recent survey by Coyle, who found clear evidence of a pattern whereby the number of women in management and professional jobs increased, but only after the pay, conditions and status had been eroded through changes in work organisation. At more senior levels, 'heavier' management structures had increased competition for a diminishing number of jobs, exacerbating the difficulties faced by women at this level.[74] Even more disturbing is the striking absence of black and ethnic minority women from even the most junior supervisory and management positions. This is despite their high level of educational attainment. Coyle suggests that this is a case where equal opportunity policies may well privilege white women at the expense of black women.[75]

In the public sector, too, the increase in the numbers of women has been accompanied by decreasing pay. In the civil service, for example, active measures to increase the recruitment, promotion and retention of women have led to a significant improvement of the ratio of women to men. In 1992, there were almost equal numbers of men and women in the non-industrial civil service and the number of women in the higher grades had improved significantly. However, this coincided with a significant decline in the relative pay of middle and higher grade civil servants.[76] In any case,

---

[72] *ibid.*, p. 23.
[73] J. Rubery and C. Fagan 'Occupational Segregation' in Lindley (ed.), above n. 9, pp. 36–7.
[74] Coyle, above n. 30, p. viii.     [75] *ibid.*
[76] Rubery and Fagan, above n. 73, p. 37.

the improvement has only marginally softened the entrenched vertical segregation of the civil service. Thus in 1992, women comprised a mere 12 per cent of those employed in the top seven grades, compared to 60 per cent in the lower level administrative group. Even those who do succeed in attaining the top seven grades (the Open Structure) tend to bunch in the lowest of these. At the highest level, women are conspicuous by their absence. In April 1992, there were no women at all in Grade 1 of the civil service; a year later, there were only two.[77]

A similar picture emerges in the professions, where dilution of job segregation has not closed the pay gap. Instead, in professions in which women have significantly increased their share, their pay continues to lag behind that of men. The legal profession provides a good example. Despite increased representation, women earn on average substantially less than their male colleagues: in 1992, female solicitors working full time received only 74 per cent of the average weekly earnings of male solicitors. In professional occupations as a whole, women in 1992 earned only 81 per cent of the average weekly pay of men.

Job segregation is particularly marked in respect of part-time workers. Women part-timers tend to work in occupational areas which are characterised by their low pay and low status and are quite different both from male full-timers and from female full-timers. In particular, women part-time workers are heavily concentrated in lower level service jobs such as personal services and sales occupations. On the other hand, few part-time jobs are available in the area of corporate management and administration or professional occupations, and many of these are temporary too.[78] Yet again, the structure of the labour market is seen to penalise women who have child-care responsibilities. The paucity of part-time jobs at higher levels means that women managers or professionals who wish to work part-time when their children are young will be forced to accept work in lower status occupations than their earlier full-time jobs.[79] That this is not inevitable is clear from a contrast with France, where part-time work is frequently used to retain women in skilled work during the period when they have young children.[80]

iv) **Education and Training**

One of the key determinants of progress in the paid labour force, apart from child-care responsibilities, is the level of an individual's educational qualifications.[81] Dex *et al* found that the percentage of women who are low paid increases as the level of education decreases. Thus relatively few of those with degrees or teaching qualifications are low paid whereas 68 per cent of those without any qualifications fall into that category.[82] The level and nature of women's educational achievements is therefore crucial. By the

---

[77] EOC, above n. 33, p. 31.      [78] Dex and McCulloch, above n. 47, p. 75.
[79] EOC, above n. 33, p. 15.      [80] Rubery and Fagan, above n. 73, pp. 34–5.
[81] *ibid.*, p. 31.      [82] Dex and McCulloch, above n. 47, p. 48.

mid-1990s, some important progress had been made, particularly at school. For example, in 1991–92, girls had higher pass rates than boys at GCSE or its Scottish equivalent. Young women are now more likely to stay on in full-time education after sixteen than their male counterparts. However, true equality between girls and boys at school has yet to be attained. As Clarke puts it: 'Girls and boys still differ in the education which they receive and the qualifications they attain. These differences foreshadow and to some extent determine further divergence between the sexes in the labour market. Girls and boys, by and large, enter different occupations with different career structures and different associated training structures.'[83]

The extent to which girls are being educated for a segregated labour market is evident from the statistics on subject choice. At GCSE level, although almost equal numbers of girls and boys attempted English and Maths in 1991–92, girls comprised less than one-third of those attempting physics. The new National Curriculum, which makes the study of a science subject compulsory until age sixteen, has diluted gender segregation at GCSE to a degree. Thus most young people now study the combined science subject. But where discrete science subjects (such as physics, chemistry or biology) are chosen, nearly twice as many boys as girls continue to do so. In other areas, segregation remains extreme: far more girls than boys take home economics, but the reverse is true for craft and technology. Nor has the small dilution of segregation at GCSE manifested at A level. In 1991–92, a large majority (69 per cent) of those taking A level English in England were female; while the opposite was true for maths, with males comprising 65 per cent. Similarly, girls comprised approximately one-fifth of those taking physics, but formed the majority of candidates in biology.[84] Such segregation has continued unabated into 1995.[85] It is striking too, that girls at sixteen tend to out-perform boys in most subjects. In languages, where girls predominate, a higher percentage of girls than boys achieved grades A to C in 1995. Even in male-dominated subjects, girls consistently perform as well if not better than boys.[86]

Nevertheless, patterns of segregation persist into higher education. In 1991–92, women comprised 46 per cent of full-time undergraduates in universities in Britain. But only 14 per cent of those reading engineering and technology and 25 per cent of those reading mathematical sciences were women. In 1995, more than twice as many women as men were studying English and French, while men outnumbered women by 4 to 1 in physics and computer studies. Even more worrying is the fact that, apart from an increase of 7 per cent in engineering, the proportion of women in the 'male' subjects remained unchanged over the decade from 1978–79 to 1988–89.[87]

[83] K. Clarke, *Women and Training: A Review*, Equal Opportunities Commission Research Discussion Series (1991), p. 4.
[84] EOC (1995), above n. 45, p. 5.    [85] *ibid.*, p. 7.    [86] *ibid.*, pp. 5–6.
[87] Clarke, above n. 83, p. 10.

The link between gender segregation in subject choice at university and gender segregation in the paid labour force is immediately apparent from statistics on the first destination of graduates. Male and female graduates work for different types of employer: in 1991, 36 per cent of male graduates in permanent employment had entered industry, as against only 15 per cent of female graduates. The opposite pattern was evident in teaching, which accounted for 24 per cent of female graduates compared to only 8 per cent of their male counterparts. Men and women also tend to be employed in different types of work, with female graduates more likely to enter personnel, medical and social work, and male graduates moving into scientific and engineering work.[88] Perceived opportunities in the paid labour force in turn affect subject choice, setting up a vicious circle. This may well be exacerbated by the introduction of student loans. As Clarke points out, women graduates have lower starting salaries and lifetime earnings expectations than men and therefore the cost of a loan is proportionately greater for women than men.[89]

For those who do not go on to higher education, the foundations of a segregated labour market are laid at the point of training. At this level, there is little evidence of an improvement in the position of women. With the decline of the apprenticeship system, the chief source of youth training outside of the education system has become the government-sponsored youth training programmes. Youth training may, however, be contributing to rather than alleviating patterns of occupational segregation.[90] In 1989, for example, the single largest occupational group for young women youth trainees was clerical work, which accounted for one-third of female trainees. For young men, by contrast, the largest occupational group was construction/civil engineering, in which women accounted for a mere 3 per cent of trainees.[91] Little had changed by 1992: while 42 per cent of male youth training students studied engineering and technology, the corresponding figure for women was still only 3 per cent.[92] A similar pattern emerges in government-funded adult training, where women in clerical, secretarial and caring occupations represent about two-thirds of the total number of female adult trainees. Few inroads have been made into 'male' occupations such as science and engineering, skilled construction, electrical and electronic trades, and vehicle trades.[93] Nor is this simply an accident: as Felstead demonstrates, the imposition of a 'market for training' as part of the government's obsession with markets has entrenched and exacerbated existing segregated structures.[94]

[88]  EOC (1995), above n. 45, p. 7.
[89]  ibid., p. 12.
[90]  Felstead in EOC, The Economics of Equal Opportunity (1995), p. 184.
[91]  Clarke, above n. 83, pp. 12–13.
[92]  EOC (1995), above n. 45, p. 7.
[93]  Felstead, above n. 90, p. 186.
[94]  ibid., pp. 188–97.

Access to in-service training is one of the keys to progress within the paid labour market, particularly in the light of rapid changes in science or technology. For women who have taken a break from paid employment for child-care reasons, there is a particular need for opportunities to refresh or update their skills. The pattern of training provision for adult employees is complex.[95] It is clear that women part-timers have substantially less access to training than both male and female full-time employees. As Clarke points out, 'since a high proportion of women spend at least part of their working life in part-time employment, and over two-fifths of all women employees currently work part-time, this is a major source of disadvantage for women in the labour market.'[96] It is not always primarily women who are thus disadvantaged. All manual workers (a majority of whom are men) and all employees in the private manufacturing sector (also a majority of men) also have relatively low access to training, as do employees in small work-places (most of whom are women). Moreover, more research is required into the quality of training received.

A particularly important area of training is for women who wish to return to the labour market after a period of full-time child-care and domestic work. Although some employers provide in-service refresher courses,[97] public provision is particularly poor. Women without an established job can only utilise existing training facilities if they are offered some assistance with child-care, if the course is close to home, and if there is financial assistance with fees. In the 1990s, the principal source of training for adults was the government scheme, Employment Training (ET), now transformed into Training for Work (TfW). Lone parents and returners to the labour market are eligible for TfW, but there are some problematic caveats. The applicant is also required to have been in receipt of income support and 'deemed available for work' for 26 weeks or more. This requires the ability to demonstrate child-care arrangements. Even if these hurdles are surmounted, a place on TfW is not guaranteed. Training providers are still required to give priority to the long-term registered unemployed, which in turn requires sufficient national insurance contributions to qualify for registration. Such a contributions record is more difficult for women than men to achieve. It is not therefore surprising that in 1992–93 only 33 per cent of adult trainees were women.[98] Higher education is out of reach of substantial numbers of women returners because they cannot afford to pay the fees; further education is more accessible, but it is likely that local management of finances will make it very difficult for further education colleges to maintain courses which do not charge fees. In any case, many colleges do not have the resources to assist with child-care.[99]

---

[95] This section draws heavily on Clarke, above n. 83, ch. 3.
[96] ibid., p. 42.    [97] ibid., p. 35.
[98] Felstead, above n. 90, p. 182.    [99] Clarke, above n. 83, p. 59.

## v) Trade Unionism

The 1980s and 1990s have been bleak for trade unions. Faced with an onslaught of restrictive legislation and massive unemployment in the traditional heartlands of trade unionism, trade unions have been unable to stem the attrition of both industrial muscle and membership. The heady days of the late 1970s, in which trade unions were able to exercise significant political and economic power, are receding fast into history. Union density overall has dipped steeply in the past two decades. At its peak in 1979, there were 13.3 million union members; by 1994 this had plummeted to 6.89 million.[100] Only one-third of all British employees are now in unions. Nevertheless, union membership remains one of the few means by which women in paid employment can act to improve their own situation and unions' attitudes towards women have changed. The blatant hostility by male trade union members towards women workers has disappeared in recent decades (see Chapter 3); instead, many unions realised that they could only stem the tide against unionism by recruiting women in non-unionised areas. The result has been a steady increase in the number of women in unions, up from 728,000 (17 per cent of TUC members) in 1933 to 2.6 million in 1994 (35 per cent of total membership). Indeed, unions have taken heart from the fact that union density among women workers held steady at 32 per cent between 1990 and 1992, while male density continued its relentless slide, from 43 per cent in 1990 to 39 per cent in 1992. Similarly, density among part-time workers held steady at 22 per cent for four years to 1992. In fact, between 1993 and 1994, the number of women members was still showing a small increase in real terms with 19,141 new women members compared with the huge loss of 422,799 or 9 per cent of men in the same period.[101]

Nevertheless, women remain in occupations and industries which are difficult to organise. Many characteristics of women's work coincide with areas of low unionisation: small work-places, part-time and marginal working, and industries such as retailing. In addition, there is substantial segregation, both vertical and horizontal, within the unions. Thus although in 1992 women formed 36 per cent of the total membership of trade unions, this membership was strongly concentrated in several unions, reflecting the occupational segregation of the work-force.[102] Of even more concern is the fact that women are seriously under-represented in top positions in unions.

---

[100] Figures are derived from B. Hepple and S. Fredman, *Labour Law and Industrial Relations in Britain* (2nd edn.), (Kluwer, 1992), para 397; *Labour Research* May 1994, pp. 9–10. EOR No. 65 (1996), p. 30.

[101] EOR No. 65 p. 30.

[102] Statistics drawn from EOR No. 53 1994, p. 44.

## II.  THE LEGAL CONTEXT

a) EMPLOYMENT RELATED LEGISLATION

As we have seen, explicit legal impediments were gradually removed throughout the century. However, it became abundantly clear to feminists and campaigners for women's rights during the post-war period that the disadvantaged status of women was so thoroughly woven into the fabric of society that more positive measures were needed. It was not until the 1970s that legislation was enacted explicitly addressing discrimination on grounds of sex in both the public and private sectors. The Equal Pay Act 1970 entitled women to equal pay for like work, and the Sex Discrimination Act 1975 made it unlawful to discriminate on grounds of sex in relation to employment, education and services. These Acts have been powerfully augmented by European Community law. Article 119 of the Treaty of Rome together with the Equal Pay Directive require equal pay for work of equal value, and have been expansively interpreted by the European Court of Justice. One important consequence has been the amendment of the 1970 Act to include the right to equal pay for work of equal value. Similarly, the Equal Treatment Directive has strengthened domestic anti-discrimination law. European Community law has also had an important influence in forcing changes in discriminatory aspects of social security law. Finally, women have been unexpected beneficiaries of EC law protecting workers when the undertaking for which they work is transferred from one employer to another.[103] Such protections have proved invaluable to the predominantly female group of workers whose public sector work has been 'contracted out' to the private sector in pursuance of government policy on privatisation (see further Chapter 7). This section gives a brief account of the legislative history of these legal instruments. A detailed discussion is found in subsequent chapters.

The industrial relations culture of post-war Britain made the principle of legislating for equal pay a controversial one. Until the 1970s, the prevailing model of industrial relations was 'voluntarist' or abstentionist, viewing industrial relations as a matter for the collective bargaining partners rather than the law. According to this model, wage levels in particular should not be the concern of the State, but of the market place or the parties to voluntary collective bargaining. The proposition that wage setting should be subject to equal pay legislation was inevitably problematic. Legislators also opposed such legislation on the grounds that to raise the pay of women would price them out of jobs, or that the implementation of equal pay would simply be too expensive. All these factors meant that equal pay

---

[103] The Acquired Rights Directive (77/187), Transfer of Undertakings (Protection of Employment) Regulations 1981.

legislation was simply not on the agenda in the immediate post-war period. Instead, equal pay campaigners concentrated on the public sector, where equal pay could be instituted without legislation, the hope being that private sector employers would follow suit. Even then, it was not until 1955 that a Conservative government conceded the principle of equal pay for like work in the civil service, teaching and local government. Nor was the principle embraced with any enthusiasm. The proposal was for a gradual implementation, over a period of six years. Within the civil service, large areas were excluded: industrial civil servants were simply omitted and the narrow definition of like work meant that highly segregated areas, such as typing, were left out.[104]

Comprehensive legislation remained elusive throughout the 1960s. This was despite international pressures. The UK government refused to ratify ILO Convention No.100 of 1951 requiring equal pay for work of equal value. The fact that the emergent European Economic Community included the principle of equal pay in Article 119 of its founding document, the Treaty of Rome, likewise made little impact (see further below). The Conservative government of the early 1960s continued to argue that equal pay should be achieved through collective bargaining rather than legislation. However, such voluntarism could not be relied upon to further the interests of women. As we have seen, many women worked in types of employment which were difficult to organise, and therefore outside of the system of collective bargaining altogether. Those women who were trade union members frequently found that their interests were ignored or even undermined by their union. When the Labour Party finally included a commitment to equal pay legislation in its 1964 manifesto, it dragged its heels for half a decade, justifying its delay by arguing that equal pay was too costly. It was only when women took direct action that some results were achieved. In 1968, three hundred women sewing machinists at Ford Motor Company in Dagenham took strike action in support of their demands for a re-evaluation of their jobs and for equal pay. Although their specific claim was not successful, they did extract a commitment to the principle of equal pay from Ford, and the widespread publicity surrounding their action increased the pressure on the Labour Government to honour its commitment to equal pay.[105] Also of major importance in the eventual enactment of equal pay legislation were the efforts of Barbara Castle, who, as Secretary of State for Employment, steered the Equal Pay Act 1970 through Parliament.[106]

The 1970 Act clearly reflected the desire of the government to take a minimalist approach, and in particular to cause as little disruption as possible to existing pay scales. First, the scope of comparison was narrow:

---

[104] See generally H. L. Smith, 'The Politics of Conservative Reform: The Equal Pay for Equal Work Issue' [1992] *Historical Journal*, pp. 401–15.

[105] A. Carter, *The Politics of Women's Rights* (Longman, 1988), p. 56.

[106] *ibid.*, pp. 115–16.

a woman could only compare herself with a man simultaneously employed by the same employer at the same establishment or another establishment of the same employer at which common terms of employment were observed. Secondly, the nature of comparable work was limited: the claimant had to prove either that she was doing the same or broadly similar work as the (higher paid) man; or that the employer had conducted a job evaluation exercise which gave the same value to her job as that of the (higher paid) man. Even if she succeeded thus far, she could be met with the 'justification' defence, which entitled the employer to argue that the difference in pay was genuinely due to a material difference between her pay and his which was not the difference in sex. The limited nature of these provisions made it clear that the chief aim of the legislation was to attack pay scales which expressly and openly set out different pay for men and women doing the same jobs. In such a case, a successful woman claimant could simply be slotted in to the relevant place in the existing male structure. Even this minimalist approach was considered to be potentially so disruptive that employers were given five years to implement the Act.

The accession of the UK to the European Economic Community in 1972, however, brought with it an unexpected impetus for change. At its foundation, the aims of the EEC were economic rather than social, and there was little reference in the Treaty of Rome to social rights. However, France, which had already instituted advanced equal pay legislation, insisted that she would be at a competitive disadvantage unless the other members were required to have similar legislation. Hence the inclusion of Article 119, requiring Member States to introduce legislation giving women the right to equal pay with men. Significantly, the provision was narrower than the ILO Convention, which required equal pay for work of equal value. Nevertheless, Article 119 lay dormant for many years. By 1971 it was clear that there was substantial non-compliance, and that sex discrimination in the EEC was rampant. It was only because of the extraordinary campaign of litigation by a Sabena air-hostess, Gabrielle Defrenne, that this provision came to life. In a series of test cases brought by Defrenne, the ECJ established that, even if a Member State had failed to legislate as required by Article 119, an individual woman in a Member State could bring an equal pay claim directly under Article 119 against her employer (be it the State or a private employer) in a court in her own country.[107] In the terminology of the ECJ, Article 119 was directly effective, both horizontally and vertically. The mid-1970s saw a parallel development on the legislative front in the European Community, due to a sudden convergence of political forces in favour of such legislation. In 1975, the Equal Pay Directive was passed, filling in the gap in Article 119 by requiring equal pay for work of equal value. It was held to be merely an explanation of Article 119 and

---

[107] *Defrenne (No. 2)*, Case 43/75 [1976] ECR 455 (ECJ).

therefore directly enforceable by an individual against both private and public employers.[108] The Equal Treatment Directive was passed in 1976, requiring measures which outlaw discrimination on grounds of sex as regards access to employment, vocational training, promotion and working conditions. This Directive is not directly enforceable against private employers but is enforceable against the State as employer.

In the UK too, the 1970s witnessed a change of attitude to labour law in general. Most importantly, voluntarism began to give way to a more interventionist style of labour law, at least on the level of individual rights. Conservative legislation in 1971, while highly restrictive on the collective level, introduced provisions on individual employment protection, such as the right not to be unfairly dismissed, which became an accepted part of the labour law structure. It was in this context that further rights for women began to appear on the statute books. When the Labour government took office in 1975, it enacted a package of individual and collective employment rights, including a right to maternity pay for six weeks at nine-tenths of the normal week's pay. This was funded by a Maternity Pay Fund, to which employers were required to contribute and from which they could claim a full rebate. Even at this stage, however, the right was only available to employees of two years standing. The Employment Protection Act also gave employees a right to return to work, providing unpaid maternity leave for eleven weeks before the birth and twenty-nine weeks after. It became automatically unfair too to dismiss an employee on grounds of pregnancy (see Chapter 5).

Whereas the momentum for the rights discussed so far derived from the EC, the more complex anti-discrimination provisions of the Sex Discrimination Act 1975 gained their inspiration from the developing jurisprudence in the United States. Although the Sex Discrimination Bill encountered hostility from the civil service,[109] it had strong support from the Home Secretary, Roy Jenkins. Both Conservative and Labour Parties were now committed to equality legislation. The Act contained several novel features. The first concerned its definition of discrimination. The Act did not merely utilise a notion of less favourable treatment on grounds of sex, often called 'direct' or 'disparate treatment' legislation. It went further and provided for situations in which formal equality of treatment might cause or perpetuate inequality of result. This concept, often called 'indirect discrimination' or 'disparate impact', was borrowed from the caselaw on race discrimination in the US, which recognised that disadvantage could be perpetuated despite facially neutral treatment. For example, literacy tests as a condition of employment perpetuate the disadvantaged status of black Americans, because they suffer discrimination in the education system. Upper age limits

---

[108] *Jenkins* v. *Kingsgate* Case 96/80 [1980] ECR 911 (ECJ).
[109] Lord Lester 'Discrimination: What can Lawyers learn from History?' [1994] *Public Law* 224.

disadvantage women who have left the labour force to have children. In recognition of such institutional discrimination, the Act contained a provision making it unlawful to impose a condition or requirement (for example of employment or promotion) which, although applied equally to men and women, was such that disproportionately few women could comply with it; it was to the detriment of the claimant; and it could not be justified irrespective of gender. As will be seen, the highly technical phraseology of this section has acted as a significant brake on its usefulness (see Chapter 7). The second feature of the Act which was novel in the context of the time was that it covered not only termination of employment, which was already familiar from the unfair dismissal legislation, but also included recruitment and promotion. Thirdly, it utilised two means of enforcement, one by individual right of action to an industrial tribunal, and the other by the Equal Opportunities Commission. This Commission is a statutory body which has the power not only to assist individuals and institute its own proceedings in respect of discriminatory advertisements and instructions or pressure to discriminate, but also to conduct a 'formal investigation' into cases of discriminatory practices (see Chapter 9). In 1976, the Race Relations Act was enacted along parallel lines to the SDA.

If the initial inspiration for the SDA had come from the US, its continuing development, like that of the EqPA, has been almost entirely due to EC law. Indeed, EC law has insulated sex discrimination laws from the hostile political climate of the 1980s and 1990s, which has witnessed a progressive undermining of both individual and collective employment rights. The inclusion of equal value in EC law soon exposed the deficiency of the UK Equal Pay Act, which only permitted a claim based on equal value if an employer had initiated a job evaluation exercise. As a result of infringement proceedings against the UK by the EC Commission,[110] the UK Act had to be amended to include an independent right to equal pay for work of equal value. It was not surprising, however, given the antipathy of the Conservative government to wage regulation, that the amendments to comply with EC law were framed in a minimalist way. Not only did the amendment retain the limited comparison to a man in the same establishment or on common terms and conditions. In addition, the equal value claim was treated as a residual claim, only operational if the earlier two provisions did not apply. The continuing distaste for the idea that industrial tribunals should set wage rates led to the requirement that the tribunal should appoint an 'independent expert' to conduct a job evaluation exercise. Moreover, the employers' defence was widened. However, EC law has continued to intervene to bolster the two Acts. In particular, a stream of references to the ECJ under Article 119 and the Equal Treatment Directive have forced a widening of the scope of the Act to include such crucial issues

[110] *Commission of the European Communities* v. *UK* [1984] Case 165/82 ICR 192 (ECJ).

as discrimination in retirement ages, occupational pension benefits and pregnancy. These issues are explored in more detail in later chapters.

The Conservative government of the 1980s has been restrained by EC law from applying its deregulatory knife to anti-discrimination law. Minimum wages law has, however, failed to benefit from such protection. As we saw from Chapter 2, minimum wages, in their peculiarly British form, had been well entrenched from the early decades of the century. However, this soon changed under Thatcherism. The antipathy of the Thatcher government to minimum wage fixing was given legal expression in the Wages Act 1986, which severely curtailed the operation of wages councils. All workers under twenty-one were removed from their remit, and wages councils were only permitted to set a minimum hourly rate and a single overtime rate for adult workers. In 1993 the whole system was abolished outright. This, as we will see, has severe implications for women workers (see Chapters 6 and 9). Other employment protection rights have been similarly undermined. In addition, the power to extend the results of collective agreements to similarly situated workers was abolished, and draconian trade union laws made it exceedingly difficult for workers to protect themselves through organised opposition.

b) SOCIAL SECURITY

The development of legislation on the social security front has been complex. The welfare system throughout the century has been designed to maintain a rigid gender-based division of labour within the family. As was seen in Chapter 2, the assumption that the husband should be the breadwinner and the wife the home-maker was given ideological legitimacy by Beveridge and continued to permeate the social security structure for most of the post-war era. The continuing strength of this ideology has been such that movements towards equality have been sporadic and deeply ambiguous. As this section demonstrates, the overt discrimination against women which continued deep into the 1970s and 1980s has been dismantled to the extent that it conflicts with EC law. However, not only do some serious gaps remain; in addition, little attention has been paid to structural or indirect discrimination. Indeed, the reforms in the direction of equality have frequently made a gesture towards formal equality while in fact entrenching structural discrimination.

Moreover, although the momentum for change has largely come from the EC in the form of the Social Security Directive, the tension between progressive social policy and the desire to limit public spending has had the effect of limiting both the scope of the Directive itself and of future development.[111] As a start, although the Directive was adopted in December 1978, Member States were given six years to implement it. In addition, the

---

[111] See S. Atkins and L. Luckhaus, 'The Social Security Directive and UK Law' in C. McCrudden (ed.), *Women, Employment and European Equality Law* (Eclipse, 1987).

scope of the Directive was limited to statutory schemes and social assistance which provided protection against sickness, invalidity, old age, accidents at work and occupational diseases, and unemployment.[112] The ECJ initially took a broad view of these categories, extending them to include invalid care allowance, although it was paid to the carer rather than the invalid.[113] However, in more recent cases, the Court has required the benefit to be directly and effectively linked to the risks specified. Most importantly, it has been held that the Directive is aimed primarily at benefits designed to guard against risks associated with employment. It thus excludes schemes which are targeted at people with insufficient resources regardless of their relationship to the employment market.[114] This means that the Directive will not prevent discrimination in benefits which are aimed simply at alleviating poverty, regardless of the recipient's link with employment.

The final section of this chapter traces the development of

(a) married women's participation in the contributory system;
(b) out-of-work means-tested provisions;
(c) in-work means-tested benefits;
(d) benefits for severe disablement; and
(e) universal benefits (i.e. non-contributory and non-means-tested).

## i) Married Women's Participation in the Contributory System

From its inception, the national insurance scheme provided for reduced contributions from married women, and correspondingly reduced benefits (see Chapter 2). Formal equality in this context was not introduced until the Social Security Act 1975, which equalised both contributions rates and benefits. The change was, however, gradual. Married women retained the 'option' of paying reduced contributions with the consequential loss of entitlement to unemployment and sickness benefit.[115] A surprising (if declining) number has continued to exercise this option. Moreover, the gesture towards formal equality did little to address the deep structural inequality which characterises the contributory system. In particular, because the availability and quantum of benefits depend on a claimant's contributions record and levels of pay, the contributory principle favours those with a continuous full-time working history. As we have seen, women predominate in the category of part-time working, and tend to have interrupted working lives. This makes it extremely difficult to meet the contribution conditions attached to contributory benefits. Similarly, since women tend to earn less than men, they are not able to build up national insurance

---

[112] Article 3 (1).

[113] Case 150/85 *Drake* v. *Chief Adjudication Officer* [1986] 3 WLR 1005.

[114] Case 243/90 *Smithson* [1992] ECR I-467 (ECJ); Cases C-63/91 and C-64/91 *Jackson and Creswell* v. *Chief Adjudication Officer* [1992] ECR I-4734 (ECJ); and see J. Sohrab 'Women and Social Security' [1994] 1 *Journal of Social Welfare and Family Law* 5.

[115] Social Security Act 1975, ss. 5(2) and 130(2).

rights through earnings-related benefits at the same pace as men. Particularly worrying is the fact that a substantial number of working women are excluded from the contributory system altogether because they earn less than the lower earnings limit. Figures from 1991 show that 2.25 million working women fell into this category; to which should be added an estimated 1.5 million women doing occasional work and home-work.[116] This is particularly problematic in old age: women's low pay and interrupted working patterns operate as a severe disadvantage to them in accruing pension rights (see Chapter 8). The difficulties faced by women are exacerbated by the abolition in 1986 of the right to claim reduced benefits if the full contributions conditions had not been met.[117] Again, the majority who experienced the effect of 'wasted' contributions in this way were married women. The change was partly justified on the grounds that those affected were likely to have a waged partner—'an example of the lack of importance attached to the principle of an independent social security entitlement for women'.[118] Finally, the indirectly discriminatory nature of the contributory system is reinforced by the new system of unemployment benefit, now called job-seekers allowance. Under the new system, yet more stress is likely to be placed on a woman's ability to prove that she has child-care arrangements on tap before she qualifies.

A more substantive move towards equality is found in the developments in respect of the allowance for adult dependants, but then only under the influence of EC law. Until 1980, the assumption of dependence continued to shape the rules governing entitlement to an extra payment for adult dependants. On the assumption that a man had the responsibility to maintain his wife, a married man was entitled to a 'dependant's allowance' for his wife, whether or not she was in paid work, provided that she was not earning above a specified limit. Conversely, it was assumed that a married woman would not be supporting her husband unless he was incapable of work; thus a married woman was only entitled to an extra payment for adult dependants or children if her husband was incapable of work.[119] This penalised women who were in fact supporting their husbands, particularly since the women's contributions were now equal to those of men. It also created a disincentive to those who wished to reverse the traditional role models. It was only because equal treatment was required by the EC Social Security Directive[120] that this was changed. Particularly positive was the fact that this was achieved by 'levelling up': married women's entitlement to spouse additions was now the same as that of married men.[121] As will be seen, this is a rare example of the achievement of substantive equality: in

---

[116] Lister, *Women's Economic Dependency*, above n. 2, p. 27.
[117] Except in the case of widows' benefits and the basic retirement pension.
[118] Lister, above n. 2, p. 32.
[119] Social Security Act 1975, s. 41(6) s. 44(1) (a); s. 44(3)(a); s. 66.
[120] 79/7/EEC [1979] OJ L6/24.
[121] Social Security Act 1980, Schedule 1.

many other contexts, the Directive was fulfilled by removing the benefit entirely, or 'levelling down'.[122] For example, in 1984, the extra allowance for dependent children, far from being extended to married women on the same terms as enjoyed by men, was simply abolished.[123]

## ii) **Out-of-work Means-tested (Non-contributory) Benefit**

Non-contributory benefits are not based on the insurance principle, which attaches entitlement to a contributions record, but on a principle of social assistance, by which benefits are targeted at those considered to be in need. Until the reforms of the 1980s, there were two main contributory benefits: supplementary benefit, designed to provide a subsistence income for those who were not in full-time work; and family income supplement, which 'topped up' the income of families on very low pay. From their inception after the Second World War, the supplementary schemes reinforced women's financial dependence on men in two ways. First, only the male partner of a married or cohabiting couple was entitled to claim benefits. Secondly, the means test was based on an aggregation of all the resources of the couple, which were then deemed to be that of the man. In other words, there was an automatic assumption that a family should be treated as one unit, with a male head of household. The distribution of resources and the balance of power between the individuals within the family were entirely ignored. It was not until 1980 that, under pressure from the requirements of the EC Social Security Directive, the rules excluding married and cohabiting women from claiming supplementary benefit and family income supplement were repealed.[124] However, the reforms introduced by the Government were highly ambiguous. Instead of using the simple 'levelling up' option, which would have extended the existing entitlement to married and cohabiting women, a new and complex set of rules was instituted to determine the claiming partner.[125] Only one partner in the family could claim, on the basis of complex rules which included recent participation in the labour force or good reasons for absence from it. Because women have more fragmented working patterns than men, it proved very difficult for women to establish themselves as the claimant partner. In fact, statistical evidence reveals that of every hundred married claimants of supplementary benefit, only two or three were women.[126] The result was that the new rules, despite being facially neutral, perpetuated the assumption of the family as a single unit with one breadwinner and a dependent partner.

---

[122] See L. Luckhaus 'Severe Disablement Allowance: the Old Dressed up as New?' [1986] *Journal of Social Welfare Law* 153 at p. 154.

[123] Health and Social Security Act 1984, s.13 and Schedule 5. There is an exception for pensioners with dependent children. See Luckhaus [1986], above n. 122, p. 155.

[124] Social Security Act 1980, Schedule 2 part I, and SI 1983/1004.

[125] L. Luckhaus 'Social Security: the equal treatment reforms' [1983] *Journal of Social Welfare Law* 325.

[126] L. Luckhaus 'Changing Rules, Enduring Structures' [1990] MLR 655 at p. 656.

It was only in 1988 when supplementary benefit was abolished and replaced by income support that couples were finally given free choice as to who should be the claiming partner.[127] This change has certainly had an impact: the number of couples in which the woman is the claimant has been rising steadily, from 1 in 2,041 in 1983 to 1 in 20 in 1990. However, in absolute terms, the figure of 1 in 20 is still low.[128] There are several reasons why this is not surprising. First, a person can only claim if she is both available for and actively seeking employment. To prove availability for employment, an applicant is required to respond satisfactorily to a pro forma questionnaire, which includes, as a matter of course, a question concerning relevant child-care arrangements should work be offered immediately.[129] Not surprisingly, this requirement is more difficult for women with children to fulfil than for men, who can usually fall back on their wives or cohabitees for child-care. The second constraint on a couple's freedom to choose relates to the right of the non-claimant partner to take up paid work without losing her benefit. Previously, the partners or wives of claimants were able to undertake paid work (below a maximum earnings limit) without obliterating the claim to income support. Underlying this was the assumption that a man's duty to maintain his wife could co-exist with her undertaking a small amount of paid employment. Under the new system, the claim is extinguished if either partner is working full-time, where full-time work was first defined as more than thirty hours a week, but has been progressively reduced so that it now stands at sixteen. If one partner undertakes paid work for sixteen or more hours a week, the family is no longer eligible for income support, but must instead claim family credit, assuming income from the paid work is low. Although some working families have benefited from this change, an unknown number will be disadvantaged because while mortgage repayments might have been covered by income support, family credit makes no allowance for housing costs.[130] In addition, the change is highly likely to act as a disincentive on claimants' partners, the majority of whom are still women, to undertake paid work.[131] In fact, as we have seen, wives of unemployed claimants are less likely to work than wives of employees. The result is to exacerbate a disturbing divide between 'work-rich' and 'work-poor' families.[132]

At the same time, the aggregation of resources of the family remains unchanged. In the case of lone parents, the assumption of women's economic dependence on men is exacerbated by the combination of this rule

---

[127] SI 1987/1968, reg. 4(3).
[128] Lister, above n. 2, p. 42.
[129] There is a limited class of exceptions to this rule.
[130] A. Ogus, E. Barendt and N. Wikeley, *The Law of Social Security* (4th edn., Butterworths, 1995), p. 463.
[131] Lister, above n. 2, p. 42.
[132] Gregg and Wadsworth, above n. 16, pp. 346–7.

and changes in the law governing the responsibility of absent fathers. This is because the absent father's responsibility extends not just to the children, but to the caring parent, who loses her entitlement to income support as a result. As Lister points out, this accentuates the contradictions between maintenance law and eligibility rules for social security benefit, particularly when the father is cohabiting with a new partner who has her own children. Whereas the benefit rules require his resources to be aggregated with those of his new partner for the purposes of claiming income support, thus assuming he is in a position to support her, the maintenance rules ignore his responsibilities to his new family and calculate his ability to pay on the basis of his whole income. As Lister points out, the 'implications of this re-inforcement of women's economic dependency on men for their personal maintenance go virtually unremarked in public debate.'[133] The problematic nature of income support is particularly stark in the light of the fact that, as a result of the difficulty in conforming to the criteria for contributory benefits, women tend to rely heavily on non-contributory and means-tested benefits.

### iii)  Means-tested In-work Benefits

The policy behind in-work benefit payments is intimately related to more general government policy on the labour market. The problem of families whose earnings from paid work are less than subsistence-level can be dealt with either through employment law, in the form of minimum wages laws, or through social security. The ideological commitment of successive Conservative governments to 'deregulate' the market makes it unsurprising that minimum wages laws were never a serious policy option. Instead, state payments to top up low incomes have been institutionalised, first in the form of family income supplement, and now under the title of family credit. Family credit, which has been on stream since 1988, is designed to provide financial help for low paid working individuals or couples who have responsibility for children.[134] Although it is not overtly discriminatory, and indeed aims to provide assistance to lone parents in particular, family credit in practice encourages reliance on a single male wage. This is because, in couples where one partner is earning, the entry into paid work of the other partner is likely to take the family over the threshold for family credit, resulting in a loss of at least 70 per cent of benefit. At the same time, an allowance of only £40 per week, increased to £60 in April 1996, is payable for child-care costs for children under eleven. Since the allowance is un-likely to cover sufficient hours of child-care, it makes financial sense for the woman to remain at home with the children and the man to seek paid work. In effect then, McLaughlan argues, family credit 'pays' the female partner to stay at home and provide child-care. Unless the woman can get a

---

[133]  Lister, above n. 2, p. 45.
[134]  Social Security Contributions and Benefit Act 1992, 128.

reasonably well paid full-time job, and so 'spring the family clear' of family credit altogether, it pays her to stay at home. The result is that nearly all of the 1 in 6 low income couples on family credit in 1992 were one income families.[135] Research also shows that in up to one-half of couples receiving family credit, these factors discourage one partner from seeking paid work. Thus, while family credit does assist lone mothers to undertake paid work, in that the benefit can be used to pay for child-care, it has the opposite effect for two partner families. Not only does this mean that the latter are destined to remain in poverty; it also has long-term effects, particularly on the non-working (usually female) partner's ability to accrue a reasonable State retirement pension (see Chapter 8).

## iv) Benefits for Severe Disablement

The complex and ambiguous movements towards equality in social security are most clearly manifested in respect of non-contributory benefits for severe disablement. A non-contributory pension for severe disablement was first introduced in 1975 to cater for disabled persons who had inadequate or non-existent contributions records and so were excluded from the contributory scheme.[136] It is deeply disturbing to note that despite its recent origin, the new benefit was structured in a deliberately discriminatory manner. In particular, married or cohabiting women were expressly excluded, the assumption being, presumably, that the vast majority depended on their husbands or partners for support and would never have wished to seek employment out of the home even if they were not prevented by their disability.[137] Indeed, the assumption of a rigid division of labour was so strong that when married women and cohabitees were later brought into the scope of the benefit, it was only on the basis that their ability to carry out housework was impeded. 'A wife with this degree of incapacity can have a most serious impact on the household budget . . . The economic value to the household of the wife's work is beyond dispute.'[138] Thus married women could only qualify for the non-contributory benefit if they could prove to be incapable of performing a 'myriad of tasks assumed to be constituent elements of "household work"'.[139] At the same time, married and cohabiting women were excluded from entitlement to the invalid care allowance, which was payable to a person who was engaged full-time in caring for a severely disabled person.[140]

The main impetus for change in social security came as expected from

---

[135] A. Marsh and S. McKay, *Families, Work and Benefits* (Policy Studies Institute, 1993), p. 48.

[136] Social Security Act 1975, s. 36.

[137] Luckhaus [1986], above n. 122, p. 157.

[138] *Social Security Provision for Chronically Sick and Disabled People* HC Paper July 31 1974, para. 43.

[139] Luckhaus [1986], above n. 122, p. 158.

[140] Social Security Act 1975, s. 37.

the EC Social Security Directive.[141] Somewhat reluctantly, the government conceded that the non-contributory invalidity pension was in breach of the Directive in excluding married and cohabiting women unless they were incapable of household duties. The pension was repealed and replaced with Severe Disablement Allowance. However, the Government refused to 'level up' by simply abolishing the household duties test and allowing married and cohabiting women to claim on the same basis as men. Reluctant to accept a rise in expenditure from £170 million to £265 million (1983 figures), it was decided instead to introduce a complex set of eligibility requirements for both men and women, which would keep spending static.[142] Again, despite the fact the new rules are facially neutral, the effect on women is marked. This is because Severe Disablement Allowance is only payable if the disability occurred before reaching twenty, the assumption being that anyone who becomes disabled during his or her working life will be able to claim contributory invalidity benefits on the basis of an accrued contributions record. Yet, as we have seen above, women face great difficulty in amassing sufficient contributions. Indeed, even the government openly acknowledged that the age bar disproportionately affects women, declaring that 'the overwhelming majority of people who become disabled whilst of working age, but who lack an adequate contribution record are married women.'[143] Even less progress was made in respect of the invalid care allowance, which excluded married and cohabiting women who were caring for invalids. It was only after a ruling by the European Court of Justice[144] that entitlement to this allowance was extended on equal terms to women who were married or cohabiting.[145]

## v) **Universal Benefits**

The final manifestation of the deeply ambiguous development on the social security front relates to child benefit. As we have seen, child benefit, in its former guise as the 'family allowance', has always been central to feminist campaigns for equality in social security. Since this benefit has always been paid direct to the mother, it has given mothers of young children a modicum of financial independence within the family. However, the notion of a non-means-tested, non-contributory benefit clashes head-on with government policy of targeting benefits at those who 'really' need them. Child benefit was therefore frozen throughout the late 1980s, and its continued existence was in jeopardy. During the 1990s, the government finally reversed this policy and committed itself to the index-linking of child benefit. Nevertheless, its real value has still not been restored: in 1992, the

---

[141] Council Directive 79/7/EEC.
[142] Luckhaus [1986], above n. 122, p. 159.
[143] DHSS *Review of the Household Duties Test* (1983), para 35.
[144] Case 150/85 *Drake* v. *Chief Adjudication Officer* [1986] 3 WLR 1005.
[145] Social Security Act 1986, s. 37 amending Social Security Act 1975, s. 37(3).

benefit was still worth only 77 per cent of its value when first introduced in 1979.[146]

## CONCLUSION

As this Chapter has demonstrated, the challenges of the present, while equally great, are different in important respects from those of the past, both in legal and in social terms. With the elimination of formal legal impediments, the liberal promise of juridical equality has finally been realised. The enactment of anti-discrimination laws has taken this further, signifying a willingness to incorporate the insights of modified liberalism. Status ascriptions embedded in welfare laws have, paradoxically, been slowest to respond, but ultimately, and on the insistence of the EU, equality is now making significant inroads. Socially, too, there has been important progress. Women's formal participation in the work-force has risen steadily, so that paid work is now the norm for most women. Birth-control is sufficiently well-developed and accessible for family planning to be a reality. Women's access to higher education has improved enormously, and the doors to professional and managerial careers are no longer barred.

None of this has, however, led to full and equal participation by women in society. A closer look reveals that, while some women have benefited from the changes, women are still hugely over-represented among the disadvantaged of society. Women, particularly elderly women, run a greater risk of poverty than men. Wide pay disparities persist, and women remain segregated in low paying, low status jobs. These contradictions have been deepened by labour market trends towards greater flexibility. Demands by employers for flexible working have facilitated the entry of large numbers of women into the paid labour force, but only on exploitative terms. The picture is one of greater polarisation between the few successful women and the remainder, rather than of a general upward trend.

It is clear, therefore, that the achievement of juridical equality is only a small step in the right direction. As the 'second wave feminists' (see Chapter 1) recognised, new and more sensitive legal tools are needed to address the deep structural causes of women's continued disadvantage. Are the anti-discrimination laws of the past 25 years sufficient for the task? This is the question posed in the coming chapters. I will argue that in fact the stubborn persistence of disadvantage is no coincidence, but is directly related to the continuing limitations of the law. In particular, it will be seen that laws attempting to address women's disadvantage continue to sub-scribe, even if in modified form, to liberal notions of rationality, autonomy, equality, individualism and State neutrality within a free market system. This makes it inevitable that their impact will be small. Because the

---

[146] Lister, above n. 2, p. 38 (95 per cent for the first child).

discussion so far has made it clear that it is at the interface between unpaid and paid work that some of the key causes of continuing disadvantage lie, Chapter 5 contains a detailed critical assessment of the law regarding pregnancy and parenthood. The book then steps over the boundary into paid work, examining pay in Chapter 6, and 'women's work' in Chapter 7. Chapter 8 examines the extent to which disadvantage extends into old age, critically analysing the law on pensions. Chapter 9 steps back from the substantive provisions and assesses the role of the law as such in advancing social change. It examines the limitations of the techniques of adjudication and enforcement, and examines possible remedial responses, including affirmative action. In the final section, Chapter 9 faces the complex question of the interaction between anti-discrimination law and the 'market', addressing in particular the opposition of free market proponents to the notion of harnessing the law to promote change for women. The book draws to a close with a brief conclusion highlighting some of the proposals for reform suggested in earlier chapters. Throughout the book, the interaction with other sources of discrimination, particularly discrimination on grounds of ethnic origin, is considered and alternative approaches, often drawn from other jurisdictions, are examined.

# [5]
# Pregnancy and Parenthood

## INTRODUCTION

The capacity to bear children is in many senses the most creative of all human potentialities. It is also a social necessity. Yet, far from being valued, women's unique reproductive function has generally been used as a pretext for stigma and exclusion from public life. The reasons for this lie deep in the history of women's subordination to men. As we have seen, throughout history, women have been portrayed as naturally and all-pervasively reproductive creatures; a convenient justification for imprisoning women in domestic life. This essentially male perspective on the role of child-birth has been a major factor contributing to the perpetuation of women's subordination.[1]

---

[1] M. O'Brien, *The Politics of Reproduction* (Routledge and Kegan Paul, 1981), p. 20.

The exponential increase in the number of women with young children in the paid labour force has dented the power of this image. But this has not carried with it the necessary alteration of working patterns and occupational structures to accommodate workers with parenting responsibilities. Instead, the boundary between paid work and family work remains rigid. We have seen clear evidence of a deepening gulf between the labour market position of women with children and those without.[2] While women without children continue to make inroads into male-dominated occupations and professions, their counterparts with children are, even today, as I hope to show, severely restricted in the type of jobs and the level of pay available to them. Indeed, it has been estimated that a woman with children in Britain loses as much as 57 per cent of lifetime earnings after 25 compared to her childless counterpart.[3] Nor is the position static: the majority of women will have children during their working lives, and will therefore find it difficult to sustain their labour market position. Yet participation in the paid workforce is no longer a matter of choice for most women. Not only do women remain primarily responsible for children; they also play an important role in providing for their children through their paid work.

Structural disadvantage is aggravated by explicit prejudice against women in respect of pregnancy and childbirth. Recent research shows that blatant discrimination on grounds of pregnancy continues to affect a significant number of women.[4] A central example is that of the Ministry of Defence, which operated an express policy of dismissing women members of the armed forces who became pregnant. This policy was specifically permitted by the Sex Discrimination Act 1975[5] and was actively applied until 1990, when the Minister of Defence conceded that it was in breach of European Community law. Between 1978 and 1990, over 6,172 women were dismissed in pursuance of this policy, leading to an abrupt and devastating end to their careers.[6] Only a handful resumed their careers in the forces: figures for the air force and army show that a mere 42 rejoined between 1980 and 1993.[7] It is impossible to tell how many women decided to forgo parenthood, or even underwent abortions, in order to avoid dismissal: Ministry of Defence figures show that between 1989 and 1993, as

---

[2] P. Elias and T. Hogarth 'Families, Jobs and Unemployment' in R. Lindley (ed.), *Labour Market Structures and Prospects for Women* (Equal Opportunities Commission, 1994), p. 92.

[3] H. Joshi and H. Davies, *Childcare and Mothers' Lifetime Earnings: Some European Contrasts* (Centre for Economic Policy Research, Discussion Paper No. 600, 1992), p. 19.

[4] For examples, see Equal Opportunities Commission *Annual Report* 1991: 27 of 161 cases granted assistance in 1991 concerned pregnancy or maternity; and see generally National Association of Citizens Advice Bureau (NACAB) *Not in labour* (1992); S. McRae, *Maternity Rights in Britain* (Policy Studies Institute, 1991), pp. 64–71.

[5] Section 85(4).

[6] Ministry of Defence *Statement on the Defence Estimates 1994* (CM 2550, 1994), para 511. Information in this section is also drawn from Ministry of Defence press releases between February and June 1994.

[7] Ministry of Defence, 28 February 1994.

many as 1,036 abortions were performed on members of the UK regular forces.[8] This is not confined to the armed forces. The number of complaints to the EOC about treatment following maternity leave rose by almost 30 per cent in 1995, becoming the second largest cause of complaints.[9]

What role, then, can the law play in protecting women against detrimental treatment on grounds of pregnancy and maternity; and in dismantling the systematic barriers to advancement facing women with child-care responsibilities? It will be seen below that substantial progress has been made in recent years, particularly as a result of developments at the level of the EU. Indeed, in the 1990s two major Directives, one on pregnant workers, and one on parental and family leave, were adopted. These developments certainly enhance the possibility for some women to become equal participants in the paid labour market. But there is still insufficient recognition of the value of children and therefore of participative parenting. Mothers who succeed in the paid workforce frequently have to do so by relying on others (usually other low paid women) to look after their children. It will be argued in this chapter that real structural change can only occur as part of a deep-seated commitment to the value of parenthood and child-care. Such change would entail more than just protection against prejudice and the facilitation of a return to paid work after child-birth. It would require a thoroughgoing alteration in the nature of work and working patterns, so that parents can become full participants both in the world of paid work and in the parenting of their children.

Part I of this chapter is concerned with the development of the law. In Part II the discussion turns to policy issues and reform.

## I.  THE DEVELOPMENT OF THE LAW

The discussion in this part begins with a brief description of the background and context, before considering in detail the nature and sources of legal protection. Two quite different legal routes have been followed: the first derives from the more general principle of equal treatment of men and women; while the second consists of a set of rights specifically focusing on pregnancy and maternity. Both of these routes are well developed in the UK and the EU, although the law based on the equal treatment principle has evolved quite differently from that based on specific rights. A third source of protection comes directly from the Welfare State.

a) BACKGROUND AND CONTEXT

The legal framework has traditionally supported the view that child-bearing is incompatible with continued participation in the formal, paid workforce. The earliest provision on maternity, namely the Factory and Workshop Act

---

[8] Ministry of Defence figures, 1994.    [9] EOC, *Annual Report* 1995.

1891, simply mandated expulsion from the work-force, by prohibiting employers in factories or workshops from employing women within four weeks of giving birth to a child.[10] There was no right to return to work after the four week period; nor were there rights to pay or other benefits during that leave. This exclusionary effect was reinforced during the inter-war years by marriage bars, according to which women were automatically dismissed on marriage, presumably because of the assumed imminence of child-birth. Such marriage bars were upheld by the courts as wholly rational.[11] A more sophisticated but equally problematic view was expressed by the architect of the Welfare State, William Beveridge. Beveridge envisaged welfare rights as playing a central role in encouraging women to remain at home as full-time mothers. Although he saw maternity benefits as expressing society's appreciation for women's work, he believed that women should be deterred from allowing paid employment to interfere with this function. This was reflected in the 1946 statutory framework: while the National Insurance Act 1946 signified important progress in providing for a maternity grant aimed at non-medical expenses, it was also openly prescriptive, stating that regulations could disentitle any woman who undertook paid work during the period of maternity payment or who 'fails without good cause to observe any prescribed rules of behaviour'.[12] The only gesture towards genuine protection of pregnancy and maternity came from the ILO, which agreed a Convention as early as 1919. Convention No. 3 requires signatories to provide a pregnant worker with maternity leave of six weeks before and six weeks after confinement; the right to benefits 'sufficient for the full and healthy maintenance of herself and her child'; the right to free medical care, and, once she is back at work, time off to nurse her child during the day; as well as protection against dismissal during maternity leave or any longer period due to illness arising out of her pregnancy.[13] However, this Convention has attracted little support. In 1992, only twenty-eight Member States had ratified Convention No. 3 and the UK was not among them.

It was not until the mid-1970s that a rudimentary legal framework began to be constructed. Two parallel structures developed. The first was based on the equality principle: the Sex Discrimination Act of 1975 made it unlawful to treat a woman less favourably on grounds of her sex than a man. The second was a set of more specific rights, including the right not to be dismissed on grounds of pregnancy, the right to return to work after a period of maternity leave, and the right to maternity pay. Although the

---

[10] Factory and Workshop Act 1891, s. 17. In the US mandatory maternity leaves were common practice. For the debate on whether legislation of this sort protected or harmed women, see B. L. Hutchins and A. Harrison, *A History of Factory Legislation* (P.S. King & Son, 1911), pp. 173–200.

[11] *Short* v. *Poole* [1926] 1 Ch. 66; *Price* v. *Rhondda* UDC [1923] 2 Ch. 372.

[12] National Insurance Act 1946, s. 14(3).

[13] Convention No. 3 (1919); broadened by Convention 103 (1952).

specific rights route is in principle an easier one for an applicant, the rights found in UK law have been limited in several crucial respects. As a start, the protection against dismissal on grounds of pregnancy was subject to a wide-ranging exception for cases in which, at the date of termination, the woman was incapable of adequately doing the work, or if she was barred by a statutory restriction from continuing the work.[14] More problematically, all the rights became increasingly inaccessible as Conservative governments raised the threshold requirements from six months' service to two years and in some cases longer. As a result many women with short service had no option but to rely on the equality principle. The result is that the general guarantee of equal treatment in the SDA has been the primary avenue of litigation in the context of pregnancy. It was only when the EC introduced its own set of specific rights in 1992[15] which, *inter alia*, outlawed the use of stringent eligibility requirements,[16] that specific rights legislation in the UK was reinvigorated. At EC level too, the equal treatment principle, found in Article 119 and the Equal Treatment Directive, has born the brunt of litigation, in this case because specific rights legislation has only been on stream since 1992. In this section, the equal treatment principle is analysed first, followed by an examination of specific rights and of the role of the State in its welfare capacity.

b) Equal or Different? The Equal Treatment Principle and Parenthood[17]

Traditional assumptions that pregnancy and maternity belong to the home, or the 'private sphere', are increasingly challenged by the exponential increase in women working in the market place, or 'public sphere'.[18] Indeed, the pregnant worker forces the law to confront the breakdown in traditional divisions between public and private. In facing this challenge, however, legislatures and courts have become ensnared in another of the dichotomies which bedevil analysis of women's rights: the equality–difference debate. As we have seen, the principle of equal treatment, like much of liberal political theory, was slow to benefit women. By classifying women as different, it was possible to deny them the rights which were deemed basic to human freedom. Indeed, the Aristotelian formula was construed in such a way that while likes should be treated alike, differences could legitimately be treated worse. In the context of reproduction, the 'difference' approach is particularly damaging. Since it is women's reproductive capacities that are emphasised as the factor which differentiates them from

---

[14] ERA 1966, s. 99.    [15] Council Directive 92/85/EEC.
[16] Trade Union Reform and Employment Rights Act 1993, s. 23.
[17] For a detailed analysis of the legal position, see S. Fredman 'A Difference with Distinction: Pregnancy and Parenthood Reassessed' [1994] 101 LQR 106.
[18] For statistics, see J. Lewis, *Women in Britain since 1945* (Basil Blackwell, 1992), p. 65; B. Hepple and S. Fredman, *Labour Law and Industrial Relations in Great Britain* (2nd edn., Kluwer, 1992), p. 181.

men, it is an easy step from here to characterise women as no more than reproductive beings, whose productive capacities are secondary. Furthermore, the process of noting only this difference between men and women tends to assume that all women are the same as each other, that all are equally fertile and desirous of reproduction. In the light of the damaging consequences of a classification as 'different', it is not surprising that women sought to demonstrate their entitlement to basic rights by arguing that they were in fact equal to men.[19] In many areas, such as that of the suffrage, equality has been a useful tool. However, in the case of pregnancy and parenthood, it has proved to be a clumsy instrument. Most anti-discrimination legislation follows a well-trodden path: those who are equal deserve equal treatment, and, conversely, those who are different may be treated differently. However, unpacking this apparently straightforward formula reveals unsuspected complexity. For example, the principle itself gives no guidance as to which of the myriad differences and similarities between individuals are relevant for the purpose at hand. As Finley argues, 'the outcome of the analysis which asks whether someone is different or the same . . . depends entirely on the characteristic or factor selected for emphasis. This selection is a highly political, value-laden choice.'[20] Yet too often no attempt is made to articulate or justify the underlying values. This approach generates particular difficulties when considering pregnancy: clearly a woman is different from a man when she is pregnant, but how significant is this difference, and what legal consequences should follow from it? It will be argued that a satisfactory solution can only be achieved by abandoning the attempt to rely on a traditional equality–difference dichotomy. Instead, it is necessary to make a conscious and explicit decision on the social value of parenthood and to formulate legal rules to reflect this.

These fundamental weaknesses in the equality principle have manifested themselves in the caselaw in four major ways. First, the equal treatment principle requires an answer to the question: 'equal to whom?' The answer supplied by anti-discrimination law is, generally, 'equal to a man'. For example, under the Sex Discrimination Act 1975, it is unlawful for an employer to treat a woman differently on grounds of her sex or marital status than a man would have been treated.[21] In the pregnancy context, this central reliance on a male norm leads straight into the awkward question of who the relevant male comparator should be. Secondly, the reach of the equal treatment principle is necessarily restricted to those who are held to be similarly situated. It requires no explanation for the type of treatment meted out to those who are not equal in the relevant ways. Thus, no justification is required for detrimental treatment in cases in which there is

---

[19] See, for example, M. Wollstonecraft, *Vindication of the Rights of Women* (Penguin Classics, 1983), p. 142.

[20] L. Finley 'Transcending Equality Theory' [1986] 86 *Columbia Law Review* 1118 at p. 1152.

[21] Section 1(1)(a).

no similarly situated male. In the pregnancy context, if no relevant comparator can be found, then detrimental treatment is in effect legitimated. The third limitation of the equality principle is that it requires only consistency of treatment between men and women, not minimum standards. In the pregnancy context, this means that a woman's rights are entirely dependent on the extent to which comparable rights are afforded to comparable men. For example, if it is accepted that a pregnant woman is similarly situated to an ill man, then she is entitled only to the rights he has. If he has no protection against dismissal or rights to sick leave, then she has correspondingly no protection against dismissal on grounds of her pregnancy or rights to maternity leave. Thus she gains nothing from anti-discrimination law. Fourthly, the equal treatment principle leads to an inadequate consideration of the question of who should bear the social cost of pregnancy and child-bearing. Because the principle translates into an obligation placed on the individual employer, the courts are prompted to require justification for placing the cost of pregnancy on that employer. But this ignores the fact that sparing an 'innocent' employer leaves the whole cost with the woman and prevents any consideration of the potential cost-spreading role of the State.

These difficulties have all been reflected in the caselaw, both in the UK and the US. It is only at the level of the ECJ that the constraints of the equality principle have been loosened. Despite the clear reluctance of the UK judiciary to depart from the perceived logic of equality, a long and complex litigation process has finally left its ECJ-inspired mark on UK law. In this section the tortuous development of the law in this direction is explored.

UK courts have been predominantly preoccupied with the first constraint of equality, the need to show that the pregnant woman has been less favourably treated than a comparable man. Early British cases took a highly restrictive view, proceeding on the basis of a literal view of the Aristotelian admonition that likes be treated alike. Not finding a pregnant man, the courts simply excluded pregnancy from the scope of anti-discrimination law. Thus in *Turley* v. *Allders Stores Ltd*,[22] the majority of the Employment Appeal Tribunal held that dismissal on grounds of pregnancy was not protected by this provision. 'In order to see if she has been treated less favourably than a man in the sense of the section you must compare like with like, and you cannot. When she is pregnant a woman is no longer just a woman. She is a woman . . . with child and there is no masculine equivalent.'[23] The result of the inability to find a relevant male comparator was to permit explicit detrimental treatment of a woman on grounds of her pregnancy. Early US cases follow a strikingly similar route. The cases of *Geduldig* v. *Aiello*[24] and *General Electric* v. *Gilbert*[25] both concerned disability insurance programmes which provided benefits in respect of sickness or

---

[22] [1980] ICR 66.    [23] *per* Bristow J at p. 70D.
[24] 417 US 484 (1974).    [25] 429 US 125 (1976).

injury, but excluded all disabilities arising from pregnancy. In both cases, the US Supreme Court upheld the programme, on the grounds that, in the words of Stewart J, 'there is no risk from which men are protected and women are not. Likewise, there is no risk from which women are protected and men are not.'[26]

Later cases took a more sophisticated view of the formula, giving up the quest for a pregnant male comparator and instead focusing on its effects on the employee's capacity to continue at work. Looked at in this light, the logical comparator is a man who is unable to work due to illness. This approach was foreshadowed by Brennan J in his dissenting judgments in *Geduldig*[27] and *Gilbert*.[28] In *Geduldig*, for example, he argued that the equal treatment principle was applicable to pregnancy, since its economic effects, such as wages lost and medical expenses incurred, were indistinguishable from the effects of other disabilities. This view was given statutory endorsement in the US in 1978 by the Pregnancy Discrimination Act 1978, which amended the equal treatment principle contained in Title VII of the Civil Rights Act 1964 so that women affected by pregnancy, childbirth or related medical conditions would be entitled to the same treatment as other persons who were similar in their ability or inability to work. In the UK, this approach was adopted in *Hayes* v. *Malleable Men's Working Club and Institute*,[29] where Waite J argued that it was not the pregnancy itself which mattered, but 'the general effect . . . upon the employee's performance at work of the need to take time off for her confinement and for periods of rest before and afterwards'.[30] This enabled the Employment Appeal Tribunal to compare the treatment of pregnant women with that of ill men. The Court of Appeal gave its stamp of approval to this approach in *Webb* v. *EMO*.[31] Glidewell LJ formulated it thus: 'To postulate a pregnant man is an absurdity, but I see no difficulty in comparing a pregnant woman with a man who has a medical condition which will require him to be absent for the same period of time and at the same time as does the pregnant woman.'[32]

In some senses, this is an extremely important development, enabling at least some pregnant women to gain protection which would otherwise have been denied them. However, it has some serious flaws. First, the need to find a male comparator has forced the analogy between pregnancy and illness. Yet pregnancy is not an illness and should not be stigmatised as 'unhealthy'. Moreover, the focus is entirely work-place oriented: it assumes that the main issue is a woman's inability to do her work; and thereby ignores the positive medical and social reasons for leave, such as the need to breast-feed and to develop a relationship with the child.[33] Secondly, the resolution of the comparator question does not guarantee any minimum

---

[26] At p. 497.    [27] Above n. 24.    [28] Above n. 25.
[29] [1985] ICR 703.    [30] At p. 708C.
[31] [1992] 2 All ER 43 (CA).    [32] At p. 52g.
[33] I. Young, *Justice and the Politics of Difference* (Princeton University Press, 1990), p. 176.

substantive rights; it merely extends whatever rights the male comparator happens to have. In particular, if there are no applicable protections in respect of illness, then pregnancy remains likewise unprotected. In fact, the use of the 'ill man' comparator did not benefit the plaintiffs in either *Hayes*[34] or *Webb*[35]: in both cases, it was held that the ill man would have been treated equally badly and therefore the claimant gained nothing from the comparison.[36]

It is only at the level of the ECJ that the flaws of the comparative approach have been recognised. Most importantly, the Court has consistently refused to accept the relevance of a male comparator. Instead, it has maintained that detrimental treatment on grounds of pregnancy contravenes the equal treatment principle simply because pregnancy is inextricable from gender. This approach was first used in the path-breaking case of *Dekker*.[37] The case was concerned with the refusal by an employer to employ a pregnant woman because its insurance company would not reimburse maternity benefits, on the grounds that her pregnancy was a condition known about at the time her employment would have commenced. Only women applied for the job; there was thus no actual male comparator. Nor was the Court concerned to find a hypothetical male comparator. Instead, it held that because only women could be refused employment on grounds of pregnancy, such a refusal constituted direct discrimination on grounds of sex, contrary to the Equal Treatment Directive.[38] The Court was clearly not deflected by the fact that the employer would, as a result of its decision, be required to bear the cost of the employee's maternity leave. Even more importantly, when *Webb* reached the ECJ,[39] the Court emphatically scotched the proposition that it was relevant to compare a pregnant woman to a man who was incapable of working for medical or other reasons. In an important acknowledgement of the uniqueness of pregnancy, it upheld the appellant's argument that pregnancy was in no way comparable with a pathological condition. A similar approach is to be found in the perceptive decision of the Canadian Supreme Court in *Brooks* v. *Canada Safeway Ltd.*[40] In this case, it was held that discrimination on grounds of pregnancy was necessarily discrimination on grounds of sex, since only women had the capacity to become pregnant. This remained true despite the fact that not all women are pregnant; the key issue was, instead, that men could never become pregnant and therefore would never be subjected to detrimental treatment on these grounds. Even more important was the fact the Court expressly dealt with questions of cost, but, unlike the covert assumptions of older cases, this Court was able to see the woman's perspective. Since pregnancy and child-bearing are

---

[34] Above n. 29.     [35] [1992] 4 All ER 929 (HL).
[36] See also *Brown* v. *Rentokil* [1995] IRLR 211.
[37] Case C-177/88 [1990] ECR I-3941.     [38] Council Directive 76/207 EEC.
[39] Case C-32/93 [1994] IRLR 482 ECJ.     [40] (1989) 1 SCR 1219.

fundamental social needs, the Court held, it was discriminatory to place the whole burden on only part of the population.

These cases demonstrate that ultimately, the equality principle can be moulded to reflect a spectrum of opinions as to the degree of protection to which pregnant workers should be entitled. This is particularly well demonstrated by the US Supreme Court case of *California Federal Savings and Loan Association* v. *Guerra*,[41] in which both sides relied on the concept of equality to further diametrically opposite aims. This case dealt with a challenge to a Californian statute which established maternity rights for women. The applicant argued that the statute offended the equal treatment principle because it gave women superior rights to men. In rejecting this argument, Marshall J, for the majority, used the equality principle in an expansive way to uphold the Californian statute. Women's basic rights to participate fully and equally in the workforce, he argued, could only be achieved by ensuring that women, like men, could have families without losing their jobs. To the extent that this might be considered to be preferential to women, the equality principle required that men be afforded similar rights to women, rather than that women be stripped of their rights. Indeed, there was no reason why employers could not afford male employees similar leave. Thus the seeds of a female rather than a male norm of comparison are sown.

These cases reflect a significant acknowledgment by the relevant judges of the value of parenting and pregnancy in society. However, it is arguable that they have moved some distance from the concept of equality as it is usually understood. The essence of the principle in both *Dekker*[42] and *Canada Safeway* was not that pregnant women should be treated equally with men, but that pregnant women should not be subjected to detrimental treatment on the grounds of their pregnancy. In the *Canada Safeway* case, Dickson CJ characterised the anti-discrimination principle as one which aimed to remove unfair disadvantage due to the fact that the costs of an activity which benefits all of society are placed on a single group.[43] While this is a perceptive and valuable conceptualisation, it is only about equality in the extended sense that all groups should equally bear the costs of parenting.

The problem with this is that the imaginative use of equality proves difficult to sustain in the face of judicial resistance. In fact, the ill male comparator has proved remarkably tenacious. In *Herz*,[44] for example, the European Court held that where pregnancy-related illness continued after the expiry of maternity leave (however short), a woman was required to find an ill man with whom to compare herself before she could claim the protection of the Equal Treatment Directive. The dangers of this reintroduction of the ill-male comparator have already been demonstrated. In a

[41]  479 US 272 (1987).      [42]  Above n. 37.      [43]  Above n. 40 at p. 1237.
[44]  Case 179/88 [1990] ECR 3879.

recent Scottish case,[45] the Court of Session held that an employer had not discriminated against a woman on grounds of her sex when it dismissed her during her pregnancy because of pregnancy-related illness. The court considered that the fact that her illness was due to her pregnancy was irrelevant: the relevant issue was that she had been treated no less favourably than a man absent due to long-term illness. In reaching this decision, the court relied on *Herz*. However, *Herz* was concerned with illness after the expiry of maternity leave; indeed, the woman had been dismissed two years after the pregnancy. To apply the *Herz* exception to illness occurring during pregnancy is to drive a coach and horses through the principle in *Dekker*.

Judicial resistance to the refashioning of equality by the ECJ has not been confined to lower courts, as is evidenced by the House of Lords' approach in *Webb* v. *EMO*.[46] In this case, the Lords shifted the focus away from equality itself onto the question of causation. In other words, it accepted the employer's argument that the woman was not dismissed because of her pregnancy but because of her inability to fulfil the needs of the business. The facts of *Webb* were somewhat unusual. Ms Webb was employed by EMO initially to provide cover for another of its employees, Valerie Stewart, who was due to go on maternity leave. It was envisaged however, that she would continue to work for EMO when her absent colleague returned. Soon after her employment commenced, she discovered that she too was pregnant. Her baby was expected at roughly the same time as that of Mrs Stewart. When informed of Ms Webb's pregnancy, EMO terminated her employment. Ms Webb brought proceedings before an industrial tribunal, claiming that she had been subject to unlawful discrimination on grounds of her sex, contrary to the Sex Discrimination Act 1975 and the Equal Treatment Directive. The tribunal dismissed her case, and her appeals were rejected by both the Employment Appeal Tribunal and the Court of Appeal. Lord Keith, with whom their Lordships agreed, appeared at first sight to be following the approach in *Dekker*, holding that dismissal on the grounds of pregnancy amounted to unlawful direct discrimination. 'Child-bearing and the capacity for child-bearing are characteristics of the female sex. So to apply these characteristics as the criterion for dismissal or refusal to employ is to apply a gender based criterion.'[47] However, in this case, 'the appellant was not dismissed because she was pregnant, but because her pregnancy had the consequence that she would not be available for work at the critical period.'[48] It is a short step from here to the 'ill male' comparator approach. Would a man have been dismissed if he would have been unavailable for work at the relevant time? The House of Lords held that a man due to have a prostate operation at the critical time would likewise have been dismissed, so that there was, under English law, no unlawful direct discrimination in this case.

---

[45] Above n. 36.   [46] [1993] IRLR 27 (HL).
[47] At p. 934.   [48] At p. 934j.

Such a narrow approach to causation is an extremely serious erosion of the *Dekker* principle. It would be unusual for an employer not to require an employee to be available for work; in almost all cases, therefore, an employer could argue that the dismissal was not because of pregnancy but because the employee would be unavailable for work when needed. This case also demonstrates the problems encountered when the questions of cost arise in the context of the equal treatment principle. There is no doubt that all the judges in the case were influenced by the perceived injustice of requiring an employer to bear the cost of maternity in these circumstances. However, because the equal treatment principle does not require explicit discussion of fault or loss distribution, the court was able to achieve its (unstated) aim of protecting the 'innocent' employer from what it considered to be an unfair cost, while not being called upon to justify placing that cost on the pregnant woman. Yet surely this too is an unfair cost? It seems clear that the pregnant woman is in the worst position to bear the cost, particularly since part of the result of the case is to deprive her of her job. The equal treatment principle gives no opportunity for exploring the relative merits of the State and the employer or a combination thereof as possible cost-bearers.

Fortunately, the ECJ in dealing with *Webb* has held firmly to the position it established in *Dekker*. The Court gave short shrift to the employer's argument that the dismissal was not on grounds of pregnancy but because she was unable to work during her maternity leave. Recognising that this would render ineffective the protection offered by the Equal Treatment Directive, it held that such protection could not be dependent on whether the woman's presence at work during maternity was essential to the proper functioning of the undertaking. Termination could not be justified by the fact that she was prevented, on a purely temporary basis, from performing the work for which she had been engaged. The fact that Ms Webb was initially recruited to replace another employee on maternity leave could not affect the answer given by the national court.

Recent cases in the EAT suggest that the ECJ's approach in *Dekker* and *Webb* is finally filtering through to UK courts. In two very recent judgements, the rights of pregnant women under the equal treatment principle were robustly asserted. Thus the EAT had no difficulty in rejecting an employer's assertion that a woman religious education teacher in a Roman Catholic school was not dismissed on the grounds of her pregnancy *per se*, but because the pregnancy resulted from an affair with a Roman Catholic priest.[49] Mummery J helpfully distinguished between two questions: the comparison element and the causation element. The comparison element was held to have been resolved by *Webb*: it was inappropriate to compare her case with that of a hypothetical man. 'Pregnant women in employment

---

[49] *O'Neill* v. *Governors of St Thomas More RCVA Upper School* [1996] IRLR 372 (EAT).

occupy a special position which attracts special protection.'[50] So far as causation is concerned, Mummery J reasserted the principle that motive was irrelevant. The question was a simple and pragmatic one: was pregnancy an effective cause of her dismissal? In this case, her pregnancy was clearly such a cause. Similarly, the EAT extended protection to a woman whose contract was not renewed when she became pregnant. Significantly, Mummery J refused to extend the exception for fixed term contracts hinted at in *Webb*, holding that such an exception would only apply if the employee were unavailable for the whole length of the contract.[51]

However, the protection afforded to women under the equal treatment principle remains fragile. Mummery J was reluctant to give the impression that pregnant women's rights are inviolable. In addition, he went out of his way to state that it was wrong to assume that if liability for sex discrimination was established, full compensation would automatically be awarded. It remains open to the tribunal to decide whether it is just and equitable to award compensation.[52]

In the meantime, some disturbing signs are emanating from the ECJ itself. In the recent case of *Gillespie*[53] a group of women claimed the right to full pay while on maternity leave. In a worrying revival of the 'difference' approach, the Advocate General took the view that Article 119 did not apply to levels of pay while on maternity leave since the situation of a man at work could not be compared with a woman on maternity leave. The Court agreed. 'It is well settled that discrimination involves the application of different rules to comparable situations or the application of the same rule to different situations. . . . [Women taking maternity leave] are in a special position which requires them to be afforded special protection, but which is not comparable either with that of a man or with that of a woman actually at work.'[54] The notion that unfavourable treatment of a woman because she is on maternity leave is not sex discrimination has been taken still further by the EAT. In a 1996 case, it was held not to be discriminatory to refuse a request to jobshare after maternity leave.[55] The male comparator unashamedly springs back to life: if men are not permitted to job-share, the argument runs, women cannot complain of discrimination.[56]

The above discussion suggests that the equal treatment principle is a complex and often clumsy medium for the protection of pregnancy and parenthood. It is only because of an implicit commitment to according protection to pregnant women that the ECJ has succeeded in fashioning a remedy from the equal treatment principle, in the face of a corresponding reluctance on the part of the UK courts. Even in the hands of the ECJ, the

---

[50] *ibid.*, at 376.    [51] *Caruana* v. *Manchester Airport* [1996] IRLR 378 (EAT).
[52] SDA 1975, s. 65(i); *O'Neill*, above n. 49, at p. 378.
[53] *Gillespie* Case C-342/93 [1996] IRLR 214 (ECJ).    [54] *ibid.*, at p. 224.
[55] *British Telecommunications plc* v. *Roberts* EOR No. 70 (1996) p. 53.
[56] It remains arguable that a case of indirect discrimination could be made out.

gains, although significant, have been limited. It has taken extensive litigation, with complex legal argument, simply to provide that dismissal or other detrimental treatment on grounds of pregnancy are unlawful. Questions concerning maternity or parental leave and other crucial entitlements are not addressed. This leads us onto consideration of the alternative route of specific rights.

c) SPECIFIC RIGHTS ASSOCIATED WITH PREGNANCY AND PARENTHOOD

At first sight at least, some of the problems of the equal treatment principle can be dealt with by moving away from an equal treatment principle to a concept of specific rights. On this approach, protection is not linked to corresponding treatment of men. Instead, pregnancy and maternity are considered as sources of entitlement in their own right. Protection from dismissal, for example, is not derived from a principle of equal treatment with a similarly situated man: instead the law specifically makes it unlawful to dismiss a woman on grounds of pregnancy. Thus substantive standards are established rather than simply a requirement of consistency. A system of specific rights is also more appropriate for the determination of duration of leave and the level and extent of pay while on leave. Unlike the equality principle, which focuses only on the bipolar relationship of employer and employee, a specific rights approach has the potential of spreading costs as between the individual, the employer and the wider community.

In practice, however, specific rights have been constrained in ways which are surprisingly similar to the limitations of the equality principle. Most importantly, as is the case for equality, specific rights do no more than reflect the political commitments of their creators. Four specific limitations can be identified. First, although the rights are independent of a male comparator, the influence of the male norm continues to lurk beneath the surface. Secondly, like the equality principle, specific rights are constrained by the market order within which they operate. In practice, higher priority is frequently given to the perceived dictates of the market, employers' needs and government economic policies. Thirdly, the rights are often inaccessible, largely because they rely on a highly individualistic enforcement process. Finally, specific rights, although of benefit to women in important respects, also contain disturbing elements of the 'difference' approach. Most importantly, by giving rights to women only, this approach has tended to perpetuate the assumption that women are primarily responsible for child-care. This is in part due to a failure to distinguish between pregnancy and parenthood. Pregnancy and breast-feeding are genuinely unique to women, and it is therefore appropriate to grant special rights to pregnant and breast-feeding women. However, this is not true for parenthood, which should be recognised as a shared responsibility of mothers and fathers. If the law is to contribute to a genuine improvement of the position of women with children, it is crucial to ensure that parenting rights are extended to both parents, and that the cost is spread among the parents, the employer and society in general.

At present, UK employment protection legislation provides for the right not to be dismissed on grounds of pregnancy, a right to return to work after a period of maternity leave and a right not to be refused reasonable time off for antenatal care. In addition, the right to maternity pay is contained in the various social security statutes. The 1992 Pregnant Workers' Directive[57] requires, *inter alia*, that Member States protect pregnant workers against dismissal, provide for maternity leave and pay and take steps to protect the health and safety of pregnant workers. The most important innovation in this Directive is its requirement that many of the eligibility criteria be removed.[58] However, the duration of paid leave established by the Directive is shorter than previously available under UK law to qualified women. The resulting complex amalgamation of UK and EU law is assessed below by considering first the extent of influence of the male norm, secondly the market order and finally difficulties in enforcement. It is worth noting at this point the contrast between these provisions and those available in the US. It was not until 1993 that there was any federal provision for parental leave on the birth of the baby. When it did come, it was gender neutral; available to either parent. But, it is limited to twelve weeks' unpaid leave within one year of the birth of the child and available only to employees employed for twelve months by employers with 50 or more workers.[59] There is also a minimum requirement of 1,250 hours worked within the preceding twelve month period.

### i) The Male Norm or Structural Inertia

The most important advantage of specific rights is that the right does not depend on those of an explicit male comparator. However, an implicit reliance on the male norm continues to act as a brake on progress in this area. The section considers first the benefits of emancipation from the direct male comparator and then moves on to examine two more subtle manifestations of the male norm.

(1) *No Male Comparator*   The contrast between the specific rights approach in the employment protection legislation and the equality principle of the SDA 1975 is plain. Whereas the SDA requires proof that the woman has been treated less favourably than a similarly situated man, the ERA 1996 (consolidating earlier provisions) provides simply that a woman is treated as unfairly dismissed if 'the reason (or if there is more than one, the principal reason) for her dismissal is that she is pregnant or any other reason

---

[57] Council Directive 92/85/EEC.
[58] Trade Union Reform and Employment Rights Act (TURER) 1993.
[59] Family and Medical Leave Act 1993, Pub. L. No. 103–3; and see A. Grill 'The myth of unpaid family leave' (1996) 17 *Comparative Labor Law Journal* 373.

connected with her pregnancy'.[60] The male comparator is entirely absent. The value thus accorded to pregnant workers permeates through to judicial attitudes. This is strikingly reflected in the contrasting House of Lords judgments in *Brown* v. *Stockton-on-Tees*,[61] a specific rights case, and the equal treatment case of *Webb* v. *EMO (No 1)*.[62] *Brown* concerned a claim by a pregnant worker that she had been made redundant on grounds of her pregnancy, contrary to the statute. In an argument which is strongly reminiscent of that in *Webb*, the employer maintained that she had not been dismissed because of her pregnancy but because she would be absent for up to eight weeks of a one-year job. Whereas the HL accepted this argument in *Webb (No.1)*, the specific wording of the statutory provision led the court in *Brown* to reject emphatically the argument based on causation. According to Lord Griffiths: 'Mrs Brown was selected for dismissal on the ground of redundancy because she needed maternity leave to give birth, and if that is not a reason connected with her pregnancy I do not know what is.'[63] Equally significant is his perception of the issues: 'I have no doubt that it is often a considerable inconvenience to an employer to have to make the necessary arrangements to keep a woman's job open for her whilst she is absent from work in order to have a baby, but this is a price that has to be paid as a part of the social and legal recognition of the equal status of women in the workplace.'[64]

Other pregnancy related rights have similarly benefited from the absence of the requirement of a male comparator. One such right is the right not to be unreasonably refused paid time off work in order to keep an appointment for antenatal care.[65] Such an entitlement is unlikely to have emerged on an equal treatment analysis; the ill male comparator model being blatantly inadequate to deal with this aspect of pregnancy. Maternity benefits too have been independent of a male comparator. Thus the central right, to a period of maternity leave,[66] is available to a pregnant worker, regardless of how men in the same employment are treated.

*(2) The Tenacity of the Male Norm*   The liberation from the male norm has been less complete when considered in its more subtle forms. The first and most important way in which the male bias of existing structures is fortified is by giving parenting rights to women only. In UK law as it presently stands, all the rights concerning maternity are available only to the mother. The result is that only women are entitled to remain at home to look after babies in their vital first few months, making it almost inevitable that mothers will be the primary carers. Financial incentives point in a similar direction. Since the mother and not the father has the right to paid leave

---

[60] ERA 1996, s. 99.   [61] [1988] IRLR 263 (HL).
[62] Above n. 31.   [63] [1988] IRLR 263 at p. 265, para 12.
[64] *ibid.*, at p. 266; and see *Clayton* v. *Vigers* [1990] IRLR 177.
[65] ERA 1996, ss. 55–7.   [66] *ibid.*, s. 71.

after child-birth, a reversal of roles is often financially impossible. Thus the existing distribution of parenting responsibilities, whereby the mother takes primary responsibility for child-care while the father continues to consolidate his position in the paid work-force, is perpetuated. This reinforcement of the status quo has unfortunately been fortified by the ECJ. In *Hofmann*,[67] a father was denied access to maternity benefits despite being the child's primary carer. He complained that he was being discriminated against on grounds of sex contrary to the Equal Treatment Directive. The ECJ rejected his case on the grounds that it fell within the permitted exception to the equal treatment principle for 'provisions concerning the protection of women, particularly as regards pregnancy and maternity'.[68] The father had argued that the derogation only applied to a strictly biological condition; it could not be said that the mother was 'naturally' better equipped to care for children. However, the Court held that the derogation went further, to include protection of the 'special relationship' between the mother and child after the birth.[69] The judgment stated emphatically that the Equal Treatment Directive was not designed to settle questions concerned with the organisation of the family or to alter the division of responsibility between parents. It was therefore held to be legitimate to reserve maternity leave to mothers. Yet this not only encourages women rather than men to stay at home with children during the early months at least.[70] It also, by emphasising the woman's special relationship with her child, has deeply problematic associations with the notion that women's child-care obligations are 'natural' and unchangeable. A small step away from this paradigm has been taken in the EU, with the adoption of a directive on parental and family leave which applies equally to fathers and mothers. However, because it is based on powers given by the Social Chapter, to which the UK is not at present a party, these new rights have no effect in the UK. The parental leave directive is explored later in this chapter.

A second way of reinforcing the male orientation of the labour market is to reserve the benefit of such rights to workers who have been able to conform to full-time, continuous working patterns until their pregnancy. Until 1994, access to pregnancy and maternity rights was severely limited by such conditions.[71] For example, the right not to be unfairly dismissed on grounds of pregnancy was only available to women who were employed for at least sixteen hours a week continuously for two years with the same employer; while women who worked for at least eight but less than sixteen hours were required to show continuous service of as much as five years.

---

[67] Case 184/83 *Hofmann* [1984] ECR 3047.
[68] Article 2(3).
[69] *Hofmann* above n. 67; for similar dicta see Case 224/84 *Johnston* [1986] ECR 1651.
[70] Germany now in fact does allow either parent to take parental leave: C. Docksey [1991] 20 IL3 258 at pp. 272.
[71] With the exception of the right to time off for antenatal care.

Those who worked less than eight hours were simply excluded.[72] The right to return to work after absence due to pregnancy or confinement required that these conditions be met eleven weeks before the expected week of confinement. Rights to statutory maternity pay (SMP) were more complex still,[73] with intricate rules on qualifying periods made even more difficult to fulfil by the exclusion of women on very low levels of pay. Thus, only those who earned above the lower earnings limit (£57 in 1994–95) qualified for maternity pay. Given the high incidence of part-time and marginal forms of work among women, as well as their generally low earnings levels, it is not surprising that, according to a survey of employees in 1988, as many as 40 per cent of women employees failed to fulfil these requirements.[74]

The emphasis on male working patterns has been significantly diluted by the Pregnant Workers' Directive. This is most apparent in the area of unfair dismissal. Most importantly, the Directive requires that all employees, regardless of length of service or hours worked, must be protected against dismissal on grounds connected with pregnancy.[75] As a direct consequence, the UK legislation was amended to delete the qualifying periods for this right.[76] It is estimated that the new provisions will benefit about 4,000 women who are dismissed or forced to resign every year. Those in skilled and semi-skilled occupations are most likely to gain, since they are more vulnerable to such dismissal than their counterparts in managerial and professional jobs.[77] However, the right is still reserved to 'employees' defined as those employed under contracts of service, which excludes many vulnerable marginal workers.

The impact of the Directive on maternity leave is more complex. As in dismissal cases, the Directive requires that leave be available to all pregnant workers, regardless of hours or service.[78] However, the substance of the EC right is weaker than that in the UK. Existing UK law entitles qualified women to a period of leave which could begin eleven weeks prior to the birth and extend for twenty-nine weeks subsequently. By contrast, the Pregnant Workers' Directive only specifies a period of fourteen weeks' leave, albeit available to all women regardless of length of service or hours worked. The UK government, in implementing the Directive, has retained the existing generous provision but continued to limit its application to women with the requisite service. The result is a two-tier system: women who cannot conform are entitled to only fourteen weeks' leave,[79] whereas those who do fulfil the old, stringent eligibility criteria have the right to twenty-nine weeks' leave after child-birth.[80]

---

[72] EPCA 1978, s. 64, prior to its amendment.
[73] Social Security Act 1986, s. 48(4) and (5).
[74] McRae, *Maternity Rights in Britain* above n. 4, p. 145.
[75] This reflects the practice in other Member States, which do not have similar threshold requirements.
[76] ERA 1996, s. 108(3b).       [77] EOR No. 47 (1993), p. 2.
[78] Article 8.       [79] ERA 1996, s. 73(1).       [80] ERA 1996, s. 79(1).

Not surprisingly, it is when we come to the price of maternity leave that eligibility criteria continue to have the greatest impact. The Directive expressly permits Member States to impose conditions on the right to maternity pay, provided these do not demand periods of previous employment of more than twelve months.[81] Although the UK government has responded by simplifying the scheme so that a single rate of Statutory Maternity Pay (previously the higher rate) is now payable to all women, it has also taken advantage of the permission to impose a service requirement. An employee is now only eligible for maternity pay if she has been employed continuously for twenty-six weeks fifteen weeks before the expected date of child-birth and earns above the lower earnings limit. In other words, a woman must already be in employment when she becomes pregnant.[82] Although the amendments are likely to benefit about 285,000 women a year,[83] there are still numerous women who do not have over forty weeks' service when their babies are due. Most problematic is the fact that the Directive did not require removal of the lower earnings limit.[84] This is likely to have a severe exclusionary effect: an estimated 20 per cent of pregnant employees earn below the lower earnings limit and are therefore excluded altogether.[85]

A third way in which the male bias of the labour force is perpetuated arises because of the myopic focus of the specific rights on the period immediately preceding or following childbirth. Even if women are protected at this stage, they may be unable to continue to participate fully in the paid work-force unless their child-care needs are accommodated on a long-term basis. Protection against dismissal on grounds of pregnancy and the right to return to work may prove hollow promises if leave is too short, the pay too low or the work is so demanding of the employee's time and resources as to leave no space for participative parenthood. In such circumstances, a woman is faced with the invidious choice of paid work with little or no time for her children on the one hand, or resignation from the job on the other. These characteristics are clearly apparent in the current legal framework. The fourteen weeks' leave required by the Directive is extremely brief: the new-born baby is still very vulnerable and closely bonded to its parents at this early age and could well still be fully breastfed. This has to some extent been mitigated by the Parental Leave Directive (see below) but the UK remains outside its scope. Interestingly, the equal treatment principle has progressed further than specific rights on this point: it has been held to be discriminatory to refuse to permit a woman to return to work part-time after maternity leave.[86]

---

[81] Article 11(4).
[82] Social Security Terms and Conditions of Employment—The Maternity Allowance and Statutory Maternity Pay Regulations 1994.
[83] EOR No. 47 (1993) p. 38.   [84] Social Security Act 1986, s. 46(2)(b).
[85] EOR No. 55 (1994), p. 38.   [86] *Home Office* v. *Holmes* [1984] IRLR 299.

The narrow focus of maternity rights has been underscored by the Employment Appeal Tribunal in the assessment of compensation for loss of future earnings in cases of dismissal on grounds of pregnancy. In the 1994 case of *Ministry of Defence* v. *Cannock*,[87] Morison J held that the tribunal should reduce the compensation if it considered that the woman would not have returned to work even if she had been entitled to. To assess the likelihood of this, the tribunal should consider specific facts, such as statistics demonstrating that the majority of women do not, in fact, return to the job in question, and that the demands of the job are such as to make it difficult for her to continue in work while at the same time participating in the care of her own children. In the case of servicewomen dismissed by the Ministry of Defence because they were pregnant, tribunals should have taken into account the fact that, having been given the chance to return to work after child-birth, only 46 per cent of servicewomen do so. 'One of the reasons why less than 50 per cent of pregnant servicewomen return to work may well be because the demands of the service are such she will have to give up a greater proportion of the pleasures and pains of parenthood than a mother in civilian life.'[88] The result of the reasoning in *Cannock* is disturbing. Instead of requiring the job to be changed to facilitate the re-entry of such women after child-birth, the EAT in effect vindicates employers who structure their employment in such a way that it is unlikely that women with young children will be able to continue with their jobs.

## ii) **Specific Rights in a Market Order**

The discussion on specific rights has concentrated thus far on the extent to which a male norm influences the nature and scope of the rights. Specific rights can also be compared with the equality principle in respect of the extent and influence of the market order. The fact that specific rights are necessarily more focused than the equality principle means that questions of cost allocation must be addressed specifically. In addition, whereas the equality principle only admits of cost spreading as between employer and employee, a specific rights framework opens up the possibility of using the State or insurance principles to spread the cost. In practice, however, the extent to which the cost has been distributed away from the pregnant worker has been limited. This is because, like equality, specific rights are shaped and constrained by the market order in which they exist. Questions of cost are therefore largely decided from the perspective of employers or governments which have other public spending priorities. Two manifestations will be discussed here: first, restrictions on the amount and availability of maternity pay; and secondly limitations on remedies for breach of rights.

---

[87] [1994] IRLR 509 (EAT).    [88] At p. 524.

(1) *Levels of Maternity Pay*   The central manifestation of the low priority given to maternity and parenthood within the market order is the low level of statutory maternity pay. As a start, as we have seen, a significant number of women are totally excluded from the Statutory Maternity Pay scheme (SMP) because of service requirements and the lower earnings limit (see above). For those who do qualify, the period of paid maternity leave is short and levels of pay during that period are low. This was particularly true prior to the Pregnant Workers' Directive, when women who qualified for the lower rate[89] received a mere £48.80 per week for eighteen weeks, six weeks of which had to be taken before the birth. Women who qualified for the higher rate of SMP[90] were somewhat better off: they could expect six weeks' pay at 90 per cent of their average earnings, followed by twelve weeks at the rate of £48.80 a week. The position has only been marginally improved as a result of the Directive: indeed, perhaps predictably, this was the issue on which most compromises were made in order to ensure its passing. As a result, the Directive only specifies a period of fourteen weeks paid leave. Even more disturbing is the fact that the clause requiring maternity pay to be pegged at 80 per cent of salary was dropped in favour of a linkage between maternity and sick pay. This revival of the 'ill male comparator' approach is ironic in the light of its vigorous rejection by the ECJ in the equality cases. It is true that the preamble to the Directive states that the association with sick pay 'must be regarded as a technical point of reference with a view to fixing the minimum level of protection and should in no circumstances be interpreted as suggesting analogy between pregnancy and illness'. Nevertheless, the linkage makes it inevitable, not only that maternity will be compensated on a relatively low level, but also that maternity is considered in the same way as illness. Moreover, this aspect of the Directive may well block progress under Article 119 and the Equal Treatment Directive. This became evident in the Advocate General's opinion in the recent case of *Gillespie*,[91] in which, as we have seen, the Court rejected the claim that it was contrary to EC equality law to pay a woman on maternity leave anything less than her full contractual pay. Although it accepted that the Directive did not apply to the case in hand, the Court was clearly influenced by the level specified in the Pregnant Workers' Directive. Thus, the Court held, it was for the national legislature to set the amount of benefit, the only control being that the amount payable should not be 'so low as to undermine the purpose of maternity leave, namely the protection of women before and after birth'.[92] The only glimmer of protection for pregnant women concerned the effect of pay rises on the level of maternity

---

[89] Twenty-six weeks, service by the fifteenth week before the baby is due and average earnings above the lower earnings limit.
[90] Two years and eleven weeks, service plus earnings over the lower earnings limit.
[91] [1996] IRLR 214.      [92] *ibid.*, (ECJ) at p. 224.

pay. The Court held that where maternity pay was calculated on the basis of pay received prior to the start of maternity leave, pay rises received during leave must be included in the calculation from the date on which they take effect.

The compromise nature of the Directive has meant that the UK law has only been marginally improved. Under the amended framework, a qualified woman[93] is entitled to six weeks' pay at 90 per cent of average earnings and a further twelve weeks at the flat rate, which was marginally increased to the Statutory Sick Pay rate of £52.50 and then to £54.55 in 1996.[94] In addition, the employee remains entitled to all the terms and conditions of employment (apart from remuneration) which would have been applicable to her if she had not been absent.[95] Significantly, from June 1994 are members of occupational pension schemes entitled to accrue full pension rights during maternity leave.[96]

While certainly an improvement on the previous set of rights, the new deal still shifts only a small proportion of the costs off the shoulders of the parent or parents. The six week period during which she receives 90 per cent of pay expires while the newborn baby is still at its most vulnerable and indeed while the mother is still recovering from the birth. This is particularly true if she chooses to begin her leave a few weeks before the due date. Furthermore, the sick pay rate of £52.50 a week is unlikely to stretch far enough to support her and her child. There is clearly an assumption that she has a partner who is supporting her financially during this period. In addition, for a woman who qualifies with less than two years and eleven weeks' full-time service, there is a hidden catch: although, in theory, she is entitled to eighteen weeks' pay, her right to return to work only lasts for fourteen weeks. Since her rights to maternity pay expire on her return to work, she is in effect only entitled to fourteen weeks' paid leave if she wishes to return to work.[97]

(2) *Remedies*   A further area which is strongly influenced by questions of cost is that of remedies. Remedies for all the rights in question have been relatively weak, reflecting a desire to prevent too great a burden on the employer. For example, the remedy for an infringement of the right to paid time off for antenatal care is merely an order by an industrial tribunal that the employer pay the remuneration the pregnant woman would have

[93] Twenty-six weeks' service prior to the fifteenth week before the baby is due and earning on average at least the lower earnings limit per week in the eight weeks prior to the fifteen week.

[94] Social Security Benefits Uprating Order SI 1996/599.

[95] ERA 1996, s. 71.

[96] Social Security Act 1989 (Commencement No. 5) Order 1994, SI 1994/1661.

[97] There is no penalty for continuing to work in the last six weeks of pregnancy: a woman can now choose to start her maternity leave period any time from the eleventh week before the expected week of child-birth. If she chooses to work until the baby is born, she does not forfeit any pay.

earned had she been permitted to take the time off. There is little deterrent value in such an award; and even the compensatory element is notional. It is not surprising, therefore, that this right is frequently ignored, and the time and effort needed to enforce it is not worth the pregnant worker's while.[98]

Until 1994, the position of a woman dismissed on grounds of pregnancy was scarcely better. Although in theory there is a statutory remedy of reinstatement, this is rarely ordered. Nor was the remedy in damages sufficiently substantial to have either a deterrent or a compensatory effect. Women's position has, however, been significantly enhanced by the European Court of Justice decision in *Marshall (No. 2)*,[99] which led to the removal of the statutory compensation ceiling of £11,000.[100] The effect has already been felt by ex-servicewomen who were discharged in accordance with the Ministry of Defence's policy of dismissing all women who became pregnant. An estimated 5,700 women were victims of this policy between 1978 and 1991 when the Ministry conceded that it was contrary to the Equal Treatment Directive and the policy was discontinued. By 1996, nearly £55 million had been paid in compensation to about 5,000 ex-servicewomen, with thirty-one receiving awards of £100,000 or more. This has not, however, extinguished the UK courts' desire to protect employers from having to bear full responsibility for their discriminatory actions. Nor has it radically changed the underlying structure whereby working patterns make it difficult for women with young children to progress in the paid labour force. In *Ministry of Defence* v. *Cannock*,[101] the EAT expressed the opinion that some of the large awards in these cases were wholly unjustified, manifestly excessive, wrong in principle and out of proportion to the wrong done.[102] The analogy with illness was turned on its head. According to Morison J, the awards were 'more appropriate for a person who has lost a career due to some continuing disability'.[103] Of greatest concern was the way he justified reimposing a cap on the amount of compensation to be awarded in a pregnancy discrimination case. As we have seen, the effect of his judgment is that the very fact that it is extremely difficult to combine parenthood with work in the armed forces is used as a reason to curtail damages awards, despite the fact that the victim has clearly been unlawfully dismissed.

Deference to employers' needs is also woven into the fabric of the rights themselves. For example, the right to paid time off for antenatal care is not an absolute right. It is merely a right not to be unreasonably refused time off during working hours to keep an antenatal appointment.[104] The reasonableness criterion allows an employer to argue, for example, that a part-time

---

[98] NACAB, above n. 4, at p. 18.
[99] Case C-271/91 [1993] CMLR 293.      [100] SI 1993/2798.
[101] [1994] IRLR 509 (EAT).      [102] At p. 525.
[103] *ibid.*      [104] ERA 1996, ss. 55–7.

worker could arrange her antenatal appointment outside working hours. In addition, the package of specific rights has never included protection against refusal to recruit on grounds of pregnancy. This contrasts with the equal treatment principle, both at the level of the ECJ and in the SDA, which extends to recruitment.

### iii) Inaccessibility of Rights

A third problem with the specific rights approach is that many of the rights are inaccessible to those who most need them. As a start, each affected woman bears the responsibility and cost of enforcing her rights by proving her case in a tribunal or court. The reluctance of pregnant women to pursue cases of denial of their rights to an industrial tribunal is well-documented:[105] added to the problems of absence of legal aid and concern about employer hostility are the physical and emotional adjustments which accompany pregnancy. The result is that the existence of a right on the statute book by no means guarantees that it may be relied upon in practice. As has already been seen, the right to time off for antenatal care[106] is a case in point.[107] Recent research also shows widespread ignorance by women of their rights.[108]

Inaccessibility of rights is worsened by complex and technical provisions for notification of the employer. The provisions for women who qualify for the full twenty-nine weeks' maternity leave are particularly complex. There are three notification provisions: the pregnant worker must notify the employer of the date of commencement of leave at least twenty-one days before that date; in addition, her employer may request confirmation of return within the last thirty-one days of her leave, in which case she must confirm her intention to return within fourteen days; and finally, she must notify her employer of her date of return at least twenty-one days before that date.[109] These notices are presumably intended to allow the employer to make the necessary arrangements; if so, research shows that such notices are of limited utility in that a substantial minority of women drop out even though they have given notice.[110] Nevertheless, the statute is framed in such a way as to make the exercise of the right wholly dependent on the precise compliance with the notification periods. As a result, courts, while critical of the provisions, have felt obliged to take a strict view: holding that the rights are lost by even a small error in compliance.[111] The stringency of

---

[105] NACAB, above n. 4, p. 18.     [106] ERA 1996, ss. 55-7.
[107] NACAB, above n. 4, p. 18.     [108] EOR No. 65 (1996), p. 7.
[109] ERA 1996, s. 80.
[110] E. Ellis 'Parents and Employment' [1986] 15 ILJ 97 at p. 100.
[111] *Lavery* v. *Plessey* [1983] 1 All ER 849; E. Ellis [1984] MLR 107. This has been mitigated recently by holding that contractual rights are undisturbed by failure to give statutory notice (*Hilton Hotels* v. *Kaissi* [1994] IRLR 270 EAT) and that the right to return exists from the time of the initial notification of an intention to return (*Philip Hodges* v. *Kell* [1994] IRLR 568 EAT).

these provisions has been somewhat eased for women who qualify only for the fourteen week leave period, but the possibility of foundering on a technicality remains. A pregnant woman in this category is required to notify her employer of the date of commencement of leave at least twenty-one days before she expects to commence her leave (or as soon as is reasonably practicable). If she intends to return earlier than the fourteen week maternity period, she must notify her employer of the date she intends to return at least seven days before that date.[112]

d) THE ROLE OF THE STATE

The discussion so far has focused on legal rights, either under anti-discrimination law or under employment protection legislation. This section moves on to consider the direct role of the State in funding maternity benefits both within and outside of the employment relationship. This role has always been ambiguous. On the one hand, public financing is essential if maternity leave is to function properly. To expect individual employers to shoulder the full burden of maternity is arguably unfair, and practically problematic, particularly if, as is commonly argued, it operates to discourage employers from employing women who might become pregnant. It is noteworthy that as long ago as 1919, the ILO, in recognition of this issue, insisted that maternity benefits be paid by the State rather than the employer. On the other hand, the State's funding powers have always been used prescriptively, for example, encouraging mothers to withdraw from the paid work-force while not affording similar opportunities to fathers. Nor have successive governments placed maternity high on the list of public spending priorities. Although the State's input has been gradually increasing, it remains small. As the EOC argued in 1982, 'in comparison with other countries, the UK has shown a reluctance to make due financial acknowledgement of the vital contribution made by childbearing women. Pregnancy appears to be viewed as a matter of individual choice which in no way merits subsidy by the State.'[113]

From their inception, State maternity payments were specifically calculated to further particular policies regarding maternity.[114] The nature of these policies and the specific means used have, however, fluctuated over the years, at times in a contradictory fashion. The earliest benefit, under the 1911 National Health Insurance scheme, was a lump sum benefit to insured workers or their wives, to pay for medical and nursing care. This was overtaken after the Second World War by the availability of free health care under the NHS. The maternity grant remained a part of the 1946 National Insurance Scheme in order to cover non-medical expenses. However, the

---

[112] ERA 1996, s. 76.

[113] Equal Opportunities Commission, *Parenthood in the Balance* (1982), p. 17.

[114] See generally A. J. Ogus, E. Barendt and N. Wikeley, *The Law of Social Security* (4th edn., Butterworths, 1995), pp. 267–75.

policy behind the grant reflected a particular view of family structure: Beveridge himself stated explicitly that the grant was not intended to cover the whole cost of maternity, 'which has a reasonable and natural claim upon the husband's earnings'.[115] In any event, the commitment to partial funding of maternity evaporated in ensuing decades. From 1969 and throughout the inflationary period of the 1970s, the grant was frozen at the derisory sum of £25. There was a brief revival in 1980, when the contribution conditions were removed from the grant,[116] enabling a further 60,000 mothers a year to qualify.[117] However, this proved to be no more than a transitional measure. The government, unwilling to meet the cost (estimated at over £70 million[118]) of restoring the grant to its 1969 value, abolished it in 1986. At the same time, it abandoned the policy of universal entitlement and, consistent with its general social security policy, focused on those in need. Claims for maternity expenses must now be made from the Social Fund[119] and are only available to those whose means are sufficiently limited to qualify as recipients of the major social security benefits, namely income support, family credit or disability working allowance. The coverage therefore contracted steeply, from universal eligibility to only about 30 per cent of births in 1992–93.[120] Even with the more focused coverage, however, the amounts paid are low: at £100, they scarcely dent the real costs of maternity.

The maternity grant was never intended to substitute for lost income. It is in the area of income maintenance that the emphasis has changed most markedly. As we have seen, Beveridge envisaged welfare rights as playing a central role in encouraging women to remain at home as full-time mothers. Although he saw maternity benefits as expressing society's appreciation for women's work, he believed that women should be deterred from allowing paid employment to interfere with this function. Thus the main provision for income maintenance, called the maternity allowance, was explicitly aimed at removing from the mother the economic pressure to continue at work for as long as possible.[121] The allowance was payable for thirteen weeks beginning the sixth week before the expected week of confinement, thus in effect insisting that pregnant women give up work six weeks before the birth or forfeit their allowance for those weeks. Like the grant, it was a contributory benefit, but only the woman's own contributions, not those of her spouse, would qualify, presumably reflecting the view that the husband should continue in paid employment to support the family.

Such a policy could not survive the overwhelming reality of women continuing in the paid work-force after child-birth. The employment pro-

---

[115] Beveridge para. 341.    [116] Social Security Act 1980, s. 5.
[117] Ogus et al, above n. 114, pp. 268.
[118] Ogus et al, above n. 114, p. 268.
[119] See Social Security Act 1986 and SI 1987/481.
[120] Ogus et al, above n. 114, p. 615.    [121] Beveridge para. 341.

tection rights introduced in 1975 (see above), including as they did protection against dismissal and the right to return to work after child-birth, were aimed at the maintenance of women's position in the paid work-force rather than their exclusion. The statutory right to maternity pay was explicitly an income maintenance provision, and the maternity allowance, which survived from the earlier period, was soon transformed to perform a similar role. The allowance, called State Maternity Allowance in 1986, now complements statutory maternity pay in that it is available to women who have been active in the paid work-force but do not fulfil the qualifying conditions for SMP. To qualify for the allowance, a woman must have been employed or self-employed for at least twenty-six weeks in the sixty-six weeks immediately preceding the fourteenth week before confinement.[122] As with SMP, the allowance is subject to a lower earnings level, excluding significant numbers of women. Indeed, only about 54,000 women were eligible in 1994–95.[123] Moreover, rates of payment for recipients of the maternity allowance are even lower than the rates for SMP. Employed women can claim the lower rate of SMP, which was a mere £52.50 a week in 1994–95; while self-employed women are entitled only to the even smaller sum of £44.25 (1994–95 figures).[124] The prescriptive tone of these benefits has been significantly moderated by the fact that the six weeks rule has been removed as a result of the Pregnant Workers' Directive. Nevertheless, the statute continues to empower the making of regulations which could disqualify the woman from receiving maternity allowance if she 'does any work as an employed or self-employed earner, or fails without good cause to observe any prescribed rules of behaviour'.[125]

Equally important has been the shift in policy behind funding arrangements. Initially, funding for SMP was considered to be the responsibility of all employers, regardless of their actual obligations to existing employees. Hence a Maternity Pay Fund was set up in 1977. It was funded by a small increase to the employers' national insurance contributions and employers could claim a full rebate for maternity pay paid out by them. However, the period from 1980 saw a gradual movement towards greater responsibility being placed on individual employers and a reluctance to place any further costs on the State. The Maternity Pay Fund was wound up in 1988;[126] employers were instead given the responsibility for administering payments of SMP, with the right to reimburse themselves through deductions from their own liability to pay national insurance contributions. Initially, employers could claim full compensation, including administrative costs.

[122] Social Security Contributions and Benefits Act 1992, s. 35 as amended by The Maternity Allowance and Statutory Maternity Pay Regulations 1994 SI 1994/1230.
[123] Department of Social Security figures.
[124] Social Security Contributions and Benefits Act 1992, s. 35(1) and (1A).
[125] *ibid.*, s. 35(3).
[126] Social Security Act 1986, schedule 4.

However, it was decided that individual employers should absorb the increased costs (estimated at £55 million) resulting from changes introduced by the Pregnant Workers' Directive. Employers are now entitled only to 92 per cent of the amount paid out in SMP. Only small employers[127] may still claim the full amount paid out plus a further 5.5 per cent for administrative costs.[128] This development is a worrying incursion on the principle that the cost of maternity should be considered a social responsibility, not one of either the individual employer or individual employee.

## II.   POLICY ISSUES AND REFORM

Any programme of reform must start with an acknowledgement of the pivotal role played by parenting in society. The traditional relegation of parenting and child-care to the 'private' sphere has been a pretext for undervaluing and stigmatising what ought to be recognised as a key social function. The exclusion of women with children from the formal workforce is clearly no longer plausible, as economic pressures on both the supply and demand sides propel mothers into paid work. In fact, the trend for mothers to return to the labour market within one year of giving birth is determinedly upward.[129] Yet it is striking that women's vigorous participation in the paid work-force has done so little to relieve them of the primary responsibility for child-care or to change the structure of the labour market. This rigid role demarcation has crucial implications for the degree of progress which women with children can make in the paid work-force. The dramatic impact on lifetime earnings (see above) is only partly a result of years spent out of the paid workforce. It also reflects the drop in status on return to paid work, and the difficulty in finding paid work which fits in with continuing child-care responsibilities. McRae's recent study of 5,000 mothers during the first five years of their children's lives showed that only 31 per cent had worked full-time throughout the period. Yet it was those who had worked full-time who were most likely to have returned to the same job and employer. Those who worked part-time were much more likely to have changed both job and employer than full-timers. Moreover, the greater their continuity, the more likely was it that the woman had been promoted or received job training. However, the combination of paid work and motherhood did not necessarily make the women happier. Indeed, only 19 per cent agreed that participation in paid work made her and her family happier, a figure which had dropped from 29 per cent in 1980.[130] The fact that women remain primarily responsible for child-care also significantly

---

[127] Defined as employers whose contributions payments for the qualifying tax year do not exceed £20,000.

[128] The Statutory Maternity Pay (Compensation of Employers) and Miscellaneous Amendment Regulations 1994 (SI 1994/1882).

[129] S. McRae, *Women's Employment During Family Formation* (Policy Studies Institute, 1996), p. xi.

[130] *ibid.*, pp. 33–4.

affects the power relations within the family. This is thrown into relief on the breakup of marriage: one of the biggest precipitants of women into poverty is divorce. Moreover, its impact is lasting: the effect of a drop in income on pension entitlements is such that elderly women constitute one of the most significant groups of people living in poverty.

A recognition of the value of parenting leads to a multi-dimensional approach to reform. Most importantly, parenting needs to be treated as the responsibility of more than just the mother. The father should be permitted and indeed expected to play an equal role. In addition, society as a whole has to take responsibility. This takes various forms, including child-care provision, flexible working time and protection against detrimental treatment. Pregnancy rights which do apply only to women need to be carefully distinguished from rights associated with parenting. I therefore begin with a brief discussion of the ways in which pregnancy rights could be strengthened. I then turn to the more complex, and more long-term, issues surrounding parenting. There are two strands to proposals for reform. The first argues for increased State-provided child-care facilities; while the second focuses on changing the structure of the work-force in order to accommodate parental involvement. The two reforms are both crucial; but their nature and interaction need careful consideration.

a) Pregnancy Rights

Pregnancy is clearly unique to women, and is best protected by a set of specific rights independent of the equal treatment principle. Freed from the myopia of the comparative approach, the law is able to address substantive protection. The removal of the qualifying period for access to rights has significantly strengthened the position of pregnant women in the workplace. However, the current set of rights is inadequate in some important respects. First, they only apply to dismissal, leaving the equal treatment principle to cover recruitment issues and detrimental treatment within the employment relationship, such as failure to promote. The existing rights need to be extended to cover such issues. Secondly, the rights are restricted to women who fall within the strict common law definition of an employee under a contract of service. Again, the SDA is wider: it includes women employed under a contract for services provided they are doing the work themselves;[131] and has a specific provision for agency workers who do not have a direct contract with the employer to whom they are sent by the agency.[132] These definitions could easily be transposed into employment protection legislation.[133] Thirdly, the rights need to be easily enforceable and attract remedies which are both a deterrent to the employer and a proper compensation for the employee. The role of the EOC in assisting individual complainants should be broadened and better resourced; better still would be access to legal aid for representation before tribunals. The

[131] SDA 1975, s. 82(1).    [132] *ibid.*, s. 9.    [133] ERA 1996, s. 230.

*Marshall*[134] case, which as we have seen insisted on proper levels of compensation, has been of great value, but decisions such as that in *Cannock*[135] need to be removed.

Finally, but perhaps most importantly, maternity leave and pay are far too restrictive. Most other European countries take the principle of income maintenance seriously, awarding women full pay or a high proportion thereof. In Luxembourg, for example, pregnant women are entitled to sixteen weeks' maternity leave at full pay, and in Denmark, to twenty-eight weeks at 90 per cent of pay.[136] Women in Italy are entitled to twenty weeks' leave at 80 per cent of their earnings; with an optional six month extension during the child's first year at 30 per cent of pay.[137] Women in Germany have the right to fifteen weeks' leave at full pay; women in France obtain sixteen weeks' paid leave at 84 per cent of their earnings and women in the Netherlands receive full pay for sixteen weeks.[138] Belgian women earn 82 per cent of their salary for the first thirty days and then 75 per cent for the remainder of the fifteen week period. Equally important is the source of funding. In Belgium in 1990, for example, it was deliberately decided to shift responsibility for funding maternity pay from the employer to the social security medical insurance system.[139] Many collective agreements and contractual provisions specify full pay during maternity leave.

As a minimum, a woman should be entitled to the package originally put forward as the draft Pregnant Workers' Directive: namely 100 per cent of her earnings during the fourteen weeks' maternity leave, although it would be desirable to increase the leave to at least eighteen weeks. Holtermann and Clarke have calculated that the net cost to the Exchequer of a scheme which entitled mothers who qualified for statutory sick pay (i.e. eight weeks' earnings at the lower earnings limit) to 100 per cent of pay for eighteen weeks would be about £529 million per annum.[140] This contrasts with the £4.2 billion planned expenditure on non-contributory disability benefits in 1992–93 alone, and the £6.7 billion planned expenditure on contributory benefits for sick people.[141]

b) Parental Policies

Far more complex and costly are parental policies. Two main components of a proper parental policy, namely child-care and provisions for leave and

---

[134] *Marshall (No. 2)* Case C-271/91 [1993] IRLR 445 (ECJ).
[135] *Ministry of Defence* v. *Cannock* [1994] IRLR 509 (EAT).
[136] EOR No. 44 (1992), p. 3.
[137] M. Biagi 'Italy' in R. Blanpain (ed.), *The Harmonization of Working Life and Family Life* (Kluwer, 1995), p. 37.
[138] S. Holtermann and K. Clarke, *Parents, employment rights and childcare* (EOC Research discussion series No. 4, 1992), pp. 78–9.
[139] Engels 'Belgium' in Blanpain (ed.), above n. 137, p. 5.
[140] Holtermann and Clarke, above n. 138, p. 37.
[141] *ibid.*, p. 49.

flexible working, are examined below. It is argued that while good quality and widely available child-care services are essential, it is also crucial to recognise and value parental participation in caring for their own children. Such a recognition requires changes in the structure of the paid work-force itself to accommodate family responsibilities.

### i) **Child-care**

Proper and easily accessible child-care is clearly a top priority in counteracting the cumulative disadvantage in the paid work-force by women with children. In a fascinating cross-national study of thirteen European countries, Joshi and Davies have shown a striking correlation between the availability of child-care and the rate of participation in the paid work-force of mothers of young children. Those countries with a low participation rate of mothers with young children were also found to have low rates of child-care provision. For example, in 1988, only 2 per cent of children under three in the UK and 3 per cent in Germany had places in publicly funded child-care. Correspondingly, the rates of participation of mothers of children under three were low in both countries: 32 per cent in the UK and 31 per cent in Germany. The contrast with Denmark and Sweden is stark. As many as 48 per cent of under three-year-olds in Denmark and 31 per cent in Sweden had subsidised day care. The participation rates of their mothers were correspondingly high: at 74 per cent in Denmark and 73 per cent in Sweden.[142] Although, as the authors acknowledge, causation may run in either direction, there is independent evidence that women do find themselves significantly constrained by shortage of adequate child-care. A survey conducted in 1988–89 found better and more extensive child-care facilities was the single most important change that women reported they would like to see to help them remain at work throughout their child-rearing years.[143] This problem is particularly acute for lone mothers, for whom the costs of care will have to be born by one rather than two incomes, and who cannot rely on some of the primary elements of the family support system, particularly that of the children's father and paternal grandparents, to provide unpaid child-care. The result is that the opportunities available to lone parents in the paid work-force are highly limited. It is not surprising therefore, that the UK has one of the lowest employment rates for lone mothers. A recent survey found that only 41 per cent of lone mothers in the UK were in employment, compared with 82 per cent in France and 70 per cent in Sweden. The report concludes that 'the very high cost of childcare creates the strongest disincentive to paid work in the UK of any of the countries studied.'[144] Moreover, there are systematic barriers within the social security system against women with difficulty finding child-care. For

---

[142] Joshi and Davies, above n. 3, pp. 39–40.     [143] McRae, above n. 4, p. 247.

[144] Family Policy Studies Centre 'The employment of lone parent families (1996); EOR No. 69 (1996), p. 4.

example, in order to claim unemployment benefit, a person has to demonstrate availability for full-time work. The questionnaire given to claimants requires evidence of child-care arrangements. This systematically restricts women's access to unemployment benefit. It is not surprising that women are substantially under-represented in unemployment figures based on the numbers who claim unemployment benefit.[145]

Despite evidence of this sort, the UK government of the 1980s and 1990s did little to increase the supply of publicly funded child-care. Reiterating its well-worn confidence in 'market forces', the government has preferred to rely on the generation of funds from voluntary sources to supplement public funding.[146] This is underscored in the 1996 consultation paper *Ideas and Options for Childcare*, in which the government explicitly states that financial responsibility for child-care rests with parents. 'Except for some specific government initiatives . . . it has been left to the market to develop services in response to parents' demands.'[147] Moreover, the squeeze on local authority spending in general has inevitably affected the ability of local authorities to provide publicly funded child-care, particularly since authorities' statutory duties are limited to the provision of day care services for 'children in need' under eight years old.[148] Child-care facilities provided by local authorities are thus generally reserved for children of parents who are in need of a place for reasons connected with the child's development, progress or safety.[149]

There have been some piecemeal government gestures in the direction of child-care provision. One was to provide an allowance of up to £50 a week for child-care costs of some participants on Government's Employment Training programme. However, although this benefited some women, particularly lone parents, its application has been haphazard, with the result that many women returners have been excluded. In addition, the incentive system built into the training system militates against women who might have difficulty finding child-care once they have completed their training: 25 per cent of the funding of the training providers depends on their demonstrated success in finding employment for trainees. Thus providers may be reluctant to train those who are unlikely to find employment because of child-care problems. This problem is reinforced by the fact that the child-care allowance is limited to the duration of training. Once the allowance is withdrawn, many women are unable to find suitable employment or to afford to take up employment offered. As Holtermann and Clarke point out, it is clearly inefficient to provide support for women so

---

[145] Holtermann and Clarke, above n. 138, p. 24.
[146] P. Mottershead, *Recent Developments in Childcare A Review* (EOC Research Series, 1988), p. 32.
[147] Department of Education and Employment, *Work and Family: Ideas and Options for Childcare* (1996), para. 6.
[148] Children Act 1989, s. 19 and Part III.
[149] Mottershead, above n. 146, p. 14.

they can take up training to re-enter the labour market, but then make it impossible for them to use the skill acquired.[150] A second small-scale government initiative was to allocate £45 million in 1993 towards providing care for school age children after school and during school holidays.[151] This is an important move in an area of gross underprovision. By March 1996, some 17,500 places had been created, and the government pledged a further £18.9 million for the next three years.[152] However, the money is administered through Training Enterprise Councils (TECs) with varying degrees of efficiency and commitment. Moreover, grants are only available to schemes in their first year of operation, assuming, against the evidence, that a scheme can be financially self-sufficient within twelve months. Finally, the level of need far exceeds the amount allocated.

The most recent government initiative, the nursery voucher scheme, suffers from similar flaws. The scheme entails the provision of vouchers worth £1,100 to parents of all four-year-old children to cover three terms of pre-school education. Parents are free to choose a nursery in the private, voluntary or State sector. Although trumpeted as a real extension of choice and diversity, the scheme is likely simply to entrench the disparities in nursery provision between the rich and the poor. Parents are free to top up the voucher in the voluntary and private sectors, but not in the State sector. This means on the one hand that well-off parents who were in any case paying for private nurseries will now be richer by £1,100; while parents in deprived areas with insufficient State provision will be unable to provide the extra funding for a private nursery place. Nor is the voucher scheme likely to stimulate further provision, since there is no new capital funding for start-up costs, training or premises.[153] In any event, as even the government admits, the scheme is unlikely to have a significant labour market effect because it covers at most three hours a day. Such short hours in fact create more difficulties for working parents keen to provide nursery education for their children. Nevertheless, the nationwide scheme costing £730 million came into effect in April 1997.[154]

So far as the EU is concerned, its impact has been disappointing. The EU policy on child-care has not been imbued with the power of a Directive, but instead simply takes the form of a non-binding Recommendation on Childcare.[155] The recommendations therein are mild and open-textured: Member States are advised to take or encourage initiatives in the provision of child-care services for parents who are in employment, education or training, or seeking employment, education and training. It does not insist

---

[150] Holtermann and Clarke, above n. 138, p. 22.
[151] EOR No. 50 (1993), p. 4; EOR No. 53 (1994), p. 6.
[152] Department of Education and Employment, above n. 147, p. 12.
[153] EOR No. 65 (1996), p. 7.
[154] Nursery Education and Grant Maintained Schools Act 1996. Vouchers were withdrawn by the new labour government in June 1997.
[155] [1992] O.J. L 123/16.

on state subsidy: it merely suggests that child-care services should be accessible and affordable to all children and parents, and that subsidies should be encouraged. More optimistic is the fact that in its Fourth Equality Action Programme (1996–2000), the Commission has committed itself to proposing measures for higher standards of care of children and other dependants, possibly within a framework directive.[156] Limited funds are available for specific projects.

Government's faith in 'market forces' and the voluntary sector has, predictably, proved unfounded. In fact private sector and employer provision is sparse. In 1994 there were only 482 employer-sponsored nurseries, and although this represented an increase from 425 in 1992, the overall figure remains minimal. Fewer than 1 child in 250 had access to a place in 1994. It is also striking that most employer-sponsored provision is in fact in the public sector. About 67 per cent in 1994 was provided by public employers, with a mere 18 per cent of nurseries provided by private sector employers.[157] Not surprisingly, employers will only consider the provision of child-care facilities if it appears commercially advantageous. It is true that employers incur costs in replacing staff who leave through lack of child-care facilities: the Greater London Council before its abolition saved an estimated £10,000 in 1984 in recruitment costs by providing a staff nursery.[158] Nevertheless, it is unusual for the commercial advantages to outweigh employers' concerns. Recent surveys have found widespread unease amongst employers, about the costs of work-place nurseries:[159] in 1990, it was estimated that it would cost £1,000 per child to set up a nursery, and running costs would be £4,000 per year or £77 per week per child.[160] Initiatives by major banks such as Midland Bank in the mid-1980s did lead to several work-place creches to meet a perceived recruitment crisis. But as soon as demographic and economic factors relieved the recruitment crisis, the nurseries were generally shut down. Midland itself abandoned its plans to set up 300 creches. As the EOC has remarked, 'Many employers understandably consider themselves to be engaged more in running their business than in setting up child-care facilities.'[161] Indeed, eleven major employers have joined together to call for greater government participation in the development of a national child-care policy, arguing that it is inefficient and unrealistic to expect individual employers to perform this function. The group, which calls itself Employers for Childcare, points out that work-place nurseries require a degree of administrative organisation and research that is beyond the resources of many employers,

---

[156] Council decision of 22 December 1995 (95/593/EC) and see EOR No. 67 (1996) p. 34.
[157] EOR No. 57 (1994), p. 5; citing (Working for childcare) 'Survey of employer-sponsored nursery provision—Britain 1994'.
[158] Labour Research Department, *Working Parents: Negotiating a Better Deal* (1992), p. 21.
[159] EOC, *The Key to Real Choice: An Action Plan for Childcare* (1990), p. 6.
[160] Labour Research Department, above n. 158, p. 20.
[161] EOC, above n. 159, p. 6

particularly small and medium-sized organisations. Reliance on employer provision, it argues, could be inimical to labour mobility, since employees may be unwilling to move from an employer who provides high quality child-care.[162] The US experience of a 'childcare market' is salutary: in 1985, out of 6 million businesses, a mere 25,000 provided some form of support for day care, and a minuscule 500 did so in the form of a work-place nursery. The result has been a 'patchwork of day care (which) has evolved in incremental steps, leaving many holes and uneven coverage'.[163] It is not surprising that the pressure group Employers for Childcare 'is convinced that central government involvement is essential to maximise the efforts of individual companies and enable businesses of all sizes to contribute towards childcare provision . . . The provision of childcare is crucial to [an organisation's] success, but it should not take large amounts of management time and skills from the development of their core business.'

Nor has the government's faith in voluntary sources as providers of childcare been underpinned by positive support. Indeed, in 1984, the Inland Revenue decided to treat employer-provided child-care as a taxable benefit in kind for directors and employees earning £8,500 or more. It was not until 1990 that an exemption was created for subsidised work-place nurseries. However, subsidised places in nurseries which are not wholly or partly the responsibility of the employer remain taxable, as do schemes such as child-care vouchers. The resulting bias towards work-place nurseries is not appropriate: many employees prefer not to bring their children into busy city centres in the rush hour; and, even with a subsidy from the employer, many employees cannot afford to pay for a place at a work-place nursery. This is particularly true for part-time workers. Employers for Childcare conclude that the taxation system poses a problem for employers because it makes it difficult to explore other, more appropriate, forms of support. It was proposed in the 1993–94 budget to introduce a new child-care allowance for those on social security benefits, in the form of an earnings disregard which would give the recipient an advantage of about £28 per week.[164] Although this is of assistance to some parents, particularly lone parents, £28 does not go very far towards the costs of a week's worth of child-minding. Moreover, as with tax deductibility in general, it does nothing to ensure that the resources exist to meet child-care needs.[165]

The result is the startling fact that the bulk of child-care is provided by family members. A survey conducted in 1984 showed that as many as 44 per cent of mothers with pre-school children used the child's grandmother for child-care and a further 13 per cent used their husbands or partners.

---

[162] Employers for Childcare, *Good Childcare Good Business* (1993), p. 9.

[163] D. Phillips, *Daycare for young children: An international perspective* [1990] cited in EOC, above n. 159, p. 7.

[164] EOR No. 53 (1994), p. 4.

[165] EOC, above n. 159, p. 11.

Their part-time counterparts exhibited a slightly different pattern, but a similar reliance on the 'domestic economy', with 50 per cent relying on husbands or partners and 24 per cent using the child's grandmother.[166] These arrangements have changed remarkably little, despite the increase in the numbers of women with pre-school children in the paid work-force. According to a 1994 study, 69 per cent of working mothers with a child under five said that their child was cared for by a relative (including partners).[167] As Holtermann and Clarke point out, this is clearly an inadequate way of providing child-care. Relatives may not always live sufficiently close, or they may have their own jobs.[168] The 1994 study also showed that 15 per cent of working mothers with children under twelve used a child-minder while 8 per cent used a day or work-place nursery. Few women (6 per cent) earn sufficiently well to be able to afford to employ a nanny to look after their children in their own home. Nor is the problem confined to pre-school children. Mothers of children at school face the difficult task of finding child-care after school and during school holidays. A 1990 study found that a startling 25 per cent of children aged five to eleven whose mothers worked full-time looked after themselves until their mothers returned home.[169] To avoid this predicament, many women choose to work only during their children's school hours, with the resulting constraints on the opportunities available to them and the pay levels on offer. Indeed, in 1994, one-third of mothers with a youngest child aged five to twelve worked only while their children were at school.

It is clear therefore that the provision of good quality child-care which is fully or partially publicly funded should be a central tenet of the programme of any government whole-heartedly committed to equal opportunities for men and women. Nor should this be limited to children under five. The absence of child-care provision for school-children during the after-school hours, half-term and vacations remains a serious constraint on women who wish to undertake paid work once their children are at school. That high levels of publicly funded child-care are a plausible alternative is evident from the experience of other European countries such as France, Belgium, Italy, Sweden and Denmark. We have seen already that provision for under three-year-olds is substantially higher in these countries than it is in the UK; and a similar pattern is evident for older children. For the age group between three and compulsory school age, as many as 95 per cent of children in France and Belgium have subsidised day care places; and comparable figures for Denmark and Italy are at least 85 per cent.[170] It is striking, however, that relatively few countries make significant provision

---

[166] Mottershead, above n. 146, p. 11.
[167] Department of Education and Employment, *Ideas and Options for Childcare* (1996), para. 16. Unless otherwise indicated figures in this paragraph derive from this source.
[168] Holtermann and Clarke, above n. 138, p. 6 and see EOC, above n. 159, p. 40.
[169] Holtermann and Clarke, above n. 138, p. 6.
[170] Joshi and Davies, *Childcare and Mothers' Lifetime Earnings*, above n. 3, pp. 6–7.

for out-of-school hours of older children. The long school day in France and Belgium has been shown to facilitate full-time employment of mothers; whereas in countries such as Germany with short school days, women are more likely to work part-time. Only Denmark appears to have developed services for children out of school hours.[171]

One of the major arguments used by policy-makers against increasing child-care provision relates to lack of resources. It cannot be denied that good quality day care is costly to provide. However, it is crucial to recognise too the costs of failure to provide such care and the important financial benefits to be reaped in the long term. Given that women in the UK forgo a large chunk of their potential lifetime earnings through child rearing, it is clear that there is a good prospect of substantial returns from reductions in benefit payments and taxation of earnings if child-care frees some of these women from such constraints in their labour market participation. Recent econometric studies show that although the initial public expenditure re-quired to establish a comprehensive child-care network is high, the flowback to the government from reduced social security payments and the increased revenue from taxation due to the growth in women's employment will exceed the cost of the state subsidies.[172] Indeed, Joshi and Davies argue that even if a 100 per cent subsidy is provided for child-care along the Swedish and French lines, 'the fiscal revenue from the woman's extra earnings more than off-sets the costs of providing childcare.'[173] Nor is it necessary for government to foot the total bill: other European countries use various formulae to share out the cost between government, parents and employers. Many employers are willing to assist in the provision of child-care, but understandably remain reluctant to take on the responsibil-ity of providing it themselves. As we have seen, Employers for Childcare argue strenuously that 'central government involvement is essential to maximise the efforts of individual companies and enable businesses of all sizes to contribute towards childcare provision.'[174] In both France and Sweden, employers contribute a proportion of costs. As the EOC points out, it is only relatively recently that employers have taken on the respon-sibility of funding pension schemes for employees: it is certainly plausible to expect child-care subsidies to be absorbed in a similar way.[175] In addition, the EOC proposes that parents be required to contribute up to one-third of the real costs, provided it is reasonably within their means.[176] In any event, the amount spent by parents on child-care has already risen sharply: the amounts paid by working mothers for child-care rose by 42 per cent between 1991 and 1994.[177]

[171]   *ibid.*, pp. 7–8.
[172]   Holtermann and Clarke, above n. 138, p. 52.
[173]   H. Joshi and H. Davies 'Mothers' human capital and children in Britain' (National Institute Economic Review, November 1993).
[174]   Employers for Childcare, above n. 162.
[175]   EOC, above n. 159, p. 10.      [176]   *ibid.*, p. 11.      [177]   EOR No. 69 (1996), p. 5.

The government has recently acknowledged that there are substantial gaps in the availability of child-care. Citing evidence that four out of five non-working mothers would go out to work if they had the child-care of their choice, the government has issued a consultative paper on child-care.[178] However, while usefully canvassing some of the key issues, the consultation paper is unwavering in its refusal to consider the possibility of government financing child-care, other than in highly limited circumstances. It is therefore unlikely that the consultation exercise will yield genuine reform.

It is important, however, not to over-estimate the potential impact of child-care provision. While it has an important role to play, child-care is intrinsically limited in its ability to affect genuine structural change. Reliance on child-care as the sole strategy for reform avoids the need to change working practices to accommodate family responsibilities. Most importantly, such reliance denies the importance of participative parenting. Most parents want to play an active part in their children's lives and should be expected to do so. The solution should surely not be simply to consign children to the care of others. Equally significantly, child-care continues to be considered a woman's job. In practice, paid child-care is overwhelmingly provided by women, be they employed in creches and nurseries or in the more informal sector as child-minders or nannies. Moreover, these jobs remain low paid and of little social status. For example, a child-minder caring for two children for forty hours a week earns less than half the average pay for non-manual women; and a nanny, who looks after children in their own homes earns barely more, at just over half the average pay for women. Neither has any prospect of promotion or career progression; sick leave and annual leave are a matter of negotiation, and may, especially in the case of child-minders, be unpaid. Most child-minders earn below the national insurance threshold and therefore neither pay contributions nor have any right to state social security benefits. Similarly, child-minders and nannies are unlikely to be members of a pensions scheme. In publicly funded nurseries or nursery schools, child-care workers generally have better pay and conditions than their private sector colleagues, and are therefore more likely to be covered by state social security and to have access to paid holidays, sick leave and pension schemes. Nevertheless, except nursery teachers, all earn below the average pay for women. Even nursery teachers, who are the highest paid staff in the under fives world, earn less than the average male non-manual worker. Possibly the worst paid are playgroup workers whose salaries, funded entirely from parental fees, tend to be so low as to be nominal.[179]

As the above discussion shows, a reliance on the provision of paid child-care as a sole strategy for reform may enable some women to escape the devaluation and denial associated with child-care. But this is only because

---

[178] Department of Education and Employment, above n. 167.
[179] EOC, above n. 159, p. 42.

they can rely on other women to take on the burden. The underlying structure is barely dented: meaningful paid work is still incompatible with meaningful parenting, and child-care continues to be considered as low status, low paid women's work. Real structural change requires a far more active accommodation of child-caring responsibilities than has hitherto been possible in the employment relationship. Most importantly, it requires proper parental leave, and flexible or part-time working for parents during the early years of their children's lives. It is to these aspects of reform that we now turn.

## ii) **Accommodating Children**

One of the root causes for the accumulating disadvantage of mothers in the paid work-force is the rigidity of the working time regime. The best benefits of paid work, including pay increments, promotion, training and pension rights, are accrued by those who are able to work full-time and continuously; and indeed are available for overtime work or mobility requirements. Although employers are increasingly advocating a 'flexible work-force', this is to enable them to save on labour costs rather than to accommodate child-care (see Chapter 4). Part-time work, homeworking, casual work and other flexible forms of work are deliberately established as cheaper options for employers and therefore carry low pay and inferior conditions of work. The result is that those who wish to compete for the better terms and conditions need to be free of child-care obligations; and conversely, those with such responsibilities are left with whatever paid work will fit in with caring work. To ensure that mothers have an equal opportunity in the paid work-force, it is therefore crucial that working patterns be changed to accommodate child-care. Such an approach requires the accommodation of breaks in continuous employment, including provision for leave both in the first year of the child's life and to cater for children's illness or other needs while they are growing up. It requires too the availability of shorter working days and weeks on terms which do not penalise the worker. Part-time work, job sharing and flexitime are all aspects of this. Crucially, such opportunities must not automatically be associated with low pay and job insecurity, and, equally importantly, they must be available to and utilised by both parents. Some of these elements are explored briefly below.

(1) *Parental Leave*   Fundamental to any programme of reform must be the availability of leave for both parents in the earliest months of the baby's life. It is at this time that a child is at its most vulnerable and when its primary attachments are formed. Although parental leave is now widely recognised in many EU Member States, the UK government prior to 1997 was opposed to such a measure. Throughout the 1980s, the UK vetoed proposals for a directive on parental leave.[180] It was only once the UK could be

---

[180] For earlier drafts, see Draft Directive on Parental and Family Leave [1984] OJ C 316/7.

bypassed, under the Social Chapter, that the Commission was able to secure the adoption of the 1996 Directive on Parental and Family Leave.[181] Indeed, the new directive was one of the first fruits of negotiations between European-level trade unions and employers' associations under the Social Dialogue procedure introduced by the Treaty of European Union at Maastricht.

The Directive gives men and women workers the right to at least three months' parental leave until an age (specified by Member States) of up to eight years. Workers who wish to exercise their rights are protected against dismissal on these grounds, and have a right to return to the same or an equivalent job at the end of the leave. In addition, rights accrued by the worker at the date on which leave starts are maintained as they stand until the end of leave. In a crucial acknowledgement of the importance of encouraging the uptake by fathers, the Directive provides that leave cannot be transferred from one parent to the other. This means that if a father does not use his rights, they are simply lost.

Despite the relatively mild tone of the Directive, the Conservative government maintained its opposition. It defended this position by drawing on the well-worn arguments that parental leave is too costly, that it will lead to an increase in unemployment and that it is best determined voluntarily between employers and employees. Moreover 'insofar as it would lead to pressures on public expenditure, this is not a priority area for public funds.'[182] Similarly, the Confederation of British Industry (CBI) has focused on the likely damage to industry's competitiveness, its adverse effect on employment levels and its failure to recognise the importance of flexibility.[183]

All of these arguments can, however, be effectively countered. So far as cost is concerned, no direct evidence has been adduced to support dire warnings of damage to competitiveness. Indeed, the Department of Employment admitted that it had not conducted any extensive research into this area, while the CBI maintained that 'costs are not easily quantifiable . . . we just know [dislocation] exists.'[184] Evidence from other countries demonstrates that the impact on employers is far from devastating. Absence due to parental leave affects a relatively small percentage of the work-force and because advance notice of leave can be given, disruption can be minimised.[185] A 1991 survey by a German institute showed that 90 per cent of companies surveyed had not experienced major difficulties, nor incurred inordinately high costs associated with parental leave.[186] Indeed, even before the Parental Leave Directive, eleven European countries had introduced parental leave, demonstrating that the cost and dislocation can easily be absorbed. In fact, most have recently improved their provision. In

---

[181] Directive 96/34/EC.　　[182] See EOR No. 1 (1985), p. 2.
[183] EOR No. 2 (1985), p. 5.　　[184] Cited in EOR No. 1 (1985), p. 2.
[185] EOR No. 66 (1996), p. 22.　　[186] ibid.

Germany, for example, a right to parental leave of twelve months, which was introduced in 1986, has now been increased to three years.[187] In France too, parental rights have improved significantly. From July 1994, all employees regardless of the size of the undertaking are entitled to take full or part-time parental leave until the child reaches thirty-six months. Leave can be taken either by the mother or the father or shared between parents.[188]

Nor can the contention that the Directive would undermine the key task of reducing unemployment be sustained. Indeed, other European countries have consciously introduced career breaks in order to increase employment. Thus in 1994, Belgium introduced a right to leave of three to twelve months up to a total of three years during the working life of most employees. It is noteworthy that this career break entitlement is not directly linked to child-caring, but the amount of money paid by the State is greater if the purpose of the leave is to look after a new born infant.[189] Denmark has also recently improved its parental leave provisions with the key aim of reducing unemployment levels by ensuring replacement staff are hired to replace those on leave. Since January 1994, Danish parents are entitled to leave of three to twelve months, which can be used at any time until the child is eight years old. Nor is the UK government's reliance on voluntary provision sufficient—in practice, there are few career break schemes, most of which are in the public sector, and some of which only apply to women, defeating the whole purpose.[190]

It is crucial to the effectiveness of parental leave schemes that fathers genuinely share responsibility with mothers. In practice, however, the tenacity of traditional role prescriptions has been reflected in a disappointing uptake among fathers. In many European countries with experience of parental leave, women remain the primary beneficiaries of parental leave. In Germany, which has a long period of leave on a low flat rate payment, the vast majority of mothers take parental leave but only 19 per cent of fathers. In Denmark in 1985, a mere 7 per cent of fathers took parental leave. Sweden has had somewhat more success, with the take-up rate among fathers gradually increasing. In the beginning of the 1990s, 38 per cent of all married fathers and 44 per cent of cohabiting fathers took some leave to care for the child in its first year. Even so, leave remained unevenly distributed: in 1992, only 9 per cent of the total amount of parent-allowance days paid for was used by fathers.[191] It is clear from these examples that uptake by fathers is closely associated with the level and duration of pay during parental leave, a conclusion which is supported by research evidence. In Portugal, for example, unpaid parental leave means that only parents who can afford to live without salary or social security can benefit.[192] By contrast,

---

[187] *ibid.*, p. 26.      [188] *ibid.*, p. 26.      [189] *Labour Research* March 1994, p. 9.
[190] Labour Research Department, *Working Parents*, above n. 158, pp. 26–8.
[191] A. Numhauser-Henning 'Sweden' in Blanpain (ed.), above n. 137, p. 99.
[192] EOR No. 66 (1996), p. 24.

in Sweden, employees are entitled to an allowance of 90 per cent of gross pay for the first 60 days, and then of 80 per cent for a further 300 days. However, paid leave is not in itself sufficient. Even in countries with earnings-related benefits, such as Finland, take-up by fathers is low, with fathers comprising only 2 per cent of takers. In Sweden too, as we have seen, fathers still take significantly less leave than mothers. This demonstrates that a further incentive is required: namely that the leave be non-transferrable as between the parents. In Sweden itself it was decided in 1994 that if the father did not use 30 days of leave at the 90 per cent rate that period would be lost to the family.[193] It is too early to assess the impact of this measure but indications are that it functions as a significant incentive.

To what extent are these priorities reflected in the Directive? Possibly its most important element is symbolic: the acknowledgement of the importance of shared responsibility for child-care. In addition, it includes at least one of the elements necessary to achieve genuine shared care: the fact that the leave is an individual entitlement which cannot be transferred from the father to the mother (or vice versa). However, it remains limited in several key respects. Of most concern is the absence of any provision for paid leave, either by the employer or through the social security scheme. Trade union pressure for paid parental leave was successfully resisted by the European-level employers' association. The best that could be achieved was a clause preventing Member States from reducing protection currently available. Thus those who already have paid parental leave may not rely on the Directive as an excuse for decreasing or removing these entitlements. For the rest, the absence of proper financial provision during the period of leave means that in practice, only those with independent sources of income can truly benefit from parental leave. As we have seen, it acts as a specific disincentive to fathers.

The Directive has three further limitations. First, the combined period of six months is relatively short, even when added to a fourteen week period of maternity leave. Secondly, the Directive allows Member States to impose a qualifying condition of up to one year's service. This represents an unwelcome retreat from the progressive position of the Pregnant Workers' Directive, which, as we have seen, only permitted qualifying periods for the purposes of paid maternity leave. Thirdly, the Directive permits Member States or the social partners to 'define the circumstances in which an employer . . . is allowed to postpone the granting of parental leave for justifiable reasons related to the operation of the undertaking.' This caveat was not present in the earlier Commission-inspired draft directives, but was a direct result of the bargaining process between the social partners. This raises a potentially serious danger inherent in using social dialogue for

---

[193] Numhauser-Henning, above n. 191, pp. 94 and 99.

legislative purposes, namely that the outcome simply reflects and entrenches imbalances in power between the two sides of industry.[194]

How costly, therefore, would it be to introduce paid parental leave in the
UK? Holtermann and Clarke examined the costs of implementing a scheme
of parental leave, based on a right to three months' leave for each parent, at
100 per cent of earnings, provided the parent had eight weeks' earnings
over the national insurance threshold. The net cost of such a scheme would
be £624 million a year (if take up was low) and £819 million (if take up was
high). As an alternative, they costed an equivalent scheme, with a flat rate
rather than 100 per cent payment. A flat rate payment would be likely to
attract fewer takers, so that the costs would range from £136 to £176
million per year.[195] These figures are dwarfed by the figure of £338 billion
which represented total income from employment and self-employment in
the UK, (including employers' social security contributions) in 1989.

Ultimately, the cost-benefit analysis of parental leave depends on the
value accorded by a government to the facilitation of participative parenting
combined with meaningful participation in the work-force. Such a commitment is already demonstrated in varying degrees in other European countries. Thus although leave in Germany is unpaid, parents are eligible for
State benefit of 600DM (approximately £267) per month in the first two
years, subject to means testing.[196] As in Germany, leave in France is unpaid
but State benefit is payable after the birth or adoption of the second child
in the family at a flat rate of 2,964F (approximately £311) a month. The
benefit is payable in part if the parent works part-time or undergoes paid
training part-time.[197] Similarly, leave in Denmark is paid: at 80 per cent of
unemployment benefit, which is itself 90 per cent of earnings, subject to a
ceiling of 2,500 KR (about £250) a week.[198] Possibly the clearest commitment is demonstrated in Sweden, which, as we have seen, has generous
earnings related benefits. Indeed in 1992, the Swedish government spent
$2.85 billion on parental leave, 1.3 per cent of the country's gross domestic
product.[199] This is not, however, a net cost: the benefits are clear. Thus in
Sweden, the participation rate of women between the ages of 25 and 49 is
the highest in the world. Since the introduction of paid parental leave, the
number of women who have terminated their employment following child-
birth has declined rapidly, with the result that 86 per cent of mothers with
pre-school aged children are employed (albeit on lower hours than men.)[200]
Moreover, paid parental leave is strongly supported by employers, who

---

[194] See S. Fredman 'Social Policy Law-making' in Harlow, C. and Craig, P. (ed.) *Law-Making in the European Union* (Sweet & Maxwell, 1997).
[195] Holtermann and Clarke, above n. 138, p. 45.
[196] EOR No. 66 (1996), p. 26.
[197] EOR No. 58 (1994), p. 6.
[198] *Labour Research* March 1994, p. 11.
[199] Grill, above n. 59, p. 380.
[200] *ibid.*, p. 381.

believe that productivity increases when workers are given the opportunity to remain at home after child-birth while retaining their links to the labour market. In addition, Swedish employers are able to reap a higher return on their investment in human capital if they do not lose trained staff on childbirth.[201]

(2) *Paternity Leave*   A less dramatic gesture towards equal parenting would be to provide for paternity leave, or leave to enable fathers to be present at the birth of the child, to share the early care of the baby, to support the mother and, where appropriate, to care for older children. As in other areas, the UK government remains implacably opposed to statutory intervention in this regard, arguing, predictably, that paternity leave is best dealt with by agreement between the parties concerned. In fact, however, voluntary provision is poor. A survey of 356 employers conducted in 1993–94 found that in fact about 69 per cent of respondents had paternity leave arrangements, and in all but two of these the leave was paid. However, such leave tends to be brief in the extreme: the median length being five days, falling to four days if local authorities and health authorities are excluded from the sample. Those employers who had not introduced paternity leave generally cited cost as the reason. However, the survey found, the cost of paternity leave to employers generally in terms of lost time is negligible, amounting to a mere 23 minutes per employee per year.[202] It would surely be a straightforward matter to ensure that all employees enjoyed similar benefits by the extension of the best practice among some employers to employers generally.

(3) *Family Leave*   The need for parental leave does not, however, end in the first year of a child's life. Working parents continue to face the prospect of illness of family members or of their carers: it has been demonstrated that family responsibilities are an important factor behind absenteeism at work.[203] In an important recognition of these issues, the 1996 Directive requires Member States to give workers the right to limited periods of time off work 'on grounds of force majeure for urgent family reasons in cases of sickness or accident making the immediate presence of the worker indispensable'.[204] It is left up to Member States to flesh out the details of this right, but in any event most European Member States already have some provision in place. In most of these countries, employees are paid in full. In Sweden, there is a right to up to 120 days' paid leave per child under twelve to cater for the child's illness,[205] a right which can be transferred to any

---

[201]  Grill, above n. 59, p. 382.
[202]  EOR No. 55 (1994), pp. 14–28.
[203]  EOR No. 27 (1989), p. 10.
[204]  Parental and Family Directive 96/34/EC cl. 3.
[205]  Numhauser-Henning, above n. 191, p. 99.

other person taking leave to care for the sick child. Portugal grants up to thirty days a year, and in Denmark, employees may take unpaid leave of up to one year with the employer's consent.[206] It is worth noting that it is unusual for employees to take their full entitlement. In Sweden, for example, parents in practice only take on average seven days leave per child. Nevertheless the UK government's opposition was, until 1997, unwavering, the official stance being that any such provision should be voluntary. However, although some employers in the UK do provide family leave, there is evidence suggesting that such provision is patchy, and could even be on the decline due to the development of more generous holiday leave provisions.[207] Those who do provide leave usually give between two and five days a year, many of them on a discretionary basis. Of even greater concern is evidence that it might be considered reasonable to allow mothers but not fathers to take time off to care for a sick child.[208]

(4) *Flexible Working*    The most fundamental change necessary to accommodate the combination of participative parenting and paid work would be to relax the rigidity of the working day and the working year. The current situation, in which flexible work is of low pay and low status, only reinforces inequalities and disadvantage. The Directive on Working Time, to the extent that it limits overtime, takes a small step in the right direction. The process is assisted too by measures to restructure working time to decrease unemployment. But such measures are only indirectly beneficial to workers with family responsibilities. Far more directly sensitive to parenting needs is, again, the Swedish measure, which gives employees with children under eight the right to shorter working days. Under the 1978 Act on Parental Leave, an employee has the right to work three quarters of full-time (normally six hours a day) while his or her children are under eight, and then return to full-time work subsequently. Equally importantly, Swedish law provides that an employee on reduced hours in these circumstances is to be considered a full-time employee with regard to employment benefits in general (albeit on pay reduced pro rata).[209] It is particularly disturbing that UK law has been rigidly opposed to such accommodation. Although a civil servant succeeded in convincing the EAT that a refusal to allow her to work part-time after her child was born was indirect discrimination,[210] the most recent case on this subject has held that it is not directly discriminatory to refuse to allow a jobshare on return from maternity leave.[211]

Nevertheless, the responsibility to accommodate child-care responsibilities through flexible working time cannot be achieved through

[206] EOR No. 66 (1996) p. 23.
[207] EOR No. 27 (1989) p. 10.
[208] EOC, above n. 159, p. 22.
[209] Numhauser-Henning, above n. 191, p.99.
[210] *Home Office* v. *Holmes*, above n. 86.
[211] *British Telecommunications plc* v. *Roberts*, above n. 55.

discrimination law on its own. A thoroughgoing policy commitment is required which relaxes the rigid boundary between work and family while at the same time maintaining terms and conditions. Only when men as well as women are encouraged to combine participative parenting with paid work on decent terms will we be on the road to true equity.

# [6]
# The State of Pay

## INTRODUCTION

The statistics on women's pay discussed in Chapter 4 show unequivocally that two decades of equal pay legislation have been unable to close the gap between the average remuneration of men and women. It is true that the effect of the Equal Pay Act 1970 was initially significant, with the differential between men's and women's full-time hourly pay jumping from 64 per cent in 1971 to 74 per cent in 1974. But since then, progress has been painfully slow. Indeed, in the twenty-two years from 1974 to 1996, the gap narrowed by a mere 5.9 per cent. Equally disturbing is the fact that women continue to predominate in the ranks of the lowest paid workers. In 1996, a troubling 39.2 per cent of women earned less than £220 per week, as against 17.5 per cent of men (see Chapter 4).

This chapter argues that the absence of real progress is no coincidence. It results from the inability of the legislation to address the institutional forces which actively perpetuate lower pay for women. As was seen in Chapter 4, job segregation remains rampant, with women predominating in low paid low status jobs, with little access to lucrative elements such as premia, training, and promotion opportunities. Women tend too to have interrupted work histories, which prevent them from accruing vested seniority rights, pensions and other job-related benefits. In addition, girls are still educated for 'women's work' and women have been less well served by trade unions than men. These forces are themselves driven by two basic causes: women's primary responsibility for child-care, and the deeply entrenched undervaluation of women's work. It is only by challenging these factors that the law could have any real impact. It is argued here that the inability to do so is a direct result of the liberal political philosophy which has shaped equal pay legislation. In particular, the legislation is fundamentally limited by its adherence to the core liberal principles examined in Chapter 1: neutrality, formal equality, individualism and deference to market forces.

The chapter begins with a brief sketch of the main provisions of the Equal Pay Act (EqPA) 1970 and the relevant EC law, namely, Article 119 and the Equal Pay Directive. These provisions are then critically analysed under the four heads noted above. The chapter then briefly turns to a separate and somewhat unexpected source of protection for women's pay, namely the EC Acquired Rights Directive.[1] In the next part, I consider minimum wages legislation, and conclude with a brief look at other legal systems with a view to sketching some proposals for reform.

## I.　EQUAL PAY LEGISLATION

### (A) The EqPA and EC Law

There are two main sources of equal pay legislation: the British Equal Pay Act 1970 and EC law in the form of Article 119 and the Equal Pay Directive. EC law dominates: not only must the Equal Pay Act be read subject to EC law, but Article 119, as clarified by the Equal Pay Directive, forms an independent cause of action, directly effective both against the State and against private employers.

---

[1] Directive 77/187 EC.

The aims of the Equal Pay Act were initially highly circumscribed, the idea being to eliminate the widespread practice of separate pay scales for men and women doing the same work. Hence the core of the Act as originally formulated gave a woman the right to claim equal pay with a man employed by the same employer in only two situations:[2] if she and he were doing 'like work'; or if their work has been rated as equivalent under an employer-initiated job evaluation study.[3] 'Like work' is defined as work of the same or broadly similar nature.[4] To its credit, the EAT, aware of employers' attempts to disguise continuing pay discrimination, was adept at recognising work as 'alike' where it was clear that differences in name or job description had been introduced to maintain the existing pay differential between previously 'male' and 'female' jobs.[5] The second head, 'work rated as equivalent', extends beyond like work but is limited to situations in which the employer has initiated an evaluation study. As noted above, the effect of these provisions was initially dramatic, but its impact was soon exhausted. Progress could only be made if the comparison was extended beyond like work.

The concept of equal pay for work of equal value had been current in international documents for some time. The ILO Convention on Equal Pay, adopted in 1951,[6] provided for a right to equal pay for work of equal value. However, it was only at the insistence of the EC that equal value was included in the UK Equal Pay Act.[7] Thus, a woman can now claim equal pay with a man doing (i) like work; (ii) work rated as equivalent under a job evaluation study; or (iii) work of equal value.[8] The equal value provisions are, however, highly complex. For example, until mid-1996 the tribunal could not do the evaluation itself, but had to refer the case to an independent expert to prepare a report.[9] Similarly, an equal value claim can be barred if a job evaluation study already exists, provided the latter is not itself discriminatory.[10]

The Act contains two crucial restrictions. First, although the claimant is free to choose her own male comparator, the scope of comparison is limited to a man simultaneously employed by the same employer at the same establishment, or one at which common terms and conditions are observed.

---

[2] EqPA 1970 s. 1(2)(a) and (b).

[3] The Act is symmetrical in that a man can claim equal pay with a woman in the reverse situation.

[4] EqPA 1970, s. 1(4).

[5] e.g. *Electrolux* v. *Hutchinson* [1977] ICR 252 (EAT); *Sorbie* v. *Trusthouse Forte* [1977] ICR 55 (EAT); *Redland* v. *Harper* [1977] ICR 349 (EAT). On the general approach of the EAT, see *Capper Pass* v. *Lawton* [1977] ICR 83 (EAT) at p. 87.

[6] Convention 100, 1951

[7] *Commission of the European Communities* v. *UK* (Case 61/81) [1982] ICR 578 (ECJ).

[8] EqPA 1970, s. 1(2) (c), added by SI 1983/1794 reg 2(1).

[9] EqPA 1970, s. 2A; the Sex Discrimination and Equal Pay (Miscellaneous Amendments) Regulations 1996 SI/438; in force from 31 July 1996.

[10] EqPA 1970, s. 2A(2).

Secondly, even if a relevant comparison has been established, it is still open to the employer to argue that the difference in pay was genuinely due to a material factor other than the difference of sex.[11] If a claim is successful, an equality clause is implied into the woman's contract, and any term in her contract which is less favourable than her comparator's is modified so as not to be less favourable.[12] The tribunal may award up to two years' arrears of pay and damages for breach of an equality clause.[13] The proceedings must be instituted by the woman to an employment tribunal within six months of the termination of the woman's employment.[14]

Article 119 is more open-textured than the EqPA, stating simply that Member States must 'ensure and subsequently maintain the application of the principle that men and women should receive equal pay for equal work'. Pay is defined broadly to include any consideration which the worker receives directly or indirectly, in respect of his or her employment from his or her employer. As originally formulated, Article 119 did not clarify whether equal work included work of equal value. This ambiguity was removed by the later Equal Pay Directive,[15] which states explicitly that the principle of equal pay requires the elimination of all discrimination on grounds of sex for the same work or for work to which equal value is attributed. It also requires that all job classification systems exclude discrimination on grounds of sex. These provisions have been considerably expanded by judicial development, as will become clear below.

## (B) The Limitations of the Law

This section contains a detailed critique of equal pay legislation in the UK and at the level of the EU. It focuses on four main sources of criticism. These are:

(a) the notion that the State should be neutral in order to permit proper freedom for individuals within the 'free market';
(b) the pivotal role of formal equality;
(c) the prominence of individualism; and
(d) the deference to managerial prerogative and State macroeconomic policies within a market economy.

### a) State Neutrality and the 'Free Market'

Equal pay legislation constitutes a direct challenge to the notion that the State should refrain from intervening in the 'free market'. More than any other area of equal opportunities, the introduction of a statutory equal pay mechanism contravenes the view that pay-setting should be the exclusive domain of the market. It is not surprising then that concerns to protect State neutrality and the free market have had a profoundly limiting effect on the structure of equal pay legislation.

---

[11] EqPA 1970, s. 1(3).   [12] *ibid.*, s. 1.   [13] *ibid.*, s. 2(5).
[14] *ibid.*, s. 26.   [15] Directive 75/117 EEC.

In the UK in the 1960s and 1970s, support for State neutrality went hand in hand with the prevailing belief in collective bargaining as the optimal means to correct imbalances of power within the market. The autonomy of collective bargaining should not, on this view, be disturbed. As Davies and Freedland comment: 'If claims to equal pay as between men and women could be used to challenge on a general basis inequities and anomalies in pay structures, the legislation might have a destabilizing effect upon industrial relations.'[16] The Equal Pay Act was therefore structured in such a way as to intervene as little as possible. Equal pay for like work was the ideal formula: the employers were simply required to slot women into an established pay structure. Similarly, equal value claims were limited to cases in which the employer had initiated a job evaluation scheme (JES) but had failed to implement its findings.[17] The message was received and transmitted by both the EAT and the CA, who repeatedly warned that tribunals should not be pay-setting bodies.[18]

By the 1980s and 1990s, the principle of State abstention from the free market had lost its collective dimension, and instead been transformed into a strident individualism. Neo-liberals asserted that the market should remain 'free' both from State intervention and that of collectivities such as trade unions. As was seen in Chapter 1, Hayek, one of the standard-bearers of this view, rejects the notion that market outcomes could be characterised as just or unjust. Instead, the market is elevated to the best protector of individual freedom. This is because a central characteristic of the market is that 'it serves no single order of ends.' Instead, it allows each individual to pursue his or her own ends 'by increasing the prospects of every one of a greater command over the various goods . . . than we are able to secure in any other way.'[19] Two conclusions are drawn from these premises. The first is that it is anathema for the State to intervene in establishing pay levels: this would amount to an insistence on a 'single order of ends' interfering with individual pursuits in pursuit of a notion of social justice which does not exist. Secondly, provided procedural rules governing exchange are followed, the market is the best method of securing the best outcome for individuals. This means that if the market produces inequalities of pay between men and women, they are inevitably justifiable in terms of women's lower productivity. This line of argument has been explicitly followed by the American writer, Posner, who argues[20] that unequal pay simply reflects differences in market worth. Women's pay, in his view, is no more

---

[16] P. Davies and M. R. Freedland, *Labour Legislation and Public Policy* (Oxford University Press, 1993), p. 214.

[17] EqPA 1970, s. 1(2)(b).

[18] See e.g. *National Vulcan* v. *Wade* (1977) ICR 455 (EAT) *per* Phillips J, *McCarthys* v. *Smith* [1979] ICR 785 (CA) *per* Lawton LJ.

[19] F. A. Hayek, *Law, Legislation and Liberty* (vol. 2) (Routledge and Kegan Paul, 1976), p. 107.

[20] R. Posner 'An Economic Analysis of Sex Discrimination Laws' [1989] *University of Chicago Law Review* 1311.

than a reflection of their lower productivity. This is largely due to their own behaviour: in the expectation of taking time out of the labour market to look after children, he argues, women invest less than men in their own human capital. In other words, Posner asserts that there is no reason to believe that sex discrimination is an inefficiency in the market. Anti-discrimination laws are thus an unjustifiable imposition on the market because they demand that women be paid more than their market worth.

The neo-liberal view has been sufficiently influential in the US to act as a brake on the development of comparable worth or equal value jurisprudence. Posner himself, in his role as Court of Appeals judge, used the neo-liberal argument in *American Nurses Association* v. *Illinois*[21] to reject a claim by nurses and typists for equal pay with men in predominantly male job classifications of comparable worth. Posner used the opportunity to give the stamp of authority to his views that the wage gap was almost entirely due to women's lower investment in their own human capital, declaring that the result of imposing a concept of relative merit would increase women's wages above their market level at the cost of impeding progress. On his view, an employer who simply paid the going wage would be justifiably surprised to discover this constituted a violation of Federal law. Nor is Posner alone in his views. In the 1980 case of *Lemons* v. *City of Denver*,[22] the tenth Circuit Court of Appeal rejected a claim by public sector nurses that the city had discriminated against them by linking their pay to private sector nurses and therefore perpetuating the chronic undervaluation of nursing work. The Court of Appeal declared simply that Title VII of the Civil Rights Act, which proscribes discrimination on grounds of sex, did not require an employer to ignore the market in setting wage rates. Five years later the Ninth Circuit Court of Appeal reiterated this view in *AFSCME* v. *Washington*,[23] in which a comparable worth claim under Title VII was again rejected. The court declared that the State could not be held to have discriminated indirectly by deciding to base payment on competitive markets rather than comparable worth. The plaintiffs attempted to turn their case into one of intentional discrimination, arguing that a discriminatory motive could be inferred from the fact that with knowledge of the historical pattern of lower wages for women, the employer continued to participate in the market, thereby perpetuating the discrimination. The court rejected this argument, declaring that mere participation in the market could not constitute direct discrimination since the State did not create the market and did not use sex-based considerations in setting wages.

In the UK, the neo-liberal view has been less influential, largely because of the constraints imposed by the EC. Indeed, equal value has been firmly entrenched as a result of EC law. Nevertheless, the legislature acted swiftly

---

[21] *American Nurses Association* v. *Illinois* 783 F 2d 716 (7th Circ. 1986).
[22] 620 F 2d 228 (10th Circuit 1980).
[23] 770 F 2d 1401 (9th circuit, 1985).

to prevent tribunals from straying into the territory of wage setting. Rather than permit tribunals to undertake the task of valuation themselves, a complex procedure was set in place, whereby an 'independent expert' was appointed to undertake the task of valuation.[24] The expert's report is only open to challenge on limited grounds. In addition, as we have seen, the right to claim equal work for equal value is barred if there is an employer-initiated job evaluation already in existence. It is only if the existing scheme can be shown to be discriminatory that the right to claim equal pay for work of equal value arises. Given the subjective nature of valuations, it is very difficult to challenge them as discriminatory. The legislature attempted to marginalise equal value even further by making it a residual right, available only if there was no like work or work rated as equivalent claim. Fortunately, the House of Lords rejected this approach on the grounds that it contravened EC law.[25]

The neo-liberal view, which is shared widely by economists, is, in any event, fundamentally flawed. Human capital theory recasts the institutional forces leading women to take primary responsibility for child-care as a rational market explanation for women's low pay. Yet the emphasis on women's free choice in terms of investment in their own human capital simply ignores the real constraints on choice faced by women. Similarly, Hayek and Posner's description of the 'free market' attributes to economic interactions a rationality and coherence they lack. In fact, market deter-mined wage structures do not accurately reflect relative productivity of workers. This can be demonstrated in at least three ways. First, investment in human capital is not necessarily rewarded with higher pay. As Corti and Dex show, highly qualified women are likely to earn significantly less than highly qualified men, while women with degrees are less likely to be in jobs which use their qualifications than men.[26] Instead of reflecting skills levels, earnings tend to be determined according to the employer's ability to pay and the level of collective organisation on the shop-floor.[27] Secondly, as was argued in detail in Chapter 4, payment structures and market rates are themselves influenced by traditional prejudices against women. Finally, the neo-liberal theory assumes that competition within the market place is perfect, so that workers will inevitably gravitate towards the job that matches their level of efficiency or skill. That this is not the case is demon-strated by segmentation theorists, who show that the labour m........ is segmented into non-competing groups. Thus the fact that some workers are relegated to a low productivity sector does not necessarily mean that they are less efficient.

[24] EqPA 1970, s. 2A(1).
[25] *Pickstone* v. *Freemans plc* [1988] IRLR 357 (HL).
[26] L. Corti and S. Dex 'Highly Qualified Women' [1995] *Employment Gazette* 115–121.
[27] C. Craig, J. Rubery, R. Tarling, and F. Wilkinson, *Labour Market Structure, Industrial Organisation and Low Pay* (Cambridge University Press, 1982), pp. 80, 84.

b) **Equality**

Possibly the most fundamental limitation on the effectiveness of equal pay legislation has been the pivotal role played by the concept of equality. Two aspects of the equality concept as utilised in the legislation have proved to be particularly restrictive. The first is that it is based on an artificial dichotomy of equality versus difference, which fails to capture the complexity of payment structures. In particular, it makes it impossible to address situations in which women are doing work of admittedly lower value than that of male employees, but the pay differential between the men and the women is far greater than the difference in value. The second constraint on equality is reliance on a norm of comparison which is heavily male-dominated. This makes it impossible for the law to confront some of the most basic causes of the pay gap, namely job segregation, the substitution of cheaper women for men, and the fact that overtime and other premia are strongly associated with male jobs. Each of these restrictions is discussed below.

i) *Equality v. Difference: The Problem of Proportionality*   Equality is uni-dimensional: it insists that likes be treated alike, but makes no pronouncement on difference. In the context of pay, this has the particularly problematic result of failing to require that differences be treated proportionately to the degree of difference. Phillips J recognised as early as 1978[28] that the Act provides no redress in cases in which the work is admittedly different, but the difference in pay between the man's work and the female's is not commensurate to the differences in work. The effect was clearly evidenced in *Maidment* v. *Cooper*,[29] in which the gap in remuneration was found to be in no way commensurate to the difference in value between the male and female jobs. Nevertheless, the fact that the woman's work differed from that of the male comparator in a small but significant detail meant that equal work had not been established and the Act was inapplicable.

The result is that the notion of equality has become fundamentally divorced from fairness in pay setting. This was openly acknowledged by Balcombe LJ in *Calder* v. *Rowntree Mackintosh*,[30] when he insisted that the brief of the tribunal was to establish equality, not fairness. In this case, an all-woman twilight shift received no premium for working unsocial hours, whereas the rotating shift, which contained 60 per cent men, received a premium to reflect both unsocial hours and the inconvenience of rotating shifts. An approach based on proportionality would have required the court to consider the possibility of adjusting the bonus to reflect only the unsocial hours element. However, the rigidity of the equality principle precluded such a response.

The problem is at its starkest when a woman does work of greater value

---

[28] *Electrolux* v. *Hutchinson*, above n. 5, p. 259.
[29] [1978] ICR 1094 (EAT).    [30] [1993] IRLR 212 (CA).

but is actually paid less than her male comparator. This was the scenario in *Waddington* v. *Leicester*[31] in which the complainant was paid less than the man she supervised. The EAT, adhering unbendingly to the notion of equality as all-or-nothing, held that the Act was inapplicable because equal work had not been established. It was in the context of such a claim that the ECJ's more flexible response became apparent. While not fully embracing proportionality, the European Court has been ready to incorporate notions of fairness into equality in order to avoid particularly absurd results. *Murphy*[32] was similar to *Waddington* in that a woman whose work had been valued higher than her male comparator complained that she was paid less than he was. The ECJ held that although Article 119 expressly referred only to equal value, the principle behind the prohibition of lower pay for equal work *a fortiori* applied to lower pay for work of greater value. Notably, the Advocate General saw this as much as a question of fairness as of pragmatism. Nevertheless, the decision explicitly rejected the idea that Article 119 requires proportional pay. This is demonstrated in the Court's award: rather than requiring that her work be paid at the appropriately higher rate, it held only that she should be paid the same as her male inferior.

A more complex but somewhat ambiguous gesture towards proportionality is found in *Enderby*.[33] In this case, speech therapists claiming equal pay with pharmacists and clinical psychologists were met with the defence that the difference in pay was justified by the state of the market. The ECJ, sensitive to the possibility that the differential might be greater than warranted by market forces, held that such a defence was only valid for the proportion of the differential which genuinely reflected market forces. However, closer examination reveals that this is not a thoroughgoing application of proportionality. Instead of addressing the problem of disproportionate differentials for work of different value, it is concerned with the extent to which work of equal value may justifiably attract lower pay.

An interesting but short-lived example of a genuine application of proportionality to pay is found in the use by the Central Arbitration Committee (CAC) of its powers under the now repealed section 3 of the EqPA. In exercising its remedial powers under the Act, the CAC was acutely aware that discrimination in collective agreements was not confined to lower pay for different work but extended to differentials which were disproportionately large relative to the difference in value. It therefore interpreted its powers as including cases in which the low rate of pay reflected a 'woman's rate of pay' rather than the real worth to the employer.[34] For example, in one award the Committee discovered that the differential between grade 6 and the all female grade 7 was three times as wide as the differential

---

[31] [1977] ICR 266 (EAT).      [32] Case 157/86 [1988] ECR 673 (ECJ).
[33] *Enderby* v. *Frenchay Health Authority* [1993] IRLR 591 (ECJ).
[34] This description is derived from P. Davies 'The CAC and Equal Pay' [1980] CLP 165 at 175.

between any other two consecutive grades in the pay structure. The solution was to require that the employer attribute pay rates commensurate to the proportionate value of the job. The sensitivity and efficacy of this approach were, however, so much at odds with the notion of equality utilised in the EqPA that the CAC soon found its approach declared unlawful. The attempt to address disproportionate differentials was considered to be an improper foray into a general wage review;[35] with the result that the CAC's role in advancing equal pay soon became otiose (see further below).

ii) *The Male Norm*   As we have seen before, equality is essentially a comparative concept. It does not dictate substantive outcomes, but merely requires consistent treatment. Not only does this preclude the possibility of challenging low pay as such; it also emphatically reinforces the male norm as the yardstick of comparison. This is manifested in three different ways. First, a woman can only use the Act if she can find a male comparator in the same employment doing equal work. Secondly, and more subtly, the equality principle favours 'male' patterns of work, to the exclusion of child-care responsibilities. Thirdly, the kind of work in which men predominate remains likely to attract greater rewards, the equality principle notwithstanding. Each of these dimensions is reflected in the caselaw.

(1)  The Male Comparator: The male norm is expressed in the EqPA in its most concrete form. The scope of comparison is highly limited: the male comparator must normally be employed by the same employer at the same establishment as the woman. The comparison can only reach beyond the woman's own establishment if the male comparator is employed at another establishment of the same or an associated employer at which, in the somewhat elusive phraseology of the Act, 'common terms and conditions of employment are observed'.[36] This dependence on a male comparator makes it impossible for the EqPA to tackle job segregation (see Chapters 3 and 4).[37] A woman working in a segregated work-place or a segregated grade within a mixed work-place is unlikely to find a male comparator doing 'like work'. Even if there are a handful of men doing 'women's work', they are in all likelihood equally low paid: men may be willing to work at a 'woman's rate' in a woman's job because they are ill; or, like students, only casually attached to the labour force; or are using the job as a route to promotion.[38] The equal value provisions allow a somewhat more expansive pool of comparison. Even in a highly segregated establishment, a woman may find a comparable male doing work of equal value. However, there are

---

[35]  *R* v. *CAC, ex p. Hy-Mac* [1979] IRLR 461 (QBD).
[36]  EqPA 1970, s. 1(6).
[37]  This is also a result of the individualism of the Act—see further section III (A) below.
[38]  J. Rubery, *The Economics of Equal Value* (EOC, 1992), p. 50.

numerous work-places where the only male workers are doing work of admittedly different value. The result is that equal value simply skirts the heartland of job segregation.

EC law, being more open-textured, has the potential to dilute the intensity of the male norm in this context. Two possible methods of addressing job segregation within the bounds of the equality principle have been raised before the ECJ. The first is the notion that if there is no man in the workplace, a woman could compare herself with a 'hypothetical' man. This possibility was raised in *Maccarthys*[39] when the Advocate General and the Commission pressed the Court to permit a woman to show that she had been treated less favourably than a man would have been treated.[40] However, the Court argued such a comparison would require comparative studies of entire branches of industry and therefore be too imprecise to be applied directly in national courts. A second means of addressing pay inequities in segregated work-forces would entail permitting comparisons between employees of different employers. This was rejected by the ECJ in *Defrenne (No 2)*,[41] largely on the grounds that direct effectiveness required greater precision than such an approach entailed. According to the ECJ, the direct effect of Article 119 could not extend beyond unequal pay for equal work 'in the same establishment or service, whether public or private', since to eliminate all discrimination, 'not only as regards individual undertakings but also entire branches of industry . . . may, in certain cases involve the elaboration of criteria whose implementation necessitates the taking of appropriate measures at Community and national level.'[42] The question was raised again in *Commission* v. *Denmark*[43] in respect of Danish law, which, like British law, is limited to comparisons within the same establishment. Advocate General Verloren van Themaat urged the Court to recognise that in sectors with a traditionally female work-force, comparison with other sectors might be necessary. Unfortunately, the EC Commission did not pursue the point before the Court, so the latter declined to deal with it. Nevertheless, a window of opportunity was left open by the reference in *Defrenne* to a possible extension of comparability beyond the same establishment to those employed in the same service. This was finally noticed and pressed upon the EAT in *Scullard* v. *Knowles*,[44] a case in which the plaintiff was the only woman employed as a unit manager by a voluntary association of local education authorities established to co-ordinate the work of colleges of further education. She sought to compare her work with unit managers employed by other councils, all of whom received higher salaries for the same or similar work. Her employer and that of her comparators were all supported and funded by the Department of Education and Employment. The EAT in a singularly important judgment accepted the

[39] Case 129/70 [1979] ECR 1275.    [40] SDA 1975, s. 1(1)(a).
[41] Case 43/75 [1976] ECR 455.    [42] Paragraphs 22 and 19.
[43] Case 143/83 EC [1985] ECR 427.    [44] [1996] IRLR 344 (EAT).

argument that Article 119 is broader than the EqPA in that it permits comparison between employees in the same service. The case was therefore remitted to the tribunal to determine whether in this case the employee and her comparators were indeed employed in the same service. The potential for revolutionary cross-industry comparisons was, however, restrained by the guidance given by Mummery J. He stressed that the industrial tribunal should examine whether the regional councils were directly or indirectly controlled by a third party (here the Department of Education and Training), the extent and nature of control, and whether common terms and conditions of employment were observed in the regional advisory councils for the relevant class of employees.[45] This limited view is in fact consistent with *Defrenne (No 2)*, which, as we have seen, did not envisage cross-industry comparisons as such.

Equally problematic is the requirement that the male comparator be employed contemporaneously with the woman. This makes it impossible for the EqPA to be used to address the pressing problem of substitution of male labour with cheaper female workers. Given the fact that 'feminisation' of work is frequently associated with decrease in pay, this is an issue which urgently needs attention. The courts were faced squarely with this issue in *Maccarthys* v. *Smith*,[46] in which a woman was paid less than her male predecessor in the identical job. Her claim under the EqPA was rejected by the UK courts. The ECJ, however, reversed this finding, holding that Article 119 does apply to non-contemporaneous work.[47] Nevertheless, this recognition of the problem of cheap substitution was seriously compromised by the ECJ's deference to economic priorities. In a wide-ranging caveat, the Court left it open to an employer to justify the difference in pay on grounds ostensibly unrelated to sex, such as a downturn in the employer's business. This possibility was soon seized upon by the EAT in *Albion Shipping* v. *Arnold*,[48] in which a man was made redundant due to a decrease in the volume of business; and the woman complainant took over his job at a substantially lower salary. The EAT stressed that while it was possible under Article 119 to compare her job with her predecessor, it was essential to consider whether economic circumstances justified the discrepancy. Yet it is highly questionable whether an employer who is unable to sustain the job at a 'man's' rate of pay should be permitted to use business arguments to justify taking on a woman at a 'woman's' pay to do the same job. In an adventurous recent judgment, the EAT took the issue somewhat further by holding, as a preliminary point, that a claimant could compare her work to that of her successor, on the grounds that this was a notional comparator 'as effective as if "actual"'.[49] However, this statement too was heavily qualified, with the EAT drawing attention to the difficulties of proof faced by the

---

[45] [1996] IRLR at p. 346.   [46] *Macarthys* v. *Smith* [1979] ICR 785 (CA).
[47] *Macarthys* Case 129/70 [1979] ECR 1275.   [48] [1982] ICR 22 (EAT).
[49] *Diocese of Hallam* v. *Connaughton* [1996] IRLR 505 (EAT) at p. 507.

applicant, and correspondingly, that the employer's defence (based on factors unrelated to sex) may be easier to fulfil.[50]

(2) Male Patterns of Work: Even a cursory examination of statistics on pay reveals that earnings potential is vastly enhanced by the ability to work long hours. Although basic pay is the major component of total earnings, additional payments such as shift and overtime payments play a crucial role in the overall pay packet. Men in Britain tend to work particularly long hours. Such hours are clearly incompatible with child-care responsibilities. As Dickens argues: 'Men in Britain work hours which at present crowd out any likelihood of taking other than a token share in family and domestic responsibilities.'[51] The pattern is self-perpetuating. Because of their responsibility for domestic matters, women's working hours, even when full-time, are significantly less than those of men. This bias towards 'male' working patterns contributes significantly to the gender pay gap, as is illustrated dramatically by the figures. In 1995, as much as 18.5 per cent of the gross weekly pay of full-time manual men was accounted for by overtime payments and shift premia, increasing the average pay packet by £53.70. The corresponding figure for women manual workers was only 9.4 per cent or (since women's average earnings are lower) a mere £17.70 extra on average per week.[52] Differential access to additional payments is further reinforced over a worker's lifetime by the system of seniority payments. Because women are less likely to have a continuous work history, they tend to be excluded from such payments.

The bias towards male working patterns is particularly evident in relation to part-time workers, 84 per cent of whom were women in 1994.[53] Not only is the average hourly pay of part-timers considerably lower than that of full-time workers, they are frequently excluded from important fringe benefits, such as the right to enter a pension or sick pay schemes. Most importantly, access to overtime premia is invariably barred, since overtime is generally only payable if a part-time worker has worked the full-time standard week.[54] Part-timers are generally excluded too from shift payments, night shift additions and premia for working weekends or bank holidays. Those part-timers who work on Sundays are frequently paid lower premia than full-timers.[55] These factors have been shown to contribute significantly to the low levels of part-time workers' pay.[56]

To what extent has equal pay legislation been able to penetrate this

---

[50] It should also be pointed out that the EAT in this case erroneously stated that the ECJ in *Macarthy's* had supported an argument in favour of a hypothetical comparator. In fact, this was the Commission's stand, and one which had been clearly rejected by the Court.
[51] L. Dickens, *Whose Flexibility* (Institute of Employment Rights, 1992), p. 61.
[52] NES 1995, A1.1, table 1.
[53] EOR No. 61 May/June 1995, p. 24.
[54] Industrial Relations Services, *Pay and Gender in Britain* (1991), p. 72.
[55] *ibid.*, p. 72.   [56] *ibid.*, p. iv.

structural bias towards 'male' working patterns? There are two stages of the analysis. First, is it acceptable to pay higher *basic* pay to a male comparator for no other reason than that he is required to work longer hours than a female applicant doing equal work? Secondly, can the law address differential access to premium payments whether related to weekly hours of work, or to lifetime patterns? So far as the first question is concerned, the UK courts were quick to equalise basic pay regardless of overtime. Thus the EAT had no difficulty in rejecting the argument that the very fact that overtime was required of the male comparator but not the woman could prevent a like work comparison of two otherwise broadly similar jobs.[57] It was much more difficult to persuade the EAT to insist on equality in basic hourly pay as between part-timers and full-timers. In *Handley* v. *Mono*,[58] women who worked fewer than forty hours a week were paid a lower basic hourly pay despite doing the same work as those who worked the full forty hours. The EAT accepted that the difference in pay was justified by the fact that part-timers contributed less to the business because their sewing machines lay idle when they were not at work.

EC law, with its more elastic definition of equality, has shown a greater sensitivity to the problems faced by part-time workers. Thus in *Jenkins* v. *Kingsgate*,[59] the ECJ specifically recognised the link between women's domestic responsibilities and their predominance among part-time workers. The Court was therefore prepared to mould Article 119 to incorporate the concept of 'indirect discrimination' (see Chapter 7), requiring equal hourly pay in cases in which it could be shown that considerably fewer women than men worked full-time. A similar analysis has been applied to the exclusion of part-timers from company pension schemes;[60] access to sick pay schemes;[61] and severance payments in cases of redundancy.[62]

The relative progress made at the first level has not been matched at the second level: differential access to overtime premia has instead proved to be a blind spot for the EqPA. *Capper Pass* v. *Lawton*[63] provides a good example. Although the EAT held that the woman's basic pay should be equal to that of the male comparator, a substantial pay disparity would remain because the men did 5.5 hours a week overtime. Phillips J declared (without substantiating evidence) that women had equal access to these payments, thereby ignoring the reality of women's relative inability to make use of such opportunities. It is true that this is less to do with the courts than with the equality principle: since the men were required to do overtime and the women were not, there could be no claim that likes were not being treated alike. Differential access to overtime cannot therefore be challenged. The

[57] *Dugdale* v. *Kraft Foods* [1977] ICR 48 (EAT); and see *Capper Pass* v. *Lawton* [1977] ICR 83 (EAT); *Electrolux* v. *Hutchinson* above n. 5.
[58] [1979] ICR 147 (EAT).     [59] [1981] ICR 592 (ECJ).
[60] *Bilka-Kaufhaus* 170/84 [1986] IRLR 317 (ECJ).
[61] *Rinner Kühn* 171/88 [1989] IRLR 493 (ECJ).
[62] *Kowalska* C-33/89 [1990] IRLR 447 (ECJ).
[63] *Capper Pass* v. *Lawton* [1977] ICR 83 (EAT).

courts have, however, stiffened this rigidity by rejecting the demand that when women do work unsocial hours they should be paid premium payments on a scale commensurate to men doing work of equal value. As we have seen, in *Calder* v. *Rowntree Mackintosh*[64] the all-female twilight shift (working between 5.30 and 10.30 p.m.) were given no premia for working unsocial hours, in contrast to shift workers doing work of equal value. The Court of Appeal, in a singularly circular argument, held that the difference in pay was justified by the difference between a rotating shift and a twilight shift. Such a justification is fundamentally gender-based, given the fact that the twilight shift was attractive only to women, probably because children could be taken care of for free by fathers, grandparents or other members of the family who would be at work during the day.

The inherent limitations in the concept of equality in addressing the ingrained bias towards male patterns of work were further highlighted by the ECJ in the recent case of *Helmig*,[65] which challenged one of the chief obstacles to equality for part-time workers, namely the lack of entitlement to overtime pay for time worked over and above part-time contractual hours. In rejecting a part-time worker's claim that overtime premia should be payable once she had exceeded her part-time contractual hours, the ECJ became enmeshed in the paradoxes of an equality approach, dependent as it is on the appropriate comparator. In this case, the ECJ compared a part-timer working overtime with a full-timer working the same number of hours within his or her ordinary contractual stint. In such a situation, the part-timer would, according to the ECJ, be paid more for doing the same number of hours. Therefore, according to this logic, upholding the claim would itself violate the principle of equal treatment. But this comparison ignores the substantive issues. Although the Court recognised that the function of overtime premia is to compensate workers for loss of leisure time and to deter employers from insisting on hours in excess of a worker's contractual hours, it did not see these issues as applying to part-time workers. Yet the personal cost to part-timers of working above their contractual hours is no less than that of full-time workers, especially since in all probability they have to make special child-care arrangements to cover the unexpected surplus. The relevant comparison should therefore have been between part-time workers doing more than their contractual hours and full-timers exceeding their contractual hours. Better still, it is arguable that the comparative approach should be dropped altogether, in favour of specific rights for part-time workers. Nor was the claim in *Helmig* outlandish: a significant minority of companies do in practice pay overtime immediately an employee has exceeded her or his contractual working hours.[66]

Equally complex is the attitude of the ECJ to cases in which a part-time worker is required to use her non-contractual time in order to obtain

---

[64] [1993] IRLR 212 (CA).     [65] [1995] IRLR (ECJ).
[66] Industrial Relations Services, above n. 54, p. 73.

training as a worker representative or to attend trade union meetings. In an important recognition of the right of part-timers to become involved in institutions of collective representation, the ECJ in *Bötel*[67] declared that it was indirectly discriminatory for German legislation to provide for only part-time pay for part-time workers attending full-time training courses as members of statutory Staff Committees. However, the Court very quickly retracted from the full vigour of this decision, holding in *Lewark*[68] that the difference in pay between full-time and part-time workers could well be justifiable on the grounds that it furthered German social policy of preserving the independence of Staff Committees from financial inducements (see further below).

The above discussion suggests that the fact that equality inevitably requires a comparison between two individuals or groups is itself one of the most fundamental problems with the concept in the context of pay. To what extent is this resolved by the more expansive notion of equality at the heart of the principle of indirect discrimination? The concept of indirect discrimination addresses situations in which equal treatment leads to unequal results. Where a requirement or condition is applied to both sexes, but in effect represents a greater hurdle to women than men, then this constitutes unlawful discrimination unless the requirement can be justified on grounds independent of gender (see Chapter 7). On the face of it, this constitutes a legal challenge which is not dependent on a woman showing that she has been less favourably treated than an appropriate male comparator. However, although more muted than in direct discrimination cases, the male norm in practice remains dominant. For a part-time worker to show that she has been the victim of indirect discrimination, she needs to prove that substantially fewer women than men can comply with the condition of full-time working. The central role of the male norm is clear, particularly in segregated occupations or work-places in which the large majority of both full-time and part-time workers are women. In such cases, part-time workers, however poorly paid, will remain without redress simply because most full-time workers are women.[69] This can be contrasted with the 1994 ILO Part-time Work Convention (No. 175), which entitles part-time workers to equal treatment with full-timers, rather than relying on a male–female comparison. Even more adventurous would be an approach based on specific rights for part-timers, independent of the rights of any relevant comparator group.

More fundamentally, the focus on equality prevents the law from addressing the underlying reasons why women congregate in part-time work. Neither Article 119 nor the EqPA demand a different distribution of child-care responsibilities, or better provision of nurseries and creches, or a

---

[67] Case C360/90 [1992] IRLR 423 (ECJ).
[68] Case C-457/93 [1997] IRLR 637 (ECJ)
[69] *Staffordshire County Council* v. *Black* [1995] IRLR 234 (EAT).

change in work expectations. The European Court in *Bilka*[70] explicitly renounced such a role, specifically rejecting the argument that Article 119 required employers to organise pension schemes to take account of the difficulties experienced by people with family responsibilities in meeting the conditions for entitlement. It is, of course, arguable that the problem of male working patterns is rooted so deeply in the division of labour between men and women in the home that it requires intervention well beyond equal pay legislation. However, a more sensitive approach within the legislative framework would at least make a start in the right direction.

(3) Men's Work; Women's Work: The third area in which the male norm continues to dog equal pay litigation is in the notion of 'women's work' or work in which women predominate and which tends to be low paid or of low status. As was seen in Chapter 3, 'women's work' is frequently similar to work which can be done unpaid in the home, such as cooking, cleaning and caring work, and is therefore systematically undervalued. Similarly, women's work is often devalued by stereotypical assumptions about their working capacity or their commitment to the labour market.

To what extent has the EqPA been able to challenge these assumptions? Certainly, the caselaw reflects some sensitivity to the issue. Phillips J in some of the early decisions warned tribunals against basing their judgments on their beliefs about suitable work for men and women.[71] In *Redland* v. *Harper*[72] the EAT rejected an attempt by the employer to avoid an equal pay claim by claiming that the only male clerical worker was a trainee manager. Particularly significant was the Court of Appeal decision in *Shields* v. *Coomes*,[73] where a male counterhand at a betting shop was paid more than his female colleague on the grounds that his presence was 'protective'. The court rejected this argument, recognising that the man's only qualification for performing a protective function was that he was a man.

However, notions of 'men's' and 'women's' work continue to influence judicial decisions.[74] The tenacity of such notions is particularly evident in relation to assumptions about the importance of 'light' or 'heavy' work. The Court of Appeal in *Noble* v. *David Gold*[75] held that women packers were not doing the same work as men packers because they were required to lift lighter boxes. The decisions contain disturbing echoes of notions of women as 'naturally' different. According to Lord Denning, the difference was not sex discrimination, but came about because of the different qualities of the two sexes. According to Lawton LJ: 'An Act of Parliament such as the SDA may try to change our attitudes towards each other but it cannot make a

---

[70] Above note 60; see also Case 184/83 *Hofmann* [1984] ECR 3047.
[71] *Capper Pass* v. *Lawton* [1976] IRLR 366.   [72] [1977] ICR 349 (EAT).
[73] [1978] ICR 1159 (CA).   [74] *Eaton* v. *Nuttall* [1977] ICR 272 (EAT).
[75] [1980] ICR 543 (CA).

woman behave like a man.'[76] What was not considered was why lifting heavier boxes should warrant higher pay.

It was not until the introduction of the right to claim equal pay for work of equal value that stereotypical classifications could come under serious fire. The revolutionary potential of this change is clear: most importantly because it asserts the right to override the determination of 'value' by the employer, and merely to undermine the male norm. This is clearly revealed in *Hayward* v. *Cammell Laird*,[77] in which a cook successfully claimed that her job was of equal value with a carpenter and a joiner in a shipyard. Thus a traditionally female job, classified as unskilled in the national collective agreement, was seen to be equal in value to skilled craftswork in traditionally male, well-unionised occupations. In more recent cases, domestic and catering assistants have claimed equal value with groundsmen and hospital porters; while clerical and sales staff have compared their work with male storekeepers and meter readers in the electricity supply industry.[78]

However, the equal value cases are far from immune from traditional assumptions. The requirement that the job be valued under various heads, including effort, skill and decision,[79] is not itself value-neutral: it is well known that characteristics of male jobs are more highly valued than those of female jobs. The law has gone some way towards addressing this problem: the EqPA recognises the possibility that the attribution of value might reflect assumptions based on the sex of the worker[80] and the Court of Appeal in *Bromley* v. *Quick*,[81] rejected the use of 'felt-fair' and 'paired comparison' systems on the grounds that these could simply reflect existing hierarchies. However, the courts both in the UK and the EC have stopped short of requiring a female rather than a male norm of comparison. This appears most clearly in *Rummler*,[82] which concerned a job classification system based on criteria of muscular effort and heaviness of work. The applicant directly challenged the male norm, by arguing that 'heavy' should be defined in relation to the female physique. The ECJ, in rejecting this argument, unrelentingly equated the male norm with objectivity. If the duties involved in the job 'by nature' required physical effort, the Court declared, it was consistent with the principle of non-discrimination to use a criterion based on 'objectively measurable' expenditure of effort. Comparison with a female norm would in itself be unlawful discrimination. Instead, equality was to be achieved by including other criteria based on qualities for which women workers had a 'natural' aptitude.

It is in collective bargaining that the real potential of equal value has been worked through. A particularly impressive collective bargaining achieve-

---

[76] At p. 551.
[77] (*Hayward* v. *Cammell Laird*) [1988] IRLR 257 (HL).
[78] EOR 58 (1994) p. 12.       [79] EqPA 1970, s. 1(2)(c) and s. 1(5).
[80] *ibid.*, ss. 2A(2) and (3).       [81] [1988] IRLR 251.
[82] Case 235/84 [1986] ECR 2101.

ment involved local authority manual workers, where a new rank order of jobs of about a million workers was completed in 1987, reflecting equal value principles. The new system of evaluation was carefully constructed to remove the inherent bias towards men in existing job evaluation systems. For example, 'skill' was extended from formal training and qualification, to include informal training and acquired experience. Similarly, under the heading 'working conditions', credit was given not just for the type of dirty work undertaken by male employees but also the kind of unpleasant conditions that caring workers, such as home helps, might have to work in. The result was a radical restructuring of the grading structure. Most notably, home helps moved from the middle of the structure to second from the top, while refuse collectors, whose collective bargaining strength had previously secured a relatively good position, moved down.[83]

However, even where equal value legislation has succeeded in piercing male status ascriptions, its progress is significantly hampered by the more slippery problem of merit payments. The growth in payment systems linked to assessments of individual performance is one of the biggest areas of change in pay over the past few years. Yet men tend to be the primary beneficiaries of such payment systems. Recent research demonstrates that in the private sector, reviews based on all-merit (rather than linked to cost of living rises) are twice as likely in male dominated than female dominated pay structures.[84] Moreover, larger budgets are allocated to all-merit reviews than merit rises paid on top of a cost of living rise.[85] In the public sector, performance related pay tends to exclude those sectors in which women are concentrated.[86] The result is that women receive significantly less by way of merit payments than men. For example in 1995, non-manual men received an average of £17.40 per week in incentive payments, over three times more than non-manual women.[87] This is of particular concern because incentive payments systems can undermine gains made by means of the concept of equal value. The seriousness of this problem is demonstrated by the experience in local government. Although basic pay was adjusted to reflect the new valuation scheme, no attempt was made to equalise access to productivity pay. The result is the startling fact that women on higher grades in the revamped local government pay scale still earn less than lower rated men.[88] For example, while the basic pay of predominantly female word processors is higher than that of male building labourers and refuse collectors, the latter have the potential to earn far more through bonus payments. Thus a word processor operator in a sample local authority

---

[83] For a fuller account, see S. Fredman and G. Morris, *The State as Employer* (Mansell, 1989), pp. 355–6.

[84] Industrial Relations Services, above n. 54, p. 42.

[85] *ibid.*, p. 43.     [86] *ibid.*, p. 51.

[87] NES 1995, Table A 1.1. This figure includes payments-by results, bonuses including profit-sharing and commission, and other incentive payments.

[88] Rubery, *The Economics of Equal Value* above n. 38, pp. 36–7.

could earn a maximum of £10,209 per annum whereas the maximum annual earnings of a refuse collector were £12,480.[89]

To what extent can equal pay legislation penetrate the male bias inherent in incentive payment schemes? The EAT's initial attitude to merit appraisal was one of strict scrutiny. Thus, in *National Vulcan* v. *Wade*,[90] it held that an appraisal scheme could only constitute a valid justification for different pay if it was unisex, jointly negotiated, fairly and reasonably operated and not left to the final determination of the employer. However, the Court of Appeal[91] was scathing in its criticism of this view. Instead, it was held that an appraisal scheme constituted a valid justification as long as it was genuine and not a pretext for concealing discrimination. The employer's previous history of paying women 85 per cent of the male rate was held to be irrelevant. EC law has been more penetrating, as evidenced in *Danfoss*.[92] The facts of the case are a dramatic illustration of the corrosive effect of merit payments on equality. Men and women on the same grade received equal basic pay, but basic pay was topped up by a system of individualised wage increases based on flexibility, vocational training, and seniority. The result of the system was that over a five year period, women in the grade earned on average nearly 7 per cent less than men. The Court held that where an appraisal scheme was based on quality of work and led to a pay discrepancy, a breach of Article 119 must inevitably have occurred. Since men and women have equal capabilities, an average differential in pay between men and women resulting from the appraisal could only be a pretext for discrimination. However, the Court was more lenient in its approach to other merit payments, such as those used to reward variable work schedules, job mobility and vocational training. Despite recognising that such payments could disadvantage women with children, the Court held that they were justifiable if the employer could show they were important for the performance of the specific duties of the worker. Since it is usually possible to demonstrate a link between such payments and the job in question, it is likely that the disparities based on merit payments of this sort will persist.

## c) **Individualism**

At all stages of an equal pay claim the focus on the individual is unwavering. The right to equal pay vests in an individual employee, who has the responsibility of bringing the complaint against her individual employer. The claim is based on a one-to-one comparison with an individual man employed by her employer in her own establishment or one with common terms and conditions. Finally, the remedy entails adjusting the individual contract of employment. This individualism was originally intended to

---

[89] Industrial Relations Services, above n. 54, p. 64.
[90] [1977] ICR 455 (EAT).
[91] [1978] ICR 800 (CA).    [92] C-109/88 [1989] IRLR 532 (ECJ).

operate as an ancillary to collective bargaining over pay. However, the strident neo-liberal ideology of the 1980s and 1990s asserts individualism both as a fundamental value and as a means to undermine collective strength. The Conservative government incessantly declared its preference for individualised pay setting, claiming that any other system simply impedes the proper functioning of the market. In practice, however, the effect is to shore up managerial prerogative in pay-setting, and seriously to weaken the effectiveness of equal pay legislation. International experience indicates that equal pay policies are far more effective when taken up by collective bargaining or other collective mechanisms for pay determination.[93]

This section considers three serious problems with the individualism of the equal pay laws. First, it sits uncomfortably with the fact that in reality payment structures cover groups rather than individuals. Secondly, it places an enormous burden on the individual, who not only has to initiate and finance litigation, but has to discover information in the sole preserve of the employer and weather any negative repercussions at work. Finally, adjudication on an individual basis creates substantial burdens on the tribunal and court system.

(i) *The Inter-connectedness of Pay*   Payment structures do not operate in a vacuum. Movement in one part of the structure inevitably affects the rest of the structure. Likewise any individual movement is constrained by pressures from other parts of the structure. Yet the equal pay laws focus only on a comparison between an individual man and woman employed by the same employer, usually at the same establishment. By ignoring the powerful influence of internal relativities, the Act has the potential to create disruptive anomalies. By ignoring external relativities, the Act seriously limits its own potential influence. European law has loosened the bounds of individualism to a degree, but its influence is still clearly felt.

(1) Internal Relativities: So far as internal relativities are concerned, the courts are haunted by the spectre of 'leapfrogging', or multiple consequential claims. A woman who has succeeded in claiming equal value with a man might trigger claims by another man in a different job and so on, thereby ratcheting up the whole payment structure. In *Hayward* v. *Cammell Laird*, for example, both the EAT and the Court of Appeal 'viewed with dismay the possibility of equality being achieved only by mutual enhancement . . . considering that mutual enhancement transcended the underlying philosophy of the Equal Pay Act and that it could have a profoundly inflationary effect.'[94] The House of Lords, although rejecting the argument in the case in hand, made it clear that the policy of avoiding leapfrogging

---

[93] ILO, p. 1.
[94] Per Lord Goff at [1988] IRLR 257 (HL), at pp. 262–3; see Popplewell J in [1986] ICR 862 (EAT); upheld by the Court of Appeal [1987] IRLR 186.

could be valid. Lord Goff stated specifically that the defence of justification would be available to prevent leapfrogging provided that there was no direct or indirect discrimination.

A different and potentially more serious manifestation of the courts' attempts to limit the ripple effects of individual claims is to confine comparisons to distinct payment structures within the establishment. Thus in *Reed* v. *Boozer*,[95] the applicant, despite being on the staff grade, earned significantly less per week than her male comparator, who was hourly paid. Although both were dispatch clerks, they had traditionally been represented by different unions and covered by different collective agreements. The employer argued that the difference in pay was justified because it arose solely out of the different pay structures. The industrial tribunal recognised that if such a justification were permitted, there would be no way to break through artificial barriers such as the difference between staff structures and hourly paid workers. The EAT, however, held that it was a valid defence to an equal pay claim to point to separate pay structures which did not discriminate internally on grounds of sex. This approach was reiterated by the EAT in *Enderby*,[96] in which speech therapists, who were predominantly female, claimed equal pay for work of equal value with the considerably better paid groups of pharmacists and clinical psychologists. The EAT accepted the employer's argument that the pay difference was due only to the fact that speech therapists' pay was negotiated in a different committee from that of the comparator groups, and that there was no prejudice to women within each bargaining committee. The EAT stressed that it was necessary for the efficient running of the business to have a stable collective bargaining structure which could not be challenged unless the bargaining process was clearly tainted by gender. This approach simply skates over the deep-seated nature of discrimination.[97] As was clear from Chapters 3 and 4, 'the practice of paying men and women according to different criteria is likely to have played a major part in the process by which these pay structures came to be established.'[98] In *Enderby* itself, the low rates of pay clearly reflected the traditional status of speech therapy as a 'woman's profession'. This was in part due to the availability of part-time work, which attracted women with family responsibilities, and in part to the fact that the pay was too low to attract men. In fact, an inquiry in 1972 established that the pay and career structure were glaringly out of proportion to the responsibilities of the job, and acted as a disincentive to recruitment, particularly of men.[99]

Fortunately, the ECJ has been more sensitive to the structural nature of pay discrimination. On the referral of *Enderby*,[100] the Court unequivocally

---

[95] [1988] IRLR 333 (EAT).     [96] [1991] IRLR 44 (EAT).
[97] Industrial Relations Services, above n. 54, p. 1.
[98] Rubery, *The Economics of Equal Value*, above n. 38, p. 32.
[99] S. Fredman [1994] 23 *Industrial Law Journal* 37.
[100] [1993] IRLR 591 (ECJ).

rejected the justification based on different collective bargaining processes, regarding it as irrelevant that there was no discrimination in either of the collective bargaining processes taken separately. This is an extremely valuable recognition of the causal link between structural discrimination and the pay gap. The ECJ's rejection of separate pay structures as a defence to equal pay claims has already had an impact in the electricity supply industry, in which female clerical workers have claimed equal pay with far better paid male manual workers.[101] It is only because women in non-manual pay structures could compare their work with manual grades that progress was achieved.

(2) External Relativities: The individualism of the EqPA is even more marked in respect of external relativities than it is for internal relativities. It is clear from empirical research that equal pay legislation can only be truly effective if it incorporates inter-firm adjustments. There are two main reasons for this.[102] First, pay levels for a particular occupation vary widely according to the type of firm. Secondly, an individual firm might find it financially impossible to implement higher pay for women unless competitors are required to do the same. Yet there is no mechanism either for inter-firm comparisons or for generalising the results of equal value claims across an industry. External relativities are expressly excluded from the scope of the EqPA by the provision requiring that comparisons be confined to an individual employer and usually to a single establishment.

The myopia of the EqPA has had particularly paradoxical results in the public sector. As we have seen, the government's ideological commitment to market forces found expression in a statutory obligation on local authorities to subject service provision to market discipline. Specified services, previously provided in-house, must be put out to tender and the contract awarded to the lowest bidder which may include the internal work-force (see further below).[103] This creates an immediate tension between internal and external relativities. Local authorities, with their tradition of collective bargaining, have better wage rates than outside contractors, particularly in female dominated sectors such as cleaning and catering. Women's position in local authorities has been further strengthened by the job evaluation mentioned earlier. Yet if the in-house labour force, the Direct Services Organisation (DSO) is to win the contract, pay levels must drop to those of outside contractors. In this situation, equal pay legislation ought to be capable of ensuring that the benefits of the job evaluation within local authorities are extended to poorly paid private sector workers. Instead it allows only internal comparisons, leaving the pay of outside competitors unregulated. The result is a no-win situation for the in-house labour groups: either they accept a drop in pay, or they claim their rights to equal

---

[101] EOR No. 58 (1994), p. 13.    [102] See Rubery, p. 53.
[103] See Local Government Planning and Land Act 1980, Local Government Act 1988, Local Government Act 1992, National Health Service and Community Care Act 1990.

pay at the cost of losing the contract and therefore their job. This problem was exemplified in *Ratcliffe* v. *North Yorkshire*.[104] In this case a local authority DSO cut the pay of its dinner ladies in order to compete with outside contractors paying subsistence wages. The dinner ladies claimed a breach of the EqPA. Focusing on internal relativities, the House of Lords held that the authority had a duty to pay the dinner ladies according to internal pay scales, determined by considerations of equal pay for work of equal value. However, the inevitable result of a successful claim was to put the DSO at a competitive disadvantage and risk the loss of the contract. The only solution is to require outside contractors to conform to the same standards, by permitting comparisons across different employers.

This problem is not confined to the public sector. It arises in all industries where sub-contracting is widespread. In many such industries, sub-contracting to specialist firms exacerbates job segregation, because individual firms are likely to specialise in job areas dominated by men or by women. For example, a cleaning sub-contractor is likely to employ only cleaners apart from a small managerial structure. The result is that the low paid cleaning workers, who are overwhelmingly women, have no opportunity to compare their pay with other cleaning workers, particularly those which have remained within the public sector. In fact, an employee of a sub-contractor might be working side by side in the same establishment with a local government employee doing work of equal value, but be unable to draw a comparison. In effect, then, any individual's right to equal pay is dependent on demarcations between employers which are beyond her control. Indeed, employers might be tempted to avoid the effects of the Act by increasing sub-contracting. It is not far-fetched to assume that this was one of the drives behind government policies to force local authorities and hospitals to contract out services which in fact are predominantly female.

The individualism of the Act extends beyond the limitation to the same employer: it insists that the comparison be confined to the same establishment. This acts as a serious brake on equal value comparisons in cases of job segregation within the same employment but at different establishments. Its effects are mitigated by the provision permitting a complainant to compare her pay to a man in a different establishment in limited circumstances. However, the provision is far from straightforward. Not only must the employer be the same or associated;[105] the complainant and her comparator must also be employed at establishments 'at which common terms and conditions of employment are observed either generally or for employees of the relevant classes'.[106] The obscurity of this formulation has resulted in complex and costly litigation with only minor gains. Possibly the

---

[104]    [1995] IRLR 439 (HL).

[105]    Two employers are associated if one is a company of which the other has control or if both are companies of which a third person has control: EqPA 1970, s. 1(6)(c).

[106]    *ibid.*, s. 1(6).

most effective use was in the local authority case of *Leverton* v. *Clwyd*,[107] which demonstrated clearly that the section can only yield intelligible results in cases of highly centralised collective bargaining. In that case, a nursery nurse working at a local authority nursery school, was, unsurprisingly, unable to find a suitable male comparator at her own highly segregated establishment. She therefore claimed equal pay with male clerical staff working at the town hall. The House of Lords, overturning the decisions of the industrial tribunal, the EAT and a majority of the Court of Appeal, held that inter-establishment comparisons could be drawn if the same terms and conditions were applicable in both establishments, the paradigm being a single collective agreement spanning both establishments. Comparison was permitted in this case, since local authority administrative, professional, technical and clerical staff (APT&C) formed a single bargaining group, which set terms and conditions for all local authority establishments. The result is to make some impact on job segregation by opening up the pathways of comparison between local authority workers employed at different sites, but who are covered by the same bargaining structure.

However, the advance *Leverton* represents is seriously weakened by rapid fragmentation of centralised bargaining. Problems arising from the trend towards devolving bargaining decisions to the level of the plant or establishment are clearly evidenced in the recent case of *British Coal* v. *Smith*.[108] In this case, an attempt was made to challenge the deeply gendered structure of the coal-mining industry, which had, until 1975, maintained separate pay scales for men and women, and which continues to operate an intense system of job segregation between low paid women workers and higher paid men.[109] Women canteen workers and cleaners found themselves at different establishments from the better paid male clerical workers and surface mineworkers with whom they claimed equal pay for work of equal value. Their claim therefore depended on being able to establish that 'common terms and conditions' were observed at the various establishments. It took a trip to the House of Lords[110] to obtain a favourable result, against a detailed and emphatic decision by the Court of Appeal. Lord Slynn's judgment includes a welcome attempt to rise above the intense technicality of the provision and achieve a result consistent with the spirit of the legislation. He rejected the contention that inter-establishment comparison could only occur if there was complete identity of terms and conditions for the comparator class as between the two relevant establishments (subject only to *de minimus* differences), on the grounds that so restrictive an approach could not have been intended. Instead, he held that the legislation was 'seeking to establish that the terms and conditions of the relevant class were sufficiently similar for a fair comparison to be made'.[111] The great advantage of such a view is

---

[107] [1989] IRLR 28 (HL).   [108] [1996] IRLR 404 (HL).
[109] Set out in [1994] IRLR 342 at pp. 345–7.
[110] *British Coal Corporation* v. *Smith* [1996] IRLR 404 (HL).   [111] At p. 408.

that the real weight of the dispute falls on the question of whether the employer can justify the difference, rather than excluding the case at this early and technical stage. This is certainly a positive development for women. However, the factual issue of whether common terms and conditions are in force remains closely tied to centralised bargaining. In this case, the factual question centred on whether local differences in access to concessionary coal and incentive payments made it impossible to argue that the employees were employed on common terms and conditions. The tribunal's decision in favour of the women depended largely on the ability to demonstrate that these payments were in fact regulated by the central collective agreement. In the many cases in which bargaining has genuinely devolved to local level, or indeed where no bargaining takes place at all, it may well be impossible to establish common terms and conditions under this provisions.[112]

(3) Amending Collective Agreements: A more effective strategy for dealing with the inter-connectedness of pay would be to move away from individualisation and permit direct adjudication over the collective agreement. It was only briefly that the EqPA contained an effective provision dealing with collective agreements. Under section 3, a collective agreement which contained explicit references to gender could be referred by a union to the Central Arbitration Committee (CAC) for amendment. If gender-based references were not removed by the date the Act came into force, then the minimum rate for men was deemed to apply to women as well. Unions, concerned in case men's minima might be 'levelled down' to those of women, were motivated to ensure that the new minimum rate be the men's. The resulting rise in the minimum rates for women had the important effect of changing relative pay rates, even over dissimilar jobs.[113] Indeed the fact that women's hourly pay rose from 64 per cent of that of men in 1971 to 74 per cent in 1977, can largely be attributed to amendments of collective agreements under section 3. However, the pervasive influence of notions of individualism combined with the desire to protect state neutrality meant that this gesture towards collectivism was half-hearted and its effectiveness short-lived. The CAC had no jurisdiction under the Act unless pay scales contained explicit references to gender: as soon as such references disappeared, it became impotent, even if an apparently neutral grade in fact masked overwhelming sex segregation. Moreover, the tool of raising women's minima to those of men was a clumsy one, ill-suited to fine-tuning complex collective agreements. As we have seen, the CAC's ambitious attempt to break out of these strictures was peremptorily terminated by the Divisional Court in *R* v. *CAC, ex p. Hy-Mac*.[114]

---

[112] See also *Scullard* v. *Knowles*, above n. 44, p. 14.
[113] Rubery, *The Economics of Equal Value* above n. 38, p. 8.
[114] Above n. 35.

More mileage can be got from EC law. The Equal Pay Directive explicitly requires that Member States make provision for declaring void or amending collective agreements which contravene Article 119. In infringement proceedings against the UK government, the ECJ held that the lack of such provision in UK law contravened Article 119.[115] However, relying on the absence of legal enforceability of collective agreements in the UK, the government acted to individualise this obligation to a point that it was no more than a token gesture. The SDA 1986 simply declared void any discriminatory term incorporated from a collective agreement into an individual contract of employment.[116] This left the burden squarely with the individual to insist on her rights, rather than using the far more effective mechanism of amending a collective agreement. It was only in 1993, under further pressure from the EC, that a mechanism was introduced whereby a discriminatory term in a collective agreement or rule could be directly challenged.[117] Even in its amended form, this provision remains intensely individualist: it is for the individual to complain to an industrial tribunal, which has the power merely to declare the term or rule to be void.[118] The far more effective remedy of amending the rule or agreement itself has been repeatedly used by the ECJ in caselaw from other countries. In the leading case of *Kowalska*, the ECJ specifically stated that Article 119 extends to all agreements which seek to regulate wage earning work collectively.[119] Equally importantly, it held that the remedy was collective: the term applying to full-time workers only should be applied pro rata to part-time workers. The Court expressly rejected the employers' argument that it was contrary to their autonomy for the ECJ to adjust their collective agreement. Real progress in the UK can only be expected if its EC commitments are more genuinely honoured.

ii) *The Burden on the Individual*   The second manifestation of the individualism of the Act is its reliance on individual complainants to enforce equal pay claims. This is extremely onerous for the applicant. Legal aid is not available for legal representation before industrial tribunals, nor are costs awarded to the successful party. As will be seen in Chapter 9, the process involves very high levels of stress in emotional and personal terms.[120] In particular, applicants find the tribunal system formal, intimidating, legalistic and slow.[121] In addition, institutional assistance for individuals is limited. Although the EOC has the power to assist test cases,[122] its

---

[115] *Commission of the European Communities* v. *UK* Case 165/82 [1984] ICR 192 (ECJ).
[116] SDA 1986, s. 6 and SDA 1975, s. 77.
[117] SDA 1986, s. 6(4B) as amended by TURER 1993, s. 32.
[118] SDA 1986 s. 6(4C).
[119] [1990] IRLR 447 (ECJ) at para 12.
[120] A. Leonard, *Judging Inequality: the effectiveness of the tribunal system in sex discrimination and equal pay cases* (London, Cobden Trust 1987); J. Gregory, *Trial by Ordeal* (HMSO, 1989); J. Gregory, *Dispensing Informal Justice* (EOC, 1993).
[121] Gregory (1993), above n. 120, p. 54.    [122] SDA 1975, s. 75.

resources are restricted. Trade union representation is of great value, but such support is not always forthcoming.[123] It is therefore not surprising that only a handful of equal pay cases are dealt with each year. The most active year was 1993–94, when a total of 780 equal pay cases were completed. But this was unusually high: only 240 were completed in 1992–93, and 418 in 1994–95. Even these figures are deceptive, since the vast majority of these cases did not reach a tribunal. Indeed, less than 6 per cent were determined by a tribunal from 1993 to 1995, and almost all the remainder were withdrawn. Even more depressing is the success rate. Of the twenty-five equal pay cases heard by tribunals in 1994–95 only eight were successful.[124] Given the huge pay disparities outlined earlier, a mere eight successfully adjudicated cases is a poor reflection on the EqPA. Nevertheless, it is heartening that the number of equal pay complaints referred to ACAS for conciliation more than doubled in 1995, rising from just 791 in 1994 to 1766 in 1995.

Some of the difficulties faced by applicants in discharging the burden of proof have been recognised by the courts. In *Danfoss*,[125] the ECJ was openly conscious of the difficulties to the applicant, particularly in cases in which it was impossible for an employee to know what criteria had been used in assigning her to a particular grade after an appraisal. In such cases, it was held, the complainant need only prove that the average pay of women on her grade was lower than that of men. The burden then shifted to the employer to show that the pay practice was not discriminatory. This approach was extended in *Enderby*,[126] where the Court declared that a pay disparity between two highly segregated jobs of equal value was sufficient to raise a prima facie case of sex discrimination. There was no need to show in addition that women were excluded by a particular condition or requirement. Again the Court's priorities were clear: 'Workers would be unable to enforce the principle of equal pay before national courts if evidence of a prima facie case of discrimination did not shift to the employer the onus of showing that the pay differential is not in fact discriminatory.'[127] This has been a particularly important development, in light of the fact that the proposed Directive on burden of proof in the area of equal pay and equal treatment for women and men has been blocked in the European Council from 1988 primarily due to the opposition of the UK.[128] The original Directive has now been withdrawn. Instead, the Commission has adopted a new draft directive on this issue under the social policy agreement, which sidesteps UK opposition. The draft directive gives legislative endorsement to ECJ caselaw, proposing that the burden of proof should revert to the

---

[123] See *Electrolux* v. *Hutchinson*, above n. 5.
[124] EOR No. 69 (1996), p. 26.
[125] *Danfoss*, above n. 92.
[126] *Enderby* v. *Frenchay Health Authority*, C-127/92 [1993] IRLR 591 (ECJ).
[127] *ibid.*, para 18.
[128] O C 176/88. For the 1996 draft burden of proof directive, see COM(96) 340 final.

employer as soon as the complainant has established less favourable treatment caused by apparent discrimination. This contrasts markedly with the stance of the UK courts, who, in a string of cases dealing with the burden of proof in discrimination claims, have rejected the notion of a shift in the evidential burden of proof once a prima facie case has been established. In a recent race discrimination case, the Court of Appeal, while recognising that it is unusual to find direct evidence of discrimination, concluded that it was unnecessary and unhelpful to introduce the concept of a shift in the evidential burden. Instead, if there is no adequate explanation for a difference in treatment, then 'it will be legitimate for the tribunal to infer' discrimination on grounds of race.[129] While the UK remains outside of the Social Chapter, this vague guidance will continue to hold sway. Nor do employers in practice appear to take their cue from EC law. Recent research shows that employers have not changed their practices to comply with the admonition in *Danfoss* that any appraisal system should be clearly understood by all involved and applied fairly and objectively. IRS found that few employers were aware of the *Danfoss* decision, and even fewer were acting upon it.[130]

iii) *The Burden on the Process of Litigation*   The third reason why individualism has been problematic is that a multiplicity of individual claims has proved impossible for tribunals to deal with rationally and efficiently. This problem was clearly illustrated in one of the earliest cases under the EqPA, namely *Electrolux* v. *Hutchinson*.[131] In this case, apart from the six applications before the EAT in the case itself, 122 were pending before other tribunals and a further 105 had intimated their intention to pursue claims. Phillips J was acutely aware even then that the process of individual litigation could not produce a coherent wage structure.[132] These difficulties, far from being addressed, have been compounded over the years, as evidenced in the very recent case of *British Coal* v. *Smith*.[133] Here a total of 1286 women in seven types of job brought claims based on 150 male comparators. Similarly, in 1994 alone North Yorkshire County Council found itself facing claims by 269 catering assistants and 280 cleaners.

Not only do cases of this type ignore the collective dimension at the cost of making nonsense of the final award, they also make it inevitable that the system becomes unwieldy and subject to unconscionable delays. In *British Coal*, the original claims were filed in December 1985; the House of Lords decision was delivered in May 1996. The EAT had pointed out in 1993 that by then only 215 applicants were still employed by British Coal. Even so,

---

[129] *King* v. *Great Britain–China Centre* [1991] IRLR 513 (CA).
[130] Industrial Relations Services, above n. 54, p. 41.
[131] Above n. 5.
[132] *Electrolux* v. *Hutchinson*, above n. 5, p. 259.
[133] [1994] IRLR 342 (CA).

only the preliminary point about the choice of comparator had been settled in 1996; the equal value report, were it to be ordered, would take at least five years to complete. Other cases have followed a similar pattern. *Enderby*,[134] which began in 1986 and went to the ECJ in 1993, was reconsidered by an industrial tribunal in December 1995 and only then referred to an independent expert to decide the equal value issue. In the meantim, legal costs incurred by the government and Frenchay Health Authority were approximately £400,000.[135] It is ten years since an independent expert was appointed to assess the claim of five hospital domestics, and the tribunal has yet to determine the equal value issue.[136] In the landmark case of *Pickstone* v. *Freemans*,[137] it took nine years for a tribunal to find that the women were employed on work of equal value, but the employer's appeal has yet to be heard. The courts have protested in a number of cases. Lord Slynn in *British Coal* v. *Smith* was scathing. 'It is clear that it defeats an essential purpose of the legislation if employees cannot enforce within a reasonable time such rights if any as they have to remedy inequality of remuneration.'[138] Both the EOC and the TUC have complained to the European Commission. However, apart from minor changes aimed at putting pressure on independent experts to complete their reports within reasonable time, the government has not responded. Instead, it has firmly rejected proposals to extend the results of individual claims to others doing like work and to appoint a full-time panel of experts. By mid-1996, despite consultations on reform, the only change which had been put in place was one permitting tribunals to proceed to decide an equal value case without referring to an independent expert.[139]

## d) **Market Forces**

The clash between the aims of equal pay legislation and market forces raises one of the most controversial issues in equal pay legislation. To what extent should equal pay be subordinated to market concerns? UK legislation has always permitted the employer to defend a difference in pay between a woman and a man on grounds unrelated to sex. According to section 1(3) of the Equal Pay Act, a difference in pay for equal work can be justified if the employer can prove that it is 'genuinely due to a material factor which is not the difference of sex'. The courts were soon confronted with the question of whether business needs or other market factors could constitute

---

[134] Above n. 126.
[135] EOR No. 66 (1996), p. 3. (The applicant's costs are not known.)
[136] *McAuley* v. *Eastern Health and Social Services Board*: see EOR No. 58 (1994), p. 12.
[137] Above n. 25.
[138] [1996] IRLR 414 at p. 405; and see also: *British Coal* [1993] IRLR 308; *Aldridge* v. *British Telecom* [1990] IRLR 10 (EAT) at p. 14.
[139] The Sex Discrimination and Equal Pay (Miscellaneous Amendments) Regulations 1996 SI No. 438; in force from 31 July 1996.

such a justification. In the early case of *Clay Cross* v. *Fletcher*,[140] an employer argued that he was justified in paying a male sales clerk more than a woman doing identical work, because the man had been paid more in his previous job. The EAT, in accepting this justification, was unable to see that it was simply perpetuating a deeply discriminatory market in which men could demand a higher price for their labour than women. The Court of Appeal, by contrast, was quite clear that extrinsic forces such as these were the very forces the Act intended to counter. According to Lord Denning, the statutory reference to a comparison between 'her case and his' meant that only personal factors should constitute valid justifications. Any other solution would be to render the Act a dead letter.

This appreciation did not, however, last long. It was at EC level that market forces were first permitted to enter into the justification defence. *Jenkins* v. *Kingsgate*[141] is best known for the very valuable recognition by the court that lower rates of pay for part-time workers constitute indirect discrimination against women. However, the same case explicitly endorsed a market forces defence. The ECJ was clearly concerned that the extension of Article 119 to include indirect discrimination could become too intensive. It thus limited the principle by holding that the employer would have a valid defence if it could be shown on economic grounds which could be objectively justified that lower pay for part-time workers was genuinely part of its business strategy.[142] Later cases have established that this defence is not confined to external market forces, but extends to internal factors, such as the employer's preference for full-time working,[143] the recognition of vocational training and seniority, and the creation of financial incentives for flexibility.[144] In these cases, the Court is clearly attempting to distinguish between sex discrimination and genuine business needs. Yet the distinction is far from clear cut. Indeed, as has been demonstrated above, discrimination may well be entirely functional to a business, whether by increasing profit margins, or by avoiding insolvency, or by placating male-dominated unions.

In partial recognition of the potential of such a defence to undermine equal pay the ECJ has insisted on a close fit between the discriminatory pay and the employer's professed business need. The test, first enunciated in *Bilka*,[145] requires an employer to show that the means chosen serve a real business need, are appropriate to achieve that objective and are necessary to that end. For example, in the case of premia for flexibility or vocational

---

[140] [1977] ICR 868 (EAT); (1979) ICR 1 (CA).
[141] [1981] ICR 592 (ECJ).
[142] Para. 12.
[143] *Jenkins* v. *Kingsgate* [1981] IRLR 228 (ECJ); *Bilka-Kaufhaus*, above n. 60.
[144] *Danfoss*, above n. 92, *Nimz* C-184/89 [1991] IRLR 222 (ECJ).
[145] Above n. 60.

training, the employer would need to prove that the extra pay was important for the performance of the specific duties of the worker. This has been adapted too for cases in which the discrimination derives from legislation or other social policy instruments. In such cases, the discriminatory impact can be justified if the means correspond to an objective necessary for social policy, and are appropriate and necessary to achieve that end.[146] This is clearly an advance on the weak standard espoused by earlier UK cases (see Chapter 8). However, the Court has left it to national courts to determine whether the defence has been made out, confining its own role to the rejection of mere generalisations such as that part-time workers are not integrated within an undertaking.[147] It is thus difficult to know what kind of defence will be accepted, and to what extent structural discrimination will thereby be legitimated.

UK law soon followed the ECJ in permitting market forces defences. In 1984 the section 1(3) defence was deliberately altered to permit non-personal, or market factors, to function as a defence in equal value claims. This was soon extended into like work claims. In *Rainey*,[148] the House of Lords held that the majority view in *Clay Cross* was unduly restrictive. In *Rainey*, as in *Clay Cross*, the court was concerned with the extent to which an employer may justify unequal pay for like work by reference to the 'going rate' which employees could demand in the market. The Greater Glasgow Health Board, in the course of setting up a prosthetic service, had found that it was impossible to fill all the advertised posts at the level of pay offered. Indeed, only women were prepared to accept the job at the rate on offer. In order to persuade the well organised and predominantly male private sector prosthetists to work for the authority, a deal was struck with the representative union by which the current private sector rate would be paid to this group only. The result was that the erstwhile private sector prosthetists, all but one of whom were men, were paid at a significantly higher rate than those who had applied in response to the initial advertisement, all of whom were women. When a woman complained that she was doing the same work as a man for lower pay, the House of Lords held that the disparity was justified by the inability to fill all the posts at the same level of pay. More generally, according to Lord Keith, in cases where there was no question of intentional sex discrimination, a difference connected with economic factors or administrative needs affecting the efficient running of the employers' business might well be relevant.[149]

The outcome of *Rainey* demonstrates the very fears expressed by Lord Denning in *Clay Cross*. No attempt was made to question why the higher paid group was almost entirely male, while the lower paid were all female.

[146] *Rinner Kühn*, above n. 61.
[147] *ibid.*
[148] *Rainey* v. *Greater Glasgow Health Board* [1987] IRLR 26 (HL).
[149] *ibid.*, p. 29.

Yet what the House of Lords regarded as mere coincidence was a clear manifestation of the fact that women's weak labour market status was being exploited to force down pay. The Council had clearly chosen to pay prosthetists on a scale which was below the external 'market rate'; and the women were in reality merely claiming to be paid at that rate. Instead of recognising this, the House of Lords suddenly switched from external to internal economic pressures. The court declared that because it would have been anomalous and inconvenient for the authority to set up a pay scale for prosthetists alone, there were sound and objectively justified administrative reasons for the decision to put prosthetists on the chosen Whitley Council pay scale. Lord Keith explicitly broadened the scope of the defence to include objectively justifiable grounds which were other than economic, such as administrative efficiency in a non-commercial concern. The result was to permit the employer to continue to exploit the fact that women are prepared to work at lower rates than men.

Two recent and far-reaching cases demonstrate both the corrosive effect of a market forces defence and a welcome glimmer of recognition by the House of Lords of the danger. In both cases, it is noteworthy that the EAT and Court of Appeal were quick to prioritise market forces over equal pay claims. By contrast, the industrial tribunal showed a greater sensitivity to the possibility that the market forces were themselves discriminatory, an approach which was helpfully endorsed by the House of Lords.

We have already touched on the first case, *North Yorkshire County Council* v. *Ratcliffe*,[150] which was concerned with the results of the government's policy of subjecting the public sector to 'market forces' by requiring local authorities to put out various services to tender. As we have seen, authorities can only keep the service in-house by forming a Direct Services Organisation (DSO) which competes for the tender. Unless the DSO wins the tender on commercial grounds, the service must be contracted out to the private sector.[151] In vulnerable and usually female dominated services such as catering and cleaning, the result has been to expose public employees to the fiercely competitive private sector market. Instead of respecting established terms and conditions under local authority collective bargaining, the process aggravates the 'race to the bottom' by encouraging both public and private sector employers to reduce pay and conditions to undercut competitors. This is frequently achieved not only by marginally lowering the basic rate, but also by eliminating pensions, overtime working and sick pay. In addition, national insurance payments can be avoided by more extensive use of part-time working.[152] Such a strategy is, of course, only possible because the overwhelming majority of employees are women whose domestic responsibilities give them little choice of employment. It is clear,

[150] Above n. 104.
[151] Local Government Act 1988 ss. 4 and 6.
[152] See Fredman and Morris, *The State as Employer* above n. 83, p. 443.

therefore, that 'market forces' themselves are fundamentally shaped by institutional discrimination against women.

In *Ratcliffe*, as we have seen, the DSO felt compelled to decrease pay below the collectively bargained rate in order to secure the contract against competition by private sector contractors which were not constrained by unions from paying poverty rates. The women affected claimed equal pay with colleagues employed in the same establishment whose work had been rated equivalent under the comprehensive local authority job evaluation scheme. In its defence, the authority argued that the difference in pay was justified by the need to compete with private contractors. The court was therefore faced directly with the question whether an appeal to market competition of this sort was an acceptable defence to an equal pay claim. Different answers were given at various levels. The industrial tribunal by a majority rejected the defence, recognising that the real reason behind the low wages in the 'market' was the fact that the labour force was 'virtually exclusively female, doing work which . . . but for the hours and times of work, that workforce would not be able to do . . . [and would] continue to do the work even at a reduced rate of pay when the alternative was no work . . .'.[153] The EAT and Court of Appeal, however, upheld the defence. The Court of Appeal in particular was unwilling to regard the market as discriminatory, and even more reluctant, if there was discrimination in the market, to use this against the Council. It was particularly impressed with the Council's argument that the alternative to decreasing pay in this fashion was redundancy. Ultimately, the House of Lords held that the tribunal had not erred in rejecting the employer's defence. The unanimous judgment contains a crucial acknowledgement that 'to reduce the women's wages below that of their male comparators was the very kind of discrimination in relation to pay which the Act sought to remove.'[154] The decision is all the more important in that it preserves the gains achieved by the local authority job evaluation undertaken in 1987 (see above).

Despite the progress made by the House of Lords, two major problems remain. The first is that, in holding merely that the tribunal had not erred, the House of Lords turned down the opportunity to make a general statement of the role of market forces defence in equal pay claims. The scope of the defence therefore remains dependent on the sensitivity of individual employment tribunals on a case by case basis. The second problem with the *Ratcliffe* case is a result of the limited nature of the Act itself. The case clearly illustrates the impotence of equal pay legislation which lacks the facility for inter-employer comparison. As was recognised at all levels in the courts, the authority was 'over the proverbial barrel'[155] because competitors were able to exploit the vulnerability of their female work-force in order to

---

[153] Cited in [1995] IRLR 441.
[154] Above n. 104, p. 443.
[155] *ibid.*

depress pay. The applicants therefore ran a serious risk that their equal pay claim would lead to loss of the DSO contract and corresponding redundancies. As argued above, however, the response should not be to permit the market forces defence, as the Court of Appeal advocated, but to insist that minimum standards apply throughout the industry. Indeed, the importance of minimum standards was recognised by the contractors themselves: in the early years of competitive tendering, the main trade association for the contract cleaning industry attempted to agree a voluntary set of minimum standards in the process of tendering for NHS contracts.[156] It saw this as a question of business efficiency, recognising that minimum standards were necessary to enable companies to recruit and retain staff of decent quality and still allow adequate profit margins. However, it proved impossible to maintain voluntary co-operation in opposition to government policy.

The strident assertion of the market forces defence by the Court of Appeal was similarly softened by the House of Lords in the highly significant case of *R* v. *Secretary of State for Employment, ex p. EOC*.[157] In this case, the EOC challenged legislation which required part-timers to work for five years before becoming entitled to redundancy payments or unfair dismissal compensation, whereas full-timers qualified after two. The government argued that the discriminatory effect was justified on the grounds that the employment opportunities of part-timers would be diminished by the imposition of additional burdens on employees. This was upheld by both the Divisional Court and by Hirst LJ in the Court of Appeal. However, the House of Lords rejected the attempted justification. Although their Lordships accepted that decreasing unemployment was a necessary aim of social policy, they held that the mere opinion of the Department of Employment did not constitute sufficient evidence to prove that the higher qualification threshold necessarily furthered this aim.[158] The courts' scepticism was soon proved to be well-founded. The result of equalising the eligibility criteria for part-time workers with those of full-time workers has certainly not been increased unemployment. To the contrary, the number of part-time jobs increased by 280,000, four times more than the previous year (1993–94).[159]

Ironically, the gradual recognition by the House of Lords of the potentially discriminatory nature of market forces arguments comes at the moment of retreat by the ECJ. Thus in the social security case of *Nolte*[160] the ECJ accepted that the exclusion of individuals on low pay working fewer than fifteen hours a week from the social security scheme was justified despite the fact that it excluded considerably more women than men. The

[156] Fredman and Morris, *The State as Employer* above n. 83, p. 443.
[157] [1991] IRLR 493 (DC); [1993] IRLR 10 (CA); [1994] IRLR 176 (HL).
[158] *Rinner Kühn*, above n. 61.
[159] EOR No. 68 (1996), p. 4.
[160] Case C-317/93 [1996] IRLR 225.

Court repeated its well-worn test, namely that a legislative measure could be justified where it reflects a legitimate social policy, and is appropriate and necessary to achieve that aim. However, the Court added that Member States should have a broad margin of discretion in choosing their social and employment policy. In this case, the social and policy aim was to foster part-time or minor employment. The Court readily held that this fulfilled its test.

This retreat was equally visible in the recent case of *Lewark*,[161] which concerned challenge of German legislation specifying that part-time employees who were staff committee members should be paid only up to the limit of their normal working hours for attending full-time training courses. The Court had no difficulty in holding that this constituted a prima facie case of indirect discrimination against women, since the vast majority of part-time workers were women, and full-time workers received full pay for attending the same training course. However, it was also quick to open the door to a wide defence of justification. The German government had argued that it was crucial to the independence of staff committees that members were honorary and unpaid, and therefore that the office should be placed beyond financial inducements. The role of compensation was merely to ensure that staff council members did not suffer loss of earnings for carrying out their duties. The Court accepted this as a legitimate social policy aim. Accordingly, if the measures chosen 'are appropriate to achieve that aim and are necessary in order to do so, the mere fact that the legislative provision affects more women than men cannot be regarded as a breach of Article 119'. The opposing social policy aim of ensuring that there was no significant deterrent to part-time workers from taking up the office of staff committee member was simply not addressed.

The caselaw examined above demonstrates that the courts are still unsure of the extent to which market forces should be permitted to deflect an equal pay claim. The glimmerings of recognition of the discrimination inherent in the market itself remain weak, and the potential for market forces arguments to undermine equal pay gains is still significant. In the face of such challenges, the case for prioritising equal pay needs to be reasserted. This debate is fully rehearsed in Chapter 9. For the present, it is worth noting that equal pay legislation is not necessarily inefficient. Employers who are permitted to cut labour costs are likely to be inefficient because they are not encouraged to find other means of improving productivity.[162] Ultimately, however, the case rests not on economics, but on social justice. As Rubery puts it:

The assumption that . . . the economy cannot afford equal value perhaps places too much emphasis on direct labour costs as the basis for competition and not sufficient

---

[161] Case C-457/93 [1997] IRLR 637 (ECJ).
[162] See also Rubery, *The Economics of Equal Value* above n. 38, pp. 75–6.

emphasis on the full development of human potential and productivity. Much of the argument that Britain cannot afford equal value in fact amounts to a statement that equal value can only be conceded once the economy has benefitted sufficiently from women accepting less than their wage work is worth.[163]

(C) PROTECTING PAY ON TRANSFER OF UNDERTAKING: THE ACQUIRED RIGHTS DIRECTIVE

A somewhat unexpected source of protection against declining pay for women comes in the form of the EC Acquired Rights Directive,[164] transcribed into UK law by the Transfer of Undertakings Regulations, known as TUPE.[165] The main effect of these provisions has been in cases of compulsory contracting out of public services, pursuant to the Conservative government's policy of introducing market pressures into the public sector.[166] Research has shown that the process of compulsory competitive tendering (CCT) has had a serious negative effect on women's pay and opportunities. A survey carried out by the EOC covering the period 1988 to 1993 found that as a result of CCT, there was a steep decline in employment, with female employment showing a more precipitous drop than men. Part-time workers bore the brunt of the fall. From the point of view of pay, the findings were dramatic: while male-dominated services have succeeded in improving both basic pay and additions, pay in female-dominated services has not generally improved and has even declined in some local authorities, particularly for part-time workers. All of the privatised contracts in the survey paid rates which were lower than the collectively agreed rates for the industry. Moreover, extra payments such as bonuses, overtime payments and unsocial hours payments for evening and weekend work were rarely paid to manual women workers.[167] A majority of contracts awarded in-house did stick to collectively bargained rates. But a significant minority (15 per cent) of DSOs which had succeeded in winning the contract, ignored the collectively bargained rates. Also contributing crucially to the reduction in pay was the fact that hours were diminished, particularly again for part-time workers. This effect, like the more direct factors, was felt more keenly by women than men. Thus the survey found that the hours worked by part-time workers in the female-dominated sectors of building cleaning and education catering were slashed. By contrast, there was no change in contractual hours of refuse collectors, in which male full-time workers predominate. The reduction in pay has had a particularly serious effect on part-time workers at the bottom end of the earnings scale. As a result of cuts in hours, premia and basic pay, many part-time workers

---

[163] *ibid.*, pp. 75–6.    [164] Directive 77/187 EC.
[165] Transfer of Undertakings (Protection of Employment) Regulations SI 1981/1794.
[166] See Local Government Planning and Land Act 1980, Local Government Act 1988, Local Government Act 1992, National Health Service and Community Care Act 1990.
[167] The figures in this section are taken from K. Escott and D. Whitfield *The Gender Impact of CCT in Local Government* (EOC, 1995).

saw their pay slip below the lower earnings limit,[168] thus excluding them from all the benefits of the national insurance system, including maternity pay, statutory sick pay, unemployment benefit and state pensions. Although no precise data could be obtained within the survey, there was clear evidence that some DSOs and private contractors, particularly in catering and cleaning, deliberately sought to keep women's wages below this threshold in order to avoid paying employer contributions. The picture of low pay and vulnerability is compounded by the growth in temporary workers. Again, the female-dominated services showed a particularly marked growth in workers employed on temporary contracts. Temporary work is not only uncertain and insecure, but frequently falls outside of the net of employment protection rights such as redundancy compensation and unfair dismissal. Nor has this pattern stabilised. Under the Local Government Act 1992, CCT is being extended into white collar and professional services. About 80 per cent of women's jobs thus pulled into the CCT web are administrative and clerical jobs in which, at present, pay rates are often well above those in private services. The competitive pressures of the outside market are bound to force down pay in this area. By contrast, many of the male jobs are in professional and technical services which are often higher in the private than in the public sector.

As we have seen, the EqPA and even Article 119 have been unable to challenge such reductions because comparisons are restricted to employees employed by the same employer. Indeed, the *Ratcliffe* case demonstrated that the best that can be achieved by the EqPA is to insist that a DSO adheres to collectively bargained rates. But because these strictures do not apply to private contractors, the only result is to risk the loss of the contract altogether. If the DSO is outbid by a private contractor, pay rates fall in any case and nothing is gained. A more promising protection is provided by the EC Acquired Rights Directive,[169] which aims to protect the pay and conditions of workers whose jobs are transferred to a different employer in the course of a transfer of the undertaking. The key substantive provisions of the Directive have the effect of transferring the contract of employment of an employee employed by the pre-transfer employer to the post-transfer employer, and with it all the rights, powers, duties and liabilities of the transferor under that contract. The effect of this, in a CCT context, should therefore be that not only must the contractor take on the employees of the public body, but the pay and conditions already applicable should continue to apply, thereby preventing an invidious race to the bottom.[170] However, the UK government was palpably reluctant to allow the Directive to undermine its ideologically driven CCT programme. Therefore, in transcribing the Directive into UK law, it inserted a caveat preventing these provisions

---

[168] £57 per week in 1994–95.
[169] Directive 77/187/EEC.
[170] H. Collins 'CCT, Equal Pay and Market Forces' [1994] ILJ 341.

from applying to transfers in the 'nature of a commercial venture'. It was thus widely assumed that contracting out by central and local government was not covered,[171] and that there was no protection against the relentless downward pressure on pay and conditions caused by the CCT process. Fortunately, the ECJ and the European Commission were determined to correct this deficiency, culminating in an ECJ decision which, *inter alia*, found the non-commercial exclusion to be an unlawful contravention of the Directive.[172] In fact, by the time of this decision, the government had already conceded the point, and the restriction was removed in 1993.[173]

The effects of the applicability to CCT of the protection afforded by TUPE are only just beginning to filter through the system and it is thus too early fully to appraise them. The provisions certainly have the potential to underpin wages in the CCT process. This potential could be significantly constrained by the fact that the Directive, like equal pay legislation, ultimately defers to economic concerns. Thus Article 4(1) states that, although the transfer itself cannot constitute grounds for dismissal, the provisions shall 'not stand in the way of dismissals that may take place for economic, technical or organisational reasons entailing changes in the workforce'. However, the ECJ has taken a robust view. In cases of dismissal just prior to a transfer, it will easily infer that the reason is the transfer. Equally helpful has been the view that a decision to decrease terms and conditions after the transfer cannot be justified on the grounds that it has taken place for economic or similar reasons. Nor is an alteration justified on the grounds that the employees have consented.[174] The result is that Collins may well be correct to argue that 'the equal pay principle is unlikely to place any significant constraint on the race to the bottom initiated by CCT. The most powerful legal control remains the Acquired Rights Directive.'[175]

## II.  ADDRESSING LOW PAY: A MINIMUM WAGE STRATEGY

The second and more wide-ranging alternative to the equality principle is a minimum wage strategy. This would fill some of the crucial gaps left by equality legislation. Instead of requiring only consistent treatment, minimum wages legislation sets substantive standards, standards which are independent of the male comparator. Low paid women therefore benefit, regardless of job segregation or generally low pay levels in their occupation. Moreover, a minimum wage which is enforced centrally by government

---

[171] Napier, *CCT, Market Testing and Employment Rights* (Institute of Employment Rights, 1993), pp. 4–5.

[172] *Commission* v. *UK* Case C-382/92 and C-383/92.

[173] Trade Union Reform and Employee Relations Act 1993, s. 33.

[174] *Wilson* v. *St Helen's Borough Council* [1996] IRLR 320 (EAT); and see *Daddy's Dance Hall* Case 324/86 [1988] IRLR 315 (ECJ); *Rask* Case C-209/91 [1993] IRLR 133 (ECJ).

[175] Collins, above n. 170.

inspectors makes it possible for women on low incomes and who lack trade union support to ensure that their rights are respected without having to bring costly and complex individual claims to employment tribunals. A minimum wage can thus reach into areas untouched by equality legislation. However, a minimum wage is only as good as the legislation which creates it. If it is set at too low a level or not properly policed, it could be counterproductive. Indeed, the experience of minimum wages legislation in the UK is ambiguous in the extreme.

This section examines the operation and impact of minimum wages legislation as it existed in the UK until its abolition in 1993.[176] Although the reason for abolition was the neo-liberal view that all minimum wage legislation is an unwarranted interference with the market, the traditional machinery can also be criticised by advocates of a minimum wage. Some of the fundamental flaws of the wages council system are set out below. The section concludes by considering more general arguments for and against a national minimum wage.

## (A) MINIMUM WAGES IN THE UK

There were two defining characteristics of minimum wages machinery in the UK, from its inception in 1909[177] to its abolition in 1993. The first was its selective nature. Instead of prescribing a floor to wages in the economy as a whole, it was targeted at selected categories of workers considered to be particularly vulnerable to low pay. The second was the attempt to use the machinery to stimulate collective bargaining. On the assumption that inadequate collective bargaining machinery was the main cause of low pay, minimum wage-fixing machinery was structured in such a way as to mirror a bargaining situation, in the hope of encouraging autonomous collective regulation. Minimum wage-fixing machinery therefore took the form of 'wages councils', originally trade boards, which were established in selected industries and consisted of employer and employee representatives together with independent persons. Councils had the power to lay down minimum levels of pay and other terms of employment for the employees within their jurisdiction. Built into the legislative structure too was the power to abolish particular wages councils when adequate collective regulation existed. The system of wages councils, having undergone several waves of expansion and contraction, covered 2.75 million workers in 1985. Wages councils have always served a predominantly female constituency: in 1992, as many as 80 per cent of wages council workers were women.[178] Among these were significant numbers of black and ethnic minority women, lone parents and wives of unemployed men.[179] Ethnic minorities of both genders were over-

---

[176] TURER 1993, s. 35.
[177] Trade Boards Act 1909, see Chapter 2.
[178] Low Pay Unit *The New Review* No. 19 (Dec 92/Jan 93, p. 13)
[179] EOC Briefing Paper *Wages Councils and Low Pay* (1992).

represented in some of the biggest wages council sectors, namely hotels and catering, and retailing.

Since 1980, however, the principles informing the wages councils system have been abandoned. The Conservative government in power from 1979 to May 1997 took the view that wages councils, far from alleviating poverty, in fact cause poverty by pricing workers out of jobs. Wages councils, on this view, 'interfere with the freedom of employers to offer and' job seekers to accept jobs at wages which would otherwise be acceptable'.[180] In pursuance of this policy, the Conservative government deratified ILO Convention No.26, which requires the creation or maintenance of minimum wage fixing machinery. It then passed the Wages Act 1986, which removed all minimum wage protection from workers under 21, prevented the establishment of new wages councils, and limited the powers of existing wages councils to setting a single minimum basic rate and a single overtime rate for all the workers within their jurisdiction. Such restrictions were, however, merely a precursor to outright abolition. The twenty-six remaining wages councils were abolished unceremoniously in 1993. The UK is now the only EU country with no minimum wage-setting machinery outside of agriculture.

While some system of minimum wage regulation is better than nothing, it is nevertheless important to point to the weaknesses of the wages councils system as it existed until 1993. Four major drawbacks are worth mentioning. First, the selectivity of the wages council system meant that inevitably, significant pockets of low pay remained unregulated. It is estimated that 37 per cent of women in non-wages council industries were low paid.[181] Nor was the system adapted to reach new areas of low pay: 'new sweated trades' such as contract cleaning were never included. The problem was exacerbated by the industry basis of wages councils, ignoring the fact that many occupations are low paid across different industries. At the same time, the system was not easily adapted to span different industries. The only attempt to address a low paid occupation across different industries was in the form of the Industrial and Staff Canteens Wages Council, which covered canteen workers, including 'tea ladies' employed in offices and factories throughout industry. But although this captured wider areas of low pay than industry based wages councils, it was clumsy to operate, covering a small proportion of each establishment's labour force, widely dispersed in small units through industry. Policing was exceptionally difficult: there were at least 24,300 establishments employing over 200,000 workers within the scope of this Council.[182]

The second problem with the wages council system was that it assumed that low pay was a temporary problem which needed only a transitional

[180] Department of Employment Consultative Paper on Wages Councils (1985), para. 7.

[181] S. Dex, S. Lissenburgh and M. Taylor, *Women and Low Pay* (EOC, 1994), p. 71.

[182] Craig et al, *Labour Market Structure* above n. 27, pp. 35–6.

remedy. Wages councils were designed to be abolished once they had achieved their aim, which was the removal of low pay by the establishment of effective collective bargaining machinery. However, even with abolition, this aim was rarely, if ever, achieved. In a fascinating study of the effect of abolition on wages and collective bargaining in six selected industries, Craig *et al* found that low pay and inadequate systems of collective bargaining persisted.[183] This is clear evidence that the problem of low pay requires a permanent protective mechanism.

The third problem with the wages councils system was its dependence on effective policing by the Wages Inspectorate. Although State enforcement is potentially more effective than individual complaints-led litigation, in practice, the system of inspection is only as good as the political will behind it. The absence of a true commitment to the wages council system led the Conservative government during the 1980s and 1990s to squeeze the resources available to the Wages Inspectorate to such a degree that it was in effect giving the signal to employers that underpayment was acceptable. In 1990, for example, 5,205 firms were found to be underpaying workers, but only seven were prosecuted.[184] The Low Pay Unit estimates that in the last years of the operation of wages councils, as many as 250,000 women in the eight main wages councils industries earned less than the legal minimum hourly rate.[185]

Finally, the wages council system was itself not free of gender bias. Prior to the EqPA 1970, wages councils followed the common practice of establishing a skill-graded structure for men, but a separate grade for women which made no distinction for women's differential skills.[186] Although the pretext for this practice was that any differentiation would cause resentment among women workers, the real effect was to reinforce, not only unequal treatment of women, but the refusal to recognise women's skills through the payment system. The practice of establishing a separate undifferentiated grade for women was discontinued after the EqPA came into force; but the absence of recognition of women's skills has had lasting effects. Nor did a unisex rate necessarily eliminate discrimination: because wages councils could only set a minimum rate, employers could continue to pay more to men than to women for work of equal value, as long as both sexes were paid above the minimum rate. Inequalities of this sort persist in respect of Agricultural Wages Boards. In 1993, for example, the Agricultural Wages Order continued to provide worse conditions for part-time than full-time workers.[187]

Nevertheless, the wages council system did have some important benefits, suggesting that a more comprehensive and properly policed system

---

[183] Craig et al, above n. 27, p. 63.
[184] Dex, Lissenburgh and Taylor, above n. 181, p. 29.
[185] Low Pay Unit, *More Crime and still no Punishment* (1992).
[186] Craig et al, above n. 27, p. 84.
[187] EOR No. 65 (1996), p. 28.

could make a real difference to the problem of low pay in women. Two important benefits may be noted. First, the gender pay gap in wages councils industries was significantly narrower than the figure for industry as a whole. In 1992, full-time manual women's average hourly earnings in wages councils industries stood at 81.3 per cent of those of men. The corresponding figure for industry as a whole was 71.5 per cent.[188] Although this is in part due to the fact that the men in the relevant industries were also low paid, it indicates that a comprehensive minimum wage could have direct effects on the pay gap. This view is supported by clear evidence showing that the dramatic decline in the level of the minimum wage relative to the average wage during the 1980s significantly contributed to the widening wage dispersion in that decade.[189] The second benefit of wages councils is that they did operate effectively to prevent wages falling to unacceptable lows. Craig *et al*, investigating the abolition of six wages councils in the 1970s, found considerable evidence of a deterioration in pay and conditions of a minority of workers, particularly those on the lowest grades and lowest levels of pay. Most of those who were underpaid post abolition were women, with part-time women workers most at risk, and in many cases pay was particularly low, at as little as two-thirds of the minimum rate.[190] Worse was predicted for the full-scale abolition of wages councils in 1993. The Low Pay Unit in 1994 reported that within a year of abolition, there was mounting evidence of dramatic falls in pay in former wages council sectors. A survey of vacancies in April and May 1994 showed that 36.5 per cent of businesses in the main wages council sectors were offering jobs at rates of pay below the Low Pay Unit's 'Minimum Rate Assessment', which was calculated by uprating the old wages council rates by the Retail Price Index. This was particularly problematic in the retail trade, where over one-half of jobs advertised were below the minimum rate assessment and as many as one-quarter were below even the old wages council rate.[191] This evidence is born out by statistics from the New Earnings Survey which suggests relative wage falls after abolition.[192] However, it is possible that the decline in wages may be less dramatic for the simple reason that widespread underpayment has been permitted by the government for many years.[193]

(B) The Case for a National Minimum Wage

Given the dominance of women among the low paid in society, it seems clear that a comprehensive minimum wage would be an essential plank in

[188] Low Pay Unit, *The New Review* Dec 92/Jan 93, p. 9.

[189] S. Machin and A. Manning 'The Effects of Minimum Wages on Wage dispersion and Employment', *Industrial and Labor Relations Review* (1994) Vol. 47, No. 2, pp. 319–29.

[190] Craig et al, above n. 27, pp. 54–5, 63.

[191] Low Pay Unit, *The New Review* No. 29 (Sept/Oct 1994), pp. 4–5.

[192] R. Dickens, S. Machin, A. Manning and D. Wilkinson 'What Happened to Wages and Employment after the abolition of minimum wages in Britain' (March 1995). Centre for Economic Performance, Unpublished.     [193] Dex et al, above n. 181, p. 88.

any agenda for reform. Such a proposal does, however, need to address the wide-ranging opposing arguments endlessly reiterated by policy-makers in the present neo-liberal climate. Four main reasons are put forward for rejecting a minimum wage. The first is that a minimum wage would simply price workers out of jobs, increasing unemployment and leading to a deterioration in the overall welfare. The second is that minimum wages do not in any event alleviate poverty, since most low paid workers do not come from poor households. Thirdly, it is argued that minimum wages are inflationary and finally that they prevent the UK from competing effectively in global markets. However, there are cogent arguments against all of these propositions, each of which will be dealt with in turn.

The argument from the 'unemployment effect' is based on the assumption that low pay is simply the true market valuation of a worker's low efficiency, productivity or value. On this argument, a statutory minimum wage forces employers to overpay such workers, thereby causing inefficiency and eventually the loss of the job. In fact, however, low pay is caused by a variety of institutional factors largely unrelated to the quality of the worker herself. Many low paid workers are members of disadvantaged groups in society, including women and ethnic minorities, who have little bargaining power. For women in particular, the constraints of child-care leave few choices, facilitating underpayment relative to value. Nor is it necessarily possible for a worker to find a job that reflects her real levels of productivity: skills are often non-transferrable as between jobs, and internal labour markets are frequently impenetrable to outsiders. As a result, as Craig et al demonstrate, low paid workers are frequently more efficient than their pay reflects. 'Low paid labour would not present such a major advantage to firms if the workers employed were of low quality or efficiency.'[194] Nor is it clear that an obligation to pay a minimum rate would simply drive employers of low paid workers out of business. Some employers could absorb the extra costs: the research of Craig et al demonstrated that in many 'primary sector' firms the availability of labour at low rates of pay was the major determinant of low wages rather than constraints on the firms' ability to pay.[195] Those who cannot absorb the cost may well be unable to justify their continued existence. To permit employers to depend for their existence on extremely low levels of pay is in fact to licence inefficiency, by easing the pressure on firms to replace out of date equipment and improve their management techniques.[196] Such employers are simply being subsidised by efficient and productive firms. It is noteworthy that in at least three of the six sectors examined by Craig et al, the employers actively opposed

---

[194] Craig et al, above n. 27, p. 76.
[195] ibid., pp. 73–4.
[196] S. Deakin, J. Michie and F. Wilkinson, *Inflation, Employment, Wage-bargaining and the Law* (Institute of Employment Rights, 1992), p. 9.

abolition of the wages council.[197] Similarly, the 1988 consultation exercise on the future of wages councils revealed a high level of support for their retention by employers.

These arguments from principle are supported by empirical evidence which disproves any close correlation between minimum wages and increased unemployment. Machin and Manning demonstrate that there is no evidence that wages councils acted as a restraint on employment in Britain in the 1980s: indeed, the data are more consistent with a positive effect on employment.[198] In similar vein, Dickens *et al* examined the proposition that the removal of wages council minimum wages would have beneficial employment effects. They found that to the contrary, abolition actually reduced the share of jobs in ex-wages council sectors, with women experiencing a more pronounced drop than men. In particular, retail distribution and hotels and catering experienced a net loss of 18,000 jobs between September 1993 and March 1994.[199] Instead, where higher wages were on offer, there were found to be more job opportunities.[200] Similarly, in the US where the federal minimum wage was significantly increased at the start of the 1990s after a decade of stagnation no negative effects on employment have been found.[201]

The second major argument used against a national minimum wage is that it has no effect on poverty. A central part of the government's case for abolition was that 80 per cent of workers in wages council industries lived in households containing at least one other earner, the implication being that these are therefore not low income households. In an explicit reversion to what should by now be a discredited view that women's earnings are merely pin-money, the 1988 Consultation Document states that wages councils should be abolished because, *inter alia*, 'most workers in Wages Councils trades are part-timers, many of them contributing a second income to the home.'[202] In fact, Dickens *et al* demonstrate that those workers who used to be paid at the minimum wages council rate and are therefore likely to suffer most as a result of abolition are also the most dependent on their own pay for their total family income.[203] Moreover, it is misleading to portray women workers as second earners: some of the poorest working households in the country are headed by women who tend to work in wages council industries. In 1990, 20.3 per cent of single parents in work were employed in wages councils industries, compared with 13.8 per cent of the general population. As Dickens *et al* point out, any reduction in

---

[197] Craig et al, above n. 27, p. 38.
[198] Machin and Manning, above n. 189, p. 326.
[199] Low Pay Unit, *The New Review* No. 29 Newsbrief, p. 4.
[200] Dickens et al, above n. 192.
[201] See Machin and Manning, above n. 189.
[202] Department of Employment Consultation Paper on Wages Councils (1988), paragraph 17.
[203] Dickens et al, above n. 192, p. 522.

earnings following abolition is likely to drive some of these workers into dependence on state benefits, which in itself increases government expenditure.[204] Finally, whether or not a low paid worker lives in a poor household, her low lifetime earnings will condemn her to poverty in old age, low earnings being the main cause of women's inadequate pensions (see Chapter 8).

A third argument used against a national minimum wage is that it would be inflationary. This assumes that differentials will be restored at least partially all the way up the hierarchy. However, this is unlikely to occur in any significant sense. Many low paid workers are concentrated in particular sectors on pay structures which have no connection with higher paid groups. Where there is some knock-on effect, it has been estimated to add no more than 2 per cent to the overall pay bill. In a recent survey of 527 firms, nearly two-thirds declared that a minimum wage (set at one-half average earnings) would not increase their organisation's pay bill; and the CBI estimates that a minimum wage at that level would add only 1.2 per cent to the total wage bill.[205] It is quite possible that improvements in productivity would more than compensate.

The final argument against a minimum wage is more global: that Britain can only maintain its international competitiveness by emulating low wage economies which appear to have flourished in recent decades. On this argument, Britain must follow the downward spiral in pay levels if it is to price British goods back into the international market. The evidence does not bear this out. Despite concerted efforts on the part of the government to drive down pay, the last two decades have witnessed a dramatic reversal of the balance of trade, from a surplus inherited from the previous government into chronic deficit. British goods are less competitive than those of Germany, which operates a high wage economy. This argument also ignores the fact that by increasing the pay of those at the top of the ladder at the expense of those at the bottom, the government has encouraged the spending preferences of the relatively better off, who tend to consume a higher proportion of imported goods, thus reducing domestic demand and worsening the balance of trade deficit.[206] Pay thresholds for those at the bottom of the pile would in themselves encourage spending, more probably on local goods and services. It would also substantially relieve the social security budget, allowing people to attain the self-respect of earning their own pay rather than relying on benefit. It is worth adding that Taiwan and Korea have both recently introduced non-negotiable minimum rates.

There are also good arguments in favour of a minimum wage. The strongest arguments are based on equity: there is no reason why the poorest in society should subsidise inefficient employers or indeed society as a

---

[204] Dickens et al, above n. 192, pp. 520–1.
[205] Low Pay Unir, above n. 1991, p. 11.
[206] Deakin et al, above n. 196, p. 9.

whole. The gap between the richest and poorest in British society has widened dramatically since 1979. As Deakin, Michie and Wilkinson demonstrate, average earnings increased by 190 per cent between 1979 and 1990, while the low paid saw their earnings rise by only 140 per cent. Since much of this difference can be accounted for by public policies such as the contracting out of services, they argue, 'this fifty percentage point difference can be regarded as a levy on the lowest paid which allowed public services to be maintained at lower real costs and/or contributed to the profits of privatisation.'[207] As we have seen, there are also strong arguments in favour of setting a floor to wages as a mechanism for enhancing labour market efficiency.

So far as women are concerned, it is clear that a statutory minimum wage will have an important impact on pay inequalities between men and women. EOC estimates show that women would comprise about three-quarters of those who would benefit from a statutory minimum wage. Such a threshold right would be particularly important in providing minimum standards for those workers for whom equal pay legislation is least effective, namely full-time ethnic minority women, homeworkers and part-time workers. The experience of other European countries is instructive. Although in all EC countries women run a greater risk of low pay than men,[208] figures based on 1980s data show that the UK had the highest proportion of low pay among women, with 20 per cent of employed women earning beneath the threshold (defined for these purposes as two-thirds of the median earning of all workers). It is striking that the countries with the lowest number of low paid workers were also the countries with minimum wage legislation. The fact that minimum wage legislation is not in itself sufficient is, however, demonstrated by Spain which, despite such legislation, came second only to the UK in the extent of low pay among employed women. Thus, as Dex *et al* point out, it is necessary to know the levels at which minimum wages are set, rather than just their existence, in order to ascertain their impact on low pay in women.[209] In addition, enforcement mechanisms are crucial. It seems clear that individual complaints should go hand in hand with an effective inspectorate, augmented by giving trade unions and other pressure groups the power to initiate proceedings on behalf of whole groups of underpaid workers.[210]

## III. REFORM

It has been seen that equal pay legislation is severely limited by its continued adherence to the problematic concepts identified in Chapter 1. In

---

[207] *ibid.*, p. 31.
[208] Dex et al, above n. 181, p. 19.
[209] *ibid.*, p. 17.
[210] For a description of the Italian system see Wedderburn [1995] ILJ 251.

particular, it is based on a notion of state neutrality which prevents decisive intervention; it uses a concept of equality which lacks substance and is tied instead to a male norm; it is highly individualistic; and it is deferent to economic and business needs. Any attempt at reform needs to overcome these limitations. Equally important is the need to shape the legal system to address the specific causes of women's disadvantage in the labour force. Characterisation of the question in these terms immediately suggests that reform must be multi-faceted. Legislation broaching the issue of pay alone will have no more than marginal impact without policies encouraging changes in the division of labour within the family (see Chapter 5), in the education and training system and in access to employment and promotion (see Chapter 7). The analysis in this section must therefore be closely tied into the rest of the book, particularly the discussion in Chapters 5 and 8.

(A) Pay Equity in Ontario

Several other jurisdictions have instituted adventurous pay equity pro-grammes which attempt to surmount some of the difficulties identified above. Possibly the most far-reaching is that of the Canadian province of Ontario.[211] The Ontario Pay Equity Act of 1987 consciously aims to correct some of the central weaknesses of equal pay legislation identified above. Thus the stance of state neutrality is abandoned, so much so that opp-onents of pay equity claimed that 'the long arm of Government will be reaching too far into the private sector'.[212] Rather than deferring to em-ployer autonomy in wage setting, the Act places a positive duty on employ-ers 'to establish and maintain compensation practices that provide for pay equity in every establishment of the employer'.[213] The initiative is thereby placed squarely in the employer's hands: each employer, whether in the public or private sector,[214] must create a plan to achieve pay equity for men and women employees. To this end, a gender neutral job evaluation study must be conducted comparing female-dominated job classes with those which are predominantly male. If employees in a male job class are found to be doing work of equal value with a female job class but receiving higher pay, the Act requires wages to be adjusted to eliminate the differential.

The Act stands out too for its striking departure from the intense indi-vidualism of the UK legislation. This is manifested in three major ways. First, whereas in the UK the burden of enforcement is left to the affected individual, the Ontario legislation is proactive, placing the onus on the

[211] See generally J. Fudge and P. McDermott (ed.), *Just Wages* (University of Toronto Press, 1990).
[212] E. M. Todres 'Women's work in Ontario: Pay Equity and the Wage Gap' [1990] 22 *Ottawa Law Review* 555 at p. 570.
[213] Pay Equity Act 1987 (chap. 34), s. 7(1).
[214] Except those with fewer than 10 employees: Pay Equity Act 1987, s. 3(1).

employer to remove discriminatory pay practices. Complaints of contraventions may be filed by a wide range of parties, including any employer, employee, group of employees or the bargaining agent representing the relevant employees.[215] Secondly, the Act moves away from a comparison between an individual woman and an individual male comparator. Recognising both that discrimination is a group rather than an individual problem and that questions of pay are essentially collective, the Act requires the comparison to be group based. The groups are, moreover, demarcated in terms of gender dominance, with a 'female' job class defined as one which is at least 60 per cent female, and a 'male' job class is at least 70 per cent male.[216] In this way, the close association between low pay and feminised jobs is addressed. Thirdly, the remedy is collective: the wage adjustment, instead of applying only to an individual contract of employment, affects the whole of the job class.

Although proactive pay equity laws have led to some significant gains for women in both the public and private sectors, the pay gap in Ontario remains. In fact, in 1993, full-time working women earned only 73.5 per cent that of men, a ratio which is worse even than that in the UK. Approximately 40 per cent of large private sector employers have not yet implemented pay equity.[217] A closer look at the legislation reveals that this is at least in part because the legislation remains bound in significant ways to liberal presumptions.

Most importantly, the Pay Equity Act is heavily deferent to market forces. This is manifested in five main ways. First, the Act explicitly lists a series of reasons which, if proved by an employer, would justify different pay for work of equal value. These include formal seniority systems, training programmes, merit systems, red circling and even skills shortages.[218] Although the Act states that seniority systems and merit compensation plans must not discriminate on the basis of gender, it is not clear whether the indirect discrimination inherent in such systems (see above) is outlawed. It is noteworthy that the skills shortage defence does not require absence of discrimination. Secondly, the employer's financial concerns are reflected in the provision limiting the wage adjustment in a twelve month period to 1 per cent of the employer's total annual wage bill until pay equity is achieved.[219] This limitation was narrowed even further by the Conservative government elected in 1995 on a platform openly hostile to State intervention in pay levels. Combined compensation payments were limited to 3 per cent of employers' 1993 payroll. Thirdly, if there is more than one male job class doing work of equal value, the women's pay is raised only to

---

[215] Pay Equity Act 1987, s. 22.      [216] *ibid.*, s. 1(1).
[217] P. Armstrong and M. Cornish 'Restructuring pay equity for a restructured work-force: Canadian perspectives': Paper presented to Pay Equity Project Conference, 1996, pp. 5–6.
[218] Pay Equity Act 1987, s. 8.
[219] *ibid.*, ss. 13(5) and (6).

the level of the lowest possible male comparator. Fourthly, even if a job evaluation scheme is purified of gender bias (and some commentators doubt if this is sufficiently strict in the Act[220]), market forces reappear at the stage of determining the actual pay for the job. Finally, the Act defers to the perceived needs of small employers by excluding employers with fewer than ten employees (although all ten need not be at the same establishment). This could well omit some of the most vulnerable women. Financial constraints have had an analogous impact in the public sector, where the costs of pay equity for agencies have not been subsidised by central government. The result has been that such agencies have found it extremely difficult to fund pay equity without cutting public services or increasing fees.[221]

Nor has the Act entirely escaped the limitations of the equality concept. Although the Act includes an important substantive underpinning to the concept of equality, by providing that an employer cannot reduce pay in order to achieve pay equity,[222] it remains tied to the need for a comparator. Until 1993, this was particularly narrow in that in order to establish a discriminatory pay practice, there had to be a male job class doing work of equal value employed by the same employer in that establishment. This meant that the extent to which job segregation could be addressed was restricted to the particular establishment. Even though the definition of an 'establishment' is more flexible than that in the EqPA,[223] there are numerous women working in all-female work-places, such as child-care centres, nursing homes or garment factories, who are unable to find a comparable male job class and so are left without a remedy. Findlay estimated that almost 50 per cent of women in work-places covered by the Act were unable to claim pay equity adjustments.[224] Nor was the Act able to address vertical segregation, that is cases in which women crowd into an all-female grade at the bottom of the wage hierarchy. Finally, like the EqPA, the reliance by the Ontario Act on the principle of equality meant that it was unable to address disproportionate differentials. Some of the equality-based defects were recognised and briefly corrected. Most importantly, the legislation was amended in 1993 to allow proxy comparisons, the aim being to assist women in female-dominated public sector work-places to find a comparator from a different work-place. At the same time, proportional comparisons were introduced. However, the proxy provisions were repealed by the 1995 Conservative government. As a result, many women cannot avail themselves of the benefits of the Act.

Similarly, the Act retains some of the strictures of individualism. This is particularly apparent in respect to the contentious issue of a 'gender neu-

---

[220] P. McDermott 'Equal Pay in Canada' in F. Eyraud et al, *Equal Pay Protection in Industrialised Market Economies* (ILO, 1993).

[221] S. Findlay in Fudge and McDermott (ed.), above n. 211, pp. 83–8.

[222] Pay Equity Act 1987, s. 9.

[223] *ibid.*, ss. 1, 14 and 15.

[224] Findlay in Fudge and McDermott (ed.), above n. 211, p. 81.

tral' job evaluation scheme. In order to overcome the fact that a collectively bargained job evaluation scheme might simply reflect the relative bargaining strength of the parties, the Act provides for disputes to be settled by an independent adjudicator, the Hearings Tribunal. The adversarial structure of the tribunal means that the process is inevitably individualised. This has been exacerbated by the decision of the tribunal not to elucidate general principles but to adjudicate the issues on a case by case basis. The result is that, although collective bargaining strength is neutralised, the process is inordinately expensive, and available only to very well financed unions which have a large enough female constituency to justify the expense.[225]

Participants in the development of the pay equity principle now acknowledge that 'the most important limitation on the legislation was the initial emphasis on individual bargaining units within individual workplaces of individual employers where individual job classes provided comparators'.[226] This resulted in the development of thousands of different plans, consuming enormous human and financial resources. Instead, it is suggested, plans should be more systematic, based on wage lines rather than job to job comparisons, and with the active involvement of trade unions. It is notable that in 1996, Quebec introduced a draft proactive Bill on pay equity, which allows comparisons between male and female jobs to be carried out in one of four different ways. These include not just a job-to-job comparison, but also a comparison of earning curves of predominantly female job classes, and a proportional comparison between a female and a male job class of different value.[227]

(B) Centralised Wage-fixing: The Australian Case

A diametrically different perspective is provided by the experience in Australia, where significant progress has been made without legislative intervention and with far less reliance on the equality approach. The key to change in Australia lies in its particular industrial relations system, with its centralised wage-fixing machinery, and a high rate of female unionisation. Change in Australia has been surprisingly recent; yet the system of centralised wage fixing has enabled its effects to be felt immediately and comprehensively. Thus from 1908 until 1970, separate pay scales were set for women and men, the principle being that a man should earn a family wage whereas a woman needed only to cater for herself. In 1969, the federal pay setting tribunal, the Australian Conciliation and Arbitration Commission, accepted the principle of equal pay for like work, followed in 1972 by a formal acknowledgement of the principle of equal pay for work of equal value. This led to the extension in 1974 of the minimum wage to women workers.[228] The results were dramatic: the minimum hourly award rate for

---

[225] Fudge at p. 74.     [226] Armstrong and Cornish, above n. 217, p. 18.
[227] ibid., p. 5.
[228] M. Thornton 'Equal Pay in Australia' in Eyraud (ed.), above n. 220, pp. 25–6.

women leapt from 74 per cent of the male rate in 1972 to 94 per cent in 1976. Actual hourly earnings rose from 68 to 81 per cent during the same period.[229] The role of the Commission (now called the Australian Industrial Relations Commission) was given statutory backing in 1993 in giving effect to Australia's obligations as a signatory to ILO anti-discrimination conventions.[230]

It is clear from this experience that a collective approach based on a centralised wage-fixing system together with a comprehensive minimum wage overcomes many of the weaknesses in both the UK and the Ontario legislation. However, there are limits to the lessons which can be drawn from the Australian context. As a start, it would be impossible to transplant the Australian system because centralised wage-fixing is now anathema in the UK. At most, central minimum wage-fixing machinery might be plausible. In any event, it is not certain that centralisation alone can guarantee progress. Fieldes, for example, convincingly demonstrates that the advances made in the 1970s were largely due to the bargaining strength of the unions, against a background of low unemployment. She also casts doubt on the extent of real progress made during the rigid centralisation of the 1980s. Much of the compression in the female to male ratio was due to a worsening of men's pay during a time of income restraint. What little gain was made by women was paid for by a reduction in real value in the pay of male employees. Yet decentralisation in the absence of real trade union power is equally ineffective. The swift movement away from centralised pay setting in the 1990s against the background of a weak trade union movement led to a decline in standards for both men and women, with women more disadvantaged than men.[231]

Moreover, a focus on the awards themselves is misleading, since it is common in Australia for employers to pay significantly more than the minimum award rate in the form of overtime payments, allowances and 'over-award' payments. Such payments are usually agreed at enterprise level, either on an individual basis or for groups represented by trade unions. It is here that discrimination against women reasserts itself. A 1992 report found that on average women receive as little as 52 per cent of the 'over-award' payments received by men.[232] Indeed, a look at actual earnings of both full-time and part-time workers reveals that women in the paid work-force in 1991 earned only 66.5 per cent of male earnings.[233] The reasons for this pattern are depressingly familiar. Enterprise level bargain-

---

[229]  Thornton, above n. 228, in Eyraud (ed.), p. 24.

[230]  Industrial Relations Reform Act 1993 (Cth), noted by M. Pittard in (1994) 7 *Australian Journal of Labour Law*, p. 170, esp pp. 194–5.

[231]  D. Fieldes 'Equal pay and decentralised wage fixing: the Australian experience': Paper given at Pay Equity Conference, 1996.

[232]  A. Chapman 'Just Rewards' in [1994] 7 *Australian Journal of Labour Law*, pp. 272–5.

[233]  C. Burton 'Job Evaluation and Pay Equity' unpublished paper presented at the National Pay Equity Campaign International Conference, September 1991.

ing clearly favours male workers, reflected in men's greater access to over-award payments. In addition, the pronounced industrial and occupational segregation of men and women has a significant influence, with women finding themselves concentrated in industries and occupations which are characterised by relatively low levels of over-award payments. This differentiation is exacerbated by the greater industrial strength of workers in male-dominated industries and occupations, which results in workers receiving group-based over-award payments. Women, by contrast, tend to receive individual over-award payments tied to subjective concepts such as merit. Finally, women form over 80 per cent of part-time and casual employees, and thus are far less likely to receive over-award payments than their full-time counterparts.[234] Fieldes argues too that even when the ratio appears to be improving, it is important to recognise the unquantified trade-offs accepted by workers, including more onerous working practices, more unpaid overtime, and an overall loss in full-time jobs replaced by part-time and temporary work.[235]

The Australian system also shares some of the weaknesses identified in all three of the jurisdictions examined here. First, in accepting the principle of equal value in 1972, the Australian Conciliation and Arbitration Commission did not invest the concept with any precise meaning. Thus it has not been necessary to challenge the male bias inherent in traditional job evaluation schemes. Secondly, job segregation has frequently been untouched, with several all-female work-forces finding themselves excluded altogether. Despite the fact that a centralised system gives ample opportunity for comparing different occupations, the 'history of work value cases in Australia reveals a marked disinclination to compare discrete occupational classifications'.[236] Indeed, the Arbitration Commission in 1985 explicitly rejected a claim by nurses that their occupations be revalued on comparable worth criteria. The reason for this was the centralised system itself: an increase for nurses carried with it the risk of stimulating other wage claims which threatened the whole centralised structure.[237] Attention in Australia is therefore turning towards the possible use of the Australian Sex Discrimination Act 1984 and to the potential for job evaluation to address the continuing discrimination against women.

## (C) The Way Ahead

It would be misleading to suggest that any particular formula holds the key to reform in the UK. Deep-seated social changes in the division of labour in the home, in the nature of women's education, training and personal expectations and in the perception of women's role in the paid work-force

---

[234] Chapman, above n. 232, p. 274.
[235] Fieldes, above n. 231, p. 8.
[236] Thornton, above n. 228, p. 34.
[237] Fieldes, above n. 231, p. 13.

are part and parcel of effective change. At the same time, the existing provisions on pay are demonstrably inadequate, and meaningful proposals for change can be made. The individualised, complaints-led system is clearly ineffective and the limitation to enterprise-based comparisons prevents the legislation from addressing widespread job segregation. Proactive job evaluation on the Canadian lines is a step forward, but is itself limited by its focus on the establishment, the difficulty in ensuring that job evaluation schemes used by employers are untainted by institutional sex bias, and the sheer complexity and expense of job-to-job comparisons in a job evaluation context.

An effective pay strategy would therefore have to move away from the limiting influences of equality, individualism, state neutrality and market forces. As a start, the concept of equality alone is insufficient to achieve substantive change: it needs to be underpinned by a proper minimum wage. A national minimum wage could be set centrally or, more flexibly, by a body along the lines of the Low Pay Commission proposed by the new Labour government. Enforcement should be in the hands both of a properly resourced inspectorate and of employees, trade unions and even other employers. Sanctions, to be effective, should have a strongly deterrent element. Part-timers, casual workers and homeworkers should all be included. Substantive change requires too that equal pay legislation, in whatever form, should specify that equality cannot be achieved by removing benefits or decreasing compensation. This is quite simply stated in both the Ontario[238] and the Australian legislation.[239]

As well as a minimum wage, a reform package would need to abandon the overpowering influence of the male norm. This must begin with a radical reworking of the concept of value. As Armstrong argues, it is not enough to redefine women's skills to fit into pre-established categories reflecting male hierarchies. Women's work requires very different kinds of skills. For example, in jobs involving the provision of services to people, the degree of skill, effort and responsibility remains invisible because there are no discrete tasks, taught skills, or visible products.[240] This leads to the assumption, which policy makers have jumped to throughout the centuries, that such work comes 'naturally' to women, and, for this reason, does not deserve high levels of pay. Men's tasks, by contrast, fit into more usual categories of formal education, independence and responsibility for others. Job evaluation can only achieve significant change if it is fundamentally reworked to reflect values such as co-operation, the ability to switch between multiple tasks, the stress in dealing with the young, the old, or the victimised, and the value of experience learned informally through the family and the job itself. Furthermore, the concept of value, refashioned in

---

[238]   Pay Equity Act 1987, s. 9.
[239]   Industrial Relations Reform Act 1993 (Cth), s. 170.
[240]   P. and H. Armstrong in Fudge and McDermott (ed.), above n. 211, pp. 114–15.

this way, would need to be severed from direct comparisons with men. Women's work must be seen as possessing intrinsic value, regardless of its similarity with or difference from men's work. Child-care workers, in nursery schools or creches, for example, should be given the opportunity to have their work revalued without having to find a man doing similar sort of work. Such a severance of value from equality would also permit the law to address disproportionality, thus meeting the needs of women in vertically segregated work-places. In abandoning the notion of 'equal value', however, it is necessary to formulate some other yardstick for determining when intervention is required. I would argue that this should be based on the principle of 'pay equity'. Although in an ideal world pay inequalities should be eradicated or diminished, the more limited aim of equal pay legislation would be to ensure that no one section of the population bears a disproportionate burden of disadvantage in the paid labour force. Pay equity would therefore denote an even distribution of inequalities in pay throughout the population. Conversely, intervention would become necessary if it were clear that a group of workers of the same sex, ethnicity or a combination of these were clustered into a low paid sector. To deal with the problem of relative low pay, such as that of women managers who on average are paid less than men, the legislation would define low pay as that relative to a narrowly defined group. Thus if it can be shown that women managers cluster at the bottom end of managerial pay, statutory intervention would be triggered even though women managers are not low paid relative to the working population as a whole. Canadian moves towards the use of earning curves and proportional comparisons provide a useful point of departure.

Any reform would also need to depart radically from the individual, complaints-led structure of present legislation. This would entail a collective solution, recognising the inter-connectedness of pay, both internally and externally. Such a solution would need to deal, therefore, with the firm's payment structure as a whole, as well as allowing inter-firm comparisons. In addition, it is crucial that the resulting pay adjustment be capable of extension to other firms or occupations. A model for this already exists, in the form of the now repealed schedule 11 to the Employment Protection Act 1975, under which the results of collective bargaining could be extended by law to other employers who did not pay the going rate. A new legislative package should also reject a wholly complaints-based system, in favour of proactivity.

How then, in concrete terms, would a reform package based on these principles work?[241] Proactivity, I would suggest, can be achieved by placing initial responsibility for change on the collective bargaining process, or, where there is no developed collective bargaining, on employers

---

[241] These proposals are based on ideas generated during discussions with other members of the Equal Opportunities group of the Institute of Employment Rights.

themselves. Thus where bargaining arrangements are in place all parties should be obliged to ensure that the final agreement advances pay equity. This should not, however, rely entirely on existing representative structures which might not incorporate women sufficiently. Thus where women are not members of the relevant unions, or are under-represented in the unions, a women's representative should be nominated to participate in the bargaining process. This participation could be strengthened by the participation of an equal opportunities officer, nominated by the EOC. Even if there is no collective bargaining, an employer should have a similar duty, when deciding on pay structures, to advance the cause of pay equity.

Adjudication should not lie with the ordinary courts, but with a body deliberately structured to deal with pay as a polycentric issue. The CAC (see above) provides a ready-made solution. Davies and Freedland describe the CAC as 'probably the most successful and innovative' of the institutions established in 1975, particularly because it placed the legal issue within the overall context of the parties' industrial relations situation, and because it sought to associate the parties as far as possible with the process of adjudication.[242] The CAC would, on this proposal, have power to intervene on the motion of any worker covered by the challenged collective agreement or payment structure, any interested union, any public interest groups, the EOC/CRE, or possibly even an interested employer. The grounds for intervention would be that an agreement or payment structure perpetuates pay inequities, or fails to make sufficient progress towards pay equity. In dealing with the matter, the CAC would be required to examine the terms with a view to determining a strategy to advance pay equity. It must have regard to a variety of factors, including the content of the jobs in the agreement or payment structure (examining the demands made on the worker in terms of skill, responsibility etc), their value to the enterprise, the levels of pay for comparable jobs in other enterprises, internal relativities, and the history of the job at issue, for example, that it has always been female-dominated, or that it has recently moved from a male-dominated to a female-dominated profession. To this end, the CAC should have extensive powers to require the employer to disclose relevant information, subject to guarantees of confidentiality. Having examined the payment structure, the CAC should then have the power to amend or adjust it in order to advance pay equity, having particular regard to the correction of disproportionate differentials, and the role of bonus payments. Given the history of judicial intervention to obstruct the workings of the CAC, its awards should be final, although if there were a separate labour court, it might be necessary to permit judicial review on limited grounds.

Part of the power of such a system would be to engage both internal and external pay relativities. It is proposed that the CAC have the power to

---

[242] Davies and Freedland, above n. 16, p. 395.

extend the award to other employers or occupations, either on its own motion, or possibly more pragmatically, on the motion of an interested party. Such an extension is common in other jurisdictions, and has a history in the UK in the form of the now repealed schedule 11 to the Employment Protection Act 1975. Clearly this requires a well resourced CAC, possibly with several divisions located in different areas. Certainly, the CAC would need its own panel of full-time job evaluation experts who could carry out the task of revaluing in a reasonable space of time.

Finally, the role of economic factors needs to be considered. The overall debate about the economics of equal value is discussed in Chapter 9. For the present, it is worth noting that the cost in other jurisdictions appears to have been easily absorbed. In Ontario, according to Todres,[243] a typical one-time adjustment for an undervalued job was 2,000 to 3,000 dollars per person. The Ontario Public Services pay equity plan yielded an average pay equity adjustment of 4,000 dollars per person. In Minnesota in the US, a pay equity plan implemented over a four-year period for 34,000 state employees increased payroll costs by only 3.7 per cent. In any case, as Rubery argues, there is no reason why women should continue to subsidise the rest of the community by their underpaid work.

Such macro-figures do not solve the micro-question of what role economic factors or business needs should play in defending pay disparities. In principle, I would argue, such factors should be disregarded on the grounds that they merely disguise and therefore perpetuate women's exploitation. There may be some room for a defence in terms of more personal factors, but seniority systems, merit award payments and productivity bonuses need to be subject to the strictest scrutiny before they are permitted to justify a pay discrepancy on gender lines. The CAC in its arbitral role should be well placed to carry out such scrutiny. At most, affordability to the enterprise should only be taken into account to the extent of permitting an award to be phased in.

A system of this sort would, it is hoped, make some impact on the gender pay gap. However, it needs to be accompanied by changes in recruitment, training, hours of work and child-care facilities if fundamental change is to follow. Some of these issues were dealt with in Chapter 5, the remainder arise in Chapters 7 and 9.

[243] Todres, above n. 212, p. 565.

# [7]
# Structural Disadvantage

## INTRODUCTION

It has been seen that women's disadvantage in the paid labour force is due to deep structural forces which are only partially tackled by equal pay legislation. If further progress is to be achieved, the law must address the powerful institutional forces which drive so many women into low paying, low status jobs and which obstruct the career paths of many others. Thus it is not sufficient to focus only on improving pay and conditions; it is also essential to facilitate women's movement out of segregated jobs, and up the promotions ladder. To do this, some of the root causes of disadvantage need to be addressed: the failure of the work-place properly to accommodate child-care responsibilities; the education and training system which shapes the expectations and opportunities of women and men in different ways; and the alarmingly high incidence of sexual harassment within the work-place. Most fundamentally, it is essential to change the expectation that women will bear the primary responsibility for parenting, care of the elderly and domestic work, whether they do in fact do so or not. These issues arise not only in the paid work-force, but also within the policy structure of the State, particularly concerning social security and employment protection legislation. Many of them have been brought before the courts in some form or other, testing the response of anti-discrimination legislation at national and EC level. As will be seen below, while significant progress has been achieved, the legislation and caselaw remain bound by the familiar strictures of equality, neutrality, autonomy, individualism and deference to business or political priorities. The chapter begins with a brief description of the provisions of the Sex Discrimination Act of 1975, together with its European counterpart, the Equal Treatment Directive. The body of the chapter is concerned with the extent to which the law can address the powerful structural impediments to women's advancement. It approaches the issue from two angles, examining first the legal conceptual apparatus and then the institutional structures with which the law must engage.

## I.  THE LEGAL FRAMEWORK

### a) The Sex Discrimination Act 1975

The enactment of a specific statute outlawing discrimination on the grounds of sex was the result of a rare consensus between the ruling Labour Party and the opposition Conservatives. Drawing its inspiration from US jurisprudence, the Sex Discrimination Act 1975 utilises two different notions of equality: the straightforward notion of equal treatment found in the direct discrimination provisions, and the more complex notion of disparate impact set out in the indirect discrimination provisions. The first notion is based on the familiar principle that likes should be treated alike. According to the statute: 'a person discriminates against a woman if . . . on the ground of her sex he treats her less favourably than he treats or would treat a man'.[1] The second notion recognises that equal treatment might produce deeply unequal results if the relevant subjects are socially unequal to begin with. Indirect discrimination aims therefore to address cases in which a practice or condition is applied equally to men and women but in fact operates to exclude a disproportionate number of women. The precise words of the statute are important: it provides that a person discriminates against a woman if 'he applies to her a requirement or condition which applies or would apply equally to a man but (i) which is such that the proportion of

---

[1] SDA 1975, s. 1(1)(a).

women who can comply with it is considerably smaller than the proportion of men who can comply with it and (ii) which he cannot show to be justifiable irrespective of the sex of the person to whom it is applied and (iii) which is to her detriment because she cannot comply with it.'[2] It should be noted that the statute also prohibits discrimination (both direct and indirect) against a married person on the grounds of his or her marital status in the employment field; but does not prohibit discrimination against unmarried persons. The Act applies equally to discrimination against men as to discrimination against women on grounds of sex.

The prohibition against discrimination does not apply generally: instead, the Act details the precise fields in which discrimination is outlawed. There are three such fields: employment; education; and the provision of goods, facilities, services or premises to members of the public. Within each field, the Act includes further detailed specifications on the grounds of action. Thus in respect of employment, it is unlawful to discriminate in selection arrangements, in the terms on which a person is offered employment, or by refusing to offer her that employment at all. It is also unlawful to discriminate against an employee by refusing her access to opportunities for promotion, transfer, training or any other similar benefits or in the way in which she is offered such access, or by dismissing her or subjecting her to any other detriment.[3] Discrimination is however lawful in cases where gender is a 'bona fide occupational qualification', defined as either that being a man is essential for the job (for example in a dramatic performance) or that the job needs to be held by a man to preserve decency or privacy, or because the job involves the holder living or working in a private home.[4]

In the education field, the Act makes it unlawful for specified educational establishments to discriminate against a woman in the terms on which it offers to admit her as a pupil; in the way it affords her access to benefits, facilities or services; or by refusing to admit her, omitting to offer her access to benefits, or excluding her.[5] Here too there are important exceptions: single-sex establishments are excluded, and, more controversially, courses in physical training.[6] Finally, so far as the provision of services to the public is concerned, it is unlawful to discriminate against a woman who seeks to obtain or use such services, by refusing to provide her with them, or by refusing to provide them on like terms, of like quality or in the like manner as to men. Such facilities or services include access to public places; accommodation in hotels; loan or other credit facilities; education, recreation or transport facilities; or professional services.[7]

b) EC LAW

The major equivalent provision in EC law is the Equal Treatment Directive,[8] promulgated in 1976. This provision is more open-textured than the

---

[2] *ibid.*, s. 1(1)(b).     [3] *ibid.*, s. 6.     [4] *ibid.*, s. 7.
[5] *ibid.*, s. 22.     [6] *ibid.*, ss. 326 and 28.     [7] *ibid.*, s. 29.
[8] Council Directive 76/207 (9th February 1976).

SDA. Its stated purpose is to put into effect in the Member States 'the principle of equal treatment for men and women' in respect of access to employment, promotion, vocational training, working conditions and, subject to some exceptions, social security.[9] The 'principle of equal treatment' is defined simply as meaning that 'there shall be no discrimination whatsoever on grounds of sex either directly or indirectly by reference in particular to marital or family status.'[10] There are narrowly defined exceptions, for provisions 'concerning the protection of women, particularly as regards pregnancy and maternity'; activities for which 'by reason of their nature or the context in which they are carried out, the sex of the worker constitutes a determining factor'; and measures which 'promote equality for men and women'. The open-textured nature of the Directive has left much scope for the ECJ to develop its own set of guiding principles, many of which have been more progressive than those developed under the SDA.

The impact of the Equal Treatment Directive on domestic law has nevertheless been less powerful than that of Article 119, the equal pay for equal work provision (see Chapter 6). This is because the Directive has been held to be effective in proceedings against the State (vertical direct effect) but not against private employers (horizontal direct effect).[11] This has been problematic for two main reasons. First, it has meant that while public employees may insist on their EC rights directly, private employees have no direct redress against their employers if their legislature fails to implement the Directive properly or at all.[12] This distinction is all the more problematic in light of the increasingly fluid boundaries between State and private employment and the consequential difficulties in creating a clear demarcation between them.[13] The problem has been somewhat ameliorated by the decision in *Francovich*,[14] a case concerning failure by the Italian government to implement the Insolvency Directive. In that case, the ECJ held that although the Directive had no horizontal direct effect, a disappointed employee could claim damages against the State for failing properly to implement its obligations under the Directive. It nevertheless remains problematic to have two such different routes depending upon whether the employer is characterised as public or private. Secondly, the absence of horizontal direct effect has meant that private employees will make every effort to bring their claims within Article 119, putting pressure on the concept of 'pay' at its centre. These difficulties have led several Advocates General to urge the abolition of the distinction between vertical and horizontal directive effect, permitting private employees to rely on the Equal Treatment Directive in the same way as their public counterparts. How-

---

[9] Article 1.      [10] Article 2(1).

[11] *Marshall* v. *Southampton and South West Hampshire Area Health Authority* [1996] IRLR 140; *Von Colson* Case 14/83; *Marshall (No. 2)* Case C-271/91 [1993] IRLR 445 (ECJ).

[12] *Duke* v. *GEC Reliance* [1988] IRLR 118 (HL).

[13] See *Foster* v. *British Gas* [1990] ECR 1-3313.

[14] Cases C-6 and 9/10 [1991] ECR 1-5357.

ever, the attempt to deepen the effect of directives in this way was rejected by the Court in the recent case of *Dori*.[15]

## II.  CONCEPTUAL APPARATUS: DIRECT AND INDIRECT DISCRIMINATION

The concept of direct discrimination, although primarily encapsulating the formal notion that likes should be treated alike, nevertheless represents a small advance on the concrete notion of equality used in equal pay legislation. Under the direct discrimination provisions, there is no need to find an actual male comparator. Instead, it is sufficient to show that the woman was treated less favourably than a man would have been treated. Direct discrimination is also stronger than the notion of equality in equal pay legislation because it eschews a justification defence. It is thus the one small enclave of the law in which there is no scope for market forces or similar arguments to trump the ideal of equality. Attempts at EC level to persuade the ECJ to incorporate a notion of justification for direct discrimination have so far been unsuccessful. However, direct discrimination is inevitably a limited concept. The hypothetical male comparator notwithstanding, the yardstick remains determinedly male. In addition, direct discrimination focuses directly on the individual, with all its attendant problems. Possibly the most problematic has been the difficulty facing an individual woman in discharging the burden of proof.

By contrast, the concept of indirect discrimination is the most sophisticated of the legal tools available to challenge structural discrimination. Tested against the familiar measures set out in Chapter 1, the concept of indirect discrimination has made important steps forward. Most important is the crucial recognition of the limits of formal equality, encapsulated in the notion that even if a criterion is applied equally to a man and a woman, the outcome might show significant disparities. Similarly, the indirect discrimination provisions offer a genuine opportunity to challenge the all-pervasive male norm. Instead of requiring comparison with a man, either real or hypothetical, the indirect discrimination provisions explicitly address the detrimental effects of 'male' norms, or requirements with which women find it difficult to comply. The most obvious examples are height and weight requirements based on the male physique. As the US Supreme Court declared,[16] height and weight criteria should not be used as a proxy for genuinely job related requirements, such as physical strength. Instead, job applicants should be tested individually for their strength, regardless of gender. The ability to challenge the male norm in this way has resulted in significant progress for women, particularly in the area of part-time working. Indirect discrimination also moves away from the rigid

[15] Case C-91/92 [1994] ECR 1-3325, concerning Council Directive 85/577/EEC.
[16] *Dothard* v. *Rawlinson* 433 US 321 (1977).

individualism of both direct discrimination and the equal pay legislation. Thus one of the chief advances made by the indirect discrimination provisions is the recognition that discrimination can often be detected only by looking at the impact on a group rather than focusing on the individual.

However, on closer examination, it can be seen that indirect discrimination continues to subscribe to the basic limiting principles. This is true even of equality: although recognising the limits of formal equality the concept does not extend to an endorsement of substantive equality. Inequalities in outcome are used as a diagnosis of discrimination; but equality of outcome is not the proposed cure. Instead, the purpose is to remove the identified barrier, the stated aim being equality of opportunity rather than equality of results. As we shall see later in this chapter, such an approach is far from sufficient even to equalise opportunities. Similarly, the departure from the male norm is not as complete as it might seem. It is still necessary to show that substantially fewer women than men can comply. The result is that in an all-female work-force, it might be impossible for part-time workers to claim discrimination. Even more restrictive is the central role played by autonomy, individualism and market forces. Each of these is dealt with below.

a) AUTONOMY

The indirect discrimination provisions in the SDA are only triggered if it is proved that women are involuntarily precluded from participation in the benefit. This is required both of women as a group and the individual woman. Thus, not only must the applicant show that the proportion of women who *can* comply is considerably smaller than the proportion of men,[17] but also that the requirement or condition is to her detriment because she *cannot* comply with it.[18] This clearly excludes from protection cases in which women have chosen not to comply. The scope of the provisions is therefore inversely correlated with the width of the definition of choice used by courts and tribunals. It has already been seen that the conceptualisation of choice depends heavily on the proponent's background philosophy. At one end of the spectrum are the neo-liberals, who argue that women's disadvantage is a result of their own choice. In particular, proponents of the human capital theory maintain that the disparity between men and women in the paid labour force is accounted for by women's choice to invest little in their own human capital in the expectation of spending time out of or only peripherally involved in the labour market.[19] By contrast, it has been a central aim of this book to expose the extent to which entrenched social systems act as constraints on individuals' freedom of choice.

---

[17] SDA 1975, s. 1(1)(b)(i).
[18] *ibid.*, s. 1(1)(b)(iii).
[19] R. Posner 'An Economic Analysis of Sex Discrimination Laws' [1989] *University of Chicago Law Review* 1311.

It has been left in the hands of the courts to imbue the statutory words with either a neo-liberal presumption of freedom of choice, or a recognition of structural constraints. Both approaches are evident. In *Price* v. *Civil Service Commission*,[20] a woman challenged the age bar of twenty-eight for applications to the civil service on the grounds that it discriminated against the many women who had their children during their twenties. The industrial tribunal held that a woman had a free choice: if she chose not to have children, she could comply with the age bar. However, the EAT recognised that such an interpretation went against the spirit of the Act. 'In one sense it can be said that any female applicant can comply with the condition. She is not obliged to marry or to have children, or to mind children; she may find somebody to look after them and as a last resort she may put them into care . . . Such a construction appears to us to be wholly out of sympathy with the spirit and intent of the Act.'[21] Instead it held that 'can comply' must be construed as meaning 'possible in practice', taking into account the usual behaviour of women.[22]

However, the recognition of constraints on freedom of choice has not always been forthcoming. In *Turner* v. *Labour Party*,[23] a divorced woman with three children complained that her employer's pension scheme was discriminatory because it provided automatic benefits for surviving spouses but not for other surviving dependents. It was accepted that because women tend to live longer than men, considerably fewer women than men could comply with the condition of having a surviving spouse. Nevertheless, the Court of Appeal rejected her claim on the grounds that she could comply with the requirement by marrying. According to Dillon LJ, 'she may not want to marry and cannot be compelled to marry, but she can marry; therefore it cannot be said that she "cannot" comply with the condition of being married at a future date.'[24] A similar approach to choice is evident in *Clymo* v. *Wandsworth*,[25] in which an employer's refusal to allow an employee to job-share once she had returned from maternity leave was found not to be discriminatory. According to Wood J, the applicant could have worked full-time, since she earned enough to afford child-care: her decision to be a participative parent was therefore one of her own choice. 'It seems clear that in trying to fit society into the framework of the statute and the statute into our society that in every employment ladder . . . there will come a stage at which a woman who has family responsibilities must make a choice. That situation was one facing this mother.'[26] The 'framework of society' which forces a choice between sustaining a responsible job and participating in the care of one's own children was not considered open to challenge.

[20] [1977] IRLR 291 EAT.      [21] *Price*, above n. 20, p. 31.
[22] For a similar approach see *Clarke* v. *Eley Kynoch* [1982] IRLR 482 (EAT).
[23] [1987] IRLR 103 (CA).      [24] *Turner* v. *Labour Party*, above n. 23, p. 103.
[25] *Clymo* v. *Wandsworth London Borough Council* [1989] IRLR 241 (EAT).
[26] *ibid.*, at p. 248.

An equally damaging reliance on choice to justify detrimental treatment is found in the US case of *EEOC* v. *Sears, Roebuck*.[27] In that case the EEOC sought to prove that Sears had discriminated against women by failing to hire women as commission-earning sales staff. The Court of Appeal rejected the claim. Statistical evidence of huge disparities between the number of men and women in these positions was dismissed on the ground that the measures failed to take account of women's lack of interest in the positions. In other words, the court accepted Sears' contention that, despite the fact that commission-earning sales staff were the elite of the staff, enjoying both higher pay and higher status than non-commission sales staff, women simply preferred not to do these jobs.

The emphasis given to women's freedom of choice despite structural constraints is not, paradoxically, echoed in cases in which a woman enlists the aid of the court to protect her freedom of choice. This is demonstrated most starkly in claims by women to a right to free choice of work despite alleged health and safety risks. In *Page*,[28] the express decision of a woman truck driver not to have children was given little weight in the decision to uphold a ban on her right to carry loads of a chemical which potentially endangered her fertility. She had argued that she had been divorced and had no intention whatsoever of having children. The tribunal countered this by holding that where there was a risk of sterility or harm to the foetus, whether in existence or likely to come into existence, her wishes could not be conclusive. The fact that her livelihood was at stake was wholly ignored in the blind assumption that all women of child-bearing age are potential child-bearers. The US case of *Dothard* v. *Rawlinson*[29] achieved a similar result by a somewhat different route. The majority agreed that Title VII protected women's right to choose whether to work in a dangerous environment (here a prison whose inmates included dangerous sex offenders). But the Court went on to hold that individual choice was overridden by wider considerations. The possibility of violence against women threatened the stability of the whole prison. That the opposite approach is plausible is demonstrated by *United Auto Workers* v. *Johnson*,[30] in which the US Supreme Court was able to recognise as discriminatory a policy which gave men but not women the choice as to whether to risk their reproductive health.

b) INDIVIDUALISM

Although indirect discrimination represents an important advance in its recognition of discrimination as a group issue rather than an individual problem, the courts remain distinctly uncomfortable with the handling of groups. Little guidance is given by the legislation, which states merely that a person discriminates against a woman if 'he applies to her a requirement or condition . . . (i) which is such that the proportion of women who can comply with it is considerably smaller than the proportion of men who can

---

[27] [EEOC] 839 F 2d 302 (1988).     [28] *Page* v. *Freight Hire* [1971] IRLR 13 (EAT).
[29] Above n. 16.     [30] 886 F. 2d. 27 (7th Circ. 1989).

comply with it'.[31] This leaves a string of questions unanswered. In particular, what is the 'proportion' a proportion of? The whole population or just a part of it? If so what part? Widely differing results can be achieved depending on which 'pool of comparison' is held to be appropriate. Worse still, a case might fail simply because, having chosen the wrong pool, the complainant is held not to have adduced the relevant evidence to prove her claim. Thus in *Kidd* v. *DRG*,[32] the applicant claimed that detrimental treatment of part-time workers was unlawful discrimination. To prove her case, she adduced figures which compared the proportion of women in the work-force as a whole who could comply with the condition of full-time working with the far greater proportion of men who could do so. This approach was rejected. Instead of the work-force as a whole, the appropriate pool of comparison was held to be all workers with young families, requiring a demonstration that the proportion of women with young families who could comply was considerably smaller than the equivalent figure for men with young families. In the absence of the relevant statistics, the claim was rejected, the tribunal refusing to accept without specific evidence the claim that more mothers of young families tended to work part-time than fathers in the equivalent position. A series of later cases demonstrates a similar use of apparently mathematical formulae to obscure the reality of disparate impact. Thus in *Pearse* v. *City of Bradford*[33] the EAT rejected the applicant's claim of indirect discrimination against part-time workers on the grounds that she had erroneously used the academic staff at a college as her pool of comparison. Figures showing that 21.8 per cent of female academic staff at the college were full-time compared to 46.7 per cent of male academic staff were held to be irrelevant. Instead, the applicant should have considered all those qualified for the post. Again, in *Jones* v. *University of Manchester*,[34] a woman claimed that it was indirectly discriminatory to set an age band of twenty-seven to thirty-five for a post as careers advisor, because significantly fewer women mature students than male mature students could comply with this requirement. The Court of Appeal overturned the tribunal's finding in her favour, on the grounds that the relevant pool was all those who had the requisite qualifications for the post, rather than all mature students. Nor was the court prepared to remedy the defect by accepting the complainant's argument that the same result would have been reached using judicially endorsed figures as had been reached using her figures.[35]

There have, however, been attempts by the judges to use the figures instrumentally to reflect the spirit of the legislation. The best example of a case in which extremely complex statistics were used in this way is *R* v. *Secretary of State for the Environment ex p. Schaffter*.[36] In this case, the

---

[31] SDA 1975, s. 1(1)(b)(i).     [32] *Kidd* v. *DRG UK* [1985] IRLR 190 (EAT).
[33] [1988] IRLR 399 (EAT).     [34] [1993] IRLR 218 (CA).
[35] For a similar example, see *Staffordshire* v. *Black* [1995] IRLR 234 (EAT).
[36] [1987] IRLR 53 (QBD).

applicant claimed that the social security scheme providing hardship grants to single parents while studying was discriminatory because only single parents who had once been married were eligible. To prove her case, she had to demonstrate that considerably fewer women than men could comply with the requirement of having once been married. Not surprisingly, statistics could be found to support both her contention and that of the respondent Secretary of State, depending on which pool was chosen. Thus the Secretary of State argued that there was no discrimination because 20 per cent of all female lone parents were never married, and 20 per cent of all male lone parents were never married. The applicant argued that the appropriate pool was not female lone parents and male lone parents, but the total of lone parents. Looked at from this vantage, it became clear that only 4 per cent of all lone parents were men who had never married, while 16 per cent of all lone parents were women who had never married. This was because women constituted 80 per cent of all lone parents. In choosing between these options, Schiemann J was able to respond to the social fact that vastly more mothers than fathers continue to take responsibility for children.[37] By ensuring that the figures chosen corresponded to the reality, he could avoid the paradoxical situation whereby the fact of institutional discrimination (women's prime responsibility for children) is used to excuse discrimination. The case is also notable in that, having found in favour of the applicants on this point, the judge did not resort to another of the technical elements to defeat it.

Similarly perceptive was the approach of the tribunal and the EAT in *London Underground* v. *Edwards*,[38] in which a woman train driver complained of unlawful sex discrimination when rostering arrangements were changed making it impossible for her, as a single mother, to look after her child in the mornings or evenings. Her case depended first on demonstrating that considerably fewer women than men could comply with the new arrangements, a task made very difficult by the fact that there were only twenty-one women train operators out of a total of 2,044, of whom only she was unable to comply. The EAT, appreciating this problem, held that in cases in which there were so few women that the figures were statistically unreliable, the tribunal was entitled to have regard to the likelihood that this was work known to be 'men's' work, and therefore to take a wider perspective, including using figures based on women in employment as a whole. Equally importantly, it held that the meaning of 'considerably smaller' could change in the light of the strength or weakness of the case for justification. Where a woman could be accommodated at little expense, the need to show a 'considerable' discrepancy in numbers was correspondingly slight, and vice versa.

[37] This insight is drawn from Dawson J in *Australian Iron and Steel* v. *Banovic* [1989] 168 CLR 165.
[38] [1997] IRLR 176 (EAT).

A similarly perceptive position was taken by the majority in the High Court of Australia in the seminal case of *Australian Iron and Steel* v. *Banovic*.[39] In this case, discrimination in the recruitment practices of the employer led to the appointment of very few women before 1980, when the policy was changed and a greater effort made to employ women. When a redundancy situation arose in 1981, the 'last in first out' method of redundancy selection was used. Not surprisingly, many women lacked the requisite seniority to escape this guillotine. In order to prove indirect discrimination under the New South Wales Anti-Discrimination Act, it was necessary to prove that there was a requirement or condition with which a substantially higher proportion of persons of the opposite sex could comply.[40] Again the figures could be moulded to fit any conclusion. If men and women were compared separately, men who could comply with the seniority requirement taken as a proportion of all men in the work-force, and women who could comply taken as a proportion of all women in the work-force it appeared that there was little difference between them: the proportion being approximately 93 per cent in both cases. However, as the court recognised, calculating the figures in this way ignored the fact that the composition of the work-force was tainted by discrimination. Instead, a pool or base group must be selected which does not itself incorporate the discrimination. It was therefore more appropriate to consider the proportion of women in the work-force as a whole who had the necessary seniority. On this approach, it became clear that the ratio of men to women who were employed pre-1981 was 15 to 1, clearly a considerable disparity.

The development of statistical analysis in US cases on direct and indirect discrimination demonstrates both the potential and the dangers of the attempt to marry a group based analysis with an essentially comparative approach. An initially enlightened approach is evident in *Dothard* v. *Rawlinson*,[41] in which minimum height and weight requirements for security guards in Alabama prisons were challenged as discriminatory. The complainant demonstrated that 33.29 per cent of women in the US were excluded by the height requirement of 5 foot 2 inches, while the minimum weight requirement of 120 pounds barred 22.29 per cent of women. The contrasting proportions for men were 1.28 and 2.35 per cent respectively. The employer challenged the use of the population as a whole as the base figure, arguing that the appropriate pool was the set of actual applicants. In the Supreme Court, Stewart J, giving judgment for the Court, had no difficulty in rejecting this argument, giving two main grounds. First, he recognised that the application process might not reflect the real pool of potential applicants because of the 'chill factor', that is applicants who are discouraged because they know they are unable to meet the height and

---

[39] *Australian Iron and Steel* v. *Banovic* [1989] 168 CLR 165.
[40] Anti Discrimination Act New South Wales 1977, s. 24(3).
[41] Above n. 16.

weight requirements. Secondly, and equally significantly, he was unwilling to reject the statistics actually chosen by the applicant, particularly where this evidence conspicuously demonstrates the grossly discriminatory impact. Only if the employer was able to offer convincing counter evidence would this aspect of the case be in dispute. On this reasoning, it would be unacceptable to reject a case only because the tribunal disagree with the choice of pool, as was the case in *Kidd*.[42]

Recent trends in the US courts have been less optimistic, with discrimination cases characterised by complex (and costly) statistical arguments accompanied by equally complex legal controversy.[43] These cases clearly demonstrate the ease with which statistics can be moulded to support a preconceived conclusion. Possibly the epitome of this process is the recent race discrimination case of *Wards Cove* v. *Atonio*,[44] in which the Supreme Court refused to uphold a finding of discrimination against an employer whose work-force was almost wholly segregated, unskilled jobs being filled predominantly by Filipino and other ethnic minority workers and skilled jobs by whites. The Court of Appeal had held that a prima facie case of discrimination had been established by demonstrating that ethnic minorities constituted a high percentage of unskilled workers and a low percentage of skilled employees. The Supreme Court rejected such an internal work-force comparison as fundamentally misconceived, on the grounds that it was 'nonsensical' to ignore the qualifications required for the differing jobs. Instead it insisted that the proper comparison should be between the racial composition of the jobs at issue and that of the *qualified* population in the relevant labour market. Most disturbing is the refusal by White J, giving judgment for the Court, to use the principle of disparate impact to correct institutional disadvantage. If the absence of ethnic minorities in skilled positions was due to the dearth of qualified workers among these groups, he declared, this could not fall within the principle of disparate impact. Otherwise, he argued, any employer who had a racially segregated work-force would have to face the possibility of being brought before the courts to justify the practice. Yet what White J depicted as a nightmare scenario is arguably the way forward. Clear and consistent segregation of women into low paying or unskilled jobs should be sufficient to trigger scrutiny and the duty to produce workable plans for employment equity.

Even if agreement can be reached on choice of pool, controversy might arise over the construction of 'considerably smaller' in the UK statute. Thus, in *ex p. Seymour Smith*,[45] the applicant was contesting the two year eligibility limit in employment protection legislation.[46] Statistics presented to the court showed that over the period of years between 1985 and 1991,

---

[42] Above n. 32.
[43] See e.g., *EEOC* v. *O & G Spring* 38F 3d 872 and *EEOC* v. *Chicago Miniature* 947 F 2d 292.
[44] *Ward's Cove Packing* v. *Atonio* 109 S Ct 2115 (1988).
[45] *R.* v. *Secretary of State for Employment, exp. Seymour Smith* [1994] IRLR 448 (QBD).

the proportion of men who could comply with the requirement (two years' continuous service at sixteen or more hours a week) ranged from 72 to 77.4 per cent, while the corresponding figures for women were in the range of 63.8 to 68.9 per cent. This meant that on average the proportion of women who could comply was about 89.1 per cent of the proportion of men who could comply.

The High Court held that this disparity was not sufficient to fulfil the statutory test, while the Court of Appeal found the opposite. The House of Lords considered that more definitive guidance from the ECJ was required. It therefore referred the case to Europe, asking the European Court to propound a 'legal test for establishing whether a measure adopted by a member state has such a degree of disparate effect as between men and women as to amount to indirect discrimination'.[47] It is submitted that any statistically significant disparity should constitute a 'considerable difference'. In a fair world without institutional barriers, it should be assumed that benefits and detriments will be evenly distributed across the genders. Statistical significance ensures that the disparity is not simply due to chance. Any further disparity ought to suffice to throw the burden of justification on the defendant.

The *Seymour Smith* litigation exposes yet another conundrum in the definition of indirect discrimination: the problem of fluctuating numbers. Lord Hoffman in the House of Lords was particularly concerned at the way in which the statistical picture changed over time, with the gap between men and women narrowing in the period after 1992. Indeed, the Court of Appeal declared only that the qualifying period was discriminatory in May 1991.[48] One of the questions referred to the ECJ, therefore, concerns the date at which it is appropriate to measure a disparity between men and women: is it when the disputed provision was adopted, or when it was brought into force, or when the employee was dismissed? It will be argued below that the only way out of this conundrum is to move away from the reliance on the concept of indirect discrimination, with its uneasy attempts to incorporate a group perspective into an essentially individualistic framework, and instead to give rights to temporary or part-time workers as such.

c) MARKET FORCES

In the last resort, the existence of disparate impact is not necessarily unlawful. Built into the law is the permission for a respondent to show that the discrimination is 'justifiable irrespective of the sex of the person to whom it is applied'. The ECJ has developed a similar defence for indirect discrimination claims both under Article 119 and the Equal Treatment Directive. The weight given to the respondent's arguments in defence is a crucial determinant of the effectiveness of anti-discrimination legislation.

---

[46] Unfair Dismissal (Variation of Qualifying Period) Order 1985 (SI 1985/782)
[47] *R. v. Secretary of State for Employment, ex p. Seymour Smith* [1997] IRLR 315 (HL).
[48] *ex p. Seymour Smith* [1995] IRLR 464 (CA) at p. 476.

Yet the notion of justifiability inevitably requires a value judgement. As Browne-Wilkinson J perceptively noted in *Clarke* v. *Eley Kynoch*, there is no generally accepted view of the relative priorities to be given to eliminating discriminatory practices on the one hand and the profitability of a business on the other.[49] As a result, the provisions have produced a range of judicial formulae, reflecting the whole spectrum of value judgements.

The origin of the test was the seminal US case of *Griggs* v. *Duke Power*.[50] This and subsequent cases set the value of anti-discrimination measures high, requiring proof that the exclusionary requirement or condition was necessary for the business of the employer or that it was essential to effective job performance.[51] Even if the employer could prove business necessity and job relatedness, it remained open for the plaintiff to argue that there was a less discriminatory alternative which would also serve the employers' business interest.[52] A similar set of priorities is clear from the UK case of *Steel* v. *UPW*,[53] in which the EAT declared emphatically that the employer was required to show both that the requirement or condition was necessary, and that no non-discriminatory alternative was available. However, the extent to which the tribunals and courts were prepared to prioritise equality issues soon waned, and the standard of justification progressively slipped. A particularly low point was reached in the race discrimination case of *Ojutiku* v. *Manpower Services Commission*,[54] in which the Court of Appeal held that an act was justified merely if the reasons for doing it were such that they would be acceptable to right thinking persons as sound and tolerable reasons for so doing. This steady decline in the standard of justification prompted Browne-Wilkinson J (as he then was) in *Clarke* v. *Eley Kynoch*[55] to express disquiet at the extent to which the matter was left to the unfettered discretion of the industrial tribunal. A strikingly similar decline in the justification test has occurred in the US. Most serious was *Wards Cove* v. *Atonio*,[56] in which the Supreme Court by a bare majority specifically rejected the view that a practice should be essential or indispensable to the employer's business before its discriminatory impact could be justified. Instead, the practice need only serve legitimate employment goals of the employer. Moreover, the burden of proof of justification, which previously rested squarely with the employer, was shifted back to the plaintiff. All the employer need do is to produce evidence of a business justification which the plaintiff must show to be invalid. Finally, if a plaintiff adduced a less discriminatory alternative, it would have to be equally effective, taking costs into account. This unabashed reversal of previous caselaw was viewed by Stevens J, dissenting, as astonishing.

Subsequent events in the US are worth noting. Attempts to reverse the

---

[49] Above n. 22, at p. 174.     [50] 401 US 424 (1971).
[51] *Dothard* v. *Rawlinson*, above n. 16.     [52] *Albemarle* v. *Moody* 422 US 405 (1975).
[53] [1978] ICR 181 (EAT).     [54] [1982] ICR 661 (CA).
[55] Above n. 22.     [56] 109 S Ct 2115 (1988).

effects of *Ward's Cove* by legislation were initially vetoed by President Bush. Two years of hard wrangling eventually produced a dilute compromise.[57] The main thrust of the Civil Rights Act 1991[58] is its reassertion that the employer bears the burden of proving the justification defence. For the rest, the Act states quizzically only that the law should continue to be as it was before *Wards Cove*. Most ambiguous is its definition of the standard of justification. Whereas *Griggs* insisted on strict business necessity, the Act requires proof that 'the challenged practice is job related for the position in question and consistent with business necessity',[59] where the terms 'business necessity' and 'job related' are defined only by reference to the Supreme Court's decisions in *Griggs* and other employment decisions before *Wards Cove*. Is this a standard as strict as *Griggs*, or has it slipped into a requirement merely that the reasons for the disparity relate to business needs? Certainly, the Bush administration declared that the standard of justification in *Wards Cove* had not been changed, although academics continue to argue that the Act gives a strong signal to the courts to adopt a more pro-plaintiff line.[60] Equally problematic is the weight given to the costs of proposed less discriminatory alternatives. In reality, cost arguments simply legitimate the continued imposition of costs on women.[61]

The signals from the ECJ have been equally complex. When indirect discrimination was first formulated, in *Jenkins* v. *Kingsgate*,[62] the defence was relatively open ended, stressing mainly the need for objectively proved reasons. This was significantly tightened in later cases. For employment related discrimination, the Court in *Bilka*[63] held that an employer must prove that the means chosen serve a real business need, are appropriate to achieve that objective and are necessary to that end. Similarly, for discrimination which derives from legislation and other social policy issues, *Rinner Kühn* stated that the discriminatory impact could only be justified if the means corresponded to an objective necessary for social policy, and were appropriate and necessary to achieve that end.[64]

On its face, this standard appears relatively strict. However, its application in particular cases varies. Until very recently, in cases before UK courts, the elimination of discrimination generally gave way in face of perceived financial advantages, however marginal, and whether accruing to a private employer or to the government. This has been achieved by gently sliding from the notion of business necessity to that of reasonable needs of an employer, and from the requirement of a tight fit between means and end, to a mere balancing of those reasonable needs against discriminatory

---

[57] For a useful description of the process through Congress, see (1992), 106 *Harvard Law Review*, p. 896.
[58] Civil Rights Act 1991, s. 105.      [59] *ibid.*
[60] (1992) *Harvard Law Review*, p. 913.
[61] (1993) 106 *Harvard Law Review*, p. 1621.      [62] [1981] ICR 592 (ECJ).
[63] *Bilka-Kaufhaus* 170/84 [1986] IRLR 317 (ECJ).
[64] *Rinner Kühn* 171/88 [1989] IRLR 493 (ECJ).

impact. Thus in *Kidd* v. *DRG* the EAT accepted that it was justifiable to make part-time workers redundant before full-timers because of the advantages set out by the employer, including fewer uniforms to launder and fewer administrative duties such as change-over briefings and recording of employees' details. The EAT, while accepting that these advantages were marginal, nevertheless held that it was unquestionably correct to say they justified the practice.[65] Equally problematic was the case of *Cobb* v. *Secretary of State for Employment*,[66] which concerned a challenge to the terms of Community Service, a scheme established to provide temporary employment for the long-term unemployed. According to Wood J the decision on justification was essentially one of balancing all the factors, where the degree of discrimination was just one consideration. Although lip service was paid to the test in *Rinner Kühn*, in fact the application of the criteria show a marked deference to the economic and administrative requirements of the State. This approach was endorsed by the Court of Appeal in *Jones* v. *Manchester*, in which Croom Johnson LJ held that the industrial tribunal had put the onus of proof too high by asking if the requirement was essential. Instead, it should have asked if the requirement fulfilled the reasonable needs of the employer.[67]

It is only very recently that the courts, led by the House of Lords, have adopted a test of strict scrutiny. In *ex p. EOC*,[68] which concerned a challenge to the qualifying periods for employment protection rights, the Secretary of State maintained that the discriminatory effect of a qualifying period was justified by its positive impact on employment creation. In particular, the five year qualifying period for part-time workers was said to maintain employment opportunities by decreasing the indirect costs of employing part-time workers. The House of Lords, true to the spirit of *Rinner Kühn*,[69] held that while the maintenance of employment opportunities was a legitimate policy, the means chosen were not appropriate or suitable to achieve that end. Not only was there insufficient evidence of an unemployment effect, the argument itself was untenable. If the reduction of indirect costs was a legitimate means, then so would be the reduction of direct costs, including cutting the pay of part-time workers. Such a policy would fly in the face of all principles of anti-discrimination law. The five year period was therefore held not to be objectively justified. An even more sophisticated approach was used in the High Court and the Court of Appeal in *ex p. Seymour Smith*. The High Court examined a variety of economic and industrial relations sources to aid in its assessment of the proposition that removing employment protection creates jobs. It concluded that there was in fact a woeful absence of any substantial probative

---

[65] Above n. 32, at p. 446.    [66] [1989] IRLR 464 (EAT).
[67] *Jones* v. *Manchester* [1993] IRLR 218 (CA) at p. 231.
[68] [1991] IRLR 493 (DC); [1993] IRLR 10 (CA); [1994] IRLR 176 (HL).
[69] Above n. 64.

material to sustain this argument, and therefore rejected the defence. This approach was endorsed by the Court of Appeal and the case now awaits the response of the ECJ. In particular, the House of Lords has asked the ECJ what material a Member State need adduce in support of its grounds for justification. In the meantime, there is clear evidence that the number of part-time jobs has in fact increased since part-time workers were given equal rights with full-timers. Between 1995 and 1996, the number of part-time jobs has increased by 280,000, nearly four times more than the previous year.[70]

It is disappointing to note that progress in the UK has not been reflected in the ECJ. The recent case of *Nolte*[71] demonstrates how easy it is to soften the rigours of the justification approach. The case concerned German social security law, which excluded individuals working fewer than fifteen hours a week and whose income fell below a given level. Such workers could not participate in the old-age insurance scheme, which also covered invalidity and sickness benefit. Despite the admitted fact that this provision excluded considerably more women than men, the Court held it to be justified. The Court claimed to be applying the *Rinner Kühn*[72] standard. But it introduced a disturbingly broad caveat by holding that, since social policy is a matter for Member States, the latter had a broad margin of discretion in choosing measures capable of achieving their social and employment policy objectives. The policy of fostering marginal employment was a legitimate one, unrelated to gender, and the State was reasonably entitled to consider that the legislation in question was necessary in order to achieve that aim. In other words the standard has been significantly diluted, from one which required objective proof of necessity, to one which deferred to the State's opinion that the measure was necessary, provided the latter was reasonable. There are clear and worrying echoes of the developments in the US after *Wards Cove* and the Civil Rights Act. It is to be hoped that in the *Seymour Smith* case, the ECJ will take the opportunity of reasserting the strict standard of justification found in the cases earlier in the decade.

The cases described above have all approached problematic conflicts of interests as requiring a solution in favour of one side or the other. A more fruitful strategy would be to consider possible compromise solutions, which could take into account the cost to the respondent of carrying the burden of rectifying a discrimination which he or she did not intend to create, while also ensuring that progress is made towards alleviating the plight of the disadvantaged group. In some American and Canadian cases, this has been formulated in terms of a 'duty of accommodation', which may not entail abandoning an indirectly discriminatory practice but instead modifying it to accommodate the needs of particular groups. The argument in favour of such a duty is perceptively stated by McIntyre J in the Canadian case of *Re*

[70] EOR No. 68 (1996), p. 4.
[71] Case C-317/93 [1996] IRLR 225 (ECJ).    [72] Above n. 64.

*Ontario Human Rights Commission* v. *Simpson Sears.*[73] Instead of applying a strict hierarchy of interests, in which one interest is held to trump others, he argued that the recognition of an inevitable conflict of interest led instead to a duty both to respect and to limit all rights: a duty of compromise or accommodation. This duty was relatively easily expressed in the case at issue, which concerned discrimination against an employee whose religious observance of the Sabbath on a Saturday conflicted with her duties to work in the employer's shop on Saturdays. In such a case, the employer was not expected to cease all Saturday working, but simply to accommodate this employee's needs. Its transplantation into cases of sex discrimination may be less straightforward, but clearly not impossible. A clear example of a case in which a duty to accommodate would have produced a more positive result was the US case of *Boyd* v. *Ozark Airlines.*[74] In this case, the Court of Appeal dismissed a claim of discrimination based on the exclusionary effect of a minimum height requirement for airline pilots. In doing so, it accepted the employer's defence, namely that the cockpit was designed in such a way that the airline could only safely be managed by a person of the requisite height. A duty to accommodate would have necessitated the adjustment of the cockpit rather than the blanket exclusion of a large number of potential employees. As Baer points out 'airplanes, like cars, are redesigned rather often—the federal Aviation Administration, more aggressive than the EEOC, tends to require such changes.'[75] Its most valuable and effective application would be to impose a duty to accommodate workers (both men and women) with parental responsibilities, by adjusting working times in a way which reflects the needs of both parties.

## III.  STRUCTURAL BARRIERS

The discussion thus far has been concerned with both the potential and the limits inherent in the direct and indirect discrimination provisions. It is now critical to consider the interaction between these conceptual tools and the social problems they address. To what extent has it been possible to use these concepts to challenge or indeed dismantle structural discrimination? This question is examined by considering three main structural impediments: (a) 'women's work' (b) education and training; and (c) sexual harassment.

a)  'WOMEN'S WORK'

Why are women disproportionately excluded from better paying or higher status jobs? Four key factors are examined in this section. First,

---

[73]  23 D.L.R. 4th 321 (1986). For a recent UK model, see the Disability Discrimination Act 1995.
[74]  568 F 2d 50 (Court of Appeals, 8th Circuit).
[75]  J. A. Baer, *Women in American Law* (Holmes & Meier, 1991), p. 89.

stereotypical assumptions about women's capabilities and role retain a tenacious hold on the labour market. Secondly, women may be excluded from an occupation on the grounds that this is necessary for their 'protection'. Thirdly, the best benefits are still strongly associated with full-time, continuous working, excluding women whose caring responsibilities have led to part-time and interrupted working patterns. Finally, and relatedly, the demands of paid work have not been sufficiently sensitive to the demands imposed by child-care and unpaid domestic work. What impact has anti-discrimination made on each of these issues? It will be argued that some change is evident, but real structural change remains a pipe-dream.

## i) **Equal or Different: Stereotypical Assumptions**

Stereotypical images of women have throughout the ages been used to justify detrimental treatment. Because women are classified as 'different' in the relevant respects, it appears justifiable to subject them to detrimental treatment. It is thus crucial that anti-discrimination law be incisive enough to pierce these stereotypes. The dangers of failing to do so were starkly illustrated in the US case of *Dothard* v. *Rawlinson*,[76] which concerned the legality of the prohibition on women prison guards being employed in 'contact positions' in Alabama prisons. The claim of discrimination was rejected by the Supreme Court. Although the Alabama prisons had deteriorated into an 'atmosphere of rampant violence, inhospitable to whatever sex',[77] it was held that women could justifiably be excluded from employment. This was because women were specific targets of assault and rape, and therefore cast as a danger to the control of the whole institution. 'Her very womanhood' declared Stewart J, giving judgment for the Court, 'would thus directly undermine her capacity to provide the security that is the essence of a [prison guard's] responsibility.'[78] The deeply problematic nature of this approach is highlighted by Marshall J, dissenting: 'This perpetuates the most insidious of old myths—that women, wittingly or not, are seductive sexual objects.'[79] The result was that women had to pay the price in lost job opportunities for the threat of depraved conduct.[80]

An equally disturbing case of stereotypes is found in the US Court of Appeal case of *EEOC* v. *Sears Roebuck*[81] in which, as we have seen, the court held that the fact that very few women were found in commission-earning sales positions in the company was due to their lack of interest in the job. The court accepted evidence which purported to prove that this lack of interest was due to women's fear of or dislike for the cut-throat competition, the increased pressure and the risks associated with

---

[76] Above n. 16.
[77] *ibid.*, at pp. 333–5 (*per* Stewart J).
[78] *ibid.*, at p. 335.
[79] *ibid.*, at p. 343.
[80] See *ibid.*, at p. 343 *per* Marshall J dissenting.
[81] 839F 2d 302 (1988).

commission-earning sales. Non-commissioned sales, by contrast, were ostensibly preferred by women because they were associated with more
social contact and friendship and less pressure and risk. As the dissenting
judge stated, women as described in the majority opinion 'exhibit the very
stereotypical qualities for which they have been assigned low status positions throughout history'.[82]

As in the US, courts in the UK have consciously struggled with the
transition from difference to equality. In his first brush with the Act,[83] Lord
Denning declared: 'Although the Act applies equally to men and women,
it would be very wrong . . . if this statute were thought to obliterate the
differences between men and women . . . The natural differences of sex
must be regarded even in the interpretation of an Act of Parliament.'[84]
By 1980, however, the Court of Appeal was openly forcing itself to put
aside such assumptions of difference. The ambivalence is however clear:
although all the judges in *MOD* v. *Jeremiah*[85] found that the men and
women were 'alike' in the relevant respects, at least two could not hide their
more instinctive responses. Thus, according to Lord Denning, 'A woman's
hair is her crowning glory. She does not like it disturbed; especially when
she has just had a "hair-do".' It was 'obviously reasonable,' added
Brightman LJ 'that women, who are more concerned with and devote more
time and attention to their personal appearance than men' should not have
to work in the extremely dirty conditions of a colour bursting shop.

The importance of piercing stereotypes has, however, slowly gained the
ascendancy, and the notion of equality reshaped accordingly. This has been
particularly apparent in denting presumptions about women's role as secondary earners within a family. In *Skyrail* v. *Coleman*,[86] a woman was
dismissed from a travel agency when she married a man from a rival agency.
The reason given for dismissing her and not her husband was that he was
assumed to be the breadwinner. This was not considered to be discriminatory by the EAT, but the Court of Appeal by a majority upheld her claim.
Significantly, Lawton LJ stated that the dismissal of a woman based on the
assumption that men are more likely than women to be primary supporters
of their families can be discriminatory. However, Shaw LJ delivered a
stinging dissent. In his view, the victim was 'excessively outraged' and the
claim was 'trivial, banal, artificial and pretentious'.[87] But the courts have
held the line, upholding a claim of discrimination by a woman who was
refused employment as a waitress because her employer considered
that women with children were unreliable,[88] and by a woman refused

---

[82]  839F 2d 302 (1988), at p. 321.
[83]  *Peake* v. *Automative Products* [1977] ICR 968 (CA).
[84]  *ibid.*, at p. 973.
[85]  *Ministry of Defence* v. *Jeremiah* [1980] ICR 13 (CA).
[86]  [1981] ICR 864 (CA).
[87]  *ibid.*, at pp. 872–3.
[88]  *Hurley* v. *Mustoe* [1981] ICR 490 (EAT).

secondment by a Welsh local authority who considered she would not honour her obligations because her husband had a permanent job in London.[89] Crucially, Browne-Wilkinson J declared in the latter case that a point had been reached where stereotypes and generalised assumptions were no longer to be considered grounds of difference.[90] Similarly, the refusal to allow a woman judo referee to referee men's national competitions[91] was held to be discriminatory, as was the denial to a woman of a position on an all-male painting team.[92] However, the ability to transcend presumptions of difference remains precarious. As recently as 1990, the Court of Appeal upheld a tribunal's rejection of a claim of discrimination by a woman who had been unable to secure a position as a site surveyor.[93] Although Neill LJ could see ample evidence of the possibility that the employer was influenced by the notion that a man would fit in better, he was not prepared to disturb the finding of the tribunal.

Not all cases of stereotyping are decided under the substantive discrimination provisions. The fact that the SDA applies only to those who are employed under a contract of service, or a 'contract personally to execute any work or labour'[94] has prevented women from asserting the right to enter some important male preserves. Thus a woman refused a position as a cab driver on the grounds of her sex[95] was excluded from the Act on the grounds that she was not employed under a contract either of service or personally to execute services. Similarly, allegations by a woman of discrimination in selection to the position of justice of the peace was rejected on the grounds that office was not contractual.[96] Again, a woman denied a renewal of an agency agreement for the distribution of newspapers previously held by her father was held to be outside of the protection of the Act on the technical ground that she did not execute the agreement personally.[97] Her allegation that the denial was because she was a woman with young children therefore went unexamined.[98]

Other exclusions in the Act have been utilised to the same effect. A woman applicant for a position as a rent officer was held to be outside of the scope of the Act on a highly technical construction of the provisions on Crown employment.[99] A woman who was denied a research fellowship at an all-male Cambridge college was unable to bring a claim of sex

[89] *Horsey* v. *Dyffed CC* [1982] ICR 755 (EAT).
[90] *ibid.*, at p. 760.
[91] *British Judo Association* v. *Petty* [1980] ICR 660 (EAT).
[92] *Grieg* v. *Community Industry* [1979] ICR 356 (EAT).
[93] *Baker* v. *Cornwall* [1990] IRLR 194 (CA).
[94] SDA 1975, s. 82(1).
[95] *Rice* v. *Fon A Car* [1980] ICR 133 (EAT): see SDA 1975, s. 82(1).
[96] *Knight* v. *AG* [1979] ICR 194 (EAT).
[97] *Mirror Group* v. *Gunning* [1986] ICR 145 (CA).
[98] The SDA definition is nevertheless wider than that under the EPCA 1978. See further below.
[99] *Department of Environment* v. *Fox* [1978] ICR 736 (EAT): see SDA 1975 s. 85.

discrimination for at least four different reasons: the fact that the college statutes excluding women were executed before the Act, the charitable status of the college, the absence of a contract of employment and the lack of direct effect of the Equal Treatment Directive.[100] A particularly problematic exception was that permitting discrimination in pursuance of statutory authority. This exception was construed so widely in *GLC* v. *Farrar*[101] as to render lawful a local authority licence forbidding women wrestlers, on the grounds that it was issued in pursuance of the authority's powers under the Local Government Act 1963. On advice by the EC Commission that this result breached the Equal Treatment Directive, the government was forced to introduce a statutory provision explicitly outlawing discriminatory conditions in licences.[102]

### ii) **Protection or Exclusion: Whose Choice?**

A particularly challenging problem for the equality–difference debate remains the question of protective legislation, or measures which prohibit the employment of women in certain jobs which are thought to pose a specific danger to women. As was seen in Chapter 2, protective legislation has been the subject of fierce controversy for at least 150 years. Although the UK was one of the pioneers of protective legislation in the nineteenth century, it was brought into the international arena by the ILO early in the twentieth century. It is therefore worth examining protective legislation in its international context. Prohibition of night-work for women was the subject of regulation as early as 1906 at the Berne Convention; and it became one of the first ILO conventions.[103] Also relatively early was Convention 45 (1935) prohibiting underground work by women in mines. Both conventions are still widely ratified: in December 1995, as many as forty-nine Member States were party to Convention 89 prohibiting night-work for women, and eighty-eight States were parties to Convention 45 (underground work).

But even the members of ILO are by no means at one on this issue. The justifiability of sustaining these conventions, particularly that of night-work, was questioned at a recent ILO conference,[103a] revealing a debate with familiar contours. Both the Committee of Experts and the workers' representatives continue to argue that protective legislation is genuinely necessary to prevent the exploitation of women. The workers' representatives argued in particular that such legislation was necessary to relieve women's double load. However, not all proponents of protective legislation have women's best interests at heart. Certainly, as we have seen, workers' representatives have frequently supported protective legislation as much in order

---

[100] *Hugh-Jones* v. *St John's College* [1979] ICR 848 (EAT): see SDA 1975, ss. 43(2), 85(1) and 51(1).
[101] [1980] ICR 266 (EAT).    [102] SDA 1986, s. 5.
[103] Convention No. 4 (1919) revised in 1934, 1948, and 1990.
[103a] ILO Record of Proceedings 1990, s. 26.

to protect men from competition by women as to protect women from exploitation. Another deeply problematic ground for supporting such legislation was articulated in the ILO debates by Egypt and Senegal, who argued vociferously that protection for women was important in order to uphold the family structure and values of their societies.

A similar spectrum of opinions is evident within the opposing camp. Many feminist thinkers dispute the benefits of protective legislation, arguing instead that the focus on difference simply legitimates detrimental treatment and exclusion. They find themselves uneasy bedfellows with both liberal and neo-liberal opponents of protective legislation. Liberals argue that equality must always be symmetrical, outlawing protective legislation for the very reason that it protects women and not men. Neo-liberal opposition comes from a very different angle. On this view, such legislation is simply an unwarranted interference with the 'free' market. The former view is well represented by several Western States within the ILO, who have now denounced Convention 89 on the liberal ground that it contravenes a symmetrical view of equality. A similar stance has been taken by the EC. The derogation from the equality principle in the Equal Treatment Directive for 'provisions concerning the protection of women'[104] has been narrowly construed by the ECJ[105] except in respect of provisions concerning pregnancy and maternity. In addition, the Equal Treatment Directive requires protective legislation to be revised when the 'concern for protection which originally inspired them is no longer well founded'.[106] More recently, the European Commission has taken a stance which is even less equivocal: a Communication issued in 1987 requires Member States to remove any restrictive legislation which limits the access of women to employment.[107] Any exception to the principle of equal treatment must, according to the Communication, be justified by reference to the 'physiological' test of the 'separate biological condition' of women; if not, they should be repealed or extended to protect all workers.

Whereas the opposition of the EC to protective legislation largely derives from a liberal view of equality, that of the UK government is determinedly neo-liberal. In 1986, most of the existing statutory provisions restricting women's hours of work or other terms and conditions of work were repealed,[108] and the Employment Act 1989 repealed or modified various other provisions requiring differential treatment of women, including the prohibition of the employment of women underground in mines and the restrictions on women cleaning machinery in factories.[109] This required

---

[104] Equal Treatment Directive (76/207), Article 2(4).
[105] *Johnston* v. *RUC* Case 228/84 [1986] IRLR 263 (ECJ).
[106] Article 5(2)(c); the first revision to be carried out by 1980: Article 9(1).
[107] *Protective Legislation for Women in the Member States of the EC*, Communication of March 20, 1987, COM (87) 105 final.
[108] SDA 1986, s. 7.
[109] Employment Act 1990, s. 9.

the UK to denounce not only ILO Conventions 31 (night-work) and 45 (underground work), but also the relevant sections of the European Social Charter.[110] An equally vociferous version of the neo-liberal view was articulated by the employers' representatives on the ILO. Their concern was clearly to remove all restrictions on night-work in order to enhance the flexibility with which they could organise their labour needs.[111]

The neo-liberals and liberals might agree in their opposition to protective legislation. But they tend to disagree fundamentally on the solution. Neo-liberals advocate the achievement of equality by 'levelling down' or removing all protection. The result is that terms and conditions for women deteriorate with no corresponding benefit for men. This has been the unwavering stance of the UK government: with few exceptions, protection for women has simply been repealed.[112] By contrast, liberal opponents of protective legislation urge that equality be achieved by 'levelling up', that is, the extension of benefits to all workers. Notably, both the EC and the ILO have taken the latter view, the EC declaring that 'equality should not be made the occasion for a disimprovement of working conditions for one sex',[113] and the ILO arguing that the promotion of equality of opportunity and treatment should not be sought at the expense of a degradation of working conditions.[114] The ILO has done more than simply declare its preference for the substantive option; in 1990 a new convention on night-work was adopted which, crucially, applies to both men and women. Recognising that the question of night-work affects all workers, both in respect of their own health and their family obligations, the Convention specifies that special measures should be taken to include minimum protection for night-workers' health and to assist them to meet family and social responsibilities.

The above discussion has concerned measures mandated by legislation. The courts have also been faced with employer-initiated policies of excluding women on the grounds that they are 'different' from men, either in terms of personal strength, sexuality or reproductive capacities. Two quite different responses are evident in the caselaw. One is both to accept the employer's judgement as to the risks to women, and to endorse exclusion as the acceptable solution. We have already seen that this was the approach in *Dothard* v. *Rawlinson*, where the US Supreme Court accepted the view that women were particularly vulnerable to sexual attacks by prisoners and

---

[110] Art 8(4)(6).

[111] ILO Record of Proceedings 1990, section 26.

[112] The prohibition on women lifting or carrying loads likely to cause injury was extended to men (Mines and Quarries Act 1954, s. 93); but prohibition of underground working for women and on cleaning of machinery which cause injury are simply repealed (Mines and Quarries Act 1954, s. 124(i) and Factories Act 1961, s. 20).

[113] *Protective Legislation for Women in the Member States of the EC*, Communication of March 20, 1987, COM (87) 105 final.

[114] ILO General Survey 1988, p. 154.

therefore endorsed the policy of excluding women from the job of prison guard. Equally problematic has been the courts' response to so-called 'reproductive hazards'. While special health and safety measures are necessary to assist pregnant women to continue in work for the duration of their pregnancy,[115] provided no detriment is attached, this is not necessarily true for all women of child-bearing age, particularly those who have no intention of bearing children. The issue arose starkly in *Page* v. *Freight Hire*,[116] in which the applicant, a woman heavy goods driver, was not permitted to drive vehicles carrying dimethylformamide (DMF) because the manufacturers had warned her employers that the chemical was dangerous to women of child-bearing age. The result was that her employment was effectively terminated. The EAT held that the employers had not acted unlawfully because they had taken the decision in pursuance of their responsibilities under the Health and Safety Act 1974, and were therefore immune under the exception in section 51 of the SDA for actions which are necessary to comply with a pre-existing law.

It is striking that in both *Page* and *Dothard* v. *Rawlinson* the risks to men were considered to be irrelevant. In *Dothard* the proper response to the inevitable attacks on both women and male guards should not have been to limit the employment opportunities of women but to take proper action against the offenders.[117] Moreover, a general improvement in prison conditions would be of greater value to all parts of society than simply attempting to exclude women. A similar pattern emerges from *Page*. Documentation from the chemical manufacturer indicated that both men and women could suffer loss of appetite, intestinal disorder, and liver and kidney problems from excessive exposure to DMF; yet the option of insisting on improving health and safety standards for all was simply not considered. The implausibility of the alternative option, that of excluding men from the work-place because of such hazards, simply underlines the ease with which women can be marginalised.

The second judicial response has been far more sensitive both to the dangers of generalisation and to the legitimacy of a solution based on exclusion of women. This is reflected in the decision of the ECJ in *RUC* v. *Johnston*.[118] In that case, the Chief Constable of the Royal Ulster Constabulary refused to renew the contracts of full-time women in the RUC reserve because he believed that if they were permitted to carry fire-arms they would be more vulnerable to assassination attempts than their male counterparts. Both the UK and the Commission argued that the provisions were inspired by a well-founded 'concern' to protect women and thus fell within the derogation for 'provisions concerning the protection of women' in the

---

[115] See Pregnant Workers' Directive 1994, ch. 5.
[116] [1981] ICR 299 (EAT).
[117] See dissenting opinion of Marshall J.
[118] *Johnston*, above n. 105.

Equal Treatment Directive.[119] The Court recognised, however, that the risks in question affected women and men in the same way. Taking the diametrically opposite approach to that of the US Supreme Court, it held unequivocally that the derogation in the Directive must be strictly construed. Women should not be excluded simply on the ground that public opinion demanded that they be given greater protection from risks which affect men and women in the same way.

In the arena of reproductive hazards, a similarly sensitive approach is found in the US case of *UAW* v. *Johnson Controls*,[120] which concerned the employer's policy of banning all fertile women from jobs involving exposure to lead. Only women who could provide medical proof of infertility were permitted to work in these jobs. The Supreme Court struck down the policy as discriminatory. Blackmun J, giving judgment for the Court, had no doubt that the policy displayed obvious bias: fertile men but not fertile women were given the choice as to whether to risk their reproductive health. This was despite clear evidence of the debilitating effect of lead exposure on the male reproductive system. However, the judgment remains tied to a formal view of equality. Instead of demanding that the work-place be made safer for both men and women, it was held to be satisfactory for the employer simply to allow women to work on the same terms, and thus subject to the same risks, as men. Far more useful would have been a 'levelling up' requirement, that is a demand that minimum safety standards be observed for all.

### iii) **Working Patterns: Flexibility for Whom?**

We have already seen that the exponential increase in the number of women in the paid work-force reflects a coincidence of supply and demand side factors. On the demand side, recent trends strongly favour a move towards flexible working patterns, allowing employers to make greater use of machinery, to match staffing to peak hours or to save labour costs in slack periods. On the supply side, jobs which do not insist on full-time, continuous working are the only option for women who need to combine domestic responsibilities with paid work. As a result, non-standard forms of work have been the main source of new employment for women over the past two decades. Indeed in 1994, as many as 5.5 million women, one-half of all women of working age, were in non-standard forms of work.[121]

The illusion of a happy fit between supply and demand is soon dispelled when the terms and conditions are examined. In fact, non-standard forms of work are populated predominantly by women on sub-standard terms and conditions. This is because, as recent research demonstrates, the introduction of flexible working is primarily aimed at meeting the business

---

[119] Article 2(3).        [120] 499 US 187.
[121] S. Dex and A. McCulloch, *Flexible Employment in Britain* (EOC Research Discussion Series, 1995), p. 132.

requirements of the employer. Although this may coincide with the needs of women with families, the shape of the job remains dependent on the employer's business purposes and might change accordingly. Indeed, Coyle's study shows that a key feature of the 1990s has been the intensification of working time, resulting from the reduction of staff levels but with an ever-increasing volume of work. 'So called flexible working arrangements in this context are often extremely inflexible. Part-time shifts and part-time hours are often structured to suit operational needs rather than those of women and families. Although job sharing and part-time working is now widespread practice, it is still rarely a real option at more senior operational levels.'[122]

This section examines the role of the law in either facilitating the exploitation of non-standard workers, or, alternatively, in protecting them. It focuses particularly on part-time workers; temporary workers and workers with fragmented work-histories; and homeworkers.

(1) *Part-time Workers* In 1995, at least 80 per cent of all part-time workers were women. Yet part-timers remain second-class citizens, working in conditions characterised by low pay, insecurity, and lack of access to contractual benefits (see Chapter 4). Outside the area of pay, discrimination against part-timers has been actively encouraged by the legislature. Until 1995, full-time workers (working sixteen or more hours per week) could qualify for rights to redundancy compensation and protection against unfair dismissal if they had worked continuously for two years.[123] However, this period jumped to five years for employees working less than sixteen hours a week; while those who worked fewer than eight hours were excluded entirely.[124] Because part-timers tend not only to work low hours but also to change jobs relatively frequently, any semblance of job security was almost impossible to amass. Such discrimination was echoed in industrial relations practice. For example, collective agreements frequently specified that part-timers should be made redundant first, and part-time workers were usually excluded from pension schemes (see Chapter 8).

Probably the most important contribution of the indirect discrimination provisions has been to challenge such discrimination. In 1994, in a decision of seminal importance, the House of Lords in *R* v. *Secretary of State, ex p. EOC* struck down the five year qualification period on the grounds that it constituted a breach of Article 119 and the Equal Treatment Directive.[125]

---

[122] A. Coyle, *Women and Organisational Change* (EOC Research Discussion Series, 1995) p. vii.

[123] Unfair Dismissal (Variation of Qualifying Period) Order 1985 (SI 1985/782).

[124] EPCA 1978, schedule 13; now amended by the Employment Protection (Part-time Employees) Regulations (1995, No. 31).

[125] *R* v. *Secretary of State for Employment, ex p. EOC* [1994] IRLR 176 (HL). Article 119 is breached by the redundancy compensation provisions and the Equal Treatment Directive by unfair dismissal provisions.

As a result, regulations were passed in 1995 repealing the hours require-ments.[126] The result is that from February 1995, all workers are treated alike regardless of the number of hours worked. It is noteworthy that the government has done more than the bare minimum in order to comply with the *EOC* case, extending protection not only to those working between eight and sixteen hours a week, but also those working fewer than eight. In addition, the hours requirements are not only removed from unfair dismissal[127] and redundancy compensation,[128] but also from other rights such as the right to written particulars of employment,[129] to return after maternity leave[130] and to time off work for trade union duties and activities.[131]

The significance of the removal of the hours qualification cannot be disputed. However, the courts have acted swiftly to limit its retrospective effects by a highly problematic interpretation of time limits. Thus when a part-time worker dismissed in 1976 attempted to claim for unfair dismissal in 1996, her claim was held to be out of time,[132] even though she had instituted proceedings within three months of the decision in *ex p. EOC*. In rejecting her claim, the Court of Appeal held that it was 'reasonably practical' for her to have presented her claim in 1976, even though it was accepted by the court that she could not be expected to have known of her rights until the case. Neill LJ held that the *EOC* case was merely declaratory of the law. Thus it was open to her even in 1976 to have simply claimed unfair dismissal, arguing that the restriction in such claims by part-time workers was indirectly discriminatory. Such an expectation of superhuman knowledge and initiative defies comprehension. While it may be true that old claims raise difficulties both practical and moral, the solution should not be sought by raising insuperable barriers, particularly since it was the action of the UK legislature in setting the qualification period which misled her. Given that the plaintiff retains the burden of proof, evidential difficul-ties will in any event make it unlikely that she will win an old claim. But she should at least have the opportunity of arguing her case.

Far more difficult are cases concerned with redundancy selection, where the best the courts can do is to influence the distribution of unemployment among a work-force, rather than to alleviate disadvantage per se. The widespread practice of making part-timers redundant before full-timers has been challenged in several cases, with mixed results.[133] Even more

---

[126] Employment Protection (Part-time Employees) Regulations (SI 1995/31), noted by A. McColgan at [1996] ILJ 43.

[127] ERA 1996, s. 108(1).     [128] *ibid.*, s. 155.

[129] *ibid.*, s. 1.     [130] *ibid.*, s. 79(1)(b).

[131] SI 1995/31, Reg 5, amending TULRECA 1992, s. 281.

[132] *Biggs* v. *Somerset CC* [1996] IRLR 203 (CA).

[133] Compare *Clarke* v. *Eley Kynoch*, above n. 22, (an agreement to make part-timers redundant before full-timers discriminatory) with *Kidd* v. *DRG*, above n. 32, (a similar agreement not discriminatory).

problematic is the well established practice of 'last in first out' (LIFO). The potential conflict of interests in this context is acute. On the one hand LIFO has been the chief means by which trade unions have succeeded in retaining some power over the process of redundancy selection. On the other hand, workers with short service, often comprising a large majority of women, are most exposed to the risk of redundancy. In general the courts have given priority to stable, predictable and agreed selection procedures, as epitomised by LIFO. In *Clarke* v. *Eley Kynoch*,[134] Browne-Wilkinson J was at pains to say that LIFO was a necessary means to achieve an agreed criterion for selection, a need which outweighed what he considered to be a minor impact. At most, it may be overturned if it perpetuates past discrimination; for example where an employer has only recently removed an exclusionary policy against women. Thus, in *Australian Iron and Steel* v. *Banovic*[135] a majority of the Australian High Court, while striking down a LIFO practice because of past discrimination, expressly supported the principle in other contexts. According to the court the discriminatory consequences should be subordinated to the employer's legitimate interest in a stable work-force, free of industrial dispute.

The above discussion shows that important progress has been made. Nevertheless, the indirect discrimination provisions remain fundamentally limited in their ability to eliminate structural barriers faced by part-time workers. This is largely because part-time workers have no rights per se. They can only expect equal treatment if they can surmount the many technical hurdles in the statute. For example, it has been necessary to convince the courts that full-time working is a 'requirement or condition' for the purposes of the statute. Several cases held that full-time working was not such a requirement or condition, with the result that part-timers foundered at the first hurdle.[136] However, the trend has fortunately been in favour of a purposive construction of these words.[137] In *Clarke* v. *Eley Kynoch*,[138] Browne-Wilkinson J was particularly concerned that the notion of a 'requirement or condition' should not be construed in a way which would defeat the purpose of the provisions, namely, the elimination of practices with a disproportionate impact.

Yet more problematic is the fact that the concept of indirect discrimination is tied to a comparison between men and women. As a result, part-timers' rights depend on proof that the impact on them as women is more damaging than that on men. Not only does this require complex statistical manoeuvres (see the discussion on individualism above). Equally seriously, it gives no useful guidance in situations in which job segregation has resulted in a work-force in which both full-timers and part-timers are

---

[134] Above n. 22.    [135] Above n. 39.    [136] *Clymo*, above n. 25.
[137] *Clarke* v. *Eley Kynoch*, above n. 22; *Briggs* [1990] IRLR 181 NICA; *Home Office* v. *Holmes* [1984] IRLR 299.
[138] [1983] ICR 165 EAT.

predominantly female. The dilemma is particularly acute when a redundancy situation arises in a predominantly female work-force. In two recent cases of this sort, the EAT responded in diametrically opposite ways. In *Clarke* v. *Eley Kynoch*[139] a collective agreement specified that part-timers should be made redundant first. All the part-time workers were women, but so were a majority of full-timers. Browne-Wilkinson J saw part-timers' rights as sufficiently important to construe the statutory formula in such a way as to strike down this practice as unlawful. However, the EAT took the opposite view in the later case of *Kidd* v. *DRG*,[140] upholding a similar collective agreement making part-time workers redundant first. *Kidd* was a particularly difficult case, since all the employees, both full-time and part-time, were women, and both the industrial tribunal and the EAT were clearly influenced by the artificiality of holding that a preference for one group of women over another was unlawful sex discrimination. Yet the reasoning only tangentially refers to this problem, relying instead on deeply problematic grounds for rejecting the claim. Despite well-known statistics demonstrating that the vast majority of part-time workers are women, the industrial tribunal, with the support of the EAT, refused to assume without evidence that more women than men were excluded by the requirement of full-time working. Indeed, the tribunal, again endorsed by the EAT, 'recognised the fact that mothers of young children are no longer conforming universally to the traditional notion that their place is in the home'.[141] This is a particularly curious statement, in that its effect was to make it all the more difficult for women with families to remain in paid work.

A more useful approach would be to move away from the generalised concept of equality and instead focus on rights for part-timers per se. This approach has been recognised in other jurisdictions. For example, in 1994, the ILO adopted a convention requiring that part-timers have equivalent protection with comparable full-time workers in specific areas such as the right to organise and bargain collectively, as well as in maternity protection, termination of employment, paid annual leave, and sick leave. Nor should it be permissible for part-timers to be paid a lower hourly basic wage solely because they work part time.[142] Unfortunately, however, by 1996, this Convention had as yet attracted no ratifications and so had not come into force. A Belgian Act passed in 1989 requires that part-time workers enjoy the same benefits as full-time workers, at least on a proportionate basis.[143]

(2) *Temporary Workers*  Women's child-care responsibilities affect not only their daily and weekly working patterns, but also their ability to work

---

[139] [1983] ICR 165 EAT.      [140] [1985] ICR 405 (EAT).      [141] *ibid.*, at p. 414.
[142] Part-Time Workers' Convention, No. 175, 1994. See too now the EC Framework Agreement on Part-Time Workers (6 June 1997).
[143] C. Engels 'Belgium' in R. Blanpain (ed.), *The Harmonization of Working Life and Family Life* (Kluwer, 1995), p. 6.

continuously. It is not surprising therefore that women are more likely than men to be in temporary jobs. Equally importantly, while male temporary jobs are predominantly full-time, the majority of women's temporary jobs are part-time (1994 figures).[144] From the demand side, the reasons why employers take on temporary workers make it inevitable that they will offer low levels of pay and job security. Temporary workers save wage costs by matching labour use to fluctuations in demand. This effect is heightened by keeping pay levels low and withholding fringe benefits.[145]

Far from protecting workers, the law has generally facilitated such exploitation. As we have seen, employment protection rights depend on being able to establish employment under a contract of service continuously for two years with the same employer. Because continuity is strictly defined, it is possible for employers to employ workers on a patchwork of temporary contracts, without accruing liability on termination. This practice has been supported by the courts.[146] Thus in *Lewis* v. *Surrey County Council*,[147] the plaintiff had worked for the council for fourteen years under a series of separate fixed term contracts, some of which were concurrent and some consecutive. The House of Lords held that she failed to qualify either for redundancy compensation or for protection against unfair dismissal. Lord Ackner was of the opinion that the facts were 'surprising if not unreal'[148] and unlikely to be repeated. This shows an astonishing lack of appreciation of modern trends towards flexibility and the consequent fragmentation of the employment relationship into different contracts. Indeed, there is evidence of a marked increase in the number of women holding several different low hours' contracts.

Nor have temporary workers as yet benefited from the progress triggered by *ex p. EOC*.[149] Most importantly, the basic two years' threshold requirement was not challenged in that case and has not been altered by the new regulations. Dex and McCulloch calculate that even after the repeal of the hours qualification, 29 per cent of women of working age, as against 22 per cent of men of working age, remain excluded.[150] It is important too that it is this which is now the subject of further proceedings. Inspired by the success in *ex p. EOC*, two private sector employees have now challenged this requirement, arguing in *R* v. *Secretary of State for Employment, ex p. Seymour Smith*[151] that significantly fewer women than men can comply with this requirement. As we have seen, the House of Lords has now asked the

---

[144] Dex and McCulloch, above n. 121, p. 36.
[145] *ibid.*, p. 22.
[146] See e.g. *Fay* v. *North Yorkshire* [1986] ICR 133 (CA).
[147] [1987] IRLR 517 (HL).
[148] *ibid.*, p. 512.
[149] Above n. 68.
[150] Dex and McCulloch, above n. 121, p. 38.
[151] *R* v. *Secretary of State for Employment, ex p. Seymour Smith and Perez* [1994] IRLR 448 QBD, [1995] IRLR 464 (CA) and [1997] IRLR 315 (HL).

ECJ to establish guidelines for determining this question. Ultimately, however, as the *Seymour Smith* litigation demonstrates, the concept of indirect discrimination is a clumsy way of dealing with the position of temporary workers. Far more appropriate would be a regime setting out specific rights for temporary workers.

(3) *Homeworkers*   Home-working remains a predominantly female phenomenon: of 662,000 homeworkers in 1993, 466,000 were women.[152] A large proportion of homeworkers are from ethnic minorities. Homeworking permits the combination of income generation with ongoing responsibility for children. Such a combination is, however, costly for the worker: low pay, isolation, and the creation of hazards and general mess in the home[153] continue to characterise homeworking (see Chapter 3). On the demand side, there are clear cost advantages to employers: labour costs can be matched precisely to fluctuations in demand, a skilled pool of workers can be maintained to respond to such fluctuations and overhead costs and factory space can be saved. Non-wage costs are also saved. Few traditional homeworkers have any fringe benefits, regardless of how many hours a week they work.

Yet this most vulnerable group of workers finds itself in a legal climate as hostile as the economic climate.[154] The repeal of minimum wages laws (see Chapter 6) has legitimated very low levels of pay. Employment protection legislation bristles with hurdles. Even the threshold requirement, proof of employment under a contract of service, has proved difficult to surmount, largely because of the sporadic and ostensibly independent nature of the work. Although homeworkers have been successful in some cases, no definite principle has been established. Thus in *Airfix Footwear* v. *Cope*,[155] a homeworker who had worked five days a week every week for a period of seven years, claimed that she had been unfairly dismissed. The EAT held that it would be highly artificial to categorise her as anything but an employee given the regularity of her service. However, Slynn J refused to lay down any general principle which would draw homeworkers as a group into the scope of the legislation, instead requiring each case to be proved on its facts. Moreover, after the Court of Appeal decision in *O'Kelly* v. *Trusthouse Forte*,[156] it has become increasingly difficult to focus on the reality of the arrangement. In *O'Kelly* the Court of Appeal insisted that a contract of services could only come into existence if the worker was obliged to accept and the employer obliged to provide work. Otherwise, the arrangement

---

[152] Dex and McCulloch, above n. 121, p. 17.

[153] U. Huws, *Home Truths: Key Findings from the National Survey of Homeworkers* (National Group on Homeworking Report No. 2), 1994.

[154] For a useful review of the position of homeworkers, see K. Ewing 'Homeworking: A Framework for Reform' [1982] ILJ 94.

[155] [1978] ICR 1210 (EAT).

[156] [1983] ICR 728 (CA).

splintered into no more than a series of daily contracts. The result is that homeworkers are required to argue their way into the legislation on a case by case basis. In *Nethermere* v. *Gardiner*,[157] for example, it was only after a trip to the Court of Appeal and the citation of twenty-two cases that an industrial tribunal's classification of two women homeworkers as employees could be upheld. Even then Stephenson LJ was at pains to follow Slynn J in *Airfix Footwear* v. *Cope* in refusing to say anything about the general position of outworkers.[158] The limitation to a contract of employment was originally intended to exclude entrepreneurs and people in business on their own account; it is ironical that it has been interpreted as excluding many of the most defenceless of non-standard workers. It is noteworthy too that in *Nethermere* the reason for the women's dismissal was a dispute over holiday pay. This is precisely the reason why the law needs to be unambiguous in its protection of homeworkers. Only if the law offers some protection against dismissal as a result of demands for better pay and conditions will any improvement be made.

The status of homeworkers is further confused by the widespread practice, endorsed by the Inland Revenue, of treating them as self-employed for the purposes of national insurance and tax. Indeed, in both *Airfix Footwear* and *Nethermere*, no national insurance deductions were made from the applicants' pay, a practice which is commonplace. However, to treat homeworkers as employees for national insurance purposes is itself problematic, because weeks in which contributions are made may not be sufficient to bring the worker over the annual threshold for national insurance protection. The only way through this morass is to include specific reference to the status of homeworkers in the relevant legislation.[159] In fact, the ILO at its 1996 Conference adopted a Convention specifically protecting homeworkers.[160] Short of this, a purposive interpretation by the courts could make important progress. An interesting precedent is the 1995 case of *Lane* v. *Shire Roofing Co.*,[161] in which it was necessary to determine the employment status of a builder seriously injured at work before liability could be placed on his employer. The judge declared emphatically that health and safety issues were sufficiently important for the courts to operate a strong presumption in favour of categorising the worker as an employee rather than as a self-employed entrepreneur. A similar approach by the courts could transform the law without the need for statutory change.

The provisions of the SDA are marginally more welcoming to homeworkers than employment protection legislation. The definition of 'employee' under the SDA is not confined to those working under a

---

[157] [1984] ICR 612 (CA).
[158] *ibid.*, at p. 627.
[159] Ewing, above n. 154, at p. 109.
[160] Report IV (2B) International Labour Conference, 83rd Session, 1996.
[161] [1995] IRLR 493 (CA).

contract of service, but extends to workers under a contract for services if they provide the service personally. However, two major hurdles remain. First, the requirement for mutuality of obligation in *O'Kelly* makes it difficult to prove the existence of an on-going contract at all, be it 'of service' or 'for services'. Secondly, even if this barrier is surmounted, a homeworker would have to prove disparate impact, that is, that the requirement or condition of working at the employers' premises rather than at home excludes considerably more women than men. The statistical difficulties of proving this cannot be underestimated.

### iv) **The Duty of Accommodation**

The discussion above concerned the halting progress towards improving the legal protection offered to flexible and marginal workers. However, improving the legal protection offered to flexible workers, while significant, is not sufficient to achieve structural change. Ultimately, structural discrimination can only effectively be challenged by legal provisions which address the underlying division of labour in the home propelling women into part-time and fragmented working. The first step in this direction would be a restructuring of working time to accommodate child-care, thus permitting both fathers and mothers to reconcile parenthood and paid work. There is some scope within the concept of indirect discrimination for such a demand. However, the cases reflect a distinct ambivalence on the part of the courts to insist on such transformation.

Possibly the most significant step in the direction of accommodation of child-care is the case of *Home Office* v. *Holmes*[162] in which the Home Office's refusal to allow a woman civil servant to return to work part-time after the birth of her second child was held to be indirectly discriminatory. Although the EAT was at pains to insist that each case should be decided on its merits, the case was significant in holding that the insistence on full-time working was a 'requirement or condition' for the purposes of the Act, and that such a demand was not justifiable. The Court of Appeal has been similarly sensitive to the potentially discriminatory effects of mobility clauses. In *Meade Hill* v. *British Council*,[163] a clause requiring the employee to be ready to move anywhere in Great Britain was held to be indirectly discriminatory the moment it was incorporated into a contract, there being no need for the employer to activate the clause. The Court took judicial notice of the fact that in practice fewer women than men could comply because they were secondary earners.

However, the technicality of the definition of indirect discrimination has enabled the EAT in several important cases to reject claims that the job should be changed to accommodate women's child-care responsibilities. Thus in *Greater Glasgow* v. *Carey*[164] a health visitor requested the right to

---

[162] [1984] ICR 678 (EAT).        [163] [1995] IRLR 78 (CA).
[164] [1987] IRLR 484 (EAT).

work on two-and-a-half or three days a week rather than five half-days because of the difficulty in arranging child-care (by the child's grand-mother) for every day of the week. Her request was rejected by the employer on the grounds that it was administratively inconvenient and that patient needs might suffer if a health visitor were not available for at least part of each day. The EAT held that the Board's decision was wholly justifiable. This failure to accommodate parents' needs is particularly dis-turbing in a profession which is overwhelmingly female: 292 out of the 296 health visitors employed by the Board were women and the management decision was taken by a woman. Still more disturbing is the case of *Clymo* v. *Wandsworth*,[165] in which a branch librarian who applied to change her full-time job into one which could be job-shared was told that her job was too senior to permit such a change. In rejecting the claim of indirect discrimination, Wood J utilised all the openings in the statutory formula. First, the insistence in full-time working was not held to be a 'requirement or condition' for the purpose of the Act. Secondly, the applicant was not found to have suffered a detriment because she was demanding a benefit, the facility of job sharing, which was simply not available to anyone of her status. Thus the fact that an inflexible practice was well-entrenched was itself used as a reason to perpetuate it. Thirdly, he held, it was not true to say that she 'could not comply' with the demand for full-time working, since she earned enough to afford child-care.

Other cases have taken a broader view of some of the constituents of the statutory formula, but still rejected or remitted the claim on other grounds. Thus, in the Northern Ireland Court of Appeal case of *Briggs* v. *North Eastern Education and Library Board*,[166] Hutton LCJ expressly preferred to give the technical aspects of indirect discrimination as wide an interpreta-tion as possible. The notion in *Clymo* that full-time working could not be a 'requirement or condition' was rejected in favour of the wider interpreta-tion in *Home Office* v. *Holmes*; as was the notion that a failure to provide a benefit such as the opportunity to job-share could not be a detriment. The court also preferred to permit the tribunal to rely on its own knowledge and experience of women's responsibility for children rather than insisting on elaborate statistical evidence. Nevertheless, the employer's defence of justifiability was upheld, the court holding that the needs of the pupils for after-school sports coaching took priority over the difficulties caused to the teacher in meeting her child-care obligations. More appropriate was the approach in *London Underground* v. *Edwards*,[167] in which, as we have seen, the plaintiff, a lone mother, claimed that the new rostering system intro-duced by London Underground in order to cut costs made it impossible for her to continue with her work as a train operator. This time the EAT

---

[165] [1989] IRLR 241 (EAT).
[166] [1990] IRLR 181 NICA.
[167] [1997] IRLR 157 (EAT).

rejected the employer's defence; holding instead that there was good evidence that London Underground could have made arrangements which would not have been damaging to their business plans but which would have accommodated the reasonable needs of their employees.

Although, as *Home Office* v. *Holmes* demonstrates, current anti-discrimination legislation has some potential for accommodating child-care, ultimately a more proactive and comprehensive policy is needed. One model for change was found in the Ontario Employment Equity provisions which required that each employer draw up an employment equity plan, detailing measures to improve the employment status of women. Unfortunately, the Act was repealed before it could have much impact in practice. Certainly real change will only be achieved if employees of both sexes have clear rights to negotiate a flexible working plan which accommodates their domestic obligations within the context of the requirements of the employer (see Chapter 5).

b) EDUCATION

Structural impediments to change are not solely caused by uneven responsibility for child-care and domestic work. They are also deeply embedded in the system of education and training. It was clear from the discussion in Chapter 4 not only that educational achievement is a key determinant of success in the labour market but also that girls and boys continue to be educated for a segregated labour market. To what extent has the law been able to reshape such education? Most successful have been cases challenging institutionalised discrimination of a formal kind. In the landmark case of *R* v. *Birmingham CC, ex p. EOC*[168] the EOC tackled the long-standing practice of Birmingham local education authority of offering 540 places at selective grammar schools to boys and only 360 to girls each year. The House of Lords held that this was unlawful direct discrimination contrary to the SDA.[169] The court had no difficulty in rejecting the education authority's argument that there had been no intention or motive to discriminate: intention or motive were held to be irrelevant. Instead, the judges stressed that the girls had lost the right to choose between different schools and had therefore been denied true equality of opportunity.

A similarly robust approach was taken by the Northern Ireland High Court in a series of applications dealing with the policy of the Department of Education in Northern Ireland to give the right to a non-fee-paying place in a grammar school to the top 27 per cent of boys and the top 27 per cent of girls in the 11-plus examinations. Because girls scored substantially better than boys at that age, as many as 422 boys were offered places on a lower score than girls who were rejected. The Northern Ireland High Court held that this was unlawful discrimination. On re-marking the papers with

---

[168] [1989] IRLR 173 (HL). The High Court decision is at [1988] IRLR 96 and the Court of Appeal at [1988] IRLR 430.

[169] SDA s. 23(1).

the aim of finding the top 27 per cent of the whole cohort, it was decided to offer places to a further 305 girls but not to withdraw the offers already made to the 422 boys. However, this created another anomaly, since there were a further 555 girls who achieved at least as well as the 422 boys. The Council's attempt to justify this on grounds of fairness was rejected: since the places were offered in the first place on the basis of a discriminatory policy, the same policy could not be used to justify further discrimination.[170] In respect of further education and training, the courts have again been quick to strike down direct prejudice and discrimination. Thus in *Grieg* v. *Community Industry*,[171] a woman trainee was refused a place on a painting team because she would not 'fit in' with the all-male team. Her claim of discrimination was upheld. Even more perceptive was the Divisional Court's decision in *ex p. Schaffter*,[172] which concerned the availability of hardship grants for single parents while studying. Prior to the case, the grants had been reserved for single parents who had once been married, the assumption presumably being that the State should not endorse unconventional family forms. In insisting that the rule be extended to include lone parents who had never been married, the court was able to facilitate upward mobility for a group of the most disadvantaged women.

However, these attacks on directly discriminatory practices are only isolated forays into the marsh of educational discrimination. Anti-discrimination law is wholly unable to address the social forces which determine girls' and boys' subject choices, resulting in a large predominance of boys in maths and science subjects and girls in arts, a pattern which is reinforced in higher education and feeds into a highly segregated job market. Nor can the law tackle differences in training, whether it is in youth training schemes which channel young women into clerical work and young men into construction and engineering; or in-service training, which is biased against part-time workers. Such deep-seated institutional discrimination cannot be dealt with by means of the individualised, retrospective, demand-side nature of anti-discrimination law. Instead, far more positive policies are required, based inevitably on a financial commitment. While still in the form of policy statements and future commitments, the European Commission Action Programme on equal opportunities has at least begun to consider directions for change in this area. The EC Fourth Equality Action Programme, to be implemented in the period between 1996 and 2000, includes a commitment to promoting a change in attitudes towards women in education. The Commission aims in particular to develop new proposals to encourage girls and boys, women and men to develop skills traditionally associated with one particular sex.[173] However,

---

[170] *Re EOC for Northern Ireland Application* [1989] IRLR 64 (QBD, Northern Ireland).
[171] [1979] IRLR 158.    [172] Above n. 36.
[173] Council decision of 22 December on a medium term action programme on equal opportunities for men and women (1996 to 2000) (95/593/EC), reproduced in EOR No. 67 (1996), p. 34. See in particular, para. 1.5.

opposition by the German government led to a halving of the budget for implementation of the programme, inevitably blunting its edge.

## c) SEXUAL HARASSMENT

### i) **Background**

Sexual harassment is problematic in a unique and corrosive way. By unceremoniously dragging the private sphere of intimate personal and sexual relationships into the public arena of the work-place, sexual harassment strips away a woman's identity as a participant in the enterprise, entitled to respect deriving directly from her humanity, and reduces her to a mere object of sexuality. As destructive as it is in ordinary relationships, sexual harassment is doubly so in the work-place, where it is imbued with the power of the supervisor or manager. Even if the harasser has no particular authority in the work-place, he has the power to make the work-place so intolerable that the victim feels compelled to leave her employment.

While always endemic, for many years sexual harassment was ignored by all except its victims. The Webbs, writing at the turn of the century, were clearly aware that the subordination of women to male workers left women vulnerable to sexual exploitation (see Chapter 2). However, their solution to what they considered to be the 'promiscuous mixing of men and women in daily intercourse'[174] was the continued exclusion of women from male-dominated jobs.[175] It was not until the 1970s that vocal feminists such as Catherine MacKinnon[176] forced the issue into the public light. Empirical research soon revealed its scale. According to surveys conducted during the 1980s in Belgium, Spain, Germany, the Netherlands and the UK, tens of millions of women in the EC suffer sexual harassment in their working lives,[177] findings which have been replicated in the 1990s in a range of different contexts. The risk of harassment is highest among groups which are already vulnerable in other ways: divorced or separated women, young women, women with irregular or precarious employment contracts, women in non-traditional jobs, women with disabilities, lesbian women and women from ethnic minorities, who suffer a particularly pernicious combination of racial and sexual abuse. Gay men and young men are also vulnerable to harassment.[178]

Despite these revelations, no specific right to protection against sexual harassment has been enacted in the UK or the EC. Instead, it has been left to the courts to fill the gap. To their credit, the courts have made significant

[174] S. Webb, and B. Webb, *Industrial Democracy* Vol II (Longmans, 1897), pp. 496–7.

[175] *ibid.*, p. 497.

[176] C. MacKinnon, *Sexual Harassment of Working Women* (Yale University Press, 1979).

[177] M. Rubinstein 'The dignity of women at work: a report on the problem of sexual harassment in the Member States of the European Community' COM V/412/87.

[178] EC *Code of Practice on measures to combat sexual harassment* (adopted on 27 November 1991) reproduced in EOR No. 41 (1992), p. 39.

progress by fashioning a remedy from the equality principle found in the SDA and the Equal Treatment Directive. However, progress has been limited, in part by the inherent weaknesses of the equality principle and in part by judicial reluctance to transcend traditional assumptions. The strengths and weaknesses of the caselaw are described below, followed by a consideration of possible alternatives.

## ii) **Judicial Progress**

Judicial recognition of sexual harassment as a species of sex discrimination was first articulated in the UK in *Strathclyde Regional Council* v. *Porcelli*.[179] Despite the absence of precedent on this issue, Lord Emslie had no difficulty in finding that sexual harassment is 'a particularly degrading and unacceptable form of treatment which it must be taken to have been the intention of Parliament to restrain.'[180] This recognition echoes developments in the US and Canada[181] where a sophisticated jurisprudence has developed. There are at least four ways in which the development of a jurisprudence on sexual harassment has been positive. First, the courts have generally recognised the central role of sexuality in transforming an interaction from an unpleasant or even bullying one into one of sexual harassment. As Lord Emslie put it in *Porcelli*, the perpetrators used 'a particular kind of weapon, based upon the sex of the victim, which would not have been used against an equally disliked man . . . [it] fell to be seen as very different in a material respect from that which would have been inflicted on a male colleague regardless of equality of overall unpleasantness.'[182] Similarly, the US Court of Appeal rejected the District Court's attempt to distinguish a claim of discrimination from one based on a woman's refusal to engage in a sexual affair with her male superior. As the court pointed out, but for her womanhood, her participation in sexual activity would never have been solicited.[183] This notion has been usefully developed in Canadian jurisprudence to include a recognition of sexual harassment as a demeaning practice, one which constitutes a profound affront to the dignity and self-respect of the victim both as an employee and a human being.[184] Secondly, the cases have recognised that the invidious nature of sexual harassment is intimately bound up with the power relations in the work-place. As the Canadian Supreme Court has put it, sexual harassment is an abuse of both economic and sexual power.[185] This does not, however, imply that sexual harassment only occurs if the perpetrator is in a superior position to the

---

[179]  [1986] IRLR 135 (CS).
[180]  *ibid.*, at p. 137.
[181]  *Barnes* v. *Castle* 561 F. 2d 983 (1977) US Court of Appeals District of Columbia Circuit, *Meritor Savings Bank* v. *Vinson* 106 S Ct 2399 (1986), *Janzen* v. *Platy Enterprises Ltd* [1989] 1 SCR 1252 (Canadian Supreme Court).
[182]  *Porcelli*, above n. 179, p. 137. See also *Insitu Cleaning Co* v. *Heads* (1995) IRLR 4 (EAT).
[183]  *Barnes* v. *Castle* 561 F. 2d 983 (1977) at p. 990.
[184]  *Platy*, above n. 181, at p. 1282.    [185]  *ibid.*

victim. In *Porcelli*, both the perpetrators and the victim were laboratory technicians. Nevertheless, the perpetrators were in a position to force the victim to request a transfer to another school. This is because, as MacKinnon points out, gender is also a hierarchy, giving men power over women over and above the authority imparted by work-place hierarchies.[186] Thirdly and of immense importance, is the refusal to make the claim depend on a finding that the victim did not consent to the advances in question. In the words of the US Supreme Court, the criterion is not whether participation is voluntary, but whether sexual advances are unwelcome.[187] In particular this is a valuable recognition of the extent to which consent can be influenced by power. Finally, courts and legislators have frequently been willing to view the problem from the perpective of the victim rather than that of the perpetrator. This is well evidenced in the development of EC law. Early attempts to formulate a definition of sexual harassment referred to conduct 'which the perpetrator knew or should have known was offensive to the victim'.[188] As Gregory notes, 'it is unwise to allow men to determine what is and what is not reasonable sexual conduct, as this is frequently at odds with women's perceptions.'[189] Representations from the women's movement led to a reformulation, focusing on the woman's perspective. Sexual harassment in this view is conduct that is 'unwanted, unreasonable and offensive to the recipient'.[190]

### iii) **Limits of Judicial Development**

The development of sexual harassment as a discrimination claim has not wholly escaped the limitations of anti-discrimination law more generally. This is manifested in three ways. First, the temptation of a symmetrical view of equality has not always been resisted. Given the absence of a right to protection against sexual harassment per se, sexual harassment cases must be squeezed into the equality principle. The courts are therefore at pains to stress that the central question remains: was the woman treated less favourably than a man would have been on the grounds of her sex? Proof that a man would have been equally badly treated would therefore be a complete answer to a sexual harassment claim. This was highlighted in *Barnes* v. *Castle*,[191] when the judge declared that a bisexual employer who harassed both men and women would be immune from suit. This line of reasoning was central to the rejection of the claim in *Balgobin* v. *Tower*

---

[186] C. MacKinnon 'Sexual Harassment: Its first Decade in Court' in P. Smith (ed.), *Feminist Jurisprudence* (OUP, 1993) 145 at p. 147.

[187] *Meritor Saving Bank* v. *Vinson* C106 S.Ct 2399 (1986).

[188] See Rubinstein, above n. 177, (1988), p. 102.

[189] J. Gregory 'Sexual Harassment' (1995) 2 *The European Journal of Women's Studies* 421 at 425.

[190] Council of Ministers, 'Resolution on the Dignity of Women and Men at Work' [1990] OJ 33 C157/33.

[191] Above n. 183, at p. 990 n. 55.

*Hamlets*[192] against an employer who took little or no action to prevent the continuing sexual harassment by one of its employees against the plaintiffs. The EAT conceded that there was no evidence as to how an employer would have responded to a complaint by a man to whom homosexual advances had been made, but was prepared to assume that a man in such a situation would have been treated no more favourably than the women plaintiffs. As a result it was held, by a majority, that, although intolerable behaviour had taken place within a sexual context, this could not constitute discrimination because the employer was treating the women no less favourably than a man would have been treated.

The second major limitation on progress in tackling sexual harassment has resulted from the fact that in the last resort, the courts are still strongly influenced by images of women as simultaneously sex objects and manipulators of their own sexuality. This is clearly manifested in the courts' attitude towards evidence directed at the woman's personal sex life. It is well known that the admissibility of evidence of a victim's lifestyle and sexual attitudes has transformed many a rape trial into a trial of the victim rather than the perpetrator. Yet the courts in sexual harassment cases have refused to bar such evidence, ostensibly supported by incantation of the 'well known principle that in sexual matters it is easy to accuse and difficult to refute'.[193] Hence in *Snowball* v. *Gardner*[194] it was expressly held that evidence about the victim's previous sexual attitudes was admissible to test her credibility and give the 'accused' a fair opportunity to test allegations. Equally problematic is the admissibility of such evidence to show that even if sexual harassment had occurred, the victim had suffered no injury to her feelings. The assumption here is that she had no dignity to protect. In this case the defendant sought to adduce evidence that the complainant had talked about her bed as a playpen. Surely this is only relevant to the act of harassment in question on the assumption that a woman who enjoys her sex life of choice is in fact fair game to any man who might make sexual advances to her, however unwelcome. Nevertheless, the approach in *Snowball* v. *Gardner* has been echoed in several cases. In *Wileman* v. *Manilec Engineering*,[195] Popplewell J explicitly recognised that a person who was happy to accept remarks of A and B in a sexual context was entitled to be very upset by remarks of C. However, he went on to hold that the tribunal was entitled to take account of the fact that she wore 'scant and provocative clothes'. In his view, 'if a girl (sic) on the shop-floor goes around wearing provocative clothes and flaunting herself, it is not unlikely that other work people—particularly men—will make remarks about it.' Hence he refused to interfere with the award of £50 as compensation for four-and-a-half

[192] [1987] IRLR 401 (EAT).
[193] *Snowball* v. *Gardner* [1987] IRLR 397 (EAT).
[194] *ibid.*
[195] [1988] IRLR 145 (EAT).

years of sexual harassment, consisting of both remarks and physical harassment. The admissibility of such evidence has, moreover, been supported by the US Supreme Court, which held in *Meritor Savings Bank* v. *Vinson*[196] that evidence of sexually provocative speech and dress was not per se inadmissible.

The continued influence of deeply ingrained images of women as sex objects is also manifested in the courts' attitude to displays of pornography in the work-place. Thus, the courts have resorted to an armoury of defences in order to support their view that exposure to pictures of nude women in sexual postures does not in itself constitute sexual harassment. The issue arose squarely in *Stewart* v. *Cleveland Guest Engineering*,[197] which concerned a complaint by a woman that her employer continued to permit and indeed encourage the display of pictures of partially clothed and nude women in her work-place. The EAT held that no unlawful discrimination had taken place because a man might have found the display as offensive as did a woman. This is wholly to ignore the power of images, which operate quite differently for women, who are purportedly represented by an image, from men, who are observers of that image. Where women are in a minority in a male-dominated culture, this we–they distinction is underlined. Unless the judiciary comes to accept that exposure to work-place pornography has more than a *de minimis* effect on women's dignity and self-respect in the work-place, such displays will continue unchallenged. Somewhat more progress is evident in the US jurisprudence, which has moved from a scornfully dismissive attitude to one of genuine comprehension. In the 1986 case if *Rabidue* v. *Osceola Refining Company*,[198] the Sixth Circuit Court of Appeal rejected a claim that sexually oriented poster displays constituted sexual harassment. Circuit Judge Krupansky held that such displays had a 'de minimis effect on the plaintiff's work environment, when considered in the context of a society which condones and publicly features and commercially exploits open displays of written and pictorial erotica at the newsstands, on prime time television, at the cinema and in other public places.'[199] This approach was vehemently rejected by a district court in the 1991 case of *Robinson* v. *Jacksonville Shipyards*.[200] In this case, extensive posting of nude women in pornographic poses was described as a 'visual assault' on the tiny handful of women skilled craftworkers in the defendant's shipyards. The court expressly disagreed with the view in *Rabidue* that such behaviour was justified by the general social context. Instead, it accepted expert evidence which showed that the presence of such images has cumulative, corrosive effects because it conveys the message that

---

[196] Above n. 187.
[197] [1994] IRLR 440 (EAT).
[198] 805 F 2d 611 (1986).
[199] *ibid.*, at p. 622.
[200] 760 F Supp 1486 (1991).

women are merely sex objects, either the victims of sexual aggression or submissive slaves rather than co-workers. Thus it cannot be squared with Title VII's promise to open the work-place to women.

The third significant limitation on progress in combating sexual harassment has been the court's reluctance to impose liability on the employer. The ease with which anti-discrimination law has been moulded to incorporate sexual harassment claims against the perpetrators thereof has been largely due to its close analogy to a tort model whereby fault triggers compensation. It is for this very reason that the employer's liability has been difficult to accommodate. In several cases, therefore, the court has refused to find against an employer unless there is evidence that the employer condoned or was otherwise responsible for the harassment. In the US case of *Barnes* v. *Castle*[201] Mackinnon J stated explicitly that an employer could only be vicariously liable if he or she knew and failed to take adequate measures to prevent the harassment continuing. Similarly, in the UK case of *Balgobin* v. *Tower Hamlets*,[202] the employer was held not to be liable because it did not actually know the harassment was occurring and had an equal opportunity policy in place. Even the EEOC guidelines specify that where sexual harassment is by co-employees, the employer should only be liable if she or he knew or ought to have known and failed to act. Protection of employers reached its heights in the EAT's decision in the racial harassment case of *Tower Boot* v. *Jones*.[203] In this case, an employee was not only subjected to verbal abuse of the most racist kind, but suffered physical assault such as being burnt with a hot screw driver. The test for vicarious liability enunciated by the EAT was the familiar tort formula that an employer was only liable for acts of employees in the course of their employment. Since this was held to be 'by no stretch of the imagination' an improper mode of carrying out authorised tasks, the employer escaped liability.[204] Fortunately, this was overturned by the Court of Appeal,[205] which recognised that the effect of the tort test was that 'the more heinous the act of discrimination, the less likely it will be that the employer would be liable'. It therefore held that the words 'in the course of their employment' should be interpreted in the sense in which ordinary lay people would understand it. However, the court expressly left it open to a tribunal to accept a defence that the employer had taken reasonably practical steps to prevent the act. The flaws in an approach so strongly wedded to fault were perceptively pointed out by the Canadian Court in *Platy*. The Chief Justice made it clear that the aim of the legislation was not to determine fault or to punish conduct. Instead its aim was remedial—to identify and eliminate

[201] Above n. 183.
[202] Above n. 192.
[203] [1995] IRLR 529 (EAT).
[204] The case was remitted to the industrial tribunal to consider if the employer was vicariously liable for a supervisor who did know what was happening.
[205] *Jones* v. *Tower Boot* [1997] IRLR 168 (CA).

discrimination. Since only an employer is in a position to remedy the undesirable effects of sexual harassment, it should be liable for all work-related actions. Moreover, 'work-related' was defined broadly to include anyone whose opportunity to harass was directly related to his or her employment position. The only faint echo of such a position is found in *Burton* v. *De Vere Hotels*[206] which held that an employer will be liable for harassment which, with the application of good employment practice, it could have prevented or reduced.

The final limitation on anti-discrimination law as a means of combating sexual harassment is its individualised, retrospective nature. Not only is it inevitably extremely difficult for a victim to adduce probative evidence of sexual harassment, in addition, the outcome is at most one of vindication and compensation, rather than a future working environment which is free of harassment. Real change is far more likely to be achieved by preventative measures and a general social stigmatisation of such conduct.

iv) **Reform**

What then are the alternatives to anti-discrimination law as a mechanism for alleviating the problem of sexual harassment? A wide range of measures has been proposed, ranging from criminal sanctions on the one hand to exhortations on employers to create a harassment-free work environment on the other. The criminal law option has been advocated by Dines and Watt, largely on the grounds of its educative and deterrent value. 'Sexual harassment is no joke and a conviction in a criminal court is a good way to make the point'.[207] Such a law does now exist in the UK, in the form of the offence of intentional harassment enacted in the Criminal Justice and Public Order Act 1994.[208] This provision makes it an offence to use threatening, abusive or insulting words or behaviour, orally or in writing, with the intent and effect of causing a person harassment, harm or distress. A constable has the right to arrest without warrant anyone reasonably suspected of committing an offence, and the sanction is a maximum of six months' imprisonment or a fine not exceeding level 5. The Parliamentary debates make it clear that the aim of the provisions is to curb serious persistent racial harassment, and its location as part of a series of public order offences suggests that the employment relationship was not their main target. Nevertheless, as was explicitly stated in Parliament, the definition is broad enough to cover sexual harassment. However, the efficacy of the criminal law in this context is doubtful. It is true that such provisions give a welcome signal that such behaviour is the subject of the most severe

[206] EOR No. 70 (1996), p. 48.

[207] J. Dine and B. Watt 'Sexual Harassment: Moving Away from Discrimination' [1995] MLR 343 at p. 363.

[208] Criminal Justice and Public Order Act 1994, s. 154, inserting a new section 4A into the Public Order Act 1986.

social censure. Nevertheless, the criminal law has several disadvantages. First, the consensus among experts in this area indicates that victims of sexual harassment are unwilling to face the publicity and risk of adverse treatment likely to accompany a formal complaint; indeed, many have no desire to destroy the career of the perpetrator provided their own work environment is harmonious. Given the known reluctance of rape victims to trigger a criminal prosecution, it is highly unlikely that victims of sexual harassment will enlist the aid of the police and the criminal law. Secondly, the problems of proof in a criminal trial are likely to be far worse than those which have already arisen in industrial tribunal cases. Not only does the provision require proof of intention by the perpetrator, a mental element notoriously difficult to prove; it also requires proof that the victim has been harassed. This is an invitation to a defendant to seek to adduce evidence of the woman's personal life and sexual attitudes in an attempt to prove that she could not have felt harassed by this behaviour. If tribunals have been quick to accept the admissibility of such evidence in complaints under the SDA, so much more so are courts with their long tradition of admitting such evidence in rape trials. Thirdly, the difficulties in distinguishing between lack of consent and unwelcome behaviour are likely to be exacerbated in a criminal court. Indeed, the very seriousness of the likely penalty may well lead the courts to opt for the narrowest construction of the offence. Finally, as is the case under the SDA, the criminal law operates retrospectively. It may act as a deterrent to future harassers, but it places no pressure on employers of harassers to institute proper preventative measures. The result is that, although Dines and Watt are possibly correct in stating that a criminal conviction may bring home the seriousness of sexual harassment, the possibility of securing such a conviction is remote.

At the other end of the spectrum is the purely exhortatory stance taken by the EC, a position which is less a consequence of principle than of political pragmatism. The very recognition of sexual harassment as a problem which requires resolution is of course a significant step forward, and it was not until 1984 that a Council Resolution of 13 December 1984 called on Member States to take steps to 'ensure . . . respect for the dignity of women at the workplace'. More specific but still cautious was the 1990 Council Resolution,[209] which affirms that 'conduct of a sexual nature . . . constitutes an intolerable violation of the dignity of the worker' if it is unwanted, unreasonable and offensive, is used as a basis for a work-related decision, or creates an intimidating, hostile or humiliating work environment. However, the substance of the Resolution is undemanding: it merely calls on Member States to promote awareness of the issue and to remind employers that they have a responsibility to seek to ensure that the work environment is free from unwanted conduct of a sexual nature. Its reference to the law is

---

[209] Council Resolution on the protection of the dignity of women and men at work, reproduced in EOR No. 32 (1990), p. 28.

similarly cautious, stating merely that Member States 'should promote awareness that [sexual harassment] may be, in certain circumstances, contrary to the principle of equal treatment' found in the Equal Treatment Directive.[210] Nor is it legally binding: a Directive on the issue appears to have been considered unattainable politically. As 'soft law', it must be taken into account by domestic courts in order to clarify Community or domestic law,[211] but none of its provisions are themselves sufficiently precise to function in this manner.

Neither of these two divergent approaches is satisfactory. An effective programme of reform would need to be two-pronged, incorporating both sanctions and preventative measures. The sanctions element is best divorced from the concept of equality. Instead of forcing sexual harassment into an anti-discrimination mould, it should be a source of entitlement in its own right. For example, the German Employees Protection Act of 1994 explicitly prohibits sexual harassment in the work-place, while a draft Luxembourg statute explicitly provides that sexual harassment constitutes a serious fault, justifying the harasser being dismissed on the spot and ordered to pay damages. In addition, dismissal for refusing to submit to sexual advances by an employer or superior cannot constitute a valid reason for dismissal.[212] Such provisions avoid the necessity of proving that sexual harassment constitutes less favourable treatment of a woman on grounds of her sex. The proposition that a man would have been equally badly treated becomes simply irrelevant. It is crucial too that evidence of previous sexual conduct be expressly excluded and that levels of damages are such as to function as a deterrent.

Such measures should be accompanied by clear duties placed on the employer to create and maintain, so far as possible, an environment which is free of sexual harassment. This entails strong preventative measures including the posting of a clear prohibition on sexual harassment and the provision of work-place complaints procedures. Other jurisdictions again provide valuable guidance. The German provision not only explicitly prohibits sexual harassment but also obliges the employer to protect its employees against harassment. Proposed legislation in the Netherlands obliges employers to elaborate a policy with the aim of barring sexual harassment in the work-place. The employer must hold regular evaluations of progress. Moreover, the victim may claim damages against the employer for failing to fulfil the duties of a 'good employer' in this context.[213] Several US states have enacted similar combinations of preventative measures and legal enforceability. For example, legislation in force in the State of Maine

---

[210] Directive 76/206/EC.
[211] *Grimaldi* Case 322/88 [1990] IRLR 400 ECJ.
[212] S. Prechal and L. Sendon, *Monitoring Implementation and Application of Community Equality Law* (European Commission, 1996), p. 55.
[213] *ibid.*, p. 55.

since 1991 requires all employers to 'act to ensure a workplace free of sexual harassment' by implementing minimum requirements. These include posting in a prominent place a notice informing employees of the illegality of sexual harassment and of the complaint process available through the Maine Human Rights Commission; and education and training of all new employees in establishments of fifteen or more employees.[214] A similar enactment in the State of Connecticut emphasises both the provision of information and the need to train supervisory employees.[215] It is accompanied by detailed regulations specifying the content of the information and training. Vermont follows suit with legislation placing an obligation on employers to ensure a work-place free of sexual harassment, and to adopt and communicate a policy on sexual harassment to that end.[216]

EU Member States have to some extent taken their cue from the EC Commission Code of Practice on measures to combat sexual harassment.[217] The Code is particularly valuable in its focus on preventative measures, stating that 'the prime objective should be to change behaviour and attitudes to seek to ensure the prevention of sexual harassment'. The Code requires an express statement that sexual harassment would not be condoned; a policy which must be effectively communicated to all employees. In addition, the Code emphasises the importance of clear and precise procedures to deal with sexual harassment once it occurs. Since most recipients simply want the harassment to stop, and may be reluctant to engage in a formal procedure, the first stage of a procedure should seek an informal resolution. If this is unsuccessful or inappropriate, a formal procedure should be established, paying due attention both to the importance of a sense of justice by all concerned and the extreme sensitivity of the matter. The Code, being attached to a Commission Recommendation, clearly falls in the category of EC soft law and should be used to guide tribunal decisions on matters such as the determination of whether an employer has taken 'reasonably practicable' steps to prevent sexual harassment as required by the SDA.[218] Its influence is gradually being felt. Thus in the valuable analysis in *Insitu Cleaning* v. *Heads*,[219] the EAT not only referred explicitly to the Code, but went on to make suggestions of future action by the employer including a procedure dealing with complaints of harassment. Nevertheless, recent research carried out by the European Commission in Member States shows 'a clear lack of progress' in the extent to which preventative action has been taken. While the EC Code was found

---

[214] Sexual Harassment Training and Education in the Workplace; see EOR No. 43 (1992), p. 25.

[215] EOR No. 46 (1992), p. 37 and EOR No. 54 p. 19.

[216] EOR No. 54 (1994), p. 20.

[217] *A Code of Practice on measures to combat sexual harassment* (adopted on 25 November 1991) [1991] OJ C 305/36; reproduced in full in EOR No. 41 (1992), pp. 39–42.

[218] SDA s. 41(3). See EOR No. 41 (1992), p. 29.

[219] Above n. 182.

to have some impact in Member States, only three (Belgium, France and the Netherlands) had enacted specific legislation requiring employers to be proactive in combating sexual harassment. The Commission is therefore actively consulting employers and unions on what further action should be taken.[220]

## IV.   FRAGMENTING AND RECONSTRUCTING

The discussion so far has been premised on the assumption of a common category of 'women'. While it is essential at the first stage of the analysis to deal with generalities, the second stage requires a more critical examination, bringing into account intersecting patterns of domination based not just on sex, but on race, sexual orientation, disability or class. The immediate result of such an analysis is the splintering of the category 'women' into diverse fragments. This section concentrates on the interaction between race and sex. The complexity of the race–sex interaction derives largely from the fact that the lines of domination are not horizontal. White women are in the dominant racial group although not the dominant gender group. White women are therefore the beneficiaries and even the perpetrators of racism. Black women, by contrast, are subject to more than just racism and sexism on their own account. They also bear what Malveaux calls the 'third burden, the burden beyond race and gender that Black women shoulder because of the labour-market treatment of Black men.'[221] Nor is it accurate to generalise about 'black' women: this category too fragments under the pressure of cultural diversity, with Asian women differing from Afro-Caribbean women, and Muslim or Jewish women differing from Christian women. Such complexity is, however, rendered invisible by statistical generalities. For example, overall trends showing a sharp increase in the number of women in the paid work-force do not reflect the experience of black women, for whom paid work has always been commonplace against a backdrop of black men's high unemployment and low earning power. Similarly unrepresentative is the familiar statistic showing a preponderance of women in part-time work. 'Women' here means 'white women'; black women tend to work far longer hours than white women.

This complex picture requires a correspondingly complex response from the law, a response which can accommodate diversity in order to achieve genuine equality of opportunity, and which can recognise subtle patterns of domination as they arise. Such a response is singularly absent in the caselaw. While the facts of the cases clearly reveal both the conflict of interests between white and black women and the diverse requirements

[220] EOR No. 69 (1996), p. 3.
[221] J. Malveaux 'Gender Difference and Beyond' in Rhode (ed.), *Theoretical Perspectives on Sexual Difference* (Yale University Press, 1990), p. 233.

stemming from cultural variety, the courts have tended to base their decisions on technical interpretations of the statute rather than sensitivity to the complexities of the situation.

This is clearly demonstrated in nursing which, being a predominantly female profession, is a particularly vivid example of the discrepant life opportunities of black and white women. A recent survey demonstrated that black nurses are significantly less likely than white staff of similar age, experience and qualifications to be in the higher nursing grades of F and G. In fact it could take them as many as five years longer to reach these grades than their white peers.[222] Yet an attempt by a black nurse to challenge the fact that she had been graded E while her white colleague had been upgraded to F failed because, in the court's view, she had brought her application out of time.[223] Balcombe LJ held that the act of discrimination complained of was simply the decision to grade the plaintiff at E rather than F. Time therefore began to run from the moment the decision was upheld by the local appeal system. He saw no reason to accept the argument that this was an act of continuing discrimination, reflected in the fact that her pay was some £2,000 a year less than Grade F pay levels. The result was that the plaintiff had no opportunity to even argue her case, although of four women working together on night duty on a twenty-five bed medical ward, only one, the white woman, was graded at F. The others, all black women, found themselves on E.

The question of cultural diversity is similarly ignored. In *Kingston Health Authority* v. *Kaur*,[224] a Sikh woman complained of racial discrimination after the offer of a place on a training course for State enrolled nurses was withdrawn when she indicated that she could only enter the scheme if she was permitted to wear trousers. Browne-Wilkinson J recognised that trousers were a requirement of the Sikh religion, so that the plaintiff would not feel respectable if she did not wear them. Nevertheless, the EAT held that the disparate impact on Sikh women was justifiable on the technical ground that the relevant regulations demanded precise compliance with uniform specifications. It is worth noting that change occurred despite the law: one month later the regulations were amended to permit trousers. A similar approach to diversity in educational qualifications has made it difficult for ethnic minority women from other countries to break into the system in the UK. This is floridly demonstrated in *Raval* v. *DHSS*,[225] which concerned a challenge of the rule that an English language O-level or its equivalent was a precondition of selection to the (relatively junior) post of clerical officer in the civil service. The plaintiff, an Asian woman from Kenya, was rejected

---

[222] S. Beisham, S. Virdee and A. Hagell, *Nursing in a multi-ethnic NHS* (1995): see EOR No. 65 (1996), p. 9.
[223] *Sougrin* v. *Haringey Health Authority* [1992] IRLR 416 (CA).
[224] [1981] ICR 631 (EAT).
[225] [1985] ICR 685 (EAT).

although she had a teacher's qualification from Kenya, was fully fluent in English and had taught in English language schools for many years. Despite a passing recognition that it may seem unreasonable to exclude a candidate with evident ability, the EAT refused to disturb the industrial tribunal's finding that this practice was justifiable.[226]

The crudeness of the legal analysis of black women's position is highlighted in cases of racial abuse. This is most clearly evidenced in *De Souza* v. *Automobile Association*[227] in which a black secretary complained of racial discrimination after she had overheard a manager instruct another manager to 'get his typing done by the wog'. The Court of Appeal rejected her claim. Far from addressing the underlying issue, May LJ concentrated entirely on whether she could be said to have suffered a 'detriment' for the purposes of the statute.[228] Instead of considering it to be inevitable that racist attitudes of this sort pollute a working environment, May LJ insisted that 'racially to insult a coloured employee is not enough by itself, even if that insult caused him or her distress'.[229] In addition, the plaintiff must show that a reasonable worker would have considered herself disadvantaged as a result. Nor did he consider it to be sufficient that the manager blatantly exhibited his racist attitudes to another manager: instead, the court held, she could only show that she had been 'treated less favourably' if he intended her to overhear the conversation, or knew or could have anticipated.

Because of the rigid boundaries between the Race Relations Act and the SDA, cases reflecting the conflict of interests between white and black women are generally dealt with as a species of race discrimination, the gender issue being entirely ignored. This is demonstrated by *North West Thames AHA* v. *Noone*,[230] in which the Court of Appeal upheld a complaint of racial discrimination by a Sri Lankan doctor who was not selected for a post as a consultant microbiologist despite the fact that her qualifications and experience were superior to those of the successful candidate. It is noteworthy that the successful candidate was also a woman, as was the consultant who had excluded Dr Noone on the grounds that Dr Noone would not 'fit in'.

The issue is more explicitly addressed in US caselaw, facilitated by the structure of Title VII, which outlaws discrimination on the grounds of 'race, color, religion, sex or national origin' within the framework of the same statute. However, the response of the US courts has been tentative. Early attempts to bring an intersectional claim based on both race and sex were unconditionally rejected. Thus in *DeGraffenreid* v. *General Motors*

---

[226] See also *Hampson* v. *DES* [1990] IRLR 302 (HL).
[227] [1986] IRLR 103 (CA).
[228] RRA 1976, s. 4(2)(c).
[229] *De Souza*, above n. 227, p. 107.
[230] [1988] IRLR 195 (CA).

*Assembly Division,*[231] a group of black women claimed that they had been unlawfully discriminated against on the grounds of their status as black women, when they were dismissed as redundant under General Motors' 'last in first out' policy. The discrimination arose because, prior to 1964, General Motors had refused to hire any black women at all. Although this policy was subsequently changed, black women inevitably failed to achieve the necessary seniority to survive a 'last in first out' selection procedure. The court refused to countenance the possibility of a claim based on the uniquely disadvantaged position of black women. In its view, this would create a 'new super remedy which would give them relief beyond what the drafters of the relevant statutes intended'. Indeed, it saw such a response as privileging black women, by giving them 'greater standing than, for example, a black male. The prospect of the creation of new classes of protected minorities, governed only by the mathematical principle of permutation and combination, clearly raises the prospect of opening the hackneyed Pandora's box.' The court dismissed the sex discrimination claim since white women had been hired prior to 1964. At the same time, it refused to consider the race discrimination claim, recommending that it be consolidated with another race discrimination claim pending against General Motors. As Crenshaw comments, this implies that the boundaries of sex and race discrimination are defined respectively by white women's and black men's experiences. Only to the extent that their experiences coincide with either of these two groups are black women protected.[232]

Far more promising is the Court of Appeals case of *Jefferies* v. *Harris County Community Action Assn,*[233] in which a black woman who was repeatedly passed over for promotion and later dismissed claimed that she had been discriminated against because she was a black woman. The evidence showed that the vacancies had generally been filled by black men or non-black women. In an important step forward, the court declared that 'discrimination against black women can exist even in the absence of discrimination against black men or white women.'[234] The court found support for this stance in the wording of Title VII, in that the reference to 'race, color, religion, sex *or* national origin' indicates a legislative intent to prohibit discrimination based on *any or all* of the listed characteristics. In further support of this conclusion, the court transplanted the principles known as 'sex-plus' from cases in which discrimination on the grounds of sex had been upheld even though directed only at a sub-group of women, such as pregnant women or women with children.

The case has certainly cut new ground, and has been followed in a

---

[231] 413 F Supp 142 (E.D. Mo. 1976).
[232] K. Crenshaw 'Demarginalizing the intersection of Race and Sex' (1989) *University of Chicago Legal Forum* 139.
[233] 615 F 2d 1025 (5th Cir 1980).
[234] *ibid.*, at p. 1032.

number of contexts. Possibly the most important concerns harassment, which is a particularly fertile field for intersectional claims, the combination of racist and sexist abuse being exceptionally pernicious. Following *Jefferies*, the Court of Appeals has held that a trial judge should aggregate evidence of racial and sexual harassment even if the evidence supports neither claim individually.[235] Nevertheless, the US caselaw remains limited. Its bare recognition of black women as a separate protected group is not based on a clearly articulated set of principles. As a result, later cases have revealed a strong desire on the part of the court to restrict the scope of the *Jefferies* doctrine. This is most clearly expressed in *Judge* v. *Marsh*,[236] in which a district court, while accepting that discrimination against black women may violate Title VII, voiced its fears that such a position 'turns employment discrimination into a many-headed Hydra'. It therefore sought to limit the *Jefferies* analysis to a combination of only two of the grounds protected by Title VII. On this analysis, only race and sex can be considered: the impact of religion or national origin cannot be addressed, let alone disability or sexual orientation. The result, as Scarborough points out, is that 'the more someone deviates from the norm, the more likely, s/he is to be the target of discrimination. Ironically, those who need Title VII's protection the most get it the least under *Judge's* limitation.'[237]

More fundamentally, the 'sex plus' analysis is based on the assumption that a black woman simply suffers a combination of race and sex discrimination. Yet the disadvantage experienced by black women is not merely the result of adding racism to sexism or vice versa; it is synergistic. As Crenshaw argues, 'the paradigm of sex discrimination tends to be based on the experiences of white women; the model of race discrimination tends to be based on the experiences of the most privileged blacks. Notions of what constitutes race and sex discrimination are, as a result narrowly tailored to embrace only a small set of circumstances, none of which include discrimination against black women.'[238] This is underlined by Scales-Trent: 'By creating two separate categories for its major social problems "the race problem" and the "women's issue"—society has ignored the group which stands at the interstices of these two groups, black women.'[239] Only by recognising a black woman as a whole person, belonging to a group with its own historical, social and economic experiences, and the synergistic nature of discrimination will true progress be made.

---

[235] *Hicks* v. *Gate Rubber* 833 F 2d 1406 (10th Circuit Court of Appeals, 1987).

[236] 649 F Supp. 770 (DDC 1986).

[237] C. Scarborough 'Conceptualising black women's employment experiences' (1989) 98 *Yale Law Journal* 1457 at p. 1472.

[238] Crenshaw, above n. 232.

[239] J. Scales-Trent 'Black women and the Constitution' (1989) 24 *Harvard Civil Rights—Civil Liberties Law Review* 9 at p. 10.

# [8]
# Enduring Disadvantage

## INTRODUCTION

A life-time of disadvantage does not bode well for a comfortable old age. Indeed, because pensions entitlements have been structured in such a way as to reflect life-time earnings, it is inevitable that the low pay and status of many women during their working life will leave them with an inadequate pension.[1] This is borne out by the evidence. While the level of poverty among old people in general gives cause for concern, its incidence among older women is strikingly high compared with that of men.[2] Nearly one in three women pensioners in the UK have pensions worth less than one-tenth of average earnings; while this is the case for only 10 per cent of male pensioners.[3] In this Chapter, it will be argued that the reasons for women's continuing disadvantage in old age are rooted deep in the legal and social

---

[1] A. Walker 'Poverty among older women' in C. Glendinning and J. Millar (eds.), *Women and Poverty in Britain in the 1990s* (Harvester Wheatsheaf, 1992), p. 182.

[2] *ibid.*, p. 179.

[3] EOC, *What Price Equality?* (1994), p. 6.

structures that have prevailed throughout the century. Recent legal developments have modified these structures in some important ways; but legal change has not necessarily signified progress. Thus although a self-conscious effort has been made to incorporate equality into the pensions framework, the notion of equality used has been formal and disconnected from substantive distributive justice. The result is that much movement has led to little change, and what change there has been has frequently been retrogressive. Part I of the chapter consists of a critical evaluation of the basic framework of pensions provision. Part II turns to a detailed critique of European law on pensions equality while Part III assesses its impact on UK law.

## I.  FOUNDATIONS OF PENSIONS INEQUALITY

The framework of the law relating to pensions has been shaped by a specific model of the family: one with a breadwinning husband and a dependent child-rearing wife. This model is not only descriptive: it also provides harsh financial disincentives to those who fail to conform. In this part, the complex detail of pension provision will be considered by uncovering the basic assumptions inherent in this model of the family. Three aspects will be examined: first, the notion that married women are and should be dependants of their breadwinning husbands; secondly, the principle that pensions should reward paid work; and thirdly, differential retirement and pensionable ages for men and women respectively.

### a)  WOMEN AS DEPENDANTS

Possibly the most influential factor guiding pensions provision since the First World War has been the notion that women are and should be dependent on their husbands. This has manifested itself in different ways within the State pension scheme and occupational pension schemes respectively. I begin with the State scheme. Here the brief glimmer of egalitarianism in the 1908 Act[4] was soon extinguished with a vengeance, to be rekindled only at the end of the century. Instead, dependence was actively perpetuated. Thus, husbands could provide dependent pensions for their wives or widows but wives could not do so for their husbands or widowers. At the same time, the law made it exceptionally difficult for married women to accrue pensions in their own right.

Dependent pensions for married women were central to the framework established by the 1925 Act.[5] This created the 'married woman's opt-out'. Married women could choose to pay no national insurance contributions and therefore gain no independent pension entitlements. Such women were instead entitled to derivative pensions on the basis of their husbands'

---

[4] The Old Age Pensions Act 1908 provided a means-tested pension of 5s a week payable equally to men and women aged seventy or over.

[5] See e.g., Widows' Orphans and Old Age Contributory Pensions Act 1925, s. 1(1)(c).

contribution record. The scheme perpetuated women's dependence in several ways. First, it excluded women breadwinners entirely, the assumption being that only married men played this role. Secondly, it discouraged married women from continuing in paid work once they had exercised the option, since paid work would not enhance their pension entitlements. Instead, the wife was wholly dependent on her husband's work record. Thirdly, the dependent wife's pension was significantly lower than the regular pension.[6] Finally, and particularly problematic, she was not entitled to any other social security benefits in her own right. This made it impossible for her to supplement the basic pension which, even for a couple, has always been scarcely sufficient to survive on.[7] Even more problematic was the absence of provision for divorced or separated women. As we have seen, divorce is the biggest single precipitant of poverty in women (see Chapter 4). Absence of pensions provision in old age simply deepened the vulnerability of divorced women. The only provision made for once-married women focused on widows: the 1925 Act introduced contributory pensions for widows, whether or not they had children. Again, however, by omitting any entitlement for women to provide for their widowers, the existence of women breadwinners was negated.

The second means of perpetuating dependence was to make it inordinately difficult for married women to accrue their own independent pensions. This came into its own after the Second World War, reflecting Beveridge's view that married women should not undertake paid work. The National Insurance Act 1946 instituted the invidious 'half-test', according to which a married woman would not be entitled to a pension by virtue of her own contributions unless she had made full contributions for at least half the period between her marriage and her retirement.[8] Failure to pass this 'half-test' led to forfeiture of all her contributions. A married man, by contrast, had only to satisfy the usual contributions conditions.[9] The alternative for a married woman was to opt out, thereby becoming dependent on her husband's contribution record. The result was a difficult choice: between dependence and a measure of security in old age, and independence on the basis of a risky reliance on the availability of paid work for half the years of her marriage. It is not surprising that the vast majority of married women opted for dependency.

It was not until 1975 that reform was contemplated. The Social Security Pensions Act 1975 was heralded as a new deal for women. In reality, although the Act made some inroads into the assumption of dependency, it left other central bulwarks untouched. Thus, significantly, the Act abolished the married women's option[10] (although women who were married or

---

[6] National Insurance Act 1946, Second schedule (16s as against 26s a week).
[7] B. Abel Smith 'Sex Equality and Social Security' in J. Lewis (ed.), *Women's Welfare Women's Rights* (Croom Helm, 1983), p. 92.
[8] National Insurance Act 1946, s. 21(5).    [9] *ibid.*, Third schedule para. 4.
[10] Social Security Pensions Act 1975, s. 3.

widowed at the time the abolition came into effect could continue to exercise it). However, the Act expressly retained the 'half-test'.[11] Given that it remained as difficult as ever to accrue a pension in their own right, it is not surprising that a large number of married women continued to opt out of the national insurance scheme and therefore remain dependent on their husbands to generate a pension for them. Indeed, as recently as 1990, there were still a hefty 1.1 million women in this category.[12] The result was that retirement pensions calculated on the husband's contribution record continued to be the norm for married women.[13] Figures from 1991 show that almost two-thirds of women in receipt of a retirement pension qualified on their partner's insurance contributions.[14]

The 1975 Act also made limited inroads into the assumption that wives could not be breadwinners or husbands dependent. Thus, it was finally conceded that a deceased woman should be permitted to benefit her husband in the same way as a deceased man could benefit his wife. The Act provided that widowers, like widows, would be entitled to a pension on the basis of their deceased spouse's contributions record.[15] However, an important discrepancy remained: whereas a widow benefited from her husband's contributions record regardless of her age, a widower was only entitled to use his wife's contribution record if he had reached pensionable age on her death.[16] In other words, the assumption of the man as provider prior to retirement prevailed. More problematic still was the absence of a provision for living wives to provide dependent pensions for their husbands. Thus until as recently as the 1995 Pensions Act, a married woman could claim a Category B or dependent pension (worth 60 per cent of an independent pension) on the basis of her husband's contribution record if they had both reached pensionable age.[17] Women could not, however, provide a pension in this way for their dependent husbands. A similarly complex picture emerges in respect of divorce. Although a woman still lost her right to a widow's pension on divorce, she could use her husband's contribution record towards her retirement pension for the years of the marriage. This was equalised in 1978 by a provision allowing a divorced man to use his wife's record in the same way.[18] However, divorced persons could still not benefit from a former spouse's entitlement to an additional earnings-related pension.[19] This was a serious drawback for divorced women who might find it difficult to amass their own earnings-related entitlement.

[11]  Social Security Pensions Act 1975, s. 28(2).
[12]  S. Hutton, S. Kennedy and P. Whiteford *Equalisation of State Pension Ages: The Gender Impact* (EOC, 1995), p. 5.
[13]  J. Reid 'New Social Security Legislation' [1976] 1 ILJ 54 at p. 58.
[14]  Walker, above n. 1, in Glendinning and Millar (eds.), p. 187.
[15]  Social Security Pensions Act 1975, s. 8.
[16]  Social Security Contributions and Benefits Act 1992, s. 50.
[17]  *ibid.*, ss. 49–50.      [18]  *ibid.*, s. 48 and see 1979/642 REG 8.
[19]  Social Security Contributions and Benefits Act 1992, ss. 52 and 53 only apply to married women, widows and widowers.

Somewhat more progress has been achieved as a result of EC law. Most importantly, it was under the influence of Directive 79/7 on Equal Treatment in Social Security[20] that the half-test was finally removed. Having been modified in 1979, the test was fully abolished in 1984,[21] just a few days before the period of implementation of the Directive expired. Nevertheless EC law remains ambiguous in its attempts to free women from the assumption of dependency. The Directive provides for the principle of equal treatment in statutory schemes, including protection against the risks of old age. However, it permits Member States to continue to operate on the basis of stereotypical family relationships in several key areas. Thus it contains an explicit derogation for provisions concerning survivors' benefits.[22] It also permits Member States to continue to grant old age benefits by virtue of the derived entitlements of a wife and to grant increases in old age benefits to husbands for a dependent wife.

The last vestiges of the assumption of married women's dependency in the State scheme are now being slowly and grudgingly dismantled. It has been particularly difficult for the law to concede that married women may indeed provide for 'dependent husbands' or that a marriage might be one of interdependence between two earning parties. The 1995 Pensions Act finally permitted a husband to claim a Category B pension on the contributions record of his wife.[23] However, even this was a reluctant concession, as evidenced by the fact that the new right only applies to women born after April 1950. Equality will therefore not be achieved until those women reach pensionable age, well into the twenty-first century. A similar point can be made in respect of widowers' pensions. The 1995 Pensions Act, in a complex amending provision, permits a widower to claim on the basis of his wife's contribution record even if he has not reached pensionable age provided other conditions are met.[24] The benefits of this are again delayed until well into the twenty-first century, with the new provisions only applying to a man who obtains pensionable age on or after the year 2010.[25]

The above discussion has focused on the painfully slow progress to formal equality in State pensions. A similar pattern is evident in occupational pension schemes. The assumption of women's dependency has traditionally been particularly strident in this sector. Thus occupational pensions, which were first developed within the public sector, were openly targeted at the salaried 'family man'.[26] Married women were barred from

---

[20] [1979] OJ L 6/24.    [21] Social Security Act 1985, s. 11.

[22] Article 3(2).

[23] Pensions Act 1995, sched. 4 Part II para. 3(1), substituting new section 48A for ss. 49 and 50 of the 1992 Act.

[24] Pensions Act 1995, sched. 4 Part II para. 3 inserting a new s. 48B into the Social Security Contributions and Benefits Act 1992.

[25] Pensions Act 1995, sched. 4 Part II para. 3 inserting a new s. 48C into the Social Security Contributions and Benefits Act 1992.

[26] The rest of this paragraph is derived from D. Groves 'Occupational pension provision and women's poverty in old age' in Glendinning and Millar (eds.), above n. 1, p. 195.

such schemes: only unmarried women could qualify for an occupational pension derived from their own earnings, while married women were expected to depend on their husbands' occupational pensions. The strength of the assumption of dependency makes it unsurprising that the only area in which provision was made specifically for women concerned widows. Thus most schemes made provision for pensions for the widows of insured men. As in the State system, however, the corresponding expectation that married women did not work to support their husbands was reflected in the absence of provision for widowers' pensions.

As occupational pension schemes spread into private sector employment, so did the basic assumptions, including the widespread prohibition of married women. The result was a disturbingly low coverage: a survey carried out in 1936 found women to comprise about 20 per cent of the total membership of private sector occupational pension schemes. Even those who did qualify were at a disadvantage: their pensions reflected their low pay, and earlier retirement. Indeed, many women were required to retire by 55.

After the Second World War, the abolition of the marriage bar triggered the increasing economic activity of married women. Nevertheless, little effort was made to include women in occupational pension schemes. It remained accepted practice for employers to require women to reach thirty before admitting them to schemes, whereas men were admitted much younger. By thirty, many women had married and left paid work to have children. Indeed, employers were often explicitly advised by the literature of the period to leave women out of pension schemes. It is therefore not surprising that in 1963, there were only 40 per cent of non-manual women and 15 per cent of manual women in private occupational schemes, compared to 80 per cent of non-manual men and 55 per cent of manual men. As in the pre-war period, the efforts of pension schemes were devoted to improving benefits available to women as widows. Also of lasting detriment to women has been the use of actuarial tables. Even where women do accrue independent pensions, statistics demonstrating that women live longer than men are used to support the assumption that women's pensions are more expensive than those of men. This is catered for by either raising the premium for women or diminishing the benefits.

An opportunity to redress the discrimination against women in occupational pensions arose with the passage of the Equal Pay Act 1970. However, the Labour government, unwilling to allow the Bill to be obstructed by opponents of pensions equality, skirted the issue. In the result, the EqPA explicitly legitimised discrimination by stating that, apart from terms relating to access to occupational pension schemes, the Act would not operate 'in relation to terms related to death or retirement or to any provision made in connection with death or retirement', where retirement was defined broadly as to include retirement on grounds of age, length of service or incapacity.[27]

It was not until 1975 that the legislature began to insist on a measure of formal equality in occupational pensions. The 1975 Social Security and Pensions Act for the first time made it mandatory for membership of a scheme to be open to both men and women 'on terms which are the same as to the age and length of service needed for becoming a member and as to whether membership is voluntary or obligatory'.[28] However, the equal access requirements were very limited in scope: only access rules about age or length of service were prohibited, leaving the employer free to continue to discriminate in respect of rates of contribution or benefit, as in cases where actuarial tables were used. Schemes were also free to discriminate in respect of other access rules such as the employee's work, marital status or earnings status.[29] For example, the employer could choose to limit the coverage of the scheme to a particular category of worker, thus in effect excluding 'women's only' categories. This stance was reinforced by the 1975 Sex Discrimination Act, which facilitated such discrimination, including as it did an exception for 'provision in relation to death or retirement'.[30] The 1975 Act also made it expressly lawful to discriminate by using actuarial tables in the calculation of annuities, life assurance policies or similar matters.[31]

EC law has proved somewhat more progressive. The 1987 Occupational Social Security Directive, Directive 87/378[32] requires for equal treatment in the provision of occupational pensions. However, it retains some crucial limitations, permitting the assumption of difference and dependency to continue. Thus sex-based discrimination in survivors' pensions is permitted until a Directive requires otherwise.[33] Moreover, although the Commission originally proposed an explicit prohibition on the use of separate actuarial data for men and women, Article 9(c) permits such use in the fixing of levels of workers' contributions for up to thirteen years after the notification of the Directive.

Despite the Directive, little further progress was made prior to 1995. The Social Security Act 1989, intended in part to give effect to Directive 86/378, included an imaginative improvement on the 1975 equal access provisions, in that it prohibited both direct and indirect sex discrimination in occupational scheme rules.[34] This meant that it covered more than just access, and made it unlawful to discriminate even indirectly. However, these provisions were not brought into force. Instead, the 1975 equal access

---

[27] EqPA 1970, s. 6(1A).
[28] Social Security Pensions Act 1975, s. 53(1).
[29] See generally Reid, above n. 13; J. Mesher 'The Social Security Pensions Act 1975' [1976] 39 MLR 321.
[30] SDA 1975, s. 6(4).    [31] *ibid.*, s. 45.    [32] [1986] OJ L 225/40.
[33] Article 9(a) and (b).    [34] Social Security Act 1989, sched. 5.

requirements were re-enacted in substantial part in 1993.[35] The only progress achieved was the provision for pension rights to continue accruing during periods of maternity or family leave, which was finally brought into force in 1994.[36] It is notable that even the 1989 Act permitted the use of actuarial calculations to justify different benefit rates in money purchase schemes. The result was that by 1992, despite some advances, there remained a significant gap between membership of occupational pension schemes for men and women respectively. Thus in that year, 62 per cent of male full-timers and 54 per cent of women full-timers were members of schemes. Of greatest concern was the fact that a mere 19 per cent of women part-timers were members.[37]

### b) Bias in Favour of Male Patterns of Work

The second reason for women's continuing disadvantage in old age is the bias in favour of male patterns of work. This bias is most clearly evident in the contributory principle, which links pension entitlements to lifetime earnings, rather than to need (means-testing) or simply to age (flat rate). The contributory principle has been at the core of both occupational and State pension schemes.[38] Because benefits in old age are dependent on lifetime earnings, this principle inevitably favours those who have worked continuously and full-time from school-leaving age until retirement, and who have achieved a reasonable status and level of earnings from their work. Such a working pattern clearly leaves no space for child-care and other domestic responsibilities. Women's continuing child-care obligations therefore directly impede the extent to which they are able to make provision for their old age.

The effects of the contributory principle are clearly visible. Figures from 1992 show that in the sixty-five to seventy-four age group, women's average weekly income of £96 is barely more than one-half of the £182 averaged by men. This difference can largely be attributed to the fact that men's income from occupational pension schemes is almost three times as much as women's. Nor is this limited to occupational pension schemes: men tend to receive State pensions which are 37 per cent higher than those of women.[39] The result is that many women are reliant on their male partner's pension scheme to underpin their standard of living in old age. Such dependency exacerbates women's vulnerability on divorce, particularly in old age.[40]

The detrimental effect on women of the bias towards male patterns of work is evident in all the complex strands of current State pension provi-

---

[35] Pension Schemes Act 1993, s. 118; see generally C. McCrudden 'Equal Treatment and Occupational Pensions' [1995] 46 *Northern Ireland Legal Quarterly* 376.
[36] SI 1994/1661.
[37] Hutton et al, above n. 12, p. 7.
[38] First provided for in the Widows' Orphans and Old Age Contributory Pensions Act 1925.
[39] EOC, *The Life Cycle of Inequality* (1995) pp. 27–8.
[40] Walker, above n. 1, p. 184.

sion, namely, the basic State pension, the State Earnings Related Pension (SERPS), contracted-out occupational earnings-related pensions, and approved personal pensions. Each of these will be dealt with in turn.

The basic State pension is the most widely applicable of the various types of pension provision. More people are eligible for the basic State pension than for any of the earnings related elements. Nevertheless, the basic State pension clearly demonstrates the continuing bias in favour of male patterns of working. Entitlement to a full pension is conditional on the claimant having paid contributions on earnings above the earnings limit for nine-tenths of his or her working life, with a reduced pension for those who do not fully fulfil these conditions. Not surprisingly, women's fragmented work histories and low earnings continue to impede their access to the full basic pension. In particular, an estimated 2 million women earn below the lower earnings limit for national insurance contributions,[41] thus finding themselves entirely excluded from old age provision. Particularly problematic are those women with earnings fluctuating around the lower earnings limit, who may find that at the end of a particular year they have not made sufficient contributions for a qualifying year, yet cannot reclaim the contributions made. Added to these two excluded groups are those women who decided in 1977 to retain their option to pay a reduced national insurance contribution and thereby forfeit their right to an independent pension. The result is a disturbingly large number of excluded women. In fact, it is estimated that by 2020 there may be as many as half of all women reaching retirement age who will still not be entitled to a full basic pension in their own right.[42]

An important advance was made in 1975 when the Social Security Pensions Act 1975 recognised the effects on pensions of the time taken out of the labour market for child-care. The Act provided that a shorter period of contributions (twenty years) would suffice to earn a retirement pension if during the missing years the contributor was 'precluded from regular employment by responsibilities at home'.[43] But the availability of this exemption, known as Home Responsibilities Protection, is limited in some key respects. Thus it is only available in years when no national insurance contributions at all have been made, excluding women who have earned sufficient in a year to attract such contributions, but who have not paid sufficient contributions to meet the qualifying requirements for a basic pension.[44] In any event, even Home Responsibilities Protection requires at least twenty years' continuous employment. Nor does the availability of a basic pension on its own suffice to ensure a comfortable old age. As a result of government's cost-cutting aims, the value of the basic pension has

---

[41] EOC, *A Question of Fairness* (1992), para. 4.3.
[42] Hutton et al, above n. 12, p. 5. A reduced pension may be available.
[43] Social Security Pensions Act 1975, s. 19(3); see now SSCBA 1992, Sched. 3 para. 5(7).
[44] EOC *A Question of Fairness* (1992), para. 4.4.

declined dramatically relative to earnings, so that by the mid-1990s, the basic State pension was worth a paltry 15 per cent of average male earnings.[45] Given the large number of excluded women, plus the large number on basic pensions alone, it is not surprising to find high levels of poverty in older women.

The basic State pension is complemented by an earnings-related element. This can be provided in a variety of ways, including the State Earnings Related Pension Scheme (SERPS), an Approved Contracted-out Occupational Pension Scheme or an Approved Personal Pension. SERPS, which was introduced in 1975, entrenches further the bias towards 'male' patterns of work, by entitling employees who have made the requisite contributions to an additional earnings-related pension, over and above the basic State pension. Inevitably, the earnings-related component reflects women's tendency to earn less than men. The disadvantage suffered by low earning women in respect of SERPS was compounded in 1986 by the change in the calculation of benefits from an average of the best twenty years to an average of all years in a working lifetime.[46] Introduced specifically to cut the cost of SERPS, this has had a particularly detrimental effect on women because it includes periods of low earnings due to part-time working or low paid work on re-entry into the labour market. It is not surprising, therefore, that women's average entitlement to SERPS payments lags significantly behind that of men. Thus in 1988, SERPS figures for women aged sixty to sixty-four were only £6.76 per week; compared with £10.29 for men aged sixty-five to sixty-nine.[47] Moreover, proposals to compensate for some of the loss by extending Home Responsibilities Protection for SERPS were not put into effect.

The main alternative to SERPS is the provision of the earnings-related element by a contracted-out occupational scheme. However, as we have seen, occupational pensions are most likely to exist in mainstream, relatively high status occupations, in which women are significantly under-represented. Occupational pension schemes are strictly premised on male working patterns. Hence women with low earnings and fragmented work histories are likely to end up with relatively small pensions. Moreover, occupational pension schemes continue to be preoccupied with the provision of widows' pensions rather than extending women's independent entitlement. This is particularly problematic for women cohabitees and divorced women. In the case of the former, rights to a share in the deceased partner's occupational pension depend on the discretion of the trustees and the rules of the particular scheme. Even more seriously, on divorce, a woman generally loses her potential right to a widow's pension and benefits. Until 1995, a court in allocating resources between the parties on

---

[45] A. Ogus, E. Barendt and N. Wikeley, *The Law of Social Security* (4th edn., Butterworths, 1995), p. 214.

[46] Social Security Act 1986, s. 18.

[47] EOC, *Your Pension Matters* (1992), p. 8.

divorce could not normally make an order which would directly affect pension entitlements. The court could make adjustments in other ways to compensate a widow for lack of access to occupational benefits in her own right; but this is at the discretion of the court. This contrasts with other jurisdictions, such as New Zealand, in which pension benefits are included in the definition of matrimonial property, and can be divided on divorce.[48] (For the position post-1995, see below.)

Pension rights can be augmented in various ways. Thus it is possible to make additional voluntary contributions to increase the final pension entitlement, a provision which is partially subsidised through tax rebates. It is now also possible to switch from occupational schemes and invest instead in an Approved Personal Pension (APP). Personal pensions have been relatively popular: by April 1993, almost 5.7 million persons including over 2 million women had APPs.[49] In practice, however, research has shown that they are only really of benefit to those who can afford to make high contributions, thus excluding the many women on low pay.[50] In both personal pensions and the additional voluntary contributions, women are placed at a particular disadvantage because of the common practice of using gender-based actuarial calculations to predict lifespan. Because women are statistically likely to live longer than men, their pensions are deemed more expensive. Hence women are frequently required to make higher contributions or are entitled to lower benefits than men. In an example given to the EOC, a company stated that for a man aged sixty each £1,000 would buy an annual pension for £122; whereas for a woman aged sixty the same sum would bring an annual pension of £113.60.[51] Such arrangements have, as we have seen, been legitimised by legislation.[52]

c) Pension Ages

Despite the extent and depth of institutional obstacles to equality for women in old age, the recent flurry of litigation has been directed almost entirely at a single issue: that of differential pension ages of men and women. Why then has the pensionable age of sixty for women and sixty-five for men become so contentious an element of the pensions framework? Paradoxically, the lower pension age for women has come to be viewed as a coveted advantage for men. Although during the years of full employment, women's lower retirement and pension age clearly operated to their detriment, modern conditions of high unemployment and compulsory early retirement have reversed this position. Currently, as many as 43 per cent of men and 68 per cent of women have already left the paid labour force by the age of sixty.

[48]  J. Eekelaar, *Family Law and Social Policy* (2nd edn. Weidenfeld & Nicolson, 1984), p. 119.
[49]  Hutton et al, above n. 12, p. 7.
[50]  See B. Davies and S. Ward, *Women and Personal Pensions* (EOC Research Series, 1992), p. 36.
[51]  EOC, *Your Pension Matters* (1992), p. 9.
[52]  Above pp. 335–6.

Pension age crucially affects the terms of early leaving. For example, compulsory or voluntary redundancy within sight of pension age usually attracts a more advantageous package than a redundancy earlier on in a worker's life. It is therefore worth examining the reasons for the age gap.

Until 1940, women and men enjoyed a common compulsory pension age, first of seventy and subsequently of sixty-five. At this stage, however, retirement was not a condition of drawing a pension. The reasons for dropping women's pensionable age to sixty in the 1940 Act[53] were complex and closely related to the basic assumptions noted above. Most prominent was the dependency issue: until 1940, a married man could only draw an additional payment for his dependent wife once both spouses reached sixty-five. This meant that if the wife was less than sixty-five when the husband reached pensionable age, the couple were required to subsist on a single person's retirement pension until she reached sixty-five. By decreasing women's age of eligibility to sixty, the Act ameliorated the harshness of this rule. Its effect was immediate: the proportion of cases in which the married couple pension rate was payable on the husband attaining sixty-five leapt from 28 to 63 per cent.[54] The Act also made a small gesture towards facilitating a measure of independence in pension rights for women. Single women had been campaigning for some time for a decrease in their pension age to fifty-five, mainly because of the difficulty of sustaining their contributions record all the way to sixty-five.[55] Single women at that time frequently left paid work to look after elderly parents, thus falling out of insurance in the same way as their married counterparts with children.[56] The new pension age of sixty was in part a compromise concession to this lobby.

On the surface, therefore, the Act appeared beneficial: it was certainly supported by the Opposition and the TUC. However, it was highly ambiguous in its effect. For uninsured women, the simpler option of dropping the age requirement altogether does not appear to have been considered. Its effect on insured women was far from wholly beneficial. As a start, the reduction in pensions age was to be financed by an increase in contributions which weighed more heavily on women than men.[57] In addition, the Act removed insured women's rights under the national health insurance and unemployment insurance schemes at sixty even if they continued in work. Given that unemployment benefit was higher than the pension, this was a significant loss. Perhaps even more disturbing was the underlying agenda, that is, to address problems of unemployment by squeezing women out of

---

[53] Old Age and Widows' Pensions Act 1940, s. 1(1).
[54] HC 357, col 1200 (20 February 1940).
[55] See HC 357, col 1412 (25 February 1940).
[56] HC vol. 357, col 1413 (21 February 1940).
[57] Men paid increased contributions of 1d as against 2d for insured women (plus 1d payable by the employer).

the labour market at sixty and to put downward pressure on women's pay.[58] Although pensions were not conditional on ceasing work, in practice, in industrial sectors, workers were dismissed on reaching pension age. This was a significant hardship, since the 10s a week pension was not sufficient to maintain a person without paid work. Yet substantive equality had few advocates in the Parliamentary debates.[59] Indeed, Mrs Adamson was almost alone in stating the argument 'for granting adequate pensions to men and women alike at an earlier age than at present. The solution of unemployment does not lie in handing out to the older women a small pension on which they cannot live and which may be used . . . to subsidise unscrupulous employers.'[60] This view remains isolated both nationally and internationally; indeed, the pattern of differential pension ages for men and women is widespread throughout Europe and was already in place in Australia in 1940.

Although in 1946 the age qualification for dependent wives was removed altogether,[61] legislation continued to entrench differential pension ages. In 1946 the right to draw a pension first became conditional on retiring from paid work,[62] with the result that the ages of sixty and sixty-five were increasingly adopted as normal retirement ages as well as pensionable ages. Differential pension ages were specifically protected by both the EqPA and the SDA.[63] Similarly, rights to claim unfair dismissal and redundancy compensation generally ceased at sixty for women and sixty-five for men.[64] European legislation followed suit: Directive 79/7 on equal treatment in social security specifically permits Member States to maintain differential pensionable ages both for the purposes of granting pensions and in respect of the consequences for other benefits.[65] Directive 86/378 allows Member States to permit differential retirement ages in occupational social security schemes until equality is introduced in state social security or until it is required by a Community Directive. This permission was utilised by the UK in the Social Security Act 1989, which allowed separate pensionable ages in occupational pension schemes until the state scheme is harmonised. However, both the EC Directives and the UK legislation have now been overtaken by caselaw developed by the ECJ, resulting in an insistence at

[58] See e.g. HC vol. 357, col 1414 (21 February 1940); and col 2151, 2155 (28 February 1940).

[59] See e.g. HC 347, col 1269 (20 February 1940).

[60] HC vol 357, col 1270–1271 (20 February 1940); see also Dr Summerskill at 2142 (28 February 1940).

[61] In 1946, provision was made for a pensioner to claim a dependant's allowance if his wife was under sixty.

[62] National Insurance Act 1946, s. 20. This link was again severed by the Social Security Act 1989, s. 7.

[63] Above nn. 27 and 30.

[64] EPCA 1978, s. 64(b)(ii), until its amendment by SDA 1986; EPCA 1978, s. 82(1)(b), until its amendment by EA 1989.

[65] Article 7(1)(a).

first on equal retirement ages and then on equal pensionable ages in all but statutory pension schemes. It is to a critical assessment of this caselaw which we now turn.

## II.  PENSIONS EQUALITY AND THE ECJ

The past ten years have witnessed a series of dramatic decisions by the ECJ on pensions equality. However, a closer examination reveals that these have not been directed, as would be hoped, at alleviating women's demonstrable disadvantage in old age. Instead, most successful cases have been brought by men claiming that they have been less favourably treated than similarly situated women. It is argued in this part that this paradox results from the ways in which the concept of equality has been formulated by the ECJ.[66] Although the meaning of equality frequently shifts with the context, the cumulative effect of the caselaw has been to sever the traditional link between equality and the alleviation of social disadvantage. Instead, equality has been fashioned in a way which tends to perpetuate existing power relations, not just between men and women, but also between employers and employees. It is therefore no coincidence that, apart from the significant exception of part-time workers, the Court's application of the equality principle to pensions has led to a further deterioration in the position of many women pensioners, while producing only minor gains for men. The main beneficiaries have instead been employers, pension funds and the State.

It has been seen that the Social Security and Occupational Social Security Directives deliberately steered clear of the marshy area of pensionable age. Legislative caution was briefly mirrored by the ECJ. The first case to contest differential pension ages, *Defrenne (No. 1)*[67] found a court reluctant to mobilise Article 119. On the grounds that the case was concerned with a social security scheme laid down by legislation, the Court held that it was not consideration from employment and so fell outside of the definition of 'pay'. Later cases by contrast saw the ECJ vigorously sidestepping both the legislative restrictions and its own test in *Defrenne (No. 1)*. Instead, by a robust and extensive interpretation of 'pay', the Court has succeeded in drawing the issue of occupational pensions into the powerful magnetic field of Article 119. In case after case, the Court has reiterated that 'pay' only excludes social security schemes or retirement pensions which are directly governed by legislation without any element of agreement and which are obligatorily applicable to general categories of workers.[68] In the seminal case of *Barber*,[69] the Court held that the equal treatment principle applied

---

[66] This section is largely derived from my previous article 'The Poverty of Equality: Pensions and the ECJ' [1996] 25 ILJ 91.

[67] Case 80/70, [1971] ECR 445.

[68] See e.g. *Ten Oever* C-109/91 [1993] IRLR 601 ECJ, para. 9.

[69] Case 262/88 [1990] IRLR 240 (ECJ).

not only to occupational pension benefits, but also to contracted-out schemes. From then on little has been excluded. Thus, Article 119 applies also to survivors' pensions,[70] supplementary occupational schemes,[71] other non-contracted-out occupational schemes,[72] public service schemes,[73] benefits on early retirement and transfer values.[74] It can be relied upon both against the employer and against the trustees of an occupational scheme, who are required to amend any provisions of a trust deed which offend the principle of equality.[75] Equally importantly, it includes the right to join an occupational pension scheme.[76] The expansive use of Article 119 has not only meant that the insistence on equality in pensions is both vertically and horizontally directly effective, but also that the exceptions and caveats in the two social security directives are inapplicable. The expansion of Article 119 has been complemented by the use of the Equal Treatment Directive, specifically to outlaw differential retirement ages.[77] Although this Directive is only directly effective against the State as employer, its impact has spread to the private sector.

Against the backdrop of a history of discrimination in pensions, the promise of equality held out by the ECJ is of enormous potential significance. The fact that this potential has not been realised demonstrates some of the central limitations of the notions of equality which emerge incrementally but not always consistently from ECJ caselaw. Three aspects will be considered here: (a) formal equality as compared with equality of results; (b) the extent of influence of the 'male norm'; and (c) the role of employers' financial interests. It is argued here that the emerging pattern reflects the Court's preference for a result which disturbs existing power relations as little as possible. In particular, the ideal of equality as a means to alleviate disadvantage has been sidelined. Instead, the financial interests of employers and pension funds have been given overriding priority over those of employees, and the interests of men have generally been preferred to those of women.

a) EQUALITY: FORM OR SUBSTANCE?

The dominant conception of equality in ECJ caselaw is a formal one, following the contours of the Aristotelian formula that likes should be treated alike. This formal conception is at times and somewhat unpredictably replaced by a substantive notion which focuses on the result, condoning unequal treatment if necessary to achieve an equal outcome. This section explores each of these conceptions as they appear in the cases.

---

[70] *Ten Oever*, above n. 68.    [71] *Moroni* C110/91 [1994] IRLR 130 ECJ.

[72] *Coloroll* C-200/91 [1994] IRLR 586 (ECJ).

[73] *Beune* C-7/93 [1995] IRLR 103 (ECJ).

[74] *Neath* C-152/91 [1994] IRLR 91 (ECJ).

[75] *Coloroll*, above n. 72.

[76] *Bilka* C-170/84 [1986] IRLR 317 ECJ, *Vroege* C-57/93 [1994] IRLR 651 ECJ, *Fisscher* C-128/93 [1994] IRLR 662 ECJ.

[77] *Marshall* C-152/84 [1986] ECR 723 (ECJ).

i) **Consistency not Substance**

Formal equality requires only consistent treatment, ostensibly remaining neutral as to the substantive outcome. Because there is no background requirement of distributive justice, formal equality is satisfied whether the two parties are treated equally well or equally badly. However, the appearance of neutrality is deceptive. A value judgement is required to choose whether to insist on 'levelling up' or to permit 'levelling down'. In making this choice, the priorities of the ECJ have shifted markedly over the years. While the earlier cases demonstrate a clear commitment to the improvement of living and working standards, the Court has rapidly moved away from the notion that equality is allied to distributive justice. Instead, a formal conception has emerged, one which is fully satisfied by consistent treatment, even if this means depriving women of their existing benefits or vested expectations. Indeed, the Court has gone further and insisted that, once a decision has been made to 'level down', equality requires that this be achieved immediately and without any transitional measures protecting women's vested interests. Only in cases where women have already received benefits does equality require the extension of such benefits to men. The result is a notion of equality which is fully consistent with an increase in disadvantage.

The earlier commitment to equality as a means of improving living and working standards emerged from the seminal case of *Defrenne (No. 2)*[78] where the Court held that Article 119 could only be satisfied by raising the pay of the lowest paid group. Any other strategy would be unacceptable because, the Court stressed, Article 119 formed part of the social objectives of the Community which aimed 'to ensure social progress and seek the constant improvement of the living and working conditions of their peoples . . . Since Article 119 appears in the context of the harmonization of working conditions . . . the objection that the terms of this article may be observed in other ways than by raising the lowest salaries may be set aside.'[79] This conception was reflected to some extent in the later case of *Marshall (No. 1)*,[80] in which it was held that it was discriminatory for the State to impose a retirement age of sixty on women when men were permitted to work until sixty-five.

The rash of cases brought in the 1990s after the *Barber*[81] decision signified a clear departure from the substantive view in *Defrenne (No. 2)*. In *Smith* v. *Avdel*,[82] the Court was confronted directly with the question of whether it was permissible under Article 119 to achieve equality by removing advantages from women. The employers in this case had decided, in the

---

[78] Case 43/75 [1976] ECR 455.
[79] Above n. 37, para. 25. See also *Nimz* Case C-184/89 [1991] IRLR 222 (ECJ).
[80] Above n. 77.     [81] Above n. 69.
[82] Case C-408/92 [1994] IRLR 602 (ECJ).

wake of the *Barber* case, that Article 119 would be fulfilled by raising the pension age of women from sixty to that of men, namely sixty-five. This entailed significant losses for women who had planned and expected to retire at sixty. It was specifically argued that Article 119 did not permit equality to be achieved by withdrawing rights from one sex. The Court disagreed. Without further explanation, it simply declared that provided equality was achieved, Article 119 was agnostic as to the specific level of pay. This position was emphatically reiterated in *Coloroll*: 'Article 119 merely requires that men and women should receive the same pay for the same work without imposing any specific level of pay.'[83] It was only in respect of discrimination between the date of the *Barber* decision and the equalisation of pensions that it was necessary to extend women's benefits to men;[84] and *Defrenne (No. 2)*[85] was recast in these terms. Three factors seem to have influenced this limited choice of 'levelling up': a practical recognition of the impossibility of withdrawing benefits already granted to women; the fact that the financial consequences for employers would be limited and well defined; and a gesture towards fault-based fairness, which requires that compensation be payable because the employer was at fault in failing to introduce equality speedily.

*Smith* v. *Avdel*[86] goes even further in its perception of equality as overridingly concerned with consistency. The Court was also asked whether Article 119 imposed any obligation on the employer to minimise the adverse consequences to women of raising pension ages. Not only was the Court emphatic in its rejection of such a view; it went further and held that any such transitional measure would in fact infringe the concept of equality. In high-sounding terms, it proclaimed: 'Equal treatment between men and women in relation to pay is a fundamental principle of Community law and . . . its application by employers must be immediate and full.'[87] As a result, it would be contrary to Article 119 for the employer to attempt to achieve equality in a progressive manner, since that would maintain discrimination. This thoroughgoing application of equality therefore strikes down all transitional measures aimed at protecting vested expectations of women after the date of *Barber*. In *Van Den Akker*,[88] the Court duly rejected the complaint brought by a group of women employed under the Shell pension scheme in the Netherlands attempting to protect their option to retain a lower pension age than men. In that case, the pension scheme had raised women's pensionable age to that of men in 1985, but had permitted women to opt to retain their lower pension age. When Shell withdrew this option, maintaining it was unlawful under *Barber*, the women argued that such a withdrawal was not necessitated by Article 119. The Court emphatically reiterated its position in *Smith*. The fact that this measure was merely

---

[83] Above n. 72 at p. 597.      [84] *Smith*, above n. 82, para. 17.
[85] Above n. 78.      [86] Above n. 82.      [87] *ibid.*, at para. 25.
[88] Case C-28/93 [1994] IRLR 616 (ECJ).

transitional did not affect the principle that equality, albeit equality in disadvantage, should be achieved immediately and in full.

## ii) **Equality of Results**

The formal notion of equality as consistent treatment is not the only conception which arises from the cases. Several cases reflect a different notion: one in which differential treatment can be justified if its aim is to achieve an equal outcome. In principle such an approach is more likely to achieve distributive justice than the formal notion. However, an examination of the cases reveals that, paradoxically, the Court's sudden shifts to a conception of equality of results have generally worsened women's position because its underlying concern, even in these cases, is not to use equality in order to redress disadvantage, but to apply equality in a way which protects the funding arrangements of employers and pension schemes.

The clearest example of a sudden switch to equality of results is *Bird's Eye Walls*,[89] which concerned a scheme in which women compelled to retire early on grounds of ill-health were paid a lower bridging pension between the ages of sixty and sixty-five than men of the same age. The employer argued that the reason for this discrepancy was in order to take account of the fact that women were eligible for the State pension between sixty and sixty-five whereas men were not. The Court held that Article 119 was not breached. Although the complainant's bridging pension was lower than that of a man of the same age, its main purpose was 'to place on an equal footing the overall financial treatment of men and women in identical situations'. It is clear that the Court has in this case suddenly moved from its endorsement of equality as consistency of treatment, regardless of overall outcome, to a notion which permits inconsistent treatment in order to achieve equality of outcome. This shift is completed by the declaration that the principle of equality would in fact have been breached (to the detriment of men) by equal treatment, that is if women had been given the same level of bridging pension as men of the same age. The immediate consequence of the unexpected move from formal equality to equality of results in *Bird's Eye Walls* was that yet again a claim brought by a woman applicant failed before the Court.

## b) THE INFLUENCE OF THE MALE NORM

As we have seen, pensions provision has traditionally operated with an inbuilt bias against those with child-care obligations and in favour of those with 'male' patterns of work. In addition, stereotypical assumptions about men as breadwinners and women as dependants have been reinforced. For example, men have always been encouraged to provide for their surviving widows, while women have been prevented from doing so. The Court has recognised

---

[89] Case C-132/91 [1994] IRLR 29 (ECJ).

and curtailed the operation of this 'male norm' in some areas. In others, however, the cases have actively underpinned this male bias. This section considers first those cases in which some inroads have been made into the male norm; and then examines those which have had the opposite effect.

There are two key areas in which the male norm has been dented: survivors' benefits and part-time workers. However, the impact in both, as will be seen, has been carefully circumscribed. So far as survivors' benefits are concerned, EC legislation explicitly reflected stereotypical assumptions about the male role as breadwinner. The Social Security Directive exempts provisions concerning survivors' benefits from the equality principle,[90] and sex-based discrimination in survivors' pensions is permitted by the Occupational Social Security Directive until a Directive requires otherwise.[91] However, in a welcome move, the Court in *Ten Oever*[92] classified survivors' pensions as pay and therefore subject to the principle of equality. The assumption of men as providers and women as dependants was thereby punctured. It is worth noting, perhaps cynically, that this is one context in which men are the direct beneficiaries of equality for women. More problematically, the decision has been made subject to the prospectivity rule in *Barber*.[93] The result is that survivors' benefits may only be claimed by men in respect of periods subsequent to 17 May 1990, so that Mr Ten Oever himself was unsuccessful.

The second area in which the bias towards male patterns of work has been challenged is in access to pension schemes. Most importantly, a stream of cases has recognised that full-time working as a condition of access to pension schemes discriminates against women, because their family responsibilities make it difficult to conform to this 'male' pattern of work. In the seminal case of *Bilka*,[94] the Court referred specifically to the difficulties encountered by women workers in working full-time. Exclusion of part-time workers was therefore held to be in breach of Article 119 when significantly more men than women worked full-time unless the employer could objectively justify the exclusion. Moreover, later cases have held that the temporal limitation in *Barber* does not apply to part-time workers' cases because employers had no reason to believe that exclusion was acceptable. These cases represent a highly significant move in favour of part-time workers: indeed, between September 1994 and June 1995, an estimated 75,000 tribunal claims were lodged by part-timers.[95] The UK government has responded by issuing new regulations,[96] which strengthen existing equal access provisions by including indirect discrimination in the list of prohibitions.

---

[90] Article 3(2).    [91] Article 9(a) and (b).
[92] Above n. 68.    [93] Above n. 69.
[94] Above n. 76 at para. 29. See also *Vroege*, above n. 76.
[95] *Industrial Relations Law Bulletin* vol. 522 (June 1995), p. 16.
[96] The Occupational Pension Schemes (Equal Access to Membership) Regulations 1995 SI 1215, s. 3.

However, the recognition that full-time working requirements have a particularly severe exclusionary effect on women is limited in three crucial ways, with the result that little impact is made on the underlying structures whereby women retain prime responsibility for child-rearing in a world in which the full-time mode of working remains dominant. The first is the formulation of the link between women and part-time working. According to *Bilka*,[97] it must first be established that a much lower proportion of women than of men work full-time. This leaves fertile ground for disputes over statistics, particularly in professions such as teaching, in which women predominate in both part-time and full-time capacities. In a recent UK case,[98] a part-time woman teacher complained that part-timers were treated less favourably than full-timers in the calculation of service for pension purposes in redundancy cases. The council employed 5934 women but only 3106 male teachers; and although a tiny minority of 45 men were employed part-time, compared to 756 women, the EAT relied instead on the respective proportions of women and men working full-time. Since 89.5 per cent of women over fifty were employed full-time, compared to 97 per cent of men, it was held that the difference was too small to found a claim under either the SDA or Article 119. Of course, a very different picture emerges if the spotlight falls instead on part-time figures, which showed that 3 per cent of men over fifty worked part-time as against 10.5 per cent of women in the same age group. These figures could well support an argument that considerably more women than men over fifty worked part-time. In fact, as this demonstrates, statistical gymnastics can simply disguise the real detriment suffered by part-time workers, the vast majority of whom are women, who remain without redress simply because they work in a female-dominated profession. This problem is likely to be particularly prevalent in the UK, since the new Regulations use the indirect discrimination formula. Far simpler and more effective would be a package which protects part-time workers as such.

The second limitation of the part-time cases concerns the Court's explicit refusal to require an employer to organise its occupational pension scheme in such a manner as to take into account the particular difficulties faced by persons with family responsibilities in meeting the conditions for entitlement to a pension. In *Bilka*,[99] it was argued that the employer should for example make sure that periods during which women workers have had to meet family responsibilities count towards the accrual of a pension. The Court, however, regarded Article 119 as restricted to the question of pay discrimination between men and women workers. Structural considerations such as the division of labour within the family are deliberately disregarded. The refusal to neutralise the effects of breaks in continuity of

---

[97] Above n. 76.
[98] *Staffordshire County Council* v. *Black* [1995] IRLR 234 (EAT).
[99] Above n. 76.

employment leaves uncorrected a crucial factor contributing towards women's disadvantage in old age.

The third limitation on the part-time cases relates to the width of the defence available to the employer. The cases all make it clear that no breach of Article 119 will take place if an employer can show that the exclusion of part-time workers may be explained by objectively justified factors unrelated to any discrimination on grounds of sex. As will be argued below, ultimately, the employers' financial interests are permitted to trump those of women employees.

The Court's ability to displace the male underpinnings of pensions law and practice, while significant, has been limited even in the above cases. Other cases have failed even to recognise the pervasiveness of such assumptions. Two examples will be used here: the first concerning male patterns of work and the second manifesting a notion of freedom of choice, which ignores the extent to which family responsibilities act as a constraint on the true exercise of such choice.

The most vivid example of a case which is based unquestioningly on a working pattern that takes no account of child-care or other family responsibilities is the *Barber*[100] case itself. In this case, a contracted-out occupational scheme provided that employees were entitled to an immediate pension if they were made redundant within ten years of their pension age, which was sixty for women and sixty-five for men. Mr Barber was made redundant at the age of fifty-two. As a result, he was not entitled to an immediate pension but only to a deferred pension with a termination payment. The ECJ held that it was contrary to the principle of equal pay to treat Barber less favourably than a woman of the same age would have been treated. At first sight, this appears to be a straightforward question of treating likes alike. However, a closer examination of the hypothetical female comparator[101] reveals her to be male in all respects except her pensionable age. This is because the Court implicitly ascribed to her Barber's own history. Barber had been employed continuously by the same employer[102] from the age of twenty to his redundancy at fifty-two. As deputy head of the Guardian's South Yorkshire claims bureau, he was in a relatively senior position. His impeccable record of continuity, relatively high status and relatively high earnings presumably guaranteed him a commensurate pension. We are given no details of the profiles of women at Barber's establishment. Nevertheless, Barber's work history is clearly one which the 'normal' woman would have been unlikely to have shared. In

---

[100]   Above n. 69.

[101]   It is worth noting that the Court has in other contexts set its face firmly against hypothetical comparators in equal pay cases (*Jenkins*) but seems to have let this one slip in because the case came to the Court as an SDA rather than an EqPA case. Contrast *Coloroll*, above n. 72, in which it was held that no comparisons could be drawn in single sex pension funds.

[102]   Originally Car and General, later taken over by the Guardian Royal Exchange.

reality, the 'female comparator' was simply Barber himself with a lower retirement age.

A second manifestation of a yardstick of comparison reflecting 'male' values is the role played by freedom of choice in the Court's reasoning. Of course, valuing choice is not necessarily inimical to women's interests. In *Marshall*,[103] for example, by insisting that women have the same retirement age as men, the Court opened up greater possibilities for autonomy for women. However, more recently, the Court has relied on a notion of autonomy which ignores the social and legal factors which heavily constrain women's choice. This is most clearly evidenced in *Bird's Eye Walls*.[104] It will be recalled that in that case, the amount of the bridging pension payable to women between sixty and sixty-five was reduced by the amount of State pension to which it was assumed women were entitled. The Court was also asked to consider circumstances in which the woman was not in fact entitled to a State pension because, as was the case on the facts before them, she had exercised the married woman's option (see above). The response was unequivocal: no breach of Article 119 took place in such circumstances. Indeed, the Court held that it would be 'irrational' to disregard the fact that she had exercised her freedom of choice in accepting the married woman's option.[105] Notions of equality and fairness pointed in the opposite direction: to take into account her real resources rather than those she might have been entitled to would give her an unfair advantage over others whose position was comparable in every other respect. This stress on 'freedom of choice' reveals an underlying assumption of economic independence and autonomy which has systematically been denied to women. As we have seen above, the married woman's option was part of a pervasive stereotyping of married women as dependants on men. It is scarcely plausible to consider the option an exercise in free choice in the light of the 'half test', which meant that independent accrual of pension rights was somewhat of a lottery. Nor did the Court consider other reasons why a woman may be ineligible for a State pension: as we have seen, a surprisingly large number of women simply earn too little to be within the national insurance system; or have not worked sufficient years to accrue a State pension.

c) The Influence of Economic Forces

In pursuing the cause of equality in pensions, the Court has found itself tangled in more than just the relationship between men and women; it has also had to deal with the other main relationship of dominance—the employment relationship. It is argued here that the thin and formalistic conception of equality which emerges from the caselaw is primarily a result of the Court's concern to leave largely unaltered the employer's prerogatives

---

[103] Above n. 77.    [104] Above n. 89.    [105] *ibid.*, at para. 29.

over its employees, and particularly to abstain from decisions which might alter the economic balance of the employer's business. This is reflected in four major ways: first its support for the achievement of equality by the removal of benefits (levelling down); secondly in its insistence on a narrow temporal limitation in cases of levelling up or extension of benefits; thirdly its formulation of the defence in access cases, and finally the use of actuarial calculations.

### i) **Support for Levelling Down**

The Court makes little direct reference to the financial consequences of its decisions. Nevertheless the decision to permit employers to achieve equality by 'levelling down' was plainly influenced by such factors. Figures for equalisation of State pension ages are controversial,[106] but UK government statistics suggest that a common state pension age of sixty would increase public expenditure on pensions by almost £7 billion in 2025, while equalisation at sixty-five would save £5 billion in that year.[107] The impact on occupational pensions schemes is likely to be commensurate. Yet the Court has permitted employers' financial arguments to swamp those of women. While estimates of the impact on women require highly complex assumptions, there is no doubt that raising the pension age of women to sixty-five will have a significant negative impact on women's retirement income, particularly in the light of the insistence on removal of all transitional protection. In particular, women who cannot secure reasonably well paid work up to sixty-five will find their pension benefits reduced because of the reduction in their lifetime earnings.[108] Moreover, the ECJ's preference for a levelling down solution will have effects beyond occupational pensions into State provision. Following the cue given by the Court, the UK government has opted to equalise State pension ages at sixty-five.[109] Research commissioned by the TUC shows that loss of five years' pension entitlement will constitute a loss of £15,000 for a woman of twenty. This figure rises to £42,000 assuming an inflation rate of 2.5 per cent up to retirement date.[110]

### ii) **Prospectivity**

When levelling down has been impossible, the Court has resorted to prospectivity to contain the financial consequences of equality. In *Barber*[111] the Court recognised that it would be impossible to insist on retrospective withdrawal of benefits from women, and hence that equality could only be achieved by levelling up. Warnings of the serious financial consequences and enormous disruption and expense of this finding were thrust before the

[106] See generally Hutton et al, *Equalisation of State Pension Ages* above n. 12, pp. 56–66.
[107] Department of Social Security, *Equality in State Pension Age* (HMSO, 1993), p. 1.
[108] Hutton et al, *Equalisation of State Pension Ages* above n. 12, p. 95.
[109] Pensions Act 1995, sched. 4 Part I.
[110] LRD, *A brief guide to the 1995 Pensions Act (1995)*, p. 22.
[111] Above n. 69.

Court, particularly by the UK government. The UK pensions industry has suggested that equality along the lines of *Barber* could cost British industry £50 billion to implement.[112] The Court responded by placing a limitation *ratione temporis*. Although phrased in terms of legal certainty, this decision was clearly strongly influenced by financial considerations. In the Court's words: 'Overriding considerations of legal certainty preclude legal situations which have exhausted all their effects in the past from being called in question where that might upset retroactively the financial balance of many contracted-out pension schemes.'[113] The precise meaning of this limitation, however, remained unclear. Did it permit claims by workers whose pension fell due after the date of *Barber*, or did it exclude all claims except in respect of benefits which accrued as a result of contributions paid after *Barber*? Later attempts to construe *Barber* demonstrate that the case was genuinely ambiguous on this point, but it is not surprising that ultimately the option was chosen which had the fewest financial consequences for the employer or the scheme. Thus in *Ten Oever*,[114] the Court declared that *Barber* only applied to benefits payable in respect of periods of service subsequent to the date of the *Barber* decision.[115] Here too, the Court specifically took into account the way in which occupational pension funds are financed. That this anxiety was shared by the Council of Ministers is evidenced by the fact that an additional Protocol was annexed to the Maastricht Treaty putting this formula of prospectivity beyond doubt.[116]

The prospectivity rule has an important caveat in the cases concerning discriminatory access requirements. *Bilka*[117] placed no temporal limitation on the right of part-time workers to equal access to pension schemes, and later cases supported this approach. This was explained in *Vroege*[118] on the grounds that the temporal limitation only concerns discrimination which employers and occupational pension schemes could reasonably have considered to be permissible owing to the derogations in the Occupational Social Security Directive. Since employers were under no such misapprehension in respect of the right to join an occupational scheme, it was held to be fair to allow part-time workers to claim the right to join retroactively from 8 April 1976.[119] However, in *Fisscher*[120] the Court held that contributions should be payable retrospectively by the women in question. This was portrayed as itself an equality issue: to hold otherwise would be to treat these women more favourably than employees who had been required to

---

[112] LRD, *Pensions and Equality* (1994), p. 8.
[113] *Barber*, above n. 69, p. 259.    [114] Above n. 68.
[115] Subject to the exception for workers who have initiated legal proceedings before the 17 May 1990. See also *Coloroll*, above n. 72, paras. 44–9.
[116] The *Barber* Protocol to the Treaty on European Union, which came into force in November 1993.
[117] Above n. 76.    [118] *ibid.*
[119] The date of *Defrenne (No. 2)*, Case 43/75, above n. 78, in which the Court first held that Article 119 had direct effect.
[120] Above n. 76.

pay contributions. In practice, of course, this functions as an effective bar to married or part-time women making use of their rights to retrospective membership, given the fact that employee contributions are worth an average of £550 per annum.[121] This is a good example of the fluidity of equality justifications: a focus on the requirement to pay contributions yields a diametrically opposite decision to a focus on whether pension benefits will in fact be available. Moreover, the Court in this case takes a static view of equality, ignoring the very real continuing effects of past discrimination. Instead, the Court has clearly been influenced by the expense likely to be incurred by employers to make good their denial of membership.

Retroactivity is further undermined by the imposition of time limits on claims under these provisions. It was held in *Fisscher* that national time limits for bringing such actions are applicable.[122] New regulations[123] in the UK apply existing EqPA time limits to access claims, so that ex-employees must claim within six months of leaving the relevant employment and existing employees from the date at which exclusion ends.[124] Any award of back-dated membership will be limited to the two year period preceding the date of the claim, while employers are only required to fund retrospective entitlement from 31 May 1995 or two years prior to the date of the claim if this is later.[125]

### iii) Defence in Part-time Workers' Cases

We have seen that the Courts' approach to equality in the part-time workers' cases demonstrates a useful recognition of women's structural disadvantage in the labour market. However, even this recognition is subordinated to the dictates of business needs. In *Bilka*,[126] it was held that exclusion of part-time workers was not discriminatory if the employer could show that the exclusion was based on objectively justified factors unrelated to any discrimination on grounds of sex. This defence is made out if the employer can show that the exclusion corresponds to a real need on the part of the undertaking, is appropriate with a view to achieving the objectives pursued and is necessary to that end. Although the standard set is relatively high, it remains true that exclusionary practices can be justified by reference to business needs. *Bilka*[127] left it to national courts to determine on the basis of the facts before them whether this defence was made out, so that it is difficult to monitor its exact impact. It is noteworthy, however, that in *Vroege*,[128] the scheme in its amended and purportedly non-discriminatory form continued to exclude workers who worked for less than 25 per cent of normal working hours. The Court was not asked to address whether this

---

[121] *Occupational Pension Schemes 1991*, 9th Survey by the Government Actuary (HMSO, 1994), p. 21.
[122] *Fisscher*, above n. 76, para. 39.   [123] SI 1995/1215.
[124] See EOR No. 62 (1995), p. 18.   [125] SI 1995/1215 regs. 5 and 6.
[126] Above n. 76.   [127] *ibid.*   [128] *ibid.*

was in itself discriminatory; it seems highly likely however that such an exclusion would be held to be justified on the *Bilka* test. This means that the most vulnerable workers could remain unprotected in old age.

### iv) **Use of Actuarial Calculations**

The question here is whether the principle of equality is breached by reliance on actuarial tables which show that women tend to live longer than men. As we have seen this widespread practice leads to the conclusion that pensions provision for women is more expensive than for men, requiring adjustment either by raising the cost of contributions or by decreasing the level of benefits payable to women. In principle, it is strongly arguable that treatment of individual women on the basis of assumptions based on an average of all women is paradigmatic of discrimination on grounds of sex. As the US Supreme Court held in *City of Los Angeles* v. *Manhart*[129] in 1978, it is discriminatory to base pension rights on a generalisation which, even if true on average, may not apply to a particular individual. Thus it was unlawful to require female employees to make larger contributions to a pension fund than male employees. A similar chain of reasoning in *Arizona* v. *Norris*[130] led to the conclusion that it was discriminatory to pay lower benefits to women based on the same contributions. Yet the use of actuarial tables in the UK has been condoned at both domestic and EC level. The SDA 1975 made it expressly lawful to discriminate by using actuarial tables in the calculation of annuities, life assurance policies or similar matters.[131] Similarly, the Social Security Directive permits the use of actuarial factors to fix differential benefit levels in defined contribution schemes. Workers' contributions may differ to take account of different actuarial calculations but only until 1999.[132]

Despite the fact that this practice has generally operated to the detriment of women, the allegations of unfair treatment have not come from women but from men. This is because, on transfer from one pension scheme to another or commutation into a lump sum pre-retirement, women may appear to be better off than men due to the fact that a larger fund has been built up in order to finance women for a projected longer period than for men. It was in this context that the validity of actuarial calculations came before the Court, first in *Neath*[133] and subsequently in *Coloroll*.[134] Both the Commission and Advocate-General van Gerven echoed the approach of the US Supreme Court, arguing strenuously that it was discriminatory to treat individuals on the basis of generalisations which may not apply to that particular individual. However, the employers were supported by no less than five governments in arguing that the use of actuarial assumptions was necessary to ensure the solvency and stability of pension schemes. It was the latter view which the Court accepted, holding that the use of sex-based

[129]   435 US 700.      [130]   462 US 1073.      [131]   SDA 1975, s. 45.
[132]   Dir 87/378: Article 6(1)(i) and 9(c).      [133]   Above n. 74.      [134]   Above n. 72.

actuarial calculations in funded defined-benefit occupational pension schemes fell outside of the scope of Article 119. It is true that these cases only strictly concerned inequality of employers' contributions to funded defined-benefit schemes.[135] However, by holding that Article 119 was not operative, the Court left actuarial calculations unregulated.[136] Moreover, in *Coloroll*, the Court explicitly held that additional benefits stemming from additional voluntary contributions were not covered by Article 119, thus permitting pension schemes in the context of additional voluntary payments to demand higher contributions or pay out lower benefits to women than men. There are therefore no proposals to amend the provisions in the Occupational Social Security Directive permitting the use of actuarial factors to fix differential benefit levels in defined contribution schemes, and the proposed amendment now explicitly permits differential employer contributions if necessary to ensure the adequacy of funds necessary to cover the cost of the defined benefits.[137]

This approach demonstrates yet again that funding concerns took priority in the ECJ's agenda. A thoroughgoing use of the principle of equality would have required strict scrutiny of an expressly sex-based practice such as this. Yet the Court did not require employers to justify the use of gender-based actuarial calculations, nor to demonstrate why alternate methods of predicting longevity, such as smoking habits, are not used. In fact, it seems clear that the use of actuarial calculations is not inevitable: many occupational pension schemes and all State pension schemes operate without them.[138] Nor can it plausibly be argued that it would be unfair to men to require them to subsidise women as a class: in reality, it is in the nature of insurance that better risks always subsidise poorer risks.[139]

The Court's general deference to employers' funding concerns was made explicit in *Neath*,[140] which held that Article 119 could not be concerned with the funding arrangements chosen to secure payment of a pension. It is noteworthy that similar concerns led the US Supreme Court, having applied equality in a thoroughgoing fashion, to restrict retroactive effect of its ban on use of actuarial tables. In judgments remarkably similar to that in *Barber*, the Court in both *Manhart*[141] and *Norris*[142] held that the financial repercussions of their findings were so great and potentially so devastating that they should only apply to benefits derived from contributions collected after the date of the respective judgments.

---

[135] *Neath*, above n. 74, p. 95; *Coloroll*, above n. 72, para. 81, p. 599.
[136] Cf E. Whiteford [1995] CMLRev. 801 at p. 830.
[137] Preliminary Draft Directive Amending Directive 86/378 EEC, Article 6(1)(i), see EOR No. 62, p. 35.
[138] See [1993] IRLR 610.
[139] See *Manhart*, above n. 129 at p. 709.
[140] Above n. 74.
[141] Above n. 129 at pp. 718–21.
[142] Above n. 130 at pp. 110–11.

## III.   THE AFTERMATH OF *BARBER*

The litigation in the ECJ has prompted important legislative adjustments. In order to bring EC legislation into line with the caselaw, a proposal[143] has now been adopted to amend the Occupational Social Security Directive so that the principle of equal treatment applies to pension ages, compensation for compulsory early retirement and survivors' benefits.[144] Similarly, the Pensions Act 1995 includes measures to incorporate the changes into UK law. As a result, the concept of equality in pensions is now centre-stage. However, the effects of equality are no less ambiguous for women in the new legislation than in the ECJ jurisprudence. This part briefly analyses the effect of the recent changes, by considering the contours of the conception of equality used. I examine first the equalisation of State pension ages, and then turn to the provisions concerning equality in occupational pensions.

a)   THE COST OF EQUALITY: EQUALISING STATE PENSION AGES

The most dramatic response to the activity of the ECJ has been the move by the UK government to equalise State pension age.[145] The Secretary of State for Social Security, Peter Lilley, described the proposals as removing 'the last glaring inequality in our treatment of men and women'.[146] But it is here that the inadequacy of a purely formal conception of equality is at its most apparent. This is because, instead of equalising pension age at sixty, the 1995 Pensions Act aims to institute a new equal pension age of sixty-five.[147] In other words, equality is achieved by depriving women of one of the few advantages which historical accident bestowed upon them. This strategy is justified by referring to the purported cost of equalising at the age of sixty. According to government figures, a common pension age of sixty would increase public expenditure on pensions by almost £7 billion in 2025. By contrast, equalisation at sixty-five actually saves money: an estimated £5 billion in the year 2025.[148]

Despite its apparent unassailability, the arguments from cost can be challenged on two grounds. First, they give off a false aura of certainty. In reality, the figures are based on a large number of assumptions about future demographic and economic trends. Since these assumptions are themselves uncertain, the costings are far from scientifically established. Secondly, and more importantly still, such figures ignore the cost to women. Yet, as

---

[143] Reproduced in EOR No. 62 (1995), pp. 32–7.

[144] Except in the case of self-employed workers, for whom the previous derogations remain applicable.

[145] Pensions Act 1995 s. 126 and sched. 4.

[146] 'Equality in state pension age' White Paper HMSO Cm 2420.

[147] The Act contains complex transition measures: women born before 6 April 1950 retain the pensionable age of sixty; women born after 5 April 1955 attain pensionable age at sixty-five and women born in the intermediate period obtain pensionable age according to a specific table of dates: Pensions Act 1995, sched. 4 Part I.

[148] Department of Social Security, *Equality in State Pension Age* (1993) p. 12.

Hutton *et al* demonstrate, the effect on women's pensions is dramatic. For women who stop work at sixty the total amount of pension received at sixty-five under the new arrangements will be about 72 per cent of the amount which would have been paid under the present system if the women had deferred claiming their pension until sixty-five.[149] Given the low level of pension already available to women, this is a serious loss. It could be argued that some of this loss will be offset by the opportunity of remaining in work until sixty-five. However, the gains are minimal. For those who are able to continue in full-time employment, the relative sum is only slightly better, increasing to 75–76 per cent of the deferred pension which could have been received under the present system. The effect of remaining in part-time work is negligible, the new pension rising to only 73 per cent of the old deferred pension.[150] Nor is it certain that women in the age group of sixty to sixty-five will find paid employment in the interim; and if they do, it may well be at the cost of younger entrants to the labour market. Hutton *et al* conclude that 'in order for women to secure even a modest State pension, the ability to secure reasonably well paid full-time employment in later life may be crucial. At present the prospects for a substantial increase in employment prospects for older women do not appear promising.'[151]

The extra burden placed on women is to some extent mitigated by the provisions entitling workers to use awards of family credit or disability working allowance to enhance their pensions record for the purposes of the additional, earnings-related pension.[152] According to these provisions, the amount of earnings in a particular year is increased by the amount of family credit or disability working allowance paid to the employed earner, provided the person earns above the relevant minimum. Given that in October 1994, 540,000 families were in receipt of family credit, these proposals have a wide potential effect.[153] However, even in optimal circumstances, the actual impact is limited, largely because of the fact that the average family credit award, at £46 per week, is relatively low, and families tend to move rapidly in and out of family credit. For example, a woman working part-time and earning just above the lower earnings limit, who receives family credit of £60 per week for two years continuously, will enhance her SERPS pension by just 92 pence a week compared to her position had family credit not been taken into account.[154]

b) Equality of Opportunity: Reforms in Occupational Pensions

The *Barber* case and its sequelae have had a more positive effect in respect of occupational pension schemes, prompting legislative moves to require equal treatment in occupational pension schemes. The Pensions Act 1995

---

[149] Hutton et al, *Equalisation of State Pension Ages* above n. 12, p. 82.
[150] Hutton et al, above n. 12, p. 84.    [151] *ibid.*
[152] Pensions Act 1995, s. 127, amending SSCBA 1992, ss 44 and 45.
[153] Figures from Hutton et al, *Equalisation of State Pension Ages* above n. 12, p. 87.
[154] The example is taken from *ibid.*, p. 88.

and accompanying regulations are specifically intended to incorporate the requirements of Article 119 into UK law. However, as will be seen, the reform has been undertaken in a minimalist sense, doing no more than is absolutely necessary to comply with EC law.[155]

At the core of the new statutory provisions is the provision for an equal treatment rule to be implied into all occupational pension schemes. Significantly, the equal treatment rule is not limited to access to pension schemes, as were its predecessors, but also requires equal treatment of men and women in the terms of the scheme itself.[156] However, possibly because of its origins in Article 119, the reform has been based on the approach of the Equal Pay Act 1970, rather than the relatively sophisticated conceptual apparatus of direct and indirect discrimination. Thus, the 1995 Act requires that the terms of occupational pension schemes apply equally to men and women doing like work or work of equal value, unless the trustees or managers of the scheme can prove that the difference is genuinely due to a non-sex-based factor.[157] This is in clear contrast to the discrimination model used by the never-implemented Schedule 5 to the Social Security Act 1989, which made it unlawful to treat a woman less favourably than a man (direct discrimination), or to impose a requirement or condition which unjustifiably excluded disproportionately more women than men (indirect discrimination). The main difference between the two approaches lies in the role of the male comparator: under the equal pay model, the Act is only effective if a woman can find a man in the same employment doing equal work. As a result, a woman working in a highly segregated occupation might be excluded from the provisions because there is no appropriate a male comparator. Most seriously, it might be impossible for a part-time worker to find a male comparator in an establishment where the full-time workers doing work of equal value are also women.[158] Under the discrimination model, by contrast, it is possible to compare the woman's position with a 'hypothetical' male. Even more importantly, the indirect discrimination provisions permit a woman to show that equal treatment might have unequal results due to the operation of institutional forces. For example a worker in a segregated establishment might have been able to establish a claim of indirect discrimination, by showing that the condition or requirement of full-time work was such as to exclude significantly more women than men, thus establishing a claim to equal pension entitlement in the absence of a justification.[159] There may of course be isolated cases in which the equal pay approach is of benefit to a claimant, an example being a case where a man doing like work at her establishment is better provided for. In

---

[155] McCrudden, above n. 35, at p. 385.
[156] Pensions Act 1995, s. 62(1) and (2).
[157] *ibid.*, s. 62(2) and (4).
[158] C. McCrudden 'Third Time Lucky? The Pensions Act 1995 and Equal Treatment in Occupational Pensions' [1996] ILJ 28 at p. 32.
[159] See e.g., *Vroege*, above n. 76.

such cases, the complex statistical manoeuvres required to establish an indirect discrimination claim could be avoided. However, such cases are likely to be unusual. It is true that she has more chance of finding a man doing work of equal value with better pension entitlements. But the difficulty of establishing that a claimant's job is of equal value to that of a male comparator is easily commensurate to that of establishing indirect discrimination. It is noteworthy that the Schedule 5 provisions have now been activated in respect of the preservation of pension rights during maternity or parental leave, so that some cases are governed by the discrimination model and others by the equal pay model.

The concept of equality in the 1995 Act also contains some important exceptions. First, and possibly most important, is the justification defence, permitting the trustees or managers of a scheme to avoid an equal treatment rule if they can show that the difference between a woman and a man 'is genuinely due to a material factor which is not the difference of sex but is a material difference between the woman's case and the man's'.[160] The standard of proof established in *Bilka* applies in pensions cases, requiring the employer to show genuine business necessity. It remains to be seen to what extent the courts will allow financial arguments, particularly those relating to the financial integrity of the scheme to function as a valid defence. Secondly, the ECJ decision in *Bird's Eye Walls*[161] is given statutory authority: that is, it is lawful to pay a larger pension to a man between sixty and sixty-five than a woman of the same age in order to compensate for the fact that he is not entitled to a State pension until sixty-five whereas she is.[162] It is ironical that in this provision a hypothetical female comparator is permitted in order to determine the amount of extra pension to which he is entitled. Thus it is lawful to pay a man the amount of State pension which 'would be payable to a woman with earnings the same as the man's earnings in respect of his period of pensionable service under the scheme'.[163] Thirdly, the ECJ's acceptance of differences arising from actuarial calculations is endorsed. Some of these permissible differences are relatively uncontroversial. Thus it is permissible for employers to be required to pay larger contributions for women than for men to take account of the actuarial calculation of greater longevity for women, if this is done in order to ensure that equal periodical benefits are paid to men and to women.[164] This reflects the ECJ's brief foray into substantive equality.[165] Other exceptions, however, permit the use of actuarial factors to justify or perpetuate women's disadvantaged position. Thus it is permissible, on the basis of actuarial calculations, to pay differential benefits to men and women in

[160] Pensions Act 1995 s. 63(4).    [161] Above n. 89.
[162] Pensions Act 1995, s. 64(2); Occupational Pension Schemes (Equal Treatment) Regulations 1995 SI 1995/3183 reg. 13.
[163] Reg. 13(b).    [164] Pensions Act 1995, s. 64(3)(a) reg. 15(1).
[165] *Neath*, above n. 74; *Coloroll*, above n. 72.

money-purchase schemes (that is schemes which relate benefits to contributions rather than to average salary) and in respect of members' additional voluntary contributions.[166] Both these exceptions may well lead to lower benefits for women. Since it is unlawful to require women to pay higher contributions than men, the assumption that women will live longer than men entails the payment of lower benefits for a longer period drawn from the same fund. The exception for additional voluntary contributions continues the trend, noted above, whereby a woman earns a lower benefit than a man for the same level of additional contributions.

## CONCLUSION

It is unfortunate that the ECJ's adventurous definition of 'pay' has not been matched with a conception of equality which is linked with a genuine commitment to the improvement of workers' living and working conditions. Instead, the ECJ has attempted to develop equality as an end in itself, against a background of minimal disruption of existing power structures. As a result, the wide-ranging application of equality has led to only limited gains, many of which have been postponed until well into the next century, while perpetuating and even deepening disadvantage in important respects. This result is mirrored in domestic law, particularly in respect of the levelling down response to the equalisation of State pension age. The new equal treatment provisions in the 1995 Act are an important step forward, although they too are hedged about with limitations. In the last resort, of course, women's disadvantage in old age can only fully be addressed by a fundamental change in the institutional barriers faced by women before they retire.

[166] Pensions Act 1995, s. 64(3)(b) and reg. 15(c) and (h).

# [9]
# The Role of Law

## INTRODUCTION

In the light of the sustained critique of the present legal structure in previous chapters, it remains to consider whether law is inevitably limited in its ability to influence deeply entrenched and deeply engendered social patterns. Can we refashion legal tools in such a way as to form part of our overall strategy for achieving the fundamental change necessary to the goal of authentic fairness? Or are we simply so entranced by the power of law, its apparent authority, impartiality and fairness, as to blind ourselves to its inescapable role of supporting patriarchy? I argue in this chapter that law must have a role in effecting change, if only because if it is not harnessed in support of progress, it frequently actively obstructs attempts to redress patriarchy. But this is not the only reason: ultimately, it is a counsel of despair to conclude that law is intrinsically and unavoidably patriarchal. Instead, it can well be empowering.[1] However, the programme of utilising

---

[1] See K. Crenshaw 'Race, Reform and Retrenchment' [1988] 101 *Harvard Law Review* 1331, pp. 1384–5.

law in support of change is a complex and risky one; and in the final analysis, is only one element of a necessarily multi-faceted approach. Most importantly, the myths that presently imbue law with its apparent sanctity must be abandoned and new premises fashioned. Law is not impartial; but nor is it sufficient to confess to partiality. Instead, as Minow argues, the law must struggle against its partiality by making an effort to understand the multitude of alternate perspectives, to recognise the impossibility of avoiding colliding realities and to shape its discourse in these terms.[2] Both the dangers and the promise are great. As MacKinnon puts it:

Law that does not dominate life is as difficult to envision as a society in which men do not dominate women, and for the same reasons. To the extent feminist law embodies women's point of view, it will be said that its law is not neutral. But existing law is not neutral. It will be said that it undermines the legitimacy of the legal system. But the legitimacy of existing law is based on force at women's expense . . . It will be said that feminist law cannot win and will not work. But this is premature.[3]

One of the first steps towards remodelling law in this way is a comprehensive reform of the present adjudicative and remedial structure. The chapter therefore begins with a critical assessment of the ways in which these structures have curtailed and even undermined the potential of the law. In the second section, I engage in the deeply controversial debate over positive action, drawing on the sophisticated reasoning in US caselaw. The chapter concludes with an examination of the interaction between law and economics.

# I. THE PRESENT SYSTEM

a) ADJUDICATION AND COMPENSATION: THE EMPTY PROMISES OF THE LAW

Judged by the litigation under the SDA and the EqPA, the impact of these statutes has been marginal at the very best. This is not only a result of the substantive weaknesses considered in earlier chapters. It is also directly related to the form of the adjudication system, and the nature and amount of the remedies available. Each of these will be considered in turn.

### i) Adjudication: The Adversarial System

Equal pay and sex discrimination cases in the employment context are litigated primarily in industrial tribunals, in the same way as other employment protection rights. There is an appeal on a point of law to the Employment Appeal Tribunal, which has the status of a High Court, while further appeals must be pursued through the Court of Appeal and the House of

---

[2] M. Minow 'Justice Engendered' [1987] 101 *Harvard Law Review*, p. 10 reproduced in P. Smith (ed.), *Feminist Jurisprudence* (OUP, 1993), ch. 9 at p. 234.

[3] C. MacKinnon 'Toward Feminist Jurisprudence' in Smith (ed.), above n. 2, p. 618.

Lords. The tribunal system was deliberately structured to provide an alternative to the existing court process, which is formal, expensive, and slow. Tribunals are subject to fewer formalities than courts: there are no complicated pleadings and tribunals are not bound by strict rules of evidence. The large number of tribunals throughout the country has made them somewhat quicker than courts, but they are still beset by inordinate delays. Finally, the distinctive characteristic of both industrial tribunals and the EAT is their tripartite structure. In recognition of the importance of first-hand experience of industrial relations, decisions are made by a legal chair (a judge in the case of the EAT) and two lay members with industrial experience, one appointed after consultation with trade unions, the other after consultation with employers' organisations. Nevertheless, despite these apparent divergences between courts and tribunals, the latter retain the core characteristic of courts—namely the adversarial system. As a result, tribunals have in practice become no more than paler versions of the ordinary courts. This is manifested in three central elements of adversarialism: the *passivity* of the adjudicative panel; the assumption of *equality* between the parties; and the focus on the *individual*. Each of these is dealt with in turn below.

In an adversarial system, the court is essentially *passive*, depending wholly on the individual plaintiff to initiate the case, bring the evidence and make the legal arguments. One result is that cases are litigated on an ad hoc and random basis, rather than according to a carefully designed strategy. Nor does a passive system elicit the best quality argument. In particular, the plaintiff is hamstrung by the difficulty in obtaining evidence which is invariably in the hands of her adversary. This is aggravated by the fact that she bears the burden of proof. The difficulties confronted by the applicant are only slightly diluted by the powers of discovery available to tribunals. In addition, the SDA provides for a questionnaire procedure prior to institution of proceedings, the answers to which are admissible in evidence.[4] However, the employer is under little pressure to respond: at most, if a respondent 'deliberately and without reasonable excuse omitted to reply in a reasonable period, or his reply is evasive or equivocal', the court or tribunal may draw any inference it considers just or equitable to draw.[5] It would be far more appropriate for a tribunal to adopt a frankly inquisitorial role.

The second characteristic of the adversarial system is that it assumes an *equality* between the parties, which belies the reality. This problem is exacerbated in the tribunal system because legal aid is not available to pay for legal representation and each party bears his or her own expenses.[6] The original motivation behind this provision was to keep lawyers out of tribunals altogether. Inevitably, however, with the increasing complexity of the law, legal representation has become more common, thereby privileging the party who can afford representation. In discrimination cases, this

---

[4] SDA 1975, s. 74.   [5] *ibid.*, s. 74(2)(b).
[6] Unless one party acts unreasonably.

problem has been mitigated by the power of the EOC to give assistance to complainants, including the funding of legal representation.[7] Assistance is available in cases which raise a question of principle, or where it is unreasonable to expect the applicant to deal with it unaided, having regard, *inter alia*, to the complexity of the case. The budgetary constraints on the Commission, however, make it inevitable that only a small number of complainants receive financial assistance from the EOC. For example, in 1993, the EOC granted legal assistance to 195 complainants, and rejected 103 requests.[8]

Finally, the adversarial system is essentially *individualistic*, processing the case as a bipolar dispute between two individuals, diametrically opposed, to be resolved on a winner-take-all basis.[9] This all-or-nothing response leaves no room for compromise or synthesis. It is only outside of the court process, in settlements, that compromise may be reached; indeed parties are encouraged to do so by the statutory provision for conciliation on request or on the initiative of an ACAS conciliation officer.[10] However, while the process of settlement may be more flexible than the court, settlement is if anything more intensely individualist than the formal hearing. Its outcome is a private matter between the parties, creating no precedents or guiding principles for society as a whole. The tension between private compromise and public adversarialism is particularly problematic in test cases, when the EOC might be eager to establish a point of principle, while the complainant wishes merely to reach an outcome.[11]

Recently, in an attempt to improve their chances of success, some complainants have tried to harness the public law procedure for judicial review. This procedure departs in significant ways from the traditional adversarial mould. Most importantly, public law remedies have effects well beyond the individual litigant. By striking down the discriminatory decision rather than focusing on the effect on an individual, judicial review can potentially change a discriminatory practice to the benefit of a whole class of present and future victims. The case of *R* v. *Secretary of State, ex p. EOC*[12] is the most dramatic example of the potential of this procedure. In that case, it will be recalled, the requirement that part-time workers work continuously for five years in order to qualify for employment protection rights was struck down under the Equal Treatment Directive. In one fell swoop, all part-time workers were able to benefit. The House of Lords rejected the Court of Appeal's view that only the affected individual had standing, and that she should pursue her case through an industrial tribunal. Instead, it

---

[7] SDA 1975, s. 75(1).      [8] EOC Annual Report 1993, Appendix 2, p. 51.

[9] A. Chayes 'The Role of the Judge in Public Law Litigation' 1976 89 *Harvard Law Review* 1281.

[10] SDA 1975, s. 64.

[11] For a survey into the levels of satisfaction of parties to the settlement process, see J. Gregory, *Dispensing Informal Justice* (EOC, 1993), p. 44.

[12] [1994] IRLR 176 (HL).

was held that the EOC had standing to initiate judicial review proceedings. Although the House also suggested that the individual affected lacked standing, the Court of Appeal in the later case of *ex p. Seymour Smith*,[13] recognised the lack of logic in such a position and held that both the EOC and the affected individuals had standing. If this is upheld, it represents a highly significant departure from the narrow individualism of the adversarial system.

Forays of this sort into the public law arena are, however, unlikely to become commonplace. The courts are fiercely protective of the judicial review procedure, making it unlikely that cases will succeed unless they are based on a claim that the courts characterise as 'public'. This means that public law is most likely to be relevant only to a complaint that primary or delegated legislation is in breach of EC law. For example, an attempt to use judicial review to quash the redundancy policy adopted by a local authority was swiftly rejected by the Divisional Court. Although conceding that judicial review would in principle be available to challenge a decision of a public authority, the court held that it would be inappropriate in this case to strike at the whole decision in one dramatic blow. Instead, each individual should litigate her own claim in an industrial tribunal.[14]

The most innovative statutory attempt to overcome the limitations of the adversary procedure is in the form of the power given to the EOC to initiate and conduct a 'formal investigation' into cases of suspected unlawful discrimination.[15] The formal investigation departs from adversarialism in several key respects. As a start, it is an active rather than passive process. The Commission has the power to initiate the investigation, thus inviting a strategic approach instead of an ad hoc series of actions. Moreover, it has strong information-gathering powers, including the ability to demand written or oral evidence and the production of documents. The formal investigation also deviates significantly from the individualism of the tribunal procedure. The power is specifically directed at a practice of discrimination rather than a particular discriminatory act against an individual. Nor is the situation characterised as an all-or-nothing bipolar dispute. Instead, the investigation is intended to be an interactive process, during which the Commission aims to secure a change in discriminatory practices through discussion, negotiation and conciliation. Its remedial powers are therefore essentially forward-looking: the Commission has the power to issue recommendations and, ultimately, if necessary, a non-discrimination notice.

However, the novelty of the procedure and the challenge it poses to deeply entrenched visions of adversarialism have led to a reaction against it by the courts. In a series of judicial review cases against the Commission for Racial Equality, which has almost identical powers, the formal investigation

---

[13] [1995] IRLR 465 (CA).
[14] *R* v. *London Borough of Hammersmith, ex p. NALGO* [1991] IRLR 249 QBD.
[15] SDA 1975, ss. 57–61.

was trammelled with a chain of restrictive procedural requirements intended to protect the employer against what was considered to be a harsh and inquisitorial procedure.[16] Lord Denning indeed went so far as to characterise the formal investigation as akin to the Spanish Inquisition.[17] The EOC has in any event never used the formal investigation in the spirit in which it was intended. It has mounted very few investigations and when it has, no coherent policy or strategic plan has been evident. Investigations have frequently been cumbersome and badly designed, leading simply to frustration and disappointment.[18] As a result, the impact of the formal investigation has been disappointing.

ii) **Remedies**

Probably the most serious failing of the adjudication process has been in the nature of its remedies. Like the adversarial system as a whole, remedies are limited first by the purported neutrality of the courts, and secondly by their focus on the individual. A direct result of the stance of neutrality is the refusal to engage actively in forward-looking reform of the kind essential to achieve a comprehensive restructuring. Thus when industrial tribunals were created, it was not thought appropriate to entrust them with an injunctive remedy. Instead, tribunals were armed with no more than the timid weapon of a recommendation. Even the recommendation is individualised: rather than reaching into structural causes of discrimination, the tribunal is merely empowered to recommend 'action appearing to the tribunal to be practicable for the purpose of obviating or reducing the adverse effect on the complainant of any act of discrimination to which the complaint relates'.[19] Tribunals which have attempted to use this power intrusively have soon been struck down. Thus in *Noone*,[20] a tribunal, having found that the plaintiff was not selected because of discrimination on grounds of race, recommended that she be offered the next available post. However, this was held to be beyond the powers of the tribunal. Instead, the Court of Appeal held, the only appropriate recommendation was to draw the attention of any appointments committee considering an application by the plaintiff to the need for compliance with anti-discrimination legislation, and to record and remind such members that the plaintiff's previous application had failed on racial grounds.[21] Moreover, an employer who fails to comply with the recommendation is treated gently in comparison with the vehemence of the sanction for contempt of an injunction. As a start, the employer may argue that he or she has reasonable justification for failing to follow the recommendation.[22] The standard of

---

[16] *CRE* v. *Prestige Group plc* [1984] ICR 473 (HL), *London Borough of Hillingdon* v. *C.R.E.* [1982] AC 779 (HL) and see generally, G. Appleby and E. Ellis 'Formal Investigations' [1984] PL 236.

[17] *Science Research Council* v. *Nassé* [1979] 1 QB 144 at 172 (CA).

[18] Appleby and Ellis, above n. 16, p. 260.

[19] SDA 1975, s. 65(1)(c).      [20] [1988] IRLR 530 (CA).

[21] See also *Prestcold* v. *Irvine* [1981] ICR 777 (CA).      [22] SDA 1975, s. 65(3).

such justification is deliberately low, permitting the tribunal to take into account practical realities, even if this means that the dismantling of the effects of past discrimination is gradual.[23] Moreover, the sanctions for failure to comply without reasonable justification are limited to an increase in compensation. Prior to 1995, this was capped by the statutory limit of £11,000.

The substitute for dynamic and interactive remedies has been an almost exclusive reliance on compensation, which satisfies the law's neutrality and individualism by granting a one-off remedy to the individual alone. Combined with the adversarial system which requires a finding that one party is 'wrong' and the other 'right', this form of remedy inevitably tempts the legislature and the courts to introduce a fault requirement. Only if the party is at fault can it be right to expect him or her to pay compensation. This was most floridly manifested in the SDA, which until 1996 stated that no compensation could be awarded in cases of unintentional indirect discrimination.[24] This restriction was finally removed in 1996, after a number of industrial tribunals had held that it contravened the Equal Treatment Directive. According to regulations which came into effect on 25 March 1996, tribunals may award compensation in cases of unintentional indirect discrimination if it would not be 'just and equitable' merely to make a declaration or recommendation.[25]

Even when fault can be demonstrated, the courts and tribunals have been unwilling to use damages in a punitive form, stressing in this context the compensatory nature of damages. This is reflected in the approach to the award of exemplary damages, in which the common law reluctance to conflate compensation with punishment has been echoed.[26] Exemplary damages have been strictly limited to two categories: (i) 'oppressive, arbitrary or unconstitutional action by servants of government'; or (ii) cases in which the wrongdoer has calculated that the profit from wrongdoing would exceed the compensation payable to the complainant.[27] Although the Court of Appeal has upheld the award of exemplary damages against a local authority for discriminating on grounds of race and sex against a black woman, this was only because the act fell within the narrow bounds of the first category.[28] In a particularly restrictive recent judgment, the EAT refused to countenance the possibility of exemplary damages against the Ministry of Defence for the dismissal of a servicewoman on grounds of her pregnancy (see Chapter 5). According to the EAT, the limitation of

[23] *Nelson* v. *Tyne and Wear Passenger Transport Executive* [1978] ICR 183 (EAT).
[24] SDA 1975, s. 66(3).
[25] The Sex Discrimination and Equal Pay (Miscellaneous Amendments Regulations) 1996 SI 1996 438, reg. 2.
[26] See *Rookes* v. *Barnard* [1964] 1 All ER 367 (HL), and *Cassell* v. *Broome* [1972] 1 All ER 801 (HL), Lord Reid.
[27] These categories were established in *Rookes* v. *Barnard* [1964] AC 1129 at 1226, and extended in the race relation context by *Alexander* v. *Home Office* [1988] IRLR 190 (CA).
[28] *City of Bradford* v. *Arora* [1991] IRLR 165 (CA).

exemplary damages to the two categories defined above meant that it could not possibly apply to a breach of the Equal Treatment Directive.[29] This was despite the fact that the ECJ has stressed that the award of damages should have a deterrent effect. A similar pattern emerges in respect of aggravated damages, which are in principle available if the respondent has behaved in a high-handed, malicious, insulting or oppressive manner in committing the act of discrimination.[30] However, in this context too, the reluctance of the courts to import a punitive element into the principles of compensation for sex discrimination is clear. Thus in *Ministry of Defence* v. *Meredith*,[31] the EAT refused to consider an award for aggravated damages to a servicewoman dismissed on grounds of pregnancy despite clear evidence that she had been advised by the medical officer that she should have an abortion if she wished to continue her career in the army. The reason, according to the EAT, was that aggravated damages were only appropriate if the plaintiff had suffered extra injury to her feelings as a direct result of the scornful and insulting behaviour. Since the complainant did not know whether the Ministry of Defence was deliberately flouting the law, this act could not have caused her extra injury to feelings.

Even on its own terms, the compensatory regime has been unsatisfactory. Until November 1993, compensation was subject to an upper limit, which frequently kept awards far below their real level. The statutory maximum, paralleling that for unfair dismissal cases, was low: it stood at a mere £6,250 in 1985, rising to only £11,000 in 1994. Tribunals generally kept awards well below the limit: in 1989–90 for example, of the fifty-five awards made, as many as twenty-four were under £750, and only eight were over £3,000.[32] It was only the intervention of EC law that forced the government and the court to consider the principles behind compensatory awards. In the path-breaking case of *Marshall (No. 2)*,[33] the ECJ struck down the statutory limit and absence of a power to award interest on damages on the grounds that it infringed the Equal Treatment Directive.[34] Most important was the Court's emphatic restatement of the principle that Member States must guarantee real and effective judicial protection of the right to equality of opportunity in a way that has a real deterrent effect on the employer. As a result, the statutory limit was removed with effect from 22 November 1993.[35] Tribunals have since that date been required to consider the quantification of damages more carefully, the measure being the tort principle of putting the party in the position she would have been in had the discrimination not occurred.[36]

---

[29] *Ministry of Defence* v. *Meredith* [1995] IRLR 539 (EAT).
[30] *Alexander* v. *Home Office* [1988] IRLR 190 (CA) at p. 193.
[31] Above n. 29.
[32] [1991] *Employment Gazette*, 305–6.     [33] Case C-271/91 [1993] IRLR 445 (ECJ).
[34] Directive 76/207, Article 6.
[35] Sex Discrimination and Equal Pay (Remedies) Regulations 1993.
[36] For a useful description of the principles see EOR No. 57 (1994), pp. 12–18.

The removal of the statutory limit has certainly had an important impact on compensation levels. A comparison of awards made by tribunals in 1993 before the lifting of the cap (21 November 1993) with the levels of awards after that date to the end of 1995 shows a steep upward movement.[37] Most dramatic were the awards in the cases brought against the Ministry of Defence (MOD) by servicewomen dismissed on grounds of pregnancy (see Chapter 5). By 1996, nearly £55 million had been paid by the Ministry of Defence to women discharged from the armed forces on grounds of pregnancy.[38] Although most were settled out of court, the seventy-three which did come before industrial tribunals received a total award of £2,589,910. The average compensation award, at £35,478, was over three times the £11,000 upper limit which had applied before *Marshall No. 2*. However, as we saw in Chapter 5, these figures are unlikely to be sustained. Although the average compensation award, excluding MOD cases, increased by 31 per cent after the cap was lifted, only 6 per cent of awards exceeded the repealed limit.[39] Moreover, while the trend remains upward, it is not nearly so steep: the 25 per cent average increase between 1993 and 1994 dropped to 14 per cent between 1994 and 1995. In any event, these figures are only high relative to the extremely low levels prior to the removal of the maximum. Even after November 1993, the average award was only £3,777, with the median standing at a mere £2,260 (excluding MOD cases). Nor are the MOD awards likely to be repeated: as we saw in Chapter 5, the EAT has now declared that the levels of awards in these cases have been 'manifestly excessive and wrong'.[40] As a result, the level of compensation awards in MOD cases halved, falling from £33,846 to £16,009.

Such low levels of compensation reflect the very low value placed by society on the removal of sex discrimination. They also mean that the incentive on women to enforce their rights is minimal. It is strongly arguable that a right without effective enforcement is in practice counter-productive: it gives the illusion of change while reinforcing the status quo. However, the government has rejected the EOC's suggested minimum award (of about £500).[41] The reason for rejection—that this would introduce a punitive element into a compensatory regime—is difficult to accept. A minimum award merely sets up a presumption that a victim of sex discrimination must have suffered some loss. In any event, the ECJ in *Marshall (No. 2)* established the principle that awards should be both deterrent and compensatory; £500 being only a gesture towards such deterrence.

Some consciousness of the specifically humiliating nature of sex

[37] Figures in this paragraph are drawn from EOR No. 57 (1994), pp. 11–21.
[38] EOR No. 66 (1996), p. 2.
[39] Figures in this section are taken from EOR No. 67 (1996), pp. 13–24.
[40] *Ministry of Defence* v. *Cannock* (1994), IRLR 509 (EAT).
[41] EOR No. 52 (1993), p. 29.

discrimination is reflected in the express provision for the award of damages for injury to feelings.[42] However, damages under this head have been kept at a level which all but negates the gesture towards respect for the dignity of victims of discrimination. Before 1988, the average award for injury to feelings was a mere £400.[43] An attempt by an industrial tribunal to use this head of damage more truly to compensate the victim by awarding £5,000 was overturned by the Court of Appeal, on the grounds that this was far out of line. In reducing this figure to £3,000, the court pointed out that the highest recorded figure was £750.[44] In the period immediately prior to the removal of the statutory maximum, the award increased marginally, averaging £1,371, with a median of £1,000. The removal of the cap on discrimination allowed this figure to rise significantly, but even with a 26 per cent rise in 1994 and 1995, the average award was still only £1,696 (excluding the MOD cases) and the median had remained at £1,000.[45] Apart from overall maxima, the courts have found other ways to limit the reach of these provisions. For example, in the sexual harassment case of *Snowball* v. *Gardner*,[46] the complainant's attitudes to sexuality were held to be relevant in determining whether she had in fact suffered hurt feelings.

The low levels of damages combined with the harshness of the adversarial system has meant that the numbers of women complaining of sex discrimination has remained low. Thus in 1993–94, a mere 1,969 sex discrimination cases were completed. Although this number doubled (to 4,052) in 1994–95, this increase is largely explained by the large number of MOD pregnancy cases. A mere 780 equal pay cases were completed in 1993–94: although a three-fold increase on the 240 litigated in the previous year, this is scarcely a good turnout. Nor was the increase sustained: in 1994–95, the number fell back to 418. Few of these cases reach a tribunal. In 1994–95, over 80 per cent of sex discrimination cases were conciliated, withdrawn or disposed of otherwise without the need for a tribunal hearing. In the same year, as many as 70 per cent of equal pay cases were withdrawn and a further 23 per cent conciliated. For the handful which do reach a tribunal, success rates are poor. About a third of the SDA cases in 1993–94, and one-half in 1994–95, were successful, with compensation being awarded in only 58 and 134 cases respectively. The success rate under the EqPA is even more discouraging. In 1994–95, applicants were successful in a mere one-third of the twenty-five cases heard by tribunals.[47]

It is instructive to compare the adversarial and remedial structures in the UK with those which have been developed in the US to deal with public law litigation. As Chayes demonstrates, the traditional adversarial model became precarious in the face of a growing body of legislation explicitly

---

[42] SDA 1975, s. 66.      [43] EOR No. 19 (1988), p. 7.
[44] *Noone* v. *North West Thames RHA* [1988] IRLR 195 (CA) at 200.
[45] EOR No. 57 (1994) p. 22; EOR No. 67 (1996), p. 17.
[46] [1987] IRLR 397 (EAT).      [47] EOR No. 69 (1996), p. 26.

modifying and regulating basic social and economic realities.[48] The adjudicative structure responded dynamically to the realisation that many public and private interactions are not bilateral transactions between individuals, but have wide social implications, rendering the bipolar structure inappropriate. The result was a transformation from what Fiss[49] calls a 'dispute resolution' model to a model of 'structural reform'. Whereas in the former, the victim, spokesperson and beneficiary are automatically combined in one plaintiff, in the latter, the roles fragment. The victim is not an individual but a group; and the spokesperson is not necessarily one of the group. Similarly, the class of beneficiaries may well be wider than the victims. A similar analysis applies to the defendant. Whereas in the dispute resolution model the defendant is both the wrongdoer and the provider of a remedy, in the model of structural reform, the wrongdoer disappears, and instead the focus is on the body able to achieve reform. In the result, the three main characteristics of the adversarial system disappear or are muted. Thus the judge is no longer a passive arbiter, but an active participant in the process, in particular of deciding whether the spokesperson adequately represents the group of victims and whether all victims are indeed represented.[50] Secondly, there is no assumption of *equality* between the parties. Instead, the imbalance of power is rectified by encouraging institutional litigators, both in the public and private sectors. In the race discrimination field, this made it possible for a public interest body such as the NAACP (the National Association for the Advancement of Colored People), encouraged by tax relief and government grants, to become the driving force behind strategic civil rights litigation. In addition, the Department of Justice was given statutory authority by the Civil Rights Act to advance anti-discrimination claims. As a result it too became one of the foremost litigators, deepening the commitment of the executive to equality. The Department has had a clear litigation programme, avoiding the problem of unplanned case by case litigation. To this is added the Equal Employment Oportunities Commission (EEOC) which, since 1972, has had the power to litigate to enforce Title VII of the Civil Rights Act. Its powers specifically include both the pursuit of individual charges and the initiation of litigation to eliminate 'patterns and practices' of discrimination. Although the EEOC has no sanctions of its own akin to the non-discrimination notice of its British counterpart, it has become a vital force in the process of challenging discrimination in the US.[51]

The modified adjudicative structure also departed actively from the *individualism* of the unadulterated adversarial system. Class actions were

---

[48] Chayes, above n. 9, p. 1288.
[49] O. M. Fiss 'The Forms of Justice' (1979) 93 *Harvard Law Review* 1.
[50] Fiss, above n. 49, at pp. 16–28.
[51] See E. Meehan 'Equal Opportunity Policies: Some Implications For Women of Contrasts Between Enforcement Bodies in Britain and the USA' in J. Lewis (ed.), *Women's Welfare Women's Rights* (Croom Helm, 1983), pp. 170–89.

developed to assist plaintiffs in cases in which an injury simultaneously affects many individuals, and involves law so complex that for any one individual to sue entails disproportionate expense.[52] The class suit is a particularly flexible type of joint action because any member of the injured group may sue on behalf of the whole group. There is no need to organise all the victims before the trial or to prove that the spokesperson is representative. Instead, participation of all plaintiffs is deferred until after the trial: all members of the group are entitled to participate in the end result, and by the same token, all share the burden of expenses on a quantum meruit basis.

The changes in the litigation structure were also strongly influenced by the nature and use of remedial powers in anti-discrimination and other public law cases. Central to this development was the creative use of the mandatory injunction, which challenged many of the premises of the adversarial system. Unlike compensation, which is retrospective, individualised and all-or-nothing, the mandatory injunction operates as a continuing constraint on future action. As a result, instead of a winner-takes-all formula, the court is actively involved in balancing the interests not only of the parties before it but those of others who are inevitably affected. This results in a change in the character of fact-finding, requiring a focus not so much on past conduct such as fault and intention, but on future consequences. To provide adequate grounds for such prospective intervention, more access to social facts and wider interest representation are required. Finally, the prospective nature of the remedy creates the incentive for parties to reach a compromise, and maintains the role of the judge in mediating, supervising and even managing the operation of the decree. Instead of litigation functioning as a private dispute settlement, it operates as a manner of carrying out a policy.[53] It is true that the result is far from perfect. There has been much debate in the US on the suitability of judges in making policy decisions of this sort,[54] and the legitimacy and accuracy of social science information.[55] Nevertheless, the fact that aspects of the change remain controversial should not obscure the essentially positive nature of these developments. An even more adventurous alternative to the adversarial procedure is that seen in proactive systems, such as in Ontario and Northern Ireland. This approach departs radically from the individualised, reactive remedial structure of the British legislation. For example, the short-lived Employment Equity Act required employers to scrutinise their own work-forces to detect inequalities and then to formulate remedial plans. Similarly, the Northern Ireland Fair Employment Act 1987 places a positive obligation on employers to work to eliminate discrimination. It is in this direction that British policy-makers should be looking.

[52] H. Kalven and M. Rosenfeld 'The Contemporary Function of the Class Suit' 1940 *University of Chicago Law Review* 8, p. 684.

[53] Chayes, above n. 9, pp. 1288–96.

[54] See the discussion *ibid.*, and in Fiss, above n. 49.

[55] See e.g., Yudof 'School Desegregation: Legal Realism and Social Sciences' in (1978), *Law and Contemporary Problems* 57.

However, little progress has been made in the UK in reforming the litigation and remedial structures. The EOC recently put before the government an imaginative set of proposals aimed at ameliorating the individualism of the current structure. As well as recommending the introduction of class actions, it was suggested that the EOC should be granted a general power to bring legal proceedings in its own name wherever it believes an unlawful discriminatory practice or act exists. On the remedial side, the EOC proposed that an equal pay award should automatically extend to other employees in the same employment doing the same or broadly similar work and that a collective agreement should be open to challenge as a whole on the application of any interested party. However, the government's response was permeated with a stubborn adherence to individualism.

The UK system of justice provides for the individual access to the law on the basis of an individual case. The introduction of class actions would serve to undermine this important principle on which the entire system of redress for breaches of employment law is founded . . . Class action is a dangerous and inappropriate tool for doing justice where an individual's right to redress depends on the actual treatment meted out to that individual, the employer's reasons for that treatment and the circumstances obtaining when the treatment occurred.[56]

The proposed extension of EOC powers to function as an institutional litigator was again seen as an unacceptable affront to the individual: 'In other areas of law, the legal system leaves it to an individual who has suffered detriment to take legal action if he or she chooses, unless a criminal offence is involved. To depart from that approach in the field of discrimination and equal pay would create a substantial difference in the manner of law enforcement between that field and others.'[57] At best, the government will continue to respond to criticism by merely tinkering with the tribunal system.

## II.  POSITIVE ACTION

The retrospective individualised nature of the present adjudicative system can be contrasted with measures which take positive action to achieve structural change. 'Positive action' can take a variety of forms, but all share the same underlying principle: the use of gender-conscious criteria in order to remedy gender-based detriment.[58] It will be argued in this section that although the theoretical problems with positive action appear intractable, they can in fact be effectively resolved. Instead, the question of positive action should be considered from a strategic perspective. Particularly in its

---

[56] 'Government Response to EOC Proposals', reproduced in EOR No. 52 (1993), p. 35.
[57] *ibid.*, p. 33.
[58] Positive action could include measures aimed at eradicating discrimination (see e.g. C. McCrudden, 'Rethinking Positive Action' [1986] ILJ 219 at p. 223) but this aspect is dealt with fully elsewhere in this book. This section focuses on gender-specific criteria, whether direct or indirect.

most intense form, that of reverse discrimination, the risks are sufficiently serious to require justification by reference to a high level of effectiveness. The section therefore begins with the theoretical debate, before turning to a consideration of the legal approach in the UK, EU and US. It concludes with a consideration of the strategic issues raised. A number of different types of positive action are examined, ranging from mild forms such as 'outreach' measures which aim simply to encourage women to apply for male-dominated jobs, to measures which deliberately give women preference over men in order to correct past discrimination or imbalances in the work-force. Also important is the strategy of contract compliance, whereby a public body uses its considerable economic powers to pursue social goals such as that of equal opportunity. It operates by the insertion of a clause into a contract between the public agency and a private contractor requiring the achievement of certain equal opportunities goals as a condition of the continuation of the contract. Since local authority and central government contracts are extremely valuable to contractors, the incentive for private employers to seek to attain the required conditions is strong.

a) Positive Action or Discrimination: The Debate

Much of the century has been spent in forcing a legal recognition of the perniciousness of gender classifications. How then can it suddenly become justifiable to permit gender-based classification to be explicitly used to remedy gender discrimination? Phrased in these terms, the theoretical problems appear overwhelming. However, the apparently inescapable logic of this question dissolves once the assumptions behind it are unpacked. Most powerful is the notion that equality is necessarily symmetrical: discrimination against men on the grounds of their gender must, on this view, be as pernicious as discrimination against women on the grounds of their gender. Yet the symmetrical assumption itself depends on prior acceptance of three of the basic liberal tenets which pervade the legal framework: *formal justice, individualism and State neutrality.*

Thus, symmetry is based on a *formal* rather than a substantive view of justice. Formal justice is an abstract concept, whose content does not vary with the historical or political context in which it finds itself. This means that the distribution of benefits and disadvantages in any particular society cannot change the content or operation of justice. It is therefore inevitably unacceptable to apply a different version of justice to a disadvantaged group from the one which applies to a privileged group. The symmetrical approach is also based on a highly *individualistic* view of society. This has two dimensions. The first dimension, the merit principle, requires that an individual should be treated according to her or his own personal characteristics or merit. Race or gender are irrelevant in the measurement of merit. The second dimension concerns fault, the principle being that individuals should only be responsible for their own actions, not for others'. This means that no individual should be held liable for social ills which are not directly her or his fault. Positive action falls foul of both these individualistic axioms: in preferring a woman over a man it ignores the merit of each, as well as imposing a burden on the man even though he is in no way responsible for the history of sex discrimination against women. Finally, the symmetrical approach assumes that the State should be *neutral*. The traditional view of State neutrality maintains that the State should be neutral as between its citizens, favouring no one above any other. The proposition that a group should be favoured on account of gender or race, even in a remedial sense, is therefore anathema. State neutrality also entails a State which intervenes as little as possible in the 'free market'. In its revived neo-liberal form, this version of State neutrality is used to oppose the use by the State or other public bodies of their contractual powers within the market to pursue public policies such as the elimination of discrimination. This necessarily outlaws the use of contract compliance.

All three of these assumptions are, however, open to question. First, *formal justice* substitutes the ideal for the reality. Because sex ought not to affect the individual, it is assumed that it does not. However, it is fallacious to assume that principles of equality and the rule of law impact in the same way on those who are privileged as they do on those who are disadvantaged. Indeed, it is simply myopic to ignore the distributive effects of models of justice: even a set of legal rules which does not aim to be redistributive has the effect of maintaining the status quo with all its uneven distributions of wealth. A similar argument can be made in respect of *individualism*. Certainly, the value of the individualistic principle should not be ignored: it is only because of a commitment to freeing individuals from status ascriptions that sexism and racism could eventually be exposed as morally and politically offensive. However, again the ideal should not be confused with the present reality. An individual's life chances continue to be strongly influenced by her or his gender and race. In order to achieve the ideal of individualism, these issues continue to demand inclusion in the legal framework. In light of this recognition, the merit principle loses its universal appeal. Instead it becomes necessary to examine whether merit itself is not permeated by gender assumptions. In fact, as has become clear throughout this book, the emphasis on formal qualifications, work experience and full-time commitment to work are merit criteria which obscure many women's real ability. The fault principle is more difficult to challenge. Positive action in its strongest form, by displacing a meritorious man by a woman, requires that an individual suffer detriment because of his sex, rather than his merit. The general response to this is that members of the advantaged group benefit from their position in a variety of ways. It is therefore fair to expect them to pay part of the cost of the solution to the problem of discrimination, provided the individual share of that cost is not too great. As the US Supreme Court stated in *Fullilove* v. *Klutznick*, 'As part of this nation's dedication to eradication of race discrimination, innocent persons may be called upon to bear some of the burden of the remedy.'[59] However, there is no easy formula for determining what is a fair cost. This is especially problematic in that race and sex are not the only sources of systematic disadvantage in society. The dilemma of the poor white compared to the middle-class black, the white woman against the black man are real dilemmas and cannot be skirted.

Finally, the belief in a State which is *neutral* as between its citizens hardly bears scrutiny. Even a non-interventionist strategy favours some groups by supporting the status quo. In any event, non-interventionism is no more than an polemical device, as is evidenced by the highly selective use of that concept even by determined neo-liberals. For example, neo-liberals wholly support State intervention to secure a 'free market', should the actors in that market choose to use their freedom in a way which conflicts with neo-liberal policies. Thus, as we have seen, the Conservative government of the 1980s was happy to use legislation to restrain local authorities from using their freedom of contract to pursue anti-discrimination policies.

It is clear from the above discussion that the theoretical difficulties of positive action quickly dissipate when a substantive, non-individualistic view of justice is taken. If the aim is to redistribute benefits in a fairer manner, then the content of justice should be determined by the actual social context. It is therefore no contradiction to argue that in attempting to remedy gender-based disadvantage, those who have suffered detriment on the grounds of sex should be treated better than those who have received benefits on the grounds of their sex. Indeed, some proponents of positive action defend the use of gender-conscious criteria by arguing that such criteria do not inevitably contradict the principle that jobs or other benefits should be awarded on merit. Instead, it is argued, the fact of being a woman may enhance the desirability of a candidate for a job or a university place where women have traditionally been disadvantaged, by providing a role model for aspirant women, or by being able to relate to clients, patients or customers with greater personal or cultural empathy.[60] In addition, the State has a positive responsibility, in the context of a political commitment to eradicating discrimination, to use all means at its disposal to promote that policy. Nevertheless, some acute conflicts of interest remain. First, it is not always clear that the action in question is indeed remedial, rather than perpetuating discrimination. Secondly, those individuals who are required to bear the cost of positive action deserve some attention. On the one hand, it may not necessarily be true that the particular white man who brings the complaint has benefited from his whiteness and maleness: questions of

---

[59]  448 US 448 (1980).
[60]  See B. Hepple 'Discrimination and Equality of Opportunity' [1990] 10 *Oxford Journal of Legal Studies* 409 at pp. 412–13; R. M. Dworkin, *A Matter of Principle* (Clarendon Press, 1985), p. 299.

other sources of disadvantage require consideration. On the other hand, even the privileged white man should not be required to carry a disproportionate burden. The debate about affirmative action should therefore take place on a strategic level. Any particular programme must be justifiable on the basis of several criteria. First, is the policy beneficial or detrimental? Secondly, who is benefiting? And thirdly, is the resulting distribution of cost fair both as between the disadvantaged and advantaged groups, and as between the two individuals in question?

b) Positive Action and the Law

i) **Three Analytic Models**

The debates discussed so far have been a vigorous part of the growing jurisprudence in this area. In order to assess the responses of the various jurisdictions, it is useful to define a spectrum of responses, ranging from the unequivocally symmetric view at the one end, to a thoroughgoing commitment to substantive justice at the other. According to the symmetric view, any action which explicitly or implicitly uses sex or race as a criterion for decision-making is unlawful, whether directed against or in favour of a disadvantaged group. One of its most articulate advocates, the US Supreme Court Justice Powell, exemplified this stance when he stated: 'The guarantee of equal protection cannot mean one thing when applied to one individual and something else when applied to an individual of another color.'[61] This model asserts the primacy of the neutrality of the law, the rights of the individual as individual, and the freedom of the market. Not surprisingly, the symmetric model rejects positive action as morally reprehensible to the same degree as pernicious discrimination on grounds of sex or race. As Abram argues: 'Without doing violence to the principles of equality before the law and neutral decision-making, we simply cannot interpret our laws to support both color blindness for some citizens and color-consciousness for others.'[62] The function of the law is limited to protecting individuals against intentional prejudice on the grounds of their race or sex. Any attempt to attach rights to group membership rather than to the individual is bound to degenerate into a 'crude political struggle between groups seeking favoured status'.[63] Nor does colour-conscious remedial action necessarily improve the welfare of the society. Relying unquestioningly on an objective notion of merit, proponents of this view consider that the use of affirmative action permits the appointment of people less well qualified and therefore less able to do the job properly.[64] Finally, it is argued that such action does not achieve its aim of helping the

---

[61] *University of California* v. *Bakke* 438 US 265 (1978).
[62] M. Abram 'Affirmative Action: Fair Shakers and Social Engineers' [1986] 99 *Harvard Law Review* 1312 at 1319.
[63] *ibid.*, p. 1321.    [64] *ibid.*, p. 1322.

needy: instead, it simply adds to the privilege of middle-class blacks or women.

At the other end of the spectrum, is the model based on substantive justice. This expressly departs from the primary tenets of the liberal, symmetric view.[65] First, it rejects the possibility of a neutral State, maintaining that a purported refusal to intervene is itself a positive statement of State support for continuing societal discrimination. Instead, the State has a duty to act positively to correct the results of such discrimination. Secondly, this model is expressly asymmetrical. Discriminatory actions which unfairly burden a historically disadvantaged group are considered to be qualitatively different from discrimination aimed to remedy that disadvantage. Thirdly, this model rejects as misleading the aspirations of individualism, maintaining that the emphasis on formal equality of individuals simply ignores the extent to which opportunities are determined by individuals' social and historical status, which includes their race and gender. The structural nature of discrimination means too that the responsibility for correcting institutional discrimination should not lie only with those to whom fault or causality can be attributed: all members of the privileged class share the duty and may be expected to bear some of the cost of remedy. Finally, the freedom of individuals in the market and the objectivity of the merit criterion are challenged: real freedom, on this model, can only be achieved by open intervention by the law to correct injustice. It is not surprising that given the radical nature of this model and the extent to which it departs from traditional values of neutrality, individualism and autonomy, its proponents have at times drawn back from its full rigour, particularly when confronted by the spectre of the 'innocent' individual, white or male, who ostensibly pays the price for remedying social ills.

Somewhere between these two extremes is the approach based on an 'equal opportunities' model. The basic principle informing this model is the recognition that true equality cannot be achieved if individuals begin the race from different starting points. The aim is therefore to equalise the starting point. Closer examination of this model reveals that it incorporates elements of each of the two more extreme models outlined above. On the one hand, it shares with the substantive model the recognition that an unbending adherence to formal justice and formal equality can in fact perpetuate actual injustices and inequalities. On the other hand, like the symmetric model, it continues to adhere to the importance of individualism. Its proponents recognise that structural discrimination distorts the life chances of individuals because of their group membership. They are therefore prepared to accept that sex- or race-based policies may be used as a transitional remedial measure. However, such breaches of the neutrality

---

[65] See also R. Fallon and P. Weiler 'Firefighters v. Stotts: Conflicting Models of Racial Justice' in C. McCrudden (ed.), *Anti-Discrimination Law* (Dartmouth, 1991) 130, at pp. 140 ff.

and symmetry of the law are only permitted to the extent that they operate to equalise the starting points of actors in the market. It is at this point that the primacy of the individual asserts itself. Once individuals enjoy equality of opportunity in this sense, they are free and therefore deserve to be treated on the basis of their individual qualities, without regard to sex or race. This model therefore specifically rejects policies which aim to correct imbalances in the work-force by quotas or targets whose aim is one of equality of outcome. Proponents of this model do not take much trouble to define 'equality of opportunity'. However, because they continue to stress the individual as the focus of legal rights their notion of equal opportunities is inevitably narrowly circumvented. Most importantly, equal opportunities policies carry no guarantee that resources will be available to ensure a genuine equalisation of starting points. It will be argued below that such a limited version of equality of opportunity has insufficient power to achieve the structural change it is held out to.

### ii) Legal Applications of the Models

(1) *The UK: Symmetry Reigns*   Possibly the clearest manifestation of the strongly symmetrical approach is found in the current legal framework in Britain.[66] Both the Equal Pay Act and the SDA are strongly symmetrical: discrimination against men in favour of women is no less unlawful than its converse.[67] This symmetry was entrenched by the majority of the House of Lords in *James* v. *Eastleigh Borough Council*.[68] According to this case, in deciding whether unlawful discrimination had occurred, the simple question to be considered was whether the complainant would have received the same treatment from the defendant 'but for' his or her sex. In the case in hand, a man of sixty-one complained of unlawful discrimination on the grounds that he was not eligible for concessionary rates for leisure facilities whereas a woman of the same age was. This was because such concessions were only available when the individual reached state pensionable age, which was sixty-five for men and sixty for women. The House of Lords held that in answering the question whether he would have been treated differently had he been a woman, an affirmative answer was 'inescapable'. The abstract, formal nature of justice epitomised in this formulation was clearly articulated by Lord Ackner when he stated: 'The reason why the policy was adopted can in no way affect or alter the fact that . . . men were to be treated less favourably than women, and were to be so treated on the ground of, *ie* because of their sex.'[69] Yet the consequences of ignoring substantive justice are clear. As Lord Griffiths recognised in his dissent, concessions for persons of pensionable age were made available because such persons are almost always less well off than when in employment and

---

[66] The Northern Irish Fair Employment Act invites a separate analysis.
[67] SDA 1975, s. 2.      [68] [1990] IRLR 288 (HL).      [69] [1989] IRLR 289 at p. 293.

less able to afford leisure and travel facilities. If women are in that position earlier than men, they require concessions earlier. Indeed, Lord Griffiths saw the possibility of finding scope within the wording of the Act to permit remedial positive action. 'What I do not accept is that an attempt to redress the result of that unfair act of discrimination by offering free facilities to those disadvantaged by the earlier act of discrimination is, itself, necessarily discriminatory "on the grounds of sex".'[70]

While the effects of differential pension ages are now being dealt with (see Chapter 8), the implications of the symmetrical principle are being felt in other important arenas. Possibly the most important concerns the gross under-representation of women in positions of power within the decision-making process, particularly in Parliament. Other jurisdictions have responded to this by permitting a certain proportion of women to be given priority over men in the process of selection candidates. In Israel, for example, which uses a proportional representation system, both major parties reserve seats for women in their lists of Parliamentary candidates. At European level, the Commission has adopted a draft Council recommendation which aims to promote more balanced participation of women in decision-making bodies of all kinds.[71] In the UK, the Labour Party decided to address the gross gender imbalance in the House of Commons by permitting women-only short-lists for Parliamentary selection as Labour Party candidates in a limited number of constituencies.[72] However, the symmetrical approach soon stifled this attempt. On a complaint by two men who wished to be considered as candidates in three such constituencies, an industrial tribunal struck down the policy as unlawful sex discrimination.[73] The case is notable for the absence of any of the sophisticated arguments found in other jurisdictions considering positive action. Instead, the tribunal regarded the matter as conclusively decided by the 'simple' answer to the 'simple' test of whether the complainant would have received the same treatment but for his sex. 'It is obvious direct discrimination on grounds of sex.'[74] Much as the structure of the statute appears to compel this response, a court less imbued with the liberal model might at least have examined the real complexity of the matter. More fundamentally still, it is highly questionable whether an issue of such constitutional importance should be adjudicated by a tribunal charged with eradicating discrimination in employment. The tribunal, however, confidently assumed jurisdiction under section 13 of the SDA, which makes it unlawful for an authority or body to discriminate on the grounds of sex in the terms on which it confers an authorisation or qualification needed to engage in a particular profession or trade.[75] It went on to declare that the long

---

[70] [1989] IRLR 289 at p. 293.      [71] See [1996] 3 EIRR 264.

[72] 50 per cent of constituencies which were either (i) marginal; (ii) new or (iii) the sitting Labour MP was not standing at the next election.

[73] *Jepson* v. *The Labour Party* [1996] IRLR 116 IT.

[74] *ibid.*      [75] SDA 1975, s. 13.

experience of tribunals in employment cases was sufficient to dispel ny doubts about their capability to adjudicate this case. However, the question is not one of capability, but of legitimacy. It is astonishing that an issue of such constitutional importance should be decided by an industrial tribunal under the banner of a provision which was clearly intended for entirely different purposes. It would have been far more appropriate to refuse jurisdiction and instead insist that the case be adjudicated as a judicial review procedure. This would at least have opened up the possibility that the case be decided on public law grounds, allowing arguments of necessity and proportionality to begin to develop. For example, a court should be asked to consider whether the response of the Labour Party was reasonable in a *Wednesbury* sense in light of the fact that women constitute less than 10 per cent of Members of Parliament. Factors to be considered included the facts that the male complainants were free to apply for short-listing in a large number of constituencies which did not maintain women-only short-lists, while a woman applying in one of the ostensibly mixed constituencies stood little chance of gaining the candidature. As will be seen below, the critical tools of analysis developed in other jurisdictions would have permitted a rigorous appraisal of the extent to which the policy aim of the Labour Party was legitimate, and the means were tailored to the end.

Such an approach is in fact endorsed in one corner of the law: that of trade union leadership. The SDA expressly permits trade unions, employers' organisations or professional organisations to reserve seats on an elected executive for persons of one sex where this is necessary to secure a 'reasonable lower limit to the number of members of that sex serving on the body'.[76] This provision was enacted in recognition of the fact that women were vastly under-represented in decision-making in trade unions. A recent survey of ten trade unions found that only two had decided to reserve seats on their executives. It was, however, notable that these two had more women on their executive bodies than any of the other unions, and believed that the presence of women facilitated the presentation of issues affecting women in particular.[77]

The second manifestation of the aversion of British law to positive action concerns the response to challenges to the merit principle. The SDA and RRA in theory include an opening for such challenges in the form of the exception whereby gender may be a requisite for a job where this is a 'genuine occupational qualification'.[78] This provision, however, is not designed to promote positive action, but instead to safeguard privacy and personal inter-relationships. For example the need for a woman employee to provide first aid for other women, to check tampax machines and to cater

[76] SDA 1975, s. 49.
[77] V. Sacks 'Tackling Discrimination Positively in Britain' in B. Hepple and E. Szyszczak, *Discrimination and the Limits of the Law* (Mansell, 1992), pp. 359–61.
[78] SDA 1975, s. 7.

for other personal and private needs of women has been upheld as a genuine occupational qualification.[79] This has been extended marginally in the race relations field to include the need for cultural empathy, but then only in cases of immediate personal interaction.[80] Any attempts to expand this into a genuine legitimation of positive action on the grounds of a radical reinterpretation of the merit principle have been firmly rebuffed. In *London Borough of Lambeth* v. *CRE*,[81] the Court of Appeal emphatically rejected the argument that one of the purposes of anti-discrimination legislation was to promote equality of opportunity by positive action. Instead, it reasserted the symmetric view of the law as aiming simply to make discrimination on grounds of sex unlawful. The personal services exception was narrowly confined to cases in which there was direct contact between the worker and the recipient.[82]

The third manifestation of the rejection of positive action in Britain is found in the attitude to contract compliance as a strategy to further equal opportunities for women. Antagonism in principle is relatively recent: contract compliance for the purposes of advancing fair wages and promoting freedom of association was well established in Britain from the turn of the century, receiving official endorsement by successive governments up to 1979.[83] It was not, however, used to advance equal opportunities for women until London local authorities set up Equal Opportunities Units to monitor and pursue their contract compliance strategies in the early 1980s. The strategy was relatively effective: the Equal Opportunities Unit of the Greater London Council (GLC) persuaded 77 out of 106 companies to institute equal opportunities action programmes in its first years of operation. However, as part of its strategy for systematically dismantling contract compliance in Britain, the Conservative government included in the 1988 Local Government Act provisions 'designed to prevent abuses of the contractual process'.[84] Among these is a specific proscription of attempts to promote equal opportunities for women by inclusion of relevant terms in local authority contracts.[85] While a limited exception for the furtherance of equal opportunities on racial grounds is permitted, the exception was deliberately confined to race, therefore leaving intact the prohibition against contractual terms forbidding sex discrimination. These provisions effectively end the possibility of even the mildest forms of contract

---

[79] *Timex Corporation* v. *Hodgson* [1982] ICR 63 (EAT).

[80] *Tottenham Green Centre* v. *Marshall* [1989] IRLR 147 (EAT); and see *Tottenham Green Centre* v. *Marshall (No. 2)* [1991] IRLR 162 (EAT).

[81] [1990] IRLR 231 (CA).

[82] SDA 1975, s. 7(2)(e).

[83] For a detailed discussion see S. Fredman and G. Morris, *The State as Employer* (Mansell, 1989), pp. 454–74.

[84] Nicholas Ridley, Secretary of State for the Environment, HC Debs vol 119. col.86 (6 July 1987).

[85] Local Government Act 1988, s. 17(5)(a); there is a highly circumscribed exception for race relations: see s. 18(2).

compliance on the part of local authorities. This is evidenced by the first major case on these provisions, *R v. London Borough of Islington, ex p. Building Employers Confederation (BEC)*,[86] in which the Divisional Court struck down as unlawful a clause in the model contract issued by Islington specifying that any contractor 'shall at all times comply with s. 6(1) (a) and (c) [no discrimination in selection for employment] and (2) (b) [dismissal or other detriment] of the SDA 1975'. The court took particular exception to the monitoring provisions in the contract, which SDA required a contractor to give the council access to documents and information proving compliance with the Act, including a breakdown of the composition of the work-force. Implicit in this is the firm rejection of the view that local authorities should be permitted to use their contractual powers to enforce the law: only the remedies specified in the Act itself are permitted, however weak. As we shall see, this contrasts vividly with the endorsement by the US Supreme Court of the right of public bodies to use their powers remedially in the race and sex discrimination field. It is also striking that contract compliance strategies are a centrepiece of Northern Ireland legislation prohibiting discrimination on grounds of religion (see further below).

Despite the strict, even myopic, adherence to the symmetrical model, UK legislation does make a small but important gesture in the direction of the advancement of equal opportunities (the second model) by permitting a degree of sex-conscious remedial action in training.[87] Thus if there are comparatively few or no women doing a particular type of work in Britain or in any particular area of Britain, it is not unlawful to afford access to training facilities to women only to help equip them for that work. Similarly, measures such as outreach measures encouraging women to take advantage of opportunities for doing that work are declared to be lawful. Finally, and possibly most significantly, it is not unlawful to give specific training facilities to those who are in special need of training because they have been fully engaged in family responsibilities. However, these provisions illustrate the narrowness of the notion of equality of opportunity they espouse. As a start, the permission to use positive action does not extend to the actual offer of a job or promotion. A woman who has participated in a women-only training scheme declared lawful by the Act stands no better chance of being offered the employment for which she has been trained than anyone else. Moreover, the measures are merely permissive rather than mandatory, and carry no commitment to government resourcing. Thus without the political will on the part of public employers, or a favourable cost-benefit analysis on the part of employers in the private sector, it is unlikely that such programmes will be mounted. In a recent survey, many organisations and trainers emphasised both the lack of

---

[86] [1989] IRLR 382 (QBD).
[87] SDA 1975, ss. 47, 48 (as amended by SDA 1986, s. 4).

resources and the lack of commitment by those in charge.[88] The paucity of women in top positions in both the private and public sectors makes it even less likely that such programmes will be prioritised; yet without such programmes it is difficult to envisage this proportion increasing. It is not surprising therefore that in practice, statutory provisions for equal opportunity have had only a marginal impact. A survey of sixty training bodies which offered single-sex training demonstrated that while some good faith attempts are being made to address the problems faced by women, 'there remain . . . terrible gaps such as lack of resources, piecemeal availability and lack of monitoring of the courses or of the students' subsequent careers.'[89] Even less optimistic is the employers' approach to training. Most worrying is the fact that all the courses run by major employers which have been evaluated were run on a full-time residential basis, with no child-care provision, and therefore excluded a substantial proportion of women employees.[90] In general, one of the most serious deficiencies in training opportunities for women is the absence of provision for training of part-time workers.[91]

(2) *The EC: Equal Opportunities*   The outlines of an equal opportunities model are clearly visible in the Equal Treatment Directive. According to Article 2(4), the Directive 'shall be without prejudice to measures to promote equal opportunity for men and women, in particular by removing existing inequalities which affect women's opportunities'. This is backed up by the recognition that 'existing legal provisions on equal treatment, which are designed to afford rights to individuals, are inadequate for the elimination of all existing inequalities unless parallel action is taken by governments, both sides of industry and other bodies concerned, to counteract the prejudicial effect on women in employment which arise from social attitudes, behaviour and structures.'[92]

It has, however, been left to the judiciary to fill in the contours of the model. Early indications were strongly symmetrical. Thus in *Integrity*,[93] Advocate General Jacobs insisted that Directive 79/7 'requires all discrimination on the grounds of sex to be abolished. Member States cannot therefore justify inequalities of treatment on the basis that the provisions at issue are favourable to women.'[94] It was not until the 1995 case of *Kalanke*[95]

---

[88]   Sacks, above n. 77, p. 380.

[89]   *ibid.*, p. 371.

[90]   K. Clarke, *Women and Training* (EOC Research Discussion Series, No. 1, 1991), pp. 63–5.

[91]   *ibid.*, p. 77.

[92]   Third recital to the preamble to Recommendation 84/635/EEC of 13 December 1984 ([1984] OJ L 331).

[93]   Case 373/89 [1991] IRLR 176.

[94]   *ibid.*, at p. 178.

that the Court itself was asked to address the issue. The case concerned one of the mildest forms of affirmative action, namely, the 'tie break' policy pursued by the City of Bremen. According to this policy, if a man and a woman with the same qualifications applied for promotion, the woman was to be given priority if women were under-represented in that grade. Under-representation was defined as existing where women did not constitute at least half the staff in the individual remuneration bracket of that personnel group within a department. When a man was passed over for a job in favour of an equally qualified woman in pursuance of this policy, he complained that he had been discriminated against on the grounds of sex. Although the German Labour Court were willing to permit such a policy, the Court struck it down on the grounds of breach of the Equal Treatment Directive.

The Court's decision epitomises the equal opportunities model. While recognising the limits of formal equality, the Court firmly set its face against substantive equality by focusing on the individual. Equality of opportunity provides a useful synthesis of these two principles. Thus, the Court held, it is permissible to take measures which give an advantage to women with a view to improving their ability to compete equally with men in the labour market. However, this does not legitimate measures which depart from the principle of individual merit. 'National rules which guarantee women absolute and unconditional priority for appointment or promotion go beyond promoting equal opportunities and overstep the limits of the exception in Article 2(4) of the Directive.'[96] Substantive equality, or equality of results, is anathema, unless it is a natural result of equal opportunities. 'In so far as it seeks to achieve equal representation of men and women in all grades and levels within a department, such a system substitutes for equality of opportunity as envisaged in Article 2(4) the equality of result which is only to be arrived at by providing such equality of opportunity.'[97] The tension between individualism on the one hand and a recognition of the limits of formal equality on the other are clearly evident in the opinion of Advocate General Tesauro. He poses the question in terms of a conflict between individualism and the anti-discrimination principle. 'In the final analysis must each individual's right not to be discriminated against on grounds of sex . . . yield to the rights of the disadvantaged group, in this case, women, in order to compensate for the discrimination suffered by that group in the past?'[98] Such a formulation of the problem makes it inevitable that the answer be in the negative. The attainment of numerical equality, he concludes, violates the right of each individual to equal treatment. In any event, on his view, equality of results will remain illusory unless it is a natural consequence of equal opportunity measures.

[95] Case C-450/93 [1995] IRLR 660 ECJ.
[96] *ibid.*, at p. 667.      [97] *ibid.*, át p. 668.
[98] *ibid.*, at p. 662.

There are three main problems with the *Kalanke* approach. First, like most proponents of an equal opportunities approach, neither the Court nor the Advocate General take the trouble to examine what an 'equal opportunities' strategy would entail, nor, more specifically, how equality of opportunity will achieve equality of results. The Advocate General alludes to measures which are superficially discriminatory but in fact aim to neutralise the effects either of specific differences between men and women, or of past discrimination, or of continuing difficulties related to women's dual role. However, no further details are given, nor are the resource implications considered. It will be argued below that equal opportunities can indeed be a powerful tool for change, but only if pursued with a thoroughgoing commitment of resources and political will to deep structural change.

The second problem with the *Kalanke* approach stems from its emphasis on the right of the individual to be treated on merit rather than according to her group membership. However, the merit principle fails to yield an answer in cases where both parties have equal merit but only one job is on offer. Certainly, in the case itself, the male applicant had no greater right to be selected than the woman. Therefore, there was no question of an 'innocent' person suffering detriment on the grounds of his sex. In such cases, a choice can only be made on the basis of a criterion not related to merit. If it is maintained that social factors cannot be used to tip the balance, it seems that only a random selection, such as spinning a coin, would be acceptable. Finally, the Court's decision to override the clear opinion of the German Labour Court is a worrying breach of the notion of subsidiarity. A case such as this should be a prime example of the deference by the ECJ to the ability of the national courts properly to gauge the legitimacy of the measure against the social and political context in which it existed.

It is noteworthy that the European Commission does not share the rigidity of the courts' approach. In a damage-limitation exercise, it issued a communication in March 1996 reaffirming the need to use, where appropriate, positive action measures to promote equal opportunities for women and men. Stressing that *Kalanke* did no more than to outlaw rigid and automatic preferences for women, the Commission takes the view that 'the only type of quota system which is unlawful is one which is completely rigid and does not leave any possibility of taking account of individual circumstances'. It thus encourages Member States to continue to adopt plans which aim to promote women according to prescribed proportions and timetables, or impose obligations in principle to recruit or promote the under-represented sex or set quotas linked to job qualifications, provided that in each case there is no automatic preference or vested individual rights. Also considered lawful despite *Kalanke* are State subventions or reductions in social security contributions granted to employers who recruit women in sectors in which they are under-represented.[99] In fact, the Commission has gone so far as to propose an 'interpretive amendment' to Article 2(4) of the Equal Treatment Directive, stating that possible measures to provide equal opportunity within the exception include 'the giving of preference as regards access to employment or promotion, to a member of the underrepresented sex provided that such measures do not preclude the assessment of the particular circumstances of an individual case'.[100] At the time of writing, the validity of the Commission's view awaits the Court's judgment in the 1997 case of *Marschall*.

(3) *The US: Symmetry* v. *Substance* It is in the US that the debate has been most sophisticated and the responses most varied. While a strong contingent of Supreme Court judges remain faithful adherents of the symmetrical stance, there has been a clear trend in favour of the substantive model. Cases in this category are characterised by a preference for substantive or asymmetric rather than formal or symmetric justice; a rejection of individualism; and an explicit endorsement of the social responsibilities of a positive, non-neutral State.

The trend began with court-ordered affirmative action programmes prescribed as a remedy in cases of proven discrimination both under Title VII of the 1964 Civil Rights Act[101] and under the Equal Protection Clause in the 14th Amendment of the Constitution. Indeed, it is noteworthy that it was the courts themselves, at district level, which quickly perceived that if cases of proven discrimination were to receive an effective remedy, affirmative action was essential. This approach was endorsed by the Supreme Court in the 1987 case of *US* v. *Paradise*.[102] In this case, on a finding by a US District Court that the Alabama Department of Public Safety had for four decades systematically excluded blacks from employment as state troopers, the court ordered that 50 per cent of promotions should go to blacks (provided sufficient numbers were qualified) until black troopers constituted one-quarter of each rank. This order was held by the Supreme Court to be consistent with the Equal Protection Clause. In particular, it clearly passed the well-established test that it should serve a compelling governmental interest in eradicating the discriminatory exclusion of blacks and be narrowly tailored to do so. Thus a substantive, outcome-oriented view was clearly preferred to one based on formal, individualised equality.

Similarly, the individualistic emphases on merit and fault have been weakened. Thus the Supreme Court soon began to accept voluntarily instituted affirmative action programmes, despite the lack of proven fault on the part of the employer. Instead, the focus is again on the social context

[99] 'Communication from the Commission to the European Parliament and the Council on the interpretation of the judgment of the Court of Justice on 17 October 1995 in Case C-452/93 *Kalanke*', reproduced in *ibid.*, p. 39.

[100] Reproduced in *ibid.*, p. 43.

[101] Pub. L. No. 88–352, 78 /stat, 253–66.  [102] 480 US 149 (1987), 107 S Ct 1053.

in which the equality concept operates: in upholding voluntary affirmative action programmes, the Court has only required sufficient evidence of past discrimination,[103] not proof of fault against the defendant. This approach is exemplified in *Johnson* v. *Santa Clara*,[104] a case which is strikingly similar on its facts to *Kalanke*. *Johnson*, like *Kalanke*, concerned a voluntarily instituted affirmative action plan for hiring and promoting women and minorities in a context of severe under-representation of both groups in the work-force. The *Johnson* plan was more flexible than that of *Kalanke*, in that the sex of a qualified applicant was only a factor among several to be considered. It was also more controversial in that a woman could be promoted even if she was marginally less well-qualified than a male applicant. More important, however, are the similarities: like *Kalanke* the aim in *Johnson* was framed in terms of equality of results, the target being to achieve a statistically measurable yearly improvement in hiring and promotion, so as ultimately to achieve a work-force of which about one-third of jobs were held by women. The plan was challenged when a qualified woman was promoted ahead of a man to the position of road dispatcher, a grade in which to date none of the 238 positions had been held by a woman. The male employee, who in fact had a marginally better test score, complained of sex discrimination contrary to Title VII. Far from facing judicial antagonism to its results-oriented focus, as did the plan in *Kalanke*, the *Johnson* policy received warm judicial endorsement. Brennan J, giving judgment for the Court, explicitly declared that it was no violation of Title VII to take sex into account in promoting a woman over a male employee where this was in pursuance of an affirmative action plan to remedy the under-representation of women and minorities in traditionally segregated job classifications.

Similarly, the US Supreme Court has rejected the neutral view of the State, instead upholding both the right and the responsibility of the State to use its public and market powers in remedying discrimination. Thus in *Fullilove* v. *Klutznick*[105] the Court upheld a policy setting aside 10 per cent of federal funds for minority businesses. Chief Justice Burger stated specifically that Congress was permitted to use its broad remedial powers in the same way as the courts could. Indeed, he stressed that in a remedial context, it was not necessary to act in a wholly colour-blind way. One of the most important results of this judicial approach has been the continued vigour of the Federal contract compliance programme, the seminal requirements of which are contained in Executive Order No. 11246 signed by President Johnson in 1965. Under this order, private firms who have contracts with the federal government may be required to institute goals for hiring and promoting women and minorities as part of an affirmative action

---

[103]   *United Steel Workers* v. *Weber* 442 US 193 (1979).
[104]   107 S Ct 1442 (1987), 480 US 616.
[105]   448 US 448 (1980).

programme.[106] Crucially, however, gender-based hiring is not required and quotas are prohibited. Thus although equality of results is the touchstone for progress, it cannot be achieved by direct reverse discrimination. The importance of the contract compliance programme is clear: in 1993, some 92,500 non-construction establishments and 100,000 construction establishments were covered. In total these establishments employed about 26 million people and received contracts of more than $160 billion.

However, the substantive model continues to co-exist with a strongly symmetrical view. The champion of the symmetrical view has always been Powell J. As he stated in *Bakke:* 'The guarantee of equal protection cannot mean one thing when applied to one individual and something else when applied to an individual of another colour.'[107] Again, in *Wygant*,[108] he used the opportunity to declare his view that discrimination on grounds of race was odious whether or not it was directed against a group that had never been the subject of governmental discrimination. Nor was societal discrimination alone a sufficient justification for racial classifications. This theme has been strongly echoed by two of the current generation of Supreme Court justices. According to Clarence Thomas J, there is a moral and constitutional equivalence between laws designed to subjugate a race and those that distribute benefits on the basis of race to 'foster some current notion of equality'. Government sponsored racial discrimination based on benign prejudice was in his view just as noxious as discrimination motivated by malicious prejudice.[109] The individualism of this model was clearly articulated by Scalia J in the same case. In declaring that the government could never have a compelling interest in discriminating on the basis of race in order to make up for past racial discrimination, Scalia J was unequivocal in his rejection of the group justice model. The notion that there can be a 'creditor or debtor race' was in his view entirely alien to the focus in the constitution on the individual.[110]

The influence of the liberal aspirations of individualism, neutrality, symmetry and autonomy remains strong enough to provoke deep unease even in those justices most committed to the substantive model. The resulting tension has led to some sophisticated compromises in US law, not found in that of the UK or EC. This is reflected in the controversies within the caselaw on two main issues: the 'innocent' third party who is discriminated against on grounds of race or sex in the process of preferring minorities or women; and the standard of scrutiny.

So far as the first issue is concerned, the vexed question of how much of a burden it is fair to expect the 'innocent' third party to bear has no easy

[106] With certain exceptions, the Order applies to Federal contractors and subcontractors with contracts of more than $10,000 per year.
[107] *Regents of the University of California* v. *Bakke* 435 US 265, 317, 318 (1978).
[108] *Wygant* v. *Jackson Board of Education* 106 S.Ct. 1842 (1986).
[109] 115 S Ct 2097, at p. 2119.
[110] *Adarand* v. *Pena* 115 S Ct 2097, at p. 2118.

answer. This is particularly so if that person is him or herself disadvantaged, for example, in terms of class. The substantive model suggests that it is acceptable to require members of the privileged groups to contribute to the cost of rectifying disadvantage; while the symmetrical model is implacably opposed to such a stance. The result has been a sophisticated and finely tuned synthesis. Thus Brennan J, frequently the mouthpiece of the substantive model, has held that the burden on 'innocent' whites or men is acceptable only in certain circumstances. These include cases in which the burden is diffuse; where it forecloses one opportunity but leaves several others open, and where it is related to the denial of future opportunities, such as promotion or selection.[111] Since no-one has an absolute right to a job or to promotion, the white man who is passed over in favour of a woman or black is not unduly burdened. However, in the highly controversial context of layoffs, where the Court is asked to 'allocate the burdens of recession and fiscal austerity',[112] the vested interests of 'dispreferred' workers to retain seniority rights and therefore remain in work have generally trumped the goals of achieving and maintaining a balanced work-force.[113] It is at this point that the compromise is achieved with proponents of a symmetrical model. Powell J, as we have seen, has declared in no uncertain terms that discrimination is odious whether it is directed against a group which had previously suffered governmental discrimination or not. Nevertheless, he has been prepared to defer to the majority view in respect of hiring goals, accepting that in such cases the burden on innocent individuals is diffused. However, seniority rights and expectations could well be the most valuable asset a worker 'owns':[114] loss of a job is therefore too serious a prospect to permit individual interests to be subordinated. The effects of this compromise are evident in *Wygant*,[115] in which a collective agreement was struck down as contrary to the 14th Amendment because it gave preferential protection against layoffs to minority employees.

The second controversial issue in US caselaw concerns the standard of scrutiny which should be applied in affirmative action cases. The Supreme Court has a well developed jurisprudence requiring 'strict scrutiny' of any classifications which burden blacks: such a classification must have a legitimate aim and be narrowly tailored to achieve that aim. Indeed, the insistence on strict scrutiny has been the cutting edge of anti-racism caselaw in the US. This raises the question: does an equally strict standard of review

---

[111] *Johnson v. Santa Clara*, above n. 104; *US v. Paradise*, above n. 102; *United Steelworkers v. Weber* 443 US 193 (1979).

[112] *Memphis Firefighters v. Stotts* 104 S Ct 2576 (1984) at 2592.

[113] Cf *Franks v. Bowmen* where the Supreme Court upheld the award of retroactive seniority to identified victims of discrimination. In this case, the court was not' convinced by the argument that this punctured the individual rights model by diminishing the expectations of other innocent employees. Instead it recognised that there will always be conflicting interests when scarce benefits are at stake, and gave priority in this context to the compensatory ideal.

[114] See also *Firefighters v. Stotts*, above n. 112.   [115] Above n. 108.

apply to racial classifications which benefit blacks at the expense of whites? US caselaw is criss-crossed with deeply conflicting judicial statements on this point. Thus in the well-known *Bakke* case,[116] both symmetrical and asymmetrical views were vividly represented. Powell J, consistent with his symmetrical stance, was unequivocal in his rejection of the argument that strict scrutiny applies only to classifications that disadvantage discrete and insular minorities. Instead, he argued, all kinds of race conscious criteria should be subject to the 'most exacting of judicial examination'. By contrast four judges (Brennan, White, Marshall and Blackmunn JJ), taking a substantive asymmetric view, held that a less stringent standard of review should apply to racial classifications designed to further remedial purposes than to pernicious classifications. On this view, it was sufficient for the policy to be 'substantially related' to the achievement of an important government objective, a standard known as intermediate review. Nor is the difference wholly semantic, as can be seen by contrasting *Fullilove* v. *Klutznick*[117] with the more recent case of *Richmond* v. *JSA Croson*.[118] In *Fullilove*, it will be recalled, the Court upheld the right of Congress to use its powers in a colour-conscious fashion to remedy discrimination. In *Richmond* v. *Croson*, by contrast, the strict scrutiny standard was applied to strike down the city's policy of retaining 30 per cent of contracting work for minority businesses. Instead of acknowledging public bodies' responsibilities for remedying societal discrimination, the Court in *Richmond* v. *Croson* confined the remedial function of states or local authorities to the eradication of the effects of private discrimination within its own legislation. It remained only to apply the same standard to Federal policy. In 1995 in *Adarand* v. *Pena*,[119] the Court came down firmly in favour of the view that even at the level of the federal government all racial classifications should be subjected to strict scrutiny. Ultimately therefore the exacting standard of strict scrutiny has won the day.

However, a closer examination of the judgments in *Adarand* reveals that the acceptance of strict scrutiny can itself represent a sophisticated compromise between the symmetrical and asymmetrical views. It is true that the substantive model was represented by Stevens J who dissented from the standard of strict scrutiny, eloquently reasserting the fundamental difference between a policy designed to perpetuate a caste system and one seeking to eliminate racial discrimination. It is true too that Thomas and Scalia JJ upheld the strict standard from a strongly symmetrical and individualistic camp. It is the approach of O'Connor J, giving judgment for the Court, which is the most interesting and represents the best synthesis of the difficult opposing views. In supporting strict scrutiny, O'Connor J was in no

---

[116] *Regents of the University of California* v. *Bakke*, above n. 107.
[117] Above n. 59.
[118] 488 US 469 (1989).
[119] 115 S Ct 2097 (1995).

doubt that this did not automatically rule out affirmative action policies. She was at pains to dispute the notion that strict scrutiny is strict in theory but fatal in fact. Provided a race-based remedy is narrowly tailored to serve a compelling governmental interest, it will pass.[120] Her view is therefore fully compatible with a continued substantive model.

The debate on the level of the standard thus far has focused entirely on the racial issue. Its effect on gender-based affirmative action is somewhat ambiguous, because the Supreme Court has never considered sex discrimination to be pernicious in the way that race discrimination is viewed. Cases of invidious discrimination against women have in fact not been subjected to the strict scrutiny test, but instead to an intermediate standard requiring only that the means 'substantially relate' to the achievement of an important governmental interest.[121] The question then is whether affirmative action programmes in favour of women are also subject to strict scrutiny. Practically, it might be awkward to apply a different standard, given that many affirmative action programmes, particularly those advanced by public bodies, refer to minorities and women in the same breath. Yet in one of the few Supreme Court decisions directly on the point, it was held that the intermediate test applied whether the plan discriminated against women or in their favour.[122] Little further discussion on this issue has taken place.

(4) *Affirmative Action: a Strategic Question*   The above discussion has demonstrated that the principled objections to affirmative action can be plausibly repudiated. Nevertheless, on a strategic level, the range and ferocity of the positions taken up in the argument about affirmative action make it essential to examine the role of affirmative action programmes for women with great care. There are three main strategic questions. First, is the plan in question beneficial? Secondly, does it achieve its aim? Finally, are the costs spread satisfactorily?

The first question, whether a gender-conscious programme is genuinely beneficial, is more complex than might be expected. Of particular concern is the danger that positive action might disintegrate into the 'difference' approach dealt with in earlier chapters. We have had enough experience of protective legislation and other exclusive policies to be profoundly wary of 'benign' gender criteria which purport to protect or benefit women, but in fact harm them. At the same time, however, the dangers of a difference approach should not be permitted to obliterate the benefits of positive action which genuinely assists women. The success or failure of sex-conscious criteria in achieving real change therefore depends on judicial perceptiveness in weighing up the costs against the risks. The complexity of the question is exemplified in the 1982 US case of *Mississippi University for*

---

[120] *Adarand*, above n. 110, at p. 2117.

[121] *Personnel Administrator of Massachussetts* v. *Feeney* 422 US 256 (1979).

[122] *Mississippi University for Women* v. *Hogan* 112 S Ct 3331 (1982).

*Women* v. *Hogan*,[123] in which a man complained that he had been the victim of sex discrimination when he was refused a place on an all-women nursing course at a State-supported university. The Court held that the exclusion of men violated the Equal Protection Clause. Both the minority and the majority judgments focused not on the theoretical arguments but on the question of whether this arrangement was beneficial to women. On the one hand, the majority depicted an all-women nursing college as positively detrimental to women, because it perpetuated stereotypes about women. O'Connor J, giving judgment for the Court, argued that the measure could not be an attempt to remedy past discrimination against women, since women had always formed the vast majority of nurses. Instead, she maintained, the policy acted against the interests of women by reinforcing the belief that nursing is a woman's profession. On the other hand, the minority insisted on the importance of allowing women the opportunity of studying in an all-women environment. Powell J, always, as we have seen, the champion of symmetry, took the opposite position in this case. He argued that the majority judgment deferred too much to conformity. Instead, diversity was a virtue: here the existence of several co-educational nursing schools in the vicinity meant that the only harm to the man was some inconvenience. This cost was far outweighed by the benefit of upholding the right to choose single sex education if desired.[124]

The dilemma between genuine remedial action and the perpetuation of stereotypes appears in stark form in social security cases. The use of gender as a proxy for disadvantage is often the most cost-effective means of targeting the needy. At the same time, there is a serious risk of creating financial incentives which perpetuate women's position as secondary breadwinners and homemakers. These complexities are well illustrated by the ECJ case of *Integrity*.[125] The case concerned Belgian national law on social security for the self-employed, which gave special concessions to married women, widows and students in respect of contributions on self-employed income. A self-employed man complained that this constituted unlawful discrimination. The Belgian government argued that the provision was not based on sex discrimination, but on socio-economic criteria, since married women, widows and students (including male students) were more likely than married men and widowers to carry on activities as self-employed persons on a subsidiary basis. The Court, in a brief and somewhat unilluminating judgment, simply upheld the complaint on the basis that married men had the right to equal treatment with married women. Advocate General Jacobs' approach was more subtle. As well as taking a

---

[123]   102 S Ct 3331 (1982).
[124]   Contrast *Commission* v. *UK* Case 165/82 [1984] IRLR 29 (ECJ), in which the ECJ upheld the UK legislation (EPA 1975 sched. 4(3)) prohibiting men from training as midwives. This provision has nevertheless been repealed; see now SDA 1975, s. 20.
[125]   Case 373/89 [1991] IRLR 176.

straightforward symmetrical line (see above), he also maintained that the assumptions underlying the legislation, namely that in all marriages the husband will be the main breadwinner, are themselves discriminatory and make no allowance for couples who wish to organise their lives on alternative lines. 'Each of the problems alluded to by the Belgian Government can be resolved in a non-discriminatory manner, so that a person's right . . . depends not on an arbitrary characteristic like sex but on objective factors such as the person's income and the amount of time he or she devotes to paid work.'[126] Such an argument correctly highlights the need for close examination of measures purporting to benefit women. Any measure giving advantages to a group defined according to gender runs the risk of over- and under-inclusiveness and may well perpetuate damaging stereotypes. However, this in itself does not imply that anti-discrimination legislation should aspire to neutrality and thereby ignore disadvantage. The risks referred to need to be balanced against the possible gains of such criteria in reducing gender disadvantage. It may well be that in social security it is too costly and administratively too complex to test each person on an individual basis. In that case, it may be more advantageous overall to define a group according to gender than not to offer the benefit at all.[127] On the other hand, the perpetuation of a stereotype may be more damaging than the overall benefit.[128]

Somewhat more subtle is the reasoning in *Commission* v. *France*,[129] which concerned infringement proceedings brought against the French government on the grounds *inter alia* that French law infringed the Equal Treatment Directive by allowing women special rights such as maternity leave, the reduction of working hours and the right to holidays for an ill child or school holidays. The ECJ in ruling against the French legislation seems to be groping towards a test akin to the US 'strict scrutiny' standard in its cryptic statement that Article 2(4) is 'specifically and exclusively designed to allow measures which, although discriminatory in appearance are in fact intended to eliminate actual instances of inequality which may exist in the reality of social life.'[130] However, in its blanket rejection of all the special rights available to female employees, it scarcely uses the instrument in the fine-tuned manner it ought to. An example of a more sensitive balancing approach is the US case of *Califano* v. *Webster*,[131] which concerned a statutory classification allowing women to eliminate more low-earning years than men for the purposes of social security retirement pensions. Although the effect was to allow women higher monthly benefits than men

[126] Above n. 125, at p. 179.
[127] A similar point can be made in respect of *James* v. *Eastleigh Borough Council* [1990] IRLR 288 (HL).
[128] Case 184/83 *Hofmann* [1984] ECR 3047.
[129] [1988] ECR 6315 (ECJ).
[130] *ibid.*, at para. 15.
[131] 430 US 313 (1977).

with the same earning history, it was upheld because women are in general unfairly hindered from earning as much as men, and the measure worked directly to remedy the disparity.

The second strategic question is whether the costs of affirmative action are spread fairly. It is in the context of lay-offs that affirmative action programmes face their most severe test. It is clearly unfair to expect a handful of individuals to bear too great a share of the social responsibility for remedying discrimination, particularly by requiring them to surrender accrued seniority rights and therefore forfeit their jobs. What then is the way through this dilemma? The perceptive judgment of O'Connor J in *Adarand*[132] is a useful starting point. As we have seen, her insistence on strict scrutiny of positive action programmes does not automatically entail the prohibition of affirmative action. Nor does it necessarily reflect a symmetrical view, equating discrimination which imposes unfair burdens on members of an exploited group and discrimination aimed at remedying that disadvantage. Strict scrutiny in the hands of a perceptive judiciary should be alive to the dangers of stigma, stereotyping and difference ideologies. At the same time, it should be based on an asymmetrical, group-based model of justice which appreciates the deep moral differences between discrimination against a group which has been subject to historical and continuing detriment on the basis of their race or sex, and programmes which aim to remedy that discrimination. Moreover, characterisation of the problem as a simple conflict of interests between a man and a woman, or a white and a black is to fall into the individualistic trap. Instead, the employer and the State could be called upon to share the burden, possibly by subsidising continued employment of both employees or helping the redundant worker to find another job.

Finally, is affirmative action effective? It is frequently argued that reverse discrimination does no more than favour middle-class women or blacks who are already relatively privileged in society. Moreover, the argument of Advocate General Tesauro in *Kalanke* cannot be lightly brushed aside: 'Formal numerical equality is an objective which may salve some consciences, but it will remain illusory . . . unless it goes together with measures which are genuinely destined to achieve equality . . . In the final analysis, that which is necessary above all is a substantial change in the economic, social and cultural model which is at the root of the inequalities.'[133] However, his rejection of positive action is too sweeping. An immensely valuable counter is provided by the Supreme Court of Canada. As Chief Justice Dickson put it in a recent case,[134] the aim of an employment equity programme (in this case setting a quota of one woman in four new hirings until a goal of 13 per cent women in certain blue collar

---

[132] Above n. 110.
[133] *Kalanke*, above n. 95, p. 665.
[134] *Action Travail des Femmes* v. *Canadian National Railway Co* 40 DLR (4th) 193.

occupations was reached) is not to compensate past victims; but 'an attempt to ensure that future applicants and workers from the affected group will not face the same insidious barriers that blocked their forebears'.[135] He identified at least two ways in which such a programme is likely to be more effective than one which simply relies on equal opportunities or the proscription of intentional prejudice. First, the insistence that women be placed in non-traditional jobs allows them to prove that they really can do the job, thereby dispelling stereotypes about women's abilities. This was particularly evident in the case at hand, in which the quotas ordered by the tribunal concerned traditionally male jobs such as 'brakeman' or signaller at Canadian National Railways. Secondly, an employment equity programme helps to create a 'critical mass' of women in the work-place. Once a significant number of women are represented in a particular type of work, 'there is a significant chance for the continuing self-correction of the system.'[136] The critical mass overcomes the problem of tokenism, which would leave a few women isolated and vulnerable to sexual harassment or accusations of being imposters. It would also generate further employment of women, partly by means of the informal recruitment network and partly by reducing the stigma and anxiety associated with strange and unconventional work. Finally, a critical mass of women forces management to give women's concerns their due weight and compels personnel offices to take female applications seriously. As the Chief Justice concluded: 'It is readily apparent that, in attempting to combat systemic discrimination, it is essential to look to the past patterns of discrimination and to destroy those patterns in order to prevent the same type of discrimination in the future.'[137]

A defence of affirmative action should not, however, over-estimate its potential for achieving change. The Court in *Kalanke* was correct in pointing out that numerical equality can be illusory if not accompanied by real equality of opportunity. At the same time, the notion of equality of opportunity itself invites scrutiny: the mere formal equalisation of the starting points envisaged by the ECJ is unlikely to have a real impact. A fully fledged equal opportunities programme requires a radical reshaping of at least two fundamental aspects of the world of paid and unpaid work. First and foremost is the insistence on a loosening of the strict separation of the family or private sphere from the market place or public sphere. This is a two-pronged strategy: on the one hand, it encourages equal sharing by fathers of parenting and family work by means of flexible working patterns, parental leave and the right to protection from detrimental treatment flowing from time out of or partially involved in the labour market. On the other hand, it facilitates the combination of paid and unpaid work for

---

[135] *Candian National Railway*, p. 213.
[136] *ibid.*, p. 214.
[137] *ibid.*, p. 215.

women, by a combination of flexible working times, maternity leave, career breaks and child-care facilities (see Chapter 5). Equal opportunities also requires a sea-change in both the quantity and quality of education and training available to women (see Chapter 4). Equalising the starting points from an educational perspective requires not only careful thought and planning, but also a high level of resource input, both of which are entirely absent from the UK statutory framework permitting women-only training in specific circumstances (see above). Instead, recent attempts to create a 'market for training' have established a funding structure in which all the financial incentives favour a perpetuation of systemic discrimination against women. The continuing and substantial segregation of women and men within government-funded training programmes is largely due to the fact that funding is explicitly related to 'success' and 'efficiency', which in this case entail ability to place a trainee in a job, and the provision of training at a low cost. Women-only training schemes targeted at non-traditional areas of women's work are therefore financially unattractive, since, by definition, it remains difficult to find jobs for women in such occupations. Similarly, programmes for lone parents are more expensive, since travel expenses and child-care costs must be provided. As Felstead demonstrates, these are only examples of a system which is shot through with discriminatory implications.[138] Nor is it sufficient to concentrate on funding: attention to the nature and substance of training is also essential. As Clarke demonstrates, training facilities are only effective if they cater for women's child-care responsibilities. Full-time residential courses, not surprisingly, are poorly attended by women, whereas courses which provide child-care, function within school hours and make transport costs available are substantially more effective. Moreover, few schemes pay attention to the environment in which newly trained women will find themselves. It is therefore essential to provide appropriate training for male workers in a relevant profession to be sure that women do not find themselves in a hostile environment.

## III.  LAW AND SOCIETY: THE INFLUENCE OF ECONOMICS

One of the key issues in the development of effective legal strategies to restructure society concerns the interaction between law and economics. Against a background of hostility by economists, it is crucial to construct a convincing case for legal intervention to enhance women's position in society. The economic case for such legal intervention will be developed on two levels. The first is ideological, challenging the theoretical assumptions which ground economists' opposition to State-led structural change. The second is strategic, justifying legal strategies in terms of their economic

---

[138] A. Felstead 'The Gender Implications of Creating a Training market' in J. Humphries and J. Rubery (eds.), *The Economics of Equal Opportunities* (EOC, 1995), pp. 177–201.

acceptability. It is crucial at this point to stress that economic arguments do not trump egalitarian arguments. Ultimately, the latter derive their legitimacy unquestionably from moral considerations of fairness and justice. However, it is important to argue that the transitional costs can be absorbed by society as a whole without severe trauma. Each of these dimensions will be discussed in turn.

a) THE IDEOLOGY OF ECONOMICS

The greatest challenge to feminist restructuring of the law comes from the resurgence of neo-classical economics (see Chapters 1 and 6). The neo-classical understanding of sex discrimination is epitomised in the work of Polachek and Siebert. Writing as recently as 1993,[139] they maintain that in a competitive market, prejudice against women would soon be eradicated. 'In a competitive market, if men were paid more than similarly productive women, some firms would be able to lower their costs by hiring women instead of men. These firms would expand their market share, bidding up the pay of women. Men's and women's wages would thus be brought into equality.'[140] Therefore, they assert, the problem of unequal opportunity cannot exist in an economy devoted to free enterprise.[141] How then do they explain the gap between men's and women's pay and opportunities which is so clearly demonstrated by the figures that they themselves use? The answer, they argue, lies in the different supply side characteristics of women. Two such characteristics are identified. The first is taste. Citing empirical studies which claim to demonstrate that women have more 'caring' attributes than men, they argue that women will supply their labour more cheaply than men to caring occupations like nursing. The opportunity to 'care' is seen as a good in itself, which compensates for the lower pay. Moreover, 'caring', unlike mathematical skill, does not in their view require an investment on the part of the worker which has to be recouped in the form of higher wages.[142] The second characteristic which sets women apart from men relates to the 'rational (family wealth maximising) division of labour in the home due to women's comparative advantage in child-bearing and rearing'.[143] A woman who intends to take time out of the labour market to care for children will tend to invest less in her own human capital when working than a person who does not intend to interrupt her career. This is reflected in occupational choice. For example, it will not seem worthwhile to embark on a job, such as trainee manager, which requires intense initial training at a relatively low starter wage, if the worker is likely to leave the paid work-force before recouping the costs in higher wages and status.

---

[139] S. W. Polachek and W. S. Siebert, *The Economics of Earnings* (Cambridge University Press, 1993), p. 141.

[140] *ibid.*, p. 141.    [141] *ibid.*, p. 171.

[142] *ibid.*, p. 206.    [143] *ibid.*, p. 166.

This line of argument makes it unsurprising that these authors reject the value of legal intervention, with some limited exceptions. 'Competition is the greatest tool for fighting unequal opportunity.'[144] Only if discriminatory employers enjoy a monopoly over the labour supply or all producers in that market have an identical distaste for women workers can discriminatory practices survive in the long run. Grudging legal intervention is permitted for market failure of the first sort, and even then the burden is on the individual to show that the market has failed, rather than vice versa. It is thus only in non-competitive sectors, such as governments and regulated monopolies, that anti-discrimination policies have a role. Equal pay legislation based on comparative worth or equal value, is particularly pernicious, interfering as it does with the natural market outcome, to the detriment of all. For example, if nurses were paid the same as computer analysts, some nurses might benefit from the pay rise, but the number of jobs would fall because there is a limited amount of money available for nursing. Worse still, pay in other, non-protected sectors would drop as laid-off nurses sought work in other parts of the economy, creating a crowding effect.

The model of the labour market which informs the above analysis dominates economics textbooks; and even feminist economists treat it as a serious analysis.[145] It has also been a central influence on government policy-making over the past two decades. However, the aura of scientific truth which surrounds economic theory is deceptive. Economics, like law, is deeply ideological. Indeed, the underlying premises of the economic model are strikingly similar to the basic liberal premises which inform much of the legal framework. In neo-liberal hands, the five foundation stones at the base of the legal edifice, namely, rationality, autonomy, neutrality of the State, individualism and equality, are imbued with a deeply market-oriented meaning. Rationality becomes the ability to maximise self-interest; autonomy denotes freedom within the market; State neutrality means lack of intervention in the workings or outcomes of the market. Society is assumed to be composed of atomistic individuals who are interchangeable market agents, and equality is simply the formal equality of individuals to enter into contracts.

All these basic premises, however, are open to challenge, even from an economic point of view. To begin with rationality. It has been seen that Polachek and Siebert accord a central role to rationality when they assert that 'much of the differences between men and women can be explained as a rational response to differences in labour force intermittency, in mathematical abilities and in tastes'.[146] Yet, even within market discourse, it has

[144] Polachek and Siebert, above n. 139, p. 171.
[145] M. Sawyer 'The Operation of Labour markets and the Economics of Equal Opportunities' in Humphries and Rubery (eds.), above n. 138, p. 40; J. Humphries 'Economics, Gender and Equal Opportunities' in Humphries and Rubery (eds.), above n. 138, pp. 73–5.
[146] Polachek and Siebert, above n. 139, p. 208.

become clear that rationality is severely circumscribed by limited information or absence of transparency. The model posited by neo-classical economists asserts that 'labour mobility and competition among firms will eradicate discrimination, and allocate labour to its most productive uses so minimising costs.'[147] But this assumes that employers can measure workers' productivity perfectly. In reality, no such measure exists. Instead, employers must make a series of estimates about workers' productive abilities in order to assign them to a particular position within the internal hierarchy. A key assumption must include the future employment stability of individual employees, particularly in order to assign pay, training opportunities and promotion prospects to different levels in the internal hierarchy. It is here that the potential for discrimination is greatest. In estimating such matters as future employment stability, employers may well rely upon a stereotypical perception of women's employment patterns, thereby assuming that it would be cost effective to assign women to low wage positions with little access to training. This creates a self-fulfilling prophecy; but is far from the optimally efficient outcome for the employer.[148]

The neo-classical notion of rationality is problematic in an even more fundamental way. Most importantly, the concept of market rationality negates the emotional and social ties which legitimately constrain the activities of individuals within the market. This negation impacts differently on men and women, to the detriment of all. For women, the denial of the value of unpaid caring responsibilities limits their meaningful participation in the market; for men, the same denial limits their meaningful participation in the family.

A similar critique can be mounted in respect of autonomy. The view that women make a rational choice to invest less in their own human capital than men presupposes that there are a range of alternative pathways available to women which are carefully weighed and discarded. This is clearly not the case. The focus on choice ignores the constraints imposed by the division of power within the family and the existence of role models. Most seriously, it ignores the obstacles in the way of a meaningful combination of paid work and participative parenting. Women, as we have repeatedly seen, are generally forced to 'choose' between caring for their children at the cost of progress in the paid work-force or progressing in the work-force at the cost of caring for their children. Modifications of the classical economic stance do make some attempt to account for the family.[149] However, these theories still consider a household as a single agent, finding it impossible to construct a workable theory of intra-household decision-making. Most problematically, their vision of human nature is too thin and stylised to

---

[147] Above n. 146.

[148] D. Grimshaw and J. Rubery 'Gender and Internal Labour Markets' in Humphries and Rubery (eds.), above n. 138, p. 130.

[149] J. Humphries and J. Rubery, above n. 138, p. 27.

accommodate the richness of emotional and aesthetic qualities which thrive within a family.

Probably the core assumption in neo-classical economics is that of individualism. It is the individual who has the fundamental right to be free and equal within the market. But this leaves out of account three crucial facets of the individual within society. First, it ignores the continuing and pervasive influence of status on the market prospects of an individual. As Sawyer argues: 'The predominance of one group in a low paying job conveys low esteem to that group, and as members of that group expect low pay there is little incentive for them to acquire training or for employers and others to provide it. The low training of the group provides a sort of justification for low pay and low status.'[150] Secondly, it disregards the community and familial ties that both enhance and constrain the individual. Such elements are, on this view, part of the 'private' sphere and should not be allowed to transgress into the public domain. Yet, as we have seen, they play a crucial role. Finally, it assumes that a legal individual is equivalent in all respects to a natural individual. This allows the company, with all its corporate economic power, to claim moral equivalence to an individual.

The assumption of a neutral State faces similar challenges. Even within the economic paradigm it is acknowledged that a *laissez faire* economy is not synonymous with perfect competition. Instead, monopolies might spring up in a pure *laissez faire* economy, requiring State intervention to maintain the competition. In an advanced economy, it is a mere mystification to posit a non-interventionist State. Even Hayek acknowledges that the State has a role in regulating the market, provided that this is limited to servicing the basic ground rules rather than interfering with the outcome. It is this selectivity of what counts as legitimate grounds for State intervention which is most problematic. Examples from eighteen years of Conservative rule abound. Thus the intense ideological commitment to rolling back the boundaries of the State and privatising public functions has necessitated State intervention on a massive scale. It is not clear why it is legitimate to interfere with local authority's freedom of contract by imposing a duty to contract according to statutorily defined rules, but not to interfere with employers' freedom to contract in order to avoid discrimination.

The ideological basis of this economic model is not the only source of challenge. It can also be criticised from within its own paradigm. It will be recalled that the neo-classical theory asserts that any differences between men's and women's pay which are not related to productivity will be corrected by the market as workers move to jobs which truly reflect their value. Thus discrimination within the market is self-correcting, and any remaining pay differences must reflect women's lower productivity.

[150] Sawyer, above n. 145, p. 45.

However, this requires a market in which at least three elements dominate. These are, first, that pay is set according to the external market rate; secondly that there are no obstacles preventing workers from moving into jobs which pay according to productivity; and thirdly that it is possible to achieve an accurate measure of productivity. However, empirical evidence demonstrates that markets do not necessarily function in the manner expected. Thus, it is clear that the whole pay difference between men and women cannot be accounted for by differences in human capital. Paci *et al*, using the economists' definition of discrimination as 'unequal remuneration of [human capital] attributes in the labour markets'[151] have demonstrated that as much as 19 per cent of the pay gap is unaccounted for by systematic gender differences.[152] This suggests fundamental flaws in each of the three assumptions of the analysis. First, pay is not necessarily set according to the external 'market' or going rate. For example, some firms may find it advantageous to pay more than the 'going rate' because it helps them elicit greater effort and therefore greater productivity from their workers.[153] In addition, many firms are influenced as much by the 'internal labour market' as the external one: empirical research demonstrates significant differences in the ways in which wages are determined and employment allocated in different parts of the economy.[154] Thus some markets (often called 'primary' markets) offer pay and opportunities which are markedly superior to those offered in other 'secondary' markets. These markets are relatively insulated from one another. This undermines the second assumption, namely that workers move to jobs which reflect their productivity, thereby achieving an equilibrium state. Such a notion is highly stylised: in reality, many workers have firm-specific skills and are tied to a firm by internal hierarchical structures which are bureaucratic rather than market-responsive. Thirdly, as has been seen, it is often impossible to achieve an accurate measure of productivity. Instead, the process of estimating productivity is frequently itself tainted by gender ascriptions.

These problems have not gone unnoticed; several new economic theories have attempted to integrate the institutional forces within the labour market into the neo-classical framework.[155] However, such theorists continue to rely on productivity as the major basis for pay-setting, even if only within the context of the internal labour market. Whereas the 'old' neo-classical theorists place their faith in competition and self-interest to weed out inefficient practices, the new recognises market malfunctions but continues to believe that individuals and interest groups will reshape institutions in

[151] P. Paci, H. Joshi, and G. Makepeace 'Pay gaps facing men and women born in 1958' in Humphries and Rubery (eds.), above n. 138, p. 87.
[152] *ibid.*, p. 87.
[153] J. I. Bulow and L. H. Summers 'A Theory of Dual Labor Markets' *Journal of Labour Economics* [1986] vol. 4 no. 3 376 at 380.
[154] Humphries, above n. 145, p. 58.
[155] Grimshaw and Rubery, above n. 148, p. 116.

response to more attractive alternatives.[156] Yet 'efficiency' is itself a value-laden term. 'Efficiency' at the level of the firm (micro-efficiency) is not necessarily synonymous with efficiency of the overall outcome, as neo-classical economists would have us believe. Not only is it well known that a low trust or unco-operative environment might lead to a 'prisoners' dilemma' or the worst possible outcome. In addition, there may be numerous alternative outcomes, leading to equilibria at different levels.[157] The level at which equilibrium is reached, far from being the mathematical outcome of objective forces, is heavily contingent on the inherited social pattern of advantage as against disadvantage. Thus given a group with little bargaining power and low social status, it might well be efficient for the economy to exploit their position by locking them into low paid jobs which carry little training and therefore lack the productive level necessary to justify higher pay. By contrast, if the law intervenes to underpin their position, for example through a minimum wage set at a reasonable level, then it becomes more efficient to train such workers, thereby improving their productivity.[158] In any event, it is crucial to recognise that institutional structure cannot always be explained in terms of efficiency: instead the historical and social discrimination which shapes such institutions needs to be openly acknowledged.[159]

b) CAN WE AFFORD EQUAL OPPORTUNITIES POLICIES?

Is it the case that equal opportunities are 'too costly' for society? Those who answer in the affirmative conveniently omit to address the unstated question: costly for whom? The costs of discrimination are at present born largely by women. But it is not only women who do so. It is also the families and dependants of women; and increasingly, this includes their unemployed husbands or partners. The assertion that equal opportunities policies are too costly also assumes that there are no corresponding benefits. Yet, as was argued above, the economic theory which asserts that anti-discrimination laws are inefficient because they insist on women being rewarded above their productivity levels is deeply controversial even amongst economists. Instead, underpaying women may well be the real cause of inefficiency. As Deakin and Wilkinson maintain, the availability of undervalued labour 'acts as a source of productive inefficiency in its own right, providing firms with a means of compensating for managerial, organizational and other forms of inadequacies . . .'.[160] Conversely, wage increases may well have a direct effect on improving productivity.[161] Similarly, firms

---

[156] Sawyer, above n. 145, p. 38.

[157] *ibid.*, p. 38.

[158] *ibid.*, p. 38.

[159] *ibid.*, p. 45.

[160] S. Deakin and F. Wilkinson 'Rights v. Efficiency? The Economic Case for Transnational Labour Standards' [1994] 23 ILJ 289 at 294.

[161] Sawyer, above n. 145, p. 42.

with family-friendly policies which succeed in retaining skilled personnel, derive a clear benefit, while those who lose such women are disadvantaged. Barclays Bank estimates that the replacement costs for women in senior clerical grades or above are as high as £17,000; while Boots puts the cost of replacing employees in less skilled positions such as sales assistants to be about £3,000 per employee. On the latter figures, a 1 per cent annual turnover of staff costs £1 million. The cost of replacing a junior manager in industry generally is thought to be £6,600, allowing for recruitment costs, training and the initial limited function of the new employee. Such costs are significantly eased by enhanced maternity leave and other specific measures: in the case of Barclays Bank, the proportion of maternity returners jumped from 33 per cent to 66 per cent; while at Boots the figure soared from 7 to 50 per cent between 1989 and 1993.[162] Other less easily quantifiable benefits are in the form of less stressed and more satisfied employees. On a more macro-economic level, as was demonstrated in Chapter 6, a low wage, low skill economy is ultimately sub-optimal because of the lack of incentive for managers to invest in training or in improved technology.

The debate about the exact costs of equal opportunities cannot be resolved in a unidimensional fashion. Much depends on the overall economic climate, the direction of government macro-economic policies, the taxation and benefit system and the legal structure. For example, the scope for enlightened equal opportunities policies is narrowed by the government-led impetus toward sub-contracting.[163] Conversely, legal requirements for minimum wages or parental leave which operate equally for all employers might reduce the adverse costs associated with competition between equal opportunities employers and those who continue to discriminate. Indeed, it is arguable that until all firms competing for good quality labour provide career breaks or child-care, the 'prisoner's dilemma' effect will prevent 'good' employers from doing so.[164] There is therefore a crucial role for the law in demanding minimum standards. Moreover, it is undesirable to leave the initiative in the hands of individual employers who are subject to the vagaries of the economy. As soon as the recession hits or the demand for labour eases, employers can be expected to abandon policies to retain women staff. Thus Midland Bank halted its programme for 200 creches in midstream, National Westminster abandoned its plans for creches, and Sainsbury's shelved its plans to try term-time working. It is well known that family-friendly policies are in general only available to employees in higher grades, and that small employers are unlikely to take any initiative whatsoever.[165] It is even more important on a macro-

---

[162] Figures from I. Breugel and D. Perrons 'Where do the Costs of Unequal Treatment for Women Fall?' in Humphries and Rubery (eds.), above n. 138, p. 160.

[163] ibid., p. 156.

[164] ibid., p. 161.

[165] ibid., pp. 162–3.

economic level that equal opportunities policies are required by statute. Otherwise, as Breugel and Perrons point out, 'there is a disjuncture between what is rational for some individual enterprises within the pre-existing gender order and what would collectively benefit employers in their need for a highly productive workforce . . . In some ways, it is a textbook case of market failure.'[166]

[166] Breugel and Perrons, above n. 162, p. 168.

# [10]
# Through the Mirage

The path to juridical equality has been steep and arduous. It has taken more than a century to reach our destination. Yet, far from having scaled the summit, we find we are just emerging from the foothills. The challenge ahead is even more formidable, in no small measure due to the fact that the signposts tend to point in the wrong direction. Equality, rationality, autonomy and neutrality, far from guiding us forward, have frequently led us round the base or even downhill.

How then do we move forward? A central task of this book has been to pierce the veil of truth and objectivity which clothes the law, exposing the partiality of its basic premises. This process has revealed a legal framework based on a paradoxical amalgam of liberal principles and pre-liberal status ascriptions, a combination which goes far to explaining the inability of the law to effect real structural change. While it is predictable that status ascriptions and stereotypes will obstruct progress, the most exacting challenge is presented by the liberal principles. Equality, rationality and autonomy are lofty ideals, signifying the heights of human aspiration. Yet, as the examination in this book has revealed, these fundamental liberal principles in fact ignore or negate many of women's central concerns. As MacKinnon puts it: 'The abstract equality of liberalism permits most women little more than does the substantive inequality of conservatism'.[1] The result is that women continue to be impaled on the age-old dichotomies, the dualisms of equality and difference, emotionality and rationality, public and private. Thus, while difference stigmatises women as primarily reproductive beings and sexual objects, equality operates by negating the value of reproduction in society. To qualify for equal treatment, women must first conform to a male norm in a world of paid work which obliterates the family. Similarly, the stigma of irrationality brands women as unreliable and unproductive workers, or as sexual objects in the work-place. Yet the recharacterisation of women as rational has frequently been used as a way of legitimating disadvantage. Women are said to have made the 'rational choice' to invest less than men in their own human capital, attracting the 'rational' market response of lower pay. We are said to have invited harassment by our clothes or our demeanour and are expected 'rationally' to ignore pornography in the work-place.

---

[1] C. MacKinnon, *Feminism Unmodified* (Harvard University Press, 1987), p. 16.

Perhaps the most complex, and most telling, is the functioning of the public/private divide. It is true that women are no longer confined in the private world of the family. Yet enhanced access to the public world of paid work has not in fact relaxed the rigid demarcation between the two spheres. Most problematically, there has been no pressure on the world of paid work to accommodate unpaid caring responsibilities. The result is to dichotomise the available roles for both men and women. Full participation in paid work is only possible at the cost of minimal participation in family work. But the flexible participation in the paid work-force essential for participative parenting is penalised by poor terms and conditions of work. Unsurprisingly, the resulting pattern is deeply gendered, with women predominating in the second category. Nor has this pattern been reconfigured by the fundamental changes in the nature of paid work. With the decline in manufacturing and the increasing importance of the service sector, full-time continuous working is no longer the dominant mode of paid work. Women are being sucked into the market to perform a variety of flexible jobs; yet the increase in quantity has by no means signified an increase in the quality of jobs. The result is that women predominate in poorly paid and insecure jobs. Similarly surprising has been the lack of impact of high male unemployment: powerful structural forces, including the built-in incentives of the welfare system, have perpetuated women's weak market position despite the potential of a full-time male carer. Nor is this the only problematic manifestation of the rigid demarcation of public and private. It also works in the opposite direction, making it difficult for women in paid work to claim a 'private' sphere within which we are entitled to be free from sexual harassment. Finally, in its traditional context of demarcating the legitimate role of the State in civic life, the public/private divide has been used to legitimate 'rolling back the boundaries of the State'. This has again operated to the detriment of women: by shifting many welfare responsibilities back to the family, such policies have deprived women of paid employment opportunities and substituted unpaid 'private' work in the family.

What role then can the law play in leading us forward? The analysis of the inherent limitations in the present legal framework makes it clear that legal instruments must be sensitively refashioned and constantly reappraised if they are to perform a positive function in the future. I have argued that at least four principles should guide such a reappraisal. First, an acute awareness of the social and structural pressures perpetuating women's disadvantage must inform any legal changes. Secondly, it is crucial to displace the principle of equality from its central position in anti-discrimination law, thereby freeing us from the stultifying influence of the male norm. Thirdly, the authority carried by arguments based on the ostensible 'rational' workings of a 'free' market must be punctured. Economic analysis is as deeply ideological as the legal system with which it interacts. Finally, and relatedly, it is essential to repudiate the notion of a neutral State. The assertion of

State neutrality merely conceals intervention of a specific and even authoritarian kind. Instead, I have argued for an express recognition of the State as the purveyor of positive values embodied in the law, values which unashamedly include the alleviation of disadvantage and the promotion of full participation by both women and men in all aspects of society, private and public.

Thus it is clear that conventional legal forms alone are insufficient, and can be counterproductive. Familiar anti-discrimination laws, based as they are on an equality principle, are inevitably constrained by the power of the male norm. I have argued in several contexts for the displacement of the equality principle by specific rights, such as the right to maternity and parental leave, the right not to be sexually harassed and the right to minimum pay. Such rights signify an explicit endorsement by the State of women's concerns, independently of their ability to conform to male working patterns or norms. Rights are also empowering, if not against an intransigent employer, at least against a neutral but law-abiding one.

However, the role of rights should not be over-estimated. Their content in practice is no more than a reflection of the current balance of political forces, and their power is diluted accordingly. In addition, they rely almost entirely on individual enforcement in a judicial system which is ridden with deterrents. Structural change requires a movement not just beyond the equality principle, but also beyond the individualism inevitably associated with rights. Given that the causes of discrimination are found deeply embedded in social structures, it is inevitable that attempts to provide redress for isolated individuals will make little impact. Instead, we need an integrated strategy which includes a wide range of social and political initiatives. Pay is a paradigm case. The deficiencies of the individualised, equality-based approach of current legislation are clearly demonstrated by the fact the gender-pay gap remains unacceptably wide. As the discussion in Chapter 6 shows, payment structures must be tackled as a whole, and in a manner which transcends a simple equal treatment paradigm, if real change is to be achieved. Nor is it sufficient to focus on payment structures; these in turn are only part of the wider social context. Even if fundamental changes are achieved in the valuation and grading of women's basic pay, disparities between men and women will reappear so long as men predominate in work for which they can demand premia payments while women predominate in marginal and part-time work and have little or no bargaining power due to inflexible family responsibilities. Real change requires far more radical intervention, in which legal forms are complemented by wide-ranging social measures opening the door to balanced participation by women in paid work and facilitating balanced participation by men in family work. Such measures require changes in working time for both men and women, a high level of child-care provision, and parental leave for both parents on sustainable levels of pay. Nor should these measures impose legal obligations on individual employers alone. It is crucial that they be seen as a community responsibility spearheaded and resourced by the State: to burden individual employers is similarly counterproductive if it acts as a disincentive to employ women with actual or potential family responsibilities.

Such broad-based social and legislative initiatives are unlikely to occur spontaneously. As ever, change will only come as a result of pressure from organised women, from women demanding greater access to policy-making processes and women refusing to accept the institutional structures dominating our lives. From a political point of view, there are clearly difficult questions to be faced: should we be demanding that women's issues be 'mainstreamed' or made the subject of special attention? Do we need gender-neutral measures, or measures targeted specifically at women? What role should affirmative action policies play and how best should education and training be restructured?[2] In what way can the diverse and even conflicting interests of different groups of women be addressed? We also need to head off the question, posed by neo-liberals and democratic socialists alike: can we afford such a wide-reaching campaign of change? Arguments against change are at their most insidious when they cite 'scientific' assertions about efficiency and productivity to support the view that change is too expensive or that women will simply price themselves out of jobs. I have argued that the scientific aura surrounding concepts such as efficiency and productivity conceals their deeply ideological basis. It is of course possible to counter these arguments on their own terms: there is certainly sufficient evidence to defend the economic plausibility of radical change. However, ultimately, the thrust of this book has been to assert unashamedly the moral and equitable grounds for paying the price for women's emancipation.

In many senses, then, I conclude with a sense of hope for the future. Having exposed the limitations of the current legal framework, it is time to begin the process of reconstruction in a new and different image. At the same time, there is no single or simple formula. While obstacles of the past are being surmounted, new and unfamiliar hurdles are springing up in their stead. The hope which is essential to drive us forward should not leave us complacent as to the magnitude of the task ahead.

[2] For the detailed discussions at the Fourth World Conference on Women in Beijing in 1996 see Lin Lean Lim *More and Better Jobs for Women* (ILO, 1996).

# Bibliography

Adonis, A., *Parliament Today* (2nd edn., Manchester University Press, 1993).

Alberti, A., *Beyond Suffrage* (Macmillan, 1989).

Anderson, B.S. and Zinsser, J.P., *A History of Their Own* vol II (Penguin, 1990).

Anon., *The Laws Respecting Women* (1777).

Aquinas, T., *Summa Theologiae. A Concise Translation* T. McDermott (ed.), (Eyre & Spottiswoode, 1989).

Aristotle, *The Politics of Aristotle* translated by E. Barker (Clarendon Press, 1946).

Armstrong, P., Glyn, A. and Harrison, J., *Capitalism since 1945* (Blackwell, 1991).

Astell, M., *Reflections upon Marriage* in Astell, M. and Hill, D. *The First English Feminist* (Gower, 1986).

Baer, J.A., *Women in American Law* (Holmes & Meier, 1991).

Baker, J. H., *An Introduction to English Legal History* (Butterworths, 1979).

Barnes, J. (ed.), *The Complete Works of Aristotle* (Oxford University Press, 1982).

Beale, J., *Getting it together* (Pluto Press, 1982).

Bergmann, B., *The Economic Emergence of Women* (New York, 1986).

Beveridge, W. H., *Unemployment* (Longman's, 1931).

Blackstone, W., *Commentaries on the Law of England* (1809) Book I Ch XV.

Blanpain, R. (ed.), *The Harmonization of Working Life and Family Life* (Kluwer, 1995).

Bowlby, J., *Child Care and the Growth of Love* (2nd edn., Penguin, 1965).

Brown, G. and Harris, T., *The Social Origins of Depression* (Tavistock, 1970).

Bryan, B., Dadzie, S. and Scafe, S. *The Heart of the Race* (Virago, 1986).

Bulmer, M. and Rees, A. (eds.) *Citizenship Today* (UCL Press, 1996).

Carter, A., *The Politics of Women's Rights* (Longman, 1988).

Clarke, K., *Women and Training: A Review* (Equal Opportunities Commission Research Discussion Series, 1991).

Clarke-Stewart, A., *Day Care* (Fontana, 1982).

Cole, G. D. H. 'Introduction' to Jean-Jacques Rousseau, *The Social Contract and Discourses* (Trans. G. D. H. Cole, Dent, 1986).

Cornish, W.H. and Clarke, G. de N., *Law and Society in England* (Sweet & Maxwell, 1989).

Coyle, A., *Women and Organisational Change* (EOC, 1995).

Craig, C., Rubery, J., Tarling, R. and Wilkinson, F., *Labour Market Structure, Industrial Organisation and Low Pay* (Cambridge University Press, 1982).

Cranston, R., *Legal Foundations of the Welfare State* (Weidenfeld, 1985).

Dahrendorf, R. 'Citizenship and Social Class' in Bulmer, M. and Rees, A. (eds.) *Citizenship Today* (UCL Press, 1996).

Davies, B. and Ward, S., *Women and Personal Pensions* (EOC Research Series, 1992).

Davies, P. and Freedland, M.R. (ed.), *Kahn-Freund's Labour and the Law* (2nd edn., Stevens, 1983).

——*Labour Legislation and Public Policy* (Oxford University Press, 1993).

Deakin, S., Michie, J., and Wilkinson, F., *Inflation, Employment, Wage-bargaining and the Law* (Institute of Employment Rights, 1992).

——and Wilkinson, F., *The Economics of Employment Rights* (Institute of Employment Rights, 1991).

Delphy, C. *Close to Home*, (edited and translated by D. Leonard) (Hutchinson, in association with the Explorations in Feminism Collective 1984).

Department of Education and Employment, *Work and Family: Ideas and Options for Childcare* (1996).

Department of Employment Consultative Paper on Wages Councils (1985).

Department of Social Security, *Equality in State Pension Age* (HMSO, 1993).

Dewar, J., *Law and the Family* (Butterworths, 1989).

Dex, S. and McCulloch, A., *Flexible Employment in Britain* (EOC, 1995).

——, Lissenburgh, S. and Taylor, M., *Women and Low Pay* (EOC, 1994).

DHSS, *Review of the Household Duties Test* (1983).

Dicey, A. V., *Letters to a Friend on Votes for Women* (John Murray, 1909).

——*Law and Opinion in England* (Macmillan, 1914).

Dickens, R. and Marning, A., "After Wages Councils", *New Economy*, Sept 1995, 223.

Dickens, L., *Whose Flexibility* (Institute of Employment Rights, 1992).

Dickens, R., Machin, S., Manning, A. and Wilkinson, D., 'What Happened to Wages and Employment after the abolition of minimum wages in Britain' (1995) unpublished.

Dworkin, R. M., *A Matter of Principle* (Clarendon Press, 1985).

——*Law's Empire* (Fontana Press, 1986).

——*Life's Dominion* (Harper Colins, 1993).

Eekelaar, J., *Family Law and Social Policy* (2nd edn., Weidenfeld & Nicolson, 1984).

——and Clive, E. with Clarke, K. and Raikes, S., *Custody after Divorce* (Oxford University Press, 1977).

Employers for Childcare, *Good Childcare Good Business* (1993).

Equal Opportunities Commission, *The Life Cycle of Inequality* (1995).

——*The Economics of Equal Opportunity* (1995).

——*Equality Management: Women's Employment in the NHS* (1991).

——Briefing Paper, *Wages Councils and Low Pay* (1992).

——*What Price Equality?* (1994).

——*The Key to Real Choice: An Action Plan for Childcare* (1990).

——*Some Facts about Women* (1994).

——*A Question of Fairness* (1992)

——*Your Pension Matters* (1992).

——*Women and Men in Britain 1993* (1993).

Escott, K. and Whitfield, D., *The Gender Impact of CCY in Local Government* (EOC, 1995).

Eyraud, F. et al, *Equal Pay Protection in Industrialised Market Economies* (ILO, 1993).

Fawcett, M., *Women's Suffrage* (T. C. and E. C. Jack, 1912).

Filmer, Sir Robert, *Patriarcha and Other Writings* edited by J. P. Sommerville (Cambridge University Press, 1991).

Finer, M. and McGregor, O. R., 'The History of the Obligation to Maintain'

Appendix 5, *Report of the (Finer) Committee on One-Parent Families* (Cmnd. 5629-1)(1974).

Fredman, S. and Morris, G., *The State as Employer* (Mansell, 1989).

Friedan, B., *The Feminine Mystique* (Penguin, 1963).

Friedmann, W. (ed.), *Matrimonial Property Law* (Stevens & Son Ltd, 1955).

Fudge, J. and McDermott, P. (ed.), *Just Wages* (University of Toronto Press, 1990).

Ginsberg, M. (ed.), *Law and Opinion in England in the 20th Century* (Stevens, 1959).

Glendinning, C. and Millar, J. (ed.), *Women and Poverty in Britain in the 1990s* (Harvester Wheatsheaf, 1992).

Gourvish, T. R. and O'Day, A., *Later Victorian Britain* (Macmillan, 1988).

Government Actuary, *Occupational Pension Schemes 1991*, 9th Survey (HMSO, 1994).

Green, V. H. H., *A History of Oxford University* (Batsford, 1974).

Gregory, J., *Dispensing Informal Justice* (EOC, 1993).

——*Trial by Ordeal* (HMSO, 1989).

Griffiths, Sir Roy, *Community Care: Agenda for Action* (HMSO, 1988).

Harlow, C. and Craig, P. (ed.) *Law-Making in the European Union* (Sweet & Maxwell, 1997).

Hayek, F.A., *The Constitution of Liberty* (Routledge and Kegan Paul, 1960).

——*Law, Legislation and Liberty (vol 2)* (Routledge and Kegan Paul, 1970).

Hepple, B. and Szyszczak, E. (eds.), *Discrimination and the Limits of Law* (Mansell, 1992).

——(ed.), *The Making of Labour Law in Europe* (Mansell, 1986).

——and Fredman, S., *Labour Law and Industrial Relations in Britain* (2nd edn, Kluwer, 1992).

Heschel, S. (ed.), *On being a Jewish Feminist* (Schocken, Books 1983).

Hill Collins, P., *Black Feminist Thought* (Routledge, 1991).

Hoggett, B. and Pearl, D., *The Family, Law and Society* (Butterworths, 1983).

Holtermann, S. and Clarke, K., *Parents, employment rights and childcare* (EOC, 1992).

Humphries, J. and Rubery, J., *The Economics of Equal Opportunities* (EOC, 1995).

Hutchins, B. L. and Harrison, A., *A History of Factory Legislation* (P.S. King & Son, 1911).

Hutton, S., Kennedy, S. and Whiteford, P., *Equalisation of State Pension Ages: The Gender Impact* (EOC, 1995).

Huws, U., *Home Truths: Key Findings from the National Survey of Homeworkers* (National Group on Homeworking Report No. 2) (1994).

Industrial Relations Services, *Pay and Gender in Britain* (1991).

Jaggar, A. M., *Feminist Politics and Human Nature* (Harvester, 1983).

Jessop, B., Bonnett, K., Bromley, S. and Ling, T., *Thatcherism* (Polity Press, 1988).

John, A. (ed.), *Unequal Opportunities. Women's Employment in England 1800–1918* (Blackwell, 1986).

Joshi, H. and Davies, H., *Childcare and Mothers' Lifetime Earnings: Some European Contrasts* (Centre for Economic Policy Research, Discussion Paper No. 600, 1992).

Kavanagh, D. and Seldon, A. (ed.), *The Thatcher Effect* (Clarendon Press, 1989).

Labour Research Department, *Working Parents: Negotiating a Better Deal* (1992).

Law Commission, *Family Property Law* Working Paper No. 42 (1971).

Leonard, A., *Judging Inequality: the effectiveness of the tribunal system in sex discrimination and equal pay cases* (Cobden Trust, 1987).

Levitas, R. (ed.), *The Ideology of the New Right* (Polity Press, 1986).

Lewis, J., *Women in Britain since 1945* (Basil Blackwell, 1992).

—— *Women in England 1870–1950: Sexual Divisions and Social Change* (Wheatsheaf, 1984).

—— *Women's Welfare Women's Rights* (Croom Helm, 1983).

Lindley, R. (ed.), *Labour Market Structures and Prospects for Women* (Equal Opportunities Commission, 1994).

Lister, R., *Women's Economic Dependency and Social Security* (EOC Research Discussion Series No. 2, 1992).

Locke, J., *Two Treatises of Government* edited by P. Laslett (Cambridge University Press, 1988).

—— *An Essay Concerning Human Understanding* (Clarendon Press, 1975).

Low Pay Unit, *More Crime and still no Punishment* (1992).

LRD, *Pensions and Equality* (1994).

——, *A brief guide to the 1995 Pensions Act (1995)*.

MacKinnon, C., *Feminism Unmodified* (Harvard University Press, 1987).

—— *Sexual Harassment of Working Women* (Yale University Press, 1979).

Maclean, M., *Surviving Divorce* (Macmillan, 1991).

Marsh, A. and McKay, S., *Families, Work and Benefits* (Policy Studies Institute, 1993).

Marshall, T. H. and Bottomore, T., *Citizenship and Social Class* (Pluto Press, 1992).

Marx, K. and Engels, F., *Selected Works* (Lawrence and Wishart, 1968).

Matthews, R. C. O., Feinstein, C. H. and Oddling Smee, J. C. *British Economic Growth 1856–1973* (Clarendon Press, 1982).

McCarthy, W. (ed.), *Legal Intervention in Industrial Relations* (Blackwell, 1992).

McCrudden, C. (ed.), *Anti-Discrimination Law* (Dartmouth, 1991).

—— *Women, Employment and European Equality Law* (Eclipse, 1987).

McRae, S., *Maternity Rights in Britain* (Policy Studies Institute, 1991).

—— *Women's Employment During Family Formation* (Policy Studies Institute, 1996).

Mill, J. S., *The Subjection of Women* (2nd edn., Longman, 1869).

Mitchell, J. and Oakley, A. (eds.), *The Rights and Wrongs of Women* (Penguin, 1976).

Morgan, D., *Suffragists and Liberals* (Basil Blackwell, 1975).

Mottershead, P., *Recent Developments in Childcare: A Review* (EOC Research Series, 1988).

Napier, B., *CCT, Market Testing and Employment Rights* (Institute of Employment Rights, 1993).

National Association of Citizens Advice Bureau (NACAB), *Not in labour* (1992).

O'Brien, M., *The Politics of Reproduction* (Routledge and Kegan Paul, 1981).

O'Donovan, K. *Sexual Divisions in Law* (Weidenfeld, 1985).

Ogus, A., Barendt, E. and Wikeley, N., *The Law of Social Security* (4th edn., Butterworths, 1995).

Okin, S. M., *Justice, Gender and the Family* (Basic Books, New York, 1989).

Owen, D., *Ethnic Minority Women in the Labour market: analysis of the 1991 census* (Equal Opportunities Commission, 1994).

Pankhurst, E., *My Own Story* (Routledge, 1914).

Patel, B., 'Racial Discrimination and Equal Pay' unpublished paper for National Pay Equity Conference 1991.

Pateman, C., *The Sexual Contract* (Polity Press, 1988).

—— *The Disorder of Women* (Polity Press, 1989).

Pennington S. & Westover B., *A Hidden Workforce: Homeworkers in England, 1850-1985* (Macmillan, 1989).

Phillips, D., *Daycare for young children: An international perspective* (Equal Opportunities Commission, 1990).

Plato *The Republic* translated by R. Waterfield, Book V (Oxford University Press, 1993).

Polachek, S. W. and Siebert, W. S., *The Economics of Earnings* (Cambridge University Press, 1993).

Prechal, S. and Sendon, L. *Monitoring Implementation and Application of Community Equality Law* (European Commission, 1996).

Pugh, M., *Women and the Women's Movement in Britain 1914–1959* (Macmillan, 1992).

Rawls, J., *A Theory of Justice* (Oxford University Press, 1972).

Raz J., *The Morality of Freedom* (Clarendon Press, 1980).

*Report of the War Cabinet Committee on Women in Industry* (HMSO) Cmd.135, 1919.

Rhode, D., *Justice and Gender* (Harvard University Press, 1989).

—— (ed.) *Theoretical Perspectives on Sexual Difference* (Yale University Press, 1990).

Roberts, E., *A Woman's Place* (Basil Blackwell, 1984).

Rosen, A., *Rise Up Women* (Routledge, 1974).

Rousseau, J.-J., *Politics and the Arts: Letter to M. d'Alambert on the Theatre* translated by A. Bloom (1977).

—— *Emile* translated by A. Bloom (Penguin, 1991).

Rover, C., *Women's Suffrage and Party Politics in Britain 1866–1914* (Routledge and Kegan Paul, 1967).

Rowbotham, S., *Hidden from History* (Pluto Press, 1973).

—— *Women, Resistance and Revolution* (Penguin, 1972).

Rubery, J. (ed.), *Women and Recession* (Routledge, 1988).

—— *The Economics of Equal Value* (EOC, 1992).

Sassoon, A. (ed.), *Women and the State* (Routledge, 1987).

Seccombe, W., 'Starting to Stop' *Past and Present* 126 (1990).

Shanley, M. L., *Feminism, Marriage and the Law in Victorian England, 1850–1895* (Tauris, 1989).

—— and Pateman, C. (eds.), *Feminist Interpretations and Political Theory* (Polity Press, 1991).

Smart, C. (ed.), *Regulating Womanhood* (Routledge, 1992).

—— *Feminism and the Power of Law* (Routledge, 1989).

Smith, P. (ed.), *Feminist Jurisprudence* (Oxford University Press, 1993).

Spelman, E. V., *Inessential Woman* (Women's Press, 1990).

Sunstein, C. (ed.) *Feminism and Political Theory* (University of Chicago Press, 1982).

Ungerson, C. (ed.), *Women and Social Policy* (Macmillan, 1985).

Vogler, C., *Labour Market Change and Patterns of Financial Allocation within Households* (ESRC, 1989).

Ware, A. and Goodin, R. (eds), *Needs and Welfare* (Sage, 1990).

Webb, S. and Webb, B., *English Poor Law Policy* (Longmans, 1910).

——*Industrial Democracy* Vol II (Longmans, 1897).

——*The History of Trade Unionism* (2nd edn., Longmans, 1920).

Wollstonecraft, M., *Vindication of the Rights of Women* (Penguin Classics, 1983).

Young, I., *Justice and the Politics of Difference* (Princeton University Press, 1990).

# Index